To the Right Reverend
Thomas Lord Bishop of

My Lord

Beeing obliged to provide my self
of a Curate to assist me in my Parishs the Forest and
Torteval in the Island of Guernesey; I humbly beg your
Lordship to permit to the Reverend M.r John Batiste de.
La Cour to preach and to admenester the holy Sacrements
in the said Island; his having been permitted to read the
Prayers by the Reverend Father in God the Bishop of
London; I know the said Clergyman to be of good Morals,
as also his Behaviour is known by several french Ministers
in London from whom he has a good Testimony: More over
he has been ordained Priest in France & he has with him
his Letters. I promise and oblige my self to pay him in
the said Parishs the Some of thirty Pounds by year besides
other Comoditys what I have accustomed to give the others
Clergy men when in my Service: And as the return of the
Fleet ander Convoy is near, and as ofter Miclemas the
Navagation of that part are with out Convoy; beeng but
few of these Sips comeing to England; wich makes me
humbly beg your Lordship Speedest dispach in favour
of this Gentleman offering my most Sincere Prayers for
the Preservation of your Lordships Life and health in
your new Deocese; and remaining in the profoundest
Respect and veneration.

My Lord

of your Lordship

Guernesey
the 28.th August
1762.

The most humble and most
obediand Servent Peter Levrier
Rector of la Forest and Torteval

Endpapers: (*left*) Certificate containing the signatures of many famous Guernseymen supporting Thomas de Sausmarez in his refusal to fight a second duel with Robert Porret le Marchant; (*right*) Pierre Levrier's letter to Bishop John Thomas asking that Jean de la Noye be appointed as his Curate.

GUERNSEY PEOPLE

Guernsey People

L. James Marr

with an introduction by
Le Seigneur de Sausmarez

and a supplement on Early Bailiwick Names by
Dr. S. K. Kellett-Smith

Illustrations arranged by
Carel Toms

Ad Insulanos Nunc et Quondam

PHILLIMORE

1984

Published by
PHILLIMORE & CO. LTD.
Shopwyke Hall, Chichester, Sussex

© L. James Marr, 1984

ISBN 0 85033 529 9

Typeset in the United Kingdom by:
Fidelity Processes - Selsey - Sussex

Printed and bound in Great Britain by
THE CAMELOT PRESS LIMITED
Southampton, Hampshire, England

CONTENTS

LIST OF ILLUSTRATIONS
(between pages 106 and 107)

FOREWORD

by Cecil Havilland de Sausmarez Esquire, M.B.E.

Seigneur du Fief de Sausmarez, Sénéchal de La Cour des Seigneurs,
and Paramount Seigneur of the Island of Guernsey

Every community should have its folk-heroes and folk villains, whether mythological or historical. How dull would English history be for schoolchildren without its King Arthur, Richard Cœur de Lion or that other Richard who is supposed to have had his two nephews smothered in the Tower of London; or French history without its Roland, its Joan of Arc or its Robespierre. Guernsey history has hitherto been sadly lacking in such fascinating figures. To how many of our schoolchildren do such names as Restauld of Jethou, the Reverend Pierre Painsec, the Bailiff William Le Marchant or even Rear Admiral Sir Thomas Mansell and Sir Peter Le Page Renouf mean anything at all?

For too many Guernsey people today the history of their island begins towards the middle of the 19th century when the early vineries were built or at the end of the German occupation. Even our present-day historians have been surprisingly unattracted by the century beginning in 1720 and ending in 1820, though this was undoubtedly the period which produced our most illustrious sons.

With the publication of James Marr's latest work, *Guernsey People*, this gap should now be filled. Intended as a supplement to his warmly praised *Bailiwick History*, it might more aptly be regarded as an introduction thereto. Its main section is devoted to close on 200 short biographies of the Bailiwick's real folk-heroes and folk-villains, of whom the earliest, St Sampson of Dol, lived in the fifth and sixth centuries A.D. and the latest, Linda Martel (an equally saintly character) from 1956 to 1961. A most happy feature of these biographies is the well-chosen introductory heading which the author has given to each one. These headings enable the reader more easily to retain in memory the name of the person concerned. There follows a further list of upwards of 70 names which are less known or more legendary. It is, however, a most valuable section as many of the persons listed were hitherto unknown to me and the anecdotes recounted about them of great interest. The third section of the work entitled 'Tables of Kinship' shows what an inbred society, for better or for worse, the inhabitants of our island have always been. I can honestly say that, having read *Guernsey People* and then having returned to read Mr. Marr's *Bailiwick History* for the second time, my opinion as to the value of the earlier work has been greatly enhanced.

Among the biographies there is a special section entitled 'Underground Resistance Heroes of the Second World War' giving a fuller treatment of the subject than is to be found in Dr. Cruikshank's official history of the occupation, covering a wider ground than the late lamented Frank Falla in *The Silent War* and in which the facts are more carefully substantiated than in *Islands in Danger*. There is every reason to regret that the many useful, as opposed to pointless, acts of passive resistance carried out during the occupation received so little recognition whether from the insular authorities, from Whitehall, or even from many fellow islanders. Mr. Marr has explained clearly and with details as yet unpublished how much valuable information was brought to England or to France by those Guernseymen who risked their lives escaping by boat, as well as how much the morale of the population was sustained by the dissemination of news sheets brought out by the valiant organisers of G.U.N.S.

This book written by an experienced history schoolteacher should be read by all schoolchildren in the Bailiwick past or present, not to speak of their parents.

Cecil H. de Sausmarez
Seigneur de Sausmarez

THE ISLANDERS

(1) 'How valiantly, manfully and steadfastly the peoples and communities of the islands of Guernsey, Sark and Alderney have stood out for us and our progenitors.'
Edward IV, 1468

(2) 'Ils sont pires que les Canibales.' *François Rabelais: 'Pantagruel', 1532*

(3) 'They would rather utter a thousand perjuries than injure a friend.'
Adrian de Saravia, 1566

(4) 'How bravelie the men of St Martyn's have behaved themselves at sea. They have brought in a prize of sixty Ton, of Amsterdam, laden with wine, tobacco, figs and rosin.'
Governor Sir Jonathan Atkins, 1667

(5) 'Wreckers and pirates by habit and tradition.' *John le Mesurier, 1747*

(6) 'Le noble petit peuple de la mer.' *Victor Hugo, 1866*

(7) 'I want to convey to the Guernsey authorities my very high appreciation of the valuable services rendered by the R.G.L.I. in the battle of Cambrai. Theirs was a wonderful performance.' *General Sir Beauvoir de Lisle, 1917*

(8) 'Stiff-necked, argumentative, francophone calvinists, with no respect for the house of Stuart.' *Jean le Pelley: 'The Knight of the Golden Tulip', 1969*

(9) 'The Occupation brought out the best and worst in all of us; but we was Guernsey people yet, and our spirit was not broken. It is the English Occupation since have broken it.' *G. B. Edwards: 'The Book of Ebenezer Le Page', 1974*

(10) 'I bet the Germans had their work cut out, keeping you lot in order.'
H.R.H. The Duke of Edinburgh, 1978

THEIR HERITAGE

'Il convient de faire remarquer qu'à Guernesey je ne sors pas de la Normandie: le meilleur moyen d'obtenir justice à Guernesey est de pousser la Vieille "clameur de haro": La descendante au 37ième degré de Rollon s'empresse de faire examiner la question par ses tribunaux, dont les juges sont payés en billets de banque portant les 3 léopards normands.'

Max Gilbert: 'Pierres Mégalithiques en Normandie', 1956

(Translation)

'It is worth noting that in Guernsey I have by no means left Normandy: the best way of obtaining justice in Guernsey is to raise the ancient "Clameur de Haro": Rollo's descendant of the 37th generation employs it to have his case examined by his courts, the judges of which are paid in notes bearing the three Norman leopards.'

AUTHOR'S PREFACE

With considerable trepidation I once again crave the indulgence of the reading public —
this time for a companion to my *Bailiwick History* which seeks to supplement 'The
Islanders' Story' in general with treatment in particular of individual participants in that
story. It is, as far as I know, the first time that anything resembling a Bailiwick biographical dictionary has ever been attempted — the sole justification I can plead for writing
it. Choice of material in a compilation such as this inevitably presents many difficulties
and in this connection I should like to make it clear that all decisions regarding inclusions
and omissions have been arbitrary, based on a personal — and consequently fallible —
assessment of whether or not the career of a dead person commands sufficient interest to
warrant being recorded; or (in the case of a living one) is such as to render him or her
memorable to future generations. I apologise for any errors of judgment my selection
may reveal, assuring anyone who might thereby feel affronted that no slight of any nature
is intended. For obvious reasons no present members of either the Royal Court or of the
States of Guernsey have been included — nor indeed of the administrative organs of
Alderney and Sark.

I should like to express my gratitude to Mrs. Margaret W. Reid of the Lieutenant-
Governor's Office for extensive help with the Tupper and le Marchant families (even
going to the length of grovelling on her knees behind the pulpit in the Town Church and
with the aid of a torch scrutinizing the memorial tablet to Bailiff William le Marchant —
and finding it to be inaccurate!); to C. H. de Sausmarez Esq., M.B.E., Seigneur du Fief
de Sausmarez, for unstinting help in connection with members of his own illustrious
family — and also for wide-ranging advice in general, thanks to which sundry blemishes in
my original draft have been eliminated; to Miss Susan Jones of Elizabeth College Bursar's
Office for information connected with several Old Boys of that school; to Mr. Emile
Digard for assistance connected with Captain Herivel and especially to Mr. Nicholas
Herivel for providing invaluable additional details regarding his father; to Mrs. Monica
Mayley for recollections of her father, Mr. C. P. le Huray; to Mr. Stanley Noel for his
kindness in according me a number of interviews centred on his late brother Mr. Cecil
Noel; to Mrs. D. W. le Pelley and Mrs. Florence Head for similar help relating to their
respective husbands; to Mrs. Frances M. Fox (*née* Stevens–Guille) for supplying most
valued information regarding the Guille family of Saint George; to Mr John Sarre for
generously making available the fruits of his research into the Ecclesiastical Court proceedings against Pierre Levrier; to the Reverend Brother Christiantian of Les Vauxbelets
for providing a plethora of detail regarding Brother Déodat; to Dr. S. K. Kellett-Smith
and Messrs. C. H. de Sausmarez, J. Stevens-Cox and T. F. Priaulx for answering my
questions about themselves; to Mr. Peter Girard for particulars of Jonathan Castle's
education; to Mr. George Bramall for informed help concerning the architect John
Wilson; to Mr. Victor Coysh for enlightenment regarding 'Tommy' Rose and also for
elucidating problems in connection with William Toplis; to the Librarian of the Local
Studies Section of the Guille–Allès Library for information regarding the founders and

to all at the Priaulx Library for help of infinite variety too extensive to tabulate — though I am particularly beholden to Mr. Bernard Hassall for his kindness in sending me, remote in darkest Hornchurch, photocopies of newspaper cuttings relating to Lieutenant-Colonel H. W. Poat; to Mr. J. E. David for a wealth of detail regarding his forbears; to the late Mr. Frank Falla for reminiscences of those involved in 'G.U.N.S.' generally; to Mrs. Megan Monk for regaling me with memories of her father (Mr. Hubert Lanyon) in particular; and to Mr. W. R. B. Giffard for the interview he granted me in connection with the Sark distributors of the same underground news-sheet. I am further indebted to Mrs. Monk for preserving for me during my absence from the island the newspaper cutting which forms the Appendix to Part III — and to Mrs. Ronald Mauger for permission to reproduce it.

Outside Guernsey I owe a debt of thanks to Roy Dotrice and his charming wife, both of whom most generously found time in their busy lives to telephone me in response to my enquiries about the career of this accomplished actor; to Dr. John Arlott, O.B.E., for information regarding himself and to Lieutenant-Colonel P. A. Wootton for providing his own *curriculum vitæ*; to the Reverend W. N. Charles Wooldridge, B.D., of the Methodist Church Conference Office for details of Sir John Leale's ordination into that church's ministry; to Mrs. M. Halford of the Shropshire County Record Office for information on Sir Thomas Leighton; to the Secretary, Victoria Cross and George Cross Association, for recounting the exploits of Sir Reginald Hart, V.C. and to Lieutenant-Colonel C. D. Darroch of the Royal Hampshire Regiment for providing similar details regarding Brigadier H. W. le Patourel, V.C.; to the Right Worshipful A. J. W. McDonald, J.P., for assistance in connection with Major A. G. Wood and Lieutenant-Colonel J. B. Pym; to Mrs. Ann Monsarrat for information regarding her late husband; to Mrs. P. M. Wilson of the Alderney Museum for clarifying the marital connections of the le Mesurier family and also for providing baptismal references to Juge Thomas le Cocq of that island, to Mrs. Iris Godfray of Mannez, Alderney, for memories of her cousin George Sharp and additionally to Hilary Carré Esq., M.B.E., Sénéchal of Sark, together with his charming wife, who, not content with filling in further details regarding this remarkable character, also generously extended the hospitality of their home to my wife and me on a hot July evening in 1983; to the Staff of Winchester Diocesan Record Office and also to Mr. J. P. Hamon, Greffier of Sark, for their helpfulness over the Reverend J. L. V. Cachemaille; likewise conjointly to the Winchester Diocesan Record Office Staff and to Doctor Jean Grant of Sark for invaluable information about the clerical brothers Jacques and Pierre Levrier; to Mrs. Brenda Hough, Archivist to the General Synod of the Church of England, for shedding further light on Bishop John Fisher and the Reverend Louis Napoleon Seichan; to the Secretary, Council of Christians and Jews, for a synopsis of the career of Dr. James Parkes; to Miss Clare Siney of Chappell and Company Limited for her help regarding Robert Farnon; to Mr. Mark Rowles (also of Chappell's), Mrs. Veronica Wood of East Grinstead and Miss Bridie Corbet of Clarebridge, County Galway, Eire, for their conjoint helpfulness in connection with Alan Murray; to A. E. Money Esq., of Radley College, for insights into Dennis Price's background; to the Royal Aeronautical Society's Librarian for providing material about Sir Alan Cobham and Henri Biard; to the Borough Librarian, Royal Borough of Kensington and Chelsea, for background details relating to Freiherr von Aufsess; to the Head of the Reading Room Information Section, British Library, for similar help with Lieutenant-General Erich Müller; to Doctor Giessler of Bundesarchiv Militärarchiv, Freiburg, and also to Doctor Rohde of

Militärgeschichtliches Forschungsamt, Freiburg, for information on Lieutenant-General Graf von Schmettow and Vice-Admiral Friedrich Hüffmeier — and last (but by no means least) to my friend Mr. E. J. Morrall of Durham University, who so kindly provided a translation thereof for one whose German fails even to match the 'small Latin and less Greek' with which Ben Jonson credited Shakespeare.

A cause of especial gratification to me is the enhancement of the value of this book resulting from the inclusion therein of the supplement on early Bailiwick names contributed by Dr. S. K. Kellett-Smith, who has brought all his habitual thoroughness and supremely conscientious scholarship to bear upon its compilation.

Finally, as with my *Bailiwick History*, I am deeply beholden to my wife Constance, without whose help the burden of proof-reading would be beyond my ability to shoulder.

For the reader's convenience the sources of quotations incorporated into the text but whose origins are not therein indicated are listed at the end of the book.

Hornchurch, 1984   JAMES MARR

PICTORIAL ACKNOWLEDGEMENTS

I should like to thank the Bailiff of Guernsey, Sir Charles Frossard, for permission to publish the picture of Sir Ambrose Sherwill by Arthur Michael, the original of which hangs in the Entrance Hall of the Royal Court House. Furthermore, I owe similar debts of gratitude to the Reverend C. V. Colman for providing the picture of Mrs. Marianne Miller; to Mr. Roy Dotrice for that of himself; to Frank Hooten Esq. for the photograph of Henri Biard; to Mrs. M. A. Murphy for that of her father Sir Abraham Lainé; to Dr. R. O. Murray of Odiham, Hampshire, for the portrait of Sir Henry Gauvain; to Stanley Noel Esq. of L'Ancresse for supplying a picture of his brother Cecil Noel; to Mr. J. Stevens-Cox for the photograph of the Reverend J. L. V. Cachemaille; to Carel Toms for those of Henry Head and Brigadier French; and to Ian Yeaman Esq. of Les Granges de Beauvoir, for the picture of Pierre de Beauvoir. I am also beholden to the Guernsey Press Company Limited for the pictures of Sir Peter le Cheminant and Brigadier H. W. le Patourel, V.C. — and to the Ancient Monuments Committee for so kindly providing those of Daniel de Lisle Brock, Victor Hugo, Peter le Lièvre, Major-General John Gaspard de Marchant, and Sir Peter le Page Renouf. For all other pictures — the lion's share — I am indebted to the generous co-operation of the staff of the Priaulx Library, to whom I am most grateful. Last, but by no means least, I should like to offer my most sincere thanks to Carel Toms for tracking down the entire collection of pictures and photographing them preparatory to publication. His contribution has been invaluable, not only as regards the efficiency with which it was accomplished, but also because of the kindliness with which it was accompanied.

As far as end-paper material is concerned, I should like to thank the Winchester Diocesan Records Office for permission to reproduce Pierre Levrier's letter to Bishop John Thomas and to C. H. Sausmarez Esq., M.B.E., for sanctioning the reproduction of the Certificate supporting his great-grandfather's refusal to fight a second duel with Robert Porret le Marchant.

Hornchurch, 1984   JAMES MARR

EXPLANATORY NOTES

1. Apart from the supplement on early Bailiwick names, this book falls into three parts of which the first attempts to cover complete lifespans, whereas the second is by way of a rider devoted for the most part to those of whom the tale to tell is of 'one crowded hour of glorious life' rather than any cradle-to-grave narrative; while the third consists of a small number of kinship tables designed to clarify the inter-family links between many of those whose deeds are recounted in Parts I and II.

2. In arranging the alphabetical order of entries in both Part I and Part II prefixes have been ignored, so that for example, 'de Vic' is to be found under 'V' rather than 'D' and 'le Roy' under 'R' instead of 'L'.

3. 'Quod vide' alone ('q.v.') refers to another entry in Part I, whereas with the addition of an asterisk ('q.v.*') it draws attention to a further entry in Part II.

4. As their name indicates, the kinship tables in Part III are NOT meant to be exhaustive genealogies, but only to illustrate the relationships between various persons featured in either Part I or Part II. Thus (for example) in Table B only two of Joshua Gosselin's fourteen children are shown — Admiral Thomas le Marchant Gosselin as he himself is the subject of an entry, and his brother Joshua as through him the connection may be established with Sir Victor Carey and Edith Carey (both of whom are also accorded entries).

5. Letter(s) in block capitals following an entry heading indicate the kinship table(s) in Part III where the person concerned is featured. Thus, for example, 'METIVIER, GEORGE (1790-1881) (C)' refers the reader to Table C alone in connection with this poet, whereas 'BRIARD, JEAN (A/F)' shows that this privateer appears in both Table A and Table F.

6. In connection with dates it must be borne in mind that prior to 1752 the year began on 25 March (this being the notional day of the conception of Christ — Lady Day — if His birth be deemed as taking place on 25 December). Consequently any date between 1 January and 24 March was at the time seen as coming within what would now be considered the previous year (e.g. 27 February — the day of Sixtus IV's Neutrality Bull — was reckoned as falling within 1480 when it was issued: yet we think of it as 1481, having grown accustomed to looking on 1 January as New Year's Day). All pre-1752 dates in this book appear in accordance with this New Style, though it must be remembered that they were not so regarded at the time.

PART I

A BAILIWICK BIOGRAPHICAL DICTIONARY

A

AFTER, VERY REVEREND JOHN (died 1573).
The last Dean of Guernsey for nearly a century.
An English divine of extreme Puritan convictions,
John After originally came to Guernsey in 1561 as
a member of the Ecclesiastical Commission
appointed to enquire into the Crown's title to the
property of minor religious foundations, so that
such property might be realised to defray the
expenses of strengthening the island's defences,
and to finance the foundation of Elizabeth College.
The crypto-Catholicism of the island's leaders led
to the Commission's scope being widened in 1562,
to include responsibility for 'the good order of
the ecclesiastical government according to the
laws and usages of our realm of England'. In the
same year Helier Gosselin (q.v.) — who had sentenced Catherine Cauchés (q.v.) and her daughters
to the stake — was dismissed from the office of
Bailiff: a move followed the next year by his
confederate Jacques Amy (q.v.) being deprived
of his position as Dean. In his place Queen
Elizabeth appointed John After (whose sphere
was subsequently extended to include Jersey,
Chausey, Alderney and Sark). Strictly speaking
After at the outset only held decanal office in
an acting capacity. Although he himself claimed
that his appointment was confirmed in 1565, the
situation was not completely regularised until
14 June 1569 when, following Elizabeth's final
repudiation of the authority of the Bishop of
Coutances over the islands in favour of that of
the See of Winchester, Bishop Robert Horne
issued his official commission to John After to
operate as Dean.

If the Queen hoped (bearing in mind the
influence exerted on Protestant sentiment in the
island by Huguenot clerical refugees from France)
that the replacement of the vacillating Amy by a
committed Puritan would bring about the 'stabilising of ecclesiastical order' within the comprehensive ambit of Anglicanism, then she was
doomed to disappointment. The new Dean
immediately showed himself to be a fanatical
Calvinist who, far from seeking to uphold the
episcopal structure of Elizabeth's 'via media',
co-operated enthusiastically with Nicolas
Baudouin of Rouen (q.v.) who had already set up
a Presbyterian organization in the Town Church

and who, at the time of After's appointment, was
arranging (with the Governor's permission) for the
election of elders and deacons and the formation
of a consistory. What was more, John After
showed such little inclination to resist the introduction of the practices of Geneva by asserting his
spiritual authority as Dean that he sat in the inter-
island Synod which assembled the year following
his assumption of office merely in respect of his
livings of Saint Pierre du Bois and Saint Martin de
la Bellieuse, on a basis of complete equality with
the other incumbents. If (as seems to be the case)
in his heart of hearts he favoured the extinction of
his office, then he was remarkably successful, for,
after death in 1573 ended his ten years as 'Doyen
fainéant', no more Deans were appointed until
the forcible imposition of Anglicanism by Charles
II nearly 90 years later!

The extent of After's uncompromising Calvinism may be deduced from the Remonstrance
sent to the Queen-in-Council in 1564 and signed
by 2,000 islanders, complaining that he forbade
kneeling in church, the observance of fast-days,
the ringing of bells at services or the tolling of the
passing bell at burials; that he administered the
Sacrament without either surplice or cope to
communicants in a seated posture and interred
the dead without proper funeral rites. Furthermore this advanced reformer, in his zeal to cleanse
the ecclesiastical Augean stables of Popery, did not
hesitate to sell brasses, books, vestments and plate
— and to appropriate the proceeds! It was said
that when Dean After took up the living of Saint
Pierre du Bois, acting on an informer's story, he
was just in time to prevent one of the churchwardens from shipping over to France the church
silver, hidden in a barrel. What the Dean himself
did with the reclaimed silver is a mystery: he
certainly did not restore it to the church. Indeed,
the petitioners of 1564 ended their catalogue of
protest with the taunt — '*Jean After, arrivé dans
l'île en 1561 peneurieux et necessiteux, avait en
trois ans reussi à s'emparer du decanat, des deux
cures de Saint Martin de la bellouse et de Saint
Pierre du bosq, et d'un prieure, avec des dimes
rentes fourments et autres commodities qui,
reunis, donnaient un revenu considerable dont il
profitait; il s'etait en dernier lieu, fait conceder*

l'île de Herm en fief-ferme. Pourtant, il ne sait ni d'enseigner ni de prêcher'.

Hostility between sheep and shepherd was mutual. In a report to Cecil in 1566 John After accused the people of Guernsey of harbouring 'murderers, thieves and whoremongers that daily fly out of Normandy' and thereby becoming so depraved that 'the Bulls from Rome be in such singular recommendation that no laws of the realm can yet pull back the unbridled sort from Rome nor the French favourers of the same'.

John After was the pivotal figure in the events which led to the islands ceasing to be *de facto* subject to the Bishop of Coutances, despite the fact that since 1499 they had been *de jure* within the See of Winchester. This anomaly had been tolerated because of the persistence of the idea that a formal separation of the archipelago from the Diocese of Coutances might impair the title of the Crown to the Duchy of Normandy! Thus, as late as 1565, after representations by the Bishop of Coutances, an Order-in-Council instructed the island authorities to ensure that all accustomed dues should continue to be paid to him. On hearing of this Order the Bishop over-reached himself, taking proceedings through his Proctors in the Royal Court of Guernsey against the Dean, claiming possession of the Deanery and the Dean's benefices on the grounds that he had not been canonically instituted by the Bishop nor paid his fees. To this Dean After retorted that he would not recognise the Bishop's claims, unless he took the oath of allegiance to the Queen and renounced papal authority. The matter was then referred to the Privy Council, which of course found the Bishop's attempt to interfere with the Queen's ecclesiastical appointments absolutely intolerable. The upshot was the Order-in-Council of 1569 which finally separated the islands from Coutances and placed them firmly under the jurisdiction of the Bishop of Winchester — a jurisdiction which persists to the present day.

'John After, having arrived in the island in 1561 penurious and necessitous, had in three years succeeded in possessing himself of the Deanery, of the two livings of Saint Martin de la Bellouse and of Saint Pierre du Bosq, and of a priory, with tithes, wheat rentes and other assets which, all told, yielded a considerable revenue of which he profited; in the last place he had himself granted the Island of Herm as a fee-farm holding. For all that, he is able neither to teach nor to preach'.

ALLAIRE, JEAN (1763-1846). *A mercilessly mercenary Midas.* The period from the Glorious Revolution to the Battle of Waterloo was the great era of privateering — an activity in which men from the Bailiwick played a prominent part, several of them becoming exceedingly rich in the process. In such ventures during the Napoleonic Wars Jean Allaire was particularly successful, thanks to the fact that he was utterly unscrupulous and perfectly prepared to stretch privateering to cover piracy in order to procure profitable prizes. The opportunities for such nefarious villainy were plentiful, as a British ship attacked by a vessel flying the French flag and manned by a French-speaking crew would naturally assume that its assailants were what they purported to be; so that all the appearances of an entirely legitimate act of war prevailed. By such deplorable devices did Allaire amass the vast fortune whereby the Fief of Sark came into the hands of his descendants, the present Seigneur (Mr. John Michael Beaumont) being his great-great-great-great-grandson.

There is a widespread assumption that this disreputable corsair availed himself of Jethou as a base from which to launch his onslaughts. If there is any truth in this belief, then such a use of the island must have been with the connivance of its tenant (Phillip de Quesnel) as Allaire himself did not acquire the lease of Jethou until 1822 — seven years after Waterloo and rather late in the day for privateering! It is, of course, possible that the island may have been used occasionally without de Quesnel's knowledge, Allaire taking advantage of the tenant's absence from time to time. From 1822 onwards Jean Allaire remained the Tenant of Jethou until his death and during his tenancy (c. 1825) the satellite islet of Crevichon was quarried for the granite of which the steps of St Paul's Cathedral reputedly consist.

In 1844, two years before Allaire's death, Ernest Le Pelley (the Seigneur of Sark) was in sore straits. For nine years silver mining ventures in Little Sark had staggered from one disaster to the next and in desperation Le Pelley raised a mortgage of £4,000 on the security of his Fief from the old freebooter, now said to be the richest man in Guernsey. Eight years later Ernest's son and successor, Pierre Carey Le Pelley, failed to meet the interest payments: whereupon Allaire's daughter Marie, the widow of Thomas Guérin Collings, foreclosed and obtained the Seignory of Sark on payment of £1,383 6s. 8d. after the mortgage and its overdue interest had been deducted from an agreed purchase price of £6,000.

The late Dame de Sercq regarded her great-great-grandfather as 'guilty of an unchristian temper, debauchery and iniquity'. As an example of her forbear's wicked and callous behaviour she cited the case of an old woman who betook herself to Jean Allaire's residence (the property called 'Le Mont Durant', now Government House) to implore mercy for her son who had been accused of sheep-stealing. It appears that Allaire and his cronies were carousing in an upper room and seizing the beldame, they pushed her down the stairs and killed her by breaking her neck. Dame Sibyl alleged that as a consequence the house became haunted, with the sound of a body bumping from stair to stair disturbing the silent watches of the night. Furthermore, she asserted that her ancestor's misdeeds had brought a curse on the premises as a result of which any closing of the driveway gates would occasion the death of the head of the household! Suffice it to say that during his occupancy of the dwelling while Lieutenant-Governor between 1925 and 1929 Lord Sackville had the staircase demolished and the drive gates removed, secretly burying a bottle of wine on the spot to remove the spell! To this day drive gates remain conspicuous by their absence. One is driven to conclude that, as with John Brown, Jean Allaire's soul — a black one — goes marching on!

ALLÈS, FRDERICK MANSELL (1818–1895). *Co-founder of the Guille–Allès Library.* The lifelong friend and collaborator of Thomas Guille (q.v.), Allès too emigrated to the United States of America as a young man and there, by industry and thrift, accumulated the wealth which enabled him to contribute massively towards the establishment of Guernsey's magnificent library — *see* 'Guille, Thomas'.

AMY, REV. JACQUES (*c.* 1500–*c.* 1586). *Guernsey's 'Vicar of Bray'.* Born in Jersey *c.* 1500 and originally ordained as a Roman Catholic priest at Coutances in 1525, this religious trimmer meekly accepted Henry VIII's repudiation of papal authority and then, on becoming Dean of Guernsey shortly after the accession of Edward VI, he slid effortlessly from the moderate Protestantism of the early years of the boy-king's reign to the extreme evangelicalism of its final months; reverted to the Church of Rome when Mary I succeeded her half-brother; and then gave lip-service to the Elizabethan 'via media' for four years from 1559, contriving to retain his decanal appointment uninterruptedly from 1547 to 1563. Thereafter for almost 20 years he embraced the island's Calvinist establishment — a ruthless opportunist who clung like a leech to the incumbency of St Saviour's through all the varying hues of the doctrinal and liturgical spectra from 1547 to 1579: and even added that of St Pierre du Bois for good measure during his last four years as Dean!

The materialistic acquisitiveness characterising Amy's cynical attitude to his ministerial office is well exemplified by the doggedness with which he attempted to establish his entitlement to sundry tithes (known as *Dimes Desertes*) from the parishioners of St Saviour's, enlisting the support of the Parochial Douzaine, the Royal Court and even the Governor himself, the better to advance his claims and line his pocket.

The episode for which this infamous time-server is notorious occurred in 1556. Anxious to display his fervour for the Roman Catholicism to which he had returned, Dean Amy brought charges of heresy against Catherine Cauchés (q.v.) and her two daughters Guillemine and Perotine — the latter the wife of David Jorés. The unfortunate women were found guilty by the Court at the prompting of the Bailiff, Helier Gosselin (q.v.) — who was also eager to show his zeal for the faith he had abjured in Edward VI's reign — and were burnt at the stake. In her death agony Perotine gave birth to a child who, on Gosselin's orders, was thrown back into the flames to burn with his mother. These gruesome details are substantiated by the terms of the petition to Elizabeth I filed in December 1558 by Catherine Cauchés' brother Matthew, who solicited the return to him, as the rightful heir, of the property (which had been confiscated) of his martyred sister and nieces. The Rev. John Fox in his *Christian Martyrdom* records that 'the dean who had been instrumental in the tragical event was committed to prison and dispossessed of all his livings'. Such retribution, however, was by no means immediate. In 1562 this clerical chameleon, by an abject recantation of Roman Catholicism, sought to survive. He petitioned the Queen, acknowledging his guilt and praying for pardon — and was still Dean when Elizabeth I in the same year addressed a warrant instructing the Ecclesiastical Commissioners appointed the previous year 'to direct order to our captain or his lieutenant *and to the dean* and certain of the jurats . . . for the good order of the ecclesiastical government'. The following year, however, he was taken into custody and replaced by John After (q.v.), one of the aforementioned Commissioners. In 1565 Amy was summoned to appear before the Privy Council at Windsor.

Although he technically remained the incumbent of St Saviour's, he was not permitted to exercise his ministry until ten years later, when he at last received a full pardon and was allowed to return to his living which he retained (now as a Presbyterian) until seven years before his death in c. 1586.

ANDROS, AMIAS (1610–1674). *A right resolute Royalist*. (A). Born in 1610, Amias Andros, Seigneur du Fief de Sausmarez, became while still a young man the Master of Ceremonies at the Court of King Charles I. Here, at the age of 27, he paid homage to the King for his Fief when he succeeded to it on the death of his father — the first recorded occasion when such homage by a Guernsey Seigneur was rendered to the Sovereign in person. Apart from similar homage paid to Charles II on 6 August 1674 by his son Edmund (q.v.), such a ceremony was not to be repeated until 1921!

Not long after the outbreak of the Civil War, Charles I in 1643 appointed Andros Bailiff of Guernsey to replace the other Royalist, Jean de Quetteville (q.v.), who had been deposed and placed under arrest by the island's entrenched Puritan establishment. This appointment was little more than a gesture, as it was obviously impossible for the new Bailiff to exercise his office. Nevertheless the same year saw him in Castle Cornet loyally standing by Sir Peter Osborne (q.v.), the Lieutenant-Governor, who was holding the fortress for the King.

At the Restoration of Charles II Andros (who has been described as one of the Merry Monarch's 'boon companions'), together with Nathaniel Darell, filed a petition to the King on behalf of the people of Guernsey, as they had supported the monarch's enemies throughout the constitutional struggle. In granting his royal pardon Charles II specifically excluded Amias Andros therefrom as he had 'no need to be included in the general pardon'. Andros returned to Guernsey in 1661 and assumed the office of Bailiff to which he had been appointed 18 years previously, exercising it until his death. He subsequently became a General (possibly the last General) of the Guernsey Militia. On his death he was buried in St Martin's church under the tower which divides the south nave from the choir.

ANDROS, SIR EDMUND (1637–1713/14). *The 'Bailiff over the Water'*. (A). Born in 1637, Edmund Andros in 1674 succeeded his father Amias (q.v.) as Seigneur of the Fief de Sausmarez.

He also inherited from his parent the office of Bailiff of Guernsey, which he held until his death. For the greater part of this long period, however, he was in no position to exercise the functions either of Bailiff or of Seigneur as he was far away on the other side of the Atlantic Ocean! In that self-same year of 1674 he became the Governor of New York, a post which he held until 1681 when he was recalled after having become embroiled in squabbles with neighbouring colonial governors — especially with Phillip de Carteret, the Jerseyman who was Governor of East Jersey. In the meantime, however, he had been knighted in 1678.

The year after his return from the New World (1682) Sir Edmund bought from Lady Elizabeth de Carteret (the widow of Sir George Carteret) for the sum of £200 the residue of her late husband's Patent whereby he had enjoyed the Lordship of Alderney. After the purchase Sir Edmund voluntarily resigned his rights to the Crown, whereupon a fresh Patent was issued in 1683 granting Alderney to him and his heirs for ninety-nine years at an annual rent of 20 marks (£13 6s. 8d.). Alderney, however, was destined to see even less of him than did Guernsey as two years later in 1685 James II on his accession appointed Sir Edmund as Governor of New England. Before leaving for America Sir Edmund delegated his powers in the island (including the command of the Alderney Militia) to Thomas Le Mesurier who through his wife, Rachel de Sausmarez, was a distant relation, Sir Edmund himself having a de Sausmarez ancestress in the person of his great-great-grandmother Judith.

In New England Sir Edmund vigorously sought to implement the policies of James II, aiming at breaking the power of the local Puritan oligarchies. As a consequence he became so disliked that in 1689 he was seized by the people of Boston and sent to England for trial. On his arrival in London, however, he was released for lack of concrete evidence against him, and three years later (in 1692) William III made him Governor of Virginia, where he remained until 1698.

At last, early in the 18th century, Guernsey saw something of its Bailiff! In the year 1704 Queen Anne created Sir Edmund the island's Lieutenant-Governor under Christopher, Viscount Hatton of Gretton (q.v.) as Governor, and he held this post as well as that of Bailiff for two years until 1706. By now he was 69 years of age and relinquished his Lieutenant-Governorship. Although still remaining Bailiff (and also, of course, 'Governor' of Alderney) he exercised neither office, but retired to London where he spent his declining years, dying in February 1714. He bequeathed the Fief de Sausmarez to his nephew John Andros provided a 'good suitable house' was built within two years — hence the present Manor House. In 1748 John's son Charles sold the manor to John de Sausmarez and the fief thereby reverted to its original owners.

ARNOLD, SIR WILLIAM HENRY, K.B.E. (1903–1973). *A Bailiff adept as administrator and negotiator.* Born at 'Le Jean', Les Amballes, on 5 August 1903, to Emma Caroline (née le Patourel), the wife of William John Arnold of Les Landes Farm in the Castel, sometime Manager of the Guernsey Branch of the National Provincial Bank, young William Henry — the youngest of the 11 children — was educated at the Boys' Intermediate School, on leaving which he entered the practice of his maternal uncle, Advocate H. A. le Patourel.

The aspiring lawyer followed this apprenticeship by going up to l'Université de Caen (La Faculté de Droit), emerging in 1923 as Bachelier-en-Droit; after which he studied at Gray's Inn before being called to the English Bar in 1926. The next year, qualified in both Norman and English Law, he was called to the Guernsey Bar and set up in practice as an Advocate of the Royal Court.

In 1930 Advocate Arnold supplemented his labours at the Bar by entering into political life with his election as one of the eight Deputies representing District Number 1 (St Peter-Port) in the States of Deliberation and of Election. He continued thus until 1940 when he joined the British Army, serving on the staff of the Judge Advocate General and rising from Staff Captain to become the head of the legal staff of the civil affairs unit with the rank of Colonel. In this capacity he landed in Guernsey at 2 a.m. on Liberation Day, having previously been responsible for preparing the whole of the defence regulations to operate in the Bailiwick in the immediate post-war period. A week later, in the company of Brigadier A. E. Snow and Judge F. G. French (q.v.) he visited Alderney, when the decision was reached that the island's heavily mined condition rendered it temporarily unsafe for any except military personnel.

Appointed H.M. Procureur in 1946, William Arnold was made a Commander of the Most Excellent Order of the British Empire in 1955 and on 11 November 1959, succeeded Sir Ambrose Sherwill (q.v.) as Bailiff. Following in the wake of so charismatic a figure inevitably

poses considerable difficulties (comparable to those experienced by Clement Attlee when he stepped into the shoes of Winston Churchill); but the new occupant of Guernsey's supreme office overcame these to such effect that three years later (in 1963) he received from Her Majesty the Queen the accolade of knighthood. The uncertainty and trepidation which beset the island as a result of the United Kingdom's application to join the European Economic Community — an application which, *prima facie*, also automatically involved Guernsey as a territory for the external relations of which the applicant was responsible — confronted Sir William with onerous responsibilities which he shouldered with diligence and supreme efficiency. Bearing in mind the old adage that 'unity is strength', he induced Jersey, Gibraltar and the Isle of Man to make joint cause with his Bailiwick in seeking alleviation of the heavy burdens which unmitigated adherence to the Treaty of Rome would entail; and it was largely thanks to his efforts that a special status of 'in but half out' was accorded to the Channel Isles when they entered into membership of the Community. His achievement in this connection was recognised early in 1973 on the occasion of an honorary Doctorate of Laws being conferred on him by Southampton University, the accompanying citation speaking of his filling 'a supremely difficult role . . . to perfection' and further commenting that 'his diplomacy has extended to the Channel Islands as a whole, even to the Isle of Man and Gibraltar, as it was he very largely who persuaded them all to speak with one voice when they shivered on the brink of the Common Market'.

Sir William Arnold was advanced to the rank of Knight Commander of the Most Excellent Order of the British Empire as one of the recipients of the 1973 Birthday Honours — a promotion awarded on the eve of what was anticipated as his retirement on his seventieth birthday during the coming August. Such a retirement, however, was not to be. The chronic heart disease from which he had long suffered abruptly claimed Guernsey's Bailiff as its victim on 21 July 1973, early in the morning at his Cobo home of 'Les Figuiers'.

d'AUBIGNY, PHILIPPE (died 1236). *The Saviour of the Isles, 'sans peur et sans reproche'.* It is largely due to the exploits of this 13th century warrior that the course of history has endowed the Channel Isles with an autonomous status in association first with the English and subsequently with the British Crown, instead of being mere off-shore French islands such as Chausey. After a two-year struggle for the control of the archipelago between 1204 and 1206 had finally left the islands in the hands of King John (q.v.), the difficult task of safeguarding Guernsey, Alderney and Herm was entrusted by the King to Philippe d'Aubigny, who became Warden of the three isles in 1207. d'Aubigny immediately gave urgent attention to the security of St Peter-Port's roadstead (so invaluable as a port of call in the communications between England and John's remaining continental lands in Gascony) and to this end pressed ahead vigorously with the construction of Castle Cornet.

The wisdom of these precautions became evident in 1212 when Eustace the Monk (q.v.) deserted John in favour of Philip Augustus of France in whose interest he seized the archipelago. By brilliant exertions d'Aubigny rapidly expelled the freebooter from all the islands save Sark, which Eustace managed to hold and which he garrisoned with a force of his followers. So impressed was John with the efficiency which d'Aubigny had displayed that he extended his responsibility the same year by making him Warden of Jersey as well as of Guernsey, Alderney and Herm.

Early in 1214 d'Aubigny was serving his King in Poitou, where John still maintained a precarious foothold. He then returned to the islands and organised an onslaught on the ex-monk's Sark garrison which met with complete success, the island being regained and many of Eustace's force being sent as prisoners to Winchester. The King promptly appointed d'Aubigny Warden of Sark also, and released the hostages he had been holding from the islands as a reward for the part many islanders had played in this operation.

It was about this time that John showed the high esteem in which he held d'Aubigny by appointing him tutor to the boy Prince Henry (the future Henry III). Thus, although he remained the Warden of the Isles, d'Aubigny now spent long periods in England. He was, indeed, present at Runnymede on that momentous 19th day of June in 1215, and as a result became one of the signatories of Magna Carta.

d'Aubigny's absence from the islands was prolonged by his going to John's support during the King's struggle with the barons after Magna Carta. Eustace the Monk took advantage of this to seize the archipelago once again on behalf of the French King in 1216, an operation synchronized with the invasion of England by the French

King's son, Prince Louis. However, shortly after John's death d'Aubigny defeated Eustace at the naval battle off Sandwich and had him beheaded on his own quarter-deck. The upshot was that the Treaty of Lambeth (1217) guaranteed the return of the islands to 'the Lord Henry of England'. Thanks to Philippe d'Aubigny's exertions, therefore, the islands were able to enjoy reasonable tranquility for the next three-quarters of a century, their possession by the English Crown being implicitly recognized by Louis IX in the Treaty of Paris of 1259.

In 1220 d'Aubigny relinquished his custody of the Isles in favour of his nephew (also called Philippe d'Aubigny) and in 1229 he left for the Holy Land in the entourage of the Emperor Frederick II (*Stupor Mundi*). There he died in 1236; he was buried in the precincts of the Church of the Holy Sepulchre.

AUFSESS, HANS, FREIHERR VON UND ZU AUFSESS (1906–). *A chivalrous foe*. Hans Max Otto Hermann Karl Gustav, Freiherr von und zu Aufsess, a nobleman whose ancestral seat is the 9th century Upper Franconian Schloss Oberaufsess near Nuremberg in Bavaria, was born on 4 August 1906 at Berchtesgaden. On 31 March 1934 he married Marie Elizabeth von Klipstein, a sculptress who hailed from Posen (then in Germany, but nowadays Poznan in Poland) who bore him two daughters. Possessed of a rare versatility of talent, the Freiherr was an expert at estate management, directing the exploitation of timber and the cultivation of crops on his lands — and at the same time was a successful lawyer. Furthermore, he had stylish gifts as a writer and showed a considerable flair as a photographic artist, producing during the Occupation a magnificent book of photographs of the Channel Islands entitled *Ein Bilderbogen von den Kanalinseln*.

This gentleman of wide culture arrived in the islands early in 1942 to serve on the staff of the Feldkommandantur (the German administrative department — replaced in May 1944 by the Platzkommandantur — responsible for civilian affairs, where he later became Chief of Administration). It transpired that between him and the late Dame de Sercq (to whom he referred in his book as 'Herrscherin von Sark') there existed a distant kinship. In the September following his arrival, much against his will and in spite of his protests, he was obliged to implement the deportation ordinance against those born outside the islands; his pleas for clemency being over-ruled as the order stemmed from Hitler personally.

In February 1943 a further order required that former officers of the British Army be deported. Major Ambrose Sherwill (q.v.) upbraided von Aufsess over the inclusion in the list of his wife and two young sons. Stung by this taunt about punitive action against women and children, the Baron appealed to General Müller (who was Commander-in-Chief — Befehlshaber — at the time) but was rebuffed. He nevertheless ignored the order as far as Mrs. Sherwill and her two sons were concerned, allowing them to stay while officially recording them as having gone to Germany. (Years later when Sir Ambrose and Lady Sherwill called on him whilst on holiday in Bavaria and asked what would have happened had General Müller (q.v.) discovered this deception, von Aufsess answered by drawing a finger across his throat!)

Towards the end of the war Freifrau 'Marilis' von Aufsess was arrested by the Gestapo after having incautiously said, 'What a pity they did not succeed' on hearing of the attempted assassination of Hitler. At the same time von Aufsess himself felt perilously insecure after the replacement of von Schmettow (q.v.) as Befehlshaber by the fervent Nazi, Vice-Admiral Hüffmeier (q.v.) — as is plain from his employment of the first person plural in his warning to the Bailiff of Jersey: '*Méfiez-vous, nous sommes des hommes suspects!*' Accordingly he made plans to escape from the islands and surrender to the Allies. Finding himself unable to carry out this project, he plotted with Freiherr von Heldorf to do away with Hüffmeier who, intransigent as ever planned to hold the archipelago as the last bastion of the Third Reich. The plot was to waylay the Vice-Admiral on one of his regular visits to his Mess at Castle Carey and there to kill him, but in this too the Bavarian baron was frustrated.

On 8 May 1945 it was Baron von Aufsess who, as Platzkommandant in Guernsey since the previous month, announced to the Bailiff and the President of the Controlling Committee, '*Der Krieg ist zu Ende, und in den Kanalinseln auch*'. For him there followed two tormenting years as a prisoner of war in England with no news of his wife, not even being able to discover whether or not she had survived imprisonment by the Gestapo. At last, late in 1947, they were re-united at Oberaufsess where the Baron resumed his career as a solicitor and attorney specialising in tax law; later becoming Director-General of the High Ducal administration of Saxe-Coburg. Some years later, grateful for the Freiherr's chivalry towards her two sons and herself, Lady Sherwill wrote in the Visitors' Book at the Schloss: 'May God bless the House of Aufsess. Now the war is over, we'll always be friends'.

B

BANKS, MAJOR-GENERAL SIR THOMAS MACDONALD ('DONALD'), K.C.B., D.S.O., M.C., T.D. (1891-1975). *The originator of the Guernsey Society who set the sea on fire!* Baptised Thomas Macdonald, but throughout his life known as 'Donald' *tout court*, this outstanding Guernseyman was born in St Peter-Port on 31 March 1891 to Margaret Elizabeth (née Roebuck), the wife of Thomas Brownsort Banks, of what was then a well-known stationery firm. After leaving Elizabeth College (where he was educated between 1899 and 1909) he crossed to the United Kingdom and entered the Post Office Department of the British Civil Service. He was 23 when the First World War broke out and he served in it with distinction, commanding both the 10th Battalion of the Essex Regiment and the 8th Battalion of the Royal Berkshire Regiment. In 1917 he was awarded both the Military Cross and le Croix de Guerre.

After the First World War Banks became the Private Secretary to four Post Masters General and in 1931 he was made Controller of the Post Office Savings Bank (as the National Savings Bank was then called). He was also responsible for such telephonic innovations as '999' and 'TIM'. In 1936 he was appointed Permanent Secretary to the Air Ministry and in 1938 Permanent Under-Secretary of State for Air. In this capacity he set up the Empire Air Training Scheme and visited Australia and New Zealand to promote aircraft production. For his services he was made a C.B. and later a K.C.B.

In the Second World War Sir Donald became Director-General of the Petroleum Warfare Department, the story of which he related in his book *Flame Over Britain*. Dramatic testimony for his success in this field is provided by Mr. Peter Fleming in his *Invasion 1940* where he recounts that Admiral Canaris had only to exhibit to the

German General Staff a purloined film showing the results of the Petroleum Warfare Department's experiment at 'setting the sea on fire' to secure the cancellation of 'Sea Lion', the invasion of Britain!

When the islands were occupied Sir Donald was greatly concerned over the welfare of refugees, feeling that there was a considerable need for an informed voice and body of opinion among Guernsey exiles that could influence the government and assist the insular authorities after liberation. With the aim of creating such a body he called together a meeting attended, *inter alia*, by Air Commodore Henry Brock, C.B., D.S.O.; Vincent Grantham, Chairman of the Chartered Bank; Major E. R. B. Ozanne and Colonel Malan. From this initiative there developed the Guernsey Society, founded in 1943 'to promote the welfare of Guernsey and to collaborate in furthering the common interests of the Channel Islands', with Sir Donald as its Chairman for the first two years of its life.

After the War Sir Donald held a series of distinguished posts, serving as a member of the International Civil Aviation Organization, the Deputy Chairman of the Air Transport Advisory Council; a Director of both De La Rue and Standard Telephone and Cable; and as Chairman of the Anglo–Chinese Chamber of Commerce. His retirement was spent at Cadnam Lodge in the New Forest, where he kept a herd of Guernseys. He died in July 1975.

BAUDOUIN, REVEREND NICOLAS (*c.* 1535–1613). *The founder of Guernsey's Calvinist system*. The scarcely veiled Roman Catholic sympathies of most of Guernsey's leading figures at the time of Elizabeth I's accession augured ill for compliance with the 1559 Acts of Supremacy and Uniformity, and for the achievement in the island of a compromise ecclesiastical settlement such as that arrived at in England. The marked local polarisation of religious sentiment led the small Protestant faction among the leading families to conclude that steps to ensure a reformed church establishment — not to mention their personal safety — had to be taken as a matter of urgency. The upshot was that at the instigation of Guillaume de Beauvoir (who was a friend of Jean Calvin himself, and was a Deacon of the English church at Geneva) a deputation was sent to Calvin asking for French-speaking pastors to tend the island's flock. Outstanding among those who came over from the Continent as a result of this request was the energetic and zealous Nicolas

Baudouin of Rouen, who in 1559 obtained the living of St Peter-Port, where he initiated the island's Calvinist system and rapidly assumed an arbitral position in Guernsey's life, secular as well as spiritual.

Treading warily at first, he initially conformed more or less to the formularies required by the Act of Uniformity. However, Baudouin soon felt secure enough to adopt a Presbyterian liturgical pattern in the Town Church. Then, with John After (q.v.) in office as a Calvinistic Dean (1563) he sought the Governor's permission to arrange for the election of elders and deacons and the formation of a consistory. The Governor — Sir Francis Chamberlayne (q.v.), a devout Roman Catholic — doubtless felt that there was little to choose between one heresy and another and accordingly gave his consent. Despite the formal remonstrance sent to the Queen-in-Council in 1564, carrying 2,000 signatures and protesting at the activities of Baudouin as much as at those of John After, the Governor's authorisation was followed in 1565 by an Order-in-Council permitting the church in St Peter-Port to follow the Geneva order provided the other parishes adhered to the Anglican rite — a proviso that was immediately to prove unenforceable because of the lack of French-speaking Anglican clergy. Presbyterianism was established and Baudouin triumphant.

The extent of the power wielded by Baudouin is well illustrated in the case of Nicolas Carey. As a result of Carey being excommunicated by Baudouin for a trivial offence he was suspended from his office as Jurat — and even when the unfortunate man had obtained letters of absolution from the Archbishop of Canterbury, the Royal Court hesitated to re-admit him to his legal functions because of the continued disapproval of the Ministers of the island's Colloque, who took their cue from St Peter Port's incumbent! It took all the prestige of the Governor, Sir Thomas Leighton (q.v.), to obtain a fair hearing of the case, establishing that Carey's offence had been minor and his excommunication had therefore been frivolous, so that at last he was reinstated as a Jurat. It is hard to exaggerate the strength of a minister's position when his denial of the Sacrament to a judge can operate to suspend him from his judicial functions!

After a quarter of a century of dominance in insular affairs, Baudouin found himself at the epicentre of a storm that was mostly of his own making, arising as it did from his entering the lists against his nominal superior, the Bishop of

Winchester. Although his office was antithetical to the fundamental Presbyterian position, Baudouin and his colleagues were prepared to tolerate their technical subordination to the Bishop, so long as he was content to pursue a policy of *faineance*. In 1581, however, an Order-in-Council provided that probate and the administration of the revenues of vacant benefices should be ordered by the Bishop of Winchester. In the light of this the Bishop (there being no Dean) appointed the Procureur, Louis de Vic (q.v.), as his Commissary to deal with wills and other ecclesiastical business. Outraged by this overt episcopal intrusion into Guernsey's Presbyterian establishment, Baudouin incited his fellow ministers in 1582 to bring trumped-up charges against de Vic.

Although himself an ardent Calvinist, this shameful exhibition of 'malice and all uncharitableness' was too much for the Governor, Sir Thomas Leighton (q.v.) and he stood by de Vic, asking the Queen's Secretary of State, Sir Francis Walsingham to deal with the matter — which ended with the Procureur being vindicated. Upon de Vic's acquittal Baudouin, professing fear for his life, sailed for England in 1583. When he arrived in London Walsingham advised him to resign his benefice in the interests of the peace of the island, and gave him a testimonial, thanks to which Baudouin was able to obtain a living in Jersey (1584). He returned, however, when tempers had cooled, resuming the incumbency of St Peter-Port in 1598 and retaining it as a revered figure until his death in his late seventies in 1613.

de BEAUVOIR, PIERRE: SIEUR DES GRANGES (1599-1678). *Guernsey's leading 'Roundhead'.*

Pierre de Beauvoir was known to contemporaries as le Sieur des Granges because of his proprietorship of the estate of that name at the top of the Rohais which had been acquired by his father Jacques in 1603. He was the scion of a family steeped in Calvinist tradition, which in an earlier generation had produced Guillaume de Beauvoir, Bailiff 1571–81, who in his youth had been a personal friend in Geneva of Calvin himself, and who had been instrumental in bringing the 'father' of Guernsey's Calvinist establishment — Nicolas Baudouin (q.v.), to the island.

No Guernseyman with such a background was likely to look kindly on the Arminian Anglicanism of the King's entourage, especially when Archbishop Laud announced in 1637 his intention of imposing on the island conformity with the requirements and usages of the Church of England. Less exalted considerations, however, also disposed le Sieur des Granges against his monarch. Besides being a landholder de Beauvoir was a prominent merchant trading with Spain and France. As such he lost heavily when Buckingham's Ile de Rhé fiasco in 1627 led Cardinal Richelieu to forbid all commerce with the islands. Lastly, he felt a strong antipathy towards the Lieutenant-Governor, Sir Peter Osborne (q.v.), sharing fully in the general resentment aroused in Guernsey in 1628 when Sir Peter attempted to use martial law to enforce a levy for the upkeep of the garrison.

When fighting started in England, therefore, it is hardly surprising that Pierre de Beauvoir emerged as Guernsey's leading anti-Royalist. He, his brother-in-law Pierre Carey, and his fellow Jurat Jacques de Havilland formed a triumvirate to act on behalf of Parliament, being styled its Commissioners. Early in March 1643 de Beauvoir called on Sir Peter Osborne in his fastness of Castle Cornet to submit and was answered on 11 March by a salvo from the fortress' guns. The Civil War in Guernsey had begun. Soon afterwards de Beauvoir arrested and deposed the Royalist Bailiff, Jean de Quetteville (q.v.).

Before Christmas arrived, however, all three Commissioners came within an ace of death. On 21 October they were inveigled by Captain Bowden, an erstwhile Parliamentary supporter who (unknown to them) had changed sides, to board his ship, *The Bramble*. They were taken to Castle Cornet where they were incarcerated in the Carey Tower. On 3 December they escaped with the help of a rope made from some flax they had found in the Tower, dashing over the rocks back to St Peter-Port at low tide — thus getting away within minutes of the arrival from England of the Royal Writ for their execution!

Just over a year later, on Christmas Eve 1644, de Beauvoir, freshly back from a visit to London, was sworn in as the Bailiff nominated by Parliament. In February 1647, however, his tenure of office was challenged by the deposed Jean de Quetteville (who was once more at large) and a tussle between the rivals ensued which was not settled until the following December when Parliament sent four M.P.s to Guernsey to confirm its nominee in power.

Nevertheless Pierre de Beauvoir's tenure of office did not in the event remain secure. Parliament gave — and Parliament could take away! It deposed him in 1651, re-appointed him in 1652 and then removed him again in 1653, issuing an Order whereby the office of Bailiff was to be held by each of the Jurats in turn for a month at a time. In 1656, however, de Beauvoir was again reinstated and held office until the Restoration, when he retired into obscurity for the rest of his days, his life being spared thanks to the General Pardon granted by Charles II to most of his father's enemies.

BIARD, CAPTAIN HENRI CHARLES (1891–1966). *Rocquaine's Dare-devil of the Skies.* This intrepid aeronaut who later in life, when employed by the States' Meteorological Station, resided for several years in a bungalow at Rocquaine, and who was destined at the age of 32 to usher in a new era in the history of the island, was born in Guildford in December 1891. Taking to the air as a youth of 19 at a time when aviation was very much in its infancy and engaging in it was still a most hazardous venture, he learned to fly in 1911 and became the holder of Aviation Certificate Number 218. Having thus qualified as a pilot, he became an Instructor with the Graham White Aviation Company.

During the First World War Henri Biard served with the Royal Naval Air Service. With the coming of peace he embarked on a career as a test pilot with Supermarine Aviation (the firm which was later to develop the 'Spitfire') and was employed in this capacity from 1919 to 1933. It was during this period that Biard achieved his greatest triumph. This was in the year 1922 when he won the Schneider Trophy race at an average speed of 145.7 m.p.h., the contest taking place in Naples. His victory prevented the Trophy being retained in perpetuity by Italy, the country which had won the two previous races at Venice in 1920 and 1921 and which would have won the Trophy outright had it secured a third successive victory. (This feat was, of course, ultimately achieved by Great Britain by the third successive British victory in 1931). Biard competed in two further Schneider Trophy races – in 1923 and 1925 – but did not again emerge the victor. In the latter year however, he covered himself with glory in another way, breaking the World Speed Record by attaining 227 m.p.h.

It was in the year following his Schneider Trophy victory that Henri Biard inaugurated a new era in Guernsey's history – the air passenger service between the island and England. The service was initially operated by British Marine Air Navigation Limited, making use of a Sea Eagle Flying Boat. Biard piloted the very first Sea Eagle to make the flight, the landing being made in L'Ancresse Bay. (It was only at a later stage that the landing place was changed to St Peter-Port).

In 1973, to commemorate half-a-century of commercial flying between Guernsey and England, a model of Biard's aircraft, presented to the island by British Airways, was unveiled in Castle Cornet Museum, where it is on permanent display to the public.

After completing his career as a test pilot, Henri Biard turned author, recounting his exper--iences in his book, *Wings*, which appeared in 1935. It transpires that one of his more celebrated passengers was George Bernard Shaw, who said he felt completely confident, even when Biard was flying upside down! The playwright thereupon presented the airman with ten shillings (fifty pence) – accompanied by an admonition to make good use of it!

Captain Henri Biard died at Dorchester on 18 January, 1966.

BLANCHFORD, REGINALD HERBERT, O.B.E., K.St.J., G.M. (1915–　　). *A life lived 'pro utilitate hominum'.* Born on 24 February 1915, to Beatrice Louise (née Zane), the wife of Harry Herbert Blanchford, Reginald Blanchford was educated at Les Vauxbelets College, where his attainments on the sports field had as their counterpart a deplorable performance in the classroom – reflecting not want of ability (as subsequent events made clear) but the lack of sufficient motivation to bestir himself. Indeed his fecklessness became a byword, and no one would have prophesied that this apparently work-shy dullard would prove to be beyond all doubt the most illustrious of the school's alumni. In despair at his son's academic record, Blanchford père removed him from school at the age of 14 in the hope of grooming him for the family business. These attempts, however, were also frustrated by a continued attitude of insouciance on the part of a lad who had yet to discover his *métier*.

At the age of 15, however, this youth of such tremendous potentiality found his vocation. In October 1930 he was involved in a near-fatal accident and his appalling experiences brought home to him the gross inadequacies of the ram-shackle provision then made by the States in its Ambulance Service, which consisted of one vehicle driven by a part-time amateur with no medical or first-aid knowledge, who also served as a volunteer fireman! His return from the very threshold of death was slow and painful, but by 1936 he had recovered sufficiently to embark on the task which he had set himself during his long ordeal. In 1934 a division of the St John

Ambulance Brigade had been formed in Guernsey, and it now acquired a recruit of peerless determination and devotion — so dedicated that it is no exaggeration to say that the existence in the Bailiwick of any ambulance service worthy of the name is due almost entirely to the tenacious efforts of this man of vision and intrepidity.

Refusing to be abashed by his junior status, Blanchford agitated until the division (which, incredibly, had no ambulance) justified its title by acquiring a second-hand conveyance. He then ran so efficient a service that in December 1939 (in anticipation of possible war-time casualties) the States handed over all ambulance responsibilities to the Brigade, promising to help with an annual grant and also with the purchase of new vehicles as and when necessary.

Having kept the services intact throughout the German Occupation by an audacious series of improvisations, Blanchford turned his attention after Liberation to improving the island's blood-transfusion arrangements, and to setting up air ambulance facilities for taking emergency cases to England. He then launched a campaign for the installation of a radio-controlled ambulance system, successfully overcoming the reluctance of the Postmaster-General to grant a licence for such an operation. On 6 March, 1947 Lieutenant-General Sir Philip Neame, V.C., the Lieutenant-Governor, formally opened the new radio-equipped ambulance station: the first in the world!

Convinced of the dire need for a marine ambulance to facilitate cliff-rescue work as well as to ferry urgent cases from the smaller islands, and undaunted by the action of the St John Brigade Council in withdrawing its support for the project when the States voted against maintaining such a craft, Blanchford turned for help to the National Round Table Association. The appeal sponsored by this organisation went so well that a converted vessel (the *Flying Christine*) was ready by July 1952. Lady Neame, the wife of the Lieutenant-Governor, in the atmosphere of official disapproval of the venture, having prudently pleaded a hitherto overlooked prior engagement, the boat was launched by the Matron of the Princess Elizabeth Hospital in a ceremony made more memorable by cabled congratulations from Lady Edwina Mountbatten of Burma, then in mid-Atlantic on H.M.S. *Surprise*.

The high-speed ambulance launch rendered sterling service in the ensuing years. However, despite massive donations made by Mr. Rupert Turner (founder of the Turner and Nowall asbestos concern) and the praiseworthy gesture of the

Sark Chief Pleas at its Michaelmas sitting in 1953 when, remembering the daring recovery of a boy's body from Grand Grève the previous summer, it voted an annual grant of £50 towards upkeep expenses, finance remained a perennial problem. Looking to the States for help was futile, as already in 1951 that body had cavilled at fulfilling the 1939 pledge to replace road vehicles — and even when cajoled by Sir Thomas Elmhirst (who became the Lieutenant-Governor in 1953) it dallied for a further 16 months before finally implementing its promises. So niggardly an attitude towards the upkeep of authorised land ambulances boded ill for the prospect of any support for a marine service, from which approval had initially been withheld in any case! Indeed by 1955 the situation had become so bad that the *Flying Christine* had to be withdrawn from service for lack of funds to pay for a refit, to help towards which the people of Sark put to shame the parsimony of the States by raising £110 5s. 0d. in a collection made in June of that year. In the event it was not until the summer of 1956 that a report on the Guernsey service, drawn up by Harold T. Ferrier, Director of Ambulances of the Joint Committee of the Red Cross and St John in London, ultimately prodded the States into assuming the fully supportive rôle which has since been maintained.

Reginald Blanchford, who had been granted the rank of M.B.E. (later raised to O.B.E.) in 1951 in recognition of his services, was accorded the Queen's Commendation in February 1957 for a daring cliff rescue the previous summer. This was followed in June of the same year by the Order of St John presenting him with its Lifesaving Medal in Gold. Finally, in November 1958 at an Investiture at Buckingham Palace, H.M. the Queen awarded this gallant islander the George Medal for what Lady Edwina Mountbatten in her congratulations called his 'great courage and endurance'.

Area Commissioner Reginald Blanchford resigned in February 1977, and the following November his outstanding work was acknowledged at the annual dinner and dance of the Guernsey and Alderney Division of the British Medical Association, when he was presented with a citation in recognition of his services. The citation reads: '1936–1977. This citation is presented to Reginald H. Blanchford Esq., O.B.E., K.St.J., G.M., by the chairman and members of the Guernsey and Alderney Division of the British Medical Association, in recognition of a lifetime dedicated to the service of mankind and in appreciation of the help he has given to the care of their patients. The finest ambulance service in the world will remain a living memorial to his work'.

LE BOUTILLIER, GEORGE (1783-1867). 'Si Monumentum Requiris Circumspice' – at Elizabeth College and the Commercial Arcades! Born in the Jersey parish of Trinity in 1783, George le Boutillier came to Guernsey at the age of 21, setting up a drapery business in the year 1804. A man of drive and verve, he almost immediately began to take a prominent part in local politics, and rapidly made his mark by agitating for improved illumination of the town. He did this to such effect that St Peter-Port is indebted to him for the initial introduction of gas lighting.

As the years went by, le Boutillier's concern for his seven children led him (in the teeth of hostility on the part of the authorities) to investigate the abuses which had reduced Elizabeth College to such a moribund condition that in 1799, five years before his arrival, it had but one pupil. Baulked by the evasiveness and duplicity of Dean Daniel Durand, the College Visitor (who was diverting the Foundation's funds in the interests of the Town Church, le Boutillier saw his chance when Sir John Colborne (q.v.), became Lieutenant-Governor in 1821. He laid before Sir John a complete plan for the reorganization of the College which so impressed the Lieutenant-Governor that (having also found the Dean, when approached, to be unco-operative and dilatory) he ordered a public inquiry in 1824. This resulted in a new charter under which a fresh and re-invigorated organisation for the establishment was set up. The decision was taken to impose an impôt of one shilling a gallon on spirits to finance the erection of a new building to the design of the architect John Wilson (q.v.). When the school was re-opened in 1826 the first two names on the register were those of the sons of Sir John Colborne. The next three, however, were those of the sons of le Boutillier: a small recognition of what the College owed him.

Four years later George le Boutillier, in association with his brother James, embarked on the stupendous venture of creating the Commercial Arcades by a pick and shovel invasion of Mont Gibel, involving the quarrying away of thousands of tons of gravel and stone: a herculean undertaking with the primitive equipment of the day. In all, 125,000 cartloads of soil had to be removed. The project was abandoned before completion, the intended glass roofing never materialising. The colossal financial burden brought ruin to this man of energy and imagination – and in 1838 he emigrated to the United States of America. In Cincinnati he built up another large and prosperous business, with branch houses run by his sons in Philadelphia and New York. Wealthy again, le Boutillier retired in 1864 to his native Jersey, where he died in 1867. He is described in the Elizabeth College Register as 'one of the greatest benefactors that ever came to this island'.

BRADBURY, ARTHUR ROYCE, A.R.W.A. (1892-1977). The English artist who became a 'semi-Serquiais'. Born near Preston, Lancashire, on 17 September 1892, and beginning as a cadet in the Mercantile Marine before taking up Art, which he studied at St John's Wood Art School, Arthur Bradbury emerged as a noted portrait painter who also did much marine work, exhibiting at the Royal Academy, the Royal Institute of Oil Painters, the Royal Society of British Artists, the Royal Institute of Painters in Water Colours – and the Royal West of England Academy, of which he became an Associate. He fell under the spell of Sark, and although he never settled in the island he paid lengthy visits to it over many years, 'commuting' between the Fief Haubert and his home at Yellow Sands, Sandbanks, Poole.

Skilled in the construction of ship models, Bradbury made one of H.M.S. Victory from timber he recovered from the East Indiaman Valentine, wrecked off Brecqhou. He also modelled several Sark fishing boats. His portrait of La Dame de Sercq (executed in 1962) furnished the frontispiece for Messrs. Ewen's and de Carteret's authoritative work The Fief of Sark: a function also performed by his study of Sark's west coast – this time for The Islands of England (a misnomer as far as concerns 'Les Iles Normandes'). He painted and drew innumerable pictures of Sark, including details of buildings and fishing craft, and some of his work provided illustrations for papers appearing in the Transactions of La Société Guernesiaise.

This esteemed artist died at Poole in the spring of 1977, leaving work on permanent display in the Imperial War Museum (Huddersfield branch), the Russell Coles Art Gallery in Bournemouth and Bournemouth Town Hall – not to mention the examples of his marine artistry which adorn the Maritime Museum at Castle Cornet.

BRAMPTON, SIR EDWARD (c. 1440-1508). Guernsey's Swashbuckling Governor. Although full governmental separation of the Jersey and

Guernsey Bailiwicks was not effected until the reign of Henry VII, yet to some extent Guernsey had distinct Crown Representatives prior to that monarch's seizure of the throne, in that from 1478 onwards Edward IV and Richard III appointed a number of 'Captains of Guernsey', all of whom were, however, technically subordinate to Sir Richard Harliston as 'Captain-in-Chief' of the entire archipelago. Among these was Sir Edward Brampton — a veritable archetype of the romantic exotic — who was Captain of Guernsey 1482-1485.

Despite his English-sounding name, Sir Edward was in fact born in Portugal of Jewish stock, his father being a blacksmith in Lisbon. His adventurous spirit soon led to involvement in the maritime vicissitudes of his native land's ally — and this in its turn resulted in his identification with the Yorkist cause in the Wars of the Roses. Settling in England in 1468, young Duarte Brandao first anglicised his name to Brandon, but soon afterwards changed this to Brampton, as the Brandon family were prominent Lancastrian supporters. Deciding to embrace Christianity and thus overcome the residential prohibition imposed on the Jews by Edward I in 1290, Brampton lived while a catechumen in the House of the Converttites (*Domus Conversorum*) in London, becoming a member of this institution to which he returned from time to time during his colourful career. Having already become known to and esteemed by Edward IV (q.v.), Brampton was accorded a signal honour in that the king consented to stand as godfather at his baptism. It was thus that he took the Christian name of Edward.

In 1469 Brampton accompanied Edward IV in the campaign against 'Robin of Redesdale' (Sir John Conyers) who had raised the standard of revolt in collusion with Richard Neville, Earl of Warwick (who was also Lord of the Channel Isles), whose antipathy to the Queen's Woodville relatives had alienated him from the King. When in September 1470 Warwick returned from France in the Lancastrian interest, and Edward IV was forced to flee to Burgundy, Brampton lay low — but he reappeared at the *Domus Conversorum* on Edward's return and fought with distinction at the Yorkist triumphs of Barnet and Tewkesbury.

In 1472 Brampton's services were rewarded by his being given the command of an armed force in the Channel and also by the grant of a number of messuages in and around the City of London (a fact commemorated by 'Brampton House' in Red Lion Square); the conveyances being in the name of 'Edward Brampton, born in the realm of Portugal'. The following year Brampton received further royal favour in being exempted from the *Nova et Parva Costuma* imposed in 1297 by Edward I on foreign merchants who thereby incurred a liability to duties 50 per cent in excess of the normal rates. By now the enterprising Portuguese had become a considerable landholder, thanks to his marriage to Isabel, widow of Thomas Tresham, through whom he obtained the life grant of wide estates in Northamptonshire which had previously been held by Tresham, but had been rendered forfeit by his high treason.

The close of 1473 saw Brampton once more wielding his sword. Earlier that year the Earl of Oxford, in alliance with the king's brother, the Duke of Clarence (who, aided by Louis XI, was again conspiring for the throne to which the Lancastrian Parliament of 1470 had said he was entitled in default of Henry VI or his issue) first landed in Essex. In the face of superior forces, the Earl took to the sea again, harrying merchant shipping and seizing St Michael's Mount on 30 September seeking to arouse Cornwall and calling on Louis XI for more help. Previous attempts to dislodge him having failed, Edward IV in December sent Brampton and William Fetherston with four ships to assault the Mount by sea and cut off the Earl's supplies. By mid-February 1474, Oxford was forced to surrender for the pardon of his life only.

By 1481 Edward Brampton was prosperous enough to be able to advance to the Royal Treasury £700 to satisfy a group of Spanish merchant creditors, in return for which he was granted permission to send wools through the Straits of Gibraltar free of export duty. The same year saw the 'Sea Dog' once again in action. During the winter of 1479-80 Louis XI, hoping thereby to keep Edward IV busy while he sought to subdue Burgundy, persuaded James III of Scotland to attack England. In the ensuing war a great onslaught was launched in the early summer of 1481 by a fleet under Lord Howard on the Scottish navy in the Firth of Forth. The action resulted in eight large ships being captured, many smaller ones being destroyed and the port of Blackness burned. Brampton commanded one of the largest ships in the expedition — 'the great carvel of Portingale' — which carried 160 sailors and 240 soldiers.

On 24 August 1482, the King appointed Brampton 'Captain Keeper and Governor' of Guernsey and its dependencies — a post which he held until 25 January 1485. King Edward was of course acquainted with Guernsey, having taken refuge in the island while still Earl of March after his flight following the Yorkist humiliation of the Rout of Ludford in 1459. Doubtless his personal knowledge of the archipelago made him alive to its importance, not only as an advanced outpost and espionage base against France, but also as a 'coign of vantage' for keeping an eye on Henry Tudor's activities in Brittany. Brampton's term of office followed closely on the King's approach to the Pope, whereby Edward IV obtained from Sixtus IV the Bull establishing the neutrality of the Channel Isles in all times of war — a status that increased markedly their value as outposts for observing any potential foe south of the Channel. As Captain of Guernsey Brampton co-operated with the equally enthusiastic Yorkist Sir Richard Harliston (his official superior in Jersey) in the cause of Richard III against the Woodville faction after the death of Edward IV. Indeed, during his tenure of office in Guernsey, he was one of the leaders of the assault made in the Downs on the fleet of Sir Edward Woodville, who was defying Richard's authority as Protector during Edward V's short occupancy of the throne. Brampton so successfully suborned the Genoese captains of most of the ships as to obtain the submission of the entire fleet, except for two vessels (one with Woodville on board) which made good their escape to Brittany and Henry Tudor. Brampton thereafter became one of the most trusted lieutenants of Richard III, from whom he obtained many gifts for his services and finally a knighthood — the first ever conferred in England upon a converted Jew.

After his patron had lost both his throne and his life to his Tudor rival, not only did the old soldier of fortune fail to die, but he stubbornly refused to fade away either! For six years his movements were elusive and mysterious, but in 1491 Brampton's continued defiance of his erstwhile master's supplanter came to a head with the emergence on the stage of history of Perkin Warbeck, claiming to be Richard, Duke of York — and, as such, the rightful king in Yorkist eyes. Warbeck owed his ability over the next six years to convince so many people of the validity of his pretensions virtually to Brampton alone. (Even James IV of Scotland gave his blessing to Warbeck's marriage with a noblewoman of the Scottish court). For a number of years before 1491 Warbeck had been in the service of Sir Edward, who had seen to it that his young protegé was thoroughly schooled in the ways and personalities of the English Court the better to

sustain his claim to the throne. Brampton obviously felt that a fake Yorkist was preferable to no Yorkist at all — and certainly to Henry Tudor whose flimsy claim rested only on descent from John of Gaunt through the bastard line of the Beauforts. So cold as to be incapable of either generosity or vindictiveness, Henry pardoned Brampton after Warbeck's overthrow in 1497 and the old mariner lived on in eclipse until death finally claimed him in 1508 — forty years after his first arrival in England.

BRÉVINT, REV. COSMÉ (died 1605). *The Church Militant Incarnate!* (G). Born at Angouville in Normandy, Cosmé Brévint moved as a young man to Switzerland, to escape religious persecution as a Hueuenot. After a spell as a schoolmaster at Neuchâtel, he served as a pastor in several Vaudois churches and eventually came to Geneva. Here he made the acquaintance of Nicolas Gosselin (the eponymous uncle of Helier de Carteret's great friend Nicolas Gosselin, later to become the tenant of Sark's Beauregard holding) who had gone to this epicentre of Calvinism from his native Jersey for fear of persecution as a Protestant during the reign of Mary I. When Helier de Carteret (q.v.) embarked on the colonisation of Sark, Gosselin prevailed upon Brévint to come to the island in 1565 to serve as its pastor and schoolmaster.

Under the energetic leadership of this man of God the church in Sark quickly achieved a high degree of organisation and discipline among its flock; and Brévint vigorously asserted its independence and its equality with the churches of the larger islands. The reputation it enjoyed was testified by a contemporary writer — *Il n'y a Eglise en toutes les Isles ny ailleurs mieux réformée ny où le peuple soit mieux gouverné et mieux reglé en la crainte de Dieu qu'en cell de l'Isle de Sercq.* ('There is no church in all the islands or elsewhere where the people are better governed and better regulated in the fear of God than in that of the Isle of Sark'.) As a consequence Brévint enjoyed a high prestige in the religious councils of the archipelago and within five years of his taking up his incumbency, Sark's importance was reflected in its being chosen as the venue for the inter-island ecclesiastical Synod in 1570.

Sark's church was technically subordinate to the Guernsey Colloque, but Brévint consistently adopted an aggressively independent attitude towards this body. In 1584 a conflict developed between the Jersey and Guernsey Colloques arising out of the transfer from Guernsey to Jersey of

Nicolas Baudouin (q.v.) and his supporters after the vindication of Louis de Vic (q.v.) the maligned Commissary of the Bishop of Winchester. Cosmé Brévint exploited this dispute to justify his refusal to attend meetings of the Guernsey Colloque, by pleading that the Sark Consistory was undecided whether to attach itself to the Jersey or Guernsey Colloque. Not until a further six years had elapsed did this 'turbulent priest' apparently yield, crossing to Guernsey in the spring of 1590 and promising obedience to the Guernsey Colloque.

A strong personality like Brévint's was unlikely to remain submissive for long, and it is hardly surprising that this change of heart was short-lived, with Sark's pastor soon reverting to the defiant demeanour which he had displayed for so many years. Eventually, however, his overbearing and abusive behaviour so incensed his own congregation that, through its Elder, Thomas Roo, it appealed to the Guernsey Colloque to discipline its minister on the grounds that he refused to accept the decision of the Sark Consistory. As a consequence Brévint was formally censured by the Guernsey Colloque in 1601 : censured but not dismissed. Old and ill though he now was, this man of iron will was not easily to be removed – and he remained at Sark's ecclesiastical helm until his death at the end of April 1605.

BRÉVINT, REV. ELIE (1587-1674). (G). *The last of the Huguenots*. The death of Cosmé Brevint left a void which proved extremely difficult to fill. Finally, after a number of infelicitous stop-gap appointments, the Seigneur, Philippe de Carteret (q.v.) came to an agreement with the late pastor's younger son Elie whereby, in return for the expenses of his theological training at Saumur being defrayed and the provision of a furnished Presbytère with adjacent grazing land in Sark being guaranteed, Elie undertook to labour in the Lord's Vineyard in the island on the completion of his studies. Thus it was that on 20 January 1612 Elie Brévint was presented to the Guernsey Colloque by Philippe de Carteret as the Minister of Sark, after which he took up his residence in accordance with the terms of his undertaking. Fate decreed that the cure of souls in the island was to remain in his hands for no less than 62 years.

In 1626 Brévint married Susanne Slowley, the daughter of the Juge of the Sark Court (q.v.*). In 1649 their daughter Anne married Jean le Gros (q.v.) whose father (also Jean le Gros) was not only the Juge of the Court, but also the head of the most powerful family in the island, now that

a triumphant Parliament had dispossessed the Seigneur. The resultant combination of the legal authority of the Court and the spiritual discipline of the minister gave this group a completely dominating position in the island.

Elie Brévint also acted as the island's schoolmaster. A Londoner who resided in Sark for a time during the Commonwealth – one F. Wearis – wrote : 'The present Minister (whom I must acknowledge a person of more Industry and parts than could be hoped for among such people) has lately begun Teach Grammar to the Children with Writing and Arithmetick, erecting a School for that purpose, so that who knows to what prodigious Learning we may have one day arrived'?

Besides his spiritual and educational ministrations, Brévint kept a notebook in which he recorded memoranda and jottings on a wide variety of topics. This manuscript was found in a loft at Le Manoir in 1860 and forms a unique source of information on Sark's affairs from 1620 to 1664. The restoration of the monarchy in 1660 brought the forcible imposition of Anglicanism throughout the Bailiwick – except for Sark! The reinstated Seigneur, Sir Philippe de Carteret, Bt. (q.v.) obviously deemed it most imprudent to attempt the removal of the incumbent who had been appointed by his grandfather and was so firmly entrenched in an island where the prestige he enjoyed was tremendous. As a result Sark remained the last bastion of Presbyterianism, not only in the Bailiwick, but in the entire archipelago : and it was not until after Brévint's death, 14 years afterwards, that Sir Philippe's son and successor (another Sir Philippe – q.v.) extended the Anglican system of church government to an island whose spiritual life had for over a century been shaped into a strict and severe Huguenot mould by a remarkable father followed by a no less redoubtable son.

BRIARD, JEAN (Floruit 1594-1616). *Guernsey's first Privateer*. (A/F). Born in Jersey, Jean Briard settled in Guernsey with his wife Rachel in 1594, buying the house in the High Street which now accommodates the Trustee Savings Bank. Into the corbelling of the side walls he had two carvings incised. One portrays Briard's Merchant's Mark and proclaims, *'En Dieu j'ai mis mon appup'* ('In God did I confide'); while the other shows the Merchant's Mark of his wife, carrying the legend, *'Et sa providence m'a conduit'* ('And His providence has guided me').

Briard conducted a lucrative trade in his ship,

La Colombe, his main cargoes consisting of fish and oil. Four years after buying the High Street property, however, he suffered a reverse, followed by the chance of realising even greater profits than hitherto — though in his case it is doubtful if any especially large gains did in the event result from this opportunity. In May 1598 Henri IV of France concluded peace with Philip of Spain at Vervins, thereby leaving Elizabeth I to continue the struggle against Spain in the Netherlands bereft of French help. Thus betrayed, the Queen issued Letters of Marque to several mariners, among whom was Briard, to employ their vessels in attacking French shipping. Jean Briard consequently emerged as Guernsey's first privateer, his forays anticipating by a hundred years the great privateering era of the 18th century.

Such authority was in fact actively solicited by Briard, who sought thereby to recoup the losses he had incurred earlier when he had had to ransom his ship and cargo to the value of 2,000 marks (£1,333.33) after seizure by privateers from Brittany (the reverse aforementioned). His initial ventures in this new role were not very successful — though possibly he enjoyed better fortune later on. Armed with his Letter of Marque Briard betook himself to Limerick, where he sought the Mayor's help in sequestering two Breton ships in that port laden with iron. This request, however, was not complied with — a refusal which elicited a reprimand from the Lords of the Council addressed to the President of Munster in June 1598.

One cannot keep a good man down, however, and seven years later (in 1605) this versatile commercial adventurer was in Spain acting as agent for Jacques de Beauvoir of Les Granges, who was engaged in the wine trade with that country. At the same time Briard continued his old fish and oil trading activities on his own account. Rendered wealthy by these ventures, Briard embarked on considerable alterations and additions to his house. The extensions he made led his neighbours to complain that their view of the harbour was obscured — a serious consideration when so much island wealth was tied up in shipping. The upshot was a *vue de justice* by the Court in 1616, when Briard was ordered to take back the jettied top floor by six inches.

Jean and Rachel Briard had a son — William — whose daughter Rachel eventually became the wife of Jean de Sausmarez (q.v.*) who as Dean of Guernsey was the key figure in the imposition of Anglicanism in the island after the Restoration of Charles II. In the long run, therefore, the house of Mammon was united with that of God!

BROCK, DANIEL DE LISLE (1762-1842). *Guernsey's Horatius*. (E). Because of Guernsey's lack of schooling facilities during his boyhood, Daniel de Lisle Brock (who was born in St Martin's) received his early education in Alderney, where he was put in the care of a private tutor in the person of Monsieur Isaac Vallant, a Swiss divine who was later (1772-85) the rector of St Pierre du Bois. After leaving Monsieur Vallat's charge Brock went to school at Richmond in Surrey, but left at the age of 14 to go to the Continent with his ailing father, who died at Dinan in 1776. In his early manhood he embarked on the Grand Tour, visiting the Mediterranean, France and Switzerland in the years 1785 and 1786.

After a stormy start to his brilliant career occasioned by the refusal in 1789 of Bailiff William le Marchant (q.v.), to confirm his election as Constable of St Peter-Port, Daniel de Lisle Brock was elected a Jurat in 1798 at the young age of 36 and rapidly acquired a well-deserved reputation as the champion of the Bailiwick's *liberté* — its charters and privileges upon which depended its survival as a political entity. He was foremost in putting up a stubborn resistance to any attempts by British ministers to override these rights, or by the British Parliament to interfere with them. On no less than four occasions between 1804 and 1810 this indefatigable Guernseyman was deputed by the Royal Court and the States to represent them in London in defence of insular privileges. The most noteworthy of these visits occurred when Brock appeared before the Privy Council to protest against attempts to impress islanders for the Royal Navy. Although confronted with as formidable an opponent as Lord St Vincent, this able advocate — with the support of Sir James Saumarez (later Lord de Saumarez) — succeeded in carrying the day.

Brock became Bailiff in 1821 at a time when further trouble was brewing, as a result of the enactment by the British Parliament of the Corn Laws which prohibited the import of grain into the United Kingdom as long as the price of British grain was not in excess of £4 a quarter. Immediately following his appointment the new Bailiff launched a campaign against the attitude of the British Government which construed the Act as applying to the Channel Isles as well as to the United Kingdom. Once again Brock was triumphant, successfully demonstrating that this claim was in derogation of the islands' status as free ports.

Brock's early years as Bailiff coincided with the drive launched by George le Boutillier (q.v.) for the reinvigoration of Elizabeth College. He co-operated enthusiastically with both le Boutillier and Sir John Colborne (q.v.) in checking the obstructive Dean Durand and in promoting the Committee of Inquiry whose findings led to the new and reformed régime in the life of the College, which was thereby resuscitated from moribundity.

In 1826, in the course of an encomium on the impressiveness of St Peter-Port, Brock had exclaimed,' *on croyait approcher la capitale d'un empire!*'; while on a previous occasion he had pinpointed the basis of the existence of this *'grande et florissante ville dans un aussi petit pays'*, emphasising that *'on doit convenir que c'est à la mer que le tout est dû'*. This perception of Guernsey's debt to the sea led Brock, when approached in 1830 by 187 merchants petitioning for harbour improvements, to put the weight o his patronage behind such projects. He favoured a breakwater to Castle Cornet to protect the road-stead and the creation of a new harbour within this shield. In the event, however, his blandish-ments evoked no response and it was not until after his death that the modern harbour came into being. He did succeed, however, in fostering the initial steps for the creation of St Sampson's Harbour — though here again it was long after his demise that the haven was completed. It is appro-priate therefore that his memorial (a plaque affixed to a 13-ft menhir) should be located at this port.

At about the same time as the merchants lodged their petition, Brock found himself involved in yet another confrontation with the British Government. This crisis of 1830–31 con-cerned the export of grain from the islands. The islanders were accused of bringing into England more grain than they could have grown them-selves and the British Customs demanded a duty on it. The indomitable Bailiff led a joint deputa-tion from both bailiwicks which proved the falsity of the accusations, and vindicated the islands' rights in respect of this valuable trade.

The following year (1832) saw Brock once again defending his compatriots — this time their right to be tried only in their own courts. A St Pancras beadle (one John Capes) had been arrested in Guernsey for dumping paupers on the island and when the St Pancras Council obtained from the King's Bench a Writ under the Habeas Corpus Act, Guernsey's Deputy Sheriff ignored it as inapplicable to the Bailiwick. Matters came to a head when the Tipstaff whom the Lord Chief Justice, disregarding Guernsey's rights, had sent to

arrest the Deputy Sheriff, was himself taken into custody! Thereupon Brock, together with the Procureur (Charles de Jersey) led an embassy from Guernsey to London to lodge a protest — and yet again emerged victorious.

In 1835 Brock 'fended off the ranks of Tuscany' for the last time. At the age of 73 this tireless leader went to London to protest against a proposed Bill seeking to deprive the Channel Isles of the right to export grain to England free of duty. The British authorities were obviously returning to the attack after their rebuff four years earlier! However the veteran campaigner once again prevailed and the Bill was withdrawn.

On his return to Guernsey Brock found a financial crisis looming. After some tentative experiments in connection with financing the building of the markets and the provision of schools, the States in the late 1830s ceased ear-marking note issues for one particular purpose at a time only, thus launching a permanent paper currency. Almost immediately, however, the Old Bank and the Commercial Bank also took to issuing notes, so that the island was threatened with a flood of paper money. By persuading the States to assert their entitlement to a monopoly issue Brock halted the incipient inflation and thereby guaranteed a stability of money values which was to endure until the First World War.

Brock died on 24 September 1842 and his funeral was the occasion for a spectacular display of esteem. It was a semi-State affair with literally thousands of people lining the route: a tribute thoroughly deserved by one whose life had been spent devotedly in the service of his island. Besides the memoral at St Sampson's, he is commemo-rated by a bust in St Peter-Port, High Street.

BROCK, MAJOR-GENERAL SIR ISAAC (1769–1812). *Guernsey's greatest soldier.* (E). Like his elder brother Daniel de Lisle, Isaac Brock, for lack of adequate local provision, was educated outside the island. At the age of ten he was sent to school in Southampton and subsequently was taught privately at Rotterdam by a French pastor who, as a Huguenot, had gone there to avoid persecu-tion. In 1785, at the age of 15½, Brock became an Ensign in the 8th Regiment of Foot, where yet another elder brother, John — who was later (in 1801) killed in a duel at Cape Town — had pur-chased a company. Five years afterwards — in 1790 — Isaac Brock purchased a lieutenancy and thenceforth promotion was rapid, with the rank of Lieutenant-Colonel in the 59th Foot being reached in 1797, at the age of 31.

In 1797 the regiment under Brock's command distinguished itself in General Moore's expedition to North Holland: and two years later — in 1801 — he enhanced his reputation by his bearing in Nelson's attack on Copenhagen, where he was second-in-command of the land forces. The upshot was that the following year, when his regiment was posted to Canada, Brock was promoted to the rank of full Colonel. Arrived in the New World, he dealt promptly and efficiently with a crisis, rapidly suppressing a conspiracy instigated by deserters at Fort George (in the area south of Lake George which nowadays is in New York State).

In 1805 he returned to Guernsey but, when relations with the United States of America deteriorated in 1806, he was hurriedly recalled to Canada. Given command in Upper Canada in 1810 (and also appointed as provisional Lieutenant-Governor of the Province) Brock, through the respect he won from them, established his ascendency over the Indian tribes under the leadership of the Shawnee warrior Tecumseh. When war broke out in 1812 Brock, now a Major-General, in his capacity as Governor of Upper Canada, was responsible for a frontier of 1,300 miles with scarcely as many men. Nevertheless, he took the offensive and marched to capture Detroit (16 August 1812) thus uniting behind him both British and French Canadians, as well as retaining the support of the Indians. For these services he was knighted on 10 October 1812, but three days later, on 13 October he fell in a skirmish at Queenstown Heights, near Niagara Falls.

Nowadays these heights are graced by a tall monument in his honour and he is also commemorated by Brock University in Ontario. In London a monument to him is to be seen in St Paul's Cathedral, while Guernsey has the Brock Memorial Chapel in the Town Church besides having two roads named after him and a plaque outside the premises of Boots the Chemists, recalling that he once lived in the building. Furthermore, the Guernsey Post Office put out a special stamp issue in 1969 to mark the bicentenary of his birth.

C

CACHEMAILLE, REVEREND JACQUES LOUIS VICTOR (1804-1877). *Sark's thalassophobic diarist and commentator*.

Born on 4 August 1804, Jacques Louis Victor Cachemaille was ordained deacon in 1834 and priest in 1835, his name appearing in the Act Book of the Bishop of Winchester among the list of Ordinands on 5 July of that year, where it is also stated that although he did not have a university degree, he was examined and found to be literate! According to a pencilled note in the Ordination Book this examination took place in either Jersey or Sark, which suggests that he was already living in the Channel Isles before ordination. As he took up the Sark living in 1835, the presumption must be that the isle of his pre-ordination domicile was Jersey.

This incumbent had in fact operated in a clerical capacity previously, having initially hailed from Geneva where he had originally become a Calvinist divine; and with disarming candour he admitted whilst in Sark that he was one of those whose compliance with Anglican requirements was no more than partial and perfunctory. In this connection he wrote: 'With only three or four exceptions, all who have filled the office of Minister of Sark, including the present Vicar, have come from France or Switzerland, have received their education at continental Universities or Colleges, and have been first consecrated to the ministry according to Presbyterian forms. Once settled in Sark they conformed in greater or less degree to the rites of the Church of England.' In view of this cleric's markedly evangelical emphasis, it is interesting to note that during his incumbency the Tractarian leader, Dr. Edward Bouverie Pusey, whilst excluded from Oxford between 1843 and 1846, inaugurated the use of surplices in the island church, when he also conducted services in English for the first time in Sark's history.

Jacques Cachemaille's residence in Sark was prolonged. An inbred aversion to sea journeys was converted into ineradicable abject fear when on 1 March, 1839, four years after taking up the island's living, he saw the ship carrying the Seigneur, Pierre Le Pelley, engulfed by a gigantic wave off l'Eperquerie and vanish from sight for ever. Thenceforth he absolutely refused to quit dry land and never left Sark for the rest of his days. His thalassophobia (which was reinforced by the 1868 shipwreck in which Mr. Andrew Giffard — the harbour engineer — and four companions lost their lives after setting out from Havre Gosselin) was to all appearances proved as only too tragically justified early in 1872 when the *Ariel*, commanded by his son Eugène Cachemaille, sailed from London for Sydney and was never heard of again.

A compulsive diarist, Cachemaille minutely chronicled his 42 years in Sark and his writings provide an invaluable source of information about the island in the mid-19th century. He arrived at the same time as silver mining commenced and gives graphic details of all the attendant circumstances, as well as of the initial hope and ultimate doom that hung over the venture. The early tourist trade is recorded, together with his disapproval of the noise and disturbance caused by the visitors. The characteristics of the islanders are scrutinised and an attempt is made to compile a glossary of the Sark Patois. Appointed by the Reverend William Thomas Collings (q.v.) to act as Deputy Seigneur during his absences from the island, the vicar's reports on his stewardship also supply further source material for the historian.

It is not beyond the bounds of possibility that this was in fact the writer's intention, as he was no mean historian himself. Residing at 'Le Manoir' (as had the various vicars since the le Pelly seigneurs moved to 'La Perronerie') he there discovered in a loft during re-thatching operations in 1860 the manuscript of the notebook which Elie Brévint had kept in a mixture of French and Latin between the years 1620 and 1664 and which had been hidden away soon afterwards, possibly as a precaution against a feared French attack during the Second Dutch War of 1665-7, when Louis XIV sided with the United Netherlands against Charles II. After having deciphered this document, Cachemaille went on to examine various records preserved at 'La Seigneurie'. From his studies there eventually emerged a series of articles on the history of Sark published between January 1874 and April 1876 which appeared in *Clarke's Guernsey Magazine* and which constitute the first attempt ever made to compile a history of the island. From these articles one learns that not long before they were written no less than ten cromlechs could still be clearly distinguished in the island. (The vicar, incidentally, was also a good photographer and, *inter alia*, has left us a picture of the cyst above Brenière as it appeared in his day.) It is also interesting to see that, as against the conventional wisdom which holds that Sark became deserted after the depredations of Bertrand de Guesclin in 1373, Cachemaille advances the opinion that records of revenues

received by Henry VI prove the island to have been inhabited and under cultivation as late as 1461! Jacques Cachemaille died in 1877 and this good man's 42 years' service to the people of Sark is commemorated by the pulpit in St Peter's church, which was erected in his memory.

CAREY, EDITH FRANCES (1864–1935). *The eminent antiquarian and folk-lore expert*. (B). This illustrious Guernseywoman was born at Morar Gwalior in India in 1864, the great-great-granddaughter (through her mother) of the gifted artist and botanist, Joshua Gosselin (q.v.). In the latter part of her girlhood her parents returned to Guernsey, settling at Le Vallon, and she became one of the first generation of pupils at the Ladies' College.

Edith Carey took up the study of local history in her early twenties to sublimate the intense emotional anguish she experienced after parental disapproval had debarred her from marrying the man to whom she had given her heart. She was encouraged in this pursuit by Sir Edgar MacCulloch (q.v.) and after his death in 1896 she edited and published his celebrated *Guernsey Folklore*. This was followed by the appearance in 1904 of her well-known work, *The Channel Islands*. This book, containing material not hitherto published, and illustrated by Henry Wimbush, was revised in 1924 and reprinted in 1930.

Edith Carey was a stalwart of La Société Guernesiaise — and indeed it was at her suggestion that in 1922 the organisation adopted this name in place of the previous cumbersome title of 'The Guernsey Society for Natural Science and Local Research'. She strengthened the influence and status of this body by raising its standards and widening its outlook, while over the years she contributed no less than 23 learned papers which were published in La Société's *Transactions*. Furthermore, she was President of La Société in 1924 and again in 1927. It was in this latter year that 'Le Semain de l'Histoire du Droit Normand' was held in Guernsey and Miss Carey delivered a number of readings on local history and customs at a selection of feudal court sites to which she conducted the delegates. Later in the same year she was elected 'Officier de l'Academie Française' and was the first foreign woman to be so honoured.

In the years following the First World War Edith Carey, in collaboration with her cousin Wilfred Carey, embarked on the compilation of the *History of the Careys of Guernsey*. Lack of time, however, prevented her from finishing the book with the help of papers left by Wilfred on his death in 1929. In the event the work was completed after she too had died by yet another cousin, the antiquarian Spencer Carey Curtis, and it finally appeared in 1938. A further posthumous volume contained a collection of hitheto unprinted essays published as a memorial to her by La Société Guernesiaise in 1936 under the title, *Essays in Guernsey History*. It is by no means unknown for intellectuals to betray endearing oddities of character and in the case of Edith Carey such a quirk consisted of a firm belief in witchcraft — on which she made herself an authority, collecting songs and stories concerned with this topic from the country parishes, whose lore provides so rich a source of accounts of the black art.

Edith Carey died on 29 May 1935, and the memorial tablet to this woman who loved Guernsey deeply and wished its history to be recorded with truth and accuracy, adjoins the Carey pew in St Martin's church. In a tribute to her memory the great French scholar, le Père Bourde de la Rogerie, said, 'She had learnt how the laws and institutions of Guernsey had not happened by chance but were the fruits of experience, and she hoped no imprudent hands would come to destroy this edifice'.

CAREY, SIR VICTOR GOSSELIN (1871–1957). *A Lamb among Wolves.* (B). Commenting retrospectively on the career of Marshal Pétain, General de Gaulle remarked in Volume II of his Memoirs (*Le Salut*, pp. 291–2) that '*son drame avait été celui d'une vieillesse que la glace des années privait des forces nécessaires pour conduire les événements*'. ('His tragedy had been that of a senescence which the chill of age deprived of the energy needed to govern men and events'.) In the microcosmic context of Guernsey a similar assessment would be appropriate in the case of Sir Victor Carey, whose misfortune it was to be confronted with a cataclysm when already at or past the psalmist's span. Yet another parallel with Pétain stems from the fact that, as the scion of a house which reputedly first came to Guernsey from Lisieux in Normandy in 1288 and whose moral standards are epitomised in the noble motto, *Sine Macula*, he appreciated as little as did the aged Marshal of France the full extent of the turpitude of the adversary with whom he had to deal — a naiveté which sometimes had appalling consequences. Thus, for example, this blindness led to his seeming to be oblivious of the hideous fate awaiting those involved when in March 1941 he ordered Inspector W. R. Sculpher (Chief of

Police) to prepare a report for submission to the Germans giving details of all Jewish persons in the island: a course of action which eventuated in the concentration camp followed by the gas chamber for Theresia Steiner (a nurse), and Auguste Spitz (a wardmaid), both of the Castel Hospital (qq.v.).

Inclined to be highly-strung and absent-minded, though gentle and kind and of innate courtesy and charm, Carey became Bailiff in 1935 at the age of 64 (and already elderly and vague beyond his years) when the unexpected death of Mr. Arthur William Bell created a vacancy which Major Ambrose Sherwill (q.v.) — who, as Procureur, occupied the post whose holder was normally regarded as heir apparent — was as yet rather too young to fill. His previous career had not been particularly distinguished. Born in July 1871 as the son of Major-General de Vic Carey and the younger brother of Edith (q.v.) the future Bailiff was educated first at Elizabeth College (1880–83) and later at Marlborough College (1885–87). Going up to the Université de Caen in 1895, he came down in 1897 with the degree of Bachelier-en-Droit and was admitted to the Guernsey Bar as an Advocate in 1898. Serving as a Lieutenant in the Royal Guernsey Artillery from 1897 to 1899, he was elected as a States' Deputy in 1900 and was appointed Receiver-General in 1912: a post which he held until his elevation to Guernsey's supreme office.

A few days before the German Occupation commenced Carey, like Malvolio, had greatness thrust upon him; a Home Office letter of 19 June 1940 commissioned him, on the recall of the Lieutenant-Governor, to 'discharge the duties of Lieutenant-Governor, which would be confined to civil duties' and to 'stay at his post and administer the government of the Island to the best of his abilities in the interest of the inhabitants'. He accordingly signed official documents as 'British Civil Lieutenant-Governor' or 'His Majesty's Lieutenant-Governor' until the Germans, towards the end of 1941, took exception to this practice; whereupon he signed simply as 'Bailiff'.

His position was indeed an anomalous one. Although retaining the post of Bailiff throughout the period of the Occupation, he remained largely in the background, effective responsibility devolving on the President of the Controlling Committee which had been formed as an emergency governmental apparatus endowed with full powers so as to give more room for manoeuvre *vis-à-vis* the Germans than would have been possible with the more cumbersome machinery of the States.

Standing aside in this way to allow the younger and more vigorous Sherwill and — subsequently — John Leale (q.v.) to carry the main burden did not mean, however, that Carey withdrew from affairs completely. He continued to preside over sessions of the Royal Court and from time to time intervened with considerable effect to deal with the Germans on matters of particular importance. The result was occasional confusion, tinged with acrimony, as to what precisely should be reserved for the Bailiff.

Part of the trouble was that — again as in the case of Pétain — Carey believed in the feasibility of an honourable accommodation with the enemy 'as between gentlemen', admitting frankly after the Liberation that 'the one thing I was keen about was that there shouldn't be any sort of resistance movement'. Accordingly there were times when he performed his functions with a punctillio verging on the excessive, issuing proclamations in his own name in terms which seemed to make him side with the occupying power — even to the extent on one occasion of using the word 'enemy' as applying to the Allied Forces!

On the other hand Carey protested vehemently over the Deportation Orders in 1942, and showed that he was alive to the flaws in Guernsey's government revealed by the experiences of adversity when in October 1943 he set up a Committee to consider how far the island's former system could cope with the strain of post-war conditions. Furthermore, when starvation threatened Guernsey in the autumn of 1944, he came forward to make indignant representations to the enemy Commandant, von Schmettow (q.v.), complaining that the Germans were using the Hague Convention to take civilian food, while ignoring the provisions which required them to keep the people fed: demonstrating moreover than the quantities being taken were much greater than the Convention permitted. He eventually prevailed upon the Germans to permit him on 5 November to apprise the International Red Cross by wireless of the plight of the islanders.

In evaluating Carey's behaviour one must not forget that he went on shouldering a thankless task up to the age of 75, not always fully realising the implications of his actions. Even the resistance hero, Frank Falla (q.v.), referring to the Bailiff's much criticised notice of July 1941 offering a £25 reward for information leading to the conviction of anyone chalking up 'V' signs or making other markings 'likely to offend the German authorities'; said that he did not blame

him, adding that he was an elderly and extremely worried man who had no choice — if he had not signed the Germans would have done so for him. The knighthood granted him in the Occupation Honours List in December 1945 had the unfortunate result of partially reviving the bitterness that had been focused upon him when conduct that was capable of interpretation as collaboration had led to his receiving an average of four letters of abuse per day. Those, however, who had been more intimately connected with him throughout the Occupation felt differently, testifying to Alan and Mary Wood (the authors of that gripping account of the Occupation, *Islands in Danger*) that 'he never baulked at meeting the Germans and backing the rest of us when necessary and that trait has always endeared him to us. We always looked upon him as a good boss and he never forgot to be kind to those who worked for him'.

For 12 years Sir Victor enjoyed the honour of knighthood. Retiring in 1946, he died in June 1957 and is commemorated for all time by the lovely cliff-top pleasance at Jerbourg, donated as his memorial to the people of Guernsey by his sons.

DE CARTERET, AMICE (1559–1631). *The scourge of the sorcerers*. (F). The younger son of Helier de Carteret (q.v.), Amice was educated at Winchester and then went up to Cambridge. On coming down at the age of 19 he married Catherine Lemprière, the heiress of the Jersey fief of Trinity. Although on the death of Helier de Carteret in 1581 Jersey's premier fief of St Ouen passed to his elder son Philippe (q.v.), Amice overshadowed his brother in Jersey public life and two years later (in 1583) he was appointed a Jurat of the Jersey Court.

On Philippe's early death in 1594 Amice became the acting Seigneur of Sark during the minority of the new Seigneur — his ten-year-old nephew who, along with the parental lands, had also inherited from his father the name of Philippe (q.v.). In this capacity Amice immediately set about easing the strained relations which had existed between his brother and the Governor of Guernsey, Sir Thomas Leighton (q.v.), making haste to arrange for the installation of the new Sark Court which had been required as long previously as 1583 by an Order-in-Council which Philippe had ignored.

The cordial and intimate relationship which Amice thus established with Leighton was to have far-reaching consequences. In 1600 the resignation of Louis de Vic (q.v.) created a vacancy for the office of Bailiff of Guernsey and Leighton, for lack of any Guernseyman he felt he could trust, recommended to the Privy Council that the Jersey-man, Amice de Carteret, should be appointed. The Jersey Court reluctantly released Amice from his duties as Jurat and in 1601 he assumed office as Bailiff of Guernsey — a post which he held for 30 years until his death in April 1631. As at the time of this appointment he was still the acting Seigneur of Sark, the links between Guernsey and Sark were much strengthened.

The new broom lost little time in sweeping extremely clean. Discarding many outdated customs and procedures, Amice initiated a codification of the laws and in 1608 introduced the system whereby the Jurats are divided into three sets of four to deal with minor cases, each quartet serving from Christmas to Easter, Easter to Michaelmas and Michaelmas to Christmas respectively. Under this arrangement — which still applies — the Bailiff and the appropriate quartet of Jurats constitute the Ordinary Court and the Contract Court, while all twelve Jurats are needed for the Full Court to assemble.

In 1610 Catherine de Carteret died and in the same year Lord Carew of Clopton replaced Sir Thomas Leighton as Governor, the new widower becoming Lieutenant-Governor. As Lord Carew was a permanent absentee, interested only in the revenues he derived from his office, Amice de Carteret sat firmly in the gubernatorial saddle, so that, being Bailiff as well, he emerged as the 'uncrowned king' of Guernsey, wielding autocratic powers which he retained for a decade, until he finally yielded the office of Lieutenant-Governor in 1620 to Thomas Andros, who held the fort pending the arrival the following year of Sir Peter Osborne (q.v.). It was during these years of Amice de Carteret's supremacy that James I, true to his maxim of 'No Bishop, no King', sought to impose episcopacy on the islands. He succeeded in Jersey, but in Guernsey the 'uncrowned king', as a staunch Presbyterian, organized such effective resistance to the change that the Crown abandoned its plans.

De Carteret was not only a fervent Presbyterian — he was also an ardent witch-hunter. Firmly believing that the ignorant or deranged beldames babbling incantations and imprecations at Le Catioric were indeed the handmaids of Satan, he proceeded against them with merciless vigour, ordering many suspects to be tortured to extract confessions. During the 30 years when as Bailiff he wielded 'the sword of the Lord and of Gideon',

77 witches were tried of whom 34 were burnt alive and 24 banished from the island. It is, alas, for this least attractive of his attributes that Amice de Carteret is chiefly remembered.

DE CARTERET, SIR CHARLES, BARONET (1679–1715). *The only Seigneur of Sark to be buried in Westminster Abbey and to have a memorial there.* (F). A fitting text to sum up the life of Sir Charles de Carteret would be 2 Samuel I:19 — 'How are the mighty fallen!' Called Charles because the king himself stood godfather at his baptism, he was knighted by James II at the age of eight in advance of inheriting the baronetcy, as a mark of gratitude for the support accorded to the king by his father, Sir Philippe de Carteret (q.v.).

Sir Charles succeeded to an impoverished inheritance on his father's death in 1693 when he was 14. Ten years later he was sworn in as the (mostly absentee) Bailiff of Jersey, but two years previously (1701) he had been faced with a revolt by his resentful tenants at St Ouen, who refused their feudal services. Although the Jersey Court found in his favour, this did not stop complaints being sent to the Privy Council regarding his frequent absences and his poor command of French. Indeed, Sir Charles was thoroughly anglicised and spent most of his time in England, being a Gentleman of the Privy Chamber.

What was more, this absentee Seigneur, despite his straitened circumstances, recklessly overspent while in London and in 1713 his mounting debts led him to seek permission to sell his fief. This permission was granted in April 1714, but before any sale could be completed Sir Charles died without issue on 6 June 1715; so that Sark passed to his third cousin (Lord John Carteret) who never visited the Channel Isles and sold the island at the first opportunity to Colonel John Johnson, one-time commander of the Guernsey garrison and one of his predecessor's chief creditors. It is ironical that such an inglorious career should be followed by posthumous honours on a scale unmatched for any other Seigneur of Sark — the sole reason for his inclusion in this dictionary!

CARTERET, SIR GEORGE (1609–1679). *Alderney's first 'Hereditary Governor'.* (F). The career of this illustrious Jerseyman had no more than a tangential impact on the Bailiwick of Guernsey, the three points of contact being Castle Cornet, Sark and Alderney. It will therefore be on this trio that the main emphasis of the following account will be concentrated.

A senior officer in the Royal Navy (where he dropped the French-sounding 'de' as an embarrassment), George Carteret invaded Jersey in November 1643 and relieved his cousin Philippe de Carteret (q.v.) who was beseiged in Elizabeth Castle by the king's enemies. This done, George Carteret planned to come to the succour of Sir Peter Osborne (q.v.), who was holding Castle Cornet for the king; and also to recover Sark (which had aligned itself with Guernsey in support of the Parliament) for his cousin, who *de jure* was its Seigneur.

In accordance with these intentions an expedition was launched in May 1644 against Sark, whither 100 men were dispatched in four boats. Unfortunately, though the minor detachment succeeded in taking the Parliamentary garrison by surprise, its leader (Captain Chamberlain) found to his dismay when the morning arrived that the main force had been repulsed and had returned to Jersey. He himself was taken prisoner by a landing party from a passing Parliamentary frigate which the Serquiais alerted by firing beacons.

Sad to say, the Sark failure was not compensated by any great success attending Carteret's plans to relieve Sir Peter Osborne. Relations between the two men were strained, so that Carteret only grudgingly supplied Osborne at irregular intervals. When the Prince of Wales arrived in Jersy in 1646 Carteret (who had been knighted the previous year) persuaded Charles that Osborne should be recalled — with the result that later that year he was replaced by Sir Baldwin Wake (q.v.*). In 1648 Sir George tried to recover both Sark and Guernsey, but each attempt was frustrated. The expedition against Sark was scattered by a violent storm; while in the case of Guernsey Carteret was foiled by the refusal of Sir Baldwin Wake (with whom his relations were little better than those he had had with his predecessor) to allow him to enter Castle Cornet with more than six men!

On hearing of the execution of Charles I Carteret immediately had Charles II proclaimed in Jersey — and the retributive dismissal of Wake from Castle Cornet quickly followed the new king's arrival in the island, where he stayed prior to his departure for Scotland in February 1650. When Colonel James Heane invaded Jersey in October 1651 Carteret held out in Elizabeth Castle until 15 December, when he surrendered after being granted safe conduct — though he failed in his attempt to obtain the return of Sark to his cousin Philippe on payment of a penalty.

When he came into his own again Charles II granted Alderney to three Jersey Royalists — Edward and James de Carteret and Clement le Couteur — for an annual rent of one mark (13s. 4d.). In the autumn of the same year these three gentlemen sold their rights to Sir George, who thereby became Governor of Alderney. The government of the island was divorced from that of Guernsey, any mention of Alderney being expressly omitted from the Letters Patent issued to Lord Hatton on his belated appointment as Governor of Guernsey in 1664. Technically Sir George Carteret held Alderney of the Crown as a feudal fief of which he was Seigneur. The attitude of the islanders, however, plus the fact that the island's governmental institutions were already well developed, meant that no Seigneur and tenant relationship comparable to that of Sark was practicable; with the result that the title of 'Governor' was employed, such a designation being rendered appropriate by Alderney's removal from the jurisdiction of the Governor of Guernsey.

The Restoration brought a shower of rewards for Sir George, quite apart from the Lordship of little Alderney. He was appointed Vice-Chamberlain of the Royal Household and a member of the Privy Council: and in addition was given the lucrative post of Treasurer of the Royal Navy. He was also granted estates in the West Country and became M.P. for Portsmouth. Steadfast in his friendship, the king prorogued Parliament in 1666 to shield Sir George when he was accused of malversation of public funds. The successful Dutch attack on Chatham, however, meant that Carteret had to relinquish his post at the Admiralty and in 1667 he was deprived of his seat in the Commons.

Of particular significance to the Bailiwick of Guernsey was the grant to Sir George in 1664 of the large tract of land in North America which he named New Jersey. Captain Nicholas Ling (q.v.) (Carteret's resident Lieutenant-Governor in Alderney) promulgated an Ordinance to the effect that all poor children, who could not be supported by their parents, should be handed over for dispatch to New Jersey to provide labour for the infant settlement. The Alderney Court approved this Ordinance, which brought a steady decline in the island's population during the next 30 years, besides establishing a contact between Alderney and the New World, to which many Aurigniais later emigrated.

Sir George died in February 1680 leaving his widow, Elizabeth, Lady de Carteret, as 'Governor of Alderney' until in 1682 she sold the residue of her late husband's patent to Sir Edmund Andros (q.v.).

DE CARTERET, HELIER (1532–1581). *The founding father of the Fief of Sark*. (F). Helier de Carteret was Seigneur of St Ouen (Jersey's premier fief) as far back as he could remember, having inherited the holding at the age of one year, on the death of his father Edouard. As he grew up his standing as Jersey's paramount Seigneur was further enhanced by the fact that his uncle (also Helier) was the island's vigorous Bailiff, who enjoyed considerable favour at Court during the reign of Edward VI and again after the accession of Elizabeth I — favour which was also extended to his nephew.

This Jerseyman's involvement with the history of the Bailiwick of Guernsey dates from 1563. The outbreak of war between England and France the previous year gave Elizabeth I cause for anxiety about the defence of the Channel Isles with the result that in May 1563 a Royal Commission was appointed to foster fortification by raising funds from the sale of confiscated church property. In June, Helier de Carteret put a proposal to the Commissioners. During his earlier years he had seen two French occupations of the deserted island of Sark (1549–53 and 1560–62). Both of these had been in time of peace, but with England and France at war Helier feared for the security of his lands at St Ouen should the enemy once again establish himself in this empty neighbouring isle. He therefore suggested to the Royal Commission that he should be granted Sark as an adjunct to Saint Ouen, in return for which he would be prepared to settle the island and defend it. In September the Commissioners obtained the approval of the Governor of Guernsey, Sir Francis Chamberlayne (q.v.) for Helier's plan and thereupon made a grant in fee-farm to him of the island of Sark and its appurtenances.

Early in 1564 Helier took an experimental party to Sark and a small area of land was put under trial cultivation, with encouraging results. He then turned his attention to other matters. In June of the same year the first inter-island ecclesiastical Synod assembled and Helier de Carteret was sent to London as its delegate to plead that if the islands were not allowed to follow the organisation and doctrine of the French Reformed Churches, the French clergy would leave and they would be bereft of anyone able to preach the Gospel in their own language. His representations were sufficiently persuasive to elicit an Order-in-Council the following year permitting the Geneva usage in the two towns. It is true that the same Order required that the Anglican rite be adhered to in the rural parishes — but in the

event this requirements was ignored because of the lack of French-speaking Anglican clerics.

The success of the 1564 agricultural experiment emboldened Helier de Carteret to take further action in Sark and in the spring of 1565, accompanied by his wife Marguerite, he established a small party of pioneer settlers on the island. June of the same year found him once more in London, this time heading a deputation to the Privy Council regarding legal appeals from Jersey Courts. While in the capital he obtained Letters Patent from the Queen on 6 August confirming the 1563 grant by the Commissioners, provided he settled Sark with 40 men, armed for the defence of the island. Seven years later (in 1572) de Carteret was again in the metropolis, heading yet another deputation from Jersey on the vexed and still unresolved problem of legal appeals. He took the opportunity afforded by his visit to report to Elizabeth I that Sark's defences were secure and the terms of the 1565 Letters Patent achieved. The Queen responded by making Sark a Fief Haubert in its own right and as a mark of her esteem sent Helier six cannon from the Tower of London, complete with ammunition and gunpowder. Sark as it exists today had come into being.

Helier had in fact already anticipated Sark's elevation to the rank of an independent fief and indeed it was his ambition that the island be acknowledged as the equal of Guernsey and Jersey and not subordinate to either. Thus the previous year (1571) he had deliberately disregarded an order to pay suit of service at the Guernsey Chief Pleas — and he continued this policy of ignoring every such summons to attend until his death.

In 1578 Helier transferred his authority in Sark to his son and heir Philippe (q.v.) as his Jersey responsibilities necessitated frequent absences from the island. The next year (1579) the ever-increasing tension in Guernsey between the Governor, Thomas Leighton (q.v.) and the island leaders led to the setting up of a Commission of Enquiry to examine the relative powers of the Royal Court and the Governor, and Helier de Carteret was appointed one of its members. He tried to bring the matter of Sark's status to the notice of the Commission — but the other Commissioners ruled that this was outside their terms of reference. Helier accordingly concluded that the focusing of attention on the fracas in Guernsey would enable Sark, without being noticed, to take assertive action which could at a later stage be presented to all and sundry as a *fait accompli*. He therefore advised Philippe to set up a separate Sark Court as an affirmation of the island's autonomy. This was done on 27 October of the same year, the genesis of the Sark Chief Pleas thus being accomplished. In effect, of course, Helier was challenging the authority of the Guernsey Court and in September 1581, after the question of the respective powers of the Governor and the Guernsey leaders had been resolved by the installation of Leighton's nephew as Bailiff, he was called to account by this body for creating a rival Court in Sark. Yet again Helier ignored the summons to attend and before any further action could be taken, he died (October 1581), leaving a most difficult inheritance for his son.

DE CARTERET, PHILIPPE (1552–1594). *The originator of 'Corvée' and 'Le Creux'*. (F). Philippe de Carteret's significance in the Bailiwick's history dates from October 1578, when his father Helier (q.v.), burdened by preoccupations elsewhere, transferred to him all seigneurial authority in Sark. A year later – in September 1579 – he received a petition from the Serquiais for the establishment of an independent island administration as an insurance against Sark being placed more firmly under the control of Guernsey. Helier having advised compliance with this request, Philippe convened a meeting on 27 October 1579 where it was decided to set up an Island Court with Edouard de Carteret (Philippe's first cousin once removed) as Bailiff, plus 12 Jurats and nine other officials – constituting between them half the male population of the island!

In January 1580, with the aim of strengthening the de Carteret position at the Court of Elizabeth I, Philippe married Rachel, the daughter of George Paulet, Lieutenant-Governor of Jersey. His father's death the following year left him in a difficult position arising out of the Guernsey Royal Court's resentment at the challenge to its authority implicit in the establishment of a Sark Court: and Philippe made matters worse by his refusal to pay the feudal inheritance due of *première saisine* to the Queen's Receiver in Guernsey, on the plea that under Norman Law he was not liable for this tax. This goaded the Guernsey Court formally to protest at the setting up of a separate court without its permission – and to dispatch the Bailiff at the head of an armed party to Sark to assert its authority. Philippe was in Jersey at the time attending to his fief at St Ouen and his deputy (Philip Messervy) failed to produce 40 armed men when called upon so to do. The island was consequently declared forfeit to the Crown and Edouard de Carteret imprisoned in Castle Cornet

for usurping the Royal Court's powers. Though later released, he was never allowed to return to Sark.

Philippe now appealed to the Privy Council and an Order-in-Council of 24 April 1583 formulated a compromise solution. Philippe was allowed to retain his position as Seigneur on payment of a reduced *première saisine* and, while Guernsey's legal supremacy over Sark was confirmed, the smaller island was given the right to its own Court of five Jurats, with the senior one acting as judge – though its jurisdiction was limited to civil cases. His position as Seigneur now secure, Philippe (to the detriment of his relations with Thomas Leighton (q.v.)) made no attempt to convene the court stipulated by the Order-in-Council, merely administering Sark through his fief court for the rest of his life.

Philippe de Carteret made three important contributions to the development of the fief which his father had founded. It was under his direction that Helier's project of creating a harbour at La Baie de la Motte by blasting a tunnel through the cliffs – hence the name of 'Le Creux' (the Hole) – was brought to a successful conclusion in 1588. He also, by an Ordinance of October 1585, established the 'Corvée' system for road upkeep, making this the direct responsibility of the tenants. His most important innovation, however, concerned inheritance legislation. According to Jersey usage, which the original settlers had assumed would apply in Sark also, the eldest son obtained his late father's house with its immediate surrounds, while the rest of the property was divided among the other children, with due safeguards for the widow. In the case of Sark, however, many of the heirs were outside the island and as, furthermore, they in their turn might sell their inheritance to anybody they liked, extreme fragmentation of the tenements was threatened, with a resultant inability to support the resident tenants, thereby imperilling the maintenance of the 40 armed men required by the terms of Elizabeth's Letters Patent. Taking advantage of the seizure by the Guernsey visitants in 1582 of many contracts of lease, Philippe, when asked to issue new contracts to confirm the titles of heirs, inserted clauses forbidding any sub-division of the land and the transfer to non-residents of any rights in the holdings; thus taking the first steps towards creating the system of inheritance which still persists in Sark.

Provisions such as these could not, however, be made retrospective and most tenants by their original contracts were free, in accordance with the Jersey tradition, to dispose of their holdings at will. Philippe's untimely death in 1594 at the age of 41 before this complication could be resolved was to prove the source of considerable difficulties in later years until definitive action was taken, 17 years after his demise, by his son.

DE CARTERET, SIR PHILIPPE (1584-1643). *The inaugurator of the Seigneur's Triezième who was captured by privateers*. (F). When Sark's third Seigneur came into his inheritance in 1594 he was but ten years of age, so that during his minority the functions of his office were performed by his uncle Amice de Carteret (q.v.). His coming of age in 1605 coincided with the death of Cosmé Brévint (q.v.), so that he was immediately presented with the difficulty of replacing this pivotal figure in the island community. After a number of unsatisfactory interim appointments (one of whom was David Bandinel, with whom he was to have further dealings at a later stage) eventually in July 1610, he undertook to pay for the training of Elie Brévint (q.v.) and to provide him with accommodation so as to obtain an acceptable successor to his father Cosmé. Elie Brévint took up the Sark incumbency 18 months later.

Besides these ecclesiastical complications Philippe found that during his minority land tenure problems had become acute. In the first place additional buildings had been erected on the various tenements to accommodate younger children — and these carried no obligation to provide anyone for island defence. This development had led the Court, shortly before Philippe came of age, to pass an Ordinance whereby only tenants of the 40 original tenements ('*Maisons de la Quarantaine*') were to have a voice in the deliberations of its legislative sessions. Secondly, the practice had spread of mortgages being raised on tenements, imperilling the ability of future tenants to meet their seigneurial dues or to subsist on their holdings. Lastly, the danger of fragmentation of holdings still threatened, despite the initial steps his father had taken to remove it.

To cope with these threats to the economic basis of the Island Settlement Philippe obtained supplementary Letters Patent from James I on 12 August 1611 whereby the raising of mortgages was prohibited and tenements were made indivisible: though they could be sold intact with the Seigneur's approval provided buyers undertook to supply an armed man for island defences. In this event one-thirteenth of the purchase price became payable to the Seigneur — the inception of '*triezième*'! This unique form of land tenure remains the basis of Sark's property law to the present day. Unfortunately, however, the Letters Patent were not registered in the Sark Court, so that the practices Philippe sought to check still continued intil his grandson put his foot down 64 years later!

After 1612 Philippe's career no longer strictly falls within the purview of the Guernsey Bailiwick's history as he was increasingly absorbed in Jersey affairs, leaving Jacques Paulet as his deputy in Sark. He was knighted on 23 February 1616-17 and subsequently acquiesced in the imposition of an Anglican ecclesiastical structure in Jersey, culminating in the appointment as Dean in 1620 of David Bandinel, who had been the Calvinist incumbent in Sark immediately after the death of Cosmé Brévint, but who had since received episcopal ordination. Sir Philippe became Bailiff of Jersey on 18 January 1626-7 and during the French War of 1628-9 he was captured by Spanish privateers and ransomed for £117 4s. 8d. Made Lieutenant-Governor of Jersey on 19 July 1634, he held Elizabeth Castle for the king when fighting broke out in 1643, dying there on 23 August.

DE CARTERET, SIR PHILIPPE, BARONET (1620-1663). *Sark's dispossessed Seigneur*. (F). Although *de jure* Seigneur of Sark for 19½ years, Sir Philippe de Carteret only had access to the fief for the last 30 months of his life. When his father died while holding Elizabeth Castle against the king's enemies in August 1643, he came into a troubled inheritance. True to its Calvinist traditions, Sark had aligned itself, together with Guernsey, in support of the very foes by whom he himself was beset in the fortress where he continued his resistance on behalf of Charles I, while his mother held on at Mont Orgueil in the same cause.

Relief came the following November when his cousin and brother-in-law, George Carteret (q.v.) seized Jersey for the king. Although an attempt to regain Sark the following year proved abortive, Philippe was rewarded for his loyalty to the Stuarts in June 1646 when he was knighted on behalf of the king by Prince Charles at a militia review held on the sands of St Aubin's Bay.

When Jersey was invaded and Elizabeth Castle finally fell to the Parliamentary forces on 15 December 1651, George Carteret failed in his attempt to regain Sark for his cousin by paying a penalty to the victors. Sir Philippe thereupon withdrew to France, where he fitted out privateers to harrass Commonwealth shipping — but he did not try to take Sark, which was defended by a captain and 30 men sent over from Guernsey. After the Restoration Charles II elevated Sir Philippe to the rank of Knight Baronet and reinstated him in his fiefs of St Ouen and Sark, of which island he was formally repossessed on 25 August 1660. The following February he also became Bailiff and Lieutenant-Governor of Jersey.

In Sark the restored Seigneur made no attempt to extend the Anglican ecclesiastical system to the island because of the great prestige of Elie Brévint (q.v.). Neither did he take any action over contracts which had been passed by the Court during the Commonwealth period and which were technically invalid for lack of his seal. What he did do was to provide for future contingencies by a small ceremony on 12 August 1661 where he formally entrusted the Seigneur's Seal to the Court for use on contracts. Fate left Sir Philippe de Carteret with little time for further action, however, as within 18 months he was dead, breathing his last on 7 February 1663.

DE CARTERET, SIR PHILIPPE, BARONET (1650-1693). *The creator of the Seneschal's Court.* (F). Because Sir Philippe de Carteret, the second Baronet, was only 13 when he succeeded his father, his mother (Anne Dumaresq) acted as Dame de Sercq during his minority, with Nicholas Richardson as her representative in the island. On coming of age in 1671 Sir Philippe lost no time in seeking to halt the fragmentation of landholdings by challenging the validity of contracts passed during the Commonwealth period in contravention of James I's Letters Patent. The gauntlet he threw down was taken up by the powerful le Gros family, thanks to whose widespread influence the Seigneur soon found himself confronted with ubiquitous total non-cooperation. Thus frustrated, Sir Philippe on 2 August 1672 obtained an Order-in-Council suspending the authority of the Sark Court brought into being in 1594 by his great-great-uncle Amice de Carteret (q.v.), on the grounds that two newly-elected Jurats had refused to take the oath of allegiance in the context of the Anglican Sacrament as required by the royal grant of pardon of 1660.

The monumental authority of the Reverend Elie Brévint (q.v.), the formidable ally of the le Gros family — to which he was connected by marriage (his deceased daughter having been the first wife of Jean le Gros) — deterred Sir Philippe from taking any more effective steps for the time

being — but on the minister's death on 30 March 1674, he sprang into action. As the new incumbent the Seigneur appointed Moise Benoist, a Frenchman who had been ordained as a priest by the Bishop of Winchester, thus finally bringing Sark within the Anglican fold after 14 years as the last bastion of Presbyterianism in the archipelago. To mark the occasion Dame Anne Dumaresq presented a chalice to the Sark church on 26 August 1675.

This done, Sir Philippe took steps to replace the suspended Court dominated by Jean le Gros (q.v.). In May 1675 an Order-in-Council created a new Sark Court consisting of a Seneschal, a Greffier and a Prévôt — all appointed by the Seigneur, whose hand was thereby considerably strengthened. This new court was installed on 15 July 1675 and has persisted to the present day.

Sir Philippe now took personal action against Jean le Gros, who had retired to his second wife's property in Guernsey, applying to the Guernsey Royal Court in 1677 to institute an enquiry into mortgages raised by this worthy in breach of James I's Letters Patent. This court action was continued against le Gros' widow after his death later the same year. The Royal Court found in Sir Philippe's favour and on 20 January 1680 the Letters Patent of James I were at last registered in the Sark Court. With the principle conceded, Sir Philippe did not try to put the clock completely back, but contented himself with the compromise agreement reached with Dame Elizabeth le Pelley, widow of Jean le Gros, in 1681, whereby the land-holdings of Sark were 'frozen' at the pattern then existing. At the same time Sir Philippe insisted that all future property transactions should involve only entire tenements in accordance with the provisions of the 1611 Letters Patent; thus finally and firmly establishing the unique land-tenure system which still obtains in Sark, whereby tenants may never divide their land nor bequeath any part of it, the whole passing to the heir by primogeniture unless sold intact during the tenant's lifetime.

The battle won, Sir Philippe withdrew from active contact with Sark and the relevance of the rest of his life to the Bailiwick of Guernsey is remote. For the record it may be said that he became Bailiff of Jersey in 1682, but was primarily concerned with events at the Courts of Charles II and James II where, after the death on 13 January 1680 of Sir George Carteret (q.v.) he became the senior representative of the family. Ever loyal to the Stuarts, he supported James II during the struggles following the Glorious

Revolution, with the result that the morrow of the Battle of the Boyne found him in such dire financial straits that in 1691 he sought Crown permission to sell his Fief. In the event he did not sell but leased all his Sark entitlements for a period of three years to Daniel Valpy *dit* Janvrin of Jersey for 3,000 livres tournois down and 1,100 livres tournois per annum. Before this agreement had run its full course, however, Sir Philippe died on 23 October 1693.

CASTLE, JONATHAN GRAHAM (1950-   ). *Guernsey's audacious ecological zealot*. Born on 7 December 1950, to Mary Constance (*née* Bussey), the wife of Robert Breedlove Castle, Jonathan Castle was educated first at La Monnaie Kindergarten in St Andrew's and subsequently at the Castel School from 1958 to 1962, when his performance in the Eleven Plus Examination was such as to earn him a place at Elizabeth College as pupil number 5813. Ending his school career just after Easter 1967, he entered the Merchant Navy, eventually qualifying as First Officer.

The daring lengths to which this Old Elizabethan was prepared to go at the dictates of his convictions were demonstrated repeatedly almost as soon as he had obtained his navigational qualifications. In the month of August 1979 the ship *Rainbow Warrior* of the Canadian Greenpeace ecological movement, under Jonathan Castle's command and with Mr. Peter Wilkinson (a director of Greenpeace) on board, was towed into Reykjavik after the Icelandic gunboat *Aegir* had swooped on her for performing what was alleged to be 'an act of piracy' 50 miles out to sea. Mr. Sigurdur Bjarnason, the Icelandic Ambassador to Britain, explained that the arrest had been made for 'doing unlawful things according to Icelandic law' whereby it was made 'difficult for our ships to kill whales'. The Guernseyman duly appeared before an Icelandic court, but survived to fight another day.

The other day came on 18 June 1980 when the *Rainbow Warrior* (the ship's company this time including employees of Independent Television News) was escorted into the Spanish port of El Ferrol by the frigate *Vicente Yanez Pinzon*, the vessel being impounded by the Spanish authorities and a guard set to watch over it. The ship had, it seemed, deliberately interfered with whaling operations 55 miles off the Spanish coast by getting in the way of the whaler *Ibsa III*. This had been done by the crew of the *Rainbow Warrior* manoeuvring several inflatable dinghies between the whaler and its prey in such a way

that firing at the whale was liable to result in injury or death for the dinghies' occupants. Although the *Warrior* was boarded after the arrival of Spanish warships, when the *Ibsa III* again chased a whale the dinghies once more moved in to protect it, only withdrawing when the warships ordered the whaler to give up the hunt. On arrival at El Ferrol Jonathan Castle faced a preliminary hearing which it was initially feared would be followed by a court-martial on a charge of 'obstructing ships in Spanish waters' where conviction would carry a minimum sentence of six months imprisonment. He was told that he would have to remain in El Ferrol for 'at least three months' awaiting trial. At the same time the Spanish naval authorities carried parts of the *Rainbow Warrior*'s thrust block ashore and set bail for release at ten million pesetas.

Meanwhile the Greenpeace organisation (which claimed that the Spaniards were hunting fin whales without restriction, despite a quota of 143 imposed by the International Whaling Commission, which Spain had joined in 1979) arranged with a small engineering firm in Millwall docks to manufacture a replacement thrust block based on the original drawings. In due course this was secreted into Spain on a Volkswagen Camper travelling from France. The 150 pound component was then smuggled on board the *Rainbow Warrior* past the three-man police guard whose attention was diverted by the crew pretending to be blind drunk. Once the block was replaced the main motor was surreptitiously tested under cover of darkness, after which 45 minutes cautious underwater work was needed to careen the ship's hull to facilitate sailing. On Saturday 8 November 1980 at 7.30 p.m. the police guard was seen to leave before the arrival of its replacement. The chance which Castle had patiently awaited had arrived. The *Rainbow Warrior* (blacked out except for essential navigation lights) immediately slid away from the quay and gingerly edged past the two forts standing sentinel over the entrance to the port. It was then found that the ship could only make seven knots and consequently it took no less than 29 hours to clear the Spanish economic zone. Fortune favoured the fugitives however, and despite a widespread naval search the Greenpeace vessel reached Jersey in safety.

The autumn of 1982 saw Jonathan Castle yet again courting mortal danger in obedience to his ideals — this time in protest against French nuclear tests in the Pacific. In command of the *Vega* he deliberately sailed his craft into the heart of the navigational danger zone surrounding Mururoa Atoll — the site of fifty underground nuclear tests since France discontinued all atmospheric testing in 1975. The French Navy seized the vessel, which was towed to Popek, taking Jonathan Castle, together with an Australian colleague (Christopher Robertson), into custody. Having made their point the two men (who by their action sought to create publicity in support of the representations whereby various South Pacific States had urged France to stop her underground tests) signed an agreement never to return to French Polynesia, in consideration of which they were released and flown to Auckland via Sydney. *Note:* Quotations in this entry are taken from reports published in *The Times* and the *Daily Telegraph.*

CAUCHÉS, CATHERINE: AND FAMILY. (Put to death July 1556). *A disgraceful episode: sorrowful simpletons sacrificed as scapegoats by scoundrels.* In his *Christian Martyrdom* the Reverend John Foxe recounts the horrifying case of the treatment meted out to three Guernsey women in the year 1556. He tells that on 27 May of that year a certain Vincent Gosset stole a silver cup from Nicolas le Conronney and then tried to pawn it for sixpence with Perrotine Massey, the married daughter of Catherine Cauchés, who lived with her mother and her sister Guillemine Gilbert. Realising that a theft had occurred, Perrotine advanced Gosset the sixpence requested, thereby securing the cup, after which she notified Conronney. Gosset, when confronted by Conronney, confessed to her guilt.

Gosset's admission notwithstanding, the case was investigated by the senior St Peter-Port constable, Nicolas Carey, who then reported finding a pewter vessel in the house where the Cauchés family dwelt. As a consequence the three women were taken into custody at Castle Cornet and when examined it transpired that, although they had come by the pewter vessel perfectly honestly; yet they had disregarded the commands of Holy Church, having absented themselves from Mass. Accordingly they were returned to custody on 1 July.

On 14 July the accused appeared before the Dean's Court; despite their undertaking that in future they would 'keep the ordinances of the King and Queen [i.e. Philip of Spain and Mary I] and the commandments of the Church' they were nevertheless convicted of heresy and referred to the Royal Court, where sentence of death was passed.

The auto-da-fé took place on 18 July at the foot of Tower Hill. As the faggots blazed Perrotine, 'her womb bursting asunder by the vehemency of the flame' gave birth to a son. On the orders of the Bailiff, Helier Gosselin (q.v.) the baby was thrown back into the fire. In Fox's words, 'the infant baptized in his own blood, to fill up the number of God's innocent saints, was both born and died a martyr'. Justifiably he goes on to remark that 'of all the singular and tragical histories in this book, nothing can be more barbarous, if anything can equal, the inhumanity of this execution'.

This terrible tale told by Fox was no fabrication, being borne out by the petition seeking redress submitted to Elizabeth I in December 1558 by Matthew Cauchés, the brother of Catherine and uncle of Perrotine and Guillemine. Furthermore, when in July 1565 the Dean and five Jurats were summoned before the Privy Council (to answer for obstreperous conduct in general and in particular for impeding the efforts of the Governor, Sir Francis Chamberlayne (q.v.) to divert chantry funds to finance fortifications) they admitted the appalling truth. The record of the proceedings states, *inter alia*, that they 'submit themselves to the Queen's Most Excellent Majesty, acknowledging their erroneous judgment as well against Katherine Cauchés and Guillemine and Perrotine her two daughters and the infant of the said Perrotine executed by fire for supposed heresy'.

It is clear that the unhappy wretches in this tragedy never had a chance, but were victims of a cynical charade staged to exonerate the Dean — the infamous Jacques Amy (q.v.) — and the Bailiff — Helier Gosselin — both of whom had conformed to the Protestant order of things under Edward VI and by this travesty of justice in which the Royal Court allowed itself to be fully involved, sought to clear themselves of possible charges of wilful support of the reformed faith — and to demonstrate their zeal for Rome — at the expense of three ignorant women of no social standing in the island, callously inculpated for their benefit.

CHAMBERLAYNE, SIR FRANCIS (died 1570). *'Tossed about with many a conflict'.* Sir Francis Chamberlayne, who became sole Governor of Guernsey on the death in 1561 of his father Sir Leonard (q.v.) was plagued for the rest of his life with defiance of his authority which he had to struggle ceaselessly to assert. The troubles besetting this harassed representative of the Crown fell into two main categories — religious and constitutional.

On the first of these issues his difficulties largely arose from the intransigence of his own co-religionists. Sir Francis had, after all, been joint Governor with his father at the time of the burning of the Cauchés family (q.v.) and even if he had not approved thereof, he had at least acquiesced in that terrible deed. It is not entirely surprising, therefore, that the local (and overwhelmingly Roman Catholic) establishment regarded with disapproval and suspicion his attempts, perfunctory though they might have been, to implement the 1559 Acts of Supremacy and Uniformity after Elizabeth I came to the throne. He himself reported to Cecil in 1562 that 'the generality here mislike the late alterations in England so as the Queen has few faithful favourers'. The state of affairs confronting him in Guernsey was succinctly expressed in the warrant issued the same year to the Ecclesiastical Commissioners: 'our subjects in our isle for lack of stabilising of ecclesiastical order be at discord and variance among themselves'.

Not only was Elizabeth's ecclesiastical polity obstructed by the leading Jurats: at the other extreme it was antithetical to the aspirations of the Huguenot clergy coming to the island from the Continent, who yearned for the 'godly order' of Geneva. Possibly (as a Roman Catholic) seeing little to choose between one heresy and another, Chamberlayne attempted to pacify such sentiment (with which the rank and file of the insular community was in sympathy) by authorising Nicolas Baudouin (q.v.) in 1563 to form a Calvinist consistory at the Town Church.

Indulgence such as this towards extreme Protestants was like shewing a red rag to a bull as far as some of the more rabid Roman Catholic Jurats were concerned – and the following April (1564) several of them went on the rampage in the streets of St Peter-Port, crying, 'Where be these Huguenots? We will have their hearts upon the points of our swords!' 'The honest sort', it seems, 'considering their estate and the might at hand', kept to their houses!

At this point religious issues became entangled with constitutional ones, to which attention now needs to be turned. Fundamentally, the constitutional confrontations stemmed from defence policy. In the early years of the reign of Elizabeth I, the war with France in support of that country's Huguenot insurgents gave rise to considerable anxiety about the defence of Guernsey and the vital St Peter-Port roadstead, despite the neutral status enjoyed by the Bailiwick thanks to the 1480/1 Bull of Sixtus IV. In this connection Sir Francis submitted alarming reports about the island's defence capacity, emphasising that normal *corvée* obligations were insufficient for putting in hand extensive refortification, and that the island revenues would not raise the money needed. In these circumstances advantage was taken of an Act of Edward VI, which gave the Crown the right to all chantries, obits and minor religious foundations. Accordingly a Commission was appointed in 1561, consisting of Chamberlayne, the Bailiff and the Jurats, which was charged with realising such property to defray defence costs. Most of the Jurats, ill-disposed as Roman Catholics towards any diversion of chantry funds to secular purposes, adopted an obstructive and hostile attitude which led the Privy Council to intervene. Thus in 1565 the ex-Bailiff and four other Jurats, together with the ex-Dean, were summoned to London. They were collectively fined £1,000 for having spent some of the money which had been collected on lawsuits against the Governor concerning the rights of the Crown – and all five Jurats, plus two others still in Guernsey, were dismissed. Their involvement both in the execution of Catherine Cauchés, her daughters and grandson, and also in the riots directed against the Huguenots in 1564 were taken into account by the Privy Council in reaching its decision.

Although the new Jurats were more amenable, the attempts made by Sir Francis to increase revenue for defence purposes by strictly enforcing the collection of Crown dues led eventually to a constitutional dispute between himself as Governor and the Royal Court. Trouble arose, when on behalf of the Farmers of the Revenue, the Procureur de la Reine took proceedings against the Dean for encroaching on Crown Rights. At this the Court (hand in glove with the Dean) confiscated the document regarding the ancient precedent on which the Crown's case rested: whereupon the Procureur refused to go on and left the Court, rendering it incapable of acting for lack of the presence of the Queen's Officers.

The Court reacted to this by imprisoning the Procureur for contempt and demanding the appointment of a new one. It also appointed representatives to go to the Privy Council, but two of these were members of the Fortifications Commission which had been set up in 1567, and Chamberlayne imprisoned them to stop them leaving Guernsey until the defence works were completed. There was now a complete constitutional deadlock, with the Court unable to sit for lack of a Procureur, and the Governor insisting that the existing Procureur be recognised and the case against the Dean prosecuted.

In these circumstances Chamberlayne begged the Privy Council to appoint a Commission of Inquiry. The eventual outcome was that the Procureur was directed to resign 'voluntarily' and the Governor to appoint a new one: while the Court, for its part, was ordered never again to refuse justice. A further, and more lasting, result was that the report of the Inquiry Commission led to the Orders-in-Council of 1569, which contained two important regulations for the future conduct of Guernsey's government. In the first place, the Governor was forbidden to imprison anyone henceforth except for military or revenue causes; while secondly, it was laid down that any future dispute between the Governor and the Bailiff and/or Jurats should be considered in conference between them, with the proviso that failing agreement within 40 days, anyone who wished could appeal to the Privy Council.

Sir Francis did not survive long to apply this reformed governmental system as he died the following year (1570), exhaused by his travails, with many of the basic tensions which had beset him still unresolved.

CHAMBERLAYNE, GEORGE (died 1590). *A traitorous ingrate*. The second son of Sir Leonard Chamberlayne (q.v.), George was granted the Island of Alderney in 1559 as a mark of the gratitude of Elizabeth I for the expulsion therefrom by Sir Leonard the previous year of the French soldier of fortune, Captain Malesart.

George, however, nullified this grant by his own actions. As a fervent Roman Catholic, he was possessed of less facility for temporising than were his father or brothers, and when the Pope excommunicated the Queen in 1570 he betook himself to Ghent in Flanders (where many years later his son — born there in 1576 and also called George — was to become the Bishop of Ypres from 1626 until his death in 1634). George *père* busied himself for the rest of his life in organizing plots against the monarch who had befriended him but whom he had repudiated, until death claimed him in 1590.

CHAMBERLAYNE, JOHN (in Alderney 1584-1591). *The Elizabethan Lord of Alderney*. The third son of Sir Leonard Chamberlayne (q.v.), despite his Roman Catholicism John Chamberlayne contrived to remain sufficiently *persona grata* with the Crown for Elizabeth I — with remarkable forbearance, after the treason of his brother George (q.v.) — to issue a Patent in 1584 whereby he was granted the Isle of Alderney

in fee simple for a down payment of thirty marks (£20) and an annual remittance of twenty marks (£13.33). The Queen seems to have been under the mistaken impression that Alderney (like Sark 20 years earlier) was deserted, as the island is described in the Patent as 'laid waste' and Chamberlayne — as in the case of Sark's Helier de Carteret (q.v.) — was required to settle at least 40 men there for its defence!

John Chamberlayne is thought to have resided in the Nunnery. He soon had the misfortune of finding himself at variance with the Aurigniais, who resented his attempt to speed the development of the island. Tension became so acute that the Governor of Guernsey, Sir Thomas Leighton (q.v.) was called upon to intervene: and the upshot was a set of Ordinances defining the respective rights of the Lord of the Manor and the people of Alderney, which have served as a model for all subsequent grants of the island.

In 1590 John Chamberlayne entered into a contract to supply the expeditionary force under the Earl of Essex which went that year to the aid of the French Huguenots in Normandy. Failing to carry out the terms of this contract, he found himself obliged to sell to the Earl for £1,000 all his rights in Alderney (26 March 1591). Retiring to his estate at Coombe near Woodstock, he passed out of the Bailiwick's history.

CHAMBERLAYNE, SIR LEONARD (1505/10-1561). *Guernsey's last joint Governorship*. Sir Leonard Chamberlayne is known to have been born at Shirburn Castle in Oxfordshire, but the date of his birth is uncertain, though it is usually considered to have been not earlier than 1505, nor later than 1510.

Although an eminent Roman Catholic, Leonard Chamberlayne contrived to be accepted as trustworthy by Rome's opponents. He played an active part in the overthrow of the Protector Somerset in the autumn of 1549 and — his religion notwithstanding — served in 1552 on the Commission for the seizure of church lands in Oxfordshire.

On the death of Edward VI in 1553, Chamberlayne immediately rallied to the support of Mary, and was rewarded by being knighted in the day after the new Queen's Coronation: 2 October, 1553. Originally sitting as Member of Parliament for Scarborough, Sir Leonard was appointed Governor of Guernsey the same year, and in the following year (1554) was re-elected to Parliament, this time as Member for the County of Oxford. In this year also the Princess Elizabeth endured her six months sojourn under duress in the custody of

Sir Henry Bedingfield at Woodstock, of which Sir Leonard was Steward. He made so good an impression on the enforced royal resident that later, as Queen, she showed marked favour to him and his family, despite differences of religious allegiance. The year after Sir Leonard took his seat for Oxford (1555), his son Francis (q.v.) also became Governor of Guernsey, holding this post together with his father. There had been several instances of shared governerships during Guernsey's history, but this twin tenure was the last recorded example of such a joint appointment.

On her accession to the throne Elizabeth I, ignoring religious differences, confirmed Chamberlayne *père et fils* in their combined office. Later the same year (1558) a French adventurer —

Captain Malesart (q.v.*) — attacked Alderney for the purpose of plunder. Being successful, he made the mistake of coming back. This time Sir Leonard dispatched an expedition from Guernsey to support a naval force under Admiral Clinton, as a result of which Malesart was captured and sent as a prisoner to the Tower of London. By way of reward Elizabeth I in 1559 granted Alderney to another of Sir Leonard's sons — George — thus starting a relationship between the island and the Chamberlayne family that was to last until 1642.

Two years after this grant — in 1561 — Sir Leonard died in Guernsey, leaving four sons and a daughter. To clarify his family's connections with the Bailiwick for the better part of a century, an abbreviated family tree is appended:

*Sir Leonard Cha iberlayne

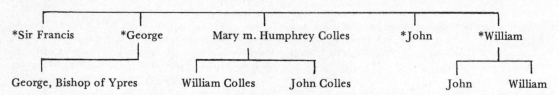

| *Sir Francis | *George | Mary m. Humphrey Colles | *John | *William |

| George, Bishop of Ypres | William Colles | John Colles | John | William |

*Persons with entries in this *Biographical Dictionary*

CHAMBERLAYNE, WILLIAM (died 1608) AND SUCCESSORS. *Catholic cuckoos in a Calvinist nest.*

Soon after the Lordship of Alderney passed in 1591 from John Chamberlayne (q.v.) to the Earl of Essex, the latter granted a lease of the Island to William Chamberlayne, brother of John and youngest son of Leonard (q.v.), whom Essex knew through his intimate friend the Earl of Southampton (the patron of Shakespeare), whose agent William was at Beaulieu in Hampshire.

William Chamberlayne accordingly crossed to Alderney, where after a time his relations with the islanders grew strained. Ultimately, in 1607, a Petition of Complaints against him was presented to the Royal Commissioners in Guernsey by Nicolas Houguez and Nicolas Simon on behalf of the Aurigniais. Obviously William, as an ardent Roman Catholic, had deliberately set out to put obstacles in the path of the establishment of a Calvinist order in the island, for the petition alleged that ever since his tenancy started in 1591 (a period of 16 years) he had failed to provide for the stipend of a minister and furthermore had seized the tithes, together with the manse, which had fallen into ruin. Not only had he by this policy reduced Alderney to an 'unchristian and

barbrous estate', but it was also asserted that the temporal welfare of the community had suffered by his having encroached on the island's common lands. The Commissioners delimited the area available for Chamberlayne's personal use as that east of a line from Le Grand Fort (Essex Castle) to Corblets Bay, plus the islet of Burhou. Moreover, he was ordered to pay a stipend of 30 marks (£20) a year to a minister — as a result of which Simon Maçon (q.v.*) — towards whose training at the Huguenot church in Southampton the Aurigniais had contributed — took over the Alderney living in November of the same year.

With William's death in 1608 the last of Sir Leonard Chamberlayne's sons disappeared from the scene, and the next generation was represented by William's two sons (John and William) and by his two nephews, William and John Colles (the sons of his sister Mary, who had married John Colles of Worcestershire). Although the lease was inherited jointly by his two sons, John elected to remain at his residence at Lyndhurst in Hampshire and only William (who had married a Guernesiaise) came over to live in Alderney, experiencing an inevitable degree of disapproval because of his religion, it being recorded that he 'was estimed among the better sort of the inhabitants of Garnezey to be a great Papist'. Nevertheless he retained the lease for many years and showed commendable powers of leadership in 1627 when alarm was caused by the threat of a French invasion. He arrayed the Alderney Militia (such as it was), armed with munitions sent by the Privy Council — but in the event the threat failed to materialise, thanks to the destruction of the attacking fleet by the Lieutenant-Governor of Guernsey, Sir Peter Osborne (q.v.).

On William's death without issue the lease passed at first to his cousin John Colles, but in 1640 this worthy made it over to his brother William for a payment of two hundred pounds. Two years later (1642) William Colles died in Alderney and the island's long connection with the Chamberlayne family (dating back to 1559) was at last severed.

LE CHEMINANT, AIR CHIEF MARSHAL SIR PETER, G.B.E., K.C.B., D.F.C. (1920-   ). *Guernsey's greatest airman*. Born on 17 June 1920 to Blanche Etheldred Wake, the wife of Lieutenant-Colonel Keith le Cheminant of Elizabeth College (where he himself received his education), the Bailiwick's future Lieutenant-Governor went from the classroom to the Royal Air Force College at Cranwell, whence he passed out under the shadows of the black clouds of war. Though mere mortals did not then know it, in the Pantheon of Olympus Ares had decreed that to Lord de Saumarez and Sir Isaac Brock (qq.v.) as Guernsey's greatest warriors on sea and land respectively, there would now be added their peer of the air!

From 1940 to 1944 young Peter le Cheminant saw war service in France, the United Kingdom, North Africa, Malta, Sicily and Italy; his gallantry earning the award of the Distinguished Flying Cross in 1943. The concluding stages of the conflict saw him in command of No. 223 Squadron, and with the coming of peace he was appointed as Instructor at Staff College — a post which he retained until 1948. This intrepid islander's fighting days were, however, by no means finished. He saw service in the Far East over the period 1949 to 1953, for the first two years of which he took command of No. 209 Squadron, winning a Bar to his D.F.C. by further outstanding courage in 1951.

After two years on the Joint Flying Staff (1953-55) this brilliant officer returned to the Far East, taking up the post of Wing Commander (Flying) at Kuala Lumpur in 1955 and remaining there until 1957. Then, after attending the Joint Services Staff Course in 1958, his career assumed the nature of a catalogue of increasingly important appointments. Following three years (1958-61) as Deputy Director of Air Staff Plans, and a further two (1961-63) commanding the Royal Air Force Station at Geilenkirchen, there ensued two years (1964-66) as Director of Air Staff Briefing before becoming Senior Air Staff Officer at the Headquarters of the Far East Air Force from 1966 to 1967 — and then Chief of Staff from 1967 to 1968, which latter year his worth was recognised by the Queen creating him Commander of the Bath.

Even higher rungs of the ladder of success were now to be scaled. Two years (1968-70) as Commandant of the Joint Warfare Establishment at the Ministry of Defence, followed by a further year 1971-72) as Assistant Chief of Air Staff (Policy) preceded the honour of knighthood conferred on this talented airman as Knight Commander of the Bath in 1972.

Sir Peter now became the British Member of the Permanent Military Deputies Group at the Central Treaty Organisation, Ankara, from 1972 to 1973, followed by two years (1974-76) as Vice Chief of Defence Staff. Thereafter for three years (1976-79) he served as Deputy Commander-in-Chief of the Allied Forces in Central Europe, during which time he was appointed Knight Grand Cross of the Order of the British Empire in 1978.

In 1980 Air Chief Marshal Sir Peter de Lacey le Cheminant became a Knight of the Order of St John of Jerusalem, and in the same year he assumed office as Lieutenant-Governor and Commander-in-Chief of the Island of Guernsey and Its Dependencies, addressing the Royal Court in Patois at the time he took the Oath. Although other Guernseymen had been Lieutenant-Governors in the past, most of them held the post conjointly with that of Bailiff, the last of these being Sir Victor Gosselin Carey (q.v.), Lieutenant-Governor from 1940 to 1945. To Sir Peter, therefore, fell the distinction of being the first Guernseyman, other than a Bailiff, to be Lieutenant-Governor since Thomas Andros held office in 1720 — over two and a half centuries previously! Sir Peter was awarded arms in 1982.

COBHAM, SIR ALAN JOHN, K.B.E., A.F.C. (1894-1973). *Guernsey's first land-based air service operator*. This world-famous aviator was born in Camberwell, on 6 May 1894, and after service in the Royal Flying Corps during the First

World War (in which he won the Air Force Cross) he took employment in 1920 with the De Havilland Company as a pilot in their air taxi service.

In 1924, with Air Ministry approval and backing, Alan Cobham undertook a survey flight to Rangoon and back to pave the way for the establishment of an air service to India — a striking achievement for those days. A further survey flight to Cape Town was made in 1925 while in 1926, with similar objectives, he few to Australia and back, landing his amphibious craft on the Thames at Westminster on his return. For these exploits he received a knighthood shortly after his return from the antipodes.

During the early 1930s Sir Alan launched his Municipal Aerodromes Campaign to induce local authorities to establish airfields. In this connection, from 1932 onwards he arranged 'National Aviation Days' in various localities to foster air-mindedness, with displays by a team of experts who performed aerobatics and provided 'joy rides'.

Keen as he was to promote the growth of local air links, this apostle of aviation was naturally attracted by the activities of the Guernsey Aero Club which (also from 1932 onwards) set about developing an aerodrome at l'Erée. At first giving help and advice, Sir Alan in 1935 with his firm Cobham Air Routes, started the original land-based air service to and from the island, employing Westland Wessex aircraft and flying between Hurn and l'Erée, where the Guernsey end of the enterprise was run by Mr. Cecil Wheadon Noel (q.v.). The first 'plane took off on Silver Jubilee Day (6 May) 1935 — which also happened to be Sir Alan's birthday! Carrying reporters from both the *Evening Press* and the *Star*, it was seen off by Sir Alan personally.

Sad to say the venture was short-lived, coming to a tragic end on 3 July of the same year. By a grim irony a service which had been beset with anxieties because of the difficulties posed by the conditions obtaining at l'Erée met its doom by one of the aircraft crashing in the Channel off Bournemouth. The pilot (Captain Ogden) was killed but the one and only passenger survived, after a gruelling time in the sea.

Sir Alan had had misgivings about the suitability of l'Erée throughout the two-month period the service was operated and (illogically, maybe, bearing in mind the circumstances of the crash which terminated it) now became thoroughly disenchanted with this little aerodrome; giving it as his opinion at a public meeting at St George's Hall that La Villaize was the only

practicable site for a modern airport. Whether or not the adage, '*Post hoc ergo propter hoc*' applied in this case, the fact of the matter is that this verdict was followed on 20 October of the same year by the decision of the States to acquire 315 *vergées* in that locality for the creation of an island airport.

By the time La Villaize Airport was opened war was approaching and Sir Alan devoted more and more of his attention to developing the technique of re-fuelling aircraft in flight. For many years he failed to evoke interest in this project — but at last it was taken up by the United States Air Force after the U.S.A. had entered the war. Thereafter Sir Alan spent the rest of his life in semi-retirement, passing part of his time in Guernsey at his house in Fort George and reaping the rewards of his many achievements. He died at Poole on 21 October 1973.

LE COCQ, THOMAS (1680–1760). *Alderney's arch-xenophobe.* When Sir Edmund Andros (q.v.), who in 1683 had been granted Alderney for 99 years, became Governor of New England in 1685, he delegated his powers in the Island to Thomas Le Mesurier of Guernsey. The distrust of outsiders which is not uncommon among small communities led to an influential section of Alderney's population regarding with disfavour the arrangement in general and Thomas le Mesurier in particular. The resultant hostility with which le Mesurier had to contend became even more bitter with the appointment as Judge of Alderney in 1704 of a highly articulate young man of intense local consciousness in the person of Thomas le Cocq, who had been born early in 1680 to Marie, wife of Richard le Cocq, being baptized on 6 February in that year. Adopting a posture which might justifiably be paraphrased as one of 'Aurigny pour les Aurigniais', le Cocq rallied behind him a substantial following of those who felt that the administration of their island by Guernseymen was an affront to its dignity. The result was a prolonged feud between le Cocq and the le Mesurier family which dragged on for many years.

Tension became acute in 1713 when George Andros inherited Alderney from his uncle Sir Edmund, who had died childless. With the prestigious Sir Edmund out of the way the 'patriots' felt that their chance had come and le Cocq organised a Petition to the Crown asking that the grant of Alderney be made over to a nominee selected by the signatories. In support of this *démarche* a polemical pamphlet was published

at the same time in London, written by the
Reverend Henry le Merveilleux, who after
appointment as the island's rector in 1706 had
become the enthusiastic lieutenant of the chauvi-
nistic judge. The publication detailed the alleged
misdeeds of le Mesurier, who answered with a
point-by-point rejoinder attacking its author. This
sally by the le Cocq faction was, however, unsuccessful. George Andros died in 1714 and by 1721
both his daughters were also in the grave, so that
Alderney reverted to George's sister Anne, who in
1704 had married John, the son of none other
than the disaffected judge's old adversary, Thomas
le Mesurier! The aboriginal Aurigniais were beset
by the hosts of Midian!

In 1729 Anne le Mesurier died and was succeeded by her son Henry le Mesurier (q.v.). Le
Cocq, however, neither flagged nor failed, but
pursued his vendetta with undiminished vigour.
After nine years tussle Henry finally asserted
himself, suspending his opponent from exercising
his functions as judge on the plea of alleged
irregularities in discharging them. Nevertheless,
le Cocq retained the actual judicial office for the
rest of his days, the duties attaching thereto being
performed over the next 22 years by judge-
delegates.

Demoting the malcontent leader did not in the
event end the confrontation. In 1744, 'worn out
with feuds of the lawless and insubordinate
Islanders', Henry handed over his Patent to his
younger brother John (q.v.) who himself three
years later (1747) fled the island, fearing for his
life! Indeed it was not until 1756 when the
privateering opportunities of the Seven Years
War provided an outlet for the bellicosity of the
Aurigniais, that there was at last security and
stability for the le Mesurier régime. This war was
still being waged when, intransigent and doggedly
unrepentant to the end, Thomas le Cocq died, a
very old man, in 1760.

COLBORNE, SIR JOHN, FIRST BARON SEATON (1778–1863). *The hero of Waterloo, who sponsored road improvement and the revival of Elizabeth College.*

Born in 1778 at Lyndhurst
in Hampshire, and educated at Christ's Hospital
and Winchester College, John Colborne entered
the Army as an ensign in 1794 and thenceforth
won every step of promotion in his military career
without resorting to purchase – a rare feat in his
day. During the campaign in the Peninsula he
distinguished himself as Military Secretary to Sir
John Moore, thanks to whose dying recommendation he obtained his Lieutenant-Colonelcy.

At Waterloo (on the morrow of which he was
knighted as a K.C.B.) the part he played in the
titanic struggle was crucial, as it was he who led
the charge which routed Napoleon's Old Guard,
thereby tipping the scales in the battle.

Six years after this hour of glory Sir John
came to Guernsey in 1821 as Lieutenant-
Governor under the Governor, George, Earl of
Pembroke. As the noble Earl was an absentee,
effective gubernatorial responsibility devolved
entirely on his subordinate, who came into a
difficult inheritance. His immediate predecessor,
Major-General Henry Bailey, had become embroiled in a confrontation with a prominant Jurat
(Jean Guille), whom he had sought to deprive of
his colonelcy in the Militia, after disapproving of
remarks he had made during a debate in the
States. Guille had refused to accept his demotion,
and the situation had become so tense that the
intervention of Lord Sidmouth as Home Secretary
was needed to resolve it. The new arrival consequently had to tread warily, but his grace and
amiability soon ensured happy relationships
between the Monarch's representative and the
island authorities.

During his seven-year term of office Sir John
made two significant contributions to the welfare
of Guernsey, the first of which concerned communications. His great precursor Sir John Doyle (q.v.)
had laid out several good roads in place of previous muddy tracks to connect St Peter-Port with
the vulnerable northern and western coasts of
the island; one of which ran through St Martin's,
the Forest and St Pierre-du-Boise to l'Erée.
Starting with the stretch now known as the Fort
Road, this highway could only be approached
from the town by the steep and constricted
thoroughfare of Hauteville. This meant that access
from the town was impeded, not only to the main
road leading west, but also to the very fortification (Fort George) which had been designed for
the municipality's protection! Sir John Colborne
eliminated this potentially dangerous inconveni-
ence, first widening La Charroterie and then
providing access both to Doyle's main highway,
and also to the fort by the construction of the
road bearing his name which scales the hillside
south of le Pont Renier.

Sir John's second memorable service to the
island was in the realm of education. After taking
up his post as Lieutenant-Governor, he lent a
kindly and sympathetic ear to the proposals of
George le Boutillier (q.v.) for reversing the decay
of Elizabeth College. Finding le Boutillier's complaints of obstruction only too well-founded, he

ordered in 1824 the public inquiry which resulted in the new and reformed charter whereby the school was resuscitated. He himself laid the new building's foundation stone on 19 October 1826; that same evening Lady Colborne marked the occasion by giving a grand ball and supper. Furthermore, at the re-opening of the school the first two names on the register were those of his two sons.

While in Guernsey Sir John had been promoted to the rank of Major-General in 1825. Three years later in 1828, to everyone's keen regret, he left the island to assume much more onerous responsibilities as Lieutenant-Governor of Upper Canada, where in 1838 he quelled a serious rebellion. Elevated to the peerage as Lord Seaton in 1839, he served as Governor of the Ionian Islands from 1843 to 1849; became a full General in 1854; commanded the forces in Ireland from 1855 to 1860 (in which latter year he attained the rank of Field Marshal); and then retired to Torquay, where he died in 1863.

COLLINGS, WILLIAM FREDERICK (1852–1927). *The Seigneur of Sark who was bizarre beyond belief.* (B). William Frederick Collings was the antithesis of his father, the Reverend William Thomas Collings (q.v.) from whom he inherited the Fief of Sark in 1882 at the age of 30. Described by an islander as 'a violent terror when he had taken drink', he seems to have inherited a penchant for carousing from his great-grandfather, the freebooter Jean Allaire (q.v.).

Entirely lacking in the military ardour which had characterised his father, the new Seigneur so neglected the Royal Sark Militia, that within five years of his inheriting the fief his parents's pride and joy had degenerated to the state of decadence summed up by a visiting journalist as 'seven dozen pairs of boots'. Thereafter (like an old soldier) it faded away, finally disappearing from the Army List in 1900. The same attitude of negligence was apparent in his refusal to spend a penny on the upkeep of his patrimony, which consequently steadily deteriorated with the passage of time. Any suggestion that maintenance be undertaken only evoked the rejoinder, 'It will last me out'.

In contrast to this seeming indifference displayed towards his responsibilities, this extraordinary man was the first Seigneur to care enough for Sark to reside permanently in it; and in 1899 he declined what must have been an extremely tempting offer when he refused to sell his fief for £30,000 (then an enormous sum) to the financial funambulist Horatio Bottomley, who planned to set up a casino in the island. Indeed, far from being prepared to sell his inheritance, he clung with tenacity to his feudal privileges. In so doing he commanded so much local support that the 1922 Sark Reform Law introducing 12 elected People's Deputies and allowing Chief Pleas to appeal to the Guernsey Royal Court against any seigneurial veto on legislation, was only reluctantly accepted, after intervention by the Lieutenant-Governor, Sir John Capper, who threatened that failure so to do would entail the forcible taking over of the island's administration.

The late Dame de Sercq described her father as 'extremely insubordinate, madly obstinate, fiercely self-opinionated and prone to outbreaks of uncontrolled rage'. On the other hand he was 'a generous man and a wonderful companion when he was with those he liked', whilst in his relations with the common people of Sark he was 'never hard on those who found difficulty in paying their rents or dues'. Compassionate towards the impecunious he might have been, but there were nevertheless many occasions when his intemperate conduct brought him before the Seneschal's Court for (*inter alia*) assault and battery, abusive language, breaking windows and firing pistols on the public highway. More than once the charges brought against him were serious enough to necessitate reference to the Royal Court in Guernsey, whither he was conducted by Sark's Prévôt. This series of cases, in which the Seigneur himself was the accused, clearly demonstrated the independence and impartiality of the Seneschal who, although appointed by the Seigneur, imposed upon him the appropriate penalties for his misdemeanours.

Despite the domineering mien he at times adopted towards her, Mr. Collings was genuinely devoted to his wife, and consequently the misadventure which befell them in April 1906 assumed tragic dimensions. They were both on board the S.S. *Courier* en route for Guernsey (and ultimately London) when she struck a rock off Jethou and sank in seven fathoms. Attempts to launch two lifeboats failed and ten out of the ship's company of 39 were drowned. Fourteen of the survivors (including Mr. and Mrs. Collings) managed to reach La Grosse Ferrière rock in a small dinghy, whence they were later rescued by the excursion vessel *Alert*. Mrs. Collings, however, was already desperately ill and was on her way to London to see a consultant. The shipwreck worsened her condition and she died a few months afterwards.

This irascible Seigneur was violently anti-clerical, and during his earlier years at the helm his *bête noire* was the Reverend Charles Vermeil (Vicar of Sark from 1877 to 1896). French by birth, this cleric's sympathies were so markedly anti-British that from time to time he demonstrated them by omitting the prayers for Queen Victoria and the royal family when conducting Matins — thus causing his enraged feudal overlord to stamp out of the church and send an immediate letter of protest to the Bishop. The incumbent would then mend his ways for a few weeks until eventually and inevitably the whole charade would be repeated! Tense though they were, however, the Seigneur's relations with Charles Vermeil were cordial in comparrison with the running fight he maintained against the next Vicar, Louis Napoleon Seichen (q.v.) — who proved no mean antagonist — for the whole period of his incumbency (1895-1922).

Towards the end of his life — in 1921 — William Frederick Collings rendered homage for his holding to the king in person on the occasion of the visit to Guernsey of George V and Queen Mary, thus becoming the first Seigneur of Sark so to do since Sir Philippe de Carteret paid homage to Charles II in Jersey in 1650. Bearing in mind, however, that Sir Philippe's homage was for St Ouen as well, the Great Eccentric emerged as the first Seigneur ever to perform this feudal obligation in respect of Sark alone.

COLLINGS, REVEREND WILLIAM THOMAS (1823-1882). *'Christian, up and smite them!':* *the clerical militant who was Seigneur of Sark.* (B). Born on 4 September 1823, William Thomas Collings was ordained Deacon in 1852 — in which year he also married Louisa Lukis, the daughter of Guernsey's famous archaeologist Frederick Corbin Lukis (q.v.) — and was ordained priest in 1853. Both ceremonies took place in Wells Cathedral, where during the intervening year of his diaconate he served as a curate. (A gross exaggeration of the humble station he thus occupied may perhaps account for the frequently repeated — but entirely false — assertion that he was a canon of that gorgeous episcopal pile: a claim which *Crockford* fails to substantiate.)

In the same year as he was ordained priest (1853) this clerk became the Seigneur of Sark on the death of his mother, who a few months earlier had acquired the fief after foreclosing on the mortgage granted in 1844 to Ernest le Pelley (q.v.) by her father, the notorious Jean Allaire (q.v.). A stark contrast to his reprobate grandfather, the new Seigneur enthusiastically and conscientiously set about doing all in his power to advance the welfare of the community in his care, seeking especially to improve the island's amenities, to provide for its defence and to encourage the lucrative tourist traffic that was then in its infancy.

In the first of these directions this man of God energetically applied himself to making up for past neglect, not stinting his own resources which he generously expended on beneficial projects. Making great efforts to establish good relations with his tenants, for whose succour he sought to summon outside aid rapidly in any emergency, he took advantage of building operations at La Seigneurie to surmount the surrounding trees for the purpose of signalling to Guernsey by the erection of the tower which the late Dame de Sercq castigated as a 'hideous Victorian excrescence'. The Seigneur's vocation naturally turned his attention to the condition of Sark's church, to which he added the chancel and also installed the low pews which still survive in place of the previous high ones. In 1855 he gave a stretch of land adjoining the church to serve as a new cemetery, the old one (adjacent to the present-day Methodist church) being by then filled up. Having thus tried to encourage virtue, he also strove to discourage vice; in the same year he persuaded Chief Pleas to sanction the construction of the island's prison! In 1864, however, the Seigneur's benevolent intentions evoked opposition rather than gratitude. His offer to donate a house for the use of the island schoomaster, provided he was an Anglican, so annoyed the strong Methodist element in Chief Pleas that the gesture was unceremoniously spurned.

It was the habit of the Reverend William Collings to leave his fellow cleric, the Reverend Jacques Louis Victor Cachemaille (q.v.) in charge as his deputy in Sark during his absences and to spend his winters in Guernsey — where, incidentally, before becoming Seigneur of Sark he had contributed generously towards the building of St Matthew's church at Cobo, providing the turret, two bells and the lychgate. In 1872 this custom nearly cost the lives of his family and himself. On 28 November the *Gosforth*, in which they were travelling, was wrecked off Herm, and only by the greatest of good fortune did the ship's company manage to get ashore on that island. As it was, the original 1565 Charter of Helier de Carteret (q.v.) which was included in the Seigneur's luggage, was lost. Luckily a copy had been deposited in the Public Record Office in London.

At the time that this ecclesiastical Seigneur came into his inheritance, Anglo-French tension had already led the British Government to embark on an extensive fortification programme in Alderney. He accordingly feared that in the event of hostilities Sark would be in the front line. Reflecting that 'when a strong man armed keepeth his palace, his goods are in peace' he took most seriously his responsibilities of commanding the Royal Sark Militia. One of his first acts as Seigneur was to persuade Chief Pleas in 1835 to appoint a paid quartermaster to look after the weapons and equipment stored in the island's arsenal. Thenceforce this warrior-priest persistently called his tenants to their military duties. Clad in the uniform of a Lieutenant-Colonel, and girt with a sword, he insisted on regular parades and shooting practice; in later years he pressed his reluctant son William Frederick (q.v.) into service as Adjudant.

In 1859 the Militia was arrayed in all its panoply for an auspicious occasion which failed to materialise. With a red carpet laid at le Creux Harbour, the force under its clerical commanding officer was drawn up to welcome what was anticipated as the first visit of a reigning British sovereign. Alas for fond hopes! An unfavourable ground swell caused the royal yacht with Queen Victoria aboard to turn about and head for Jersey, speeded by a salute fired from the guns of the loyal Serquiais. A further 98 years were to elapse before a reigning monarch actually set foot on the island.

The silver mining operations which had ruined the le Pelley family had also ushered in the island's tourist trade, thanks to the Sark Mining Company's policy of encouraging visits of inspection to the mines as a means of publicity. The Reverend Seigneur realised the great potential of this trade for Sark's prosperity and deliberately did his best to foster it. As an attraction for the visitors he had the 'Window in the Wall' look-out blasted through the cliff above Port du Moulin. He also encouraged hotel development, and both the Dixcart and the Bel Air (destroyed during the German occupation) were built during his time — the former patronised by Victor Hugo (q.v.). Within six years of his becoming Seigneur, tourist traffic had increased to the point where a worthwhile revenue could be derived from charging a Landing Tax, which was imposed for the first time in 1859.

In the winter of 1865–66 great gales destroyed the breakwater in la Baie de la Motte. Although he initially favoured developing l'Eperquerie as a harbour, this Seigneur of the Cloth deferred to majority opinion and, eager to maintain (and indeed extend) Sark's tourist trade, appointed Mr. Agnew Giffard as engineer-in-chief, in charge of the construction of a new harbour (le Creux Harbour) financed by an *impôt* on spirits. There was to be a tragic sequel to the creation of this improved haven, as in October 1868 Mr. Giffard and four companions lost their lives when their ship foundered en route for Guernsey.

The Reverend William Collings died in March 1882 and Sark mourned the loss of a devoted, capable and benevolent Seigneur.

DE LA COUR, JEAN (died 1591). *Guernsey's Elizabethan benefactor.* Ringing phrases such as Tennyson's reference to 'the spacious times of great Elizabeth' tend to divert attention from the fact that the second half of the 16th century was a period of rampant inflation, the ravages of which in Guernsey were exacerbated by the disappearance of the religious Confraternities, of which there had long been several in each parish succouring the sick, old and needy. These, however, were swept out of existence by the Royal Court in 1547, the reformers in their zeal deploring them as besmirched with the taint of Popery. Furthermore, despite a Royal Court Ordinance of 1566 (requiring parish constables to apprentice impoverished children) and another of 1588 ruling that the aged poor should be subsidised from the alms of the 'temple' of their parish, present-day techniques of financial manipulation designed to cushion humble folk against price rises were unknown, and severe distress resulted.

In that same year of 1588, the plight of the unfortunate aroused the compassion of Jean de la Cour, one of the Jurats of the Royal Court. By a deed of gift this Good Samaritan started the 'Bien des Pauvres Donataires de Monsieur Jean de la Cour', leaving a property in Hauteville, two plots of land and 15 quarters of wheat *rente* with instructions that the income deriving from these assets was to be distributed at the discretion of the Court, particularly to those who had suffered by fire, to assist them in rebuilding. Since its inception the de la Cour Fund (which still exists, though now greatly increased by legacies and donations) has helped the victims of pirates and also mariners who had suffered shipwreck. The Fund was also intended to aid orphans to find a trade.

Although Jean de la Cour's death in 1591, leaving no issue, extinguished an old island family which in 1443 had provided the Bailiff-cum-Sub-Warden (Thomas de la Cour) and a further

Jurat in Jean's father Nicolas, this generous man's charity to the distressed has ensured the immortality of his name.

COYSH, VICTOR HUBERT (1906–   ). *The devotee of Alderney who was determined to be a Guernseyman.* Victor Coysh was born on 24 April 1906 to Florence, the wife of Frederick William Coysh, a draper of the Commercial Arcade whose ancestors came from the West Country, whence the new-born baby's great-grandfather had sailed to Guernsey from Lyme Regis in the early 19th century. The family lived in a commodious Georgian house with a magnificent garden in Hauteville, and was sufficiently affluent to employ two servants and a gardener.

He was educated initially at Kingsley House Kindergarten and subsequently (1915) at the Intermediate School, moving thence to Elizabeth College in 1920. Young Victor Coysh hoped that on leaving school in 1923, at the age of 17, he would be able to take up teaching as his career. This aspiration was frustrated because of lack of funds, the financial position of his parents having worsened to the extent that their home in Cambridge Park Terrace (whither the family had moved from Hauteville) was opened as a guest house to eke out resources. The school-leaver therefore took up a clerical post with Advocate Ambrose Sherwill, but before long forsook this position for another with the granite merchants John Mowlem and Co., as his poor command of French militated against his prospects in a lawyer's employ. During this period he also performed his service in the Militia, in the band of which he played as a clarinetist.

With affairs going from bad to worse Coysh *père* and *mère* decided to leave Guernsey and seek better fortune in Bournemouth. Victor wished to remain behind but parental insistence, coupled with his inability at this stage of his life to support himself, compelled him to go as well in 1926. Like General MacArthur when driven out of the Phillipines, he vowed to return; but unlike MacArthur he did not have a vast army at his beck and call and so took rather longer about it! Nevertheless, unhappy in England where he kept body and soul together in an occupation which at best could only be described as dull, Victor Coysh's love for his native isle was, if anything, increased by his absence from it – and he was determined, with true 'donkey' persistence, to remain a Guernseyman come hell or high water! His unwavering resolve to get back to the island was so strong that it even led to his breaking off

an engagement to marry a young woman who preferred to stay in England. As a device to ameliorate his exile be brought out – at his own expense – his first publication, entitled *Unknown Guernsey*. He also made repeated visits to the island, on one of which (in 1930) he joined La Société Guernesiaise.

Marrying a Guernsey bride (Miss Leila Carey) at the outbreak of war, the newly-weds' joint intention of settling in the island was frustrated by the German occupation. After the Liberation, however, this 'Guernseyman by insistence' managed to obtain a transfer from his employers – the Bournemouth Gas Company (not as yet nationalised) – to the Guernsey Gas Light Company; and at last returned to his birthplace – crossing in so violent a gale that the *Isle of Jersey* was forced to seek shelter first at Spithead and then at Cherbourg, taking three days on the voyage from Southampton. The next year his insular identity was triumphantly confirmed by his election to the Council of La Société Guernesiaise.

In 1947 the returned exile found his true *métier*. After having read his first paper before La Société Guernesiaise – 'The Guernsey Fishing Boat' – he wrote the *Press Guide to Guernsey* and was subsequently offered employment as a reporter on the *Guernsey Press*. He had become known to the management through his articles both in La Société's *Transactions* and also in the *Review* of the Guernsey Society: of which he had become a founder member in 1942.

Happily leaving the uninspiring ambience of the Gas Company, Victor Coysh embarked on a career full of variety for which nature had manifestly designed him. Among assignments too numerous to tabulate, he covered the Queen's visit in 1957 and lunched at the Old Government House Hotel in the same room as Her Majesty; he became Chief Reporter in 1958 and covered the visit of Princess Alexandra (to whom he was presented) in 1968. In 1970 he was appointed to membership of the States Historical Committee, set up to assist Dr. Charles Cruickshank in the preparation of his official history of the German Occupation; and in 1971, on the eve of his retirement, he was invited to attend the Court of Chief Pleas, where the Bailiff summoned him to his Bar and thanked him for his journalistic services over so many years.

These years, however, had been full of incident apart from events connected with his profession. During them he had written *Swastika Over Guernsey* and the Sark *Official Guide*; he was one of the original sponsors of the Saumarez Park 'Guernsey Kitchen' which was opened in 1952. He was elected to the Council of the Guernsey Society in 1954; and helped to create the National Trust of Guernsey (to the Council of which he was then elected) in 1960, in which year he had also published his illustrated book *Guernsey*. In 1966 he was elected President of La Société.

Victor Coysh's years of retirement have also been fruitful. His journalistic duties had frequently taken him to Alderney, for which island he had developed a deep and abiding attachment. An Aurigniais (Ernest Biggs) once said of him, 'He has one hobby and that hobby, for many years, has been Alderney'. Already while still labouring as a reporter his affection for Alderney had received recognition in his being granted honorary life membership of the Alderney Society in 1967; while three years later there appeared his *vade mecum* for anyone visiting the island — *Afoot in Alderney*. After retirement, however, he set out to give full treatment to the 'Cinderella of the Isles' and the result was his thorough and absorbing book, *Alderney* which was published in 1974. His *History of the Royal Guernsey Militia* followed in 1977. Finally, still indefatigable and heedless of the passing of the years, Victor Coysh at the age of 72 produced in 1978 in collaboration with Carel Toms (q.v.) a fascinating pictorial record of the Bailiwick prior to 1914, entitled *Guernsey Through The Lens*. A further (post-1914) *Guernsey Through The Lens Again* was published in 1982, following hard on the heels of *Sark: The Last Stronghold of Feudalism*. Furthermore, Victor Coysh became a life member of La Société Serquiaise which he helped to found in 1975 and in 1983 his *Visitors' Guide to Guernsey, Alderney and Sark* was published. As for the future, who knows?

D

DALRYMPLE, GENERAL SIR HEW WHITE-FOORD, BARONET (1750–1830). *The Lieutenant-Governor beset by embarrassing allies.* He entered the army as an ensign in 1763 at the age of 13 and rose steadily until he became Colonel of the Grenadier Guards in November 1790. Hew Dalrymple was promoted to the rank of Major-General in October 1794, and in March 1796 was appointed Lieutenant-Governor of Guernsey, a post he retained until 1802. On taking up his appointment he became the first Lieutenant-Governor to occupy the building now known as the Old Government House Hotel, which was bought that year from Nicholas le Mesurier for £2,750 — and continued as the residence of successive Lieutenant-Governors until 1857.

During his term of office the Lieutenant-Governor was confronted with a ticklish variant of the not unfamiliar problem of the disconcerting guest — and on this occasion an involuntary one as well. The difficulty arose in 1799 when a Russian force fighting side-by-side with the British in Holland sustained a defeat and had to be evacuated. The Bill of Rights precluding their landing in the United Kingdom, they were quartered in the Channel Isles awaiting the breaking of the ice to enable them to return through the Baltic to Russia. Six thousand men were quartered in Guernsey in barracks at Delancey, as well as at l'Ancresse and the Vale Castle.

Although General Sedmoratzky and his officers, in honour of Czar Paul's birthday, staged a grand ball at the Assembly Rooms where the principal inhabitants and the officers of the garrison were entertained, trouble arose with the soldiery following the deaths of several hundreds of a fever contracted in the Dutch marshes, the victims being buried in a small cemetery below the Vale Castle, part of which survives to the present day. The demoralised survivors took to drinking raw spirits and their conduct deteriorated alarmingly. One soldier was committed for rape, but was acquitted on the grounds of insufficient evidence; while another, caught stealing vegetables on a farm, was fired at and wounded — some reports said killed — by the farmer.

This incident incensed the whole Slav force, and it was feared that the Russians might revenge themselves on the inhabitants generally. With only a small garrison of regular troops available in the island, Dalrymple needed to exercise all the tact and make all the conciliatory gestures of which he was capable, as well as enlisting the efforts of General Sedmoratzky also, in order to prevent an ugly situation from developing. When the Russians eventually embarked the guns of Castle Cornet were kept loaded and ready to prevent any re-landing: and the whole population of the island heaved a sigh of relief — not least the Lieutenant-Governor!

Replaced in Guernsey in 1802 by Sir John Doyle (q.v.) and promoted to Lieutenant-General, Dalrymple assumed command of the Gibraltar garrison in 1806 and in 1808 gained notoriety (together with the Jerseyman, Lieutenant-General Sir Harry Burrard, Baronet) as a signatory to the infamous Convention of Cintra, whereby the French, after being defeated by Wellesley at Vimeiro, were allowed to evacuate their troops from Portugal for conveyance back to France in British ships. Although never again entrusted with a command in battle, Dalrymple was nevertheless promoted to full General in 1812 and created a Baronet in 1815. Sir Hew Dalrymple died in 1830.

DAVID II, KING OF SCOTLAND (1324–1371).
The boy-king whose vengeful attacks prompted the development of the Militia. David, the son of Robert the Bruce, inherited the Scottish throne on the death of his father in 1329 when he was a mere five years of age. Seeing in the infancy of the formidable Bruce's heir an opportunity to recoup its fortunes, the rival Balliol faction initiated action ultimately destined to prove traumatic for the Bailiwick of Guernsey. Sailing from the Humber with the tacit support of Edward III, they defeated David's forces at Dupplin Moor in 1332, with the result that Edward Balliol was crowned King at Scone. Soon afterwards, however, Balliol was driven from Scotland again and fled to Edward III who, now coming out openly in his support, marched north, took Berwick-upon-Tweed and defeated David's supporters at Halidon Hill in 1333. Edward Balliol was replaced on the throne as the puppet of Edward III, who was recognised as Lord Paramount of Scotland. David (by now nine years of age) sought asylum with Philip IV in France; and once installed in the Château Gaillard, the boy-king in exile plotted revenge, encouraged by his royal host who, pursuing the traditional policy of his house sought the discomfiture of the English with the ultimate aim of ejecting them from Gascony.

Scope for revenge was offered by the Channel Isles, rendered vulnerable by the decay of their defences stemming from prolonged neglect by the rapacious henchmen of the vampiric Sir Otto de Grandison (q.v.), who had died the year before Bruce's son came into his troubled inheritance. The plums being thus ripe for the picking, young David — now 12 — sailed in the autumn of 1336

for the islands, where his forces were reported to have committed 'arson, murder and divers other atrocities'. Sark and Alderney, utterly bereft of defence, suffered the worst damage. David's forces, however, were not able to establish themselves firmly and withdrew to France. In May of the following year Edward III, as a precaution against a further anticipated attack by David, ordered Sir Thomas de Ferrars (the Warden of the Isles) 'to levy and array all men capable of bearing arms and to form them into companies of thousands, hundreds and twenties' — one of the decisive stages in the evolution of the island militias. The title, '*Vingtenier*', given to Sark's junior constable, is an echo of the designation of a commander of a company of 20 at that time.

David regained his throne in 1338 when Edward III's preoccupation with the early campaigns of the Hundred Years War deprived Balliol of his prop. David was, however, taken prisoner by the English after his defeat at Neville's Cross in 1346 and remained 11 years in captivity. Released in 1357 on an undertaking to render homage to Edward III and to pay a ransom, he reigned ineffectively until his death in 1371.

DAVID, JOHN WINTER (1837–1903); DAVID, JOHN (1867–1928); DAVID, JOHN MARK (1910–1965).
A family providing St Cecilia with three generations of disciples. The David kindred's long association with Guernsey's musical life was inaugurated by John Winter David, who was born in 1837 to Susan Winter, the wife of John David, a sea captain and committed Methodist who forbade all alcohol on his ship, where daily prayers were *de rigueur* — but whose mother-in-law ran a wine shop! A church organist from his twenties until his death in 1903, as well as functioning as a choir master (first at the Town Church and then at the Vale church) from the age of 30 onwards, this music lover was also bandmaster to the North Regiment of the Royal Guernsey Militia from 1865 to 1894. In addition, he composed various hymn tunes, such as 'Marienlyst' and 'Longwood', to which 'Captain of Israel's host, and Guide' and 'Lead Us, O Father, in the paths of peace' respectively are usually sung — melodic orisons more familiar in Protestant Noncomformist circles than elsewhere within the Christian fold. Originally designed to accompany carollings in French (to the cadences of which they are by rhythm and metre more suited), these scores were written while David was organist at la Chapelle Méthodiste Française

in Victoria Road — and before his move (denominational and linguistic as well as locational) to St Barnabas at that church's opening in 1874. Yet another hymn was written for him by Victor Hugo (q.v.) with whom David was friendly, despite the disparity in their religious outlooks.

A Douzenier of St Peter-Port's Cantonal Douzaine Number Four from 1884 to 1898, John Winter married Mary Ann Mauger, who on Christmas Day 1867 bore him a son — John David — who carried on the Orphean tradition established by his father. After a spell as an assistant master at the Boys' Intermediate School, John David joined his parent at the Receiver-General's Office where he became Assistant Receiver-General in 1912. He had previously (in 1904) been appointed clerk to Elizabeth College, to the duties attaching to which he added in 1917 those of secretary to the States' Educational Council, retaining both posts until his death on 27 October 1928. He too served as a Douzenier in his case the Douzaine of Canton Number Three of St Peter Port.

Although by career a civil servant, John David by inclination resembled his parent, in being dedicated heart and soul to the service of Phoebus, and especially to music of the orchestral and choral variety. Organist at a succession of churches from his teens until his death, he took over from his father in 1888 the presentation at the Ozanne Hall of a series of concerts (usually devoted to oratorios) and thereby nurtured the development of the chrysalis from which there emerged in 1896 the Guille-Allès Choral and Orchestral Association: a body destined to sustain an interest in and a love for the best in music, both sacred and secular, until enthusiasm waned after death had deprived the organisation of the inspiration which emanated from its sponsor's very being. After such assiduous nursing, one may easily imagine how proud a day it was for John David when the combined choir and orchestra he had fostered was conducted in person by Samuel Coleridge-Taylor (1875–1912) in a rendering of his composition, 'Hiawatha's Wedding Feast', at St Julian's Theatre on Tuesday 23 March 1909. David was also an ardent supporter of the initiative of Dean Samuel Falle in Jersey which led to the institution in 1908 of the Jersey Eisteddfod, and thenceforth agitated tirelessly for the establishment of comparable artistic and musical sessions in Guernsey in friendly contest with those of the sister island — efforts which, after maddening delays, finally achieved success in November 1921 when the inception of the Guernsey Eisteddfod brought to birth an annual

competitive festival which rapidly became the principal musical event of the year with mutual rivalry stimulating a very high standard of attainment. In this connection he added to his other labours that of being Eisteddfod secretary, shouldering this extra burden until his death in 1928. He and his father are jointly commemorated by a memorial tablet in the south transept of the Town Church which reads: ' "He hath put a new song in my mouth." In loving memory of John Winter David, 1st organist of St Barnabas Church 1874-1902; also of his son John David, organist of this church 1924-28.'

John Mark David, who was born to John David's wife Annie Margaret le Pelley on 8 July, 1910, grew up to be a votary of Poseidon as well as of Apollo, following in his great grandfather's footsteps and serving in the Merchant Navy (in his case as a radio officer) throughout the Second World War — during which he was one of the ship's company of 72 on board the S.S. *Empire Banner* (6,699 tons) when she was torpedoed and sunk on 7 February 1943, about 30 miles northeast of Tenés in Algeria while en route for the Allies' forward base port of Bône (nowadays Annaba) conveying 3,800 tons of tanks and motor transport. All were saved. A holder of both the 1939–45 Star and the Atlantic Star, the sea continued to lure him after ill-health had forced him to quit the Mercantile Marine in 1945 and he developed a particularly keen interest in local shipping which animated him for the rest of his days. Inheriting his father's commitment to 'the food of love', however, John Mark David had set up in business as a music dealer in 1932 and to this pursuit he returned after the war, supporting his family thereby from then on. His two main predelictions were reflected in his non-professional activities, where on the one hand he became the Vice-President of the Guernsey Eisteddfod Society, while on the other he served on the local committee of the Royal National Lifeboat Institution and was also a vigorous advocate of the establishment of the Maritime Museum at Castle Cornet.

A constable of St Peter-Port from 1959 until his death, John Mark David was earnest in good works and energetic in cultural promotion, serving on the Council of the National Trust of Guernsey and on that of La Société Guernesiaise. He was president of the latter body for the years 1958 and 1959, the while collaborating with J. P. Warren (q.v.) in preparing the paper entitled, 'More About Elisha Dobrée's Diary and Weather Journal'. He was also a member of the Ancient Monuments Committee and of the Guille-Allés

Library Council as well as of the St Peter-Port Hospital Board. By a quirk of fate he died on his father's birthday — Christmas Day, 1965.

DÉODAT ANTOINE, FRÈRE DES ÉCOLES CHRÉTIENNES (1878-1951). *The builder of Les Vauxbelets Chapel.*

Born near Nantes on 18 July 1878 to Josephine Giraudineaud, the wife of Joseph Treilhaud, young Antoine Treilhaud grew up a sensitive lad of a retiring nature, reluctant to obtrude himself. Extremely devout, he expressed the desire at puberty to be ordained and consequently sought admission to a seminary. Despite his unblemished character and manifest sincerity, however, it was found that an inbred reticence and a degree of modesty verging on the excessive rendered him unfit to shoulder the responsibilities devolving on a priest.

The rejection of his candidature for the priesthood led this youth in his piety to consider joining the fraternity of laymen devoted to the education of boys founded by Jean-Baptiste de la Salle in 1680 and known as 'The Brothers of the Christian Schools'. He accordingly became a postulant of the Order at Nantes on 5 October 1894, when he was just over 16 years of age, and two months later, on 8 December, he was officially 'robed' as a Novice of the Order. Within ten months, however, the trait of hesitancy in his personality which had already caused him to be adjudged unfit for priestly office, halted the normal course of progress in the profession he now wished to embrace. Quailing at the prospect of committing himself even to temporary vows, he held back, unsure of his vocation and — no longer a novice as that term is usually understood, but not under vows either — hovered for the next seven years (until 1902) in the anomalous position described as that of 'Novice employé'.

By now young Monsieur Treilhaud was 24 years of age and, steeling himself to summon up the resolution needed for such a step, he became provisionally professed by taking his first temporary vows. Thereafter, racked by misgivings such as had assailed the centurion who had solicited a cure for his sick batman — 'Lord, I am not worthy' — Brother Déodat Antoine (as he was now known by courtesy though still not fully inducted into the Order) remained 'temporarily' professed until 1938 when he had attained the age of sixty !

It was during this prolonged period of 'impermanent' commitment that Brother Déodat on 5 December 1913, came to Les Vauxbelets — where he was to remain for over a quarter of a century. Soon after his arrival the sight of the lovely wooded slope behind the house put into his mind an idea which was to find expression in what became an all-absorbing pursuit over many years. From early youth this gentle soul had been intensely moved by the contemplation of the experiences which Bernadette Soubirous testified as having been vouchsafed to her in 1858 when, in the words of that great Anglican scholar Charles Williams, 'at Lourdes the waters sprang for healing under the direction of the Anthropotokos'. Now here, on the site of this pretty valley, Déodat decided to build a replica of the grotto where the 14-year-old girl had been convinced she had seen and spoken with the Mother of her Saviour — and also of the church which was later erected above it. This man of unassuming and verecund temperament had found his life's work !

Déodat set to work in March 1914, building with clinkers and heavy stones a chapel so tiny that on the evening of its completion it evoked caustic comment. Deeply hurt, the builder spent the following night pulling down the structure and replacing it before dawn by evergreen shrubs. He soon resumed his labours, however, and the grotto was finished and officially blessed on the day that the First World War broke out ! Brother Déodat immediately crossed to France for military service but ill-health led to his return one month later. During the war he replaced his original demolished edifice by another measuring nine feet by six and accommodating four people. This was visited in 1923 by the Bishop of Portsmouth (to whose jurisdiction all Roman Catholic churches in the Channel Isles are subject). The Bishop expressed disappointment at being unable to get his somewhat rotund frame through the doorway, remarking that otherwise he would have authorised the saying of Mass in the building. Déodat's reaction to this episode was to destroy his second attempt in September 1923 and to commence the construction of the chapel decorated with pebbles, ormer shells and broken pieces of pottery on which he worked until the Second World War and which still stands today.

All this time the designer and builder of this remarkable labour of love had remained no more than a provisional member of the de la Salle Order, his profession still only 'temporary'. He had now reached his sixtieth birthday and it was obvious that to one of such shyness and reserve the prospect of being the cynosure of all eyes while making final vows in a public ceremony would be quite simply unendurable. With this in mind the Bishop of Portsmouth, an understanding and sympathetic shepherd of his flock, made arrangements for this diffident man of such artistic bent to be professed privately in the very shrine he had built – a rite that was performed on 14 September 1938.

Within a year Europe was again plunged into war and Brother Déodat, his health now seriously impaired, returned to Nantes where he spent his declining years surrounded by the misery occasioned by the enemy occupation of his beloved France. Six years after the conflict ended he died in Nantes on 21 November 1951, aged 73. By the time of his death it had become apparent that he qualified for the divine response postulated by the Founder of his Faith as granted to the publican who, beset by a similar sense of personal unworthiness, dared venture no further than the threshold of the temple. As far as worldly esteem is concerned the regard accorded to this self-effacing coenobite is beyond doubt. Not even the founder of the Christian Brothers' Order – Jean-Baptiste de la Salle himself – is known to anything approaching the size of the public which has become acquainted with this humble and obscure brother who meekly served in a menial capacity, rendering obedience to superiors now long forgotten. As the centenary of his birth drew near the extent of his renown and of concern for his achievement was amply demonstrated when, following the discovery towards the end of 1977 of an imminent danger of subsidence; this major threat to the survival of his masterpiece was removed by a flood of donations enabling under-pinning and restoration work to be put in hand with minimum delay.

DOTRICE, ROY LOUIS (1923–   ). *A remarkable career: from under-age aviator to Thespian of renown*. Born on 26 May 1923 to Neva (*née* Wilton), the wife of Louis Dotrice, Roy Dotrice was educated first at Dayton Kindergarten in Rocquettes Road and subsequently at the Intermediate School, which he left in 1939, taking a junior position with the firm of Langlois and Company in the Bordage. When the German Occupation threatened, young Dotrice, accompanied by his mother and brother, betook himself to Plymouth on board a granite-carrying ship connected with his employer's business. In England, bereft of any means of support the family sought relief; Roy was provided with a railway voucher and 30s. to enable his brother and himself to go to Manchester, to the vicinity of which many Channel Isles refugees were at that time being despatched.

Arrived at their destination, the two brothers found themselves in a workhouse! The only escape was to find employment and the future West End star obtained work as a junior clerk with a firm of handkerchief manufacturers. While this post provided release from the workhouse, it was not one which made it possible to sustain life, as it only brought in 10s. 6d. a week – and bus fares alone came to 6s. 0d.! The Guernsey Donkey, face to face with destitution, made his way to a recruiting station, gave his age as 18 (it was in fact 17) and joined the Royal Air Force.

Although he did not realise it, in thus volunteering for flying duties with Bomber Command, Roy Dotrice was taking the first steps on the path to his life's career behind the footlights. Between the night of 11 February 1942 and the morning of 13 February the German battleships *Scharnhorst* and *Gneisenau* made a dash up Channel from Brest to reach home waters at Kiel. At the end of the month the two vessels were subjected to heavy air attack. In Volume Four of his War Memoirs (*The Hinge of Fate*, Chapter XV), Sir Winston Churchill records that 'on the night of February 27th the *Gneisenau* was hit in dock at Kiel and, although we did not know it at the time, was so heavily damaged that she played no further part in the war at sea'. During the course of this operation a magnificent Guernseyman in a flying machine was shot down while not yet 19 years of age and as a consequence spent the rest of the war as a prisoner in Germany. It was his participation in amateur dramatics to while away the weary years of captivity that first awakened this intrepid islander's interest in the theatre.

Freed by the Allied victory, Roy Dotrice made his first public stage appearance in a revue called *Back Home*, which was performed entirely by ex-prisoners of war in aid of the Red Cross. During the immediate post-war decade there followed the not unusual drudgery of an interminable round of repertory theatres. Then in 1955 he formed the Guernsey Repertory Theatre Company, directing and appearing in its various productions at the Little Theatre (alias Central Hall) until 1957. He followed this up by joining the Shakespeare Memorial Theatre Company (later renamed the Royal Shakespeare Company) in July 1958, becoming one of its long-term contract players in 1961.

In January 1967 at the Hampstead Theatre Club Roy Dotrice appeared as John Aubrey in the one-man production entitled *Brief Lives*. The following December he made his first Broadway appearance in this same part (his favourite) at the John Golden Theatre. Back in London a year later he yet again appeared in this part at the Criterion Theatre as from February 1969 for a run of 213 performances — a world record for a one-man show. He also played the same part on television and on the strength of it was voted 'Television Actór of the Year'. Another television appearance was in the Harold Pinter play, *The Caretaker* (which won an Emmy Award when shown in the U.S.A.). An hilariously funny televised series came from the pen of the late A. P. Herbert under the title of *Misleading Cases*, in which Roy Dotrice played the rôle of a litigious geriatric who invariably emerged triumphant from highly convoluted involvements in a court where the part of the judge was taken by Alistair Sim. Of all his television performances, however, the one of outstanding significance for this gifted player was that where he was cast in the rôle of the novelist's father in *Dickens of London*. He was only able to do so thanks to efficacious spiritual healing whereby a cure was effected for a hip injury which otherwise would have precluded his participation in the production: an experience which confirmed his faith in such therapy wrought by enlisting divine aid.

After the opening in 1978 of the new museum in Candie Gardens, Roy Dotrice provided the commentary accompanying the Visual Aid feature centred around Le Clameur de Haro which was made for exhibition in the establishment's small auditorium. Four years later — in February 1982 while he was playing the elegantly sinister putative husband opposite Nyree Dawn Porter in *Murder in the Mind* at the Strand Theatre — this accomplished actor consented to become joint Patron with His Excellency the Lieutenant-Governor of the Guernsey Arts Council. In the same year too, one distinguished Guernseyman did honour to another in the broadcasting of a series of readings by Roy Dotrice from that masterpiece by Gerald Basil Edwards (q.v.) — *The Book of Ebenezer le Page*.

DOYLE, LIEUTENANT-GENERAL SIR JOHN, BARONET, G.C.B., K.C. (1756–1834). *Guernsey's most popular Lieutenant-Governor*. Entering the army as an ensign in 1771 at the age of 16, John Doyle saw service in the American War of Independence as a young officer, distinguishing himself at the Battle of Brooklyn, and also at Germantown, where he was wounded. Later in the conflict he was appointed Brigade Major under General Cornwallis.

With the coming of peace Doyle entered politics and was elected to the Irish Parliament as the Member for Mullingar. In 1796 he became Secretary at War in Ireland. He was destined ere long, however, to take up the sword once more. The French Revolutionary War had broken out in 1793 and in 1797 the Commander-in-Chief in Ireland was forced to resign after his outspoken condemnation of General Lake's mail-fisted 'disarming of Ulster' in the wake of the uprising following the abortive French assault at Bantry Bay the previous December. Doyle accompanied Abercrombie when the latter was subsequently posted to Egypt and commanded a brigade in the campaign which culminated in the French defeat at Alexandria (21 March 1801) when Abercrombie was mortally wounded.

By now Doyle had earned sufficient renown to be promoted to the rank of Lieutenant-General, and in 1803 he was sent to Guernsey as Lieutenant-Governor when the resumption of hostilities after the Peace of Amiens placed the island in imminent danger of invasion. He was to stay at this post until 1816 and although technically subordinate from 1807 onwards to George, Earl of Pembroke (who became Governor that year) Doyle remained effectively at the helm, his superior being an insouciant absentee.

The new Lieutenant-Governor addressed himself vigorously to the urgent problem of the island's security. He immediately set about improving the Militia, seeing that it was better equipped and insisting on the implementation of a training programme, appointing his nephew (Colonel John Milley Doyle) as its inspector. At the same time he drew up a major defence plan, to finance which he prevailed upon the States to vote the unprecedently large sum of £30,000 for supplies. The plan embraced the entire coast from La Salerie in an anti-clockwise direction to Fermain Bay, the defence of St Peter-Port being left to Castle Cornet and the still uncompleted Fort George. Doyle planned that every vantage point on the low-lying coast from La Salerie to Grande Havre was to be used to accommodate a battery of guns, while similar gun emplacements were to be erected between Grande Havre and Grandes Rocques — whose fortifications were to be supplemented by a powder magazine. Farther down the west coast parapets were to be thrown up at Houmet and l'Erée and battery sites constructed, while the ancient Rocquaine Castle (Fort Grey) was to be repaired and guns placed at strategic points on the rising ground above the bay. Finally, to complete these western defences, the old castle at Pezeries was to be repaired, the parapet strengthened and a powder magazine installed.

Although one would have thought the unscalability of the cliffs from Pleinmont to Petit Bôt to be such as to provide automatic-defence, Doyle took no chances but insisted on the erection of watch houses at the high points of La Prévôté, Les Tielles, Mont Herault and Pleinmont. Thereafter three vulnerable bays remained — Petit Bôt, Saints and Fermain. In each case Doyle required the erection of ramparts of stone at least 12 feet in height, supplemented by trenches and parapets. Batteries were also built on the cliffs.

Having dealt with primary defence, Doyle later turned his attention to its major ancillary — communications. Realising the inadequacy of the road system for the rapid movement of troops and guns to any threatened part of the coast, he drove two new roads through the island from St Peter-Port in 1812 — one to Vazon, and one to l'Erée — and in so doing set the pattern for Guernsey's present network. To finance this work Sir John hit upon the idea of draining the Braye du Valle and selling the reclaimed land. In this fashion he killed two birds with one stone, for, by uniting the Clos du Valle with St Sampson's he removed any possibility of the northern islet being used by an invading force as a base for further attack.

During his term of office John Doyle was created a Baronet in 1805 and was also elected to the United Kingdom Parliament as the Member for Newport, Isle of Wight, holding this seat for the two years 1806 and 1807. By the time of Napoleon's defeat Guernsey's Lieutenant-Governor had attained tremendous popularity and his recall in 1816 (occasioned by post-war staff reductions) took place in the teeth of emphatic remonstrances by the States, which body urged vehemently, but unsuccessfully, the case for his retention in office.

Sir John returned twice to Guernsey after relinquishing his appointment. The first occasion was in September 1823 when, accompanied by his nephew Sir John Milley Doyle, he arrived on board the *Royal George* — the second steamship ever to visit the island. (The first, the *Medina*, had called three months earlier.) He did not, however, land, although he sent a message assuring his Guernsey friends that all his heart and soul were with them. In 1826 he returned and this time came ashore to a rapturous welcome. He disembarked at the St Julien Rock and the populace, taking the horses out of the carriage that awaited him, hauled it in triumph over the rough surface of the Deschamps Causeway to the town.

Sir John Doyle died in London in 1834, but this paragon among Lieutenant-Governors has never been forgotten in the Bailiwick where his memory is perpetuated by a road, two forts (one in Guernsey and the other in Alderney) and a group of dwellings at l'Ancresse on the site of the barracks he established — not to mention a column at Jerbourg which, although destroyed by the Germans in the Second World War, has since been replaced by a commemorative obelisk.

DRAKE, REVEREND FRANCIS MACKWORTH (1901-   ). *The creator of the Chapel of Christ the Healer*. Born in 1901, the Rev. Francis Drake went up to Oxford in the wake of the First World War as an Exhibitioner at Exeter College, obtaining his B.A. in 1924 and his M.A. in 1932. He taught for some time and then, after receiving his theological training at Wycliff Hall, Oxford, was ordained deacon in 1940 and priest in 1941 — in both cases by the Bishop of Lichfield. Having entered Holy Orders, he served as Chaplain to Wrekin College, Wellington, from 1940 to 1945. He then went out to India, where he had been appointed as headmaster of the Bishop Colton School at Simla — a position he held from 1945 to 1949.

In 1950 Fr. Drake, armed with permission to officiate within the Diocese of Winchester, came to Guernsey to take up the post of Principal of La Monnaie School in St Andrew's. He retained this appointment for the next ten years — years which were to prove the most traumatic and crucial of his life. During the autumn of 1955 this priest, brought to a state of intense spiritual awareness as a result of his son Robin's long and painful terminal illness, had a mental vision of a tiny church with a square tower in the chicken run behind La Monnaie house. As a result of this experience he persuaded his friend, Clifford Moullin, an architect, to design a miniature church, although he had no money to pay for it. Six months later Fr. Drake was told of a local donor who was prepared to defray all construction costs, on condition of remaining anonymous. Accordingly the work was put in hand, the builder being Marcel Flouquet. On 9 May 1957 the chapel, built of pink and blue Guernsey granite, was dedicated to Christ the Healer by the Bishop of Winchester. Prayers are said daily for the sick whose names are deposited in a box in the porch.

During the course of his son's illness Francis Drake had frequently been in contact with Dorothy Kerin at Burrswood — indeed, it was at her prompting that he had approached Clifford Moullin for plans for his projected church — and in 1960 he went to Groombridge where he served as Chaplain to the Burrswood Nursing

Home and Healing Centre until 1962. Back in Guernsey he spent four further years (1964–68) as Warden of La Monnaie Home for Rest and Healing, which he himself had established. For his retirement this man of God chose the peaceful surroundings of the old cottage of Le Grée, at Le Gron, St Saviour's.

DUNCAN, JONATHAN (1799–1867). *Herm's paradoxical figure: an archaeological vandal cum historian.* Jonathan Duncan, who played so prominent a part in the history of Herm in the mid-19th century, was a person of wide culture and varied talents: lawyer, entrepreneur, historian, journalist, financial polemicist and student of religious beliefs. Yet at the same time he was capable, at the dictates of profit considerations, to connive at the wholesale mutilation and indeed obliteration of priceless archaeological treasures, to the impoverishment of the very heritage which constituted his field of study as an historian: a strange contradiction.

Born in 1799, Duncan was called to the Bar shortly after coming down from Cambridge (Trinity) in 1821. He did not, however, practise for long, as in 1824 he forsook London for the Channel Isles, entering into a 14-year agreement with Lieutenant-Colonel the Honourable John Lindsay (q.v.) for their joint exploitation of Herm's granite, whereby — with uncharacteristic incaution — he advanced substantial sums on this speculative venture. Although soon disillusioned by Lindsay's inefficiency and dilatoriness, he inexplicably extended both the agreement and the size of his commitments. In 1825 he contributed further to the business by his invention of a horse-drawn timber-press, which he later converted to crush granite — doing so with such efficiency as to make it cope even with Herm's exceptionally hard variety. Despite orders for Herm stone for the construction of the East and West India Dock Roads, however, the enterprise remained in a bad way and Herm was held 'en saisie' by the States of Guernsey (a major creditor) after Lindsay's death while still an undischarged bankrupt in 1826,

Undeterred by his predecessor's experiences, Duncan took the island on hire and by 1829 was able to inform Lindsay's widow (who was also his notional mother-in-law: he had married her late husband's natural daughter in 1828) that Herm was prospering, with granite sales large enough to warrant the opening of additional quarries and the provision of accommodation for 270 workmen — whereby, incidentally, he became responsible for the erection of most of the buildings still in the island today.

In 1830, with a view to promoting further capital investment, Duncan formed a partnership with Geoffrey Martin and Ebenezer Fernie, trading as the Herm Granite Company. The installation of an iron railway and the existence of a harbour capable of taking ships of 250 tons burthen, made it possible to export six hundred tons of granite daily. It was during this period that Duncan, evincing no compunction over his action, ordered the demolition of La Pierre aux Rats Menhir so as to provide a 100-ton block of stone which, though intended to form the base of the Duke of York's Column in Waterloo Place, was not in the event so used. By order of the States of Guernsey, Duncan replaced this Menhir (which mariners had long used as a sea-mark) by the existing obelisk. (This wilful destruction of a prehistoric religious relic by 'Hyde' Duncan is even more astonishing when one reflects that it closely followed the appearance in 1830 of 'Jekyll' Duncan's scholarly work *The Religions of Profane Antiquity*. Yet it was but a prelude to further wanton plundering — under similar commercial motivation — of Herm's megalithic remains left, right and centre!)

Despite a misleading semblance of profitable trading, with Herm's stone exported (*inter alia*) for King William's Steps between the Mall and Carlton House Terrace, the Granite Company was dissolved in 1836, and Duncan was declared bankrupt in 1837. Managing (thanks most likely to his legal knowledge) to evade the worst consequences of this development, Duncan went into dignified retirement in Guernsey, editing the *Guernsey and Jersey Magazine* and delivering lectures at the Mechanics' Institute. Between the years 1841 and 1843 he produced his celebrated *History of Guernsey* — almost totally avoiding therein any mention of the isle of his misfortunes! (It may also be noticed in passing that his credulous acceptance of the claims made in the spurious 'Dédicase des Eglises' detracts from the quality of an otherwise painstaking compilation.) He then betook himself to London where he contrived to live out the rest of his life in comfortable circumstances, emerging as an impassioned advocate of currency reform; in which capacity he repeatedly denounced S. J. Loyd's monetary system and the 'silly sophisms' of Sir Robert Peel in *Jerrold's Weekly News*. In the same vein he wrote in 1847 *The National Anti-Gold Law League*.

Thus, with his reputation as a savant enhanced by such publications as *An Historical Dissertation* on the *Mythology and Hieroglyphics of the Ancients* and *The Religious Wars of France*, Jonathan Duncan died, a respected citizen of the metropolis, in 1867.

DUQUEMIN, CYRIL (1909–). *Macte virtute.* See *Underground Resistance Heroes of the Second World War.*

E

EDWARD IV, KING OF ENGLAND AND LORD OF IRELAND (1442-1483). *A grateful Royal refugee.* Born in Rouen in April 1442 to Cicely (*née* Neville), the wife of Richard Duke of York, Edward was inescapably involved in the tragic struggles between the White Rose of York and the Red of Lancaster. These arose from his father's maternal descent from Edward III's second son Lionel of Clarence which gave him a title to the throne as good as – if not better than – that of Henry VI (born the month after Edward and succeeding to the throne three months later). The latter was descended from Edward III's *third* son John of Gaunt; and Edward's claim was incomparably better than that of the ambitious Beauforts (of the bastard line stemming from Gaunt's liaison with Katherine Swynford) who, represented by Edmund Beaufort, Duke of Somerset, sought power through the manipulation of the feeble-minded monarch.

Four years after the York–Beaufort rivalry had erupted into open warfare with the Battle of St Albans, the 17-year-old Edward (who at the time was the Earl of March) was among those fleeing for their lives after the defeat of his father's supporters at the Rout of Ludford in October 1459. Accompanied by his mother's kinsman the Earl of Warwick (later to achieve fame as 'The Kingmaker' and who since 1449 had been Lord of the Isles) he sheltered at Nutwell, near Newton Abbot in Devonshire, with Joanna Dinham, a widow whose son procured a ship in which the fugitives sailed for Guernsey, where they found asylum until they eventually reached the English town of Calais. Not one to allow services rendered to go unrewarded, Edward (after the Crown had been placed on his head by the Yorkist victory at Towton in March 1461 following on the death of his father at the Battle of Wakefield the previous year) granted Joanna the custody and marriage of a royal ward, plus a present of £80 to distribute among her tenants and servants. As for those to whom he was beholden in Guernsey, the area they inhabited, to the south of Anneville, was carved out of the Ducal desmesne to form

le Franc Fief au Gallicien, 230½ *vergées* in extent, the tenants of which were freed for ever from the payment of all feudal dues.

Hard on the heels of Edward's triumph at Towton, Jersey was seized in May 1461 on behalf of Pierre de Brézé, Comte de Maulevrier, Grand Seneschal of Normandy. This was most likely done in the Lancastrian interest with the connivance of Brézé's cousin Marguerite of Anjou, the warlike queen of Henry VI and Edward's inveterate foe. In 1468 the French were driven out again by one of Edward's most fervent supporters, Sir Richard Harliston, who was aided by forces he had picked up in Guernsey en route. This help in the liberation of the sister island prompted the king to grant the Bailiwick a Charter confirming its privileges and immunities, in which he stressed 'how valiantly, manfully and steadfastly the said peoples and communities of the said islands of Guernsey, Sark and Alderney have stood out for us and our progenitors, and what great dangers and losses they have sustained for the safety of the same islands and for the recapture of our Castle of Mont Orgueil'.

The most important manifestation of Edward's solicitude for the welfare of the Isles (his personal knowledge of which alerted him to their usefulness for observing any potential foe south of the Channel) came with the accord he reached with Louis XI of France in the course of the tortuous 1479 negotiations for a marriage between the infant Dauphin and Elizabeth of York, whereby each undertook to regard the archipelago as neutral in the event of further war between their two realms. To reinforce and consolidate this compact Edward sought papal patronage for the agreement – an application which eventuated in the epoch-making 1480/1 Bull of Sixtus IV (q.v.) which accorded to the islands a neutral status that was to endure for 200 years.

Cannily perceiving that guaranteed neutrality would enhance the value of the islands as advanced outposts for keeping an eye on Henry Tudor's activities in Brittany, Edward in August 1482 appointed his trusted intimate Edward Brampton (q.v.) as 'Captain, Keeper and Governor' of Guernsey and its dependencies. The king's death the following year at the early age of 41 robbed the islands not only of a monarch *in loco ducis*, but also of a grateful and benevolent patron.

EDWARDS, GERALD BASIL (1899–1976). *A Guernseyman of genius: impecunious exile and writer of outstanding calibre.* The posthumous publication in 1981 of the novel, *The Book of Ebenezer le Page* (written throughout in 'Guernsey English' and acclaimed by the eminent author John Fowles as 'a portrait and memorial that must surely become a classic of the island') brought to public notice in Guernsey a native-born littérateur of rare talent who, deliberately seeking obscurity, had remained unknown throughout his life.

Born on 8 July 1899 to Harriet (*née* Mauger), the wife of Thomas Edwards, a quarry-owner in the Vale, Gerald Basil Edwards by his own admission tended to shun company, finding it difficult to associate with other people -- especially with women: 'all my relationships with women have been a fight to the death'. This trait in his temperament is also highlighted in a contemporary's description of him as 'a real loner, an odd sort of character who never had any friends'. Yet from the pen of this eremitic personality came what one reviewer has hailed as 'undoubtedly the finest novel ever written about the Bailiwick'.

Starting his education at the Hautes Capelles School, Gerald Edwards in 1909 won a scholarship to the Boys' Intermediate School, whence he went to Vauvert as a Pupil Teacher in 1914. By now the First World War had broken out and in 1917, with his 18th birthday behind him, Edwards joined the Royal Guernsey Light Infantry. Because of his tender years he never saw action and the Armistice found him at Portsmouth as a Sergeant-Instructor in gunnery. After demobilisation he spent four years (1919–1923) at Bristol University, but no details survive of what he read there.

It would seem that Gerald Edwards retained his Guernsey residence throughout his time at the university and returned to the island on coming down. In 1924, however, his mother died and his father, on re-marrying in 1926, deliberately took steps to disinherit his son in favour of his new wife. In an emotional turmoil at this parental rejection, Edwards left Guernsey to seek his fortune elsewhere. Never again was he to be domiciled in the island of his birth. Going to London, he worked for the University Settlement of Toynbee Hall and also joined the Workers' Educational Association as a lecturer in English Literature and Drama. He also appears to have put in a spell with the Bolton Repertory Company, for which he wrote a number of plays -- all of which he subsequently destroyed!

At some point between 1926 and 1930 Gerald Edwards married, but his innate difficulty in relating to other people meant that although it produced four children, the marriage was not a success. It was still limping along in 1930 when he and his wife lived in Hornsey where in a tenancy agreement he gave his profession as 'author'. By 1933, however, it had finally broken down and Edwards travelled for a time in Holland and Switzerland, earning his living by his pen with articles, poems and plays — all later consigned to the flames.

With the coming of the Second World War Edwards took up an appointment in an employment exchange and thereafter remained in the civil service until his retirement in 1960. Like many a Guernseyman he yearned to spend his declining years in his native isle, but Guernsey is no place for anyone subsisting on an exiguous pension who is denied the right to occupy local market premises! Exiled by the slender nature of his means, Gerald Edwards betook himself first to Wales (1960–61), then to Penzance (1961–64) and Plymouth (1964–67) before finally settling in Weymouth (handy for visits to Guernsey) from 1967 onwards.

During these wanderings the involuntary exile conceived the idea of a trilogy of novels depicting life in the island of his birth. The three parts he envisaged as *Sarnia Chérie: The Book of Ebenezer le Page*, *Le Boud'lo: The Book of Philip le Moigne* and *La Gran'mère du Chimquière: The Book of Jean le Féniant*. Edwards told his daughter that while he was in Plymouth he completed the first draft of *Ebenezer le Page* and half of *Le Boud'lo*. His ultimate aim seems to have been not only to evoke the Guernsey atmosphere but also to portray the damage done to the traditional insular life-style by the modern developments he disliked so much, such as the 'finance industry' and — especially — tourism, which he deplored as 'an incubus that saps the natural and spiritual vitality of the island', contemptuously referring to tourists as 'pests'.

Over all this period, however, Edwards made no attempt to obtain publication of his work, about which he displayed symptoms of manic depression. Living in a small room described by a witness as 'like that of a monk' so frugally that his landlady said that all he possessed could be packed in a small suitcase, he most likely would have gone to the grave with nothing to show for his efforts but for the friendship and sympathy of Edward and Lisa Chaney (to whom he dedicated *Ebenezer*) whose encouragement led him completely to re-write his masterpiece between 1973 and 1974. Drafts for the rest of the trilogy he destroyed, at the same time accepting stoically repeated rejections of *Ebenezer* by one publisher after another.

Gerald Edwards died of a heart attack on 29 December 1976. His body was cremated and its ashes scattered at sea.

EUSTACE THE MONK (executed 1217). *The ravisher of the Isles.* Forsaking the cloister to become a soldier of fortune, this notorious pirate was eventually appointed Seneschal to Renaud Dammartin, the Count of Bologne. Around December 1203, however, after a quarrel with the count, he took to the forest at the head of an armed band and, in true Robin Hood fashion, harrassed his enemy's followers and despoiled his property — though in his case it is highly unlikely that any benefit accrued to the poor! After about a year of such defiance of his erstwhile master, the ex-monk was captured in January 1205 and sent to be tried at the French court. On the way there, however, he eluded his escort and, disguised as a Templar, fled to England where, in the Spring of 1205 he sought the protection of King John (q.v.) to whom he offered his services, swearing fealty and surrendering his wife and daughter as hostages.

The previous year — in the summer of 1204 — King Philip Augustus of France, as a result of the capitulation made at Rouen by Pierre de Préaux (q.v.*), had acquired control of the Channel Isles, which he garrisoned with troops under the command of a castellan named Romerel. Realising the importance of the archipelago (and especially of the roadstead of St Peter-Port) for the main-tenance of communications with his remaining mainland territories in Gascony, John was anxious to effect its recovery and decided for this purpose to avail himself of the services of his new protégé. Thus in August 1205 Eustace, with 30 ships supplied by the English king, set out for the Channel Isles and overcame the resistance of Romerel's forces in furious combat in which he himself figured prominently, fighting first with an axe and later with a dagger. The islands were then devastated, with 'nought left to burn'. Rather late in the day came a Writ issued in September 1205

(and apparently addressed to Eustace) requiring the recipient to maintain peace in the islands and cause no damage! Possibly with a view to restrain-ing the excesses of this renegade religious, John seems (according to the *Histoire des Ducs de Normandie*) to have made him an informal grant of the islands.

This *de facto* control did not in the event last for long, as the indications are that by the follow-ing December the archipelago was yet again in the hands of Philip Augustus: and when John contrived once more to regain the islands (May 1206) Geoffrey de Lucy became Warden of Guernsey and Hasculf de Suligny of Jersey. There is a likelihood, however, that Eustace retained a foothold for his entourage and himself in Sark. At all events, although the monk-turned-corsair held lands in Norfolk, there is evidence that he was based outside England, as in both May 1206 and April 1208 he was granted safe conducts to visit that country — and later events suggest that Sark could well have been his *pied à terre*.

In the autumn of 1212 there came a breach between Eustace and King John, to whom the adventurer owed 20 marks. The smallness of the sum involved makes one suspect that the debt was the occasion, rather than the cause, of the dispute, which possibly stemmed from steadily increasing tension over a prolonged period. What-ever its cause, the freebooter by way of reaction to the rift proceeded to seize the islands (nomi-nally on behalf of Philip Augustus!) and, although expelled by Philippe d'Aubigny (q.v.) he managed to retain control of Sark. It was not until two years later — October 1214 — that the rebel was dispossessed of Sark by d'Aubigny, who sent his brother and uncle, together with 'fourteen ser-geants' as prisoners to Winchester.

By March 1215 all was forgiven and forgotten. Desperately seeking support wherever he could find it in the deepening crisis preceding Runny-mede, John released the prisoners and made his peace with Eustace. It is to be hoped that he remembered that whosoever sups with the Devil must needs use a long spoon, for by mid-September of the same year the forsworn monk had deserted the king and joined the rebellious barons in the civil strife which followed Magna Carta. Then, after the arrival in England in June 1216 of the Prince Louis (the son of Philip Augustus who sought to obtain John's crown for himself) Eustace yet again seized the Channel Isles, ostensibly on behalf of the young prince, though the indications are that he acted independently as the villanous marauder he was. Hoping to find rich fishing in troubled waters, Eustace then made ships available to Philip Augustus to ferry across the Channel supplies for his son's forces. In August 1217, however, Nemesis struck. His ships were intercepted by Philippe d'Aubigny and in the ensuing Battle of Sandwich Eustace was defeated. Retribution was swift. D'Aubigny, staunch as ever in the Plantagenet cause, had this treacherous brigand executed on his own quarter-deck.

F

FALLA, FRANCIS WALTER (1911–1983). *Macte virtute*. See *Underground Resistance Heroes of the Second World War*.

FARNON, ROBERT JOSEPH (1917–   ). *The Donkey Serenader who came to live with the Donkeys*. Born in Toronto in 1917, this accomplished musician, and islander by adoption, had by the tender age of 14 learned to play every instrument in the orchestra – though the trumpet was his forte. Thus in 1934, when no more than 17 years old, he was already playing lead trumpet and writing choral arrangements for the Canadian Broadcasting Commission's Orchestra led by Percy Faith. Three years later (when still only 20) he assumed the leadership of the orchestra on Faith's departure for the United States.

In 1942 Robert Farnon joined the Canadian Army, where he was immediately seen as the Maple Leaf's counterpart to Glen Miller. He was consequently made conductor of the Canadian Army Orchestra, and with the rank of Captain brought it over to England in 1944, building up a formidable reputation. After the war Farnon stayed in England, and established himself in public esteem with his Concert Orchestra's 'Journey Into Melody' broadcasts during 1946. In addition he wrote several scores for his own and other orchestras, including 'The Donkey Serenade', 'The Bells of Saint Mary's' and 'Pagan Love Song'; while for his publishers (Chappell's) he built up a large 'Mood Music' Library.

At the same time this versatile Canadian composed serious music. He had already (at the age of 22) written his 'Symphony in D Flat' in 1939 and further works which are in some ways reminiscent of Delius and Debussey followed – especially his 'Ottawa Symphony'. During the 1950s, however, Robert Farnon made his greatest name in films, providing music for such Anna Neagle-Herbert Wilcox pictures as *Spring in Park Lane* and *Maytime in Mayfair*, as well as for such Ivor Novello productions as *King's Rhapsody* and *The Dancing Years*. On the strength of these successes Warner Brothers in Hollywood signed him up, but after several unsatisfactory experiences arising from his irritation at the cinema capital's penchant for pandering to puerility, Farnon decided that henceforth he would only accept assignments in films that appealed to him personally.

In the mid-1960s this famous man of music became one of the people in the Island's story when he settled in Guernsey, acquiring with le Fief de la Velleresse de la Fallaize not only the notional obligation dating back to the 12th century to keep watch against the island's foes, but also a shelter offering escape from the pressures of a busy life in films, recordings and broadcasting – as well as the labours of composition.

FISHER, RIGHT REVEREND DOCTOR JOHN (1748–1825). *The first Anglican Bishop to visit the Bailiwick*. Born in 1748 at Hampton in Middlesex, the son of John Fisher, Prebendary of Salisbury, this future Bishop was educated first at Peterborough and later at St Paul's, before going up in 1766 to Peterhouse, Cambridge, as a pensioner on a Pauline exhibition.

Taking the degree of B.A. in 1770, he was ordained deacon the following year and priest two years later – on both occasions by the Bishop of Winchester. Then, having taken the degree of M.A. the year he was priested (1773), John Fisher followed this up by taking his B.D. in 1780 and being awarded his D.D. in 1789. Having in the meantime been appointed as tutor to the royal children (with particular responsibility as preceptor to the Prince Edward, who was later to be the Duke of Kent and father to Queen Victoria) and also a Chaplain to King George III, Fisher served as a Canon of Windsor from 1786 to 1803, in which latter year he was elevated to the episcopacy with his consecretation as Bishop of Exeter. In 1795 he was charged with superintending the education of Princess Charlotte of Wales and in 1807 was translated to Salisbury, in which See he remained for the rest of his life.

In 1818 Doctor John Fisher conducted the first episcopal visitation of the Channel Isles since the Reformation, crossing in the 46-gun frigate *Tiber* and coming in the stead of Dr. Brownlow North, Bishop of Winchester, who was too frail and deaf to undertake the journey. (Dr. North did, however, compose a special sermon for the occasion, based on 1 Corinthians 1:X — 'that there be no divisions among you; but that ye be perfectly joined together' — which, because of his inability to deliver it, was published in English and French under the title of *Uniformity and Communion*.) Although the archipelago had been placed unequivocally within the Diocese of Winchester by Order-in-Council in 1569, the survival of a Huguenot Establishment in Guernsey until 1660, followed by the persistence of Calvinist sentiment in defiance of Charles II's imposition of Anglicanism, had hitherto rendered impolitic any overt assertion of the Church of England's episcopalian structure. Sleeping dogs had therefore been allowed to lie for the one and a half centuries that had passed since the appointment of a Dean in the person of Jean de Sausmarez (q.v.*) had signalised the formal establishment of the Anglican system at the Restoration. The post-Waterloo influx of English settlers had, however, modified the ecclesiastical climate and it is significant that one of the main events during this prelate's stay in Guernsey was the consecration of the church of St James the Less which had been built expressly 'for the celebration of Divine Worship in the English tongue', there being no church at that time catering for those without a knowledge of French. The idea of providing such facilities had been conceived by Sir James Saumarez, Baronet — later Admiral Lord de Saumarez (q.v.) — in 1807 as a means of reducing friction between the island and the garrison.

During his visit Dr. Fisher also consecrated the present-day Torteval church, erected to replace its neglected predecessor, which had fallen into ruin. Furthermore he conducted the first confirmations to have been performed in the Bailiwick since its divorce from the Diocese of Coutances in Tudor days. Over the intervening period the Anglican requirement of this rite as a precondition of admission to the Holy Communion had been ignored. In its place the Presbyterian system of examination of potential communicants by the Consistoire had been retained, with the rector and churchwardens making up an unofficial Consistoire for this purpose. In this connection Doctor Fisher also administered the sacrament of confirmation in Sark and Alderney, travelling to the latter island on board Governor John le Mesurier's yacht *Vigilant* and being accorded a 13-gun salute on both arrival and departure.

Dr. John Fisher died on 8 May 1825 and was buried at St George's Chapel, Windsor. A further four years were to elapse before the islands were first visited by their own Bishop (of Winchester), in the person of Doctor Charles Richard Sumner in 1829.

FOWLER, HENRY WATSON (1858–1933) and FOWLER, FRANCIS GEORGE (1870–1918). *The literary and lexicographical brothers of St Pierre du Bois*. These two gifted sons of Caroline (*née* Watson), the wife of the Reverent Robert Fowler, were born in 1858 and 1870 respectively. Henry, the eldest of the couple's eight children, was born in Tonbridge and educated at Rugby whence he went up to Oxford (Balliol) with a scholarship in 1877. After coming down he taught for a short while at Fettes and then at Sedbergh from 1882 to 1899. In this latter year, resigning his post at Sedbergh after a dispute arising from his refusal, as a conscientious agnostic, to prepare his pupils for confirmation, Henry took lodgings in Chelsea, living meagrely on a small inherited income and swimming daily in the Serpentine, whatever the state of the weather.

In the meantime Henry's younger brother Francis George, after reading Classics at Cambridge (Peterhouse) between 1889 and 1892, had entered into a partnership with a tomato-growing friend in Guernsey, where he built a granite cottage adjacent to his partner's house near St Pierre du Bois church. Here Henry joined Francis in 1903, putting up a companion cottage adjoining his brother's. He then entered upon a spartan routine, starting each day with an early morning run to Rocquaine (so regular that the people at La Planque would say as he passed by, '*V'la Mister Fowler, i' y' est huit haëures*' — and it always was!) A swim at the bay and a return run was followed by his toilet, breakfast, work for the rest of the morning, lunch (provided alternately by each brother), a rest, a frugal tea, more work and finally a cold supper before going to bed.

Living thus, the two brothers cooperated in producing in 1905 a four-volume translation of the *Dialogues of the Gods* and the *Dialogues of the Dead* of the second century Greek writer Lucian of Samosata: and followed this up with their joint authorship of *The King's English* in 1906. The year 1908, however, brought a change of circumstances as on his 50th birthday (10 March) Henry married Jessie Marian Wills, the superintendent at the Alexandra Nursing Home. Although marriage brought a somewhat less ascetic life-style the brothers' combined labours continued, issuing in the appearance of *The Concise Oxford Dictionary* in 1911. On 11 April of that year Francis too entered wedlock, taking to wife Una Jane Mary Maud Godfrey, the daughter of John Roger Godfrey, an artist of Petit Bôt.

Then came the First World War. Although 56 years of age at its outbreak, Henry's mind was so exercised by the violation of Belgium and the peril to Britain that in April 1915, a month after his 57th birthday, he represented himself as being only 44 (*splendide mendax*) and enlisted in the 23rd Royal Fusiliers (the 'Sportsmen's Battalion'). Francis accompanied him, also lying about his age. After nine months training the two brothers were sent to the front, but almost immediately — at the end of January 1916 — they were returned to the base at Etaples as being over age. Here Privates H. W. and F. G. Fowler protested vehemently at being obliged to waste their time and their abilities performing menial tasks which they resented, having joined the Army to fight.

These protests — coupled with a severe attack of gout — procured Henry his discharge and he was invalided out of the Army in May 1916. Then, after spending a term at Sedbergh and putting in some time on munitions work, he returned to his literary labours. Francis too was invalided from the forces, but he was much less fortunate than his brother. The rigours of Army life brought on tuberculosis as a result of which he died in 1918. His name appears on St Pierre du Bois War Memorial.

Back in Guernsey Henry and Jessie settled in at Le Moulin de Haut, near the point in the Castel where Candie Road abuts on la Rue à l'Eau — and here Henry set about completing a project started by his brother and himself before their enlistment. This was *The Oxford Pocket Dictionary*, which was finally published in 1924, carrying a joint preface written in 1917 before the death of Francis.

The years of happy domesticity at Le Moulin de Haut came to an end in 1925 when the lease ran out and the Fowlers decided to move to England, because of Jessie's constant need of specialist medical attention unobtainable in Guernsey. It transpired that she had cancer. Thus they left for Hinton St George near Crewkerne in Somerset where in 1926 Henry produced his magnum opus — *A Dictionary of Modern English Usage* — much of which had been compiled while still living in the Castel. Her terrible disease finally claimed Jessie Fowler as a victim in October 1930 and Henry followed her to the grave just over three years later — on Boxing Day 1933.

FRENCH, FREDERICK GEORGE (1889–1962). *Alderney's Judge in the years of adversity.* Born in December 1889 and educated at the City of Norwich School, Frederick George French was on the point of beginning a scholastic career when the First World War intervened and he joined the forces. During the conflict and its aftermath French spent eight years in the Indian Army, a member first of the 36th Sikhs and later of the Burma Military Police. He saw service on the North-West Frontier at the time of the Mohmand Rising, in Mesopotamia with the Kut Relief Force and also on the Chinese Frontier, earning the 1914–15 Star and the India General Service Medal with Bar (Burma).

On laying down the sword Mr. French served in the Education Department of Burma as a Divisional Inspector of Schools, coupled with a part-time post as a lecturer at the University of Rangoon. In 1929 he was appointed to membership of the Niven Committee on Technical and Vocational Training, on which he was Government Secretary; and in 1931 he was nominated Education Member of the Government Committee on Law Reform relating to juvenile delinquency. Before this latter year was out, however, he was recalled from the Civil Service to the Military Police Service during the Burma Rebellion, in connection with which he was gazetted the thanks of the government.

With the coming in 1935 of the new constitution providing for Burma's eventual separation from India (finally effected on 1 April 1937), Mr. French retired from the service and took up residence in Alderney where, with his ship the M.V. *Ranger*, he was able to indulge his favourite sport as a yachtsman. His retirement was interrupted in November 1937 when he was asked by the government of Malta to advise and assist with the reorganisation of the teaching of English in the islands' schools.

In the summer of 1938 Frederick George French was appointed Judge of Alderney on the death of Major R. W. Mellish and entered on a term of office destined to prove traumatic to an extent never experienced by any of his predecessors — or, for that matter, by his one and only successor either! Before two years were up he had to cope with unprecedented peril as the German

Army cut through France like a hot knife through butter. His testing time had come.

On 9 June 1940 a pall of smoke darkened Alderney's skies and during the following days the islanders' fears increased as the sounds of battle became audible by day and flashes of gun-fire visible at night. The evacuation of the troops stationed in the island which commenced on Sunday 16 June so augmented the alarm that French addressed the people in church, seeking to maintain calm by emphasising the very temporary truth that the units being withdrawn were going to Guernsey! The next day, however, finding himself stopped in the streets by people 'in obvious panic', he telegraphed Guernsey for permission to use his initiative and, getting no reply, asked the officer commanding the last batch of departing troops to explain Alderney's plight to the Lieutenant-Governor.

At last receiving a telegram from the Lieutenant-Governor on 19 June giving him *carte blanche* to do as he thought best, French formed a four-man Executive Committee of three Jurats who had kept their heads plus himself as President. When two ships called later the same day, one detailed to pick up Poilus who had managed to get over to the island, and the other children together with their teachers, the Judge insisted that only the categories specified should sail — but the next day he sent a fishing boat to Guernsey with a request for evacuation facilities. An unfortunate misunderstanding arising from the reply to this message received from Ambrose Sherwill (q.v.) on 21 June led French, after consultation with the Executive Committee, to decide to appeal directly to the Admiralty, asking for ships to evacuate the whole of the population. He then assembled the islanders on the Butes and explained what he had done. The ships requested arrived at first light the next morning and the entire popula-was embarked after obstructing the airfield and destroying the wireless transmitter.

Once arrived in England Frederick French resumed his military career, taking up an appointment at the War Office and rising to the rank of Brigadier. His responsibilities in connection with Alderney, however, continued as he was in constant touch with the Voluntary Relief Committee, composed exclusively of Alderney people, which was set up in London, elected by a postcard vote of evacuee Auriginiais. Periodical subsequent postcard votes enabled the committee to be apprised of the opinions of the refugees and to obtain their approval for its actions. Furthermore, the members of the Alderney States were

likewise consulted by post and their approval obtained for measures proposed by the committee. Thus the judge remained the lynch-pin in a device for the administration of an exiled community unique in British constitutional experience. In 1943 this continuing concern for Alderney led Brigadier French to advise the Home Office that a major pioneering effort would be needed after liberation to put the island back on its feet. Pointing out that many of the younger evacuees might well be reluctant to return, that several of those who did so would be old and requiring care, and that it would take time for farmland to be made productive again, he emphasised the desperate need for a carefully 'planned replantation'.

On 16 May 1945 Judge French accompanied a detachment from Guernsey's liberating force which went to Alderney to accept the German surrender; and he immediately decided that, being so heavily mined, the island was as yet unsafe for any save military personnel. He returned, however, early in December at the head of a reconnaissance party and by the middle of the month 100 refugees had been repatriated, followed by two more parties before the end of the year. By July 1946 nearly 700 Alderney folk were back in their native isle.

French had given up an important and highly responsible post at the War Office in order to lead his people back to Alderney. However, we have it on impeccable authority that 'a prophet is not without honour, save in his own country' and the returning Auriginiais, gazing upon their devastated homeland, murmured against their judge as did the Children of Israel against Moses for leading them away from subjection (but neverthelss security) in Egypt. Furthermore, the Brigadier's austere and realistic approach to the problems of rehabilitation did not endear him to the happy-go-lucky islanders — and matters were made worse by the fact that his onerous war-time duties had brought on a duodenal ulcer which at times made him rather peremptory in his manner, addressing public meetings with the salutation, 'People!' rather than 'Ladies and Gentlemen'.

French's unpopularity reached a peak over the means he employed to allocate furniture lacking any clear title to its possession. He had all such effects deposited on the Butes and at the blowing of a whistle everyone rushed to seize what he or she could, irrespective of rightful ownership — an unseemly episode that came to be known as 'The Battle of the Butes'. This incident was grist to the mill for William Herivel, a member of the Alderney States and the judge's most bitter opponent, fiercely resenting what he interpreted as autocratic rule. It was largely his persistent and merciless criticism that led French to resign in 1947. He withdrew, embittered, into private life, devoting himself to writing Elementary English textbooks for use in colonial schools.

Frederick George French died far from Alderney: at sea while on holiday in 1962. The memory of his wife, who had pre-deceased him, is preserved both by a memorial tablet in Alderney's Anglican church and by the name given to a room (the Ann French Room) included in the Island Hall.

G

DE GARIS, MRS. MARIE (1910-   ). *The gifted philologist and historian of St Pierre du Bois.* Born in St Pierre du Bois on 15 June 1910, as Marie le Messurier, the daughter of Edwin John le Messurier and his wife Elsie (*née* le Cheminant), Mrs. Marie de Garis (whose husband Wilfred died in 1962), spent her childhood in a home where Guernsey's ancient Norman–French language was the only tongue employed, so that she did not learn any English until the time came to attend school as a pupil at St Pierre du Bois School, followed by the Ladies' College. While by no means alone in having such a background, Marie de Garis was certainly unique in the life-long scholarly interest she took in her ancestral idiom, and in the enthusiasm with which she devoted herself to ceaseless efforts to secure its preservation against the relentless encroachments of anglicisation in Guernsey — not only in the realm of speech, but also in social attitudes and ways of life. Undaunted by the magnitude of her task in an age when the older generation was progressively being replaced by another whose members had spent their childhood as refugees in England and consequently knew no tongue other than English, this authoress of several papers of philological interest also became the capable and committed Secretary of the Philology Section of La Société Guernesiaise and in 1967 composed an *English–Guernesiais Dictionary* which evoked a brisk demand and was soon out of print.

In the autumn of 1982, as a worthy means of marking the centenary of La Société Guernesiaise (of which she became President the following year), Marie de Garis produced a veritable tour de force with her *Dictiounnaire Angllais–Guernesiais* — a much-enlarged revision of her 1967 book which also contained a Guernesiais–English section and constituted the most comprehensive work on the Island's ancient variant of the Langue d'Oil ever to appear. Far from confining herself to a mere list of word-equivalents, the accom-

plished lexicographer also embodied in this magnum opus a great deal of information on insular laws, customs and folk-lore — as well as indicating the distinctions in locution between the Higher and Lower Parishes.

During the 1970s a surge of nostalgia developed in the island for the 'Guernsey-English' of yesteryear — which was employed to such effect by Gerald Basil Edwards (q.v.) in his *Book of Ebenezer le Page* — and not a few voices were raised urging that attempts be made to save it from extinction. It is hardly surprising that Marie de Garis, with her passionate attachment to the genuine language of old, should show scant sympathy for such aspirations. Delivering the Report of the Philology Section at the Annual General Meeting of La Société Guernesiaise held in February 1981, she dismissed 'Guernsey-English' as 'only a transitional mode of expression employed by Guernesiais speakers, not very proficient in English, translating their thoughts from one language to another, uncaring and unmindful of the differences of structure, intonation, idiom and phraseology between the two tongues', and she therefore concluded that ' "Guernsey-English" is, in essence, English pressed into the Norman-Guernesiais mould. As such it has no future for it has no past'.

Linguistic labours cannot, however, be said to have exhausted Marie de Garis' valuable endeavours in the cause of maintaining Guernsey's cultural heritage. No mean historian, a selection of historical and sociological articles flowed from her pen and in 1970 there appeared her diligently compiled and high informative *Story of St Pierre du Bois Church*. Her fellow-islanders are also indebted to her for having unearthed a haunting tale of the tribulations of true love in the account of Marie Robilliard, who, having at last proved the truth of Virgil's dictum that 'Omnia vincit amor', in 1600 became Marie Martel (q.v.*) despite the opposition of the island's ecclesiastical establishment. Folklore also claimed her attention and a series of articles on this theme which appeared in the *Review* of the Guernsey Society was followed by the publication in 1975 of her well-researched *Folklore of Guernsey*.

A person of intense parochial patriotism, Marie de Garis served as an energetic Leader of St Pierre du Bois Residents' Association and in this capacity was prominent among those who in May 1980 crossed swords with Lieutenant-Colonel Patrick Wootton (q.v.) over his refusal to pay rates on Lihou Island. Summing up this lady's career as a whole, anyone with the temerity to adapt Holy Writ might well exclaim, 'Behold une Guernesiaise indeed, in whom there is no guile!'

GAUVAIN, SIR HENRY JOHN, F.R.C.S. (1878–1945). *The Hippocrates from Alderney*. Born in Alderney on 28 November 1878, to Catherine Margaret, the daughter of Jurat Peter le Ber and the wife of William Gauvain, the island's Receiver-General, Henry Gauvain was educated at Tonbridge High School and subsequently at King's College, London. Later a scholar at Cambridge (St John's), he went in 1902 to St Bartholomew's Hospital as senior science scholar, qualifying in 1906 and proceeding to the degrees of M.D. and M.Ch.(Cantab) in 1908.

In the same year as he graduated Gauvain took up the post of medical superintendent of Lord Mayor Treloar Cripples' Hospital and (subsequently) College at Alton in Hampshire, his work rapidly earning for this establishment an international reputation. Alive to the educational needs of his charges, he enlisted the aid of Lloyd George, thanks to whose persuasiveness when bringing the matter before Parliament, Alton in 1912 made its mark as the first hospital to provide schooling for its juvenile patients: hence the addition of the words, 'and College' to the title of this institution. After Gauvain's death this institution was split, the Hospital (with a fine portrant of Sir Henry in its Treatment Centre) being separated at the inception of the National Health Service in 1948 from what came to be known as the Lord Mayor Treloar College for the Education and Care of Disabled Boys and Girls. At a marine branch of the hospital opened at Sandy Point, Hayling Island, in 1919, Gauvain demonstrated the remarkable benefits of sea-bathing in conjunction with heliotherapy in the treatment of tuberculosis; while later (in 1925) his hospital became the first to have a properly equipped light department.

The author of numerous papers on surgical tuberculosis, hospital design and heliotherapy, Gauvain was appointed consulting surgeon to the King Edward VII Welsh National Memorial Association for the Treatment of Tuberculosis; to the London, Essex and Hampshire County Councils; and to King George's Sanatorium for Sailors at Bramshott. He was also President of the Electrotherapeutic and Diseases of Children Sections of the Royal Society of Medicine and Vice-President of the National Association for the Prevention of Tuberculosis. Knighted for his services to crippled children in 1920, Sir Henry was elected a Fellow of the Royal College of Surgeons in 1927 and in 1936 was awarded the Distinguished Service Gold Key of the American Congress of Physical Therapy. His experience in surgical tuberculosis was second to none and his professional skill was matched by a kindly personality and abundant charm.

During the Second World War Sir Henry founded the Overbury Court Residential School for evacuated Belgian cripple children, and also rallied to the succour of his fellow islanders in distress by serving as President of the Alderney Evacuee Relief Committee. Sad to say, he did not survive to see the liberation of his birthplace, dying at Alton on 19 January 1945.

GEOFFREY OF ANJOU, DUKE OF NORMANDY (1113–1151). *The Duke of Normandy who laid the foundations of insular liberties*. Born in 1113, Geoffrey Plantagenet – so known from the sprig of broom, *planta genesta*, which he wore when riding – married Matilda, daughter of Henry I of England and widow of the Emperor Henry V, in 1128, when he was 15 years of age: eleven years younger than his bride. Tall, fair and lean, with quick eyes revealing an impetuous nature, the English king's new son-in-law was fiercely energetic and skilled in the art of war; his superb memory and ready wit earning him a reputation for learning unusual for his day. He was also possessed of the violent temper of his house (reputedly stemming from a demon ancestress) which once prompted St Bernard of Clairvaux to remark, 'From the devil them came: to the devil they will go'. The year following his marriage (1129) Geoffrey took over the County of Anjou from his father (Fulk V) on the latter's departure for the Holy Land and four years later (in 1133) his wife gave birth to a son, Henry (later King Henry II of England).

In the summer of 1135 a second child (Geoffrey) was born of the marriage, to be followed in the August of 1136 by yet another son – William.

The previous December, however, Henry I had died and Matilda, to whom her father had exacted an oath of allegiance from the entire baronage, found herself obliged to fight for the claims of herself and her son against her cousin Stephen of Blois who, oath notwithstanding, now seized the English throne (and proclaimed himself Duke of Normandy to boot) as the only surviving grandson of the Conqueror.

While England endured the purgatory of 'nineteen long winters', turmoil in Normandy also followed the death of Henry I, with Geoffrey (as the champion of his son, rather than on his own account) engaged in a prolonged struggle against Stephen in the course of which he swallowed Normandy bit by bit 'as if it were an artichoke'. Eventually the fall of Rouen to his forces in 1144 led to an alliance with Louis VII of France, under the terms of which Geoffrey paid homage to him for Normandy, of which he thus became Duke. He retained the ducal coronet until January 1150 when he made over the Duchy to his son Henry — who thus became Duke of Normandy four years before ascending the throne of England. A major result of these vicissitudes was the severance of the link between Normandy and the Kingdom of England which had been established by the victory of Duke William II (The Bastard) at Hastings in 1066.

This period of divorce from the English Monarchy was an especially important one for Guernsey, which had been brought entirely into Geoffrey's hands as a result of two developments in the course of the conflict. Firstly, Roger, Vicomte of the Cotentin (who held half of Guernsey) had been killed (1138) fighting for Stephen — and had left no heir. Secondly, the holder of the other half of the island, Ranulf, Earl of Chester, 'whose hand, like Ishmael's, was against every man', had sided at times with Stephen, thus rendering his Norman feifs forfeit. To advance the interests of his son Henry, Geoffrey needed both to win the support of the church and also to consolidate the military strength of Normandy in preparation for an attack on England: and the action he took in these circumstances may partly be inferred from two Papal Bulls — despite the fact that they appeared after his relinquishment of the ducal throne. In 1150 a Bull of Pope Eugène III confirmed the monastery of Mont St Michel in ownership of 'whatever you possess in the island'. A further Bull issued in 1155 by Adrian IV (alias Nicholas Breakspear, the only English Pope) spoke more specifically of the monastery holding a quarter of the whole island.

In making Mont St Michel a partial restoration of Guernsey lands taken from it by Duke William II in 1042, Geoffrey had to take care to avoid alienating the powerful lords whose support would be needed if England were ever to be invaded in furtherance of his son's title to its throne. Accordingly the award to the monastery was confined to scattered non-arable wasteland as part of a comprehensive reallocation of landholdings in the island. Furthermore, the system was instituted of one consolidated feudal payment in respect of holdings — later to be called the 'King's Farm' — which not only carried exemption from servile obligations, but also guaranteed political liberties under local law. Thus the islanders' entitlement to trial in their own courts and their immunity from arbitrary exactions stem from the implementation of Duke Geoffrey's policies. In addition, the probability is that from the same period dates their exemption from military service outside the islands except 'that they will go with the Duke of Normandy, if need be, when he goes in person to recover England'. As the late Professor le Patourel pointed out, such a proviso would only be of relevance at the time Geoffrey was planning an invasion of England to promote his son's claim to the English throne. Lastly, the increase in the ducal holdings in the island resulting from Geoffrey's confiscations and reallocations increased the importance of the Guernsey Ducal Court, and led to Guernsey having a Vicomte of its own responsible to the Sénéchal of Normandy, instead of sharing one with Jersey: the first step on the road to the attainment of a distinct political personality and ultimately to the enjoyment of local autonomy,

Having caught a chill after bathing in a pool when much over-heated following a long ride on horseback on a sultry day, Geoffrey died on 7 September 1151. On the evidence of the developments outlined above, the conclusion is inescapable that the consequences for Guernsey of the career of this scion of 'the Devil's Breed' were of an importance hard to exaggerate.

GIFFARD, WILLIAM REGINALD BOUCHARD (1912-   ). *Macte virtue*. See *Underground Resistance Heroes of the Second World War*.

GILLINGHAM, JOSEPH JOHN (1901-1945). *Macte virtue*. See *Underground Resistance Heroes of the Second World War*.

GOSSELIN, HELIER (*c.* 1517-1579). *A Bailiff of barbaric brutality*. (E). He was born in Jersey as the son of Thomas Gosselin, who by 1521 was a Jurat in that island's Royal Court, and a member of a family which was one of the first in the archipelago to embrace the teaching of the Reformation. Helier Gosselin came to Guernsey in 1540 and married Perotine, the daughter of Francis Henry, by whom he had a son, Nicholas – who later (in 1565) was foremost among those co-operating with Helier de Carteret (q.v.) in the colonisation of Sark, where Havre Gosselin is named after him – and a daughter, Collette – who became the ancestress of the Reverend Thomas le Marchant (q.v.*) and also of John Tupper of Cap la Hogue fame (q.v.*). Helier's being of marriageable age shortly after his arrival in Guernsey, considered in conjunction with his known date of death, would suggest 1517 as a likely year of birth.

Of undoubted ability, Gosselin soon became prominent in local affairs, being sworn Procureur on 7 September 1546 and appointed Bailiff three years later, his commission of 12 October 1549 styling him 'Honourable' – a grim irony when later events are borne in mind. The religious *bouleversement* brought about by the accession of Mary I in 1553 made him anxious for his office and, hastily accommodating himself to the Roman obedience, he assiduously sought to establish good relations with Sir Leonard Chamberlayne (q.v.), the Roman Catholic Governor whom Mary appointed on ascending the throne.

Helier's attempts to ingratiate himself with the Marian régime did not stop at mere sycophancy – which, contemptible though it may be, would appear as praiseworthy when compared with the depths to which he in fact sank. Eager to rid himself of the slightest suspicion of any lingering taint of apostacy, he connived with Dean Jacques Amy (q.v.) in bringing to the stake Catherine Cauchés (q.v.) and her two daughters on a charge of heresy – and further demonstrated his zeal for Rome by giving the monstrous order that the baby boy to whom Catherine's daughter Perotine gave birth in her death agony should be thrown back into the flames which were devouring his mother. By this infamous deed Gosselin placed himself in the ranks of such as Judas Iscariot, Salome, Geoffrey de Mandeville, Heinrich Himmler, Ilse Koch and Idi Amin, who are remembered for all time for acts of surpassing villainy and cruelty.

When the Crown passed to Elizabeth I, Helier again sought to retain his position by once more emulating the chameleon, forsaking the Papal allegiance which he had been to such pains to assert under her half-sister. In 1562, together with seven Jurats, Dean Jacques Amy and the Procureur (Thomas Effard) he petitioned the Queen, acknowledging culpability and seeking pardon. He was deprived of his post in December of that year and, although elected a Jurat of the Royal Court on 5 March 1564, received an order from Windsor 15 months later 'to make repayre hither unto us with all convenient speede'. Yet again this despicable wretch was dismissed from office and not until 10 years had passed was he pardoned. He died in December 1579.

GOSSELIN, JOSHUA (1739-1813). *Guernsey's polymath extraordinary*. (B/D/E). Joshua Gosselin was born in November 1739 as the scion of a house which in the 16th century had produced Nicolas Gosselin, foremost among the original settlers in Sark (after whom Havre Gosselin in that island is named) and – less reputably – Helier Gosselin (q.v.) the infamous Bailiff who ordered the new-born son of Perotine Massey *née* Cauchés (q.v.) to be cast into the flames that were consuming his mother. He showed artistic talent in boyhood and while still young also developed the wide and varied interests whereby he was to distinguish himself as botanist, conchologist, and antiquarian, as well as acquiring fame for his outstanding gifts as a painter.

Of independent means and thus free to devote himself to service rather than the quest for gain, Gosselin took up a commission in the Guernsey Militia in 1758, remaining for the next 40 years in this force in which he was promoted to full Colonel in command of the North Regiment in 1789. Ten years after joining the Militia (1768) he was elected as Greffier to the Royal Court – a post which he retained until 1792. During his term in this office Joshua displayed no small measure of courage in defying the orders issued in 1775 by the overbearing Bailiff, William le Marchant (q.v.), to deny registration to any contracts coming from the feudal Fief Courts. Bearing in mind the spirit of the age, it is obvious that compliance with the Bailiff's requirements would have constituted a most revolutionary procedure and Gosselin justified his refusal to connive in this attempted curtailment of Seigneurial powers so eloquently that his action in continuing to grant registration to such contracts was upheld by the Jurats, and ultimately (in 1777) by the Privy Council.

As a botanist Gosselin made the earliest recorded and most comprehensive list of wild flowers in Guernsey, as well as amassing a collection of dried plants in the form of an herbarium (which, rediscovered in recent years, is now housed in a special cabinet donated by La Société Guernesiaise). Furthermore, beginning in 1767, he made copious lists of garden plants and shrubs. Conchology also attracted his attention and from early youth he collected and listed a vast assortment of shells from Guernsey's beaches, compiling an index of no less than 114 species.

In the realm of antiquarianism this embodiment of cultural versatility made numerous drawings and plans of prehistoric monuments, not only in Guernsey but also at Trelach in South Wales. In addition he visited and studied Stonehenge. The Royal Society of Antiquarians published an account by him of what at the time were thought of as 'Druidical' remains in Guernsey. Indeed, it was the plans and records of the island's dolmens made by Gosselin in the early 19th century which initially aroused Frederick Corbin Lukis's (q.v.) interest in archaeology — with whom this man of parts cooperated in the pioneering excavations of La Varde in 1811.

Intimations of Joshua's penchant for art were manifest at the tender age of 10 in a paper-bound book containing grey wash drawings of human figures, the cover of which is inscribed 'Livre à dessiner à Josue Gosselin: le 30 juin 1750'. In his superb water colours, over 200 of which are still in existence, he is fastidious about detail — yet nevertheless his work reflects a tremendous sense of composition. Especially noteworthy are his study of St Peter-Port as seen from Castle Cornet (1793) and that of Castle Cornet and the adjacent islands which he painted from his house in Glategny Esplanade in 1775. In every case the colours are as fresh and unfaded as on the day of painting thanks to the pictures being secured in a portfolio by his grandson Thomas William Gosselin — for whom John Wilson (q.v.) built 'Springfield' in La Petite Marche (now Queen's Road) — who collated his grandsire's work.

By his wife Martha le Marchant, whom he married in July 1761 and who survived him by 3 months, Gosselin became the father of 14 children, of whom only 4 outlived him. Some of them went to live in England and this led to repeated journeys across the Channel by their parent from 1784 onwards. On one such visit in May 1813, whilst staying in Hertfordshire with his second son, Captain (later Admiral) Thomas le Marchant Gosselin (q.v.) following to the end his wide range of pursuits, this veritable polyhistor died, his remains being buried in Bengeo churchyard, on the outskirts of the county town.

GOSSELIN, ADMIRAL THOMAS LE MARCHANT (1765–1857). *Guernsey's nonagenarian Admiral*. (B). The second son of Joshua Gosselin (q.v.), Thomas le Marchant Gosselin entered the Royal Navy in 1778 at the age of 13, his first ship being the *Actaeon* (Captain Boteler). The War of American Independence was raging and the following year young Gosselin was serving on H.M.S. *Ardent* when she was captured off Plymouth by the combined French and Spanish fleets (16 August 1779). After being ransomed he was appointed in October 1780 to the *Barfleur* — the flagship of Sir Samuel (later Lord) Hood — and thereafter saw frequent action, above all in the engagement off Dominica in April 1782.

The 1783 Peace of Versailles ushered in a somewhat pedestrian period in this young officer's career and it was not until 1787 that he reached the rank of Lieutenant. However, the outbreak of the French Revolutionary War once more accelerated advancement. After his promotion to Commander in April 1793, in March 1794, on board H.M.S. *Kingfisher*, Gosselin participated in the capture of a French convoy off Belle Ile; and the following year saw him engaged in waters adjacent to the Channel Islands, when he commanded H.M.S. *Syren* during operations off the coasts of Normandy and Brittany under Sir Richard John Strachan. These forays resulted in a large number of enemy coasting craft being captured or destroyed. Gosselin was appointed Captain in July 1795. Three rather uneventful years ensued at the end of which, in 1798, he took charge of a convoy to Jamaica and, once in the Caribbean, took part in the reduction of Surinam in 1799.

The resumption of hostilities after the Peace of Amiens saw Gosselin sailing as flag-captain to Admiral Cornwallis in 1804 and commanding the inshore squadron off Brest in 1805; after which he served in the Channel Fleet (1806–7) in command of H.M.S. *Audacious*. Involvement in the Peninsular Campaign followed. In 1808, carrying on board a distinguished fellow Channel Islander in the person of the expedition's Commander — the Jerseyman, Lieutenant-General Sir Harry Burrard, Baronet (1755–1813) — together with his staff, Captain Thomas Gosselin convoyed a large force of troops to the Tagus; and later (in January 1809) he covered the embarkation of the Army under General Sir John Moore at Corunna: a service for which he received the thanks of the British Parliament. In March of the same year he was married to Sarah Hadsley, of Ware Priory, Hertfordshire, by the Archbishop of York, at St James's, Piccadilly.

Thereafter, although Gosselin saw no further service afloat, he nevertheless became a Rear-Admiral in 1814, a Vice-Admiral in 1825 and finally an Admiral in 1841, by which time he was 76 years of age. Yet he still had 16 years to live, dying at Bengeo near the town of Hertford in 1857 at the ripe old age of ninety-two.

DE GRANDISON, SIR OTTO (c. 1238–1328). *A bold and resourceful warrior: but a callously vampiric exploiter.* In the year 1258 Count Peter of Savoy (who, as the uncle of Eleanor, the Queen of Henry III, had connections at the English Court) came to London bringing with him young Otto from the town of Grandson, on the shores of the Lake of Neuchâtel. The youth, who was 20 or thereabouts at the time, was the orphaned son of the count's protégé, Peter de Grandson.

By 1268 the Burgundian parvenu had become Sir Otto de Grandison, one of the knights of the Prince Edward, under whom he had fought in 1256 at Lewes and Evesham during the struggle against de Montfort. He later accompanied the prince on Crusade when his royal master decided to follow in the steps of St Louis, who had taken the Cross for the second time in his reign. After Louis' death of the plague in Tunis they both landed at Acre in May 1271. The following year, having survived an attempt on his life, the prince decided to make his will and in it he named de Grandison as executor. The probability is that when the news of his father's death reached Edward, Sir Otto accompanied the new king to England, landing at Dover on 2 August 1274. Thereafter he was almost constantly employed as a trusted and confidential servant, the king writing that there was 'no one about him who could do his will better'. The royal favour brought wealth and influence to de Grandison, who was granted wide estates in Ireland as well as in England.

In November 1275 Edward I appointed Otto de Grandison Warden of the Isles on condition of the payment of an annual 'farm'. Fourteen months later, however, in January 1277, he received the Isles as a free grant for life 'on account of his intimacy with the King, of his long and faithful service from an early age and in acquittance of debts incurred in the King's service'. With the style and title of *Dominus Insularum* Otto thereupon had his own silver seal made, similar to the king's Privy Seal. Having received his grant 'in acquittance of debts incurred' the Lord of the Isles regarded his governance of the archipelago as providing him with a sponge to be squeezed. His many preoccupations precluded his presence in the islands, and the upshot was a rigid and unsympathetic régime on behalf of a rapacious absentee lord which caused widespread resentment. Otto's desire to dominate the Isles dovetailed with the wishes of the king, for while the royal favourite sought to exploit, his patron wished to extinguish insular privileges, bringing the archipelago under centralised control. Of this, more later.

Meanwhile, entrusting the Channel Isles to underlings, de Grandison busied himself in other aspects of the king's service. In the summer of 1227, together with John de Vesci, he commanded the force which overran Anglesey in the course of the campaign against Llewelyn, thereby cutting off the Welsh prince from his food supplies and thus expediting his surrender. Then the following January he was sent with Robert Burnell (Edward's Chancellor) to settle the king's affairs in Gascony. They administered that Duchy with viceregal powers. This assignment concluded, Sir Otto made for Rome, entrusted with a confidential mission to the Papal Court during 1280 and 1281. De Grandison was barely back from Italy when Llewelyn renewed his defiance of Edward I, and Otto in the spring of 1282 resumed his Anglesey command. When peace was made he was appointed Justiciar of North Wales (March 1284). With all these responsibilities it is small wonder that he had no time to pay any personal attention to the Channel Isles.

In July 1290 Sir Otto received the Cross at the hands of John Peckham, Archbishop of Canterbury and set out for the Holy Land to prepare for Edward's intended arrival there. The king in fact never undertook the Crusade but de Grandison fought with great gallantry in the defence of Acre (March to May 1291), escaping to Cyprus at the last moment as the town fell. He stayed in Cyprus for three years, after which he took part in a campaign in Armenia, finally returning to England in the spring of 1296. Thereafter for 10 years he was employed in a series of diplomatic missions arising out of Edward I's dispute with Philip the Fair over Gascony — a dispute, incidentally, which had led the king in 1294 to take the Isles, because of their exposed position, into his own hands. They were not restored to Otto until 1298, after which he remained Lord of the Isles until his death 30 years later. Otto is known to have been with Edward at Lanercost in the autumn of 1306 (when his royal master was once again in the field against the Scots) but when the king died the following July he withdrew to his birthplace and resided at Grandson for the rest of his days.

By the time the Lord of the Isles withdrew to Burgundy, however, disaffection in the Isles themselves had become acute. Otto's perpetual absence had necessitated the adaptation of insular administration with sub-wardens carrying out executive functions, and bailiffs judicial ones. At first there was little to choose between these two types of functionary, who were hardly more than two wings of the same bird of prey. De Grandison's deputies in the islands invariably made his personal interest their chief concern, and the situation was even worse when Otto was in distant lands as the local underlings then took orders from his attornies who acted with robot-like insensitivity on their master's behalf. As time went by, however, the bailiffs, who were usually recruited from the ranks of the island gentry and thus were imbued with local patriotism, came to constitute the focus around which centred the growing resistance to de Grandison's depredations — with the result that the Bailiff eventually came to be the foremost authority in each island, enjoying an ever-increasing prestige.

Once Otto was installed in office, both monarch and overlord saw in the manipulation of the judiciary a means of attaining their ambitions — that of the king to centralise and that of de Grandison to exploit. Thus they combined in pursuing a policy which eventuated in a series of General Eyres which was to prove a most potent threat to local autonomy. Edward I and his two successors saw in the infiltration and ultimate domination by English judges of the judiciary in the islands a possible means of annexing them to the Realm (as distinct from the Crown) of England. This prospect arose from the fact that the courts were the main *legislative* authority in the early 14th century, so that once English jurisdiction had been established in the archipelago's courts, the islands would become virtually as much part of England as the Isle of Wight. Furthermore, as medieval legislation often appeared to forbid something when in reality it meant that the activity in question could not be indulged in without a licence that had to be paid for, it followed that court rulings constituted an ideal means of raising money time and time again — which was exactly what Otto required of the islands.

These judicial visitations were essentially occasions for straining the law in Otto's favour with a view to extracting every possible penny from the inhabitants. Somebody could be fined for almost every action. If the accused were convicted, he would obviously be fined — and if he were not convicted, then his accuser (possibly a jury of presentment) would be fined for false accusation. Furthermore, by the issue at these sessions from 1309 onwards of Quo Warranto Writs (i.e. writs requiring the islanders to explain and prove by what warrant they claimed their rights and privileges) Edward II was obviously trying to apply to the islands the device whereby his father had successfully curtailed local privileges in England — this provoked further intense resentment.

There was one occasion, however, in 1320 when the Bench was occupied by local magnates sitting together with the Jurats. This session not only hanged one of de Grandison's most notorious henchmen — Gautier de la Salle (q.v.*) of 'Bailiff's Cross' fame — but in addition some of his other officials were fined and ordered to return property which they had fraudulently acquired, while judgment was also delivered that the ancient 'laws and customs' should continue to be enjoyed by the islanders. These findings led to a petition from the islanders for Otto's removal and were followed by an episode which clearly exemplifies the emergent power of the bailiff as the champion of insular assertion. In 1321 Gerard d'Oron — Otto's nephew (q.v.*) — was appointed as sub-warden and, finding the islands in open revolt against his uncle's extortionate rule, withdrew to Sark. Later, however, he returned to Guernsey and attempted to unseat the bailiff (John le Marchant), whereupon the Bailiff and the court threw him into jail! Nothing could show more clearly than this does how local grievances were finding a focus in the Bailiff and the Jurats of the court. The affair makes it clear that the Bailiff now had a distinct identity — so distinct indeed that he, as the representative of the judicial authority of the Lord of the Isles, had thrown the representative of his administrative authority (and his nephew to boot) into prison.

Confronted with these repeated demonstrations of defiance by his vassals Otto decided on personal intervention. Although at least 85 years of age (and possibly older) he travelled from Lake Neuchâtel to the islands, arriving in June 1323 and staying most likely until 23 December of the same year when he seems to have accompanied Gerard d'Oron who on that date left Guernsey to go on Edward II's behalf to Burgundy and Savoy. It is hardly surprising that the General Eyre which was convened during his stay quashed the 1320 judgments, and that it was deaf to the Jurats' plea that Gerard d'Oron's appointment was invalid for lack of instructions to rule according to local 'laws and customs'. This *volte-face* caused general alarm, from the Seigneurs who feared for their holdings to the common people enduring fines and petty acts of oppression — while all the inhabitants resented their traditional rights being regarded as a franchise to which they had to show a title. Otto certainly appeared as a monstrous, if distant, ogre. Even his death in 1328 failed to allay the fears he had inspired.

Such was the Burgundian overlord who was the arbiter of the Islands' fate for over half a century. While it may possibly be argued in his defence that his personal courage is beyond question and that constitutional troubles were more in evidence than individual wrongs during his long incumbency, yet it is hard to gainsay the assessment of the late C. L. Kingsford in his authoritative monograph, *Sir Otto de Grandison*:

> 'The administration of the Channel Islands during these fifty years was an unfortunate experiment in the rule of dependencies and reflects little credit either on Otto or on the home government'.

LE GROS, JEAN (1616–1677). *Sark's 'overmighty subject' who became the progenitor of the island's second dynasty of Seigneurs.* (G). Born into a family of Serquiais rendered rich and influential by its successful participation in the hosiery trade, Jean le Gros was appointed Prévôt in 1643 at the same time as — consequent upon Parliament having deprived Sir Philippe de Carteret (q.v.) of the fief of Sark — the authority of the Seigneur was vested in his father (Jean senior) in his capacity as Juge of the court. As his brother Benoist was simultaneously elected a Jurat, the le Gros family thus emerged as the most powerful group in the island. This position was further strengthened by Jean's marriage in 1649 to Anne, the daughter of the redoubtable Minister Elie Brévint (q.v.). The resultant combination of the legal authority of the court and the spiritual discipline of the formidable incumbent enabled the group to run Sark's affairs as it wished — and the family exploited to the full this situation for its own benefit. In defiance of the Letters Patent obtained in 1611 from James I by Sir Philippe de Carteret (q.v.) tenements were dismembered, mortgages contracted and new houses built: all authorised by a court dominated by the very clan which derived most advantage from these transactions.

With the departure in April 1659 of Captain Richard Winne (the Parliamentary Captain of the Island garrison) Jean le Gros was appointed Captain of the Sark Militia by Colonel John Weaver (the Parliamentary Lieutenant-Governor in Guernsey) with orders 'to keep the Isle for His Highness the Lord Protector of England' — i.e. Richard Cromwell, as Oliver had died the previous September. By maintaining a tactful silence about this commission after the restoration of the monarchy had procured Sir Philippe de Carteret's reinstatement the following year, le Gros contrived to retain his post as Prévôt and even to succeed his father as Juge when the latter died in April 1661. On the death of Sir Philippe himself less than two years later, the minority of his heir (who was only 13) enabled the new Juge to retain his stranglehold over Sark's affairs. His wife Anne had died in 1657 and in 1664 he married Elizabeth le Pelley of Guernsey (with whose family his own had long-established commercial links forged through their mutual engagement in the hosiery trade), thus consolidating his position and improving still further his economic prospects. Well might the new Seigneur, rendered impotent by his youth, have reflected ruefully on Sir John Fortescue's warnings of the 'perillis that mey come to the Kyng by ouer myghtye subgettes'.

Then came the confrontation. On coming of age in 1671 the young Seigneur took vigorous steps to assert himself, first obtaining an Order-in-Council in 1672 suspending the Sark court on the grounds of the Jurats' refusal to take the Oath of Allegiance in the context of the Anglican Sacrament as required by the Royal Grant of Pardon of 1661; and later obtaining a further Order in 1675 abolishing the court entirely and replacing it by the Seneschal's Court such as exists doday. Having thus unseated Jean le Gros, Sir Philippe took action against him in the Royal Court of Guernsey, whither the ex-Juge had withdrawn to his wife's property in the Castel (see *De Carteret, Sir Philippe, Baronet, 1650–1693*) and after the defendant's death in 1677 he continued the litigation against Elizabeth *veuve* le Gros — with whom the Seigneur finally agreed to accept the existing pattern of land-holding in Sark providing that the terms of the 1611 Letters Patent were observed in future.

The Seigneur seemed to have triumphed, but in the long run the dead man may be said to have won the fight! The de Carteret fortunes never recovered from the losses incurred in supporting James II against William III: and these straitened circumstances were exacerbated by the profligacy of Sir Charles de Carteret (q.v.), so that when he inherited the fief on the death of Sir Charles, Lord John Carteret sought to sell it at the first opportunity. Sark thus passed our of de Carteret hands in 1720 and after being held by Colonel John Johnson followed by James Milner, Esquire, was purchased shortly after the latter's death in 1730 by Jean le Gros' daughter, Susanne. As she had married her cousin Nicolas le Pelley, this purchase inaugurated the line of le Pelley Seigneurs (with La Seigneurie at the le Gros home of La Perronerie rather than at Le Manoir established by the de Carterets), which was to last until 1852.

GUÉNAULT OF LANDÉVENNEC, SAINT AND ABBOT (505?-590?). *The Apostle of Alderney*?

The question of when and by whom Alderney was converted to Christianity constitutes one of the major unsolved mysteries of the Bailiwick's past. Apart from the completely spurious and utterly unconvincing figure of St Vignol (q.v.*) the main claimant to the honour of this achievement is found in the person of St Guénault (alias Winwaloe or Guénolé) who is said to have taken the Faith to Alderney from Sark at the start of the last quarter of the 6th century.

This saint's Feast Day falls on 3 March. Of his origins and career, however, there are two conflicting accounts, one stating that he was born in Wales and became a disciple of St Sampson (q.v.), while another places his birth at Ploufragan in Armorica whither his parents (Francan and Gwen) had migrated from Britain. It is thought that at the age of 15 he was taken by his father to the monastery on the island of Lauré presided over by the Abbé Budoc, who many years later sent him to found at Landévennec near Brest another monastery of which he ultimately emerged as Abbot. Here he is believed to have died in extreme old age.

Yet another variant of the tradition claims that Guénault had evangelistic aspirations, desiring to visit Ireland but being dissuaded therefrom in a vision by his contemporary St Patrick. Such inclinations towards missionary activity could possibly have led to his reputed visits to the Channel Isles — though the version of his life story which depicts him as a disciple of St Sampson would obviously more easily account for his alleged presence in the archipelago. St Guénault's cult is widespread in Brittany and the attractive chapel dedicated to him in the countryside near the Bréton commune of Trevou–Treguignec is a replica of an ancient shrine built before 1030.

DE GUÉRIN, LIEUT.-COL. THOMAS WILLIAM MANSELL (1861-1929). *A noteworthy soldier,*

public servant and savant. (B). Born at Le Mont Durand on 23 January 1861, to Margaritta Sarah Collings (*née* Mansell), the daughter of Rear-Admiral Sir Thomas Mansell, K.C.H., K.S.S.* (q.v.) and the wife of Lieutenant-Colonel Elias Thomas de Guérin of the Royal Guernsey Militia, young Thomas William entered Elizabeth College at Easter 1873, but left later the same year because of the grave anxiety occasioned by his poor state of health. Thenceforward he continued his education under private tuition.

Despite this sickly boyhood, in 1879 at the age of 18 de Guérin joined the 1st Regiment of the Royal Guernsey Light Infantry as a Second Lieutenant, after which a steady rise brought him to the command of the Regiment with the rank of Lieutenant-Colonel in 1897 — a position he held until 1904, when he retired from active military life — though he served as Militia aide-de-camp to the king from 1905 until his death.

Besides his activities in the Militia, Lieutenant-Colonel de Guérin also directed a large business as a timber merchant in La Charroterie, with an extensive bakery also operating on the same premises. After a political initiation as a Douzenier of Canton Number 1 in St Peter-Port, he was elected to the St Peter-Port Central Douzaine in 1900 and re-elected in 1906, becoming a Constable of St Peter-Port in 1907. He was sworn-in as a Jurat of the Royal Court on 6 June 1908 with the result that, because of the constitutional arrangements then obtaining in the island, he automatically became a member of the States as well — in which capacity he made invaluable contributions to insular administration. Over the years Jurat de Guérin served on many committees, including (*inter alia*) the Ancient Monuments' Committee and those responsible for the Lukis Museum, the Priaulx Library and for investigating the vexed question of the fate of the Militia in the light of the British government's withdrawal of financial support. In this connection he delivered a memorable address on the history of the Royal Guernsey Militia when the States debated its future in December 1928.

The Honorary Curator of the Guille-Allès Museum (which was rearranged and classified under his supervision), Lieutenant-Colonel de Guérin scarcely had an equal among his contemporaries — apart from Miss Edith Carey (q.v.) — as an historian, emerging as a recognised authority on the customs, laws and historical development of the Bailiwick. It is hardly surprising, therefore, that he was regarded as an invaluable member of La Société Guernesiaise, of which he was President for the period 1911-12 and again for 1925-26. Prominent among the many papers he prepared and read to La Société were 'Feudalism in Guernsey'; 'Our Hereditary Governors'; 'Le Colombier at Torteval'; 'Sieges of Castle Cornet'; 'Megalithic Culture in Guernsey'; 'Excavations in Alderney'; 'Early Constitutional History'; 'The Human Figure in the Déhus Dolmen'; and 'The Statue Menhir at St Martin's'. This redoubtable scholar was also a member of the Huguenot Society and of La Société Jersiaise, in connection with which he took the keenest interest in the excavations at La Hougue Bie. As a consequence of these pursuits his unexpected death on 19 February 1929 gave rise to as acute a sense of dereliction in academic quarters as was felt in Bailiwick political circles.

*K.C.H. = Knight Commander of the Hanoverian Guelphic Order; K.S.S. = Knight of Saint Sylvester.

GUILLE, JEAN (1788-1845). *Guernsey's Bailiff who was cashiered from the Militia.* (C). Born in 1788 at St George in the Castel, the nephew of Esther Guille and thus the first cousin of George Métivier (q.v.), Jean Guille was elected a Jurat in 1809, when he was only 21 years of age. He had already, four years previously, been commissioned as a Captain in the Militia, and the year after ascending the Jurats' Bench he became the Colonel of its North Regiment. At the time he gained this promotion the Lieutenant-Governor was Sir John Doyle (q.v.), who six years later was replaced by Major-General Henry Bayley — a gubernatorial change which was destined to imperil the continuance of Guille's regimental command.

This eventuality resulted from an unfortunate confrontation between Jurat Jean Guille and the Lieutenant-Governor over the period November 1818 to February 1819. Taking exception to remarks made by the Jurat in the course of a States' debate on 25 November 1818 when he criticised as excessive the level of expenditure on the Militia now the Napoleonic Wars were over, Bayley deprived Guille of his colonelcy of the North Regiment. Alleging that this action by the Lieutenant-Governor, penalising him in his military capacity for what he had said in his administrative one, infringed the privileges of the States, Guille declined to acknowledge the validity of his demotion, and this clash of wills persisted until the following February when the Home Secretary — Lord Sidmouth — resolved it by an Order-in-Council requiring Guille on the one hand to withdraw his refusal to accept his dismissal

and General Bayley on the other to reinstate him.

Having survived this contretemps, Guile was appointed honorary aide-de-camp to the king when the Militia was made 'Royal' by William IV in 1831 — and subsequently Inspector of Militia also. Then in 1835 Jean Guille, Seigneur des Fiefs Fantome et Canelly, became Lieutenant-Bailiff under Daniel de Lisle Brock (q.v.) as Bailiff. On succeeding Brock in January 1843 after his predecessor's death the previous September, Guille had to resign his Militia appointments as being incompatible with the office of Bailiff. He had, incidentally, never been admitted to the Bar and was one of the last non-lawyers ever to hold Guernsey's supreme office.

Guille's period in office was destined to be short and difficult. The year before he became Bailiff a new Lieutenant-Governor had arrived in Guernsey in the person of Major-General William Francis Patrick Napier, C.B. (q.v.), and the Island's civil head found himself once again embroiled with the monarch's representative, who adopted a consistently disdainful and hostile attitude towards him. It is possible that Napier was already predisposed against Jean Guille before he ever set foot in the Bailiwick, as in his younger days Major-General Bayley had been his patron and mentor — and it is an entirely credible supposition that the disciple had taken over the prejudices of the master. In any case, poor Guille did not long survive to contend with this domineering adversary. Towards the end of May 1845, being in poor health, he went to Plymouth hoping that the change would do him good. On 3 June however, he died. Thousands of people gathered outside the gates of St George and at the Castel churchyard on the day of the funeral, where the procession itself numbered no less than 500 mourners.

GUILLE, THOMAS (1817-1896). *Guernsey's 19th century missionary of culture.* Born in the Forest Parish on 17 May 1817, Thomas Guille while still only 14 sailed in 1832 for New York, where Daniel Mauger (an old friend of the family) was already installed as a house painter. Arrived in the New World, young Thomas became apprenticed to his fellow Guernseyman in his business. Two years later, in 1834, he was joined in the U.S.A. by his boyhood playmate, Frederick Mansell Allès, who was 18 months his junior, having been born on 18 October 1818. Not only did the two friends thrive as house painters and decorators, prospering exceedingly and becoming wealthy men; but in addition Thomas Guille took pains to educate himself, accumulating several hundred volumes of standard works by the age of 20.

Visiting Guernsey in 1851, Guille advocated the formation of parish libraries in a series of newspaper articles, but nothing definite was done until a second visit in 1855, when the Guille Library Committee was formed and Guille's book collection divided into five sections placed in charge of friends with the idea of their being exchanged in rotation — but this was not in fact done.

In 1867 Guille returned to Guernsey for good and brought all the books to a central dépôt in St Peter-Port, save for a Reading Room in St Martin's which he personally superintended for three years, after which he concentrated upon the central establishment. This proved to be a thankless task as his fellow-islanders evinced little desire to avail themselves of his services. Prospects improved, however, when his old friend Frederick Allès came to his aid in 1881. Between them they bought from the States for £900 the old Assembly Rooms for conversion into a Public Subscription Library in 1883, better access being provided by the creation in 1886 of the present Market Street entrance.

The Guille-Allès Library had been born, but neither Guille nor Allès felt that they had attained their main objective. Over the entrance in the French Halles they had placed the combined motto and exhortation, *Ingredere ut proficias* ('Enter that thou mayest profit'). Far from profiting, however, the working classes whom Guille and Allès, as self-made men, hoped would be the main beneficiaries of their efforts, could not even be prevailed upon to enter! A similar lack of interest was displayed towards the Museum which the two colleagues established on the floor above their library. Nevertheless, undeterred and true to their commitment to the promotion of self-advancement, these benevolent associates in 1884 founded two scholarships at the Boys' Intermediate School (which had first opened its doors to pupils the previous year) thus inaugurating the scholarship system in the island. In the same year Thomas Guille became the second President — in succession to Edgar MacCulloch (q.v.) — of the Guernsey Natural Science Society, as La Société Guernesiaise was known in its early days.

In an attempt to attract proletarian patronage and on the assumption that a middle-class milieu acted as a deterrent, Guille, in the year of Allès' death (1895) founded the Artisans' institute in a building adjoining Les Poids de la Reine given by the States for the purpose. Because of his own death the following year (1896) Guille was spared the realisation that this venture too was doomed to a mediocre fate. It dragged on with indifferent success until the Second World War when it was finally killed by the persistent apathy of those for whom it had been designed. The library, however, survived as a major boon to the island, with a marked expansion of the clièntele following the replacement of the subscription system by a free lending service in 1981 — 98 years after its foundation!

H

HART, GENERAL SIR RICHARD CLARE, V.C., K.C.B., K.C.V.O. (1848-1931). *The author of Guernsey's Golgotha.* Born in 1848 at Scarif in County Clare, Ireland, Sir Reginald Hart achieved glory on 31 January 1879 when his gallantry earned the award of the Victoria Cross in the course of that year's Afghan expedition. After four years (1902-1906) as Commandant of the School of Military Engineering, General Hart was Commander-in-Chief in South Africa from 1912 to 1914 before assuming office as Lieutenant-Governor of Guernsey for the period of the First World War.

A strict teetotaller with a keenly developed sense of chivalry, the new Lieutenant-Governor deplored the fact that by dispersing its manpower in various branches of the Forces (and particularly the Royal Irish Regiment) the Bailiwick as such was condemned to win no battle honours. He therefore proposed the raising of a unit with specific local identification to gain glory in combat, the States having, for the duration of hostilities, relinquished the ancient right of exemption from service beyond the islands' shores. This suggestion was put forward with sufficient persuasiveness to procure its acceptance and the upshot was the creation of the wartime Royal Guernsey Light Infantry consisting of a 1st (Service) Battalion, in which a total of 2,280 men served in the field at various times, plus a 2nd (Reserve) Battalion in

Guernsey, which was about 1,700 strong at the hour of the Armistice. The Lieutenant-Governor proudly patronised his brainchild and in the Spring of 1917 presided over and addressed a grand parade at L'Ancresse Common where the Service Battalion was presented with drums, bugles and company flags -- all provided by the women of Guernsey. Furthermore, his nephew (Lieutenant-Colonel A. H. S. Hart–Synnot) commanded the Service Battalion for a while after Lieutenant-Colonel H. J. de la Condamine had been invalided following the Battle of Cambrai in November 1917.

The consequences of thus concentrating a large proportion of the manpower of Guernsey, Alderney and Sark in a single unit were, however, catastrophic (as is testified by the carnage reflected in the appalling death roll recorded on the Island War Memorial) and many, in the anguish of their grief, bitterly resented the gallant General's quixotic impulses. It is said that while awaiting the departure of the ship carrying him away at the end of his term of office, he indicated the Doyle Column and expressed a fear that the Guernsey people would never similarly commemorate him - only to be told to be of good cheer as they would most likely build a pub and call it the *White Hart*! Such is the story: *se non è vero è ben trovato*! By then 70 years of age and having done his war-time duty according to his lights, the hero of the Afghan campaigns went into retirement at Bournemouth, where he died in October 1931 at the age of 83.

HATHAWAY, SIBYL MARY, D.B.E. (1884–1974). *The legendary 'Double-Dame' of Sark*. (B). The elder of two daughters born to Sophia, the wife of the Seigneur of Sark, Frederick William Collings (q.v.) Sibyl Collings was brought up by her eccentric father as though she were a boy, with no concessions made to female frailty – not even to the disability she suffered from having legs of different lengths – so that she grew up to be tough, resilient and self-reliant.

She was destined to stand in considerable need of these qualities. When she was 17 her irascible parent, taking exception to her association with Dudley John Beaumont and berating her as a 'damned virago', literally threw her out of the house at dead of night clad only in a nightdress. The following morning she was found cowering in a hedge by the self-same young man, who had been alerted by Mrs. Collings. Leaving Sark the next day, the couple were married soon afterwards at St James's, Piccadilly. Although he survived the First World War unscathed, Dudley Beaumont

succumbed to the 1918 influenza epidemic while his wife was pregnant with their seventh child, leaving her with the problem of supporting the six survivors (one had died in babyhood). Appeals to both her father and her father-in-law having fallen on deaf ears, the young widow took up employment with the Y.M.C.A. in Cologne and thus obtained not only an income but also a roof over the heads of her three younger children and herself – and later over that of her eldest child also.

Becoming Dame of Sark in 1927 and describing herself as *'un vrai Serquais'*, Sibyl Beaumont promised that *'avec l'aide de Dieu je ferai tout mon possible pour le bien et la prosperité de l'île'*. Making good many years of neglect by her predecessor proved hard work, and in the early autumn of 1929 La Dame set out for a holiday in the U.S.A. In London en route she met Robert Woodward Hathaway, who wooed her so assiduously on her return from the New World that at the beginning of November they were married at St Marylebone Church -- before the self-same altar where the wedding of Robert Browning and Elizabeth Barrett had been solemnised. By this marriage Robert Hathaway technically became the Seigneur of Sark -- and indeed, he regularly attended Chief Pleas in this capacity. His wife, however, invariably accompanied him 'to give advice', so that effectively she remained at the helm. She also made good use of her husband's American connections, which facilitated further trips across the Atlantic devoted to promoting valuable publicity for Sark by lecture tours.

The quality of Mrs. Hathaway's leadership was highlighted in the days preceding the German occupation. Announcing that she herself would remain in Sark, she called on all native-born islanders to do likewise — and they did! During the war (which brought its quota of personal anguish, with her eldest son — Francis William Lionel — being killed in an air-raid in Liverpool in May 1941 and her husband being deported to a Detention Camp in Germany in February 1943) La Dame provided a magnificent example of dignity in defeat. Although she was later accused of excessive affability with the local enemy hierarchy, she in fact made a point of never going to the Germans but always insisting on their coming to her. Once they had arrived, she made no attempt to adopt a suppliant posture, but instead dominated her interlocuters, castigating them in their own language (picked up in the Cologne days) with caustic remarks such as, 'You can't do that: I won't allow it!' Furthermore, in the last grim months of the Occupation she organised a raid on German grain stocks and also amassed a secret hoard of potatoes, thereby saving many Sark families from starvation during the cruellest winter of the War. Her ascendency was particularly manifest just after the Liberation when, seeing no British troops were instantly available, Mrs. Hathaway 'took over' the defeated German garrison, supervising their clearing up of the island and disposing of land mines.

With the coming of peace La Dame resumed her lecture tours in an endeavour to boost Sark's post-war recovery by yet again promoting its tourist trade. In 1949 the Hathaways had the honour of entertaining H.R.H. the Princess Elizabeth, together with H.R.H. the Duke of Edinburgh, who officially opened the island's new harbour at La Maseline, which had been in gestation since before the War. In the same year Mrs. Hathaway became an Officer of the Order of the British Empire.

These honours, however, came in the wake of grief, as her eldest child (Bridget Amice) had died the previous year at the age of 46: and within five years of receiving the O.B.E. she was to suffer a further bereavement with the loss of her husband only a few days after their Silver Wedding. Further trials awaited. Within a decade she had to endure the agonising spectacle of yet another daughter (Douce Alianore Daphne) slowly succumbing to cancer compounded by alcoholism, finally dying in 1967. In all these sorrows she sought assuagement in hard work and the discharge of her duties on the island.

In July 1957 history was made by the visit of Her Majesty the Queen and the Duke of Edinburgh: the first time a reigning monarch had ever set foot in Sark. During the course of the visit the Ceremony of Homage was performed at a special session of Chief Pleas held in the Boys' School. Never before had a Seigneur or Dame of Sark rendered homage on the island's own soil. In 1965 (the quatercentenary of Elizabeth I's original Charter to Helier de Carteret) additional honours were bestowed on Mrs. Hathaway when, in a ceremony at Buckingham Palace, the Queen created her a Dame Commander of the Order of the British Empire. Sark's feudal Mistress had become what she herself described as a 'Double Dame' (Empire and Sark)!

Within four years, however, it looked as though there would be no quincentenary to celebrate in 2065. Irked by the Kilbrandon Commission's intrusion into her island's affairs and wearied by the persistent slackness so sadly apparent in Sark's administration, Mrs. Hathaway in July 1969 addressed Chief Pleas in monitory vein, complaining that even its own members often broke the very laws they had made; that public houses staying open beyond the licensing laws' generous limits of 8 a.m. to 11 p.m. had led to hooliganism; and that lack of respect for traffic regulations by the growing number of tractors was ruining the island's placid atmosphere to the discomfiture of the economically invaluable tourists, whom she had been at such pains to attract by her publicity efforts. Then came the bombshell! La Dame announced her intention to surrender her Charter to the Crown 'in somewhat the same way as the Hereditary le Mesurier Family did in Alderney' — with the recommendation that the government of Sark be taken over by Guernsey.

This 'abdication' threat certainly 'made the Sark people sit up and look into their affairs'. The enforcement of regulations was rapidly tightened up and before the year was out the rather indulgent William Baker was replaced as Seneschal by Mr. Bernard Jones who, as a Guernseyman, was divorced from local coteries. The following January Mrs. Hathaway relented, announcing that she had been persuaded 'by an enormous number of letters and requests' to retract what she had said.

Although peace reigned once more, reform was in the air and the moves were initiated which were to eventuate shortly after La Dame's death in married women obtaining rights broadly equivalent to those of wives in the rest of the Bailiwick. As for Mrs. Hathaway, she remained in unchallenged supremacy for the rest of her life. Bereaved once again in 1973 with the death of her second son (Cyril John Astley), she gave her approval early in 1974 for the stage presentation of William Douglas Home's play *Dame of Sark* and looked forward to meeting Celia Johnson, who was to play the title rôle. This was not to be. In July 1974, very suddenly. she died, deeply mourned by an island which she had benevolently dominated for almost half a century.

HATTON, CHRISTOPHER, FIRST VISCOUNT HATTON OF GRETTON (1632-1706). *The Governor who was blown up.* When Christopher, second Baron Hatton, arrived in Guernsey in the summer of 1670 to take up his appointment as Governor he met with a chilly reception, it being recorded that 'not a gunn was heard for a wellcome usually given to anybody that comes from the King'.

This frigid attitude displayed by the islanders arose from bitter memories of his father, the first Baron Hatton (1606-70 and Governor of Guernsey from 1662 to 1665) whom Clarendon dismissed as 'a person of great reputation, which in a few years he found a way utterly to lose'; and who, not content with debarring from office such Commonwealth supporters as Pierre de Beauvoir (q.v.), Pierre Carey and Jacques de Havilland, rapidly provoked intense resentment by referring to Castle Cornet as his 'Palace' and by abusing all local dignitaries, from Bailiff Amias Andros (q.v.) downwards, as 'factious robbers and thieves'. The upshop was (despite a pathetically transparent attempt in 1664 to ingratiate himself with the insular community by appointing his two sons as Captains in the Militia, a massed parade of which he inspected at Les Grandes Mielles) that repeated complaints of his dishonesty and arbitrary interference with the course of justice eventually compelled Charles II to recall him in the autumn of 1665. Thereafter, though Hatton technically retained the governorship (the reversion of which had been granted to his son) effective gubernatorial authority for the next five years was in the hands of Colonel Sir Jonathan Atkins. Following his suspension he gave himself up to debauchery, forsaking his family for the lewd company of Scotland Yard revellers in London, with whom he recklessly squandered his substance before dying at Kirby in Northamptonshire in July 1670.

The new Governor was no stranger to Guernsey. After being appointed a Gentleman of the Privy Council by Charles II in 1662, he and his brother Charles had accompanied their father to the island, where not only had he held a commission in the Militia but also in October 1664 had compiled a report on the state of Guernsey for submission to Colonel William Legge — and furthermore had temporarily acted as Governor during the absence of his father in February 1665. (Among his responsibilities at that time, incidentally, had been the custody of the distinguished prisoner General John Lambert (q.v.*) whose daughter Mary was his sister-in-law, being the wife of his brother Charles.) He now set about overcoming his initial handicaps. The man whose 'unparalleled prudence and application repaired the shattered estate of his family' also succeeded in transmuting suspicious hostility into warm affection; all hearts being won by his kindliness, his concern for the people's prosperity and his love of flowers — manifested especially in his cultivation of the Guernsey Lily.

Two years after assuming office, Lord Hatton was involved in a tragedy. On 30 December 1672, lightning struck the keep and the magazine in Castle Cornet. The resultant explosion not only destroyed the keep (which was never replaced) but also killed both Cecilia Lady Hatton and Elizabeth the Dowager Lady Hatton — the Governor's mother. Despite being blown, while still in his bed, on to the battlements, Lord Hatton himself miraculously escaped injury -- and by a further quirk of fate his infant children, although occupying the same room as their mother, also survived the disaster. This accident of history gave additional impetus to an already nascent political trend whereby the rôle of the Governor was gradually assuming a more constitutional complexion analogous to that of the Sovereign whose vicegerant he was. As a result of the calamity the monarch's representative now came to live among the islanders for whom he was responsible, rather than in splendid isolation in an offshore fortification: a development which ultimately led to a more intimate relationship and greater rapport with the island authorities. Lord Hatton remained a widower until 1676, his second wife being Frances, the daughter of Sir Henry Yelverton of Northamptonshire.

Appointed Custos Rotulorum for his native county of Northamptonshire in 1681 (an office he retained until 1689), Guernsey's Governor was advanced to become Viscount Hatton of Gretton in the County of Northamptonshire on 11 December 1683. At the time of the Glorious Revolution, with its accompanying ejection in Guernsey of his Roman Catholic Lieutenant-Governor (Colonel John Legge), Viscount Hatton behaved with marked circumspection. When approached in November 1688 with a view to his participation in an attempt to secure Plymouth for James II, he refused (on the plea of ill-health) to be associated with any such enterprise.

As things turned out, however, the Orange triumph was to lead to Lord Hatton being confronted with the problem of a disaffected people before a further twelvemonth had elapsed. To remove all impediments to the pursuit of his struggle against Louis XIV, William III repudiated the long-standing neutrality of the Channel Isles — and as a corollary Guernsey was garrisoned and its sea-approaches patrolled by the Royal Navy. Friction between the soldiers of the garrison and the local population rapidly issued in widespread discontent. A pamphlet entitled *The Complaint of the Inhabitants of the Island of Guernzey* shows that on 6 August 1689 the

Guernsey leaders alleged 'that they were compelled to raise a general tax to provide quarters for such officers and soldiers as cannot be lodged in public houses, and among them, for divers inhabitants who have enlisted as soldiers, and have habitations of their own; also that they were much oppressed by the soldiers not paying their landlords at the removal of quarters'.

When this complaint was passed to him by the Privy Council, Viscount Hatton on 24 August directed that no more islanders were to be recruited and that those already recruited were to be discharged as soon as possible and meantime were to lodge with their own families; that five sols per week billeting money should be paid to householders upon whom soldiers were quartered; and lastly that commissioned officers were to pay for their quarters out of their own pockets, with the right of complaint to the Bailiff and Jurats if they felt that they were overcharged. These instructions, unfortunately, were not completely implemented with the result that further complaints ensued: but these were dealt with by the Privy Council itself.

During the rest of Lord Hatton's term of office the participation of John Tupper (q.v.*) with his ship *Monmouth Galley* in the 1692 Battle of Cap la Hogue ushered in the great era of privateering. In addition, Guernsey experienced serious outbreaks of smallpox in 1692 and 1705. Christopher, Viscount Hatton, died in September 1706.

DE HAVILLAND, SIR PETER (1747-1821). *The 'John Wilkes' of Guernsey*. (D/E). The chequered political career of George III's *bête noire*, John Wilkes (1727-97), is closely mirrored in that of Sir Peter de Havilland who, like his famous contemporary on the other side of the Channel, progressed from being a baulked placeman, resentfully defiant of authority deemed to be despotic, emerging later in life as a pillar of the Establishment. Scion of a house originating at Haverland near Valognes in Normandy which, settling in the island in 1176, had during the 17th century provided in Jacques de Havilland one of the Commissioners appointed in 1643 to govern the Bailiwick in the parliamentary interest (see 'de Beauvoir, Pierre'), Guernsey's Crusader for Right was born in 1747 and after completing his education at the Université de Caen, was admitted an Advocate of the Royal Court in 1770.

In 1774 expectations of advancement in his career in the shape of appointment as Comptroller were frustrated when the post of Junior Law Officer was given to the Bailiff's nephew, Thomas

de Sausmarez (q.v.). As a result de Havilland, embittered against Bailiff William le Marchant (q.v.), rapidly became conspicuous in the ranks of his adversaries. Thereafter, even if motivated partly by disgruntlement, this disappointed lawyer nevertheless came to be widely regarded by his fellow islanders as a champion of their liberties against the autocratic pretensions of the Bailiff.

In 1775 the hostility between the two antagonists issued in Peter de Havilland being suspended by Le Marchant from functioning as an advocate as a punishment for 'insolent conduct towards the Chief Magistrate in the Royal Court'. Aghast at this blatant victimisation, the Jurats refused to try any more cases until the young attorney was reinstated. The Privy Council in response to an appeal, ordered the lifting of this suspension. As, however, the Privy Council also deplored the Jurats' action in holding up all court business, they resigned en masse by way of protest, thus initiating a prolonged confrontation with the Bailiff (see 'Le Marchant, William'). Thereafter de Havilland persistently opposed the Bailiff who, in correspondence with the Privy Council conducted in May 1799, named him as prominent in a local 'Faction' allegedly working to 'foment discontent'.

By the latter part of 1783 the animosity of the bailiff obliged de Havilland to leave Guernsey for Exeter, giving up his practice as an advocate – in which his clientèle had dwindled alarmingly as a result of the rareness of any success achieved by his pleas in a court presided over by his enemy. In 1785, however, the exile returned and was elected as a Jurat of the Royal Court – in which capacity he became six years later the central figure in an episode which ended in the complete humiliation of the overbearing Bailiff. A sensational course of events was initiated in 1791 by Jurat de Havilland bringing an action for slander against the Bailiff, who had accused him of swearing a falsehood in an affidavit submitted to the Privy Council. In addition de Havilland refused to resume his seat as a Jurat until his honour had been vindicated. By the cunning use of delaying tactics Le Marchant contrived to prevent any hearing taking place until November 1795, when the court – despite the Bailiff's attempts to intimidate it – found for de Havilland and awarded him damages of 1,000 livres tournois. Refusing to pay, Le Marchant belaboured with a cane de Havilland's brother Martin who, in his capacity as Prévôt, called on him in April 1796 with the information that, in default of payment, sundry executions had been made on his property. This behaviour eventuated in the bailiff being so severely disciplined by the Royal Court the following month as to induce an outlook on his part sufficiently chastened to ensure that he trod the path of constitutional rectitude for the rest of his term of office.

In 1795, while this drama was still in progress, the marriage was solemnised between the Procureur, Thomas de Sausmaraz (q.v.) and Catherine, the daughter of Jurat de Havilland and his wife Emilia Tupper — who the self-same year became the aunt of the baby destined to earn fame as Guernsey's pre-eminent historian, Ferdinand Brock Tupper (q.v.). As a result of this union, Peter de Havilland emerges as one of the ancestors of the present (1984) denizens of Sausmarez Manor — witness the second Christian name of the current Seigneur du Fief de Sausmarez — Cecil Havilland de Sausmarez, M.B.E. (q.v.).

Three years before this wedding Peter de Havilland had taken a step whereby he gave the initial impulse to the creation of his own lasting memorial. This was the purchase in 1792 of a set of fields between the Grange and Lower Vauvert whereon this enterprising Jurat, with a legacy for his children in mind, embarked on the development of what was to become known as the New Town — a project which was not fully completed until some time after his death. The testimony of his great-great-grandson reveals that in this complex Sausmarez Street (the road-sign's omission of the second 's' is an error) was named after his daughter-in-law Elizabeth (whose father — such are Guernsey's marital relationships — was also his son-in-law) and Havilland Street after himself; while the thoroughfare midway between them derived its name from his brother John — whose canonisation at the hands of cartographers from John Wood of Exeter with his 1843 'Plan of St Peter's Port' onwards, is completely lacking in warranty. Union Street was so named in honour of his marriage and George Street after his brother-in-law. He and his family (who had previously lived in the Rohais) moved into one of the earlier houses to be erected: 'La Maison de la Ville Neuve' (now Number 8, Sausmarez Street), which was built in 1804.

Peter de Havilland — who fostered the adoption in the islands of the telegraph system originated in France by Claude Chappe (1763–1805) in 1792 (and featured prominently by Alexandre Dumas in *The Count of Monte Cristo*) whereby messages were signalled from station to station by the movement of shutters and semaphore arms (a memento

of which remains in the cliff-top signalling tower after which is named the adjacent Telegraph Bay in Alderney) — was in 1810 appointed bailiff in succession to Robert Porret le Marchant (the son of his old rival) and during his time as Guernsey's civic head he had the honour of knighthood bestowed upon him by the Prince Regent at an Investiture held on 6 March 1817. This award gave recognition to his valuable services in general and in particular to the enthusiasm with which he lent support to the road schemes of Sir John Doyle (q.v.), to finance which he raised a public subscription in the teeth of strong opposition from the powerful le Marchant family, including the Lieutenant-Bailiff, Eleazar le Marchant. Four years after receiving the accolade — in April 1821 — Sir Peter died in office at the age of 74.

HAYWARD, SIR CHARLES WILLIAM, C.B.E. (1892–1983). *Jethou's philanthropist.* Born in 1892 in Wolverhampton and educated in that town's St John's School, Sir Charles Hayward pursued a successful business career from early manhood to the age of 81. Rising rapidly to the board room, he first became a company director in 1920 and thereafter held a variety of directorships in a miscellany of enterprises, including firms engaged in engineering, farming and horticulture. In 1932 he became Chairman and Managing Director of Electrical and General Industrial Trusts Limited. He followed this up by his appointment in 1936 as Chairman and Joint Managing Director of Firth Cleveland Limited and its component companies, and held both these highly responsible positions until 1973.

Made a Freeman of the City of London in 1938, Charles Hayward became a member of the Post Office Advisory Council in 1952 and in 1961 established the Hayward Foundation. This organization (of whose Trustees Sir Charles assumed the Chairmanship) was set up to help medical students and also to provide care for the elderly poor in difficulties. Becoming an Honorary Fellow of the Institute of Ophthalmology in 1967, this generous benefactor was made a Commander of the Most Excellent Order of the British Empire in 1970 and in the same year he was also appointed an Honorary Fellow of the Royal College of Surgeons.

The following year (1971) the fee-farm lease of Jethou was put on the market by Mrs. Susan Faed at an original asking price of £45,000 (which included £5,000 for furnishings, motor launch, livestock and sundry effects). Charles Hayward (who had just become a widower on the death of his wife Hilda Arnold whom he had married in 1915 and who had borne him a son) thereupon purchased the lease (though in the event, he paid £91,000), under the terms of which the tenant is required to pay an annual rental of £100 to the Crown and in addition to arrange his own electricity, water, sewage and transport systems. The next year (1972) he married Elsie Darnell (his former secretary) and the year after that was appointed Honorary Fellow of Keble College, Oxford and also a Knight of Grace of the Order of St John. In the 1974 New Year's Honours List there appeared the name of Mr. Charles William Hayward, C.B.E., to whom the Queen had granted a knighthood 'for services to the elderly'. This honour was followed by Sir Charles becoming an Honorary Doctor of Laws of Birmingham University in 1975.

Following the arrival in Jethou of Sir Charles (who had also, *inter alia*, become a Vice-President of the Wildfowl Trust) the Bailiwick benefited enormously from personal charitable ministrations as well as from those of his Hayward Foundation. From these sources there flowed handsome donations to the transport section of the St John Ambulance Brigade; a gift of £10,000 to the Arun Lifeboat appeal; and addition to Le Platon Nursing Home consisting of a day room for the residents together with a bathroom and a small ward; and extensive refurbishing of the Guille–Allès Library in connection with its conversion from one run on a subscription basis to one providing a free lending service in 1981. A happy by-product of this last-named benefaction was the perpetuation of Sir Charles' name by the Reading Room devoted to Local Studies being dubbed the 'Hayward Room'. Sir Charles died in Jethou on 3 February 1983.

HEAD, HENRY GEORGE (1899–1969). *The firebrand of La Ville Roussel de Bas.* Born at Les Baissières on 21 May 1899 to Mary Susannah (*née* Ozanne). the wife of George Head (a farmer) and educated at Melrose School, Henry George Head, who has been described as 'a tough wiry little man with the curiosity of a magpie', earned his living in early manhood as a trader in electrical goods, eventually becoming the local representative of the Hoover concern.

In 1930 Henry Head married Florence Emily le Feuvre of Sark. The couple in the years following their wedding resided in Guernsey, however, and during the German Occupation, when it was no longer possible to earn a living in the electrical goods business, Head supported his wife and himself by working as an insurance agent on behalf of the island branch of the Brittanic Assurance Company; while in the immediate post-Liberation period he tried his hand as an auctioneer.

In 1947 came the event which was to lead to Henry Head's name reverberating throughout the Bailiwick. Mrs. Florence Head inherited the Sark Quarantaine Holding of 'La Ville Roussel de Bas' and the couple thereupon moved to the Fief Haubert, where Henry immediately qualified for a seat in Chief Pleas as proxy for his spouse. In this assembly he rapidly became known as 'the stormy petrel' because of his fulminations against entrenched privilege and what he interpreted as gross inequity in the details of insular administration. Appointed as Sark correspondent for the Guernsey and Jersey newspapers and supplementing this by free-lance contributions to several English journals as well, Head rapidly acquired so thorough a mastery of Sark's laws as to understand them far better than most other members of the island legislature. He thus emerged as a veritable thorn in the flesh of the establishment, an indefatigable advocate of reform, in the campaign for which he was staunchly backed by Mr. Hubert Lanyon (q.v.).

In a very real sense these 'radical twins' may be regarded as having initiated Sark's 1951 Reform Law. Towards the end of 1949 Head's investigations established unequivocably that no confirmatory Order-in-Council had ever ratified the 1922 Sark Government Law, whereby for the first time in history provision had been made for the inclusion in Chief Pleas of elected deputies of the people. The consequence of this omission was that Sark's legislature lacked any legal basis for its existence! The Privy Council hurriedly issued a directive provisionally authorising Chief Pleas to function pending the enactment of appropriate legislation: legislation which in the event took the form of the 1951 Reform Law which is the basis of much of Sark's present-day Constitution.

Shortly after the passage of the Reform Law Head (who on 3 October 1951 had been elected as Sark's Constable at the Michaelmas Sitting of Chief Pleas) gave rein to his puckish sense of humour to the discomfiture of La Dame. Telephoning 'La Seigneurie' he asked who was responsible for, or could lay claim to, wreckage on the island's shores. Mrs. Sybil Hathaway (q.v.), thinking that Poseidon had yielded up highly valuable flotsam, immediately asserted her rights — only to find that the wreckage consisted of a dead whale for the disposal of which her own claim now rendered her responsible! Her tormentor, however, demonstrated the absence of any malicious animosity underlying his behaviour by the considerate way in which, a little later, he took pains to avoid embarrassing his victim in the dead whale episode by waiting until she was out of Sark before seeking any Court Order to restrain Mrs. Douce Briscoe (La Dame's alcoholic daughter) from the somewhat unseemly conduct in the island's bars to which she was prone.

Once again backed by Hubert Lanyon (who, *inter alia*, was a fellow-member of the Land Reform Committee) Henry Head, maintaining that Sark's laws were 'wrapped up in cobwebs of decay' so that they would 'bedevil any lawyer in office', set out to establish the precise extent to which the island's feudal regulations permitted the Serquiais to buy plots for building. He claimed that these investigations revealed many unauthorised alterations to tenement boundaries — some of recent date.

In 1958 Head and Lanyon called for a Royal Commission to look into what they alleged to be grave irregularities in Sark's administration, with especial reference to the way in which the Douzaine raised the Direct Tax to finance poor relief. Scornfully describing the method employed as being 'By grace or by God', Henry Head asserted that the amount paid by any individual depended on 'whether your face fitted' and stressed the urgent need for a fairer system. These allegations provoked a letter of protest sent to the *Guernsey Evening Press* and bearing the signatures of 148 Serquiais — and in the event no Royal Commission was appointed, while the alternative suggestion of an Investigatory Committee manned exclusively by Channel Islanders was turned down by Chief Pleas. Nevertheless, as time went on, it was conceded that Head's complaints did not lack substance and many of the faults he indicated were subsequently rectified.

By 1960 the health of the 'stormy petrel' began to fail. There being no children of their marriage to inherit their holding, his wife sold to Mr. Herbert Holborrow the tenement of La Ville Roussel de Bas, which had been continuously in the hands of her family since Helier de Carteret (q.v.) originally granted it to Pierre le Feuvre in 1565. The couple then left Sark (where, besides all his other cares, Henry Head had also been the inspector charged with responsibility for precautions against the Colorado beetle) to return to Guernsey for their years of retirement: years during which the old campaigner fought his last battle — a losing one — against the ravages of cancer, to which he finally succumbed on 15 June 1969. Before death claimed him, however, the veteran radical contributed frequent letters to the *Guernsey Evening Press* containing witty and satirical accounts of States' Meetings; and in 1967, defying the relentless march of his dire disease, he sought and obtained election to the States of Deliberation as Deputé du Peuple for St Peter-Port.

When taking his leave of the Fief Haubert, Head reiterated his old strictures, complaining at the lack of proper Rules of Procedure in Chief Pleas and alleging that anyone attempting to raise in that body any topic distasteful to La Dame would be shouted down by the Seneschal. By way of retort Mrs. Hathaway after his departure claimed that the quaintness of Sark's laws attracted visitors; emphatically denied that she was a despot; and went on to remark that there had been two men who had wanted to alter the Constitution, 'but they didn't get anywhere and now one has left the island and the other has lost almost all his trade'. That 'they didn't get anywhere' is debatable: a neutral onlooker could easily be forgiven for forming the impression that the 'stormy petrel' exerted an influence that will long endure. Ironically his crusading zeal was eventually justified by none other than his main adversary — La Dame herself — who in the very year of the irrepressible gadfly's death was so exasperated by the irresponsibility displayed by many members of Chief Pleas as to threaten to surrender her Patent as a ploy to bring them to their senses!

HERIVEL, CAPTAIN SYDNEY PECK, C.B.E., D.S.C. (1890–1970). *The Founding Father of modern Alderney.* Born at Malmesbury in Wiltshire on 17 February 1890, to Lucy Jane (*née* Yoxall), the wife of William Herivel, Sydney Peck Herivel (who in adult life was affectionately known as 'Toby' by his host of friends) came of an old Alderney family, his father (himself an Aurigniais by birth) having left the island some years earlier in search of wider opportunities.

After receiving his education at Grove House School in Highgate, young Sydney Herivel went into business in London, but at the same time, sharing fully the national pride in the Fleet which was so pronounced in Edwardian days, he joined the Royal Naval Volunteer Reserve and consequently was called up for service immediately on the outbreak of the First World War. Commissioned in 1915, he served throughout the conflict with such distinction as to return to civilian life in 1919 as an Officer of the Most Excellent Order of the British Empire.

During the inter-war years Sydney Herivel pursued a career in the City connected mainly with insurance broking, and on 31 July 1925 he married Miss Edith Beatrice Leesmith who later bore him a son — Nicholas John Maitland. He still maintained his membership of the Royal Naval Volunteer Reserve, however, and thus was recalled for active duties when the Second World War broke out in September 1939. Attaining the rank of Commander, he was awarded the Distinguished Service Cross in 1941 in recognition of his bearing the previous year during the evacuation of the British Expeditionary Force from Dunkirk and, serving for the whole of this grim struggle, he did not resume civilian status until 1949.

By this time the Herivel family's ancestral island home had been liberated, but was prostrate after the ravages of enemy occupation, the effects of which (with any possibility of a restraining influence by a resident civil administration having been precluded by the total evacuation of 1940) had been so exacerbated as to produce utter destitution. The situation called for drastic political changes involving *inter alia* the abolition of the office of Juge — the traditional 'uncrowned king' of Alderney who presided over both the States and the Court of Law in its two manifestations (Ordinary and Chief Pleas). (Commander Herivel's kinsman, William Herivel, by his implacable opposition to Judge Frederick French (q.v.) had been largely instrumental in procuring that worthy's resignation in 1946.) In place of this system the Government of Alderney Law, 1948, ordained a separation of powers as between the Legislature and the Judiciary, the court sitting under a chairman and the States assembling under a president elected by universal suffrage who was also to be regarded as the island's civic head.

To shoulder the responsibilities of this new office the electorate chose Commander Herivel, who, after demobilisation, had settled at Les Mouriaux House and he accordingly became the first President of the States of Alderney on 1 January 1949; as such rapidly emerging as 'Mr. Alderney', personifying in an inimitable manner the island whose unflattering reputation as the archipelago's 'Cinderella' he countered by remarking that this beautiful but unfortunate maiden had two ugly sisters! He was also widely acclaimed for his unrivalled knowledge of local conditions, his charm, and his stubborn determination to put Alderney back on its feet as quickly as possible after the ordeal of the war — an ambition so fully and efficiently realised as to prompt *The Times* on 15 January 1970 to refer to him encomiastically as the 'anchorman of the island's post-war economy'. His outstanding contributions earning him advancement to the rank of Commander of the Most Excellent Order of the British Empire in the 1953 New Year's Honours, Commander Herivel was repeatedly voted back to his exalted station, surviving the technical invalidity of his 1969 re-election and described in *The Times* report of his retirement as combining in his person the qualities which, had he been in England, would have ensured him success as a Parochial or District Council Chairman, coupled with an ability to handle the Home Office and to entertain the Queen.

A member of the Royal Channel Islands Yacht Club, Patron of the Alderney Society and President of the Alderney Branch of the Royal British Legion, Sydney Peck Herivel was in 1966 promoted from the rank of Commander to that of honorary Captain in the Royal Naval Reserve (with which the R.N.V.R. had by then been merged) and in June 1970 a plaque commemorating his long service to the island was unveiled in the Alderney Court House. By then 'Mr. Alderney' was over 80 years of age and despite the defiance he hurled at senescence, sickness, stress and strain, the sands were running out. On 16 August of that year Edith Herivel died and ten days later her husband (who had watched his wife's funeral from an ambulance) tendered on the grounds of deteriorating health his resignation which the States of Alderney reluctantly accepted. The very next day — 27 August 1970 — Alderney's first States' President followed his wife to the grave, dying in the Mignot Memorial Hospital. An era of the island's history had come to an end.

HEYLYN, REVEREND PETER (1600-1662). *The Islands' first annalist.* In 1656 there was published in London a book bearing the lengthy title *A Full Relation of Two Journeys: The one into the Main-Land of France, the other into some of the adjacent Ilands.* Part Two of this publication concentrates on the Channel Islands and is headed, *The Second Journey, containing a Survey of the Estate of the two Ilands of Guernezey and Jarsey, with the Isles appending.* The author of this wordily-entitled chronicle was the Reverend Peter Heylyn, who, born at Burford in Oxfordshire in 1600 and educated locally, had gone up to Oxford at the tender age of 14 in 1614 and, taking his B.A. in 1617, had been elected a Fellow of Magdalen in 1618 before proceeding to his M.A. in

1620. Taking Holy Orders in 1624, as a High Churchman Heylyn consistently maintained the affinity between 'Ecclesia Anglicana' and this historic Catholic Church. After travelling in France in 1625, he was married in 1628 to Laetitia Heygate, of Hayes in Middlesex — and in March of the following year he came to the Channel Isles as Chaplain to the force sent under the command of the Governor of Guernsey, the Earl of Danby, to augment the islands' defences against France, whence it was feared that an attack might be mounted based on St Malo.

As the first book ever written devoted specifically to the Channel Isles, the importance of Heylyn's *Survey* is hard to exaggerate. From it one learns of the contemporary value attached to St Peter-Port's roadstead nestling under the shelter of Cornet — 'the principall honour and glory of this Iland, I mean Guernezey, is the large capaciousnesse of the harbour, and the flourishing beauty of the Castle'. The Militia, however, did not impress this observer: 'Their trained band consists of only 1,200 and these, God knows, but poorly weaponed'. Heylyn goes on to tell of insular government: 'in the art of Government a little Empire doth nothing differ from a greater; whereupon it is, that even these small Ilands, in imitation of the greater Kingdomes have also their "Conventus ordinum", or assembly of the States'. The perquisites of the resident Lieutenant-Governor — Sir Peter Osborne (q.v.) — also receive his attention, when he talks of the 'bignesse' of the pike found in La Grande Mare at Vazon and reserved for his consumption: and then describes Jethou (kept as Sir Peter's game reserve) as possessing 'some few fallow deer and a good plenty of conies'. Furthermore, he gives details of the main industry of the day — 'The principall commodity which they use to send abroad, are the works and labours of the poorer sort, as Wast-cotes, Stockins, and other manufactures made of wool, wherein they are exceeding cunning'. Despite their 'works and labours', however, the lot of 'the poorer sort' was often dire and Heylyn was appalled that 'children were continually craving alms of every stranger'.

As a clergyman visiting islands where Jersey had been brought to conform in a perfunctory and resentful fashion to Anglicanism, but where Guernsey still adhered to its Presbyterian system, Peter Heylyn naturally gave considerable attention to religious matters. He affirms that the government meant to reform the church in Guernsey, but was initially prevented by the distractions first caused by the breach with Spain and then by the

French War of 1627-29. Later on the Edinburgh Prayer Book Riots of 1637 frustrated William Laud (Archbishop of Canterbury since 1633) who, Heylyn claims, had actually selected a person with knowledge of the islands to conduct a visitation prior to archepiscopal action. In this connection it is interesting that the inference which may be drawn from another publication by the same author (his *Cyprianus Anglicus* written in defence of Laud) is that the 'person with knowledge of the islands' was none other than Heylyn himself. He was certainly closely identified with the Laudian school, becoming a court chaplain on his return from the Islands in 1630 on the strength of Danby's recommendation to Laud, and the following year being appointed a Prebend of Westminster. In 1633 he prepared the case against William Prynne and played an important part in bringing about his conviction by submitting a list of quotations from the outspoken Puritan's *Histriomastix*. In the same year he obtained the benefice of Alresford in Hampshire, where he lost no time in introducing full Laudian ritual, while in 1636, at the behest of the king, he answered the scruples of the Puritans with his *History of the Sabbath*.

Eluding arrest by Parliamentary forces on the outbreak of the Civil War, Heylyn joined the king at Oxford and subsequently, though impoverished by the seizure of his chattels at Alresford, he and his wife lived at Winchester until it fell in 1646. Fleeing in disguise, he finally settled in 1648 at Minster Lovel in Oxfordshire, where he was let be by Cromwell, who winked at his private celebrations of Anglican rites and suffered him to publish his *Survey* in 1656 and even a *Vindication of the Church of England* in 1657. Acting as sub-dean at the Coronation of Charles II on 23 April 1661, Heylyn died on 8 May 1662 and his body was buried in Westminster Abbey.

HÜFFMEIER, VIZEADMIRAL FRIEDRICH (1898-). *The Führer's formidable fanatic.* Born in June 1898 at Kunersdorf near Wriezen (north-east of Berlin), Friedrich Hüffmeier was appointed Adviser to the Naval High Command (Europe) in May 1938 and stayed at this post until August 1939 when for a short while (until September) he became Naval Liaison Officer to the Army General Staff. He then served as a Naval Staff Officer until May 1941, when he was given command of the light cruiser *Cologne*, of which he remained captain until March 1942. In April of the same year he took command of the battleship *Scharnhorst* (now back in home waters after her dash up Channel from Brest the previous February): a command which lasted until October 1943 when (fortunately for him as the vessel was sunk two months later) he was appointed Chief of Security at Naval High Command – a post he kept until June 1944.

It was at this point that Friedrich Hüffmeier came to the Channel Isles in supreme charge of all naval units in the archipelago. Tall and burly in appearance, his superficial geniality hid a fundamental rabid fanaticism – as was manifested by the speed with which he organised study courses in National Socialism for the men under his control. Within a few weeks of Hüffmeier's arrival the Allied breakout in France had converted the islands into remote offshore redoubts linked with the main bulk of the German forces by no more than perilous and infrequent air communications. This fervent exponent of the 'Herrenvolk' cult, aspiring to be a big fish in a small pond, argued vehemently that the Commander-in-Chief – Lieutenant-General Graf von Schmettow (q.v.) – did not react with sufficient audacity to this situation: and reported accordingly to higher authority.

Hüffmeier's aggressive stance won favour even from Hitler himself, but any proposal to make him Commander-in-Chief (*Befehlshaber*) in von Schmettow's stead came up against the difficulty that there were ten times· as many military personnel as naval in the islands, so that the appointment of a naval Befehlshaber would give rise to intense resentment among the troops. As a compromise, therefore, Hüffmeier in September 1944 was made Chief of Staff ·to the Commander-in-Chief, so as to enable him to exert 'naval influence' on von Schmettow.

Having got his foot inside the door, Hüffmeier pushed! Launching a relentless campaign to supplant von Schmettow, he repeatedly and cogently advocated draconian measures to prolong the islands' capacity for resistance 'by means of drastic confiscation and by severely reducing consumption'. He thus rapidly emerged as the 'power behind the throne', his hand strengthened by his promotion to the rank of Vice-Admiral on New Year's Day 1945 – with the upshot that the status of Graf von Schmettow (with whom Hüffmeier by now was barely on speaking terms) steadily degenerated to that of a figurehead until he was removed on 'health grounds' (though he had not needed to consult a doctor for 15 months) on 27 February.

Once in the saddle, the Vice-Admiral – a ruthless upholder of the New Order – committed himself to hold the insular fortresses come what may, persuaded that if he stood firm as a latter-day Leonidas defending a new Thermopylae, the archipelago could be used as a bargaining counter at any peace conference that might be convened. Determined to keep the garrison fed, even if every single civilian had to succumb to starvation, he placed his faith in maintaining and extending the production of milk, butter and cheese from the island herds – hence his opposition to any slaughter of cattle – supplemented by a massive cultivation of vegetables. His proclamation to the troops on assuming command left no room for doubt as to his attitude and intentions:

> 'I have only one aim: to hold out until final victory.
> I believe in the mission of our Führer and of our
>   people.
> I shall serve them with immutable loyalty.
> Heil our beloved Führer!'

This unrepentent Nazi (who ordered the captain of the Red Cross ship *Vega* to fly his flag at half-mast when the news came of Hitler's suicide) certainly led a charmed life, surviving a plot to abduct him by Monsieur L. V. Lambert (the French consular agent) and another to assassinate him by Barons von Helldorf and von Aufsess (q.v.). It is indeed conceivable that he might have achieved his ambition had his men been efficient herdsmen and market gardeners: but instead he found himself in command of 30,000 starvelings and semi-invalids, with no will left to resist. Even so, as late as 6 May 1945, with Germany in collapse and the territory held by Karl Doenitz, as Hitler's successor, not extending beyond the confines of Flensburg, Hüffmeier planned a raid on Granville for the following day – and only cancelled it on direct orders from the Grand Admiral himself. This still-born operation is a reminder that, thoroughly unpleasant though he was, the Vizeadmiral was unquestionably a great naval commander – witness the success of the February 1945 attack on this same seaport which, although prepared by his predecessor, was executed under his direction.

Having instructed his men to salute British officers after they had landed – but to do so in the Nazi fashion(!) – Hüffmeier signalled on 7 May that, on orders from higher authority (Doenitz) his representative would meet the Allies off Les Hanois at noon on 8 May. He only sent a junior officer, however, whom he had merely authorised to discuss armistice terms – with the warning that, failing such discussions, he would open fire on the British ships should they remain within territorial waters! When the next morning his Second-in-Command, Major-General Heine, finally signed the Instrument of Surrender, the Vizeadmiral did not hand over his sword (which he had taken the precaution of destroying) and furthermore candidly admitted that he had also deliberately incinerated all Wehrmacht records. Turned over as a prisoner of war to the Commander of H.M.S. *Faulkner*, the truculent satrap of the last outpost of the Third Reich remained in captivity until October 1947. The following April he was formally discharged from the Navy and retired into the obscurity of private life.

HUGO, VICTOR MARIE (1802–1885). *The literary lion of Hauteville House.* Born at Besançon in February 1802, Victor Marie Hugo spent his infancy in Italy and Spain (whither military duties took his father, who was one of Napoleon's generals) and later in Paris, where at the age of ten he wrote verses which already foreshadowed his tremendous talent.

As a young man he rapidly rose to the head of the new Romantic School in literature and became a member of the Academie Française. In 1845 he was made a Peer of France by Louis Philippe. At heart a republican, however, Hugo was elected to membership of both the Constituent Assembly and of the Legislature after the fall of 'Le Roi Citoyen' had ushered in the Second Republic in February 1848, emerging in debate as an eloquent defender of political freedom.

It was this commitment to the principles of constitutional liberty that led Hugo, after Louis Napoleon's coup d'état of 2 December 1851, to quit France and (via Belgium) to make for what he described as '*des morceaux de France tombés à la mer et ramassés par l'Angleterre*' settling in Jersey in 1852 as a leading figure among the 200 or so 'proscripts' who had fled from the iron hand of their country's new master.

An especially prominent 'proscript' was the Polish-born Zénon Boleslas Swietoslawski (1811–75) who had taken an active part in the overthrow of the Bourbons in 1830 and who, once in Jersey, founded the Republican newspaper, *L'Homme*. On 10 October 1855 there appeared a letter in the correspondence columns of this publication vilifying Queen Victoria for her state visit to Napoleon III. This forthwith provoked a characteristically forceful reaction on the part of the British Prime Minister (Lord Palmerston) who — obviously with Franco–British cooperation in the Crimea in mind — wrote on 12 October to Sir George Grey (the Home Secretary) proposing that

all French refugees be deported from the Channel Isles and brought to the United Kingdom where they could do less harm. The fiery British leader continued, 'We are not doing Justice by our faithful and zealous Ally the Emperor of the French, by allowing a knot of his mortal Enemies to be plotting within an hour's sail or row of his Shore'. As an immediate measure he told Grey to enquire into the possibility of prosecuting *L'Homme* and also to set agents to watch the refugees.

The upshot was that Jersey's Lieutenant-Governor expelled the triumvirate editing the offending paper — and Hugo too when he protested against this step! Thus he came to Guernsey where he was granted asylum despite Palmerston's fulminations — or maybe (bearing in mind the Bailiwick's touchiness over any utterance in derogation of its autonomy) because of them! After a temporary stay at l'Hotel de l'Europe (between Quay Street and Cow Lane), Hugo moved to Hauteville. First renting Number 20 lower down the road for a year, a payment of £1,000 in 1856 procured 'Hauteville House' (donated in 1927 by his descendants to the city of Paris) which, as a skilful and practical craftsman in all forms of woodwork and with a passion for bric-à-brac, he transformed into a veritable museum of treasures. His mistress, Juliette Drouet ('Juju'), who had originally occupied Number 44, later took over Number 20 (now called 'Friends' House') and guests at select dinner parties were presented to '*Madame la mère de mes enfants*' and '*Madame mon amie*'.

Prominent among such guests was Georges Métivier (q.v.), the Patois poet and etymologist with whom the eminent exile was on Christian name terms, helping him with the production of his *Dictionnaire Franco-Normand*. Such friendship with an islander was exceptional, however, as by and large Hugo did not get on particularly well with the Guernesiais, whom he described as consisting of 'those content to ramble round their gardens and those content to ramble round the world'; and who, for their part, tended to ignore him, regarding their involuntary guest as an eccentric. Those who knew about it did, however, admire his charitable generosity in giving a dinner to the poor children of the vicinity every Thursday from 1863 onwards. Remembering the proximity of Cornet, Pedvin and Cliff Streets, there must have been a lot of them!

During Hugo's stay in Guernsey there occurred the distressing episode of his second daughter Adèle's infatuation with an officer of the garrison, whom she followed to Nova Scotia. (In this connection it is interesting to note that over a century later — in 1975 — this poignant affair of the heart was portrayed in a film, many sequences of which were shot in Pedvin Street.)

In the study at the top of his house of refuge, through a window of which he could on a clear day see his beloved France, Hugo stood at a plain shelf of black walnut, writing *Les Misérables* (1862) and *Les Travailleurs de la Mer* (1866). In the opening paragraphs of this novel (set in Guernsey) the Great Man rather carelessly made his heroine (Déruchette) walk down the coast road approaching the town from St Sampson's and turn *LEFT* to go inland! Lastly, near the end of his sojourn in the island (1869) he wrote *L'Homme Qui Rit*. In the meantime the tedium of exile was relieved by periodical holidays in Sark — '*le plus merveilleux poème de pierres qui surgisse de la surface des eaux*' — staying at the *Dixcart* Hotel (then known as *Gavey's*).

After Napoleon III's defeat at Sedan, Hugo (who had become a legendary figure during his absence) returned on 4 September 1870, weeping over France's humiliation at the hands of Prussia. Despite his advanced years he played a prominent part in the ensuing siege of Paris (in the course of which his son Charles died of apoplexy), steeling the city's will to resist by personal example and inspiring declamation. Although his stance made him the darling of the Left, he nevertheless deplored its lapses into intemperance; and after Paris had fallen, disgusted by the excesses of the Communards (whom he rebuked for their vandalism) the septuagenarian republican idealist withdrew to Brussels with a new mistress (the 18-year-old Marie Mercier), later moving to Vianden in Luxembourg. Subsequently Hugo returned thrice to Guernsey (where he had retained ownership of Hauteville House), coming in 1872 and writing *Quatre-vingt-treize* during his stay; once more for a week only in 1875 and yet again in 1878 to convalesce after illness. Eventually settling in Paris, he died in that city in May 1885 and his body was buried in the Panthéon.

On the eve of the outbreak of the First World War Victor Hugo's statue was unveiled in Candie Gardens, its plinth inscribed with the littérateur's gratitude to the people of Guernsey, as expressed in the dedication of *Les Travailleurs de la Mer* — '*Au rocher d'hospitalité et de liberté, à ce coin de vieille terre normande où vit le noble petit peuple de la mer, à l'Ile de Guernesey, sévère et douce.*'

LE HURAY, CYRIL PETER (1890–1959). *A talented and versatile expositor: teacher, novelist, feuilletonist and author of a lucid Bailiwick Vade Mecum.* Born in Hauteville on 1 June 1890 to Elizabeth Mary (*née* Blanche), the wife of James Raymond le Huray, Cyril le Huray was educated at St Martin's School, whence he moved to the Pupil Teachers' Centre for an apprenticeship in the profession of his choice prior to going up to King Alfred's College in Winchester, where he qualified as a schoolmaster in 1910.

After holding an appointment at Sheerness for a short while, le Huray took up a post at a school in Cambridge, where he remained until 1917, indifferent health precluding any combatant service in the First World War. While at Cambridge he was registered as an Extra-Collegiate undergraduate of that city's famous university, reading Horticulture and graduating as a Bachelor of Arts in 1915, being advanced to a Master of Arts three years later. By them he was serving at the Salt School in Bingley (then in the West Riding, though now in the Metropolitan County of West Yorkshire), whence in 1921 he moved to Dunstable Grammar School, where he taught Modern Language and remained for the rest of his career.

During the German Occupation the death occurred in 1943 of Le Huray *père*, who had enjoyed the usufruct of Le Bordage at La Bellieuse since the demise of his wife several years previously. Having thereby come into his inheritance, Cyril le Huray returned to Guernsey in the wake of the Liberation, retiring early because of the persistence of poor health. Despite this disability he soon attained prominence in island life, holding office first as Constable of St Martin and subsequently spending many years as St Martin's Douzaine Representative in the States, where he served on the Natural Beauties Committee and also as President of the Civil Defence Committee. In addition he was a member of the Town Hospital Board.

It was, however, in the sphere of academic and literary activity that this gifted Guernseyman's retirement was particularly distinguished. Joining La Société Guernesiaise immediately after his return to the island, he was elected to its Council in 1951 and became its president for the years 1953 and 1954. Besides contributing several papers to La Société's *Transactions*, le Huray also made his mark as a novelist, writing *Death for a Holiday* and *Our Fathers That Begat Us*. The latter was published under the nom-de-plume of 'San Martinez', a pseudonym whereby he also signed a series of articles appearing in the

Star newspaper — articles which provided the basis for his major work, *The Bailiwick of Guernsey*, comprising an exhaustive *coup d'oeil* of the Bailiwick embellished with a wide variety of historical allusions. The victim of a brain tumour, Cyril Peter le Huray died at the Town Hospital on 8 October 1959.

I

IRVING, LIEUTENANT-COLONEL PAULUS AEMILIUS (*c.* 1725–1796). *The Lieutenant-Governor with a mutiny on his hands!* In the year 1770 Sir Jeffrey (later Lord) Amherst was appointed Governor of Guernsey. He assumed office at a critical juncture. Unrest in the American colonies was increasing in scale. Indeed, the very year of Amherst's appointment saw the frustration of British attempts to placate the colonies by repealing the Import Duties Act, as the continuance of the imposts on tea as the sole exception to repeal, provoked the troubles culminating in the Boston massacre. With France as a constant potential enemy on the other side of the Channel, Guernsey in those days possessed considerable importance as a 'frontier fortress' — the last place where George III's government wanted to risk any emulation of American behaviour. Accordingly Amherst sought to place the island's administration under a firm and dependable hand and to this end prevailed upon the king to appoint as Bailiff the forceful and dominant William le Marchant (q.v.). To make assurance doubly sure the Governor nominated as his Lieutenant to be domiciled in the island another 'strong man' in the person of Lieutenant-Colonel Paulus Aemilius Irving.

Lieutenant-Colonel Irving had been born into a family whose seat was at Woodhouse, Dumfries, *c.* 1725 (judging by his son's known year of birth being 1751) and had a successful career in the Army behind him, having particularly distinguished himself as a Major commanding the 15th Foot in scaling the Heights of Abraham and assaulting Quebec under General Wolfe in 1759. He was Guernsey's Lieutenant-Governor from 1770 to 1783, and throughout this period gave Le Marchant his full moral support in the imposition of an authoritarian régime — even instigating some of the policies adopted. Inevitably, the autocratic conduct of the Bailiff led to protest and it was largely thanks to Irving's backing that Le Marchant was able to survive in office.

The new Lieutenant-Governor both made history and created a deep impression almost as soon as he took up his appointment as he brought over with him his private carriage: the first four-wheeled vehicle ever to be seen in the island, where many thoroughfares were too narrow to provide passage for such a magnificent equipage. As a psychological aid to establishing ascendancy through inculcating awe it was invaluable.

The great paradox of Irving's term of office was that although fate decreed that he would indeed have to quell unrest in Guernsey, the insubordination did not prove to be on the part of the islanders over whom he had been placed as a resident policeman. Shortly before he relinquished his appointment he had to deal with a mutiny among the troops at Fort George which broke out in March 1783. The mutineers were Irishmen of the 104th Regiment (about 600 in number) who seem to have been incited by a group of discharged men from the 83rd Regiment who had recently arrived from Portsmouth. Initially, Irving tried to deal with the situation by attempting pacification, yielding to the demand made by the rebellious soldiery that the gates of the still uncompleted fort should be left open so as to permit them to come and go at their pleasure. The temporary respite procured by this concession was short-lived. Late in the afternoon of 24 March the men started to fire on their officers, compelling them to vacate the fort. The Lieutenant-Governor at once decided that the time had come to use force. At midnight he advanced on the mutineers at the head of the 18th Regiment of Foot (The Royal Irish) who had remained loyal, supported by the Militia. A parley produced no solution as the insurgents refused to surrender. Desultory shooting on the part of the rebels continued until 4 a.m. when Irving himself was fired on. He then gave the order for the fire to be returned and the Militia units were moved to so threatening a position that the mutineers, realising that they were outnumbered and out-manoeuvred, submitted.

After leaving Guernsey Lieutenant-Colonel Irving became the Lieutenant-Governor of Upnor Castle, commanding the Medway estuary in Kent — and there he died in 1796.

J

JERVOIS, SIR WILLIAM FRANCIS DRUM-MOND, G.C.M.G., C.B. (1821-1897). *The designer of Alderney's Victorian forts*. Born in Cowes in the Isle of Wight and privately educated at Gosport and Woolwich, William Jervois entered the Royal Military Academy in 1837 at the age of 16 and was commissioned in the Royal Engineers two years later. Posted in 1841 to the Cape of Good Hope, Lieutenant Jervois was employed in the construction of defensive posts against the Kaffirs, and the next year he was appointed Brigade Major of a force sent to the Orange River to control the Boers. Following several years spent on the construction of military roads and bridges, he made a survey of Kaffirland in 1847 which proved of great value in subsequent campaigns; after which he returned to the United Kingdom in 1848, highly commended by the Governor of the Cape of Good Hope.

The year after his return Captain Jervois (as he now was) assumed command of a company of sappers and miners which he took with him in 1852 to Alderney whither he had been sent to plan and supervise the construction of the system of forts intended as protection for the great naval base at Braye whereby the island was being converted into 'the Gibraltar of the Channel'. These defence works aroused considerable interest far and wide and even Queen Victoria herself, together with the Prince Consort, paid a visit of inspection in August 1854. In accordance with the custom of such occasions, Jervois was awarded a brevet majority to mark the auspicious event.

In connection with these fortifications the comments made by Victor Coysh (q.v.) in his book, *Alderney*, are illuminating. He remarks that Jervois 'allowed his artistic taste to get the better of strictly military needs at times. In consequence, one finds medieval embellishments, such as arrow slits and machicolations, battlements and moats, more in keeping with the defences of Elizabeth I than those of Victoria. The finest quality dressed stone was used and care was taken to use stone of different shades, thus vastly improving the appearance of the forts. The setting, of course, further enhanced their appearance. In fact, the military architect had the time of his life in Alderney!'

Whether the architect had the time of his life or not, his display of castellar artistry in Alderney made a good impression and in 1856 Major Jervois became Assistant Inspector-General of Fortifi-cations at the War Office. In 1857 (when Anglo-French relations were strained following the discovery that the explosives in the bomb thrown by Orsini at Napoleon III were made in England) he was entrusted with preparing plans for the defence of London, and in 1859 he became Secretary to the Royal Commission on the Defences of the United Kingdom.

A triumphant 30-year period ensued. In 1863 Lieutenant-Colonel Jervois became a Companion of the Order of the Bath and was also sent to North America to report on defences in Canada and Bermuda. Although his recommendation that iron be used in fortifications encountered considerable opposition, Jervois successfully persisted in his advocacy of this hitherto unthought-of method and after several years in the New World went to India in 1871 and 1872 to advise on defences in the sub-continent. Made Knight-Commander of the Order of St Michael and St George in 1874, Colonel Jervois was in 1875 appointed Governor of the Straits Settlements, where he rapidly quelled unrest in Perak as well as submitting the report on which the defences of Singapore were based. Sent to advise the Australian colonies regarding defensive dispositions in 1877, Major-General Jervois was in 1878 made a Knight Grand Cross of the Order of St Michael and St George and then from 1882 to 1889, with the rank of Lieutenant-General, held office as an extremely popular Governor of New Zealand. Finally, after his return to the United Kingdom, he was in 1893 appointed Colonel-Commandant of the Royal Engineers. Sir William Jervois died at Virginia Water in 1897.

JOHN, KING OF ENGLAND, LORD OF IRELAND, DUKE OF NORMANDY AND AQUITAINE, COUNT OF ANJOU (1167-1216). *The bestower of insular constitutional privileges*. Among students of English history there have of recent years been a number of attempts to rehabilitate this monarch, who traditionally has been vilified by such writers. As far as the Channel Isles are concerned, however, no such exculpation is necessary, as it has long been commonly accepted that in his dealings with them (to which alone this entry has reference) King John appears in a distinctly favourable light, manifesting wisdom and far-seeing diplomacy in his willingness to accord local privileges as a fair price for securing the loyalty of the people in what had become an extremely valuable part of his domains.

His defeat on the Norman mainland brought home to John the essential truth that the situation of St Peter-Port roadstead on the main route to his remaining possessions in Gascony rendered vital the security of the Channel Isles. He therefore made particularly vigorous military efforts to dislodge Philip Augustus from the archipelago in a struggle between 1204 and 1206 during which the French king seized it at least once and most likely twice. Having finally emerged vitorious from this tussle, John realised that to ensure the permanent retention of the islands the attitude of the inhabitants was crucial and that they accordingly would have to be placated to the fullest possible extent. Hitherto the islands had been connected with mainland Normandy by a chain forged of four main links — tenurial, economic, ecclesiastical and administrative — and in regard to each of these links the king, so as to avoid straining the islanders' allegiance, sought to follow whenever possible a policy of continuity modified by no more than minor safeguards.

As far as the tenurial link was concerned John had little choice, a complete rupture being rendered inevitable by the logic of events. During the period of débâcle in continental Normandy the islands were in chaos, rent by factional feuds, not only between rival claimants to properties, but also between the supporters of John and those of Philip Augustus, to whom allegiance had been given by no less than 14 fief holders with land in what later became the Bailiwick of Guernsey. Consequently, although the islanders after their initial ambivalence ultimately threw in their lot with him — doubtless influenced by local leaders who saw a chance of gaining independence from their feudal superiors on the Norman mainland — John took no chances, but seized hostages from leading local families and expropriated his opponents' holdings in the islands. Only after several years had passed without any further overt acts of treachery on their part did John seem to grow more confident about the dependability of the islanders — especially after they had helped in the ejection in 1214 from Sark of Eustace the Monk (q.v.). Thus, when he released his hostages subsequent to this operation, he specified that he did so 'because we trust fully in your loyalty'.

On the economic level John made no attempt to sever the links with the mainland, to which fresh and salted fish, livestock and sundry animal products were normally exported and from which were imported millstones, timber, wine and salt. He did, however, impose duties on the exports

from the islands: not as a punitive measure but primarily to ensure adequate supplies for the garrison which fear of Philip Augustus obliged him to maintain in the archipelago.

Ecclesiastically the links between insular and continental Normandy were very strong indeed, there being no less than 12 Norman religious foundations with holdings in what is now the Bailiwick of Guernsey, of which those of Mont St Michel were the most extensive and widespread. Thus in the monastic sphere mainland influence was paramount. Furthermore, the islands formed part of the Diocese of Coutances (Archdeaconry of Bauptois).

It was plain that the loyalty of the islanders towards the Norman church was unwavering; and John recognised this fact, acquiescing in the mainland church's retention of its insular holdings — and in the continuance of the spiritual jurisdiction of the Bishop of Coutances: an accommodation that persisted until the reign of Elizabeth I. Thus, although the king confiscated Norman ecclesiastical holdings for a short while, he not only restored them but also resumed payments to the mainland religious houses from his 'ducal' revenues in the islands: and continued them even after he had become an excommunicate!

On the administrative plane the king was also most conciliatory, seeking as far as possible to maintain the '*status quo ante bellum*' refraining from any annexation of the islands, but regarding them as part of the royal domain outside the realm and appointing Philippe d'Aubigny (q.v.) as warden to administer the archipelago as a 'royal peculiar' on his behalf. In so doing John in fact laid the foundations of the islands' political status, as the device of treating them as a possession of the King of England, but separate and distinct from his Kingdom of England, rendered their relationship with England comparable to that between Hanover and the United Kingdom in the period 1714 to 1837 — a principality united with another in the person of the prince only. This relationship has persisted, with the Lieutenant-Governor as the modern-day counterpart of the Warden.

A potent means of preserving loyalty is to accord judicial autonomy. An enquiry conducted in 1248 by the Warden (Drew de Barentin) revealed that John had allegedly 'instituted twelve sworn Coroners to keep the pleas and rights pertaining to the Crown'. From this statement stemmed the belief that the islands were indebted to John for the original appointment of Jurats: but more recent investigation has shown it to be highly probable that the king in fact adapted an earlier institution to new needs. Nevertheless the fact remains that the free election by the people of judges and magistrates chosen from among themselves has been prized from antiquity and it matters little whether John inaugurated the arrangement or sponsored its continuance and development: either way he was placing the responsibility of judicial office in the hands of local dignitaries and thus in the long run fostering the attainment of autonomy.

In view of all these considerations, small wonder it is that King John, regarded in England as an oppressor from whom concessions had to be wrung by force of arms, has over the years been seen in the islands in the guise of a realist and a benefactor.

JONES, BARRY CUTHBERT (1893–1981). *The distinguished actor-manager of Le Catioroc.* Born on 6 March 1893, to Amelia Hammond (*née* Robilliard), the wife of William John Jones (soap merchant), and educated at Elizabeth College, Barry Jones had just arrived at his majority when the First World War broke out. He immediately offered himself for military service, initially in the Royal Guernsey Light Infantry and subsequently in the Royal Irish Fusiliers — and did not return to civilian life until February 1921. At one point in the conflict he commanded a platoon of Serquiais, making him very popular in later years in Sark — where *Appointment with Venus* (in which he appeared) — was filmed.

Jones was no sooner out of the army than behind the footlights, making his first stage appearance on 29 March 1921 at the Grand Theatre in Leeds, where he took the part of the Clerk of the Court in the production of Sir Frank Benson's company of *The Merchant of Venice.* Later the same year he went to the U.S.A., where his first New York appearance took place in 1924; so that Barry Jones had the somewhat unusual experience for a British actor of treading the

boards on Broadway before having been seen on the West End stage.

In 1928 Jones formed a partnership with Maurice Colbourne, with whom he toured Canada and the U.S.A. until 1931. In this latter year the partners re-crossed the Atlantic and once back in Britain undertook the management of the Ambassadors' Theatre, where the Guernsey actor · at last — made his first London appearance. On his return from the New World Jones extended and improved the cottage (a former watch house) he had acquired in 1923 at Le Catioroc and to which he thenceforth often returned to relax and recuperate from the stresses of a busy actor-manager's life, filling it with curios collected far and wide. Noteworthy among the many parts played by Barry Jones during the thirties was the title rôle in the successful West End production, *Charles the King.*

On the outbreak of the Second World War this accomplished actor set out on a tour of Canada under the auspices of the British Council. Then in 1941 he toured the U.S.A. with Gertrude Lawrence to raise funds for British War Charities. Before the year was out, however, Barry Jones forsook the stage to don uniform for the rest of the war; first becoming a special constable in London and a twelvemonth later (at the end of 1942) joining the Royal Naval Volunteer Reserve — although by now nearly 50 years old. Discharged from the R.N.V.R. in October 1945, this patriotic islander still continued making himself available for National Service, working with E.N.S.A. until the end of 1946 and devoting himself to the entertainment of the troops stationed in Austria, Italy and Germany.

From 1950 onwards Jones supplemented his stage work by embarking on additional careers in radio plays and films and later in television plays. In 1968 and by now 75 years of age, this grand old man of the theatre retired to his retreat at Le Catioroc, spending the evening of his life back in his much-loved native isle and dying there in 1981.

K

KELLETT-SMITH, DR. STANLEY KIRBY, M.R.C.S., L.R.C.P. (1916–   ). *The historian of Herm and Jethou.* Born in Eastbourne in November 1916 and educated at Cheltenham College,

Stanley Kellett-Smith in 1933 entered St Thomas's Hospital as a medical student. Qualifying during the midst of the Second World War, he was commissioned in the Royal Army Medical Corps in 1942 and saw service in the United Kingdom, Algeria, Tunisia and Greece before leaving the Army with the rank of Major in 1945.

In 1946 Dr. Kellett-Smith came to Guernsey, taking up a practice in which he remained until 1975. In 1976 he retired to Glategny Esplanade. We have it on impeccable authority that 'they that be whole need not a physician, but they that are sick'. During his years in Guernsey, however, his massive contribution to insular historical research gave the 'whole' as such cause as the sick to be thankful to this particular physician. This contribution was especially noteworthy in the case of Herm and Jethou, about which Dr. Kellett-Smith is justifiably recognised as a peerless authority. Years of painstaking investigation are distilled in his typescript notes on these twin islands available for consultation by all and sundry in the Priaulx Library (of the council of which he became a prominent member). In addition to these notes the student has also been provided with lucid and well-researched articles on 'Quarrying and Mining in Herm and Jethou' (which appeared in the 1961 *Transactions* of La Société Guernesiaise) and 'Restauld of Jethou' (in the same publication for 1964). A further miscellany of articles on these two islands may also be seen in various numbers of the Guernsey Society's *Review* between 1961 and 1980. Outstanding among these is the pair of monographs (in the Spring and Summer 1980 numbers) dealing with those two contrasting 19th century moulders of Herm's

destiny — Lieutenant-Colonel the Honourable John Lindsay and Jonathan Duncan (qq.v.).

Even those not particularly interested in Herm and Jethou will find themselves indebted to Dr. Kellett-Smith if they seek information on the ancient history of the entire Bailiwick. His scholarly 'Old Names of the Channel Islands' (which appeared in La Société's *Transactions* for 1962) was reinforced by 'Further Observations on Channel Islands Names with Particular Reference to the Helgi Lays' (same publication 1968). Sandwiched between these two there came, with the publication of 'The Corsican Plaque' in 1963, a critical and cogently argued appraisal of the arguments for and against regarding Basiel, son of Turbel (q.v.*), as the first identified Guernseymen. Then, moving right across the ages to the 19th century, one finds the masterful article on 'The Guernsey Cholera Epidemic of 1832', which appeared in the 1980 *Transactions*.

Not allowing his services to stop at the written word, Dr. Kellett-Smith always proved generous with verbal and personal advice to anyone seeking help to further his or her investigations or projected publications. The word 'doctor' comes from *doctus*, the past participle of the Latin *docere*: 'to teach'. The implications of this derivation apply with singular aptness to this asclepiad, the value of whose educational contributions on the historical plane it would be hard to exaggerate. Most deservedly did he earn the gratitude of the island of his adoption.

L

LAINÉ, SIR ABRAHAM JAMES, K.C.I.E. (1876–1948). *A distinguished Guernseyman of principle and honour — and a passive resister of the highest order.* Born on 26 August 1876 to Rachel (*née* Mahy), the wife of Abraham Lainé, Abraham *fils* was educated at Elizabeth College from 1889 to 1895, whence he went up to Oxford (Pembroke), winning a Goldsmiths' Exhibition in 1896 and gaining honours in Moderations in 1899.

On coming down from the University Lainé entered the Indian Civil Service with his appointment as Assistant Magistrate and Collector in Bengal in 1900, four years later being transferred thence to Assam with the rank of District Commissioner. A steady climb up the ladder of advancement saw him Assistant Commissioner in 1912, Deputy Commissioner in 1915 and Second

Secretary to the Government of Assam in 1922. In the same year he became a member of Assam's Legislative Council, remaining as such until 1930 when he was promoted to the grade of Chief Secretary to the Government of Assam, made a Companion of the Order of the Indian Empire, and appointed a Member of the Assam Executive Council. This membership he retained until 1935 when he was made a Knight Commander of the Most Eminent Order of the Indian Empire and became Acting Governor of Assam. He did not, however, retain this post for very long as he retired later the same year, being by them 59 years of age.

Returning to Guernsey, Sir Abraham was elected a Jurat of the Royal Court in 1938, becoming also President of the States Ancient Monuments Committee. In the same year he was appointed President of the Essential Commodities Committee on its formation as the war clouds gathered. Two years later, as enemy occupation loomed, Sir Ambrose Sherwill (q.v.) chose him as Vice-President of the Controlling Committee and also its member responsible for food supplies. His wisdom and wide experience proved invaluable in both capacities. The Germans regarded him as a man to be reckoned with and on two notable occasions he showed that no fear of the occupying power would deter him if he felt that a vital principle was at stake.

The first of these occasions is recounted by Sir Ambrose Sherwill in his unpublished memoirs. On 23 October 1940, the Royal Court registered the German Military Administration's anti-Jewish measures, nearly all Jurats consenting thereto in the mistaken belief that no Jewish persons were left in the Bailiwick. One voice, however, spoke out in the name of humanity and decency. Sir Ambrose wrote, 'The honour of refusing to concur in its registration fell to Sir Abraham Lainé who, when called on as a Jurat to vote on the matter, openly and categorically refused his assent and stated his grave objections to such a measure. This courageous act of his should never be forgotten.'

The second occasion arose when Sir Abraham, as President of the Essential Commodities Committee, protested vehemently against the instructions emanating from the Feldkommandantur that the whores in the German Army brothels should be given extra rations, regarding such a requirement as rank injustice. Although overruled, Sir Abraham had nevertheless, once again, made a stand in the name of fair play and civilised standards of conduct. Sir Abraham's home of Le Gardinet in the Castel having been requisitioned by the Germans, he moved to 'Thistlewood', Choisi, St Peter-Port, remaining there after the Liberation. Here this Guernseyman of mettle and nobility of spirit died on 22 February 1948.

LANYON, HUBERT HENRY (1903–1981). *Macte virtute*. See *Underground Resistance Heroes of the Second World War*.

LEALE, REVEREND SIR JOHN (1892–1969). *A Daniel in the lions' den!* Born on 14 January 1892, to Amelia Susan (*née* Bird), the wife of John Leale of Le Grand Pont, and thus into a family owning a well-known hardware business in St Sampson's, John Leale was educated at Elizabeth College, subsequently going up to Cambridge (Jesus). Indifferent health precluded his participation in the First World War (he was invalided out

of the Militia after a short spell of service) and he entered the Methodist Ministry. After his ordination at that church's Manchester Conference in 1918 he subsequently served at Wesley Hall, Great Ancoat Street, Manchester, remaining in England until his mid-thirties.

This man of ascetic temperament returned to Guernsey in 1928 on the death of his father and rapidly made his mark. By 1934 he achieved the distinction (at the age of 42) of being appointed a Jurat; and when enemy occupation was imminent it was Leale who suggested the formation of the Controlling Committee as a more flexible organ than the States for day-to-day dealings with the Germans. Originally its member responsible for Economics and Finance, he became its President after the Feldkommandant's announcement on 24 December 1940 banning Ambrose Sherwill (q.v.) from all public office because of his involvement in the episode of the British agents Hubert Nicolle and James Symes (qq.v.).

Taking absolute integrity and unlimited patience as his watchwords in the responsible and delicate position in which he found himself, Jurat Leale pursued through thick and thin a policy of maintaining correct relations with the occupying power. Consequently he deprecated activities such as running an underground newspaper or smuggling out intelligence about German dispositions – and after the war was over commented on the failure to honour those who had defied the enemy in such fashion by saying, 'It might be difficult for a Government which is a signatory to the Hague Convention to recommend honours for those who broke the Convention'.

In his 'Report on Five Years of German Occupation', submitted to the States on 23 May 1945, Leale shrugged off criticism by the riposte, 'It's easy to talk big when you have no responsibilities on your shoulders'. Moreover, he dismissed the practicability of subversive action, remarking, 'Guernsey was in fact an impossible place in which to indulge in underground activities. Any attempt on these lines brought retribution on the population and it was generally realised that getting other people into trouble is a doubtful way of displaying one's patriotism'. Elsewhere in his account of his stewardship he made clear beyond all doubt his own concept of the type of demeanour appropriate to the circumstances by stating quite frankly – 'One of our main functions was to soften the impact of German Orders when they were harsh'. Consequently he made no bones about the fact that 'we espoused the Hague Convention "for better, for worse, for richer, for poorer, in sickness and in health" ' — while, towards the end of the same speech he claimed, 'Our behaviour gave them no cause for severity'.

In the Honours List published on 12 December 1945, 'The Rev. John Leale, Jurat of the Royal Court' was granted a knighthood in recognition of 'services during the enemy occupation of the islands'. With the implementation of the Reform Law in 1948 he became a Conseiller and in 1953 was appointed Lieutenant-Bailiff: a post he retained until 1967 when he reached the age of 75. In 1960 Sir John was also appointed Acting President of the States and in this position too he remained until reaching the age limit. Sir John Leale did not long survive retirement from public life, dying aged 77 in July 1969.

LEGG, ERNEST (1903–1972). *Macte virtute*. See *Underground Resistance Heroes of the Second World War*.

LEIGHTON, SIR THOMAS (*c.*1528–1610). *A doughty but dubious Elizabethan; despotic or dutiful?* Thomas Leighton was born in Shropshire to Jocosa, wife of John Leighton of Wattlesborough Esquire, who, after bearing her husband six daughters, was delivered of three sons in succession. Of these Thomas was the second. As his elder brother Edward is variously recorded as being either five or seven years of age at the time of their father John's death in 1532, the birth of Guernsey's future governor must have fallen at some point in the period 1526–30 — and most likely 1528–29 (years which would allow for Edward being only five at John's death and also leave time for the birth of the third son, Charles, prior to his father's demise). Thomas married Elizabeth Knollys (sometimes referred to as Cecilia) who, born in 1542, was through her maternal grand-mother Mary Carey *née* Boleyn) the great-niece of Anne Boleyn and thus first cousin once removed to Elizabeth I, to whom she was a Maid of Honour. By her he had a son (Thomas) and a daughter (Elizabeth).

It has been alleged that Leighton was involved in the 1554 Wyatt Plot against Mary I, but his connection with this ill-starred venture cannot have been more than tenuous and his very survival points to his having extricated himself well before the fatal *dénouement*. What is certain is that he achieved great distinction in the French War of 1562–63, breaking through with great daring to invested Rouen, of the defence of which he and his pikemen were thereafter the mainstay. Wounded and taken prisoner when the town

finally fell, the French out of regard for his valour exchanged him early in 1563; whereupon he participated in Warwick's desperate defence of Le Havre, which ultimately failed as the garrison fell victim to the plague faster than reinforcements could be poured in to replace the dead.

Thomas Leighton landed in Guernsey to assume office as Governor on Whit Sunday (14 May) 1570 and was appalled at the weak and unsatisfactory nature of the defences, which were 'far owte of good order', while the Militia was so ill-equipped 'as in my Lyffe I never saw worse'. He addressed himself particularly to strengthening Castle Cornet and eventually, after persistent efforts over a quarter of a century, he succeeded (working with the eminent military engineer Paul Ivy) in building an outer sheath around the old fortress and incorporating therein polygonal bastions — at that time the very latest technique in castellar construction. Defraying the enormous expense thus incurred ultimately led to the Governor becoming embroiled with the local hierarchy on the issues of royal revenue, the nature of local law and the status of neutrality. Leighton's policy was to finance re-fortification by levying a duty on all goods (foreign or not) arriving in foreign ships. He obtained a Royal Warrant in 1571 to authorise his adopting this course of action, and the Privy Council upheld him despite the protests of merchants (both in England and in Guernsey) whose pockets were thereby depleted.

Leighton, as an ardent Puritan, started off with the advantage of being in tune with Guernsey's Calvinist Establishment, and as a result enjoyed an initial honeymoon period in his relationships with the insular authorities. These placid years were interrupted by two lengthy absences from the island. Regarded as especially well informed on French affairs, he was sent to France on special embassies in 1574 and 1578. It was after the completion of the latter assignment that the Governor found himself for the first time up against serious trouble in Guernsey. He was to learn that religious accord availed him little when the Guernesiais felt that their ancient privileges were under threat. Popular disturbances in 1578 obliged the Bailiff and Jurats to take refuge in Castle Cornet. As a result they applied to the Privy Council for a Commission 'to bring the people to better obedience'. At the same time, some other Guernsey people appeared before the Privy Council alleging that they were wronged touching their liberties and the administration of justice. Accordingly a Royal Commission was appointed (including Leighton in its membership) to examine the whole question of the respective powers of the Royal Court and the Governor and also 'defects touching the jurisdiction of the Bailiff and Jurats'.

In the event the self-same Bailiff and Jurats (possibly in the hope of thereby obtaining a reduction in the dues levied by the Governor) joined forces with the complainants, testifying to the Commission that Leighton was to blame for all disaffection, by misgoverning tyranically, imprisoning without trial and pressing Guernsey-men to take ship against pirates in spite of their privileges exempting them from service outside the island. These representations notwithstanding, the Privy Council ruled in Leighton's favour, forbidding the Bailiff and Jurats 'to intermeddle in anything touching Her Majesty's rights'. When unrest continued Leighton, claiming that the fundamental cause of resentment was his action in putting a stop to trade between the Guerne-siais and the pirates, sought the removal of the main trouble-makers — and ultimately obtained the dismissal of the bailiff (William de Beauvoir), his brother (a Jurat) and Nicholas Martin (another Jurat). It seems that basically the disturbances stemmed from distress caused by the decline of trade resulting from the Wars of Religion in France. Hence — in all probability — the anxiety to trade with pirates: strange conduct from God-fearing Calvinists!

Leighton's triumph over William de Beauvoir, although clinched by the installation as Bailiff of his nephew, Thomas Wigmore, was not to prove the end of his troubles. The dust had not yet settled when he found himself at loggerheads with Guernsey's ecclesiastical establishment. An Order-in-Council of 1581 provided that probate and the administration of the revenues of vacant benefices should be ordered by the Bishop of Winchester. In the light of this, the bishop appointed the Procureur — Louis de Vic (q.v.) — as his commissary to deal with wills and other ecclesiastical business. Outraged by this episcopal intrusion into their Presbyterian establishment, the ministers in 1582 brought trumped-up charges against de Vic. Ardent Calvinist though he was, this shameful exhibition of 'malice and all uncharitableness' was too much for the Governor, who stood by de Vic, asking Walsingham to deal with the matter — which ended with de Vic being vindicated. Upon de Vic's acquittal Nicolas Baudouin (q.v.), the 'founder' of Guernsey Calvinism, professed fear for his life and sailed for England in 1583. On the recommendation of Walsingham he took a living in Jersey in 1584. The following year (1585) three other ministers also left for Jersey after a search of their houses ordered by Leighton. The clergy had been brought to heel.

Although Leighton thus upheld the power of the Crown against ecclesiastical defiance (which was never repeated for the rest of his term of office), yet within five years he was once more embroiled with the Royal Court. The occasion for the dispute occurred in 1586 when the Governor seized four French ships in St Peter-Port, believing them to have Spanish goods on board. The Royal Court immediately declared the seizure invalid on the grounds of Guernsey's neutrality. Leighton, however, declined to release the ships, and the Court appealed to the Privy Council. The Council upheld the Court's ruling and instructed Leighton that no such arrest should again be made to the prejudice of the island's privileges. At this juncture, however, Leighton complained to the Privy Council that the Bailiff (his own nephew Thomas Wigmore) and the Jurats had taken advantage of the dispute to levy slanderous charges of tyranny against him — and the upshot was that Wigmore and the Jurats were summoned to London in 1587. To present the case for the Governor the Queen's Procureur, Louis de Vic, also went to London where, the accused having hired two men to murder him, he was attacked in Westminster and left for dead, but recovered. As a consequence the Bailiff and the Jurats were consigned to the Marshalsea, de Vic's chief assailand (a scoundrel by the name of Rousewell) was set in the pillory in Guernsey and de Vic himself was appointed as the new Bailiff. Leighton was vindicated and triumphant.

The instalation of the dependable de Vic as Bailiff ensured greater stability and, furthermore, the Governor was away from Guernsey for prolonged periods between 1587 and 1595. When the Armada threat loomed he was sent to Hampshire and Dorset and later to the east coast of England as one of the commissioners appointed to supervise local defence arrangements and to advise Lords-Lieutenant. He then took part in a great conference with Burleigh, Raleigh and others, to consider general defence strategy — and when the crisis came in July Leighton and Sir John Norris were made Joint Chiefs of Staff to Leicester as Commander of the Army at Tilbury. In recognition of these services Elizabeth I bestowed the honour of knighthood upon Guernsey's Governor. In 1591 a further call on his services led to another absence, this time until 1595. He was sent as adviser to the Earl of Essex, who had taken command of the English army sent to Normandy in support of Henri de Navarre during its struggle for the French throne.

In 1597, however, fresh troubles arose. Taking umbrage at an alleged remark by Nicholas Carey that when the queen died he would pull the Governor by his ears out of Castle Cornet, Sir Thomas reported the matter to the court — and was so infuriated when Carey was acquitted that he submitted to the Privy Council that 'these Jurats ought to be punished so as to learn them to take a greater regard in matters that concern Her Majesty'. Nine Jurats were sent to London, of whom three old adversaries of the Governor (Nicolas Martin, William de Beauvoir and Jean Effard) were detained. Their accusations against Leighton were found by the Privy Council to be malicious and defamatory, and they were required to acknowledge this in writing before the Council and also in a public assembly in the island.

Although Sir Thomas had finally triumphed in his various confrontations with the island's establishment, his position was challenged anew after the accession of James I when the conclusion of peace with Spain and the end of the French Wars of Religion (by reducing the islands' importance as frontier fortresses and thereby removing the urgent necessity of the Governor's paramountcy) favoured a more assertive attitude on the part of the local hierarchy. The upshot was that two petitions were forwarded to the king (in 1604 and 1607), and the obvious intensity of insular dissatisfaction led the Privy Council to appoint a Commission, whose recommendations issued in an Order-in-Council in 1608. This Order-in-Council restricted the power of the Governor and enhanced the position of the Royal Court and of the States. The Governor's prerogative was circumscribed by his being required to consult the Royal Court before taking actions of an administrative nature previously regarded as being unquestionably within his competence. In his declining years Leighton was suffering the fate of Ozymandias!

The conventional wisdom over the years has regarded Sir Thomas Leighton as an autocratic and oppressive Governor who disregarded insular liberties and kept the people down by main force. The hard fact of the matter is that he sought to extract money from local pockets — the very thing that had brought endless trouble to his precedessor, Sir Frances Chamberlayne (q.v.). 'Who steals my purse, steals trash' announced Iago — but he was no Guernseyman, and to deny the

Guernseyman's possession of an acute money sense is to fly in the face of facts. Moreover, local opinion saw no sufficient reason for financial sacrifice to pay for fortification. The entire archipelago had enjoyed neutral status for a century and the internationally-minded Guernsiais saw in this neutrality their best protection and 'wished rather to be friends of all than enemies of any'. This in fact was the crux of the matter, leading Leighton as a Shropshire-born English patriot afflicted by the xenophobia endemic in Albion, to stigmatize the Norman islanders with their cosmopolitan outlook as 'a people cowardly in their courage and somewhat too kind to the French' and to promise that 'I will keep them Her Highness' subjects *maugre* their hearts'. Loyal to the trust reposed in him by his sovereign, bluff Sir Thomas lacked tact and tried to drive Guernseymen rather than lead them, forgetting that he was dealing with Donkeys! Maybe his shade four centuries later was hovering over the Duke of Edinburgh when His Royal Highness remarked to the Serquiais, 'I bet the Germans had their work cut out keeping you lot in order!'

LEVRIER, JACQUES (died 1752) and LEVRIER, PIERRE (died after 1796). *Two mysterious clerical brothers, one of whom championed colonial independence and raised the Clameur de Haro in the House of God.* In Sark's old cemetery adjoining that island's Methodist church there stands a defaced tombstone which reads:

'Ici gissent les corps du Rev. M. Jaques Levrier Ministre de cette isle décédé le 16 . . . de Dame Magdelaine . . . son epouse décédée le 22 . . . de Pierre Levrier leur fils décédé le 19 . . . Comme aussi celui de Dame Marie Papot mère du dit M. Levrier décédée le 22 Avril 1761.'

'Jaques (sic) Levrier Ministre de cette isle' was privately ordained deacon, with a further ordination as priest following immediately afterwards on 29 December 1751, by the Bishop of Winchester (the Right Reverend Benjamin Hoadley, D.D., a celebrated controversialist who, left a cripple after illness in youth, was obliged to preach in a kneeling posture for the rest of his days). An ordination in 1751 would imply birth c. 1727–28, especially as his brother Pierre was old enough to become Vicar of Sark in 1752 and was also still alive in 1796, so that he seems likely to have been born in the late 1720s: a consideration which suggests a birth of proximate date for Jacques.

The extremely rare telescoping of the two ordinations: the private nature of the ceremony; and the fact that it occurred most unusually in the middle of the Christmas season, rather than being delayed until the far more customary Petertide since early Advent had been missed, all points to the proceedings being regarded as an emergency. The records also indicate that on the very same day the new priest was licensed to officiate in the island of Sark and herein lies a clue as to the reason for the hurry. The Seigneur of Sark, Daniel le Pelley, was presumably in urgent need of a replacement for the new incumbent's predecessor, the Reverend Vital Privat, and it is a reasonable assumption that representations had been made to the Bishop via the Dean of Guernsey (the Very Reverend John le Mesurier) for the ordination of the Seigneur's nominee with all possible speed, so as to fill the vacancy in the island's living with the minimum delay. The qualifications on the part of Levrier which led Daniel le Pelley to make this particular choice remain obscure, as all that is known about this appointee's background is the purely negative information that he is not listed in *Alumni Cantabriensis* or *Alumni Oxoniensis*: a revelation which is hardly surprising in the case of a Frenchman!

Accompanied by his wife and son — and most likely his mother and brother too — the new Vicar of Sark lost no time in taking up his duties and fate may well have decreed that one of the first of these would be to conduct a funeral, as Daniel le Pelley died on the morrow of Jacques Levrier's arrival, leaving his 18-year-old son Pierre as the new Seigneur. The man of God's turn to meet his Maker was soon to come as well, a harsh destiny bringing the incumbent to the grave within a few weeks of his Seigneur, with his wife Magdelaine and his son Pierre following within the next decade — at any rate before the demise in April 1761 of his mother Marie (*née* Papot), whose name appears last on the epitaph. It should be borne in mind, however, that in the absence of concrete evidence as to precise dates, the sequence here postulated is no more than conjectural and it is of course possible that the priest might have predeceased his patron. The only certainty is that both were dead before Spring was out.

At this juncture Jacques' brother Pierre (after whom his son had presumably been named) contrived to obtain appointment to the island living left empty by this death in the family. How Pierre came to be sacerdotally qualified is not clear. Although when he was indicted in 1794 he

was described in the Acts of the Guernsey Ecclesiastical Court as 'a Priest or Minister in Holy Orders of the Anglican Church', the hard fact is that no record of his ordination exists in the Winchester Diocesan Archives — nor for that matter in those of any other diocese south of the Thames. It is true that occasionally island livings were filled by apostate Roman Catholic clergy — such as Louis Napoleon Seichan (q.v.) 150 years later — who stood in no need of Anglican ordination, being already possessed of orders recognised as valid by the Church of England; but this was obviously not so with Jacques Levrier, who sought and obtained Anglican ordination (and was married to boot), so that the presumption must therefore be against such being the case with his brother either. It could, however, be relevant to remember that during the 18th century the wide umbrella of the Church of of England sheltered several Huguenot conventicles, with special provision applying whereby Calvinist clergy lacking episcopal ordination were permitted to minister to these congregations provided they received the sanction of the bishop in whose diocese they were geographically located. Bearing in mind Sark's strong Calvinist traditions — the legacy of a century's sway held by Brévint *père et fils* (qq.v.) — and the unenthusiastic attitude of the Serquiais towards even the markedly evangelical brand of Anglicanism which Sir Philippe de Carteret (q.v.) had introduced in 1675, it is not beyond the bounds of possibility that Pierre could have been a Pastor of l'Eglise Reformée de France who obtained episcopal authorisation to officiate in what was virtually a Huguenot congregation *de facto*, even if Anglican *de jure*. In this connection it is significant to note that the curate referred to in a later paragraph is described as 'ordained in France', 'known by several French Ministers in London' and 'permitted to read the prayers by the Reverend Father in God the Bishop of London': a delineation suspiciously suggestive of an 'authorised Huguenot'. Furthermore, if Daniel le Pelley did indeed outlive Jacques Levrier the likelihood of such indulgence being extended to Pierre is increased, as the representations of a distraught and very sick Seigneur, urging the claims of a cleric — the brother moreover of his deceased predecessor — who was available but technically debarred from assuming office, might well have induced Dr. Hoadly to tolerate the irregularity implicit in the appointment requested.

Whatever the new incumbent's credentials might have been, however, relationships between him and Elizabeth le Pelley (who, as the mother of the new Seigneur, operated as Dame de Sercq during her son's minority) rapidly proved to be remarkably reminiscent of those between Mrs. Proudie and Obadiah Slope in *Barchester Towers*, speedily degenerating from initial patronage to subsequent implacable hostility. Construing Pierre Levrier's behaviour as unbecoming of a clerk in holy orders, La Dame promptly dismissed him — only to find that the vicar, supported by his congregation, refused to leave. At this Elizabeth le Pelley locked both pastor and flock out of the annexe at Le Manoir which did duty as a church. It is plain that things had come to this pass by October 1752, as on the 25th of that month Philippe Dumaresq, the tenant of Le Clos de Dixcart, brought an action in the Island Court against La Dame for closing the footpath from Dixcart Valley used by the worshippers on their way to services. La Dame refused to budge and by her intransigence imposed on Sark what effectively amounted to an Interdict — a state of affairs which lasted for three years. As a result of this the inhabitants (who had to cross over to Guernsey to get married) complained to the Dean, who thereupon summoned Elizabeth *veuve* le Pelley to attend his court to justify her conduct on pain of excommunication. La Dame (who by her actions had virtually excommunicated herself in any case) refused to go, holding that the building used for worship was her private property which she was entitled to lock up if she so wished — and further maintaining that the minister was the personal chaplain of the Seigneur and thus held office at the Seigneur's pleasure.

In 1755 Pierre le Pelley came of age and John le Mesurier returned to the attack, asserting his authority as Dean and ordering the Seigneur, on pain of 'excommunication majeure', to arrange for Divine Service to be performed in Sark forthwith. Bowing to the storm, Pierre invited François Guillaume Durand, rector of St Sampson's and vicar of the Vale, to come and conduct Divine Worship in the island. This was done on 14 December 1755, but half-way through the service Levrier rushed into the building and raised the *Clameur de Haro*, thereby stopping the proceedings and automatically bringing the whole matter within the jurisdiction of the Royal Court of Guernsey. The Royal Court vindicated Levrier on the grounds that the Seigneur's possession of the advowson of the living did not carry with it the right of dismissal. The incumbent's victory, however, proved to be a Pyrrhic one, as the following year the Seigneur, egged on by his

mother, prevailed upon the Sénéchal to declare Levrier *persona non grata* and to issue an order to the Prévôt and Connétable to deport him from the island for causing a public mischief! There is no evidence of the victim of what seems a monstrous injustice (and which apparently brought no legal reprisals) making any further efforts to defend himself. Accepting his expulsion with apparent docility, he quietly left and temporarily disappeared from view.

Two years later Levrier re-emerged. On 1 April 1758, following the resignation of Andrew Migault, he was presented to the livings of the Forest and Torteval, his formal admission and institution ensuing on the 4th of the same month. Retaining this cure of souls for several years, he applied to the new Bishop of Winchester (the Right Reverend John Thomas, D.D.) on 28 August 1761, to authorise the appointment of Jean-Baptiste de la Noye as curate to assist him (and describing him in the terms referred to above), but during 1765 he vanished. On 15 September 1785, Lieutenant-Colonel William Brown (the Lieutenant-Governor) wrote to the Governor (Field-Marshal the Lord Amherst), reporting that 'Piter Levrier' (as he had signed himself in his letter to the bishop asking for a curate) had been absent from the parishes in his charge for 20 years, adding that it was thought he had gone to America, where he had reputedly fought on the side of the colonists against the British in the War of Independence. On 23 September Amherst passed on this information to the bishop (by then Dr. Brownlow North), who replied on 25 September by saying that a suit should be brought against Levrier if his deprivation was required, and that careful enquiries should be made to ascertain whether he had ever visited Guernsey, and if he had provided for his parishioners by paying a curate to officiate during his absence. Finally, after an incredibly long additional delay of almost 11 years, a letter dated 22 June 1796, informed the bishop that sentence of deprivation had been pronounced after a year's suspension, and requested episcopal ratification thereof. Proceedings in Guernsey's Ecclesiastical Court against this enigmatic cleric (plus the subsequent year's suspension) had in fact dragged on from 3 November 1794 to 17 June 1796, with the inferential corollary that the 'careful enquiries' advocated by the bishop had been so prolonged as to take up the period September 1785 to November 1794.

There is no further sight of this extraordinary man after this point. Why he betook himself to the New World is a mystery — but the conclusion seems inescapable that he must have remained for the rest of his days in what had become the United States of America.

LE LIÈVRE, PETER (1812-1878). *The versatile genius of Hauteville*. Born in April 1812, Peter le Lièvre was educated at Elizabeth College which he attended from 1825 to 1829, a period initially coinciding with and later immediately following upon the school's resuscitation from moribundity procured by the efforts of Georges le Boutillier (q.v.) aided and abetted by the Lieutenant-Governor, Sir John Colborne (q.v.). Later in life (from 1850 to 1855), le Lièvre was one of the directors of the college.

By profession a wine merchant, with premises first in le Marchant Street and subsequently on the Esplanade just north of le Tourgand, le Lièvre was by inclination a man of wide culture, geologist, naturalist and — above all — artist, noteworthy for his exquisite drawings on the one hand and his arresting paintings on the other, examples of which are to be seen at Castle Cornet and the Candie Museum and Art Gallery respectively. His drawings not only show the island's numerous dolmens, but in addition several of them are the subjects of some of the well-known Moss Prints of the 1830s; while many of his paintings depict the magnificent coastal scenery of Sark and Guernsey.

Peter le Lièvre was also a most competent designer, as anyone gazing on the Town Harbour can see at a glance, as the two lighthouses at its mouth are both designed by him — possibly as an activity ancillary to his responsibilities as a member of the Harbour Construction Committee. (He was, incidentally, also a member of the committee with oversight of the erection of the markets.) Further evidence of his abilities as a designer is manifest in the Town Church, where the pattern of the organ pipes was his conception.

Alive to his social obligations, Le Lièvre served with distinction in the Militia, rising to the rank of Lieutenant-Colonel in the Royal Guernsey Artillery; sought to aid those intent on self-improvement by helping to found the Mechanics' Institution in 1832 and working until 1871 as its treasurer; and was for many years a churchwarden of the Town Church and treasurer of its Sunday schools.

Peter le Lièvre made little attempt to lay up for himself 'treasure on earth where moth and rust doth corrupt'. A bachelor all his days, he lived with his two spinster sisters at No. 17 Hauteville - a house with accommodation in no way comparable to that provided in the dwelling of his refugee literary contemporary farther up the road on the other side, but rendered dark, chilly and dank by the steep rise of the ground behind it which resulted in the back garden being on a level with the upper storeys. Content with this spartan abode and unsuccessful in his candidature for a seat on the Jurats' Bench, this talented and engaging islander (who died at the relatively young age of 66 in 1878) has nevertheless left indelible 'footprints on the sands of time'. The man and his work were commemorated by the Guernsey Post Office in its special stamp issue for Christmas 1980.

LINDSAY, LIEUTENANT-COLONEL THE HONOURABLE JOHN (1762-1826). *Herm's tragic tenant: a man of vision beset by concepts beyond his competence*. Born in March 1762 as the eldest son of Lord Balcarres, the Honourable John Lindsay grew into a high-spirited and ardent youth who, choosing the army as a career, entered the Royal Artillery Regiment, being subsequently transferred to the 73rd Highlanders. As a young lieutenant he was present at the massacre when the city of Kanchipuram was sacked during the course of the onslaught against the British of Haidar Ali (1780-81). One of only 14 survivors out of his entire battalion, he was taken prisoner and was incarcerated for four years at the enemy capital of Seringapatam — though he did have the compensatory satisfaction in 1792 of taking part (now as a captain) in the reduction of the same town by General Cornwallis. After service in France in 1795, followed by promotion to the rank of lieutenant-colonel, the Honourable John Lindsay in 1800 married Lady Charlotte North, the daughter of Lord North, Earl of Guildford, and Lady-in-Waiting to Queen Charlotte. Then — despite the fact that the French Revolutionary War was still in progress — he retired from the army.

Almost immediately thereafter Lieutenant-Colonel Lindsay seems to have succeeded in establishing an amicable *ménage à trois*, the daughter born to his mistress (the widowed Mrs. Colebrook Cooper) in 1802 being named Charlotte after his wife, who also consented to be the baby's godmother! Furthermore, Lady Charlotte remained a loving wife and also a good friend of Mrs. Colebrook Cooper, deeply concerned over the welfare of Charlotte and of the other two children borne for Lindsay by his leman — John (1805) and Harriet (1807).

In 1808, when Lindsay and his *ménage* went to live in Bermondsey, there came the first indication of the money troubles that were to plague him for the rest of his days. In order to obtain £650 ready cash, he undertook to furnish its provider (John Edwards) with an annuity of £110. Within five years his financial affairs had deteriorated to the point where the gallant Lieutenant-Colonel feared recovery proceedings and even the possibility of imprisonment. To escape these embarrassments he approached the Tenant of Herm (Pierre Mauger) in 1813 through the medium of a mutual acquaintance (Major Bourne) with a view to acquiring the lease of the island and hence a haven of refuge from the dreaded lawsuits.

Negotiations with Mauger dragged on for two years, with an increasingly desperate Lindsay twice anticipating their conclusion by raising money with Herm as collateral. In November 1814 he borrowed from his father-in-law (Lord North) £1,200 at five per cent quoting Herm as security. Then in the early months of 1815 an extraordinary sequence of events was initiated by John Edwards selling his annuity. In no time it changed hands again, ending up in the possession (of all people) of Mrs. Colebrook Cooper; whereupon Lindsay promptly redeemed the bond from his inamorata in return for the title deeds of his Bermondsey property and the potential rights in Herm which he had still to acquire (and which were pledged to his father-in-law in any case!). In the meantime (in January 1815) Lindsay had obtained from his legal adviser in Guernsey — none other than Le Procureur du Roi, Thomas de Sausmarez (q.v.) — a categorical assurance that he would be safe from his creditors in Herm. Spurred on by this incentive, Lindsay pursued his negotiations with Pierre Mauger with renewed vigour and finally the lease of Herm was registered in his name on 28 July 1815. He immediately installed Mrs. Colebrook Cooper (together with the children of their liaison) in the island as his agent.

The Honourable John Lindsay had become the Tenant of Herm, but he does not appear to have paid for the lease — at any rate, not the full consideration to which he was committed. By February 1816 Pierre Mauger was dead and his son, John Mauger, was pressing for the outstanding balance. In no position to make any such settlement, Lindsay cast around for fund-raising expedients, approaching Major-General Bayley, Lieutenant-Governor of Guernsey, with the proposal that Herm be used as a settlement to which felons might be transported and claiming that the island was capable of accommodating 1,000 convicts. In October 1819 Lord North contacted Thomas de Sausmarez, seeking repayment of his £1,200 loan. Such redemption was of course entirely behond Lindsay's means; and yet, despite his pecuniary entanglements, Herm's Tenant the following February (1820) launched a madcap (and in the event abortive) scheme for the erection on the top of the island of a large mausoleum to commemorate George III!

Although the Honourable John's relations with his brothers had always been distant, his sister (Lady Anne Barnard) had remained his confidante throughout all the vicissitudes of his troubled career, and in May 1820 she appealed to their father on her brother's behalf. The upshot was that Lord Balcarres advanced a loan to his 'impulsive' son on condition that the principal would not be repaid during Lindsay's lifetime (there was no need to fear that!) and that he would not 'part with any of his Herm interests' (for which, even at this date, he still had not paid in full!). His father's loan gave Herm's Tenant a breathing space in which to investigate further possibilities of raising revenue. In a correspondence with Major-General Bayley conducted between August 1820 and March 1821 he first sought the services of one non-commissioned officer and 15 men to help in the building of a pier and later submitted grandiose proposals for the construction of a vast harbour incorporating Balvoir Bay, urging the value of such an installation as a naval base near a potentially hostile France. He even solicited the good offices of the Lieutenant-Governor in seeking a loan of £750 from the British Parliament to help pay for harbour works — yet again proposing Herm as security!

John Lindsay now started directing appeals to the Home Secretary, Sir Robert Peel, seeking aid in May 1822 to exploit Herm's plentiful granite deposits by being provided with convict labour. He followed this up by buying a crane (possibly that still to be seen on Herm's pier), but by the end of the year matters reached their nadir, with his affairs being promulgated at the Bar of the House of Lords. Nevertheless he approached Peel yet again the following March, pleading that his agricultural prospects had been ruined because of Guernsey's ability, as a territory not subject to the Corn Laws, to import grain from abroad. Consequently he requested a loan of £1,200 at four per cent with — needless to say — Herm once again as collateral. Sir Robert did not respond and June 1823 arrived with John Mauger still not fully paid for the lease of the island sold by his father eight years previously.

Then — for a time — Fortune smiled. The granite boom, destined to lead to a rise in Herm's population from 37 in 1821 to 191 in 1831, was getting into its stride. Encouraged by a large order to supply stone for Rennie's London Bridge, Lindsay embarked on an extensive capital installation programme and recruited labour from Scotland. He was also — at last — supplied with the non-commissioned officer and 15 men requested of Major-General Bayley two years earlier. Things were still going well in November 1824 when the Honourable John arranged with Jonathan Duncan (q.v.) for the latter to buy all Herm stone for 14 years, making his own arrangements for sales to third parties — and furthermore to put up an investment of £1,500. In return Lindsay promised to pay Duncan five per cent of the first £1,000 profit and thereafter 33 per cent.

By the following March, however, a disillusioned Duncan was pleading with Lindsay to bestir himself to fulfil a contract for stone for Somerstown in London. Nevertheless, despite his disappointment Lindsay's new partner quite inexplicably extended their mutual agreement a fortnight later and put up a further £2,000 to boot! A contract to supply granite for the Turnpike Trust signed in November 1825 seemed to augur well, but fundamentally Lindsay's affairs were now in an irremediable muddle, with total debts amounting to no less than £13,000.

In March 1826 Lieutenant-Colonel the Honourable John Lindsay died in London, utterly bankrupt, the island of which he was tenant 'en saisi' by the States of Guernsey. Death had rescued him from a situation beyond his power to rectify. Surely a fitting valedictory, epitomising his career, would have been: 'Ah, but a man's reach should exceed his grasp, Or what's a heaven for?'.

LING, CAPTAIN NICHOLAS (1599-1679). *The poacher who turned gamekeeper.* (A). Born in 1599 and already 43 years of age when Charles I raised his standard at Nottingham, Nicholas Ling nevertheless at once made himself available for service with the Parliamentary forces, fighting at Edgehill in 1642 (where he was wounded) and later being taken prisoner by the Royalists at Brentford. Released as a result of an exchange of prisoners, Ling was transferred to Guernsey which, with its Calvinist traditions, was staunch in the Parliamentary cause. In 1643 Captain Ling was placed in command of the small garrison in Sark and as a result was the next year once again — briefly — a prisoner of the Royalists. This

occurred at dawn on 27 May 1644 when an assault organised by Sir George Carteret (q.v.) was launched against the island. A small Royalist company headed by Captain Chamberlain took the defenders by surprise and seized Ling in his bed — but were themselves taken prisoner later in the day when, left in the lurch by the second Royalist contingent which had failed to make landfall, they were overpowered by a landing party from a Parliamentary frigate which had been alerted by distress beacons lit by the womenfolk in Little Sark. The experience of this sally led Parliament to order the following November that a permanent garrison of 30 men under Captain Ling's command should be maintained in the island.

Nicholas Ling so conducted himself in Sark that in January 1651, by which time he had commanded the garrison for seven and a half years, he was presented with a testimonial by the islanders. Encomia, however, butter no parsnips, and in 1652 poor Ling addressed a petition to Parliament, complaining that he had received no pay since his arrival in the Channel Isles and consequently was falling into want, together with his wife and children.

In 1656 Captain Ling was transferred to Alderney to assume responsibility for the government of that island on the Lord Protector's behalf and also to command its Militia in place of Pierre le Febure (q.v.*). At the Restoration he adroitly changed his allegiance to become an ardent Royalist and thus contrived to retain his position in Alderney, with Sir George Carteret (who held a grant of Alderney from Charles II) appointing him as his resident Lieutenant-Governor. By now an islander by assimilation, Ling (who had become a widower) further emphasised his local identity by marrying into Guernsey's prestigious (and Royalist) Andros family. The first 'Governor' to live in St Anne — the Chamberlaynes (q.v.) having resided at Longy — Nicholas Ling built the first house on the site which is today occupied by the Island Hall. He it was who in 1669 promulgated the Ordinance whereby destitute children were sent to Sir George's colony of New Jersey. Remaining in Alderney for the rest of his days, he died there in 1679.

LIST, HAUPTSTURMFÜHRER MAXIMILIAN (1910- ?). *The Schutzstaffel sadist of Sylt.* Of the four earthly hells established in Alderney during the Second World War the worst was indubitably the camp called Sylt located south of the island's airport, the horrors of which may be adjudged from the fact that a transfer thereto was the punishment most dreaded by the occupants of the other installations, familiar though they were with systematic brutality. Originally built by the Organisation Todt in August 1942 to house forced labour, it was taken over in March 1943 by Baubrigade (Construction Brigade) No. 1 of the S.S. under the command of Hauptsturmführer (Captain) Maximilian List.

Described by Jurat T. X. H. Pantcheff as 'the proud senior representative of an élite corps, a key executive arm of a repressive authoritarian régime, used to the exercise of arbitrary power', Maximilian List was born in Munich on 9 February 1910, the son of Andreas List, Burgomaster of that city. By civilian profession an architect, List had been an ardent Nazi long before Hitler's appointment as Chancellor, joining the Storm Troopers in 1930 as one of the earliest members of the brutal Totenkopfverband (The Death's Head Formation), his enlistment number being the prestigiously low one of 4791. Steeped in the Herrenvolk culk, he went to considerable pains in answering the questionnaire accompanying his application for admission to the S.S., giving the names and dates of his ancestors as far back as 1736 as proof of his pure Aryan blood. In a further application submitted in 1937, for permission to marry, he stated that although his relations were Roman Catholics he himself did not share their religious beliefs.

Decorated for services performed in the occupied Eastern Territories after the invasion of the U.S.S.R. in June 1941 (one shudders to think what those services must have been), List was attached to the S.S. Headquarters in Berlin in 1942, and then served in the Oranienburg and Sachsenhausen Concentration Camps near the German capital before moving to Alderney in March 1943. He immediately had a châlet built for himself outside Sylt's boundary fence, linked to the camp's interior by an underground passage (which still survives) through which he could come and go unnoticed, thereby epitomising his policy of keeping himself aloof from the dire deeds perpetrated under his command. Thus Herr Wilhelm Wernegau (a Sylt survivor) testified many years later that 'List never personally killed or whipped anyone with his own hands – he only gave the orders and others did this'. The cumulative effect of such orders may be deduced from the fact that by June 1943 only 800 prisoners remained alive out of the 1,100 who had been in the camp when he had assumed command the previous March. Indeed the fortification con-

struction schedule was so badly upset by the malnourished state of the workforce that the island commandant required Sylt's commander to treat his prisoners less severely and to increase their rations – an order which List had the temerity to disregard.

By the end of June 1943 200 of the inmates of Sylt were too weak to work, most of them reduced by starvation to an advanced state of tuberculosis. Maximilian List's reaction to this state of affairs was to decide to ship the invalids to Neuengamme near Hamburg for extermination in that Concentration Camp's gas chamber. So ill were the poor wretches thus consigned to be put down like unwanted animals that by the time the transport left Alderney on 5 July 50 of them had died already – whereupon List with callous efficiency arranged for an empty wagon to be attached to the train conveying the victims from Cherbourg onwards into which could be placed the bodies of those who died en route.

Then the unexpected happened. Despite their desperately sick condition (so strong is the will to live) some of the victims with their bare hands contrived to make a hole in the floor of the cattle truck in which they were travelling and ten of them got away by dropping through it while the train was in motion. A further two escaped by profiting from the confusion after the train had stopped and their comrades' flight had been discovered. Tried by an S.S. Court Martial in the autumn of 1943 for permitting this escape, List candidly admitted the depletion of his labour force wrought by death, claimed that staff shortage compelled him to send off the transport with minimal guards, and said that he felt no guilt over the escapes as everything had been done which could have been done. He was acquitted.

Maximilian List continued his régime of coldly calculated cruelty at Sylt until 15 April 1944, when he left Alderney for Oslo, appointed to the Staff of the S.S. 'Nord' Headquarters. His stay in Norway was short, however, and after a brief visit to Berlin during which he was promoted to the rank of Sturmbahnführer (Major), he was posted to Italy on 20 July 1944. From Italy he eventually returned to Berlin and was in that city at the end of April 1945. On 1 May with Germany in collapse, he was paid a year's salary (1,414 Reichmarks) and set about planning how best to evade retribution for his career as a merciless jailer of the Thrd Reich. Well aware of being a wanted man because of the numerous murders for which he was responsible in Alderney (and doubtless elsewhere also), List planted false documents showing that he had been killed in Italy — and thus made good his escape.

In the case of this war criminal Justice proved to be not only blind, but gullible as well. Even after a full investigation of the misdeeds perpetrated in Alderney no effort was made to bring him to book because of the belief that he was dead. It was not until 1974 that his survival became manifest, the records of the German Public Prosecutor showing that in that year Maximilian List, formerly of S.S. Baubrigade 1, gave evidence in a Hamburg Court! The indications are that at the time of writing (1984) this monster of depravity is still alive.

LOVERIDGE, SIR JOHN HENRY, C.B.E. (1912-   ). *A Bailiff of sterling worth.* Born in August 1912 to Vera Lilian, the wife of Henry Thomas Loveridge, Guernsey's future bailiff was educated at Elizabeth College and during his youth was well-known as a footballer, playing for the Athletics Association Football Club. (In later years, incidentally, Sir John, who always retained his fondness for sport, became a keen golfer who also enjoyed swimming.) Originally embarking on a career in the island's bureaucracy, during the German Occupation he rendered signal service as Secretary to the Essential Commodities Committee. The value of his labours in this capacity was recognised after the Liberation when at the end of 1945 George VI made him a Member of the Most Excellent Order of the British Empire.

On the morrow of Liberation Mr. John Loveridge (as he then was) married Madeleine Melanie, the daughter of Eugene Joseph Tanguy and shortly afterwards deciding on a legal career accordingly went up to l'Université de Caen. Qualifying in English Law as well as le Droit Normand, he was called to the Bar at the Middle Temple in 1950 and was admitted as an Advocate of the Royal Court in 1951. He soon made his mark, being appointed H.M. Comptroller within three years of first coming to the Guernsey Bar (1954). While in this office Sir John served in the Royal Air Force Volunteer Reserve from 1954 to 1959. In 1960 he rose to the position of H.M. Procureur and held this post until 1969. During his term as the Chief Law Officer of the Crown his worth was accorded further recognition in 1964 when he was advanced to become a Commander of the Most Excellent Order of the British Empire.

Appointed Deputy Bailiff in 1969 (in which capacity he drafted the Report of the States'

Constitutional Relationships Committee on constitutional relations between the Bailiwick and the United Kingdom), he succeeded Sir William Arnold as Bailiff on the latter's death in 1973 and thereafter exercised Guernsey's supreme office with assured authority, coupled with affability and kindliness. After being appointed a Judge of Appeal for Jersey in 1974, Sir John received his knighthood in 1975, in which year he was also made a Commander of the Order of St John of Jerusalem. Sir John retired in August 1982, respected and admired by the island he had served so well.

LUKIS, FREDERICK CORBIN (1788-1871). *Guernsey's great archaeological pioneer.* (B). Frederick Corbin Lukis was born in 1788 to Sarah Lukis (*née* Collings) the wife of John Lukis who, during his son's boyhood built the existing Lukis House facing the Grange — financed by the profits reaped from privateering and wine *entrepôt* ventures. As was frequently the case among well-to-do families at the time, young Frederick developed wide interests in various fields, including science, natural history, botany, geology and conchology — but it was his outstanding work in the realm of archaeology which was destined to perpetuate his name.

This interest was initially aroused by the sketches of prehistoric remains drawn by Joshua Gosselin (q.v.), who was an elderly cousin, Frederick Corbin's great-aunt Catherine having married into the Gosselin family. It was stimulated to fever pitch by the joint venture in which the two of them cooperated in unearthing La Varde Dolmen in 1811 — in which year the young zealot also sketched the megalithic tomb at La Platte Mare ('L'Autel des Landes').

What now became his life's work was based entirely on self-instruction: a fact which, considered together with his lack of the modern techniques of excavation which were barely nascent at the time, makes his achievement truly remarkable. Hindered rather than helped by his contemporaries (whose attitude hovered between indifference and hostility) he conducted a desperate struggle to preserve the Bailiwick's heritage of dolmens and menhirs; his independent mind, with its refusal to accept theories without full verification, establishing (contrary to the general belief of his day) that the former were tombs and not 'Druids' altars'. Meticulous in his approach to his self-imposed labours, he compiled a comprehensive record of his excavations in six volumes of manuscript written between

1853 and 1863, a record now kept in the Candie Museum and Art Gallery.

Thanks to Lukis' efforts numerous dolmens were saved from damage and their contents preserved: many of them now being stored in the Island Museum. In the year 1837 he discovered cyst near La Mare ès Mauves and also made the first scientific investigation of the Déhus Dolmen; with La Rocque Qui Sonne and the Mare ès Mauves megalithic complex being excavated shortly afterwards. An example of the vandalism against which he was forced to wage incessant war is furnished by the case of Le Creux ès Faies at L'Erée to which Lukis turned his attention in 1838, only to find to his consternation that it had been filled with rubble on the orders of the officer commanding Fort Saumarez as a means of preventing drunken troops from hiding there. He followed this up in 1839 by excavating Le Trépied Dolmen at Le Catioroc, and restoring the westernmost capstone which he found in a collapsed condition. In addition to his work at Le Creux ès Faies Lukis in 1838 also excavated extensively in the interior of the church remains on Lihou Island, as well as investigating the domestic structures west of it, of which he left a sketch. His drawings of the church (made when the Priory buildings were much more complete than they are now) suggests a late 12th century choir of elaborate construction.

Frederick Lukis did not confine his attention to Guernsey, but was active throughout the Bailiwick. He knew of the cyst above Brenière Bay in Sark and regarded it as man-made, but left no further written record. He hurried to Alderney when the fortifications programme was launched in the 1850s in the hope of saving what he could from obliteration. Unfortunately, however, despite his efforts to preserve some sort of record for posterity, large numbers of burial chambers, cysts and even whole cemeteries were destroyed before any adequate examination could be undertaken or records compiled.

In Herm the cup to drink was, if possible, even more bitter. Thanks to the support of a large band of helpers, including several members of his own family, Lukis uncovered a number of megalithic sites, though the records of these discoveries are rather inadequate — due, no doubt, to the intense pressures under which he was working. His task was indeed a formidable one, beset with difficulties. Not only did the ubiquitous quarrymen litter many sites with iron spikes and tools, but they trampled clumsily over skulls just unearthed and in their fecklessness mutilated some of the burial chambers. Particularly enraging was the fact that 'the workmen of Herm had orders to break up surface rocks whenever they found them suitable for dressing as square blocks'. The inevitable result was the destruction of many dolmens — not to mention the loss of La Pierre aux Rats.

Lukis never allowed his absorbing passion (in connection with which he became a Fellow of the Society of Antiquaries) to interfere with the discharge of his obligations as a Guernseyman. He so acquitted himself in the Guernsey Militia (which became 'Royal' during his time of service) as to attain the rank of full Colonel — and he was, moreover, appointed as aide-de-camp to the Lieutenant-Governor. He also showed a lively sense of his social responsibilities in the patronage he gave to the Mechanics' Institution on its foundation in 1832 by consenting to be its first President, seeing in this new organisation a means whereby youthful artisans would be encouraged to follow the path of self-advancement through study which he himself had trodden.

In 1813 Frederick Lukis married his first cousin (his mother's niece) Elizabeth Collings, who bore him four sons and three daughters — all of whom cooperated with their father in his pursuits, the sons helping with excavations and the daughters (especially Mary) recording the discoveries in oils and water-colours. One of his daughters (Louisa) married her cousin the Reverend William Thomas Collings (q.v.), and thereby the eminent archaeologist emerges as the great-great-great-grandfather of the present (1984) Seigneur of Sark. As for his sons, two of them (Dr. Frederick Collings Lukis and the Reverend William Collings Lukis) conjointly excavated La Platte Mare Tomb ('L'Autel des Landes') in 1837–38; while another son (Captain Francis du Bois Lukis) discovered and excavated the Sandy Lane Cyst in 1872. It was, furthermore, this son who in accordance with his father's wishes, bequeathed to the island on his death in 1907 the Archaeological Museum his parent had built up, at the same time making available for the nominal sum of less than £100 the family home in the Grange to accommodate it. The Museum's contents now form part of the collection displayed in the Island Museum at Candie.

Frederick Corbin Lukis died in 1871 and his body was buried in the vault in Candie Cemetery built by his brother-in-law — Sir William Collings (q.v.*), the donor of the Sir William Collings Fund for the relief of distress — for his wife (Lukis' sister Margaret) who had died in 1852.

M

MACCULLOCH, SIR EDGAR (1808–1896). *An erudite Bailiff; authority on folk-lore and founding father of La Société Guernesiaise.* Born in 1808, Edgar MacCulloch came of an old Scottish family which had moved to Guernsey in Charles II's reign after its position in its native Galloway had been rendered untenable by persistent attachment to the cause of the proscribed Covenanters who, meeting in illegal conventicles implacably hostile to the episcopacy re-established in the Kirk by the Act Recissory of the Edinburgh Restoration Parliament, were relentlessly hunted down and dragooned. (The same family, incidentally, was later involved in the first bank established in Guernsey – MacCulloch, Allaire, Bonamy and Company – which failed with heavy liabilities during Edgar's infancy in 1811).

Initially attending the school in La Plaiderie run by the Reverend Philip Hayes (Elizabeth College at the time being moribund), the youthful MacCulloch continued his education by spending the years 1824 and 1825 at an academy in Brussels considered of great merit and to which several other Guernsey boys were sent during this period. He subsequently acquired a final polish by plucking the flowers of enlightenment from the hedgerows of experience during a two-year sojourn in France between 1825 and 1827.

Always a staunch churchman (despite his family's Covenanting background) Edgar MacCulloch was actively involved in the projects resulting in the building of the churches of St Barnabas and St Stephen – and in addition paid out of his own pocket for the installation in 1869 of the restored font at St Martin's. Indeed, the first public office ever held by Guernsey's future Bailiff was that of rector's warden at the Town Church.

Elected as a Jurat of the Royal Court in 1844, MacCulloch sat on the committee responsible for the erection of the Victoria Tower in 1848 – and to this day his name may be seen among those recorded on the plaque inside the entrance to this architectural extravaganza. Two years later, in 1850, he succeeded Peter le Lièvre (q.v.) as president of the Mechanics' Institution – the name of which was soon afterwards altered to the Mechanics' Institution and Literary Society, because of the increasingly bourgeois complexion of this organisation. Three years after that he held the post of States' Supervisor when the foundation stone of the new harbour was laid.

After being elected Lieutenant-Bailiff in 1869, Edgar MacCulloch in 1873 persuaded the States to acquire its first 'ancient monument' by buying the near-derelict Chapel of St Apolline – a purchase which in all probability saved this 14th-century shrine from irredeemable collapse. Then in 1882 he played a leading part in founding La Société Guernesiaise (initially known as the Guernsey Society of Natural Science) and became its first President. His portrait was accordingly featured in the special stamp issue made by the Guernsey Post Office in 1982 to mark the centenary of this worthy body – which was further signalised by affixing a plaque to his residence in Le Pollet, now a shoe shop.

In 1884 MacCulloch was appointed Bailiff and thereafter held Guernsey's supreme office with great distinction until ill-health brought his retirement in 1895. His term of office is commemorated by his coat of arms, together with his motto, *Vi et Animo* ('By manhood and with Spirit'), adorning the Bailiff's pew in the Town Church.

In 1886 Edgar MacCulloch's great qualities and innumerable services received their due reward when he was accorded the well-deserved honour of knighthood. In the same year Sir Edgar gave yet further proof of his kindliness and humanity by persuading the States to vote £200 to supplement private contributions and thus enable the Model Yacht Pond to be constructed on the Castle Emplacement to provide the youth of the island with 'healthy, innocent and amusing recreation'.

Eager to serve the island he loved in every way open to him, Sir Edgar was for many years a Gunner in the Royal Guernsey Militia Artillery and was also indefatigible in promoting educational and cultural activities. A prominent authority on education for half a century, he constantly sought to encourage the teaching of French in the hope of thereby countering the ever-increasing threat to the preservation of the Bailiwick's traditional life-style posed by the relentless march of anglicisation. He was also a member of the London Antiquarian Society, La Société d'Antiquaires de Normandie and of the Folk-lore Society. He twice represented the island at the Congress of the Bréton Association, on the second occasion at Vitré reading a paper on relations between Vitré and Guernsey.

In line with these interests Sir Edgar over the years had assiduously collected details of local traditions, beliefs, customs and superstitions which formed the basis of the work by which he will be remembered for all time — his magnum opus, *Guernsey Folk Lore*. Seen through the Press after his death by Miss Edith Carey (q.v.) — whose interest in local history had first been aroused by its author — this remarkable compilation is an indispensible *sine qua non* to any appreciation of the richness of Guernsey's heritage.

MACCULLOCH, DR. JOHN, M.D., F.R.S., F.L.S., F.G.S. (1773–1835). *A distinguished Guernseyman and eminent geologist.* Born on 6 October 1773 to Elizabeth (*née* de Lisle), the daughter of Jurat Thomas de Lisle and the wife of James MacCulloch (whose extensive interests embraced not only banking in Guernsey but also commerce in Brittany), the baby destined later in life to become the uncle of Sir Edgar MacCulloch (q.v.) — the son of his brother Thomas — grew into a precocious, withdrawn and thoughtful boy. After schooling in Cornwall, first in Plympton, later in Penzance and finally (1787–1790) at Lostwithiel Grammar School, John MacCulloch studied medicine at Edinburgh (where he formed a close friendship with Walter Scott — later Sir Walter), graduating *Medicineæ Doctor* on 12 September 1793 with a thesis on electricity.

It was at this juncture that MacCulloch's father not only lost his business in Brittany as a result of the French Revolution, but lost his liberty also, finding himself imprisoned during the Jacobin 'Reign of Terror'. Finally obtaining his release, he lost no time in quitting France and thereafter settled in Cornwall. In quest of security after this decline in his family's fortunes, MacCulloch entered the Royal Regiment of Artillery as assistant surgeon: and it was while serving in this capacity that he earned sufficient repute as a botanist — another of his many accomplishments — to merit election as a Fellow of the Linnean Society on 21 April 1801. In 1803 came a change of occupation, his scientific acquirements leading to his appointment as Chemist to the Board of Ordnance. He remained at this post until 1807, when he set up in medical practice at Blackheath, becoming a Licentiate of the College of Physicians on 30 September 1808. Then once again financial disaster befell his family with the failure in 1811 of Guernsey's first bank — MacCulloch, Allaire, Bonamy and Company. Obliged by this reverse yet again to seek employment and a guaranteed income rather than practising on his own account, John MacCulloch accepted a commission from the Board of Ordnance to conduct a survey in Scotland with the object of determining which kinds of rock could be most safely employed in powder mills. His career as a geologist had begun — and for the next ten years he travelled extensively in Scotland, accumulating a vast store of scientific observations. He had already, however, been interested in this branch of science for a number of years and had become a member of the Geological Society on 5 February 1808. Indeed, in the same year that he undertook his Scottish survey MacCulloch contributed to the very first volume of the fledgling Society's *Transactions* with a paper entitled, 'An Account of Guernsey and the other Channel Islands' — his first important geological study. In his admirable work *The Landscape of the Channel Islands* Mr. Nigel Jee provides a rer inder that on this occasion the learned Guernseyman behaved in typical 'absent-minded Professor' fashion, having to admit when delivering his paper that he had mislaid the specimens which he had collected in the archipelago and was thus compelled to confine himself to a verbal description of the islands and their rocks! Despite this embarrassing 'first performance', however, he was elected president of the Society for the year 1816-17.

In 1814 Dr. MacCulloch was appointed geologist to the trigonometrical survey and also became a lecturer on chemistry and mineralogy at the Royal Military Academy, Woolwich. He later held a similar appointment at the East India Company's College at Addiscombe near Croydon — and in 1820 he was nominated physician to Prince Leopold of Saxe-Coburg (later — in 1830 — king of the Belgians). In the same hear he was elected a Fellow of the Royal Society. Commissioned in 1826 to prepare a geological map of Scotland, he worked on this project until 1832, in the meanwhile finding time to complete by 1830 a work running to three octavo volumes entitled *Proofs and Illustrations of the Attributes of God, from the Facts and Laws of the Physical Universe; being the Foundation of Natural and Revealed Religion*. Publication was withheld, however, owing to the simultaneous appearance of the *Bridgewater Treatises* — a set of eight essays on 'The Goodness of God as manifested in the Creation', written by contenders for the award of £8,000 left in his will by Francis Henry Egerton, Earl of Bridgewater (1756–1829) for the best monograph on this subject. Consequently it was not until after this gifted islander's death that (in accordance with the terms of his will) this theological magnum opus saw the light of day.

In the early summer of 1835 and by now in his 62nd year, Dr. MacCulloch somewhat surprisingly married a certain Miss White. A few weeks later — on 21 August — when on holiday with his wife near Poltair in Cornwall, he was thrown from his phaeton, thereby sustaining compound fractures necessitating amputation of his right leg. He endured the ordeal with exemplary fortitude, but only survived the tortures of surgery by a few hours. His body was buried at Gulval, a village near Penzance. Thus bravely died a Guernsey savant of whom Jonathan Duncan (q.v.) said in his *History of Guernsey*: 'The variety of his acquirements was not less remarkable than their extent. Allusion has been made to his knowledge of medicine, geology, mineralogy, chemistry and trigonometry. He was also well acquainted with theology, astronomy, zoology, botany, physics and the mechanical arts. He was skilled in architecture. He drew well and has left an immense number of drawings. He was a good musician and his musical compositions show that he was conversant with the theory as well as the practice of the science'. Justifiably did the peerless geologist Sir Charles Lyell (1797–1875) in his obituary notice speak of John MacCulloch as 'unrivalled in the wide range of subjects of which he displayed great talent and profound knowledge'.

MACHON, CHARLES NICHOLAS (1893–1944). *Macte virtute*. See *Underground Resistance Heroes of the Second World War*.

MAGLOIRE OF DOL, SAINT AND EVANGELIST (*c.* 500–*c.* 586). *The patron saint of Sark*. According to a *Life of Saint Magloire*, most likely dating from the tenth century and liberally overlaid with myth and fable, Sark owes its conversion to Christianity to the work of this missionary, whose festival falls on 24 October and whose birth is variously placed at Vannes in Armorica and Glamorgan in Wales. His mother appears to have been Afrella, a Welsh princess and wife of Umbrafel, the son of an Armorican lord named Emyr Lhydau and allegedly the paternal uncle of St Sampson (q.v.), of whom Magloire thus emerges as a first cousin.

St Magloire (also known as Maelor or Mannelier) is held to have been entrusted in his youth to the care of St Illtyd at Llantwit in Glamorgan and subsequently to have become a monk and a companion of St Sampson, who is reputed to have ordained him and taken him to Armorica. After many years cooperation with his cousin in evangelistic labours St Magloire is deemed to have

succeeded him as Bishop of Dol — a claim which is highly suspect. The story goes that while in Dol Magloire was visited by the 'Chieftain of Sark' who, in gratitude to the saint for being healed of a skin infection, made a grant to his followers and himself of part of the island. This 'Chieftain' is frequently identified with Count Loyesco — probably synonymous with le Comte l'Oiseau, the legendary Lord of Jersey (which island Magloire is also said to have visited, delivering its people from a 'dragon', in return for which he was granted land there as well). In this connection the tale is told that in Sark Magloire cured the daughter of a nobleman named Nivo of dumbness — and it is interesting that the late Dame de Sercq in her *Notes on Feudal Tenure* (1928) lists as one of the 'Lords of Sark' 'Nivo: A.D. 550', to which she adds 'Comte l'Oiseau: A.D. 580 (Probably a descendant of Nivo)'.

Thus invited (and apparently giving up his See, exchanging the rôle of abbot for that of bishop), Magloire is stated to have landed in Sark about 565, accompanied by 62 monks, and to have set up a religious house in the valley still called La Moinerie. For grinding grain the fraternity built a watermill lower down the valley, damming the stream to obtain power. Echoes of these coenobites' activities are heard in the name 'L'Ecluse' ('The Dam') given to the Quarantaine House in this vicinity, while the inlet at the foot of the valley is still called le Port du Moulin. From this centre the saint is believed to have set about converting the surrounding islanders, presumably also crossing to Herm and Jethou where he is credited with building a chapel on the Pierre Percée Reef (then above sea level). Its ruins may have survived as late as 1833, as in his *Topographical Dictionary* published that year Samuel Lewis mentions 'portions of an ancient building, thought to have been a chapel belonging to a hermitage existing here in the sixth century'.

Magloire is thought to have died in Sark on 24 October 586 and to have been buried there. According to the *Acta Sanctorum Octubris* his body remained in the island for 264 years until 850 when six monks at the behest of the Bréton Prince Nominöe carried it to Léhon (near Dinan), where its reinterment led to the foundation of the famous Royal Priory of Léhon. Eventually, so it is said, his remains were moved yet again to a final resting place in Paris. The date of 850 is significant as it coincides with the massacre of Sark's monks and the destruction of their monastery at the henads of marauding Norse pirates (who were possibly led by the bloodthirsty

Jarl Hasting) which is known to have occurred around that time. Indeed, the existence of the monastery and its despoliation by the sea-dogs are the only incontestable facts in the entire saga of Sark's saint1

MANSELL, REAR-ADMIRAL SIR THOMAS, K.C.H. (1977-1858). *The Guernseyman who captured 170 ships*. (B). Born in Guernsey on 9 February 1777 to Martha (*née* Price), the wife of Thomas Mansell, Thomas Mansell *fils* entered the Royal Navy in January 1793 — a month before his 16th birthday — initially serving on board the frigate H.M.S. *Crescent*, commanded by his illustrious fellow-islander Captain James Saumarez (q.v.). Two years later (in March 1795) he followed Sir James Saumarez (as he had by then become) to H.M.S. *Orion*, aboard which he took part in the running fight off L'Orient in June 1796, the Battle of Cape St Vincent in February 1797 and the Nile action of August 1798.

Promoted by Nelson in the wake of the Nile victory to be acting Lieutenant of H.M.S. *Aquilon*, Mansell later served in the Channel. In 1806 he was engaged in the struggle to wrest back from the Dutch the Cape of Good Hope, which three years previously had been returned to them by the Peace of Amiens. After this campaign Sir Home Popham sent him back to the United Kingdom in command of an armed transport. A further period of service under Sir James Saumarez ensued, aboard, successively, H.M.S. *Diomede*, H.M.S. *Hibernia* and H.M.S. *Victory* — until on 17 September 1808 this officer of promise was given command of the sloop, H.M.S. *Rose*, in which during the following May he participated in the capture of Anholt in the Baltic.

Recognition of this gallant Guernseyman's worth came in 1812 when Czar Alexander I presented him with a diamond ring in acknowledgement of his achievement in piloting a Russian squadron through the Belt (the narrow waters cutting through the Danish archipelago and linking the Baltic with the Kattegat); while during the same year Charles XIII of Sweden invested him with the Order of the Sword 'in testimony of the esteem in which he held his services'. In 1813 Mansell commanded H.M.S. *Pelican* off the north coast of Spain and on 7 June 1814 he was advanced to the rank of Post Captain (i.e., one commanding a ship of 20 guns or more, as distinct from an officer merely enjoying the courtesy title of Captain), it being stated that while in command of the *Rose* and the *Pelican* he had

captured at least 170 enemy vessels (some of them privateers of force).

Although the coming of peace removed further opportunity for distinguishing himself, Captain Thomas Mansell was nevertheless in 1837 nominated Knight Commander of the Hanoverian Guelphic Order and accorded the accolade of knighthood. Sir Thomas was made a Rear-Admiral on the retired list on 9 October 1849 and he died at his residence in the Grange on 22 April 1858.

In 1806 Lieutenant Thomas Mansell (as he then was) married Catherine, the daughter of John Lukis and the sister of the famous archaeologist Frederick Corbin Lukis (q.v.). She bore him four sons and four daughters, among whom one son (Arthur Lukis Mansell) commanded the survey ship *Firefly* in the Mediterranean and rose to the rank of Vice-Admiral; while one of the daughters (Margaritta Sarah Collings Mansell) became the wife of Lieutenant-Colonel Elias Thomas de Guérin, Royal Guernsey Militia, and the mother of Lieutenant-Colonel Thomas William Mansell de Guérin (q.v.), the highly esteemed scholar and administrator.

LE MARCHANT, MAJOR-GENERAL JOHN GASPARD (1766-1812). *The dunce who founded the Royal Military College*. (D). John Gaspard le Marchant was born in 1766 to Maria Hirzel, the wife of John le Marchant (late of the 7th Dragoons) and into the branch of this family (one of the most dominant in Guernsey's life in the 18th century) domiciled at La Haye du Puits, the Castel property acquired from its previous Andros owners in 1674. His grandfather was Thomas le Marchant of le Manoir ès Marchants and Lieutenant-Bailiff of the Bailiwick, while his mother was the daughter of Count Hirzel de Gratian, Maréchal du Camp of the Swiss Guards in the service of France.

The island's lack of educational facilities in his boyhood led to young John being sent to a boarding school in Bath, where he was adjudged by his schoolmaster to be the greatest dunce he had ever met! It would seem, however, that his low level of attainment reflected fecklessness rather than inability; after his return home the lad became studious and with the help of the family butler (an American loyalist of no mean learning) rapidly made good past neglect.

In 1781 at the age of 15 John le Marchant was appointed an ensign in the Wiltshire Militia. Possessed of the turbulent temper endemic in his house — and particularly exemplified by his kinsman Bailiff William le Marchant (q.v.) — the tyro had barely donned uniform when he called out his Colonel for allegedly insulting him! He was indeed fortunate in having a commanding officer of compassionate understanding who overlooked the effrontery and smoothed things over.

Transferred (still as an ensign) to the 1st Royal Foot in February 1783, the young subaltern spent a number of years in garrison at Gibraltar. While home on sick leave after a bout of yellow fever, he married Mary, the daughter of Jurat John Carey — a union which caused consternation in the two families as both bride and groom were under age. The newly-wed swain was quickly sent back to his regiment. The alarm, however, was groundless as the marriage proved to be happy and fruitful, with the eldest son (Carey) later becoming aide-de-camp to his father.

Eventually Le Marchant was transferred to the Queen's Bays. Here he attracted the notice of George III with whom he became a great favourite. After serving with the Bays in the Flanders campaign of 1793-94 he was in 1795 transferred yet again — this time to the 16th Lancers — on attaining his majority. It was about this time that Major le Marchant devised a system of cavalry sword exercises which, after approval by the Duke of York (the Commander in Chief), were described by their inventor in his *Cavalry Sword Exercises* published in 1796. He also suggested a new sword pattern which in 1797 was adopted by the Blues. Lord Cornwallis (Master General of Ordnance) presented Le Marchant with a sword in recognition of his efforts, on the strength of which he was promoted to Lieutenant-Colonel and transferred once more to the 7th Hussars quartered near Windsor.

It was at this juncture that Le Marchant made the main contribution whereby he earned military immortality, submitting plans to the Duke of York in 1799 for the establishment of the Royal Military College. This was ultimately founded in 1802 and Le Marchant became its first Lieutenant-Governor. He remained at this post for nearly nine years, during which time over 200 officers (including many of Wellington's Peninsula staff) passed through his hands. Originally the college had a senior department at High Wycombe and a junior one at Great Marlow, though both were later moved to Sandhurst.

In 1810 Le Marchant was promoted to Major-General and given command of a brigade of heavy cavalry in the Peninsula. He was present at the capture of Ciudad Rodrigo and also at Llevena in April 1812. On 22 July at Salamanca, with the abandon he had habitually displayed since his wife's death the previous August, Le Marchant

(who cut down six of the enemy with his own hand) led a charge of 800 horse against 5,000 infantry, scattering the enemy and taking 1,500 prisoners. At the climax of the engagement he was shot in the groin and died almost immediately, being hastily buried in a nearby olive grove. In recognition of his invaluable services a monument to his memory was set up in St Paul's Cathedral and a pension of £1,200 settled on his family.

LE MARCHANT, WILLIAM (1721-1809). *'L'Etat, c'est moi!': The irascible Bailiff who sought to ride roughshod over his fellow islanders' rights and privileges.* (D). Born on 3 October 1721 into the family which (apart from the 12-year period 1758-1770) provided Guernsey with its Bailiffs continuously from 1728 to 1810, William le Marchant erupted into public life in 1754 when he was elected a Jurat by the unanimous voice of the States of Election — a very rare occurrence. Ten years later, in 1764, he was appointed H.M. Receiver after making his mark by the publication of his monograph *The Rights and Immunities of Guernsey*, which helped to resolve the differences between the island's merchants and the British government over taxation questions.

In 1770 this thrusting and assertive personality was appointed Bailiff on the recommendation of the Governor (Lord Amherst) who saw him as the ideal local 'strong man' to complement the Lieutenant-Governor — Lieutenant-Colonel P. A. Irving (q.v.) — in placing in reliable hands the government of an invaluable frontier fortress adjacent to a potentially hostile France. Four years after his assumption of office — in 1774 — the Procureur, John de Sausmarez, died and Le Marchant, seeing a chance to consolidate his power and influence, persuaded Lord Amherst to appoint as the new Procureur his eldest son Hirzel le Marchant. He also procured the post of Comptroller for his 18-year-old nephew Thomas de Sausmarez (q.v.), the son of the previous Procureur by his second wife (Le Marchant's sister Martha). By these machinations the Bailiff aroused the hostility of Matthew de Sausmarez (the son of the late Procureur by his first wife and who, having been Deputy Procureur to his father, expected to succeed him) and also a young Advocate called Peter de Havilland (q.v.) who aspired to be Comptroller.

The first chickens thus hatched came home to roost in 1775 when de Havilland (who had made no secret of his resentment) was suspended by le Marchant from his practice as an Advocate because of his alleged 'insolent conduct'. The Jurats thereupon refused to try any more cases until de Havilland was reinstated and later resigned en bloc (1776) by way of protest against further arbitrary decisions made by the Bailiff without consulting them. At the ensuing meeting of the States of Election Matthew de Sausmarez (who, having a seat thereon as a Constable for St Martin's, saw an opportunity for revenge on the Bailiff) successfully urged the re-election of all the Jurats who had resigned. The Bailiff's refusal to accept the validity of this vote was overruled by the Privy Council, which ordered that the Jurats be duly pronounced re-elected. Apart from four who had refused to resume office they were accordingly reinstated. Le Marchant had been rebuffed and De Sausmarez' ploy to humble him had succeeded.

In January 1777 Matthew de Sausmarez renewed the attack on his enemy, persuading his fellow Parish Constables to join with him in protesting against the practice of the Bailiff in ordering the Sergent of the court to carry out arrests (a duty properly appertaining to the Prévôt) without consulting his colleagues on the bench — thereby clearly exceeding his powers. The Constables in a body presented themselves at the Bailiff's chambers on 24 January, when (in the words of the Order-in-Council of 11 November 1778) 'instead of meeting that reception which their publick character and respectful behaviour naturally claimed, he began by insulting them, but particularly the Petitioner, by accusing him of Perjury'. De Sausmarez brought an action against the Bailiff 'pour l'avoid affreusement insulté' — and the Privy Council, with a recent suit in mind, ordered le Marchant (despite his protests) to recognize the court's competence to try the case although he personally was involved. Le Marchant remaining obdurate, a further Order-in-Council was issued and the case eventually heard in March 1781 when de Sausmarez was awarded 425 livres tournois (c. £30) damages for calumny.

The lawsuit on the basis of which the Privy Council ruled the Royal Court competent to hear a case involving the Bailiff had been taken out by le Marchant himself in 1777 against Isaac Dobrée, whom he accused of 'calumny' for stating in public that his (the Bailiff's) record of the previous year's proceedings of the States of Election where the Jurats had been re-elected en masse, was invalid. By this action le Marchant established the precedent that the Royal Court

could try cases to which he was a party — and furthermore, he also antagonised his nephew, the Comptroller Thomas de Sausmarez, who was then seeking the hand of Dobrée's sister Martha. Nine years later (1786) the animosity between the two men became mutual as a result of the Comptroller's vigorous defence of one Zacharias Mahy, held by le Marchant to have committed perjury when giving evidence during the trial of a Methodist named Thomas Hallowris accused of subversive activities. The following year (1787) the Bailiff's son Robert Porret le Marchant was elected a Jurat, and the prestige of the family was further boosted when the old Manoir ès Marchants was replaced by the building which now constitutes the St Peter-Port Constables' Office — erected as a fitting residence for the holder of Guernsey's supreme office. How little the old Adam in this office-holder was quenched was demonstrated the year after that (1788), when le Marchant gratuitously launched an attack on the opponents of the autocratic pretensions of his Jersey counterpart, William Charles Lemprière.

The confrontation between uncle and nephew, Bailiff and Comptroller, came to a head early in 1789. The previous year le Marchant had dug a well over which he had erected the pump, a later version of which is still to be seen at the foot of Rue le Marchant. This water-supply he offered to the parish of St Peter-Port for 5,600 livres tournois (£400), towards which an affluent landowner (Richard de Beauvoir) was required by the Chefs de Famille of the parish to contribute 1,500 livres turnois (c. £107). In face of de Beauvoir's protest at such a levy the Royal Court re-valued the pump at 4,200 livres turnois (£300) as a result of which de Beauvoir's contribution was reduced to 1,100 livres turnois (c. £78). To placate the Bailiff the St Peter-Port Douzaine resolved that the £30 difference between de Beauvoir's old and new contributions should fall on the parochial taxpayer, with the senior Constable responsible for collecting this sum. Seeing a wonderful opportunity of making political capital out of opposing a decision which appeared to favour the rich against the poor, le Marchant appealed against it, but before the appeal could be heard the Constables' term of office expired. To keep his appeal alive the Bailiff sought by persistent prevarication to postpone *sine die* the assumption of office by the new Constable-elect, even going to the length of taking advantage of a Regulation of 1607 (never before invoked) which entitled him to defer implementing any court ruling for 40 days should unanimity among the

Jurats be lacking — as could always be relied on, thanks to his son's presence on the bench. In the course of altercations arising in the court consequent upon the devices he was employing, Le Marchant accused de Sausmarez of having '*malversé*', adding '*qu'il avait agi contraire à son serment*'. The upshot was that the Comptroller and the would-be Constables took the matter to the Privy Council which, by its findings of June 1791, sat neatly on the fence, requiring the Bailiff to swear-in the new Constables forthwith but also ruling that his remarks to Thomas de Sausmarez, though couched in excessively severe language, nevertheless only amounted to a reprimand and therefore were not defamatory. On the other hand the Privy Council disallowed le Marchant's claim to the right of delaying for 40 days the execution of any decision of the court where the Jurats were not unanimous.

During all these years the feud with Peter de Havilland had continued unabated. Forced in 1783 to give up his practice as Advocate as his pleas rarely succeeded with le Marchant in the chair, Peter retired to Exeter, but returned to the fray in 1785 when he was elected a Jurat. In 1791 battle was joined with the Bailiff accusing his old adversary of having sworn falsehoods in an affidavit submitted to the Privy Council. De Havilland immediately brought an action for slander and refused to resume his seat as a Jurat until his honour had been vindicated. Le Marchant contrived by delaying tactics to prevent any hearing taking place until late November 1795 and even then tried to overawe the court by announcing his intention of obtaining from the Lieutenant-Governor a military force to escort to Castle Cornet Jurat de Jersey, who was presiding in the cause — and followed this up by brandishing a knife in the courtroom: according to one account under de Jersey's very nose!

Despite these attempts at intimidation the court found for de Havilland and awarded him damages of 1,000 livres tournois. The Bailiff, however, refused to pay and still excluded de Havilland from his seat as a Jurat. Not content with defying a subsequent Order-in-Council to reinstate his antagonist, he assaulted the Prévôt and bruised him with a cane when the latter was sent to him to signify that in default of payment of the damages awarded to de Havilland certain executions had been made on his property. At the end of a tense session in May 1796 the Royal Court fined le Marchant 300 livres tournois and sentenced him to 15 days imprisonment in Castle Cornet, remitted to house arrest for the same

period after the Bailiff had given his word of honour to abide there. When reinstated later that summer, it seems that at last the old despot had been tamed, his remaining years in office from then until 1800 devoid of further alarums and excursions. Relinquishing office to his son Robert Porret le Marchant in 1800, William le Marchant retired into private life, dying on 16 October 1809.

DE LA MARCHE, REVEREND JEAN (1585–1651). *Envoy plenipotentiary cum puritanical prig*. De la Marche was of Burgundian origins, his eponymous great-grandfather, after forcible ejection from the ancestral home at Marcenay in the Côtes d'Or by the troops of Charles the Rash in 1477, having ended a subsequent nomadic existence by settling in Guernsey, where evidence survives for his residence in July 1505. Jean de la Marche was born to Michelle (*née* Vering), the wife of Hellier de la Marche, on 6 August 1585. He appears to have received his early education at 'La Grande Ecole' (Elizabeth College), whence he went up to Cambridge in July 1604. Coming down early in 1608, he declined the Colloque's invitation temporarily to undertake the charge of Elizabeth College, being anxious to pursue his religious studies. Helped by a grant from the States he went to the Theological College at Saumur where he took his degree of Master of Arts, after which he was called to the Ministry on 6 August 1613 (his 28th birthday), being installed minister of the two parishes of St Andrew's and the Forest on the following 5 September. In January 1617 he married Esther de Beauvoir, whereby he inherited through his bride's late mother Collette Careye, the Carey Estate of La Ville au Roi.

Of considerable attainments, Jean de la Marche emerged as one of the most active members of the States and in November 1617 was entrusted with a most delicate mission on the outcome of which the future of Guernsey's Huguenot Establishment depended. True to his maxim, 'No Bishop, no King', James I was intent on imposing Anglicanism in the Channel Isles — a policy which, in Jersey, was to meet with success in 1620 with the appointment as Dean of David Bandinel. An opportunity to achieve a like success in Guernsey seemed to arise in 1616 when Thomas le Page of St Martin's appealed to the Court of Arches against the excommunication imposed on him by Simon Herne, the incumbent of that parish, for refusing to live with his wife. Summoned to this court, Herne instead pleaded his cause in London before Lord Carew (Guernsey's absentee Governor). Thanks to Carew's representations, the king himself took cognisance of the matter, and on the strength of this Herne returned to Guernsey without attending the Court of Arches. An infuriated Archbishop Abbot then (July 1617) excommunicated Herne, whereupon the States decided to appeal directly to James I against such attempted infringement of their privileges, and at the same time to petition him to confirm the island's right to exercise the Presbyterian discipline; sending de la Marche as their envoy. So successfully did Jean de la Marche plead with the king that on 20 November James delivered to him a letter confirming the continuation of Guernsey's ecclesiastical system. Thenceforce the minister of St Andrew's and the Forest was the hero of the hour. Made chaplain of the garrison at Castle Cornet in May 1623, he was again appointed in February 1625 (New Style) as one of a delegation sent to the King-in-Council to seek permission for the export of wool to Guernsey, free of customs duty – and was transferred by the Colloque to the prestigious living of the Town Church on his return. In September 1626 came another embassy when he was among those chosen to go to England to seek the confirmation of Guernsey's privileges from Charles I on his accession. He was, furthermore, elected a member of the committee appointed in August 1628 to supervise the repairs of the island's fortifications in view of the war with France. In addition he was frequently made auditor of the accounts of the States and chosen to serve on several committees.

At this juncture, however, de la Marche overreached himself. Insistent on the assertion of what he deemed to be his rights, in November 1626 he boldly claimed from the Governor (by then no longer Lord Carew, but the Earl of Danby) the restitution of the tithes based on tobacco and grassland appropriated by the Crown at the Reformation, taking out a lawsuit against the farmer of the Royal Revenue, Pierre Careye. In 1628 he stepped up his campaign by attacks from the pulpit, using Galatians VI, 6 as a vehicle for a disquisition on 'la doctrine des Dîmes prediales' (grassland tithes) and thereby so offending his Consistory that it forbade further addresses on this theme. Oblivious, however, of the hornet's nest he was stirring up around himself, Jean de la Marche proceeded to launch a personal attack on a fellow cleric of whose lax conduct this virtuous but self-righteous paragon disapproved, publicly deploring at a session on the Colloque in January 1632 the 'abominable drunkenness'

of Joshua Slowley, Master of Elizabeth College and Chaplain to Castle Cornet. A year later Slowley retorted, maliciously accusing the critic of his morals of treason and heresy for preaching that tithes taken by the Crown were due to him by Divine Right.

The upshot was that de la Marche was imprisoned in Castle Cornet from February to September. It is interesting that while incarcerated he had his last attack (in May) of 'une maladie langoureuse' from which he had suffered for several years. In September he was released on condition of appearing as and when required to answer charges levelled against him and also to proceed with his appeal. Accordingly, in November he appeared several times before Sir Peter Osborne (q.v.) who had been deputed by the Privy Council to examine the whole matter – and the following February (1634) left for England to prosecute his appeal. In this connection he saw the Earl of Danby in April – but returned at the end of July 'n'ayant jamais peu (sic) obtenir l'examen de mon affaire'. Within ten days the Colloque deprived him of the incumbency of the Town Church and appointed him to St Andrew's.

In September 1636 de la Marche was summoned to Castle Cornet to appear before Danby (who was paying a brief visit to the island), together with the four ministers who had done duty for him during his imprisonment and absence in England and whom he was required to pay for these services. He however declined so to do and persisted in this refusal despite repeated demands until eventually (in June 1640) the Colloque disallowed further applications, thus bringing de la Marche's prolonged purgatory to an inconclusive end.

In the meanwhile de la Marche had the previous December submitted a proposal that advances be made to the Jersey Church (by then run on Anglican lines) with a view to reconciliation. This was acted on a year later when the Colloque voted to send Samuel de la Place (who in 1620 had replaced Herne as Incumbent of St Martin's) to Jersey to negotiate reunion. Then in March 1641 de la Marche was sent, together with de la Place, as deputies to Parliament to make representations concerning the church in Guernsey. He composed for the occasion a Treatise on Revelations XVIII, 17 which much impressed the parliamentary leaders. Although a sermon delivered in the French church in Threadneedle Street the following February was so intemperate in its abuse of episcopacy as to antagonise the resident minister (Dr. Primrose) who preached against it the next Sunday, de la Marche was nevertheless in April 1642 chosen by Parliament as one of the 24 ministers selected to take part in the Assembly of Divines at Westminster convened to examine the government of the church. A year later — after the post had been held briefly by Louis Herault following Dr. Primrose's death in December 1642 - he was appointed as minister of the French church in May 1643, ousting his pro-Royalist predecessor. In this capacity he inveighed mercilessly against the king and queen, excommunicating any who protested — and became so intemperate in his anathemas against all objectors to his views as to foment a near riot, with a 100 malcontents beseiging the church in January 1646, obliging the Lord Mayor to intervene to calm the tumult. Although a superficial reconciliation was finally achieved, the accord remained fragile and eventually a large segment of the congregation became permanently estranged from the church. Only his sudden death on 14 October 1651 restored unity to the distraught French church whose more moderate members had viewed with dismayed distaste de la Marche's attitude at the time of the trial and execution of Charles I.

So died a Guernseyman of undoubted talent and sincerity, but also one of sanctimonious intolerance, a prophet of hate for those he saw as God's enemies: in short a 17th-century Puritan of the deepest hue.

MARTEL, LINDA (1956–1961). *An extraordinary child of intense spiritual perception and an instrument of paranormal therapy.* Born at Amherst Maternity Home on 21 August 1956 to Eileen Ethel (*née* Allchin), the wife of Royston James Martel, a commercial traveller of St Sampson's and later of George Street, St Peter-Port, Linda Martel was not initially expected to survive, suffering from hydrocephalus, spina bifida and a consequent paralysis of the legs. The baby was therefore hastily baptised for fear of an imminent demise.

This gloomy prognosis notwithstanding, Linda lived and the abnormal expansion of her head was arrested a year later with the insertion of a catheter to draw off fluid from the cranial cavity. Thereafter her remarkable awareness of the supernatural became increasingly apparent. From time to time this prodigious child was vouchsafed visions of Our Lord and of the Blessed Virgin ('the Pretty Lady'), with a bright light on various occasions of this nature being visible in her room to those outside. Yet despite these experiences (or maybe because of them!) the inspired little

girl at all times objected vehemently to being taken into any church.

As soon as Linda was able to speak she began her career of healing, telling those benefiting from her ministrations that they would recover — assurances which frequently proved to be well-founded. Furthermore, some of those relieved of their ailments were themselves accorded visions — one of these being personally known to the present writer. At last there came the day in mid-October 1961 when the phenomenal five-year-old announced that 'her Jesus' was soon to come for her. A week later, on 20 October, she died and her body was buried in St Sampson's churchyard.

Then commenced a series of healings from beyond the grave. Victims of the most painful afflictions found that their sufferings melted away when portions of the child's clothing were applied to the affected parts of the body. One such (an acquaintance of the present writer) was able to walk around normally without any discomfort after having been told in the wake of an accident causing severe multiple leg injuries that his agonising condition was irremediable and that never again would he be able to move without crutches. Even visits to the little girl's grave were in several cases found to be therapeutically efficacious. A whole series of such cures had taken place by the time that Charles Graves wrote *The Legend of Linda Martel* in 1968 — and the evidence is that they by no means stopped at that point. When approached for his views on these phenomena the distinguished Anglican priest-cum-pathologist-cum-don-cum-consultant, the Reverend Dr. Martin Spencer Israel, M.B., M.R.C.Path., D.C.P., replied that he saw Linda as 'a very advanced soul who came into incarnation in the greatest humility to reveal Christ to her compatriots in prayer, counsel and healing'; and he went on to say that to him everything concerning her was 'a source of infinite wonder and thanksgiving'. Guernsey would appear to have its own Bernardette Soubirous.

MARTEL, LIEUTENANT PHILIP, M.C. (1914–). *The spy from the jeweller's shop.* Born to Lily (*née* Roger), the wife of Thomas Martel on 17 December 1914, Philip Martel was educated at Elizabeth College, on leaving which he became a shareholder in the family jewellery concern trading as 'Roger's' in the Commercial Arcade. To equip himself to the full for this type of business, he studied watch-making in Geneva and sight-testing in London, where he obtained the

Diploma of the Spectacle Makers' Company. In the years between leaving school and the outbreak of war Philip Martel volunteered for service in the Royal Guernsey Militia, in which force he developed by disciplined application the attributes of stamina and fortitude which were to stand him in such good stead later on.

On the outbreak of war Philip Martel was among those affected by the general mobilisation of the Militia, on which the defences of Guernsey devolved after the withdrawal of the Regular Army garrison. When all militiamen in January 1940 were given the option of returning to civilian life for the time being or offering themselves for the British armed forces, Mr. Martel — in common with several of his comrades — joined the Hampshire Regiment, where, thanks to his pre-war military training, he was soon commissioned.

The episode which was to immortalise Philip Martel began on the night of 9 July 1940, when, together with Second-Lieutenant Desmond Mulholland (q.v.) he set off from Devonport in Submarine H.43 (escorted for the first part of its journey by H.M. Trawler *Indian Star*) in the second stage of Operation 'Anger' charged with reconnoitring in advance of a full-scale Commando Raid (Operation 'Ambassador') scheduled for the night of 12-13 July. The two subalterns were landed at Le Jaonnet, with Martel's particular duty, after spying out the lie of the land, being to meet and guide a section of the 'Ambassador' raiding party at Petit Bôt on 12 July — but to go on subsequent nights to Le Jaonnet to be picked up should the raid not take place.

'Ambassador' was in fact postponed and when it did occur two nights later the torch flashes of 'D' in morse code sent out as instructed by the young men were mistaken by the Commandos for enemy signals, with the result that they immediately withdrew. The two agents were stranded and on the run, Martel suffering acutely from the fact that, lacking rubber-soled shoes, he had to go barefoot to avoid detection after curfew, so that his feet were soon sore and bleeding. Having sheltered once with his sister in Queen's Road, he refused to return for fear of compromising her and eventually broke into a deserted house in St Martin's to steal clothing and a razor (as his beard growth was making him conspicuous). After failing to get away in a fishing boat which they stole at Perelle, the two fugitives made a hazardous trip to Sark on the same ship as a group of German officers, but found escape from that island to be impossible. Deciding to give themselves up, they contacted Major Ambrose

Sherwill (q.v.) who at great personal risk provided them with old Militia uniforms before reporting their presence to the German Commandant's Chief of Staff. Thus saved from being shot as spies, the two subalterns were treated as prisoners of war.

Released at the end of the conflict, Philip Martel was awarded the Military Cross for his exploit. He returned to civilian life in Guernsey and to the family jewellery business, finally retiring in 1979. On 27 October 1968, however, he briefly resumed his military rôle when, once again as Lieutenant Philip Martel, he was one of the officers in reserve at the impressive service in the Town Church when the Militia Colours, following restoration, were presented, re-dedicated and laid up.

MATCHAN, LEONARD JOSEPH (1911-). *The tycoon of Brecqhou*. Born in a Fulham back street on 26 March 1911 to Elsie Harriet (*née* Greenleaf), the wife of George Matcham, a sewing-machine engineer, Leonard Matchan (who quoted his recreation as 'Work') came in his achievements to typify the traditional self-made man. Educated at Trinity School in Croydon, he in due course became a Fellow of the Association of Certified and Corporate Accountants and a holder of the Joint Diploma in Management Accounting Services. He then started on a career which ultimately saw him controlling an international complex of companies with an annual turnover of £100 million, having at one time or another successfully involved himself in a bewildering miscellany of ventures embracing (*inter alia*) cosmetics, mink farming, fashion, engineering, plastics, hotels, fruit machines, publishing, professional football and speedway racing.

Marrying Kathleen Artis in 1933, Matchan by the age of 25 (in 1936) had become Vice-President and European General Manager of Max Factor Incorporated of Hollywood, California — a position he held until 1949. To this he added the Presidency of the Toilet Preparations Association from 1940 to 1948, before practising as an accountant from 1950 to 1955. Cope Allman International Ltd. (of which he became Honorary Life President) was built up by him from the takeover of a Birmingham firm making coffin furniture and earning about £800 profit per annum. Although an expert on company law and until 1979 Chairman of Guarantee Trust of Jersey Limited, he was paradoxically of left-wing sympathies. Leonard Matchan stood as the Labour Party candidate for Poole, Dorset, in 1951 — and, although unsuccessful, was the only Labour candidate to increase his vote in a General Election which was calamitous for his party.

In April 1966 this millionaire with a reputation for getting his own way arrived in Brecqhou (an island free even from Guernsey taxation) already assured of La Dame de Sercq's *congé* to buy its tenancy. Offering £40,000 in response to the price of £125,000 sought by the agent, he eventually settled for £46,000 with farming equipment thrown in. As tenant of Brecqhou Matchan automatically qualified for the seat in Chief Pleas appertaining to the Quarantaine Holding of La Moinerie de Haut, allocated to a previous lessee of the island (Mr. Angelo Clarke) by La Dame in 1929 — and as a member of Sark's legislature he was soon involved in an imbroglio arising from his use of a Gazelle helicopter to carry him to business meetings in England, France and Jersey. Dislike of the noise caused by the aircraft, plus the fact that the internal combustion engine (tractors apart) is in any case outlawed in Sark, led to a proposal that it be banned. Denying that Sark's prohibition on the internal combusion engine applied to Brecqhou, the Tenant of La Moinerie de Haut warned that should the use of the machine be forbidden on the grounds that Brecqhou was integral to Sark, then he would insist on Sark maintaining its small neighbour's roads and also paying the sixpence-a-tail (now 2½ pence per tail) bounty on rabbits — which in that case would apply to Brecqhou as much as to Sark proper — in respect of the islet's three million coneys. Matchan's arguments prevailed and Chief Pleas voted him permission to use the helicopter for his lifetime, on the understanding that he would not overfly Sark itself — unless on an errand of mercy such as taking over a veterinary surgeon or lifting a sick or injured person to hospital in Guernsey in bad weather.

His special status thus secured, Leonard Matchan set about establishing himself as monarch of his small domain, complete with the appurtenances of power. Obtaining from Mrs. Sibyl Hathaway (q.v.) the coveted — and unique — right to keep a bitch, he issued his own conveyance stamps in six denominations from one pre-decimal penny to two shillings until 1969 when the States of Guernsey assumed responsibility for the Bailiwick's postal services, and refused to tolerate any infringement of its monopoly. In addition the Matchan coat of arms — two seagulls, a wave and three trefoils — was incorporated for Brecqhou, with La Dame's permission, into Sark's Standard, with authorisation for it to be flown from the flagpole of the little island where an indefatigable magnate continued to rule a vast industrial empire through a battery of telephones.

LE MESURIER, HAVILLAND (1758-1806). *The Guernseyman who helped to beat Napoleon by keeping the Army fed.* (A). Born in Guernsey, the youngest son of John le Mesurier I (q.v.) and the uncle of John le Mesurier II (q.v.), Havilland le Mesurier obtained a scholarship at Winchester in 1770, but resigned it the next year — at the ripe old of age of 13! He spent the next few years in a 'mercantile connection' with his father and his brother Peter (q.v.): the 'next few years' corresponding with the golden age of privateering.

In 1782 Havilland married Eliza Dobrée in Guernsey prior to joining a large mercantile firm at Le Havre. Thence he moved to London, but after suffering in the commercial dislocations arising from the war crisis of 1793, he accepted the post of 'adjudant commissary-general of stores, supplies and storage' with the forces on the Continent under the Duke of York (Commander in Chief). During the winter of 1794-95 he was employed as acting commissary-general of the army in the course of the retreat through Holland and Westphalia to Bremen, the efficiency with which he discharged his duties earning subsequent high commendation. On his return to England in 1795 he entered into business with his brother Paul le Mesurier (q.v.) as 'P. and H. le Mesurier, of Austin Friars, Merchants' — and maintained this interest until his death, over and above his military commitments. During the invasion alarm of 1798 Havilland was appointed commissary-general of the Southern District; while holding this post he introduced a new plan of supply embracing the establishment of scattered depôts of stores, each in charge of a 'reserve commissary' — a plan warmly approved by Sir Charles (later Earl) Grey.

Havilland le Mesurier resigned in 1800 in protest at being placed in a secondary position contrary to express stipulation. He was, however, reinstated by Addington in March 1801 and sent to Egypt to superintend commissariat arrangements for the army returning from that country: duties which subsequently involved service in Malta and Naples. Out of his experience he wrote a number of works on commissariat organisation. By now his health was failing and he died at Westminster in March 1806.

LE MESURIER, HENRY (1713-1779). *The originator of Braye Harbour.* (A). On the death in

1729 of Anne le Mesurier (*née* Andros) her 16-year-old son Henry succeeded to the grant of Alderney which his mother, consequent upon the deaths of her brother George and his two daughters, had inherited from her uncle Sir Edmund Andros (q.v.) who had died childless. For the next century he and his successors continued to be known as 'Hereditary Governors' of Alderney (please see 'Carteret, George') although – as was pointed out by the late Maurice Ouseley, sometime Secretary of the Guernsey Society – the title was a local conceit, Privy Council papers invariably referring to the holders of the Patent issued to Sir Edmund by Charles II (and subsequently renewed) as 'fee-farmers' of the island.

The youthful 'Governor' came into a troubled inheritance. Ever since the death of Sir Edmund Andros in the year of Henry's birth, his grandfather (Sir Edmund's Lieutenant), his uncle and his father had, one after the other, been plagued by the implacable hostility of the group of Aurigniaias led by the Judge Thomas le Cocq (q.v.), who bitterly resented rule by outsiders. This feud continued unabated until finally, in 1738, Henry asserted his authority and on the grounds of alleged irregularities in their performance, contrived to obtain le Cocq's suspension from the exercise of his functions – though he still retained the office of judge until his death in 1760.

Before le Cocq received his *congé* Henry, seeking to stimulate Alderney's trade, revived a 1608 proposal of William Chamberlayne (q.v.) to construct a harbour at Braye to replace the old one at Longy which had been rendered increasingly useless as a result of silting. Accordingly in 1736 he obtained a grant of a portion of the common lands at Braye for houses and warehouses in return for the construction of the roughcast breakwater which still survives to the present day. Shown on I. H. Bastide's contemporary Ordnance Survey as the 'New Peer'[*sic*], it is now known as the Old Jetty.

Although le Cocq no longer operated as Judge, the removal of the enemy commander did not bring with it any dispersal of his troops, and le Mesurier found himself increasingly defied by the all-but-ungovernable Aurigniais. Finally, in 1744, he exchanged his Patent of Alderney with his brother John for lands in Guernsey, saying that he was 'worn out with feuds of the lawless and insubordinate Islanders'. Settled in Guernsey, he married Marie Dobrée and their daughter Martha later became the wife of Peter Perchard (q.v.), Lord Mayor of London 1804-5. Later in life

he prospered greatly from entering into a partnership with his brother John le Mesurier (q.v.) in privateering ventures. Henry le Mesurier died in 1779.

LE MESURIER, JOHN (1717-1793). *Alderney's 18th century condottiere*. (A). The younger brother of Henry le Mesurier (q.v.), from whom he took over the Patent of Alderney in 1744, John le Mesurier almost immediately found himself (like his predecessor) confronted with exasperating intransigence on the part of the Aurigniais; and in 1747, saying he had 'reason to fear his life in danger', he fled to Guernsey, seeking the protection of the Royal Court, which confirmed his sitle of Governor and forbade the States of Alderney to assemble in his absence.

Prospects improved immeasurably with the outbreak of the Seven Years War in 1756. The privateering opportunities presented by this conflict and the ensuing War of American Independence not only diverted the bellicosity of the Aurigniais, but also proved to be extremely lucrative in the profits they yielded, so that John and Henry – his brother-cum-partner – prospered exceedingly; so much so that in 1763 he exchanged the Patent for a new grant of 99 years. At the same time he used some of his gains to enlarge the Georgian residence which occupied the site of the old house built by Captain Nicholas Ling (q.v.), converting it into Government House – it is now the Island Hall – while some years later (in 1779) the family moved in to the newly-completed Les Mouriaux House – latterly the abode of the President of the States of Alderney. In 1767 he added to the old church the Clock Tower (the only part of the structure still to survive) and in 1770 he provided the island with its first Court House in La Rue des Héritiers (now Elizabeth II Street).

Although from the early 1770s onwards delegating most of his functions to his son Peter le Mesurier (q.v.), John nevertheless was far from being reduced to a cypher. Still with a finger in the privateering pie, he and Henry made a record haul in 1779 when their ship *Resolution* brought in prizes to the value of £134,589. In 1786, incensed at the prospect of what he saw as a subversive heresy contaminating the island, he threatened to deport the Methodist missionary, Dr. Adam Clarke, to the Casquets if he dared set foot in Alderney. The threat, however, was not carried out and the following year John Wesley himself (q.v.*) preached at Braye and slept overnight at the *Diver's Inn*.

1. Sir Edmund Andros (1637-1714), Seigneur de Sausmarez, Bailiff of Guernsey, Governor of New England, New York and Virginia.

2. Sir Donald Banks (1891-1975).

3. (*above left*) Henri Biard (1891-1966), aviator and winner of the Schneider Trophy, 1922.
4. (*left*) Reg. Blanchford (1915-   ), taken from *Samaritan of the Islands* by Don Everitt, 1959.
5. (*above*) Daniel de Lisle Brock (1762-1842), Bailiff 1821-42.

(*top right*) Rev. J.L.V. Cachemaille (1804-77).
(*top*) Edith Frances Carey (1864-1935),
storian.
(*right*) Sir George Carteret (1609-79).
inted c.1667 by Lely. Original in St Ouen's
anor, Jersey.

9. (*left*) Sir Peter le Cheminant (1920-   ),
Lt.-Gov. of Guernsey, 1980.
10. (*below*) Rev. W.T. Collings (1823-82),
Seigneur of Sark, 1853-82.

(*above*) Roy Dotrice (1923-   ).
(*above right*) Sir John Doyle (1756-1834),
Gov. 1803-16, c.1797.
(*right*) Brigadier F.G. French, Judge of
Alderney, 1938-47.

14. (*above left*) Sir Henry Gauvain (1878-1945).
15. (*above*) Lt.-Col. T.W.M. de Guerin (1861-1929).
16. (*left*) Sir Peter de Havilland (1747-1821), from a miniature.

18. Capt. Sydney Peck Herivel (1890-1970). President of Alderney States 1949-70.

17. Henry Head (1899-1969).

19. Victor Hugo (1802-85). Resident in Guernsey, 1855-70.

20. (*opposite*) Sir Abraham Lainé (1876-1948).

26. Marianne Miller (née Carey (1826-1912). Found ress of Cobo church.

27. Mrs Margaret Neve (1792-1903). On her 109th birthday.

28. (*above left*) Cecil Noel (1897-1941) as a Corporal in the Royal Flying Corps.
29. (*above right*) Sir Peter Osborne (1584-1653). Royalist defender of Castle Cornet.
30. (*left*) Rev. James Parkes (1896-1981), architect of Jewish/Christian rapprochement.

31. Brigadier H.W. le Patourel V.C. (1916-79).

32. Sir Peter le Page Renouf (1822-97), Egyptologist.
33. (*opposite*) Admiral Lord de Saumarez (1757-1836).

34. Sir Ambrose J. Sherwill (1890-1968), Bailiff 1946-60, painted by Arthur Michael

35. Ferdinand Brock Tupper (1795-1874), eminent historian.

John's last noteworthy action occurred in 1790, when he endowed Alderney's first school. He died, aged 75, in 1793, after having held the reins of Alderney's government for nearly half a century.

LE MESURIER, MAJOR-GENERAL JOHN (1781-1843). *Alderney's last 'Hereditary Governor'.*

(A). The son of Peter le Mesurier (q.v.), John was appointed an Ensign in the 132nd Highlanders in 1794 at the age of 13 — but was soon transferred to the 89th Foot (the unit in which he remained for the rest of his military career), becoming a Captain-Lieutenant in 1796. In 1798 he served with a flank battalion commanded by Colonel Stewart in the course of the Irish rebellion: while the following year found him in the Mediterranean, where in 1799 and 1800 he participated in the blockade and capture of Malta under General Thomas Graham, and also in the subsequent occupation of Messina. After serving in the Egyptian campaign of 1801 (including the battles before Alexandria, the defence of Rosetta and the surrender of Cairo) he returned to Ireland at the Peace of Amiens (1802). On inheriting the grant Alderney at his father's death in 1803 he retired on half-pay with the rank of Major, and while on the half-pay list (where he remained for the rest of his life) he eventually attained the rank of Major-General. In 1804 he married his first cousin Martha, the daughter borne by his maternal aunt Martha to Peter Perchard (q.v.), who became Lord Mayor of London in the autumn of the same year.

Peter le Mesurier had left his son a troubled inheritance. Not only was he rebuffed by the officers of the 300-strong Regular Army garrison stationed in the island, who received instructions from the Guernsey Command not to recognise the military authority of the Alderney Governor (who was only a half-pay Major after all) but he also fell foul of the Alderney Jurats by assuming the title of Seigneur. Four Jurats refused to pass a contract in which he was so designated and John's appeal to the Privy Council to enforce recognition of his title was rejected in 1814. In the meantime vigorous action to suppress smuggling taken by the British government in 1808 had brought distress to Alderney — and this was later made worse by the removal of the garrison after Waterloo. The financial burdens on the Governor became so onerous that in 1823 John wrote to the Treasury offering to surrender his grant of the island on payment of suitable compensation. In 1824 the British Treasury offered £700 per annum for the rest of the lease (i.e. until 1862). John accepted this offer and surrendered the island in 1825. He retired to Berkshire and died at Bradfield Place, near Reading, in May 1843.

LE MESURIER, PAUL (1755-1805). *The first Guernseyman to become Lord Mayor of London.*

(A). Born in Guernsey in February 1755, on reaching his majority in 1776 Paul le Mesurier entered into partnership with Nicholas le Cras (a merchant of Walbrook in London) and soon became well-known as a prize agent during the War of American Independence which was then being waged. In 1780 he joined the first voluntary military association to be formed in England and rose to be a Colonel of the Honourable Artillery Company in 1794.

As a shareholder in the East India Company, Paul le Mesurier was so active in opposing Fox's India Bill of 1783 that he was appointed a director of the company. Furthermore, the reputation he gained also brought him election as M.P. for Southwark at the general election following the defeat of the Bill. He became Alderman of Dowgate Ward of the City in October 1784, was Sheriff of the City of London in 1787 and entered on his term of office as Lord Mayor of London in November 1794. In this office he lavishly entertained Lord Cornwallis, the Governor-General of India, when His Excellency was presented with the Freedom of the City the following month.

In 1795, while still Lord Mayor, Paul formed a business partnership with his brother Havilland le Mesurier (q.v.), which lasted until his death ten years later. Paul le Mesurier died in December 1805 and was buried in the churchyard of Christ Church, Spitalfields.

LE MESURIER, PETER (1753-1803). *The Alderney Militia's Godfather.*

(A). The eldest son of John le Mesurier I (q.v.) and the father of John le Mesurier II (q.v.), Peter le Mesurier acted as Lieutenant to his father from about 1770 onwards, being responsible for the construction of Les Mouriaux House in 1779. As deputy for his parent, Peter in 1777 set about reorganising the Alderney Militia (which he stated to be 217 strong) on an efficient basis, making service and drills compulsory for all men between 16 and 60 years of age. The British government helped by supplying 200 stands of arms, and later in 1781 uniforms — hitherto worn only by officers at their own expense — were adopted for all ranks.

Peter himself claimed in correspondence with the War Office to have spent £500 out of his own pocket on barracks and other contigent expenses associated with this reorganisation.

Despite John le Mesurier's opposition Methodism had mushroomed in the island, the sect's first chapel being built in 1790 and Peter, succeeding to his father in the same year (1793) as the French Revolutionary War broke out, found himself confronted with two problems posed by this widespread Wesleyanism, the first of which arose from Methodist sabbatarianism issuing in a refusal on the part of the faithful to participate in Sunday Militia drills. Peter solved this by creating a special company for these 'conscientious objectors' which drilled extra hours on weekdays — a unit derisively referred to by non-Methodists as 'l'Armée de Gédéon'. The second development called for the exercise of considerable tact on his part. The flight from revolutionary France of priests who refused to take the oath demanded by the 'The Civil Constitution of the Clergy' brought no less than 124 religious refugees to Alderney and Peter, with his marked Protestant prejudices of the strong Methodist element in mind, had to tread warily. He took in the emigrés and treated them with kindness, but insisted on Mass being said in private only, for fear of hostile reactions to any overt manifestation of Popery.

Peter le Mesurier's military preoccupations were to have woeful consequences. In 1795, while superintending the mounting of a gun, he was seriously injured by the fall of a cannon, his thigh being fractured and several ribs broken. He never recovered fully from this mishap and, dragging on for the next few years as a semi-invalid, died in the year 1803.

MÉTIVIER, GEORGE (1790–1881). *Guernsey's leading literary luminary: Franco-Norman lexicographer and 'national poet' of the Island.* (C). Outstanding among poets specialising in the Norman tongue, George Métivier was born in 1790 in Fountain Street, St Peter-Port — and was of French descent, his grandfather (the Reverend Jean Métivier, a pastor of l'Eglise Réformée de France) having sought refuge from religious persecution first in Holland and then in Guernsey. Conforming in a perfunctory way to Anglicanism — as did so many of his fellow clerics along the lines described by the Reverend Jacques Louis Victor Cachemaille (q.v.) — Jean Métivier became curate and later (in 1752) rector of the Castel church.

Jean Métivier's second wife (Elizabeth Carey) bore him a son, Jean-Carey Métivier, who in 1794 succeeded Thomas de Sausmarez (q.v.) as H.M. Comptroller and whose wife (Esther Guille) bore him five sons — of whom George was the second — before his death in 1796 at the age of 38. The young widow's straitened circumstances were relieved by her father, Jean Guille, giving her and her sons the shelter of his home at St George in the Castel. Here George Métivier grew up, learning the Patois as well as French: and later being sent to a private school to learn English. Thus, despite his urban birth, he came proudly to identify himself as a Catelain (a Castel parishioner).

Leaving Guernsey on the morrow of Waterloo, Métivier for a time studied medicine at Edinburgh University, but eventually gave it up in favour of languages, history and poetry: in connection with which his residence in Scotland had given him a familiarity with Robert Burns, whose influence is apparent in some of his 'Rimes' — notably 'Madlon Vidamour' and 'L'vier Colas'. He then tried a career in commerce, but finally surrendering himself to the Muse (which, like Love in the hymn, would not let him go), he devoted himself to poetry and linguistics for the rest of his days.

George Métivier returned to Guernsey in 1842 after an absence — occasional short visits apart — of 26 years. Loving the isle of his birth, he made a study of the development, history and morphology of its language: which he saw as a genuine remnant of Norman–French rather than — as do at times the superciliously ignorant — dismissing it as the mere prattle of uncultured yokels. His poems, displaying considerable powers of observation, reflect fantasy and tenderness, recording popular superstitions, describing 'les amours rustiques' and employing idioms expressing the bucolic humour of Guernsey countryfolk. During his exile *Les Rimes Guernesiaises* appeared in 1831 and prominent among his subsequent poetry collections are *Les Fantaisies Guernesiaises* and *Poesies Guernesiaises et Françaises*.

Over and above his poetic work, George also engaged in a prolonged correspondence with Frederick Corbin Lukis (q.v.), exploring the etymological derivation of the names of the megaliths investigated by the archaeologist — and displaying thereby a formidable knowledge of several languages old and new. He was also an intimate of Victor Hugo (q.v.), who enthusiastically cooperated with him in the preparation of his *Dictionnaire Franco-Normand*.

This dictionary, ultimately published in 1870, was undoubtedly Métivier's *chef d'œuvre*. On the strength of it he was visited by Prince Louis-Lucien Bonaparte (the brother of Napoleon III) who was regarded as a great scholar, and at whose request George translated the Gospel according to St Matthew into the Norman tongue. The repute his lexicon earned for its author prompted the Lieutenant-Bailiff, Mr. (later Sir) Edgar Mac-Culloch (q.v.) to comment in 1877 — 'As are all true Guernesiais, I am proud of our poet George Métivier and it is with pleasure that I see that his original genius, his remarkable talents and his profound scholarship find admirers outside his fellow countrymen'.

After the publication of his dictionary, it was plain that the sands were running out for Guernsey's great man of letters, who, although a bachelor all his life, is nevertheless thought to have loved and to have been loved over a period of many years, one of his last poems being a touching farewell to this mysterious and unidentified Beatrice from her Dante. A devout Christian, Métivier accepted the approach of death with resigned equanimity and one of his bardic disciples — Denys Corbet — thus described his passing in 1881: *'Resigne content de son sort — Le Sage s'incline et s'endort.'*

The remains of Guernsey's great poet were buried in St Martin's churchyard, in a tomb bearing the Métivier coat of arms. A detailed and informed appreciation of this gifted islander is to be found in the fascinating study in depth of the man and his work flowing from the pen of Mr. Peter Girard (and appearing in the 1980 *Transactions* of La Société Guernesiaise) reference to which will be richly rewarded.

MILLER, MARIANNE (1826–1912). *The foundress of Cobo church*. This committed and resourceful woman was born Marianne Carey, the youngest child of Major-General Peter Carey and his wife Julia, in July 1826. In 1831, when she was five years of age, her family went to live in the Isle of Wight, staying there for the next eight years — until 1839. Over this period, however, they paid an annual summer visit to Guernsey and it was during one of these holidays that Marianne formed in her mind the resolution that was to lead to her name meriting indelible inscription in the island's annals.

Young Marianne being very fond of Cobo, a highlight of each summer sojourn was a picnic on the beach there arranged to coincide with her birthday by way of a special treat. On one such occasion in the early 1830s the child felt tired as the three-mile walk from Havilland Hall drew

near its close and — being treated with indulgence not only as it was her birthday but also because she was considered to be delicate — she went to rest awhile on La Rocque de Guet near the watch-house erected during the War of American Independence. Looking down from this vantage point on the cottages of the fisher-folk below her, compassion welled up in the little girl's heart for their inhabitants, who had over two miles to walk to get to their parish church of St Marie du Castro. She mulled for some time over their plight and then went to her father, saying how much she pitied these poor people having to go so far each Sunday, and announcing that she wished to build a local church for them at Cobo. Amused by what he regarded as no more than an infantile fantasy, General Carey temporised, giving the stock answer employed by parents throughout the ages — that he would have to see about the matter later on when Marianne was older.

The father might thereupon have dismissed the matter from his mind — but not the daughter. When she indeed was older — much older: 17 in fact — she once again approached her father with the idea which by now had hardened into a fully matured scheme in her mind. This time the project received her parent's blessing provided its initiator did not use her beautiful singing voice to raise money for its realisation. It was 1843 and 11 years were to elapse before Marianne's plans came to fruition — years of intense effort beset with repeated difficulties: but the resolute Miss Carey was indefatigable.

After starting her fund-raising activities in a small way by selling pictures, Marianne consulted her ailing sister Caroline who arranged to leave £200 on her death which occurred soon afterwards. In remembrance of their daughter her parents matched this with a further £200, while Marianne herself managed to find £300. Parading the begging bowl before her relations (including her uncle Nicholas Carey, the Dean of Guernsey) brought in further sums and eventually £1,600 was accumulated. This was enough to build a church but as yet there was no land available to accommodate it. A site, however, was donated by Mr. de Beaucamp of Cobo and Marianne's godmother, Mrs. Thomas Carey (*née* Manning and the sister of the Cardinal) offered to build a vicarage, while the Reverend William Thomas Collings (q.v.) presented the turrets, two bells and the lychgate. At the same time the Reverend Lord de Saumarez and Colonel the Honourable St Vincent Saumarez undertook to provide the churchyard.

Yet more problems arose, however, An endowment fund of £2,000 was seen to be needed so that from its investment proceeds the vicar's salary could be found. With the help of Dean Carey this too was also gradually amassed. A whole array of formalities then had to be observed, as Marianne's church would be geographically located in the Castel parish, so that the rector's assent for the excision of a separate ecclesiastical parish from his territory had to be sought. Furthermore, the Church Building Commissioners had to be satisfied that the project had ample justification and the approval of the Bishop of Winchester was also required. These hurdles surmounted, the foundation stone of the church was laid on St Matthew's Day (21 September) 1852 — and on 6 December 1854, when Marianne was 28, the church of St Matthew was consecrated by the Right Reverend Vincent William, Bishop of Mauritius. In the presence of the women the child's dream was fulfilled.

Marianne Carey married Dugeld Stewart Miller of the 7th Foot (the Royal Fusiliers). Despite her girlhood reputation for being delicate she survived to the advanced age of 86, dying in 1912. For many years no more than a photograph in the church commemorated her, but in 1963 an oak chair bearing her family crest (and designed to be used by visiting clergy) was dedicated as a memorial to this devoted Christian of energy and determination.

MONAMY, PETER (1680/1-1748/9). *The marine artist 'second only to Van de Velde'*. Although thought by Jersey's great historian the late George Reginald Balleine (quoting Horace Walpole's *Anecdotes of Painting*) to have been born in Jersey *c.* 1670, the evidence stemming from the researches of the painter's descendant, the eminent art historian Charles Harrison-Wallace, places Peter Monamy's birth to Dorothy (*née* Gilbert), the wife of Pierre Monamy, in London during January 1681 — his baptism taking place at St Botolph's Without Aldgate on the 16th of that month. It also suggests that he was of Guernsey origins, the scion of a family which, settling in the island in the mid-16th century (witness the inscription on the support beam fronting the Savings Bank in High Street, reading, '*La Paix de Dieu soit ceans, fait le 18 Octobre 1578 de part André Monamy*': '"May the Peace of God be within these walls" Done the 18 October 1578 by André Monamy'), in 1643 provided in his grandfather André one of the 12 Commissioners governing the Bailiwick during the Civil War in the Parliamentary interest; and furthermore indicates that 1670 was the year in which his father Pierre (described as a 'seafaring rogue') seems to have left for London — the city in which it is beyond doubt that his son was initiated into his *métier*.

Horace Walpole somewhat condescendingly dismissed any such training vouchsafed to Monamy as being confined to learning the first rudiments of drawing from a sign-and-house painter on London Bridge — and the plain fact is that he was appriced from 3 September 1696 until 1 March 1704 to William Clark, who in 1687 had been appointed Master of the Painter-Stainers' Company and became a City Constable in December 1696. The tyro's first independent commission was to help decorate a gallery in the Vauxhall Pleasure-Gardens, on the wall of which he painted pictures of 'Admiral Vernon's Capture of Porto Bello', 'The Taking of the San Joseph', 'The Victory of the Mary Rose over Seven Algerine Pirates' and 'Sweet William's Farewell to Black-eyed Susan'. These were soon recognised as far from an ordinary sign-painter's work and the repute their quality earned for the artist led to the ill-fated Admiral Byng employing him to decorate his coach with ships and naval trophies.

Yearning to paint on canvas, Peter Monamy took as a model the work of the younger Van de Velde, whom Charles II had brought to England to be a Court Marine Painter — and did so to such effect that pictures by the two artists have occasionally been confused, a Monamy in the Dulwich Gallery being for long attributed to the Dutchman, one of whose paintings in Hampton Court was for a time labelled 'Monamy'. Specialising in nautical scenes, in which he displayed a detailed knowledge of ships, with not a rope out of place and the smallest details of vessels and their rigging meticulously accurate, Monamy delighted in battle-pieces, many with Channel Island associations, particularly 'The Taking of the *Princesa*' by Captain Thomas Durell of Jersey, 'The Capture of the *Mars*' by Captain Philip Saumarez (q.v.) — a work which now hangs at Sausmarez Manor — and 'A Ship in Distress', representing the loss of the *Victory* in the Race of Alderney. The portrayal of such subject matter reflects the fact that, though living in London, the Monamy family maintained its island connections, Peter's uncle Andrew (a partner of Daniel le Febvre) having applies in August 1687 to Guernsey's Governor — Christopher, Viscount Hatton (q.v.) — for a licence to trade with the Bailiwick in wool (to which commodity salt had been added by 1696).

Praised by experts such as Samuel Redgrave (1802-1876), the famous art commentator, and Edward Keble Chatterton (1878-1944), an informed writer on the sea and ships, for his precision of touch and delightful colouring, Monamy has been criticised for trying to paint on too large a scale, his work being at its best on a moderate-sized canvas. Though never of the topmost rank, he is regarded as holding an assured place high among the lesser masters, with his most popular pictures (despite his concentration on marine paintings) depicting scenes only partly consisting of sea-scapes — as exemplified by 'The Embarkation of Charles II at Scheveningen', housed in the Dublin Gallery.

Monamy lived during his later years at Westminster in Old Palace Yard, where he died in poverty early in February 1749, his burial at St Margaret's, Westminster, being recorded on the 7th of the month. His widow Hannah (née Christopher) was left in such reduced circumstances that 18 months later, on 27 July 1750, 'The Household Furniture, Pictures, China, &c. of Mr. PETER MONAMY, Sea Painter, Deceased', was 'sold by AUCTION By JOHN HEATH By Virtue of a Distress'. In 1761 the Incorporated Society of Artists voted ten guineas to Hannah out of the proceeds of their first exhibition at Spring Gardens. A portrait of her husband, etched by the little-known artist Bretherton, hangs in the Museum of La Société Jersiaise. It bears the eulogistic inscription, *'Petrus Monamy, Navium et Prospectum marinorum Pictor: Vendeveldo Soli Secundus'.*

† MULHOLLAND, JOHN DESMOND (1919-1945). *A gallant Guernseyman whom the Fates used ill.* Born at Wandsworth on 17 July 1919, but brought to Guernsey as a child, he was educated first at Les Vauxbelets and subsequently at Elizabeth College, Desmond Mulholland (the 'John' was otiose) volunteered — in common with Philip Martel, Hubert Nicolle and James Symes (qq.v.) — for service in the Royal Guernsey Militia after leaving school. Qualifying as a barrister at Gray's Inn before the war, he joined on its outbreak the Duke of Cornwall's Light Infantry, in which regiment he was commissioned.

On the night of 9 July 1940 Mulholland accompanied Second-Lieutenant Philip Martel (q.v.) on Operation 'Anger' (in his case ordered to meet and guide the 'Ambassador' Commandos at La Moye Point) and — apart from being spared the agony of bleeding feet as he had with him a pair of rubber-soled shoes — thereafter shared in

† MOULLIN, THOMAS (1831-1927): see p. 173.

the adventures of his fellow-agent (see Martel, Philip).

Although, like his comrade, he was released at the end of hostilities, poor Desmond Mulholland did not long enjoy his freedom. After surviving his adventures as a spy and nearly five years in a prison camp, he went on holiday to Brighton where, by the cruel whim of destiny, he met his death as a result of taking a bath. On 3 September 1945 (the exact anniversary of the outbreak of the war in which he had displayed such courage) he was overcome by fumes from a gas heater in a hotel bedroom, where he was found dead a short while later: a tragic end to a brave man's life of promise.

MURRAY, MAJOR ALAN ROBERT (1890-1952). *The Guernsey-born soldier and songster.* Alan Robert Murray was born on 2 November 1890 in Queen's Road (still, incidentally, referred to in the birth record as 'La Petite Marche' despite the lapse of 44 years since the change of name) to Florence Catherine Elizabeth (née Barlow), the wife of Lieutenant-Colonel — later Major-General — Robert Hunter Murray (who at the time was Deputy Assistant Adjutant General). He was educated at Malvern College, whence he went up to Cambridge (Pembroke). Shortly before the outbreak of the First World War he joined the Seaforth Highlanders at Shorncliffe, sailing almost immediately for India. In 1917 he took part in the campaign in Mesopotamia and the Armistice found him in Egypt on the staff of Field Marshal Allenby. Then, rejoining his regiment, he served in Northern Ireland, where he became aide-de-camp to the Duke of Abercorn, the Governor of the Province. In the mid-1930s indifferent health compelled Major Murray to resign his commission.

Although the army had been his career Murray is remembered more for his musical labours than for martial prowess. He was not only a composer, but also an accomplished performer on the piano, organ and violin. Of the 113 songs he wrote — the royalties on which in 1982 still came to between £500 and £700 per annum — the best-known is undoubtedly 'I'll Walk Beside You' (of which he wrote the music with Edward Lockton contributing the lyric). This appeared in 1936 and rose to a peak of popularity in 1939. A film was based on it and Alan Murray went to Hollywood to collaborate in its production. Other successful titles include 'Madame Jeanette', 'Spoils of War Mission', 'Too Tired to Sleep' and 'Wandering Player'. Murray also enjoys the distinction of having composed a national anthem: that adopted by Iraq in 1933 and retained until the revolution which overthrew the king in 1958. Shortly before his death he composed his last ballad, 'The Happy Waltz'.

Alan Robert Murray (who remained a bachelor and during the Second World was a B.B.C. news commentator to the Middle East as well as serving in the Crowthorne Home Guard in Berkshire) collapsed and died at Nairn in Scotland on 29 May 1952, leaving several of his manuscripts to the Royal Academy of Music, of which he had been a director.

N

NAFTEL, PAUL JACOB (1817–1891). *The Guernsey artist who won international repute.* Regarded as possibly the greatest artist that Guernsey has ever produced, Paul Jacob Naftel was born on 10 September 1817 into a Quaker clock-making family of St Saviour's whose 'grandfathers' inscribed 'Thomas André Naftel à Guernesey' are much esteemed, being as reliable now as when new. Paul, however, took no interest in the family business but, completely self-taught, took the post of drawing master at Elizabeth College, where he stayed for over 30 years. As time went by he distinguished himself more and more by his pictures of the Bailiwick, among which that of the Quay at St Peter-Port is usually considered his masterpiece. Yet, famous though he became, this gifted Guernseyman (who lived at Grange Villa, St Peter-Port) had the nobility of soul to superintend the drawing classes for sedulous proletarian seekers attending the evening courses organised by the Mechanics' Institution.

Naftel became an Associate of the Society of Painters in Water Colours in 1850, and was elected a Member in 1854. In August of the same year when Queen Victoria and the Prince Consort came to Alderney to inspect the progress of work on the Naval Base, Naftel (who had already portrayed the Royal Visit to Guernsey in 1846) was commissioned to paint this scene also.

Between 1850 and 1889 he exhibited over 500 works comprising pictures of the Lake District and other parts of northern England in addition to those of the Bailiwick. As a result he gained international renown even before he left Guernsey in 1870 for London — where, before he died, over 60 of his paintings were shown at the Naftel Gallery of the Fine Art Society in New Bond Street.

Paul Naftel died at Twickenham on 13 September 1891 — three days after his 74th birthday. A belated tribute to him in the *Elizabethan* magazine for June 1898 included this accolade: 'Few more remarkable instances of pure native genius exist of late years in the annals of Guernsey, and none have left a more undying fame than the subject of this memoir. Gifted as he was by nature, he has left many hundreds of imperishable works for the pleasure and enjoyment of his countrymen both in Guernsey and in the larger outside world.'

NAPIER, GENERAL SIR WILLIAM FRANCIS PATRICK, K.C.B. (1785–1860). *A controversial figure: chivalrous champion of the weak or paranoic megalomaniac?* Born at Celbridge, County Kildare, in December 1785, William Napier entered the Army as an Ensign in the Royal Irish Artillery in June 1800. At the suggestion of Sir John Moore he took a lieutenancy in the 52nd Regiment in 1803 and the following year obtained a captaincy in the 43rd Regiment — which was part of Moore's own brigade.

Only 17 when the short-lived Peace of Amiens ended in 1803, Napier's record in the ensuing Napoleonic War was outstanding. Present at the siege of Copenhagen in 1807, he particularly distinguished himself in the Peninsula between 1808 and 1814, showing endurance and courage of the highest order (above all at the Coa River engagement) and being wounded on several occasions — once (at Casal Novo in 1811) with a bullet near the spine which brought him to the very verge of death. While on convalescent leave he married in February 1812 Caroline Amelia Fox, the niece of the famous politician Charles James Fox — and two years later, his constitution permanently impaired by his many wounds and the rigours of service, he returned to England once more as a brevet Lieutenant-Colonel. Despite ill-health, however, Napier left for Belgium on learning of Napoleon's escape from Elba, but was too late for Waterloo. Nevertheless he served with the Army of Occupation and on retirement from the active list in 1819 was made a Companion of the Bath.

In 1823, at the suggestion of Lord Langdale,

Napier started his *History of the Peninsular War* which, running to four volumes, was finally finished in 1834. These 11 years of toil had produced a classic of the English language, characterised by impartial admiration of the heroes of both sides, as well as by the spontaniety of its style. While still at work on this magnum opus, William Napier was promoted to full Colonel in 1830. Though he declined a seat in the Commons, feeling debarred therefrom by his poor health, meagre means and large family, yet he displayed marked political awareness and — as would be expected of one married into the Fox family — was very democratic in outlook in an age when democracy was distrusted as a danger to the State. Loud in defending the weak and denouncing oppression and wrong, he took even the great Duke of Wellington to task after the Chartist Bull Ring riots in Birmingham, stressing that, deplorable though the behaviour of the rioters undoubtedly was, yet the treatment meted out to them was excessively severe.

In February 1842 this St George locked in perpetual combat with the Dragon of Tyranny was promoted to Major-General and appointed Lieutenant-Governor of Guernsey and its Dependencies. The *Dictionary of National Biography* represents him as arriving on 6 April keen to throw himself heart and soul into his duties, but almost immediately finding much to discourage him. Alleging that the defences were wretched, the Militia in need of complete reorganisation and the administration of justice scandalous, it goes on to claim that, despite local obstruction, General Napier devised a defence scheme which, after approval by a committee of artillery and engineer officers sent from London, was partially executed. It is then asserted that the Lieutenant-Governor reorganised and rearmed the Militia and powerfully influenced the States to adopt a new constitution whereby feuds between town and country, which hitherto had impeded improvements, were set at rest. Finally it credits Napier with procuring a Royal Commission to enquire into the island's civil and criminal laws, the recommendations of which tended to remove many evils in the administration of justice.

In the Bailiwick, however, things have never been seen in such rosy hues and the period of office of the hero of the Coa River and Casal Novo is usually regarded as verging on the disastrous. In matters military, Napier in 1844 complained to Whitehall about the inadequacy of the gun carriages supplied to the Militia — but this, of course, was the responsibility of the British government

rather than the States of Guernsey. The Militia numbered 7,796 out of a total population of 26,706 when he took office. In May of the next year he arranged for the appointment to each Militia Regiment of an Assistant Inspector together with drill sergeants 'receiving pay from the Secretary at War', the five assistant inspectors forming part of His Excellency's staff. This, presumably, constitutes the 'reorganisation' of the Militia referred to by the *Dictionary of National Biography*. The following October tension between the Lieutenant-Governor and the Militia was highlighted when five Lieutenant-Colonels and five Captains resigned their commissions, preferring to serve in the ranks, and declaring themselves determined to take every legal means of being relieved of the disgrace of holding a commission in the Guernsey Militia under existing circumstances. Things were even worse in 1844 when Napier, fearing assassination, prevented the Militia from celebrating the Queen's Birthday. Two Militia Officers stood trial for conspiracy, but were acquitted. In 1845 Captain J. C. Guerin of the 1st Regiment was dismissed by the General on the grounds that it was not in the public interest that he should hold a commission: he was reduced to the ranks.

As far as civil affairs are concerned, the 'new constitution' ending feuds between town and country allegedly adopted thanks to Napier's 'powerful influence' obviously refers to the 1844 'Loi relative à la Réforme des Etats'. This measure replaced Constables in the States by Douzaine Delegates and made provision for delegates from St Peter-Port's four Cantonal Douzaines to attend as well as from its Central Douzaine, thereby giving greater representation to the parish with the biggest population which contributed the lion's share of the island's revenue. The Lieutenant-Governor's 'powerful influence' however, was far less responsible for this reform than the indignant remonstrances made by the town's *chefs de famille*.

It is true that a Royal Commission did investigate the island's criminal law (but *not* civil) in 1847. It is also a fact that this Commission reported that the Jurats could in one capacity issue Ordinances with the force of law and in another execute these laws of their own making — a marriage of legislature and judiciary which on the political analysis of le Baron de Montesquieu was a recipe for tyranny. It is also true, however, that the Commissioners admitted that powers theoretically so unlimited were in fact never abused, so that the Guernesiais were content with their lot. Indeed, one may remark parenthetically that the huge crowds two years previously at the funeral of Jean Guille (q.v.) had provided eloquent testimony of the affection with which the people of Guernsey regarded their 'oppressors'. No 'evils in the administration of justice' were therefore removed — in fact, no concrete results whatsoever sprang from the Commission's report.

If on the whole General Napier as a committed liberal regarded Guernsey's governmental system as essentially oligarchic he was of course right — but then the same could also be said of the United Kingdom. The suffrage for the election of Douzaines and hence of Constables (the only representative element in the States at the time of his arrival) was confined to taxpayers (i.e., property-owners in the context of the taxation system of the day): but this section of Guernsey's population corresponded to the middle classes in the United Kingdom who — even in post-Reform Bill Britain prior to the enfranchisement of the urban proletariat by Disraeli's 'Leap in the Dark' of 1867 — alone elected the Commons. Moreover, the House of Commons in Parliament was still to a large extent subservient to the unelected House of Lords, as were the Constables (and subsequent Douzaine Delegates) in the States to the unelected Rectors and indirectly elected Jurats. By the standards of the day, therefore, Guernsey's system gave little cause for complaint.

Furthermore, high-handed conduct and contumelious treatment of local officials ill behoved an impassioned advocate of reform. Yet Napier insisted on regarding the Bailiff and Jurats as ignorant civilians whose powers could easily be over-ridden by his military authority and prestige as the Queen's Representative. The 'folie de grandeur' with which he seems to have been afflicted may be inferred from his diary note concerning his reception on first arriving in the Bailiwick: 'I smiled and bowed and spoke my acknowledgements, conversed and did King'. His resultant overbearing demeanour first led to a clash in 1843 when he saw fit to expel a Frenchman named Le Conte from Guernsey on his own account, without deigning to refer to the island authorities. The upshot was a tense interview between the General and Jean Guille, made even tenser by the Lieutenant-Governor's refusal to enter into any discussion with the Bailiff while the Jurats were present. Not surprisingly, the interview was inconclusive and relationships between Napier and the Royal Court became extremely strained.

A further action by General Napier in 1844 constituted a deliberate defiance of Guernsey Law, in that he took it upon himself to issue a free pardon to a soldier (Private Fossey of the 48th Dépôt) whom the Royal Court had sentenced to two months imprisonment for assaulting a visiting English couple (Mr. and Mrs. Clark). Contemptuously ignoring the court, Napier went in person to the prison, insisting on Fossey's immediate release — and when the jailer demurred, sent to Fort George for troops to compel compliance. Private Fossey was then released and the unfortunate jailer found himself prosecuted before the Royal Court for disrespect to the Lieutenant-Governor: he was, however, acquitted. These repeated manifestations of arbitrariness provoked the Royal Court into sending two petitions to the Queen (supported by a memorial from the islanders), submitting that the Lieutenant-Governor should observe the rights, privileges, customs and laws of the Bailiwick. Thanks, however, to Napier's friendship with the Duke of Wellington, Guernsey's pleas fell on deaf ears, the Privy Council ruling that the Lieutenant-Governor had the right to deport aliens without the consent of the court, though the Jurats were entitled to be consulted. It was also ruled that the jailer should have released Private Fossey without delay, but he should not have been threatened with the use of force.

Before these judgments had been delivered there came the bombshell. In May 1844 a force of 600 men was landed at St Peter-Port from troop transports 'to quell the island's insurrection', Napier being convinced that there was a conspiracy afoot against his life, with five bottles of champagne offered to anyone who pushed him off the Pierhead to drown! Over 12,000 outraged islanders assembled at a protest meeting at the New Ground (now Cambridge Park) to consider the statement that 'imputations have been recently thrown upon the loyalty of the inhabitants of the islands' and General Sir Thomas Saumarez (q.v.) was chosen to carry a loyal address across the Channel to the Queen.

In August 1846, at the suggestion of Sir George Grey (the Home Secretary) Queen Victoria herself took a hand in the dispute, paying a surprise visit to Guernsey accompanied by Albert, Prince Consort. Pointedly snubbing Napier, whom she refused either to receive on her yacht or visit at Havilland Hall, Victoria landed the following day and was accorded a tumultous reception which made the loyalty of the Guernesiais plain for all to see. Just over a year later Sir George Grey vigorously represented to Wellington the desirability of replacing this unpopular Lieutenant-Governor. Appearances were maintained by Napier being allowed to resign at the end of 1847, and the pill was coated with sugar when the following May he was made a Knight Commander of the Bath in the Queen's Birthday Honours List, and in addition was given the Colonelcy-in-Chief of the 27th Regiment.

In 1849 this old war horse of undeniable bravery (but also of apparent schizophrenia) retired to Scinde House at Clapham Park, where in 1851 he published his *History of the Administration of Scinde*, which was much praised by Carlyle. One of the generals selected to carry banderoles at Wellington's funeral in 1852, he was promoted to full General in October 1859 and died the ensuing February, Lady Napier following him to the grave within six weeks. Both bodies were buried at Norwood.

NEAME, LIEUTENANT-GENERAL SIR PHILIP, V.C. K.B.E., C.B., D.S.O., D.L. (1888-1978). *The Lieutenant-Governor of the Years of Recovery.* Born at Faversham, Kent, on 12 December 1888 and educated at Cheltenham College, whence he proceeded to the Royal Military Academy at Woolwich, Philip Neame entered the army in 1908 and by 1914 had attained the rank of Captain. During the First World War he served with the 15th Field Company, Royal Engineers. He was mentioned in despatches no less than five times in the course of the conflict, as well as being awarded the Victoria Cross for his outstanding gallantry in 1914, followed by the Distinguished Service Order in 1916. In addition he was appointed Chevalier de la Légion d'Honneur and won both the French and Belgian Croix de Guerre.

This brilliant military career was continued during the inter-war years, commencing with an appointment directing the staff at the Staff College, Camberley from 1919 to 1923 (when he published his *German Strategy in the Great War*) followed by service in India with King George's Own Bengal Sappers and Miners from 1925 to 1929. There ensued a spell at the Imperial Defence College from 1930 to 1932, after which Philip Neame became General Staff Officer Grade I of the Waziristan District of India (during which time he went in 1936 to Lhasa as a member of a political/military mission) before a return to the United Kingdom to take up the appointment of Commandant at the Royal Military Academy, Woolwich, during 1938 and 1939 — in which latter year the value of his services was accorded

recognition by his being made a Companion of the Most Honourable Order of the Bath.

The Second World War saw further feats of daring on the part of General Neame. After serving as Deputy Chief of the General Staff, British Expeditionary Force, 1939-40, he commanded the joint British, Australian and Indian forces opposing Rommel's first attack in Cyrenaica in 1941, operating so far forward that he was taken prisoner by the enemy. With the confusion accompanying the fall of Mussolini in 1943, however, this intrepid soldier succeeded in escaping from captivity in Italy.

Appointed Lieutenant-Governor of Guernsey and its Dependencies at the Liberation and created a Knight Commander of the Most Excellent Order of the British Empire in 1946, Sir Philip for the next eight years presided over the Bailiwick's recovery, his efforts making a massive contribution towards the rehabilitation of the islands — with especial emphasis on Alderney, utterly devastated by the foe. With the brave and resourceful Ambrose Sherwill (q.v.) installed as Bailiff, the prostrate Bailiwick was thus provided with a vigorous and energetic partnership to nurse it back to health. Extensive political changes characterised his period of office, Guernsey's system of government being reformed and Alderney's transformed out of all recognition. Besides extending a somewhat cautious patronage to R. H. Blanchford (q.v.) in his efforts to extend and improve the Bailiwick's Ambulance Service, His Excellency, as Commander-in-Chief, was particularly enthusiastic about reconstituting the Royal Guernsey Militia as a 100-strong Royal Marine Commando, with a permanent staff of instructors provided by the Royal Marines. In the event, however, although a small arms range for use by the projected unit was constructed at L'Ancresse at a cost of £4,000; the envisaged annual cost of £12,500 (plus the expense of craft maintenance) ultimately precluded the materialisation of this Marine Militia — and Guernsey's ancient force became no more than a memory enshrined in the exhibits at the Castle Cornet Museum which the Lieutenant-Governor opened in 1953. Later the same year Sir Philip (who during his term of office had written his autobiography, *Playing with Strife*) relinquished his appointment. After a quarter of a century's retirement he died at Sittingbourne in his natal county of Kent on 28 April 1978.

NEVE, MARGARET ANN (1792-1903). *Guernsey's nearest approach to Methuselah!* (C). This famous Guernsey lady was born Margaret Ann

Harvey in the Pollet on 18 May 1792 — as is testified by her baptismal entry in the records of the Town Church. Her father, John Harvey, was later (1813) a churchwarden at the same church — the only one in St Peter-Port at the time — while her mother Elizabeth (*née* Guille) was the daughter of Richard Guille of Saints (died 1790) and his wife Mary Mourant. On the distaff side, therefore, Margaret Ann stemmed from the Saints branch of a well-known Guernsey family — the branch which in the 14th century had produced in Jacques Guille one of the leaders of the rising against the French Occupation Forces reputedly commanded by Madoc of Wales (q.v.*).

At the age of 15 Margaret Ann sailed for Bristol, where she was educated at the renowned school in that city operated by the Misses Cottle. These ladies had many literary and social connections, thanks to which young Miss Harvey during her schooldays made the acquaintance of Charles Lamb (1775-1834) and William Hazlitt (1778-1830) — as well as of Charles-François du Périer Dumouriez, the French General who, with the frustration of his plans on the morrow of his victory over the Prussians at Valmy in September 1792 to use his army to overthrow the National Convention, thereafter ruling in the name of Louis XVI, had defected to the Austrians after defeat at their hands at Louvain in March 1793, settling in England after temporary sojourns in Germany and Switzerland, supported from 1800 onwards by a British government pension.

On 18 January 1823 Miss Harvey married John Neve of Benenden in Kent. The reception took place in Rouge Huis House to which before daybreak the bridegroom had to trudge through deep snow after a stormy crossing from Weymouth. During their honeymoon the Neves went to Brussels and Margaret Ann visited the field of Waterloo, where she collected as a memento either a metal epaulette featuring the imperial cypher (an 'N' surmounted by a crown) or a belt buckle worn by one of the Imperial Guards: the accounts differ. Thereafter the couple lived at Tenterden until John Neve died in 1849. There were no children of the marriage. His widow returned to Guernsey and settled with her spinster sister at Rouge Huis — a property then more extensive than now, embracing the present Rouge Huis Avenue and continuing along the side of Brock Road as far as the site where the Boys' Intermediate School was built in 1893.

Besides being an accomplished musician, Mrs. Neve was fluent in French and Italian as well as having a working knowledge of German and Spanish and also a sufficient command of Greek to be able to read the New Testament in that tongue. As a widely travelled woman these linguistic abilities were of considerable use to her. She visited Spain, where she stayed for five months well before any railways had been introduced into that country and as the years went by advancing age failed to deter her from venturing afar. In 1884, at the age of 92, together with her 89-year-old sister, she went to Cracow (then in Austria–Hungary) to see Kosciusko's monument — after which she extended her journey by visiting Russia.

Mrs. Neve's energy was verily phenomenal. Up to the age of 106 she never missed her walk down to the markets and back each Saturday; while every Sunday, as a devout Evangelical Anglican, she walked to Holy Trinity church and back. Although during the last five years of her life her hearing failed and walking became difficult, yet nevertheless, at the age of 108 she still pottered around her garden with a light spade. Similarly the annual treat which she gave to the children of the Town Hospital continued until she was well over her century. *Guernsey Through The Lens* (a publication which appeared in 1978) contains a photograph taken a week after her 109th birthday, accompanied by her signature and the dates of both her birth and of the photograph (1792 and 1901) all written by herself.

Margaret Anne Neve died on 4 April 1903. A lifespan stretching from the reign of George III to that of Edward VII had embraced eight years and 228 days in the 18th century (18 May 1792 to 31 December 1800), 100 years in the 19th century (1 January 1801 to 31 December 1900) and two years 94 days in the 20th century (1 January 1901 to 4 April 1903). She was 44 days short of attaining the age of 111 years. Her body was buried in the Cimitière des Frères, where her twin-headed white family vault surrounded by iron railings may still be seen through the cemetery gate, on the right of the central path.

NICOLLE, HUBERT FRANK, M.C. (1919-   ). *A Guernseyman of daring who doubly diced with death.* Born on 23 November 1919 to Elsie May (*née* Hubert), the wife of Emile William Nicolle, and educated at Elizabeth College, Hubert Frank Nicolle volunteered for service in the Royal Guernsey Militia before the Second World War and, on the disbandment of that force in Febraury 1940, joined the Hampshire Regiment, where he was granted a commission. The events that were to immortalise Lieutenant Nicolle's name began on

5 July 1940 when he agreed to go to Guernsey on an espionage assignment, after having been warned that he would be shot if caught. Accordingly the following evening (6 July), he embarked at Devonport in Submarine H.43 (Lieutenant G. R. Colvin) which for the first stage of its journey was escorted by H.M. trawler *Lord Stanhope*. He had been ordered to conduct a one-man reconnaissance as the first phase of 'Operation Anger' in preparation for 'Operation Ambassador' — which was then envisaged as a full-scale Commando raid. In particular he had to learn about the numbers and disposition of German troops.

After a 24-hour journey Hubert Nicolle paddled ashore from the submarine in a canoe on the night of 7–8 July landing at Le Jaonnet at 1 a.m. on 8 July. After clambering up the cliff he made his way to his parents' home in Town, knowing that his father (Emile Nicolle) as Secretary to the Controlling Committee, would obviously be well-informed about local conditions. It also transpired that his parents' neighbour (Mr. H. H. Collins, the Manager of Le Riche Stores) supplied the Germans with rations and so knew their ration strength — 469 in Guernsey and 11 in Sark — as well as troop locations. Furthermore his uncle, Captain Frank Nicolle, was Assistant Harbour Master and so able to give details regarding shipping movements. Lastly, a friend, Thomas Mansell (whom Hubert had contacted en route for the Town from Le Jaonnet) reported on aircraft arrivals at the airport: two troop carriers and a reconnaissance 'plane. Armed with this knowledge he returned to Le Jaonnet before curfew on the evening of 7 July and then lay low above the bay until at 1 a.m. on 8 July, he made his rendezvous with Lieutenants Martel and Mulholland (qq.v.) to whom he passed on his information before embarking for a return to England and the warm congratulations he so richly deserved.

For most people one such exploit would have been enough: but not for Hubert Nicolle. At 3 a.m. on 4 September 1940, he landed with Lieutenant James Symes (q.v.) at Petit Port, having travelled by motor torpedo boat from Portland in accordance with a directive issued by Winston Churchill to plant agents so as to obtain the best possible information regarding German forces in occupied territory. The two spies were briefed to gather information regarding the general situation in the island. After sheltering with his Uncle Frank at La Ville au Roi and obtaining the required information, Nicolle rejoined Symes to rendezvous with the boat at Petit Port on the

night of 5–6 September. The naval craft failed to arrive either that night or the following two, after which the two young men returned to Petit Port no more for fear of detection as the moon was waxing. Realising that they were marooned, they attempted to get away from Bordeaux harbour with the connivance of Captain Fred Noyon (q.v.), but this scheme was frustrated by a German order concentrating all fishing craft at St Peter-Port following the escape to England of a party of eight men on Friday 6 September.

To avoid compromising their relatives and friends, the two subalterns spent a great deal of time hiding in Elizabeth College cricket pavilion, where they were helped by the groundsman, William Allen. Towards the end of September an attempt to rescue them came to nothing when Captain John Parker, landing at La Corbière in an attempt to contact them, unluckily ran into the arms of a German anti-aircraft detachment and was taken prisoner. Fortunately for him, he was in uniform. Meanwhile, Major Ambrose Sherwill (q.v.) had by now learned of the presence of the two agents through Hubert Nicolle's father Emile. A cat-and-mouse game then ensued with the Germans — who had been made suspicious by the capture of Parker. Eventually the Guernsey Commandant, Major Bandelow, conveyed to Sherwill that if any British soldiers in the island surrendered they would be treated as prisoners of war, with a deadline at 1800 hours on 21 October. Five minutes before the expiry of the time limit the two young officers gave themselves up wearing uniforms purloined by Frank Nicolle from an overlooked stock stored at the harbour. They had been on the run for six and a half weeks.

Prolonged questioning at Fort George followed, with Nicolle's interrogation on one occasion lasting for 14 hours. The day came when his interrogator revealed that he knew about the July activities and, remarking that he was no more than a dirty spy, informed him that he would be shot. Both young men, together with those who had helped them, were dispatched to solitary confinement in the Cherche Midi Prison in Paris and were only saved from the firing squad by the sense of military honour of the Befehlshaber, Graf von Schmettow (q.v.), who asked to be relieved of his post if the promise made by Bandelow on his behalf were not honoured. He also appealed through his immediate superior — Count Brockdorf — to Admiral Canaris, Chief of Counter-Intelligence, on whose orders the lives of the two subalterns were spared, while those who had helped them were released.

Liberated at the end of the war and awarded the Military Cross for his gallantry, Hubert Nicolle at first took an appointment as a civil servant in the States' Insurance Department, but later forsook this in favour of working as the island representative of the Sun Life Assurance Company of Canada — in which employment he remained until retirement. In his spare time he made himself responsible for compiling a Roll of Honour of those from his old school who had fallen during the war. On 27 October 1968 his military glories were briefly revived when he was one of those selected to bear the Royal Guernsey Militia Colours at the ceremony at the Town Church where they were presented, re-dedicated and laid up.

NOEL, CECIL WHEADON (1897–1941). *The Daedalus of L'Erée.* Born at Les Hubits on 6 February 1897, to Edith Mary (*née* Wheadon) the wife of Arthur Abraham Noel, and educated at Elizabeth College, Cecil Wheadon Noel was still only in his 'teens when the First World War broke out. Nevertheless, he immediately volunteered for the Forces, becoming a motor mechanic trainee — and later an air fitter — in the Royal Flying Corps. With a flair for mechanical engineering, he gave a number of lectures on this topic whilst stationed in Oxfordshire, one of which was heard by H.M. King George V.

Qualifying as a pilot with the rank of Flight-Sergeant, Cecil Noel went to France where he saw 18 months' service flying DH.9 bombers and being awarded La Croix de Guerre by the French for his exploits. He was then commissioned and returned to England, spending the rest of the war as a flying instructor at Turnhill in Somersetshire.

Back in Guernsey after the armistice and still only in his early 20s, the ex-bomber pilot found that he could not settle down to any one pursuit, with the result that the ensuing decade was characterised by incessant experimentation in one ephemeral interest after another. At first he applied for a patent for an internal combustion engine with a revolving induction camshaft, taking premises in Town to develop this brainchild — only almost immediately to neglect it in favour of opening a garage in the Bordage in association with his younger brother Stanley Noel, providing repair services for motor cycles and cars.

Discarding this occupation in its turn, Cecil Noel left Guernsey again, going to Loughborough College in Leicestershire (which at that time specialised in engineering courses) with the intention of reading for a London University external degree in engineering. Once more, however, restlessness prevailed and when the firm of Ashwell and Nesbitt offered him a post investigating the production of gas from vegetable waste, he promptly forsook his studies and left Loughborough to chase after this new will of the wisp. Needless to say, it was not long before he wearied of gas from waste also, deciding instead to go in for the manufacture of lapping machines for procuring exact measurements: only to return to Guernsey a few months later attracted by yet another transient enthusiasm in the form of radio and earning a living by making, selling and repairing wireless sets (which were still in their infancy). His intimates were not surprised when before long this gave way to trying his hand at chromium plating!

Then came a chance to get back into the air and with it an interest which at last was to prove permanent. In association with Advocate H. H. Randell, Cecil Noel founded the Guernsey Aero Club and started looking around for a suitable site for an airfield. At the same time, in cooperation with Harold le Parmentier, he designed and constructed Guernsey's first island-built aeroplane, 'The Wee Mite'. Three years from the original discussion of the project in 1930, the aircraft was in flight. The first attempts were made from the beach at Vazon on 12 February and 16 February 1933. Relying on no more than an absurdly low-powered ABS Scorpion 30 h.p. engine, Noel only managed to life his plane a man's height from the ground for a distance of a few yards. Nevertheless she was airborne, the practicability of his plans had been proven and flights by land-based aircraft from Guernsey soil had been pioneered. Then on 10 April now powered by a nine-cylinder radial Salmson engine and with a 30-foot wingspan, 'The Wee Mite' made her first sustained flight at heights varying between 1,000 feet and 2,500 feet from her starting point at Vazon Bay and passing over Pleinmont, Town and L'Ancresse before landing again. Finally a grand demonstration flight around the island was made on the following 15 September (uncannily anticipating the day seven years later when the Battle of Britain was to reach its climax), with the home-made aeroplane attaining a top speed of 93 m.p.h. Meanwhile — in 1932 — what was felt to be suitable land for an aerodrome was found at L'Erée and Advocate Randell negotiated its purchase in quarters. Once acquired, however, the land needed draining and Noel energetically directed his efforts to this task. It was not long before he was flying from the partially-completed field not only his 'Wee Mite', but also a twin-cockpit biplane in which he provided 'flips' for those who had an urge to sample the joys of aviation – one of whom was the present writer.

One of the major difficulties at L'Erée was presented by a hillock dividing the northern portion of the projected aerodrome from its southern counterpart. As long as this hillock remained only the southern half could be used. Matters stood thus when Sir Alan Cobham (q.v.) started his 'Cobham Air Routes' service to Hurn near Bournemouth on Silver Jubilee Day (6 May) 1935, with Cecil Noel (who by then was the officially accredited Guernsey Aero Club's Manager at L'Erée) supervising the Guernsey end of the enterprise.

Although after the abrupt end to his venture following the crash of one of his aeroplanes to the west of the Isle of Wight, Sir Alan became disenchanted with L'Erée and publicly advocated the creation of an airport at La Villiaze, Cecil Noel persisted in his attempts to promote the Aero Club's little aerodrome – and with a view to furthering the operation of a passenger service to England in conjunction with Olley Air Services, pressed ahead with arrangements for the expansion of L'Erée's facilities by the removal of the hillock. On 8 February 1938, a gigantic explosion rent the air as an attempt was made to blast away the offending geographical feature – but alas, although some sizeable chunks of rock were dislodged the hillock as a whole proved obdurate

and still stands defiantly at the present day! When the following year Sir Kingsley Wood opened the States' airport Cecil Noel bowed to the inevitable and in accordance with the maxim, 'If you cannot beat them, join them', accepted the post of Assistant Airport Control Officer at La Villiaze.

This was on 6 May 1939: four years to the day since Cobham Air Routes had started its service from L'Erée. Within four months the Second World War had broken out and Noel, although by then 42 years of age, once again donned uniform, serving with the Royal Air Force as Airport Control Officer at St Eval Royal Air Force Station between Wadebridge and Newquay in Cornwall. Here on 25 January 1941, he offered to stand in as Duty Officer on behalf of a friend who was particularly anxious to be free that evening. So it was that Cecil Wheadon Noel was present when the aerodrome was subjected to a heavy attack by the enemy, in the course of which he was killed. Thus died a Guernseyman of imagination, verve and daring.

NOYON, CAPTAIN FREDERICK WILLIAM, S.G.M. (1879–1962). *Macte virtute*. See *Underground Resistance Heroes of the Second World War*. Besides his wartime exploits, this son of the Vale Parish (who was born on 20 January 1879 and followed the sea from the age of 14, becoming fisherman, pilot and master mariner) was awarded Lloyd's Sea Gallantry Medal when, as master of the *Foam Queen*, he rescued the crew of a ship which had gone aground in the Thames Estuary. He died suddenly on 11 May 1962.

OSBORNE, SIR PETER (1584–1653). *Castle Cornet's Cavalier*. The son of Sir John Osborne and his wife Dorothy (*née* Barlee), Peter Osborne on attaining manhood inherited the office of Keeper of the Privy Purse to the king which had been in his family since Elizabeth I's original grant of it to his grandfather (also Peter Osborne) at Christmas 1551. Knighted on 7 January 1611 Sir Peter in 1614 married Dorothy, the daughter of Sir John Danvers and the sister of Henry Danvers, Earl of Danby. Outstanding among their children was their daughter Dorothy (1627–96), who was the authoress of the famous and lively *Osborne Letters* written to her true love (Sir

William Temple) the plentiful contemporary allusions of which make their perusal most rewarding.

In March 1621 James I appointed Danby as Governor of Guernsey for life, and the Earl used his influence to procure for his brother-in-law the position of Lieutenant-Governor, together with the reversion of the governorship should be (Danby) be the first of the two to die. On assuming office one of Sir Peter's first actions was to review the Guernsey Militia, which at the time was 1,157 strong; subsequently issuing the following orders to the force:

'Orders to be observed by the Captaynes and severall companies: That upon the sighte of any fleete, horses with saddle to be sent to the Towne from each parish.

'That the ordnance in all places throughout the Island be sufficiently mounted and viewed by the Captaynes.

'That there be good draught ropes and tackling for all the ordnance, to remove them upon occasion.

'That there be a sufficient store of drumes, and these serviceable and fitt.

'That all Captaynes and Lieutenants carry partizans, and every Sergeant a halbert.

'That beacons be made ready, and fired upon all occasions of alarme.

'That everyone repayre speedily with his armes to the place of rendezvous upon the alarme being given, and presume not to depart from his cullers without his Captayne's order and leave'.

As a staunch Anglican, Sir Peter tended to be out of harmony with Guernsey's Calvinist establishment, but nevertheless tolerable relationships obtained during his first years in office, especially as he was away fairly often, sitting in the parliaments of 1623–24 and 1625 as member for Corfe Castle in Dorsetshire. Tension between Lieutenant-Governor and inhabitants became acute, however, in 1627 when, as part of the measures taken to strengthen the Channel Isles in view of the Ile de Rhé campaign, Osborne brought over a body of 200 soldiers to Guernsey. While the need for the presence of such a force was soon manifest by a French attack on Alderney (which was foiled by Sir Peter's vigorous action in dispersing the invasion fleet) yet intense resentment was aroused in the Bailiwick by the fact that because of the king's chronic impecuniosity, the islanders were obliged to raise large sums for the payment and upkeep of this garrison. In 1628 the Lieutenant-Governor alienated the Guernesiais still more by attempting to impose martial law to enforce this contribution. Additional reinforcements arrived in 1629, making the burden even more onerous. Among the new arrivals there came as chaplain the Reverend Peter Heylyn (q.v.), whose pen has provided such valuable source material for the historian.

The mutual animosity engendered by these contretemps persisted and reached its dénouement on 4 March 1643 when Pierre de Beauvoir (q.v.), as a Commissioner acting on behalf of parliament, called on Osborne to submit. Like 'Kentish Sir Byng', Sir Peter 'stood for his King, bidding the crop-headed Parliament swing' and on 11 March

from his fastness in Castle Cornet opened fire on the Town, thus starting an intermittent bombardment which over the next eight and a half years would make Fountain Street, High Street and the Pollet untenable. The Civil War had begun in Guernsey.

The tussle between Royalist castle and Roundhead island rapidly proved to be a stalemate — which was not materially affected one way or the other by the capture of the island leaders in October 1643 and their escape the following December (please see 'de Beauvoir, Pierre') Osborne from his redoubt was able to prevent shipping from entering or leaving the Town Harbour, so that it was not long before the islanders began to feel the pinch. On the other hand, Sir Peter — who became Governor of Guernsey de jure on the death of Lord Danby in January 1644 had no effective authority beyond the castle where, to add to his difficulties, he had to contend with a mutiny occasioned by his striking one of his gunners with the flat of his sword. Furthermore, his ability to hold out depended on the support and supplies he received from George Carteret (q.v.) in Jersey. Unfortunately relations were strained between Jersey's Lieutenant-Governor and the castle's gallant commander (whose demeanour amply justified the assessment of Royalists in 1066 And All That as 'wrong but romantic'), so that Carteret only grudgingly supplied Osborne at irregular intervals. In response to the besieged Cavalier's expostulations that 'My stores are exhausted and I am like to be lost' and that 'It shall be your fault if the Castle falls into other hands', the Jerseyman, demanding payment for supplies delivered, retorted that 'every tub should stand on its own bottom'.

The antipathy between the two leaders meant that Sir Peter's days were numbered when Charles, Prince of Wales, arrived in Jersey in April 1646, after having been driven out of the West of England by Fairfax. George Carteret (who had been knighted in 1645) enjoyed tremendous prestige with the young prince, and he cogently argued the case for the recall of Osborne — with the upshot that later in the year Sir Peter surrendered his governorship to Sir Baldwin Wake (q.v.*). He went to England, but finding the Royalist cause in disarray and the king a prisoner of the Scots, he retired abroad. Sir Peter Osborne died in 1653.

OWEN OF WALES (c. 1330–1378). *The vivid personality who led La Déscente des Aragousais.* Born about 1330, Owen of Wales is stated by Froissart to have been the son of Aymon or

Edmund, a Welsh prince wrongfully put to death by Edward III. It seems, however, that his true father was Thomas ap Rhodri (c. 1295-1363), a nephew of Llywelyn ap Gruffydd — which would have meant that this colourful character, as the illustrious Llywelyn's great-nephew, was consanguineous with the Welsh princely line, thereby apparently vindicating his claim to be the rightful heir to the Princes of Wales.

A soldier of fortune, Owen seems to have entered the service of Philip VI of France while still quite young, earning for himself, as 'Yevain de Galles', an outstanding reputation as a mercenary leader. Although he came to England in 1365 to take possession of his late father's manor of Tatsfield in Surrey, he returned to France in 1366 — and was deprived of his estates in England for adhering to the king's enemies when Charles V repudiated the Treaty of Brétigny in 1369.

Owen having spoken much at the French court about his hereditary claims as lineal successor of Llywelyn, Charles V conceived the idea of exploiting his pretensions by utilising them to foment a diversionary insurrection in Wales. With this in mind, a fleet set out from Harfleur in 1370, preceded by a notable proclamation setting out Owen's claims — but came to nothing, being forced back by bad weather. Two years elapsed until all was again in readiness, so that it was not until May 1372 that another expedition set sail, this time with the intention of joining forces with a Spanish fleet (sent by the Castilian King Enrico, who was indebted to Charles V for his throne) in the vicinity of the Channel Isles for a combined assault on the Welsh coast. It was the failure of the Spanish force to arrive at the rendezvous which caused the attack to be diverted against Guernsey.

Owen landed at Vazon Bay (most likely on 15 June 1372) at the head of a force which, according to Froissart, was 4,000 strong. Against him Edmund (or Aymon) Rose, the sub-warden under Walter Huwet, Warden of the Isles, was able to muster 800 men, consisting mostly of the local Militia of feudal levies reinforced by some 80 English men-at-arms and archers who had been sent over from St Sauveur-le-Vicomte as a precautionary measure when news of Owen's preparations had first reached English ears. The outnumbered defenders were gradually forced back, finally giving battle on the plateau where Elizabeth College and the adjacent streets are now located —an area which, until the mid-19th century, was known as 'La Bataille' and which still contains a passageway by the name of Battle Lane. Froissart says that the Guernseyman left 400 dead on the field before they yielded, withdrawing into the town and the defences of La Tour Beauregard.

Meanwhile, Owen's ships had sailed round the island with the intention of attacking St Peter-Port from the sea, but this project was frustrated thanks to the protection of the sea approaches afforded by Castle Cornet, to which they therefore laid siege. The invaders also had to contend with another centre of resistance at the Vale Castle which they also invested and wherein Rose himself stubbornly held out. During these sieges, probably to find payment for his men, Owen sent pillaging parties to Sark and Jersey, in both of which islands they laid waste many farmsteads. Meanwhile Castle Cornet was proving well-nigh impregnable, Owen finding it to be 'strong and well purveyed with good artyllary, so that it was not easy to be wonne'. Thus Owen still had failed to take it when he was reccalled by the French king, with orders to go to Santander to arrange a joint Franco-Spanish attack on La Rochelle. He therefore lifted the siege and departed.

Six years later Owen met his death. That he was considered a serious menace to England is suggested by the circumstances of his assassination (obviously with English connivance) in 1378 at the hands of John Lamb, a Scot who had wormed himself into his victim's confidence.

The Guernsey ballad recalling this incursion is called 'La Déscente des Aragousais', suggesting an assault by Aragonese. This apparent discrepancy might be accounted for when it is recalled that Owen's operation was planned in collusion with Spanish forces with which he intended to link up to the north-west of Guernsey. It is not impossible, therefore, that a Spanish liaison contingent might have been included in the force which sailed from Harfleur — and its presence among the invaders (some of its members perhaps being taken prisoner) could have created the impression that the enemy was Aragonese.

OXENHAM, JOHN (1852-1941). *The story-teller of Sark*. Born in Manchester as William Arthur Dunkerley and educated at Old Trafford School whence he went up to his native city's Victoria University, this famous novelist's nom-de-plume of John Oxenham ultimately became his recognized appellation, certainly by long usage and possibly also by deed poll.

John Oxenham's early years after coming down from the University were spent in business. He lived for a time in France and travelled widely in Europe, Canada, the United States of America and East Africa, after which he turned to publishing. In collaboration with Robert Barr he introduced to Great Britain the weekly *Detroit Free Press* while later, together with Barr and Jerome K. Jerome, he launched *The Idler* and subsequently – this time with Jerome alone – the weekly *To-Day*. By the time he reached his mid-forties, Oxenham decided to forsake publication in favour of writing, thus embarking on a career as author in which, besides poetical works and books devoted to biographical philosophical and religious themes, no less than 42 novels were to flow from his pen, the first of which, *God's Prisoner*, appeared in 1898.

John Oxenham resided intermittently in Sark for many years during the reigns of Edward VII and George V, drawing from its magnificent scenery, wild beauty and turbulent history inspiration for a quartet of novels set in the island and dealing with various episodes in its past. Although somewhat marred by the author's infuriatingly inaccurate persistence in describing the islanders as English, all four stories are packed with action and never fail to hold the reader's attention. The first of the series, *Carette of Sark* – featuring Napoleonic War privateering and smuggling centred on Les Boutiques Caves and with Torode of Herm modelled on the notorious Jean Allaire (q.v.) – appeared in 1907. It was followed the next year by *Pearl of Pearl Island* (an Edwardian romance with the betrothed inamorati face to face with death when caught in the vicious Pointe de Jeu current and wherein the course of true love runs the smoother thanks to Sark's autonomy). Set in silver-mining days, with a prematurely aged Vicar Cachemaille (q.v.) and L'Etac – confusingly designated as L'Etat – serving as the. hero's refuge from a lynch-mob, *A Maid of the Silver Sea* was published in 1910: and finally, after a prolonged interval, 1924 saw *The Perilous Lovers* – an idyll pitched in the period immediately preceding the colonization of Sark by Helier de Carteret (q.v.), who is credited with a knighthood and also with cutting the tunnel at Le Creux which was of course actually dug by his son Philippe (q.v.). In the meantime – in 1908 – in collaboration with William Toplis

(q.v.), the prestigious *Book of Sark* was produced in a sumptuous edition limited to 500 copies, each of which was individually autographed by both author and artist.

Oxenham's verse publications started with *Bees in Amber*, which he published on his own account in 1913, defiantly and triumphantly ignoring the prophecies of gloom of his usual publishers; while during the First World War over eight million copies of his 'Hymn for the Men at the Front' were sold. After the First World War the author, a man of deep Christian conviction, wrote a succession of books dealing with the life of Our Lord, beginning with *The Cedar Box* in 1924. John Oxenham married Margery Anderson of Greenock who bore him a daughter. Mrs. Oxenham died in 1925. He himself died in Worthing in 1941 at the advanced age of 89.

OZANNE, SIR EDWARD CHEPMELL, K.B.E. (1852-1929). *The only Bailiff to be dubbed knight in Guernsey*. Born on 15 December 1852 to Martha (*née* Chepmell), the wife of Dr. John Ozanne, Edward Ozanne was educated at Elizabeth College, whence he went up to the Université de Caen. Here he gained his Bachelier-en-Droit in 1873 and became Licencié-en-Droit in 1874. Admitted as an Advocate of the Royal Court on coming down from the University, he was appointed Comptroller in 1877 and served in that capacity until 1895 when he took up the post of Procureur – a post which he retained until his elevation to the office of Bailiff in 1915.

Besides presiding over the Bailiwick's destinies for the greater part of the First World War, Edward Ozanne also had the unique experience of receiving the accolade of knighthood from the sovereign on Guernsey soil. This occurred when he was made a Knight Commander of the Most Excellent Order of the British Empire on the occasion of the visit to Guernsey paid by Their Majesties King George V and Queen Mary on 11 July 1921.

Sir Edward resigned the following year, and after seven years retirement he died on 15 March 1929, leaving behind as a permanent memorial his invaluable reference work *Recueil d'Ordres en Conseil d'un Intérêt Général enregistrés sur les Records de l'Ile de Guernesey depuis 1800*.

LE PAGE, JOHN (1913-). *Macte virtute.* See *Underground Resistance Heroes of Second World War.*

LE PAGE, THOMAS (1915–). *Macte virtute*.
See *Underground Resistance Heroes of the
Second World War*.

PAINSEC, REVEREND PIERRE (*c*. 1580–*c*.
1647). *A 17th-century Calvinist cullion*. (A). The
austere ethical standards of Guernsey's Huguenot
Establishment in the 16th and 17th centuries were
not always reflected in the lives of the faithful –
and even the ranks of the clergy were not entirely
devoid of those who fell by the wayside. Prominent among such clerical weaker vessels are Pierre
le Roy *dit* Bouillon, dismissed from the living of
St Pierre du Bois in 1593 for having seduced his
servant girl; and Joshua Slowley, the crapulent
chaplain of Castle Cornet whose drunken roister-
ing was reported to the Island Colloque in January
1632 by Jean de la Marche (q.v.) – on whom the
peccant pastor a year later wreaked a terrible
revenge, indicting him with alleged treason.

If, however, any trophy were to be awarded
for persistency and versatility in departing from
a state of grace, then it would without doubt go to
Pierre Painsec. Returning to Guernsey early in
1605 after having been educated for the ministry
at the expense of the parish of St Peter-Port (a
fact which suggests that birth must have been *c*.
1580), this clerical black sheep was appointed
minister of the Castel and St Andrew's, with
instructions also to assist the aged Nicolas
Baudouin (q.v.) of the Town Church at the quar-
terly catechisms and celebrations of the Holy
Communion in that 'Temple'. In theory, at any
rate, he also took over temporarily the cure of
souls in St Saviour's (whose incumbent, Daniel
Dolbel, the same year unexpectedly died).

The extent to which the new appointee actually
performed these various functions is problematical. As far as his help in the Town is concerned,
this he refused to continue in October 1605 on
the plea that he had not been paid. Although he
withdrew this refusal under threat of suspension,
Painsec in fact still failed to carry out these
duties. As a result he was summoned in December
before the Colloque, where the discussion became
increasingly recriminatory until eventually the
elders of St Andrew's and the Castel informed the
Colloque of Painsec's prolonged neglect of his
clerical functions in either parish, the *fainéant*
excusing himself on the alleged grounds that
neither of the two Consistoires concerned had
provided him with adequate sustenance. The
Colloque thereupon suspended Painsec until he
should repent and admit his fault. Not, however,
until the following April was any apology forth-

coming, the penitent then being reinstated on
condition of public confession of his culpability
in the 'Temples' of St Peter-Port, St Andrew's
and the Castel. Moreover, once again he officially
shouldered further responsibility, taking over for
the time being at the Vale parish after the death
of Jeremy Valpy.

In May 1610 Painsec again appeared before the
Colloque for having 'grievously molested' his wife
(Elizabeth Andros). As at the time it was permis-
sible to discipline a wife with a rod not thicker
than the little finger providing the chastisement
did not go *'jusqu'à l'effusion du sang'*, the assault
must have been severe to merit censure. The
erring cleric was ordered to make public confession of his guilt from the pulpit, both as a minister
and as a husband, including a declaration that the
sentence imposed on him was a just one.

His many frailties notwithstanding, shortage
of clergy led to Painsec being appointed to St
Peter-Port to succeed Baudouin on his death in
1613. In 1625, however, on Jean de la Marche's
assumption of office in the Town, he was transferred to the Castel. During his incumbency of
that parish he was involved, together with Joshua
Slowly, in several drunken brawls, in the course of
one of which (in October 1633) he might well
have strangled Slowley had he not been restrained
by one Grimes, the servant of Captain Nathaniel
Darell – the deputy of the Lieutenant-Governor,
Sir Peter Osborne (q.v.).

Frequent indulgence in unseemly behaviour
did not, however, appear to be any bar to Painsec's
advancement. By 1633 he had been elected a
Jurat of the Royal Court and he was also among
those who deputised for Jean de la Marche during
this zealot's captivity – services for which he
demanded payment at a hearing conducted by the
Earl of Danby (the Governor) in September
1636. The reprobate accordingly continued on
his merry way, and reports of his profanities had
become so widespread by Christmas 1639 that
the Colloque appointed a panel of ministers and
elders to look into the matter. However, Captain
Darell disapproved of this step and locked up the
Castel 'Temple' where the enquiry was scheduled
to be held.

The following Easter, with Darell still persisting
in his opposition to an investigation, Painsec
openly boasted in a tavern that he had long since
given himself to the Devil and that he there and
then reaffirmed this commitment – throwing in
further impious remarks for good measure. At this,
Darell changed his mind, convoking on 10 April
1640 an extraordinary sessions of the Colloque

before which Painsec was formally accused of blasphemy. He was convicted, and then condemned by Darell to be excommunicated and deposed from the ministry. The elders, however, urged that he be merely suspended from office, and in this attitude they commanded sufficient support to carry the day. The Devil certainly seemed to be looking after his own! Thus Painsec retained the Castel living until his death *c.* 1647, when he was replaced by Thomas le Marchant (q.v.*).

PARKES, REVEREND DOCTOR JAMES WILLIAM (1896-1981). *Guernsey's Anglican priest who strove for rapprochement between Christ's followers and His nation.* Born on 22 December 1896 in St Andrew's Parish to Annie Katherine (*née* Bell) the wife of Henry Parkes, a grower residing in La Route des Fauconnaires, James William Parkes was educated at Elizabeth College and, although only in his 'teens with the First World War broke out, made his way to England and, armed with sufficient scholarships to cover four years in Oxford later on, volunteered for the British army. His misgivings over destroying life rather than saving it were resolved by his becoming a Gas Officer (i.e. a specialist in anti-gas precautions). Demoblised in the spring of 1919, Captain Parkes (as he had then become) went up to Oxford (Hertford) the following autumn. While there he founded a student international assembly which became part of the League of Nations Union, and incurred intense opprobrium by supporting an invitation to 12 German students to visit the university for a month. His life-long commitment to eirenics had begun.

After graduation James Parkes took holy orders, but he never held a living. The path he did take on coming down was to join the staff of the Student Christian Movement as its International Study Secretary. His activities came to the notice of William Temple (from 1929 Archbishop of York and later — 1942 — Archbishop of Canterbury) who lent his support, calling for regular reports on what this idealistic young man was doing. The ensuing correspondence continued until Temple's death in 1944.

From 1923 to 1925 Parkes spent the summer months travelling in Europe, and was deeply moved by the despair and moral isolation of postwar Germany. In 1925 at an international student Christian conference in Switzerland he was asked to take the chair in a discussion on the Jewish question. He was so appalled by the venom and false innuendoes of the opening speech that he intervened, refusing to accept such a discourse as an introduction to a debate among Christians, and saying that he would call on no one else to speak until this address was withdrawn. After 20 minutes silence fraught with tension the speaker rose and said that his utterances had not been intended as antisemitic. Parkes accepted this and the conference continued.

Convinced by this experience that he was dealing with the greatest sin in the church's history; and seeing antisemitism as a Christian creation, stemming from regarding Judaism as the now dead and discredited precedessor of Christianity rather than a living and sincerely practised religion, James Parkes threw himself into ceaseless efforts to promote through joint study and research a better rapport between these two related monotheistic faiths. He thus emerged as a pioneer in the field of Christian/Jewish dialogue, persuaded that mutual understanding would heal the breaches created by ignorance and prejudice. It was in large measure due to his inspiration that in 1942 there had come into existence the Council of Christians and Jews, pledged to 'a common effort to fight the evils of prejudice, intolerance and discrimination between people of different religions, races and colours, and to work for the betterment of human relations, based on mutual respect, understanding and goodwill'.

Besides accumulating a vast library, the contents of which he made available to serious students, Dr. Parkes also wrote extensively in connection with the cause to which he gave his life. *The Foundations of Judaism and Christianity* (dealing with the spiritual equality of Christians and Jews) appeared in 1960, to be followed the next year by *A History of the Jewish People. Antisemitism*, published in 1963, provided a detailed examination of the psychology involved in this age-old prejudice; while in 1969 there came *Prelude to Dialogue* — an impassioned plea for discussion between equals as the best means of reaching a creative solution of the Christian/Jewish dichotomy.

Dr. Parkes was never domiciled in Guernsey permanently after his Oxford days, though he repeatedly visited his birthplace, and towards the end of his life emphasised that it was being a Guernseyman which explained his sympathy and understanding for small peoples in a raging world of self-interest. Joining the Guernsey Society practically at its inception, the articles he contributed from time to time to its magazine, *The Review*, were much appreciated. On coming down from the university he lived near Royston in

Hertfordshire, moving in 1964 to Iwerne Minster near Blandford Forum in Dorsetshire. Shortly before his death, in a conversation with Leonard Goss, General Secretary of the Council of Christians and Jews, James Parkes talked about his plans to return to Guernsey for the rest of his days — but this was not to be. The Reverend Dr. James William Parkes died in Dorset in August, 1981.

PARKINSON, PROFESSOR CYRIL NORTH-COTE, M.A., Ph.D., F.R.Hist.S. (1909–). *The triple Seigneur of academic and literary versatility.* He was born on 30 July 1909 in Barnard Castle, County Durham, to Rose Emily Mary Curnow, the wife of William Edward Parkinson, A.R.C.A., an artist with social aspirations beyond his pocket who died when his son was 16. Cyril Parkinson was brought up in York and educated at that city's St Peter's School, whence he went up to Cambridge (Emmanuel) where he read history, hoping to become a naval historian. To this end he wrote what came to be recognised as the definitive biography of Edward Pellew, Viscount Exmouth, Admiral of the Red, which, published in 1934, helped its author to gain a Ph.D. at King's College, London. The following year Emmanuel elected him to a Fellowship which he at first hoped might lead to a Chair enabling him to establish a school of maritime studies. This, however, proved to be a vain expectation and he realised that in adopting naval history he was proposing a subject which nobody really wanted. Consequently, after writing *Trade in the Eastern Seas* in 1937 he discarded his early ambitions and in 1938 took the post of senior history master at Blundell's School, Tiverton.

The outbreak of war wrenched Parkinson away from Blundell's, first to teach at the Royal Naval College, Dartmouth. He then had a varied experience in the forces, serving at one time or another with the Royal Navy, the Army and the Royal Air Force. After a taste of the Navy at Dartmouth in the early months of hostilities, he was commissioned in the Queen's Royal Regiment in 1940 with the rank of captain and thereafter served as an instructor at an O.C.T.U. until 1942 when he was attached to the R.A.F. for a twelvemonth. Then, after promotion to major, he spent the rest of the war on the General Staff at the War Office.

With the return of peace Dr. Parkinson took up an appointment as a history lecturer at the University of Liverpool, staying there from 1946 to 1950, when he began an eight-year career as Raffles Professor of History at the University of Malaya in Singapore, devoted mostly to training future administrators. He combined these academic labours with acting as correspondent for the *Manchester Guardian*, reporting on the civil strife with which the country was plagued prior to the attainment of independence in 1957. It was during his time in Singapore that his *War in the Eastern Seas* was published in 1954. On leaving Malaya he spent two years as a Visiting Professor — in 1958 at Harvard and at Illinois and California in 1959 and 1960.

Although its author considered *East and West* — a comparison of oriental and occidental civilisations and political attitudes published in 1963 — to be his most important book (with others such as *The Life and Times of Horatio Hornblower* coming later, not to mention his two plays and — from 1973 onwards — a series of novels), it was without doubt the appearance in 1958 of *Parkinson's Law, the Pursuit of Progress* (his brilliant serio-comic tilt at bureaucratic malpractice) which brought him fame and fortune. Virtually overnight every schoolboy knew that 'work expands to fill the time available for its completion and subordinates multiply at a fixed rate, regardless of the amount of work produced' — and when this was soon followed by similar widespread awareness of the dictum that 'expenditure rises to meet income' his days of eminence — and affluence — may indeed be said to have commenced. Not only were honours showered upon him, with Maryland University awarding him an honorary Doctorate of Laws in 1974 and Troy State University in Alabama first appointing him Professor Emeritus in 1970 and then bestowing upon him an honorary Doctorate of Literature in 1976; but also the flow of royalties from his books became the flood whereby Dr. Parkinson was enabled in the late 1950s and early 1960s to establish himself as a Guernsey Seigneur three times over.

Cyril Northcote Parkinson emerged not only as Seigneur du Fief de Beauvoir (with its Seigneurie at Les Câches) but in addition as Seigneur de Mauxmarquis and also as Seigneur d'Anneville (together with its dependencies of Fauville and la Croûte Bouilleuse), the Seigneurie of which he refurbished practically to the point of reconstruction after having languished for many years as a cowshed. The enthusiasm with which he identified himself with the island of his choice was emphasised by the title and subject matter of his first play — *Helier Bonamy* — the opening performance of which took place in Guernsey in 1967. Much the same may be said of his second play — *The Royalist* (1969) — which also had its initial staging in Guernsey. Furthermore, taking obvious pride in his feudal status, Professor Parkinson took the opportunity afforded by his presence at a session of La Cour des Chefs Plaids des Fiefs d'Anneville et de Fauville held in April 1980 in the ancient building restored by the Seigneur from a state of dereliction, to stress how strongly he deplored the erosion of seigneurial links with the sovereign, maintaining that those favouring such a development were 'sawing away at the bough of the tree on which they and we are sitting' and further insisting, 'I am a royalist, like my Andros predecessors in the Fief, and my wish would be to strengthen, not weaken, the bonds of loyalty'.†

LE PATOUREL, BRIGADIER HERBERT WAL-LACE, V.C. (1916–1979). *Guernsey's 'verray parfit gentil knight'*. Born in June 1916, the son of Mr. H. A. le Patourel, H.M. Procureur, 1929–34 and the younger brother of Professor John le Patourel (q.v.), 'Wally' le Patourel (as his friends knew him) was educated at Elizabeth College, on leaving which he embarked on a career in banking. Once his schooldays were behind him, he volunteered for service in the Royal Guernsey Militia, and it soon became clear that his aptitudes accorded far more with the métier of the soldier than with that of the banker. An outstanding subaltern, he was chosen to carry the King's Colour at the Coronation of George VI in 1937 when a Colour Party and 25 militiamen went to London for the occasion under the command of Major E. M. Langlois. It was thus hardly surprising that as the war clouds gathered this young man of martial spirit finally quit banking and went into the army, serving with the Hampshire Regiment.

The event which was to make Le Patourel's name resound in the courts of Ares took place on 3 December 1942. This was the fourth and final day of the battle for the control of the Tebourba Gap (20 miles to the west of Tunis) which had started at dawn of 30 November. At 1000 hours on that day enemy parachute troops of the Sturm-gruppe 'Koch' started to attack the whole of the positions held by the much depleted second battalion of the Royal Hampshire Regiment. Most of the fire was directed at the battalion's left flank. After about an hour Major le Patourel, who was commanding 'Z' Company, reported that enemy forces had established themselves, after a furious battle, on positions lately occupied by a company from another unit and were bring-ing heavy machine gun and mortar fire to bear on his left-hand section post on Point 186. Assault

detachments from 'Z' Company were despatched and succeeded in reaching the top, but were unable to retain the position owing to heavy casualties from enemy fire.

It was in the course of a desperate attempt to clear the enemy from the high ground on the battalion's left that Major le Patourel displayed the heroism which earned him the Victoria Cross. The citation accompanying the award reads — 'This officer then personally led four volunteers under very heavy fire to the top in a last attempt to dislodge several enemy machine guns. The party was heavily engaged by machine gun fire and Major le Patourel rallied his men several times and engaged the enemy, silencing several machine gun posts. Finally when the remainder of his party were all killed or wounded, he went forward alone with a pistol and some grenades to attack enemy machine guns at close quarters and from this action he did not return . . . Major le Patourel's most gallant conduct and self-sacrifice, his brilliant leadership and tenacious devotion to duty in the face of a determined enemy were beyond praise'.

It was believed that Major le Patourel was killed — and indeed his Victoria Cross was awarded posthumously. It was discovered later that he had been seriously wounded and taken prisoner. Freed as the Allies drove deep into Germany, the hero of Tebourba accompanied the Home Secretary, Mr. Herbert (later Lord) Morrison on his post-Liberation visit to Guernsey on 14 May 1945; the Minister later reporting to the Cabinet that 'as can be imagined, his reception was tumultuous'.

A distinguished peace-time military career ensued. Promoted to Lieutenant-Colonel, Le Patourel served as an instructor at the Quetta Staff College in India immediately after the war, returning to England in 1948 as an instructor at the School of Infantry at Warminster, where he stayed until 1950. From 1950 to 1953 Le Patourel served with the Parachute Regiment in the United Kingdom, Cyprus and the Suez Canal Zone, becoming the Commanding Officer of that Regiment's 14th battalion in 1954. The years 1957 to 1959 saw him in Washington, D.C. as General Staff Officer to the British Joint Services Mission, while in 1960 he assumed the responsibilities of Deputy Commander of the Army of Ghana. Finally, before retiring from the army with the rank of brigadier, le Patourel served as Deputy Commander of Number 43 Division District during the years 1961 and 1962. On 27 October 1968, he repeated the duty first dis-charged 31 years previously when he once again

† His status as a triple Seigneur was, however, transferred into that of a dual one by his sale in January 1984 of le Fief d'Anneville to Mr. and Mrs. Kevin Lycett.

paraded as a Guernsey Militia Colour-bearer: this time at the nostalgic ceremony at the Town Church where the Colours of the now defunct Militia were presented, re-dedicated and laid up.

Although a frequent visitor to the isle of his birth, Wallace le Patourel never resided permanently in Guernsey after joining the army. While in Warminster between 1948 and 1950, in October 1949 he married Miss Babette Beattie, who bore him two daughters, and after his retirement from the army the couple settled in Somersetshire at Chewton Mendip. Here Brigadier Herbert Wallace le Patourel, V.C., died in September 1979.

LE PATOUREL, PROFESSOR JOHN HERBERT, M.A., D.Phil., F.B.A. (1909–1981). *Guernsey's eminent medievalist.* Born in 1909 to Mary Elizabeth (*née* Daw), the wife of Mr. Herbert le Patourel (later — 1929 to 1934 — H.M. Procureur), John le Patourel, the elder brother of Brigadier Wallace le Patourel, V.C. (q.v.), was educated at Elizabeth College whence he went up to Oxford (Jesus) on a scholarship in 1928. Fascinated from boyhood by history, Le Patourel on coming down from Oxford took a post as lecturer at University College, London, subsequent to which he became reader in Medieval History at London University. While at the University of London he wrote his first book, *The Medieval Administration of the Channel Islands*, which was published in 1937.

During the Second World War, as a member of the Channel Islands Study Group, John le Patourel was one of the contributors to the informed symposium, *Nos Iles*, produced by that body. He was also a member of the Guernsey Society from its inception and of La Société Guernesiaise throughout his adult life. After the war he was appointed Archivist to the Royal Court of Guernsey and at the same time took the chair of medieval history at Leeds University, retaining this professorship until his retirement in 1979, when the university granted him a Research Professorship. As a consequence he made his home at Ilkley, remaining there until his death. In 1949, as literary executor of Arthur John Eagleston, C.V.O. (q.v.*), he prepared for the press that writer's *Channel Islands Under Tudor Government*. His own *Building of Castle Cornet* was to follow in 1958.

Professor Le Patourel's special interest was centred on the Channel Isles and their relations with France — a theme investigated in his paper, 'Guernsey, Jersey and Their Environment in the Middle Ages', published in the *Transactions* of La Société in 1974. The whole subject was thoroughly explored in his last major work, *The Norman Empire*, which appeared in 1976. Mrs. Jean le Patourel shared many of her husband's interests and in the summer of 1952 they conducted a joint excavation and examination of the ruins of Lihou Priory, later to be followed by a further 'dig' — this time Castle Cornet. With no trace of the lofty academic about him, John le Patourel was unfailingly generous with valuable help and advice to the less well informed who sought his aid. This erudite and kindly islander died suddenly in July 1981.

LE PELLEY, ERNEST (1802–1849). *'Silver and gold have I none'.: The Seigneur who mortgaged Sark.* (G). The second son of Pierre le Pelley II (q.v.) and his wife Anne de Jersey (to whom he was born in 1802), Ernest le Pelley inherited the Fief of Sark when his elder brother Pierre le Pelley III (q.v.), his predecessor as Seigneur, was drowned in March 1839.

Besides the fief, the new Seigneur also inherited a moral commitment to provide a new school site (as stipulated in his brother's unsigned will), and in addition financial commitments to the Guernsey and Sark Mining Company. The first commitment he discharged (as the present-day junior school bears witness), but the second commitment broke him. Ever more powerful and expensive pumping equipment was needed as deeper and deeper veins were worked in frustratingly disappointing searches for the elusive silver, of which only £4,000 worth was obtained at a cost of £34,000. To clear existing debts and to finance the purchase of more pumping machinery, Le Pelley in May 1844 borrowed from Jean Allaire (q.v.) £4,000 with his fief mortgaged as security. The euphoria occasioned soon afterwards when a vein of ore was struck worth £600 per ton turned to despair in 1845, when the ceiling of the lowest gallery collapsed and the workings were flooded.

Overwhelmed by this disaster and with all he possessed mortgaged to the hilt, Ernest le Pelley died in October 1849. In 1829 he had married Amelia Carey and their son, Pierre Carey le Pelley, inherited obligations he was utterly incapable of discharging. Accordingly in 1852 Marie Collings *née* Allaire, the daughter and heiress of Jean Allaire (who had died in 1846) foreclosed the mortgage securing her father's loan to Ernest, thereby acquiring Sark for the family which still holds the fief for £6,000 less £4,000 initially advanced and £616 13s. 4d. overdue interest — a net payment of £1,383 6s. 8d.

LE PELLEY, JURAT IL CAVALIERE JEAN (1899-1982). *An accomplished internationalist and distinguished public servant.* Born in October 1899 in Genoa (whither his father's professional commitments had taken his parents) to Mary Ann Victoria (*née* White), the wife of John Quertier le Pelley, Jean le Pelley was educated at the Boys' Intermediate School and subsequently at Elizabeth College, on leaving which he embarked on a career in banking. With this in view, he left Guernsey for the City of London, where he was enrolled in the Foreign Department of the Midland Bank and also – to widen his experience – in that of La Banca Commerciale Italiana.

The First World War was then in progress and as soon as he was old enough (by which time the titanic struggle was approaching its end) Jean le Pelley offered himself for service in the Royal Naval Volunteer Reserve, where he carried with him his insular identity, recording in later years that 'as a naval rating I wore a Guernsey in winter'.*

On demobilisation from the forces Le Pelley returned to his birthplace where his maternal grandfather, John White, ran a shipbroking business. It was during his stay in this seaport, in 1924, that he entered into employment with the National City Bank of New York – which later added the qualification 'First' to its title and later still became, as 'Citibank', the second largest bank in the world. This concern – in which he eventually became an assistant vice-president – he was to serve for the rest of his working life. He remained in Italy until 1938 when, on Mussolini's sequestration of the banks in that country, he was entrusted with closing down the Genoa and Milan branches before being transferred to the London office. Here he became a manager accountant (a title which goes with the authorisation to sign documents on the bank's behalf) and stayed at this post throughout the war, his responsibilities including assuming charge of accounts of enemy nationals whose assets had been seized by the Bank of England. During this period he supplemented his professional duties by putting at the nation's service his considerable linguistic abilities (he was fluent in seven languages), scriptwriting and broadcasting propaganda in French, German and Italian on behalf of the Department of Political Warfare, as well as transmitting cryptic coded messages to underground resistance movements.

During the immediate post-war period Jean le Pelley was required by his employers to assess and periodically report on the confusingly fluid situation in European countries, and on their contortions to recover from the ravages of the terrible conflict. Then, in 1949, he went to New York to spend a year at head office devoted to study. He then took a roving commission based on Paris, but which also involved extensive travel throughout the continent, in the course of which he opened branches in Brussels, Milan, Amsterdam, Geneva, Athens and Frankfurt, as well as undertaking the preparatory work for the establishment of branches in Zurich and Rome. While in Paris he also headed the American Common Market Counselling Service – designed to help American corporations fearful of being excluded from European markets as a result of the Treaty of Rome – and in this capacity made valuable contributions to the development of Italo-American financial and industrial relations. With an area of responsibility extending from Lisbon to Athens and from North Africa to Paris, he travelled extensively in Africa and the Middle East as well as in Europe, and became well known in financial circles connected with the Vatican, the United Nations Educational, Scientific and Cultural Organisation, the Food and Agriculture Organisation, and the North Atlantic Treaty Organisation.

Forty energetic years in the world of international banking came to an end in 1964 when Jean le Pelley decided to return to Guernsey (where he had inherited a house) for his retirement. He himself in 1971 described his reactions to his return home:

'Now after a lifetime spent, not exactly on the seven seas, but certainly in several continents, I found myself back in Guernsey, getting once again attuned to its changeable seas, its vast dramatic skies and flying clouds (like something in an old Dutch seascape), the damp winter fogs, the glorious autumns, the warm summers that tempt you into the boat; and the chill run home after the sun has set'.*

The years back in Guernsey were fruitful ones of ceaseless activity. His erstwhile employers continued to call on him from time to time between his retirement and 1974 to deal with special problems as and when they arose – calls resulting in lengthy visits to Beirut, Rome and Milan. In the island itself, his qualifications were quickly recognised and his services were consequently eagerly sought for the States' Ancient Monuments Committee, and as a member of both the Council and the Executive Committee of the National Trust of Guernsey and as Treasurer of the Court of Seigneurs – not to mention La Société Guernesiaise where, after a lifelong fascination with history, he became Secretary of the Historical Section in succession to Mr. Victor Coysh (q.v.) and was moreover elected President in 1970, thereafter serving as a vice-president. A life-long member of the Society of Nautical Research, Le Pelley had already earned repute as a naval historian, in this capacity writing book reviews for the *Mariners' Mirror* and maintaining regular contact with La Musée de la Marine in Paris, the Whaling Museum in Nantucket, and the Maritime Museums at Cape Cod and Greenwich — the last-named of which at the time of his death he was assisting in the compilation of a catalogue of maritime memorials throughout all the Channel Islands. Not surprisingly, therefore, he was a member of the joint Jersey–Guernsey Advisory Committee on a projected history of Channel Islands Shipping, in connection with which he worked closely with the relevant research team at London University right up to his death.

His integrity and considerable abilities led to his election as a Jurat of the Royal Court in July 1967, an office in which he served until reaching the age limit in October 1974. During this period he also became Honorary Consular Agent for the Italian community in the island, following which (in 1971) Jean le Pelley was appointed to the Order of Merit of the Italian Republic, with the rank of Cavalière: his active interest in Italian affairs over many years thereby receiving recognition. He also served on the Post Office Committee which negotiated the transfer of postal and telecommunication operations from the British G.P.O. to the States of Guernsey, having previously sat on an earlier committee which had investigated the feasibility of Guernsey shouldering such an undertaking. In addition, he was a member of the Council and also on the Management Committee of the Guille–Allès Library, as well as being a Trustee of the Priaulx Trust for the teaching of the French language in schools. Throughout his retirement Le Pelley was a Director of Kleinwort Benson (Guernsey) Limited and also of Citibank (Channel Islands) Limited.

In his young and middle years a keen mountain climber (and as such a member of the Alpine Club), and also a first-class skier who continued to tramp about mountains on foot well into his 70s, Jean le Pelley's earthly pilgrimage of diligent application to every task in hand was brought to a close on 25 September 1982 when death finally robbed his fellow-islanders of his warm personality and wise counsel.

*Both quotations are taken from an article entitled 'The Guernsey Frock' in the Guernsey Society's *Review*, Volume XXVII, No. 2.

LE PELLEY, PIERRE (1763-1820). *The Seigneur of Sark who was faced with revolt*. (G). He was born in 1763 to Martha (*née* Careye). His eponymous father eight years before his birth had been the young Seigneur involved in the affair of Pierre Levrier (q.v.). Pierre le Pelley succeeded to the Fief of Sark on the death of his parent in 1778 when he was only 15 years of age. During his feudality he found himself confronted with a sustained attack on his rights dating from 1789 onwards, which stemmed both from the militancy of Methodism and also from the anti-feudal ferment generated by the French Revolution.

The defiance with which he had to contend centred around his *droit de multure* (milling monopoly) and the tenants' *corvée* obligations. In connection with the first of these issues, Thomas de Carteret, tenant of La Forge, threw out a challenge in 1796 to the Seigneur's milling rights by erecting his own windmill and subsequently refusing either to obey le Pelley's order to demolish it or to appear before the Seneschal's Court when cited by his adversary. Arrested by the Seneschal and brought before the Royal Court of Guernsey, de Carteret won his case, the Royal Court ruling in May 1797 that the Seigneur was not entitled to deprive a tenant of the right to possess a mill provided it was for his own use exclusively. The opposition being emboldened by this judgment, Pierre's own mill was set alight by an unknown arsonist the following October, soon after which yet another private mill was built in Little Sark to avoid the hazardous crossing of La Coupée.

As for the *corvée*, the resentment of the poorer tenants over these obligations (which their circumstances compelled them to perform in person while their richer counterparts were able to employ substitutes) found expression at a meeting of Chief Pleas in November 1803, when a resolution that road upkeep should be the responsibility of contiguous house-holders was carried by 22 votes to 11. However, the refusal of the Seneschal to register this decision for lack of Seigneurial consent (Le Pelley being in Guernsey at the time) was vindicated on appeal in November 1804 by the Guernsey Royal Court, which thus implicitly upheld the Seigneur's right of veto. The disgruntled tenants retorted by refusing to work on the roads of Little Sark if their holdings were in Great Sark, and vice versa; while both groups declined to provide labour on La Coupée, alleging that it was not a '*grand chemin*' within the terms of the Roads Ordinance of 1585. This impasse was not resolved until 1812 when a compromise was reached whereby the tenants agreed to work on La Coupée, in return for a contribution from the Seigneur towards the cost of the undertaking.

Pierre le Pelley found a more fundamental threat to his authority posed by the rapid growth during his Seigneurship of a righteously assertive Methodism, the adherents of which formed the spearhead of the ever-increasing opposition to his feudal powers. Their chapel (completed in 1796) became a centre for formulating hostile action against the Seigneur, and for planning vigorous opposition in Chief Pleas to the levying of *impôts* for defraying some of the expenses of the Established Church. By way of riposte le Pelley sought to re-establish the status and prestige of the Anglican church, by obtaining a grant of £400 from the fund set up by the British government in 1817 to promote the erection of Anglican churches to counteract the spread of Wesleyan influence. He used the money to help finance the construction of St Peter's Church to replace the inadequate outbuilding at Le Manoir which hitherto had done duty as Sark's place of worship. The foundation stone was laid in 1820, but Pierre died before the work was completed.

LE PELLEY, PIERRE (1799–1839). *The Seigneur of Sark infected with 'Silver Rush' fever*. (G). This third Pierre le Pelley in a row to be Seigneur of Sark inherited the fief in 1820 at the age of 21. He immediately attempted a policy of pacification aimed at healing the strained relationships which had developed between Seigneur and tenants in the time of his father Pierre II (q.v.). Besides seeking to involve the tenantry in the new Anglican church (then nearing completion) by selling pews, which then became integral parts of the tenements of the purchasers, he also sought public approval by donating land to the north of the church for a school, to finance which he negotiated a loan from the States of Guernsey on his own initiative. Similarly, in 1832, although personally in favour of building a new prison in conformity with an Order of the Royal Court of Guernsey, he nevertheless let sleeping dogs lie rather than antagonise the tenants who had opposed the project in Chief Pleas. By 1835 Seigneur tenant relationships had become completely amicable and Pierre was able, without incurring any animosity, to arrange the purchase from Jean le Feuvre of the holding of La Moinerie de Haut, later demolishing the house and adding

the grounds to the gardens of La Seigneurie. (He also by this purchase acquired an additional vote on Chief Pleas which was enjoyed by successive Seigneurs until 1929 when it was made over to the Tenant of Brecqhou by Dame Sibyl Hathaway (q.v.).)

In 1833 Le Pelley was approached by John Hunt, a mining surveyor, for permission to exploit silver deposits in Little Sark. After initial hesitation, he acceded to the request and also took up ten shares in the 'Guernsey and Sark Mining Company' as the venture was called — further increasing his commitment when an additional lode was discovered at Port Gorey in 1836. Convinced that wealth beyond the dreams of avarice was virtually within his grasp, he drew up a will in 1837 donating to the island a site near Le Manoir for a further school. The dream was fated to turn into a nightmare — but Pierre le Pelley was spared the realization of this. On 1 March 1839 he was drowned en route for Guernsey in a terrible scene off Bec du Nez, witnessed by the vicar, the Reverend John Louis Victor Cachemaille (q.v.).

PERCHARD, PETER (1729–1806). *Guernsey's Dick Whittington who found the streets of London paved with silver as well as gold*. (A). During the 18th century the silversmiths of the Channel Isles earned a reputation for a high level of craftsmanship, and several of them went to England, where they achieved considerable success. One such was Peter Perchard, a prosperous silversmith belonging to an old-established family of St Pierre-du-Bois and born in that parish in 1729. Peter learned his trade from his uncle Matthew Perchard, a jeweller and goldsmith in London's famous Hatton Garden, who died in 1779, leaving what in those days was the enormous sum of £30,000.

After his uncle's demise Peter continued to thrive, being installed as the Prime Warden of the Goldsmith's Company for the period 1786–87 and later being appointed as Sheriff of the City of London in 1793. He served as President of St Bartholomew's Hospital from 1804 onwards and on 9 November of the same year he was invested with the dignity of Lord Mayor of London. He died in January 1806 — a mere ten weeks after the end of his term of office.

Peter Perchard married Martha, the daughter of Henry le Mesurier (q.v.) and the first cousin of Paul le Mesurier (q.v.), one of his predecessors as Lord Mayor of London. His daughter Martha married Major-General John le Mesurier (q.v.), the last 'Hereditary Governor' of Alderney who, as the son of her mother's sister Marie, the wife of Peter le Mesurier (q.v.) was her first cousin. A memorial in the Town Church commemorates this distinguished Guernseyman, whose body (in common with those of his wife and four children) is buried in St Mary, Abchurch, so that his remains fittingly repose in the heart of the city over which he presided as civic head.

† POAT, LIEUTENANT-COLONEL HARRY WALL, D.S.O., M.C., Croix de Guerre (1914–1980). *A Guernsey Galahad of talent and vision*. Born at Baubigny on 15 June 1914 to Eliza Emma (*née* Jones), the wife of Frank Wall Poat, he was thus a member of a family long associated with horticulture. In 1884 his grandfather Jean Poat (1837–1908) had been the first person to grow tomatoes (in a span house) as a main crop rather than as a mere sideline to grape production. Harry Wall Poat was educated at Elizabeth College whence, realising that merely following traditional methods of cultivation would no longer suffice in an increasingly competitive economy, he went up to Reading University to read for a Bachelor of Science degree in agriculture, the better to equip himself for a career as a grower. On coming down he raised a loan to finance the construction of a small vinery which he worked himself — but he had only just cleared the debt thus incurred when his career as a horticulturist was rudely interrupted by the outbreak of the Second World War.

In this titanic struggle Harry Poat was to achieve glory. Already commissioned in the Royal Guernsey Militia, on its disbandment shortly before the German Occupation he joined the King's Own Scottish Borderers and was soon — albeit briefly — back in Guernsey, being a participant in the ill-fated 'Operation Ambassador' launched against the island's south coast in July 1940. He then went to the Middle East, where ere long he was active with the Special Air Service Regiment, fighting with this unit through Africa, Sicily and Italy. He was subsequently parachuted into France for liaison work with the Maquis. Then, in Germany, Lieutenant-Colonel Poat (as he had become) commanded the Forward Light Reconnaissance Unit which pressed as far north as Kiel in the van of the 6th Airborne Division. On the cessation of hostilities and the disbandment of his unit he became second-in-command of the London Scottish, retaining this post until demobilisation. His gallant and distinguished services during the conflict received recognition in his appointment by King George VI as a Companion of the Most Distinguished Service Order and in his

being awarded the Military Cross. He was also decorated by France with the Croix de Guerre.

Having returned to Guernsey in the wake of the Liberation, Lieutenant-Colonel Poat was on 1 January 1949 elected with a record poll as Peoples' Deputy for St Sampson's. Operating in this capacity as a member of the Housing Authority and also on the Tourist Committee, Military Service Committee and Outdoor Assistance Board, he held office until 21 December 1951, when the pressure of his family business debarred him from seeking re-election. Continuing, however, to render public service as President of the Central Committee of the Royal British Legion, he was honoured by the Queen in December 1953, being appointed as aide-de-camp to Her Majesty — the last Guernseyman ever to enjoy this distinction. Later, on 30 June 1971, his sterling qualities and great abilities procured his choice by the States of Election as a Jurat of the Royal Court in succession to Mr. A. V. Dorey and thereafter, both as a Jurat and as an acting-magistrate (which he became on 26 January 1975) he made a most valuable contribution to the administration of justice in the island.

This contribution was abruptly terminated on 14 October 1980 (appropriately, for a warrior of the Norman Isles, the anniversary of the Battle of Hastings). This warm-hearted and generous man, who showed never-failing concern for his employees and who at the time of his election to a juratcy was described by Conseiller Roydon Falla as 'a man with a disciplined mind in war and peace', fell victim to lung disease (fibrosing alveolitis) and died a few days after returning to his home at Millmount, Candie, from a course of medical treatment in the United Kingdom.

PRIAULX, OSMOND DE BEAUVOIR (1805–1891). *The benefactor of Cavendish Square*. Born in March 1805, Osmond de Beauvoir Priaulx read law at Cambridge, but never practised as 'he found himself above the necessity of earning his livelihood' (*Star* obituary notice, 17 January 1891). By prudent investment, he became even richer and indulged to the full his passion as an avid bibliophile, accumulating a vast library of thousands of volumes which filled his London home in Cavendish Square. Although resident in England, Osmond Priaulx had a great love for Guernsey, which he visited frequently. His knowledge of the island's old families was boundless, and by diligent investigation he made himself an authority on any genealogical question connected with the insular community.

† PHILLIPS, THOMAS (1635–1693): see p. 173

In 1859 Osmond bought Candie House (built *c*. 1780) from his brother Joshua — to whom it had been sold many years previously by Peter Mourant (q.v.*) — and ten years later he followed up this purchase, by offering to endow Guernsey with a public library. After the acceptance of this offer by the States in April 1869, Priaulx in December 1871 presented both house and grounds to the States 'for the use of the inhabitants of the island' provided the sitting tenant (Sir Peter Stafford Carey, who was Bailiff from 1845 to 1883) enjoyed security of tenure for life. Sir Peter died in 1886.

In 1880 Osmond Priaulx endowed the proposed library with investments worth £9,500 to finance its upkeep, stipulating that the money should be held by Trustees for the benefit of the Institution. In March 1887 the States voted £2,000 for alterations at Candie House, which was thereupon converted by Amias Charles Andros (1837–98) to accommodate a reference library. At the same time Priaulx agreed that the remainder of the estate should become the absolute property of the States — consent which eventuated in the opening of the public Pleasure Gardens of Candie. Later that year this generous donor 'placed his books, the solace of his life, in this Library and gave them for ever to the people of Guernsey'. The Institution was opened to the public in 1889, since when it has afforded free of charge to all and sundry research facilities of incalculable value. The extent of Priaulx' munificence may be appreciated when it is borne in mind that the value of the gift of Candie Estate and the book collection came to £15,000 at 1891 prices — equivalent to well over £300,000 at the time of writing 90 years later.

Osmond de Beauvoir Priaulx died on 15 January 1891 and in accordance with the terms of his will, his body was cremated at Woking. He had for many years been an earnest advocate of this method of disposing of human remains which at the time met with the disapproval of the great majority. An urn containing his ashes reposes in the library, for the existence of which the people of Guernsey will be forever in his debt.

PRIAULX, THOMAS FREDERICK DE LA MARE (1906-   ). *The genealogical sage of St Saviour's*. This outstanding historian, with a name and lineage (coupling Priaulx and de la Mare) redolent of Guernsey, was, paradoxically, born in the Isle of Wight. Needless to say, his parents were Guernsey folk and he was only a few months old when the family returned to the island. Educated at Les Vauxbelets College, he grew up a thorough Guernesiais, learning to speak in the Patois through conversations with his grandfather's farm workers — that being the only tongue they understood.

On leaving school, Mr. Priaulx spent some years working in an advocate's office in Court Row, from which experience he became intimately acquainted with insular procedures, practices and customs — information which was to prove invaluable as the basis of his academic work later in life. In 1931 Frederick Priaulx (the 'Thomas' being otiose) joined La Société Guernesiaise. At that time interest in La Société was at a low ebb, and as a consequence every encouragement was given to younger members. Thus it was that the new recruit came into contact with such enthusiasts as William Rolleston, Spencer Carey Curtis, Mildred Brock, Vera Carey, Ralph Durand and — above all — Edith Carey (q.v.), all of whom were very generous in imparting their knowledge on local subjects to younger newcomers. It was only after a prolonged seminar sitting at the feet of these cognoscenti that Mr. Priaulx in the mid-1950s ventured to contribute to La Société's *Transactions* with a paper on cider-making in Guernsey. Several further papers followed, whereby Frederick Priaulx gained his well-deserved reputation as a distinguished authority on island lore.

Being born outside the Channel Isles placed Frederick Priaulx in the category affected by Hitler's Deportation Orders. He was accordingly deported in the autumn of 1942 to Germany, where he was interned until freed by the Allied victory. After the war was over, Mr. Priaulx became a member of the Guernsey Society which had been formed during the conflict and, in response to the urging of Professor E. B. Moullin, began writing articles for its magazine, *The Review*. At first concentrating on genealogical matters and local family histories, these essays later dealt with a variety of social customs, topics and practices, many of which by the time of writing had fallen into disuse. The leading contributor to the investigation entitled *The Guernsey Farmhouse* which the Guernsey Society published in 1963, Frederick Priaulx (who, *inter alia*, became assistant editor of its magazine) was elected to its governing council and later became a vice-president of the Society.

These valuable services to the Guernsey Society did not involve any neglect of La Société Guernesiaise, to the *Transactions* of which he continued to provide papers and of the Historical Section of which he became secretary. Furthermore, as would be expected of one with Frederick Priaulx' veneration of Guernsey's traditions, he became Sénéchal of the Fief des Eperons and also of the Fief Mauxmarquis, besides being Vavasseur of the Fiefs Janin Besnard and Canteraine. In addition Mr. Priaulx, who has remained a bachelor all his days, served both as Douzenier (1947-51) and Constable (1939-42) of his home parish of St Saviour, the informed history of the church of which also flowed from his pen.

PYM, LIEUTENANT-COLONEL JOHN BEVILLE (1866-1916). *The notorious fomenter of discord in the Militia.* On 19 May 1899, the Lieutenant-Governor, Major-General Michael Henry Saward, returned to Guernsey after attending a conference at the War Office in London convened as a result of widespread insubordination in the North Regiment of the Royal Guernsey Militia. He had taken with him a petition signed by 90 militiamen, which read as follows:

> *'A Monsieur le Colonel J. Leale:*
> *'Nous les soussignés, membres du Regiment du Nord, vous prions de bien vouloir accuellir notre requête, ayant été longtemps assujétis à un point de tyrannie et frappé par des amendes continuelles sans en connaître la raison; et, comme juenes gens frappés d'une loi sevère ne nous donnant aucune privilege de nous défendre.*
> *'Nous vous prions bien d'avoir la bonté de reconnaître notre loyauté et notre vouloir de faire notre devoir, autant qu'il est requis de nous.*
> *'De nous proteger contre la tyrannie dont nous avons été assujétis pendant le temps de service du present adjutant, sous le commandement duquel il nous est impossible de faire notre devoir.'*

> 'To Colonel J. Leale:
> 'We the undersigned members of the North Regiment, beg you to be so good as to give ear to our petition, having for a long time been under tyrannical subjection and hard hit by continuous fines without knowing the reason why; and are thus like young people penalised by a severe law not giving us any right to defend ourselves.
> 'We ask you to be so kind as to acknowledge our loyalty and our willingness to do our duty as much as is required of us.

> 'Also to protect us against the tyranny to which we have been subjected during the period of service of the present adjutant, under whose command it is impossible for us to do our duty.'

The source of *'la tyrannie dont nous avons été assujétis'* was John Beville Pym, who, born at York on 16 November 1866 and having chosen a career as 'a Jolly, 'Er Majesty's Jolly, soldier and sailor too', was at the time a Captain in the 2nd Royal Marine Light Infantry, holding an appointment in Guernsey under an arrangement arrived at in 1873, whereby a professional adjutant and permanent staff were to be attached to each Militia Regiment. While no doubt technically efficient, Pym was a martinet who failed to appreciate the difference between paid regular volunteer soldiers, and unpaid conscript quarrymen and labourers who were unenthusiastically parading after a hard day's work. Punishing minor breaches of military discipline by fines, he showed his contempt for the men on parade by abusive language, which was keenly resented. The upshot was a refusal to drill, at first by 74 men but later by considerably larger numbers, who on one occasion ostentatiously marched from Baubigny Arsenal to Bulwer Avenue where, removed from the presence of the detested Pym, the mutineers drilled under their regimental commander, Colonel J. Leale, cheering him as he rode home after the parade.

When 14 ringleaders were given a month's imprisonment, their comrades organised a fund to support their families. So inflammatory were some of the speeches made at a mass meeting held at Les Capelles Chapel after their release that Pym was sufficiently alarmed to demand police protection, with the result that a member of the St Peter-Port Constabulary was posted to guard his residence at No. 2 Ross Place, Mount Row. Ultimately, in a further attempt to enforce discipline, the Royal Court sentenced 40 more insubordinates to a month's solitary confinement – the trial being accompanied by demonstrations outside the prison and the Court House as well as in the vicinity of Baubigny Arsenal. In the hope of avoiding further public demonstrations at the time of release, the prisoners were discharged the evening before their term of imprisonment was up. They left their clothes behind, however, and called for them *en masse* the next morning. A crowd quickly gathered and the 'martyrs' marched back to St Sampson's in a triumphal procession, being welcomed at their destination by blasts from the siren of a ship in the harbour.

Under cover of a further Militia reorganisation the same summer (whereby the North Regiment lost its identity on the merging of the various regiments into two infantry battalions) the overbearing adjutant was quietly removed and the trouble — which had threatened to engulf the entire Militia — was at last smoothed over. The episode, however, was far from forgotten and *'Pas Pour Pym'* remained a family saying in the northern parishes right up to the inter-war years.

As for the egregious Pym himself, the slow climb up the ladder of promotion which is so often the peace-time lot of the professional officer, had by the outbreak of the First World War brought this 'kind of a giddy harumfrodite' to the rank of Lieutenant-Colonel — still with the 2nd Royal Marine Light Infantry. The bad health with which he was by then beset put service in the field out of the question, and the result was that his contribution to the war effort was confined to administrative duties connected with ordnance supply. Although thus spared the rigours of campaigning, his condition steadily worsened and in the late autumn of 1916 it brought him to an early grave. Lieutenant-Colonel John Beville Pym died at Edmonton shortly after his 50th birthday in mid-November of that year.

Q

DE QUETTEVILLE, JEAN (1582–1648). *The Royalist Bailiff who steadfastly defied the Roundheads.* Born in 1582, Jean de Quetteville was appointed as a Jurat of the Royal Court in 1616, at the age of 34. Eight years later — in 1624 — he became H.M. Receiver, from which post he was promoted to the supreme dignity of Bailiff in 1631, thus entering on a term of office which was destined to prove memorable.

When Charles I hoisted his standard at Nottingham, Guernsey's entrenched Calvinist establishment made inevitable the Bailiwick's adherence to the cause of his enemies. Jean de Quetteville, however, true to his oath on taking up his duties as Bailiff, remained loyal to the crown. The result was that in 1643, at the instigation of Pierre de Beauvoir (q.v.), he was deprived of his office and placed under arrest for conniving in the exploits of George Carteret (q.v.), who managed to run the blockade and get supplies through to Sir Peter Osborne (q.v.), who was holding Castle Cornet for the king. The senior Jurat, Jean Bonamy, was then sworn in as Judge Délégué *'pendant l'absence de Jean Quetteville, Ecuyer, Bailli'*. As de Quetteville was under arrest (he was subsequently shipped to England and imprisoned for a time in Hurst Castle) *'pendant l'absence'* was expected to be of indefinite duration. While he was incarcerated Pierre de Beauvoir was sworn in as Bailiff as parliament's nominee on Christmas Eve 1644.

However, in February 1647 Jean de Quetteville, showing considerable spirit, returned to Guernsey and insisted that he alone had the right to perform the duties of Bailiff. He proceeded to convene the States a number of times as a display of his rightful authority, in defiance of the vociferous opposition raised by de Beauvoir on each occasion. In these circumstances Lieutenant-Colonel Robert Russel, the Parliamentary Lieutenant-Governor, persuaded the court in March to declare that the office of Bailiff should be treated as vacant until the differences between the rival claimants had been settled. As a consequence Jean Careye was sworn in as Juge Délégué and each rival Bailiff found himself barred from the court over which he claimed the exclusive entitlement to preside. In the autumn four members of parliament were appointed to investigate the contretemps and (hardly surprisingly) the upshot was de Beauvoir's confirmation in office, signalised by his presiding over a sitting of the court early in December. Worn out by the struggle, the doughty champion of Stuart legitimacy, now in his mid-sixties, died the following spring, the king's man to the end.

DE QUETTEVILLE, JEAN (1761–1843). *The missionary of Methodism.* An inscription in the vestibule of Sark's present Methodist church (built in 1925) shows *'pierre fondamentale numero 36'* as being *'à la memoire de Jean de Quetteville, fondateur de l'œuvre de Sercq et natif de St Martin, Jersey'*. Born in Jersey in 1761, Jean de Quetteville was educated in Winchester (though not at that city's famous public school). Although confirmed while at school, de Quetteville nevertheless experienced a period of acute depression as an Anglican, feeling himself besmirched with the 'filthiness and superfluity of naughtiness' which

St James had exhorted the faithful to 'lay apart'. Conditioned by this spiritual disquiet, his religious climacteric came in 1784 when John Wesley (q.v.*), in response to the appeals of Methodist soldiers garrisoned in Jersey, sent over a bilingual preacher, Robert Carr Brackenbury. The latter's exposition of the Wesleyan message completely won over the guilt-ridden Jerseyman, who immediately joined the newly-established Methodist Society as an able and enthusiastic convert.

The following year, the first whisperings of Methodism reached Guernsey when islanders who had been involved in the Newfoundland cod fisheries returned home, bringing their newly-acquired faith with them. Deciding to take advantage of this situation, Brackenbury in 1786 sent over de Quetteville who, thanks to the disgruntlement of the Guernesiais with the Anglicanism which had been imposed on them from without, found a fertile soil for the spread of his teachings. 'Mon Plaisir', the house of Henry de Jersey (whose daughter Susanne married de Quetteville in 1788) became the headquarters of the movement — Wesley himself preaching from an adjacent mounting-block during his visit to the island in 1787.

Despite the large numbers of his converts, de Quetteville suffered considerable persecution. While he was preaching in a house in the Vale a mob broke in, seized him, and dragging him to the parish boundary, literally kicked him into St Sampson's. Against this assault the victim appealed to the court in vain — and indeed, further mal-treatment was to follow. Bad eggs and dung were hurled at the preacher, who was also drenched with bucketfuls of water. In 1788 he was arrested on the charge of causing disunion in families, but the witnesses giving evidence in the case disagreed in their testimony, with the result that the court discharged him. Indeed, the venom thus displayed against de Quetteville was counter-productive. Even William le Marchant (q.v.), who was far from being mild and gentle in temperament and whose anti-Methodist attitude had been manifest in his severity two years previously against Zacharias Mahy (in the case of Thomas Hallowris) was nevertheless so disgusted by this blatant attempt to inculpate de Quetteville, that he extended his patronage to the struggling Methodist Society, coming the following year to inspect the foundations of their first chapel, which was being built on land belonging to him in La Rue le Marchant.

De Quetteville paid frequent visits to Alderney — where Methodism had been introduced in 1787 by one of his co-religionists, Adam Clarke — and in 1789 he turned his attention to Sark, where he preached in the kitchen of 'Clos à Jaon', the property of Thomas Mollet. One of his audience, Jean Vaudin, the tenant of La Ville Roussel (who was described by de Quetteville as *'illitré et croyant aux sorciers'*) offered a site adjoining his house for a chapel. Called 'Ebenezer Chapel', the building was completed in 1789, whereafter Methodism took a strong hold in the island, becoming a thorn in the flesh of the Seigneur, Pierre le Pelley II (q.v.).

Ordained into the Methodist ministry in Jersey in 1791, de Quetteville was sent to Paris, but at the outbreak of the French Revolutionary War, he returned to the Channel Isles in 1793. In 1795 he published a collection of 467 hymns in French, mostly by himself: a veritable psalmodic *tour-de-force*. Thereafter he exercised his ministry in the isle of his birth. Jean de Quetteville died in 1843.

R

RENOUF, SIR PETER LE PAGE (1822-1897). *A talented and versatile academic, theologian, oriental linguist and Egyptologist.* This gifted Guernseyman, who was born on 23 August 1822 to Mary (*née* le Page), the wife of Joseph Renouf, was educated at Elizabeth College, whence he won a scholarship to Oxford (Pembroke), going up in 1840 with the intention of reading theology preparatory to taking Holy orders in the Church of England. Soon after entering on his studies this brilliant islander (who had formed a strong friendship with John Henry Newman) became active in the Oxford Movement and soon emerged as the anonymous author of some of the famous *Tracts for the Times.* After the condemnation of the Tractarians by Oxford University in 1841 Peter Renouf, perceiving the step as required by the logic of his position and with sufficient moral courage to take it, forsook the established church for the Papal Obedience and was received into the Roman fold at St Mary's College, Oscott, on Easter Day 1842. Stoically accepting the abrupt termination of his career at Oxford which his conversion entailed (the University's facilities being restricted to Anglicans) Renouf embarked at Oscott on what was to prove his life's study of Oriental languages, together with theology and philosophy. In making his submission to Rome he had preceded his famous friend and contemporary by three years, Newman not following in his footsteps until 1845.

After travelling widely on the continent while employed as a tutor by the de Vaulchier family of Besançon between 1846 and 1855, in the latter year Peter Renouf complied with the request of his friend John Newman, and gave his services to the new Catholic University of Ireland established at Dublin. Initially lecturing in French literature and the history of philosophy, he was appointed to the chair of ancient history before the year was out — with the professorship of eastern languages subsequently added.

He held his professorship from 1855 to 1864, and during these years Renouf studied Hebrew, Arabic and Sanskrit with a view to embarking on an extended examination of ancient historical documents. With the help and encouragement of his wife, Ludowika la Roche of Frankfurt, whom he married in 1857, Peter Renouf emerged as one of the most conscientious and reliable Egyptologists of his day, setting about the stupendous task of a complete and consecutive translation of the *Book of the Dead*. Furthermore, in 1863 he published in the University's literary journal, *Atlantis* a defence of his much-loved science against the attacks made on it by Sir George Cornewall Lewis, completely disposing of all objections to the method of deciphering hieroglyphics developed by Jean François Champollion — who from his study of the Rosetta Stone discovered during Napoleon's expedition to Egypt, had perceived that their interpretation rested on the realisation that the inscriptions combined signs representing ideas and others representing sounds.

In 1864 Peter le Page Renouf left the Catholic University (though he retained the honorary title of Professor of Oriental Languages) in order to take up an appointment as one of Her Majesty's Chief Inspectors of Schools. He held this post for over 20 years, during which period nearly all his spare time was devoted to Egyptology, with especial attention to his self-imposed labour of collecting and annotating various texts of the *Book of the Dead*. In 1875 he made a notable contribution to Egyptology with the publication of his *Elementary Grammar of the Ancient Egyptian Language*. In the same year he supplemented his studies by a lengthy visit to Egypt

when, accompanied by his wife, he minutely examined many monuments, painstakingly translating their hieroglyphics. On the basis of the extensive knowledge and experience thus acquired he was requested by the Hibbert Trustees in 1879 to deliver a series of lectures on 'The Religion of Ancient Egypt'. In the meantime, however, he had incurred the censure of the Roman Catholic ecclesiastical hierarchy with the appearance in 1868 of the monograph *The Condemnation of Pope Honorius* in which he attacked the concept (not yet elevated into a dogma) of papal infallibility. The publication was promptly placed on the Index Librorum Prohibitorum.

In 1885 Peter Renouf relinquished his school inspectorate on being appointed as Keeper of Egyptian and Assyrian Antiquities at the British Museum, and two years later he was elected President of the Society of Biblical Archaeology. Retiring in 1891, he was knighted in 1896, thus being accorded an honour which, though amply deserved, had been long withheld because of the regrettable prejudice against those of his persuasion which was so prevalent in the 19th century.

In the summer of 1897, while back home in Guernsey on holiday, Sir Peter overtaxed his strength, and although at first he seemed to recover, he went into a decline on his return to London and died on 14 October of the same year. In accordance with his wishes, his remains were brought back to his native isle and they now lie in the crypt of St Joseph's church on Cordier Hill.

RESTAULD OF JETHOU (c. 995–c. 1060). *An enigmatic figure: probably a sea-dog.* By the terms of an undated 11th-century charter preserved in the library at Avranches, a certain Restauld, 'one-time ship master of Duke Robert of Normandy' ceded the island of Jethou (referred to by its earlier name of Keteou) to the Abbé de Mont St Michel and his brethren on condition that he 'may be worthy to be counted and numbered as their brother and fellow for ever'. The Duke Robert of the Charter was most likely Duke Robert I. (q.v.*).

A clue as to the identity of this donor is to be found in another charter of the year 1020 or thereabouts, whereby Duke Richard II (996–1026) donated various properties in the Cotentin to the Abbey of Marmoutiers at Tours, including 'a quarter of Buistotville, which quarter Restauld now holds'. By a further proviso specifically relating to 'the quarter that Restauld now holds', it is laid down that after his death the Abbey is to 'possess it completely free for ever'. (It is, incidentally, Restauld's being of an age to be a landowner in 1020 that indicates his birth as possibly around 995; while it is the confirmation by Duke William II in a manuscript of 1062 of the Abbey's enjoyment of the title promised it after Restauld's demise which suggests that he died prior to this date — presumably *c.* 1060.)

On the basis of the evidence provided by Duke Richard II's charter, Restauld emerges as a substantial landowner early in the 11th century — a status at that time normally synonymous with being a warrior of eminence. The likelihood is, therefore that Restauld was a prominent corsair among the Norse community established around Cap La Hague, which was not fully brought under the control of the Dukes of Normandy until the early 11th century. From this area he would have been in a highly strategic position at the entrance to the Race of Alderney. The probability is that Duke Robert I ('The Devil'), who reigned from 1027 to 1035, was helped by Restauld when storms dispersed his naval expedition against Canute in 1030 (perhaps also in his subsequent campaign against the Duke of Brittany) and about 1034 gave Jethou to him for services rendered. The gift would have been very welcome, considering Jethou's usefulness to such a pirate leader who already controlled the eastern side of the Race of Alderney, for with ships based on this island as well as in the Buistotville vicinity, he would have been able to close the passage of the Race. Restauld probably donated Jethou to Mont St Michel about 1055 when his life was drawing to its close, presumably in the hope of thereby atoning for his misdeeds and thus averting the terrors of hell-fire — but also possibly as a ploy to promote a *corrody* (i.e. a contractual maintenance provision by the monastery) to give him security in his declining years.

Fuller details may be gleaned from the masterly investigation in depth into the career of this intriguing character made by Dr. S. K. Kellett-Smith (q.v.) in the 1964 *Transactions de la Société Guernesiaise.*

DE ROCHES, JEAN (14th century). *The founding father of the Militia?* Jean de Roches played a prominent part in island life in the mid-14th century, being joint Sub-Warden from 1326 to 1328 (sharing office with Raoul Basset de Drayton 1326-27 and with Robert de Norton 1327-28), and afterwards becoming Warden of the Isles on the death of Otto de Grandison (q.v.) in 1328, retaining the post until 1330. His attempts to make good the prolonged neglect of insular defence by de Grandison's rapacious henchmen (as a result of which the castles were partly in ruins, without arms or stores) were hampered by lack of funds — Otto having sucked the islands dry. Furthermore, he reported in 1328 that Alderney was incapable of being defended, while Sark's lack of landing facilities made it immune from attack, so that it stood in no need of defence: an assessment which the sad lessons of experience were to prove to be over-sanguine. As for Guernsey — and Jersey too, for that matter — a plenitude of landing places induced vulnerability, but de Roches considered that as long as Castle Cornet — or Mont Orgueil — was well garrisoned, it could be used as a springboard for expelling any force which might effect a temporary occupation. Hence his anxiety over his inability to find the twopence per head per day which he was committed to pay the 50 men guarding Castle Cornet whom, pending the receipt of funds from the king, he said he was placating *'par beles paroles'.*

Jean de Roches is usually regarded as the main midwife at the birth of the Island Militias, the earliest indications of the islanders participating in measures for their defence being provided by the trained bands ('*le power del pais*') this Warden raised to repel Norman pirates; while additional evidence stems from the accounts he submitted in 1330 — his last year of office — which include expenditure on a hogshead of wine given to Guernseymen who spent two days and two nights keeping watch in Castle Cornet against further sea-raiders.

Although relinquishing his Warden's post in 1330, de Roches must have remained in a position of no mean responsibility, as five years later (in 1335), while Henry de Ferrers and William of Montacute were Wardens, his duties involved yet another stage in Militia development. In the tense period preceding the following year's raid by David Bruce (q.v.) — a period of which he himself said, '*Nous ne savions lequel nos sumes de pees ou de gerre mes en la meer nos ne trovoins qe gerre*' ['We do not know whether it is peace or war, but at sea we find nothing but war'] — de Roches received orders to array the men of the islands and to take such measures as he thought fit for their defence. The full birth of the Militias was thus accomplished.

ROSE, FLIGHT-LIEUTENANT THOMAS, D.F.C. (1895-1968). *The famous air ace and energetic 'live-wire', who lent powerful aid to Alderney's*

post-occupation recovery. Born on 27 January 1985, at Chilbolton in Hampshire, 'Tommy' Rose (as he was always called) joined the Royal Flying Corps on the outbreak of the First World War, and fought with distinction both in this service and subsequently in the Royal Air Force, shooting down more than 12 enemy machines, and being awarded the Distinguished Flying Cross for his gallantry.

On his retirement from the Royal Air Force in 1927 Flight-Lieutenant Rose (who, *inter alia*, was a keen rugby football player) flew all over the world as a commercial pilot in the course of a long association with Phillips and Powis Aircraft Ltd. of Reading. He later became a test pilot for Miles Aircraft Ltd., remaining in this employment throughout the Second World War. During the inter-war years, he won the King's Cup Air Race in a Falcon Six aircraft designed by F. G. Miles on 7 September 1935, flying at an average speed of 176.28 m.p.h. over a 356 miles course of seven laps of the triangle Hatfield–Broxbourne–Henlow. He was, furthermore, the runner-up in the same contest in both 1934 and 1936 – in which latter year he also flew to the Cape of Good Hope in 3 days, 17 hours and 37 minutes, thus breaking the record which Amy Mollison had held since 1932. Leaving Lympne at 12.25 a.m. on 6 February he arrived at Cape Town at 6.02 p.m. on 9 February.

After the Second World War 'Tommy' Rose became the General Manager of Universal Flying Services Ltd. This concern operated flights to Guernsey in 1947, carrying both passengers and freight, and it might well have been this contact with the Bailiwick which brought its attractions to the notice of the intrepid aviator – for the very next year he settled in Alderney with his wife, retiring from Universal Flying Services in 1949. Managing first the Grand Hotel and later the Marais Hall Hotel, the air ace rapidly proved in a practical fashion his love for his island of adoption, his jovial personality and zest for public work being of incalculable value in Alderney's stern post-war uphill struggle and his efforts earning him both affection and respect.

Elected a member of the States of Alderney, 'Tommy' served on the Inter-Island Advisory Council, and as Chairman both of the Estates and Agricultural Committee and of the Publicity and Entertainments Committee. He was also a member of the Harbours and Transport Committee, while his interest in welfare work led to his serving on the Public Assistance Committee as well. He additionally operated as an Alderney

representative at meetings of the Guernsey States of Deliberation. When death claimed him on 20 June 1968, Alderney mourned a well-loved figure who had taken the island to his heart, serving it devotely for 20 years with unflagging fervour.

LE ROY, PIERRE (1600–1675). *The 'Samuel Pepys' of Guernsey.* (F). Born in 1600, Pierre le Roy, whose home was at Les Tilleuls in the Castel, was the school master of St Martin's School for many years and – from 23 October 1660 – also clerk (*lecteur*) of the parish. He married Anne Brett, the daughter of Ursula Brett, *née* de Vic, who was first cousin once removed to Louis de Vic (q.v.) Procureur and Bailiff and also ward (after her father's death) of Jean de Vic (q.v.) the Greffier and Procureur who was the father of Sir Henry de Vic (q.v.). Anne bore Pierre two sons, Guillaume and Josué, both of whom in emulation of their father became school masters – though in their cases in the Castel parish (where in March 1653 Guillaume was also appointed verger and parish clerk). Guillaume's son – another Guillaume – likewise followed in the same footsteps.

Pierre le Roy's fame rests on the diary that – like his English contemporaries Pepys and Evelyn – he kept for many years. Over two centuries after his death it was edited and published by the Reverend George Edward Lee, rector of the Town Church from 1881 to 1912. This diary is especially valuable for the insight it gives into the period covering the Civil War, the Commonwealth and the Restoration, describing (*inter alia*) the surrender on 19 December 1651 of Castle Cornet by Colonel Sir Robert Burgess (q.v.*) and specifically mentioning that the defenders of the fortress had been reduced to 55 in number. Besides the fascinating glimpses of day-to-day life provided by this journal, with information on the development of Guernsey's educational facilities, one also learns of the prominent part played in island life by the Militia, a 'grand muster' of which is recorded as having taken place in 1656 at Les Grandes Mielles, with details given of the numbers attending from each parish to make up the total parade of 1,418.

After a life of dutiful service to the community, Pierre le Roy died 1675.

DE LA RUE, THOMAS (1793–1866). *Undoubtedly Guernsey's greatest entrepreneur.* Thomas de la Rue, founder of the famous firm of international extent which prints Guernsey's postage stamps and with ramifications embracing, *inter alia*, the 'Security Express' delivery service, was born at Le Bourg in the Forest parish on 24 March 1793 in the house with a dower addition standing behind a post box on the side of the road opposite 'Le Perron du Roi'.

In 1803, at the age of ten, young Thomas was apprenticed to a printer and publisher named Joseph Antoine Chevalier. In 1811, his apprenticeship completed, he was engaged by Thomas Greenslade as editor (at the age of 19) of a new newspaper called *Le Publiciste*, which was first issued in September 1812. The following year de la Rue left Greenslade to start his own newspaper – *Le Miroir Politique* – which he continued to issue after going into business in 1815 with his brother-in-law, publishing *La Liturgie*, illustrated with engravings on steel.

Apart from *The Star* (Guernsey's first English language newspaper, which first appeared in 1813) all newspapers had been in French since the advent of the very first – *La Gazette de L'île de Guernescy* – in 1789. There was now a proliferation of them and de la Rue felt that the market was saturated. With the comment, '*C'est trop peut-être pour cette île*', he sailed for England in 1816 to seek wider scope for his talents.

In London he became engaged in the manufacture of straw hats, as well as entering the stationery business with two partners, producing the first de la Rue playing cards in 1831. When straw hats went out of fashion in 1835, de la Rue's inventiveness led him to introduce bonnets of embossed paper, which were a great success for a time, and led him into the ornamental paper trade. Thus arose the house of de la Rue and Sons. In 1838 the firm produced a special gold edition of *The Sun* newspaper to commemorate Queen Victoria's coronation, while the year 1851 saw de la Rue acting as deputy chairman to the paper, printing and bookbinding class in the Great Exhibition.

De la Rue's forbears had come to Guernsey as Huguenot refugees from France and, with this ancestry in mind, the French acknowledged his achievements by creating him Chevalier de la Légion d'Honneur in 1855. In the same year the firm secured the contract for printing the Great Britain fourpenny carmine postage stamp, following this up in 1859 with a further contract to print three denominations of currency notes for Mauritius.

The extensive use of sulphate of barytes as a pigment was initially introduced by de la Rue and the white enamel used on superior types of playing cards is a barytes white. Among his other innovations, de la Rue introduced several new printing inks, and invented the embossing of book-binders' cloths and paperhangings. He also patented the fixing of iridescent film on paper. Thomas de la Rue died on 7 June 1866, after which the firm passed into the hands of his son, Warren de la Rue, who had been born in Guernsey in 1815.

S

SAMPSON OF DOL, BISHOP AND SAINT (*c.* 485–*c.* 565). *The patron saint of Guernsey.* The fact that Sampson of Dol (whose feast day falls on 28 July) is revered in South Wales and Brittany as well as in Guernsey most likely reflects the odyssey which brought him to the island's shores. Although Clovis (466–511), the leader of the heathen Franks, embraced Christianity in 496, his kingdom was split up at his death between his four sons, among whom Childebert was allocated Neustria (Normandy). The savage ensuing struggles between Childebert and his brothers led to the devastation and depopulation of Armorica (Brittany). The residual and impoverished Armorican population consisted of Celts and it was natural that the Christian Celts of Britain, themselves hard-pressed by the pagan Anglo-Saxon invaders, should see in the half-empty land of their cousins a harbour of refuge. The overwhelming probability is that St Sampson was included among these refugees fleeing across the Channel.

Born in Wales, *c.* 485, to Amon of Dyfed and his wife, Anna of Gwent, young Sampson was dedicated to God while a student in the monastic school at Llantwit in Glamorgan, presided over by the illustrious St Illtyd (*c.* 475–525: festival 6 November). In early manhood he retired to Caldey Island (offshore from Tenby), where he was later joined by his father, becoming abbot of the island's community on the death of his predecessor, Piro. Sampson subsequently undertook a missionary journey to Ireland, after which he left Caldey and retired with Amon to the Severn Valley. Before long he was consecrated bishop by St Dyfrig (Dubricius) and, following a vision telling him to go overseas (how picturesque a way, incidentally, of accounting for the flight of a refugee) he travelled through Cornwall (visiting the Scilly Isles, one of which is named after him) and then — *c.* 520 — took ship for Armorica. Thence he embarked on his missionary travels to the Channel Islands, being said to have landed in Guernsey about 530, establishing a wooden chapel in approximately the same position as the present church dedicated to him. From this base he set about a mission to the islanders, whose practice of the faith embraced by their forefathers early in the fifth century had long since become adulterated by pagan recidivation. On his return to Armorica St Sampson is held to have helped in the restoration of the rightful prince Judual, who overcame his rival, Conmor, in 555. Sampson then visited Paris, where Childebert nominated him Bishop of Dol — though as no settled diocesan organisation existed in the area at the time, such a designation would have been at most a purely honorary one. Guernsey's patron saint is probably identical with the '*Samson, peccator, Episcopus*' ('Sampson, sinner, Bishop') who signed the Acts of the Council of Paris in 557. He is believed to have died in 565.

While it is plain that much said about Sampson is suppositive, the marked probability of a substratum of truth in the accounts was indicated by Professor John le Patourel (q.v.), who pointed out that there is in Guernsey a church dedicated to this saint; that this church was in existence certainly in the 11th century (1030) and possibly earlier; and that it is most unlikely that such a dedication would have been made by the people of Norse ancestry who then comprised the population.

SANTANGELO, DOMENICO EUSANIO, L.C.R.M. (Liège) (1882-1970). *Guernsey's foremost musician.* Destined to play a dominating part in the cultural life of Guernsey, Domenico Eusanio Santangelo was born on 12 July 1882, at San Vincenzo, Campobasso, Molise, Italy, to Norina Tartaglione, the wife of Giuseppe Santangelo. Early in life he showed such pronounced musical promise as to induce his parents to move to Antwerp in Belgium, to enable him to be taught the violin by his elder brother Michele, the practice of whose profession had taken him to that city.

The upshot was that by 1891 he was a pupil at a school in Antwerp run by the Brothers of the Order of Jesus, whence he went on to the same town's Ecole de Musique to study under the famous Belgian composer Pierre Benoit. Then at the age of 16 he became a student at the Con-servatoire Royale de Musique at Liège — at that time the most renowned institution in the world for stringed instruments — where he studied under Oscar Dossin and emerged as a Licentiate, gaining the degree of Baccalaureatus Musica.

On leaving the Conservatoire, Domenico Santangelo toured Belgium as the leader of a string quartet. In 1901 he was heard by the well-known Signor Bonifaco, Music Director of the *Russell Hotel* in London, who persuaded him to move to the British capital to serve as the hotel's principal violinist. Three years later he terminated this engagement to join his brother Michele for a professional assignment at the *Pomme d'Or Hotel* in Jersey — and while there he was asked by Lady Otway in 1906 to come to Guernsey to play in a charity concert she was organising at St Julian's Hall. Thus it was that this gifted young man of 24 arrived in the island that he was to make his home for the rest of his life, becoming a Guernseyman in every sense save the natal one.

On his first arrival 'Santy' (as he came to be affectionately dubbed throughout the island) took up a post for several years with Wilfred Shirvell at the *Channel Islands Hotel* (latterly known as the *Savoy*). Just before the outbreak of the First World War, however, he was appointed musical director at St Julian's Hall (later entitled St Julian's Theatre, and afterwards transformed into the Gaumont Cinema). Here he formed a string ensemble (the Santangelo Orchestra) which for many years played there, its functions including the provision of musical accompaniment for silent films. It also featured in entertainments elsewhere in the island. The resident manager of the theatre (George A. Deighton) having written a poem originally called 'Dear Guernsey' and subsequently renamed 'Sarnia Chérie', Domenico Santangelo set it to music and thus provided Guernsey with its nearest approach to a 'national song' — as well as further popularising the questionable belief that such was the Roman name for the island.

With the demise of silent films, the Santangelo Orchestra came to an end in 1929, but the following year the Guernsey Orchestra rose like a phoenix from its ashes and gave regular performances under the Santangelo bâton at Candie Gardens Auditorium which featured prominently in insular cultural life during the ensuing decade. Known from 1937 onwards (when a States' subsidy commenced) as the States of Guernsey Orchestra, it kept up the islanders' spirits during the German Occupation and continued playing in the post-war period as well.

The main inspiration behind the formation of the Guernsey Music Society in the 1920s, this keen supporter of the Eisteddfod was also an active Rotarian and a Director of the Guernsey Amateur Dramatic and Operatic Company. He died in the isle he had made his own, where he had brought so much pleasure to so many, on 13 February 1970, respected and esteemed throughout the community.

DE SARAVIA, ADRIAN (1531-1613). *The first Principal of Elizabeth College.* Adrian de Saravia was born in 1531 in Hesdin, Artois (then in the Spanish Netherlands, though now part of France), his mother being Flemish though his father was of Spanish origin. Both his parents embraced Protestantism and young Adrian, brought up in the Reformed faith, was trained for its ministry and became a pastor in Antwerp, where he took a part in drawing up the Walloon Confession of Faith. Later, with the help of Jean de Marnix, Sieur de Toulouse, he formed a Walloon Church in Brussels.

In 1560 the underlying religious tension in the Low Countries – springing from Spanish (i.e. Roman Catholic) overlordship of a largely Protestant community – erupted into serious trouble, causing de Saravia to flee for his life. Thus it was that he came to Guernsey, whither many other continental Calvinist clergy were currently making their way and where the following year (1561) he married a Guernesiaise, Catherine Allez. In 1563 Elizabeth I set up the college which bears her name in the fond (but vain) hope that it would exert a pro-Anglican influence in an island increasingly leaning to Presbyterianism, and de Saravia was appointed the first headmaster of the new foundation. For his sustenance he was assigned 'eighty quarters of wheat rente, large measures, to be drawn from Her Majesty's Receiver's Office in the said Island annually on the Feast of St Michael the Archangel'. Furthermore, each pupil was expected to present him with 21 *sols tournois* every New Year. The disciples of Geneva, however, were not the only anti-Anglican elements in the island, as many leading families remained attached to Roman Catholicism. Thus two years after taking up his appointment de Saravia reported to Cecil that in the April of the previous year 'on the day when peace was proclaimed a drunken and seditious gathering led by one of the Jurats went about cursing the Huguenots and were ready to turn their arms against their own countrymen if any of the professors of the Gospel had come in their way'.

The year after his appointment at Elizabeth College, Adrian de Saravia became assistant minister to Nicolas Baudouin (q.v.) at the Town Church, where the observances of Geneva were first practised in the island. The Artesian academic was, however, not happy in Guernsey, of whose people his opinion was poor, considering that, 'made of fraud', 'they would utter a thousand perjuries rather than injure a friend' and bewailed 'the vicious life led openly by evil-doers', fearing that 'if they were left to their own devices we should find them more barbarous than any Turks'. He considered that the common people, though downtrodden, 'have grown so hardened to their sufferings that they have lost any feeling of them. And so the Jurats lord it over them like so many dumb cattle'. Moreover, his logical mind was affronted by the local legal system, which evoked the comment, 'I cannot say that the laws are broken, for they have no laws. They boast about their ancestral customs, but they are changed from day to day at the will of inexpert judges'. Feeling as he did, it is hardly surprising that in 1566 de Saravia proposed returning to the Continent. Cecil, however, having been approached by Sir Francis Chamberlayne (q.v.) prevailed upon him to remain. He accordingly stayed on in the island for two more years, until in 1568 he became the master of the Grammar School in Southampton.

Eventually returning to his homeland, de Saravia in 1582 became Professor of Divinity at the University of Leyden, but in 1587 the discovery of a political plot in which he was implicated forced him to flee to England. Although lacking episcopal ordination, his appointment the next year as rector of Tattenhill in Staffordshire was made possible thanks to the attitude exemplified in the dictum of Archbishop Bancroft (1544-1610) that when bishops could not be had, then ordination by presbyters must be deemed lawful. Adroitly accommodating himself to the Anglican *via media*, de Saravia returned the compliment by composing a treatise in defence of episcopacy which appeared in 1590.

So it came about that the Calvinist-trained Netherlander lived out the rest of his life in England, a pillar of the established church. Appointed both a prebendary of Canterbury and vicar of Lewisham in 1595, de Saravia became very friendly with the great Anglican philosopher of *Ecclesiastical Polity* fame, Richard Hooker (1554-1600), to whom on his deathbed he gave absolution and administered the last sacrament. Made a prebendary first of Worcester and then of Westminster in 1601, in 1604 he dedicated to James I a Treatise on the Holy Eucharist; while in 1607 he was nominated one of the translators of what (after its publication in 1611) came to be known as the Authorized Version of the Bible; with particular responsibility as a member of the committee entrusted with the Old Testament from Genesis to the Second Book of Kings inclusive. Installed as rector of Great Chart in Kent in March 1610, he breathed his last on 15 January 1613 and his body was buried in Canterbury Cathedral, where his second wife Margaret Wüts (Catherine Allez having died seven years previously) caused a monument to be erected in his memory.

SAUMAREZ, JAMES, ADMIRAL LORD DE SAUMAREZ (1757-1836). *Guernsey's undoubted greatest naval hero*. (D). Before the Germans razed it to the ground in 1943, Delancey Park was dominated by an obelisk inscribed: 'To James, First Baron de Saumarez of Guernsey, G.C.B., K.B., D.C.L., Admiral of the Red and General of Marines, B. 1757, D. 1836. This Memorial was erected as a tribute of admiration by his fellow-countrymen, 1877.'

Born in St Peter-Port in March 1757 to Carteret (*née* le Marchant), the wife of Matthew Saumarez, James Saumarez – who was the posthumous nephew of Philip de Sausmarez (q.v.) – entered the navy as a midshipman in 1770 at the age of 13, and was immediately posted to the Mediterranean where he served for five years until returning to home waters in April 1775. In October of the same year, aboard H.M.S. *Bristol*, he sailed for North America, taking part in the disastrous attack on Fort Sullivan on 28 June 1776. At a later stage in the War of American Independence, he took command in February 1778 of the schooner H.M.S. *Spitfire*, but she was burned at Rhode Island the following August to prevent her falling into enemy hands. Back in the European theatre, the young Guernseyman served for two years (1779-1781) on H.M.S. *Victory*, at that time the Channel flagship. He then recrossed the Atlantic in 1782, seeing service in the West Indies on board H.M.S. *Russell*, which warmly engaged the French flagship, *Ville de Paris*. With the 1783 Peace of Versailles, however, Saumarez was placed on half-pay and returned to Guernsey, remaining there (apart from brief interruptions in 1787 and 1790) until the outbreak of the French Revolutionary War in 1793.

The exploits of James Saumarez in this war and the ensuing Napoleonic Wars brought him his glorious immortality. He first caused island hearts to swell with pride in the spring of 1793 when, with the rank of captain in command of H.M.S. *Crescent* (the crew of which was composed almost entirely of Guernseymen) he captured the French frigate *La Réunion* (36 guns) off Cherbourg, thereby earning the honour of knighthood. Christmastide of the same year saw Sir James engaged in a daring errand of mercy. On the 27th of the month he commanded five warships which escorted into Guernsey ten transports of Roman Catholic refugees from the Jacobin Terror.

In 1794 a plan to invade the archipelago and put paid to the Channel Island privateers was drawn up by Lazare Carnot, the Committee of Public Safety's 'Organizer of Victory'. The upshot was that on Sunday 8 June 1794, a most exciting naval action took place off the west coast of Guernsey. Sir James Saumarez had been sent out from Plymouth with a small squadron to reconnoitre the strength of the enemy naval forces in the area of St Malo, where intelligence reports suggested that an expeditionary force of 20,000 was assembled for the invasion of the islands. Saumarez had three frigates (H.M.S. *Crescent* – which was under his direct command – H.M.S. *Druid* and H.M.S. *Eurydice*) together with five small vessels. Off the north-west of Guernsey he sighted two French ships of the line and three frigates, so that his effective force was three to five. This soon became two, for H.M.S. *Eurydice* was a slow sailer and he ordered her to make for harbour to avoid capture. To aid her escape, *Crescent* and *Druid* steered north-east, drawing the French away from *Eurydice*, which was sailing south-west. The wind being from the north-east, Saumarez put about to the south-west as soon as *Eurydice* was safe, and crowded on sail. Ordering *Druid* to hold her course, he edged *Crescent* to the shore, drawing the foe under the fire of the shore batteries. Again putting about, he sailed north, across the enemy line. Capture seeming certain to them, the French closed, but Saumarez had a Guernsey pilot, Jean Breton, who made straight for Vazon Bay, giving the impression that he meant to beach the ship rather than be captured. The French gave up the chase and were astonished to see *Crescent* escape through the narrow channels in the reefs off the bay. As they went through this needle's eye Saumarez asked Breton if he were sure of his sea-marks. 'Quite sure sir', replied the pilot, 'for there is my house and your house in line'.

After distinguishing himself at Cape St Vincent in 1797 and serving as Nelson's seonc-in-command at the Nile in 1798, Sir James Saumarez was appointed rear-admiral in 1801. In June of the same year he was created a baronet. After inflicting a crushing defeat on the French and Spanish off Gibraltar in July, he was nominated a Knight of the Bath, given the Freedom of the City of London, presented with a Sword of Honour, awarded a pension of £1,200 and voted the thanks of both Houses of Parliament — the great Nelson being lavish with his praise when the vote was proposed in the Lords.

In 1803 Saumarez assumed command in Guernsey waters. The renewal of the war after the Peace of Amiens saw the islands in imminent danger, with Napoleon fulminating against them because of their privateering exploits. In these circumstances Sir James was placed in command of the squadron based on St Peter-Port with orders to defend the islands and also to blockade the enemy fleet under Genteaume in Brest. The efficiency with which he discharged these duties played an important part in frustrating Napoleon's plans to invade, not only the Channel Isles, but Britain as well. While engaged in these operations Saumarez destroyed a flotilla of enemy gunboats due to sale from Granville to the invasion assembly point at Boulogne.

In March 1808 Saumarez was given command of a squadron sent to the Baltic, originally to support the Swedes against the Danes and Russians. He maintained control of the Baltic for five years, and by affording communications by sea to the Russians (now Britain's allies) which were, of course, denied to the French, he helped to bring about Napoleon's *débacle* in 1812. In recognition of his services he was presented by the Crown Prince of Sweden with a diamond sword valued at £2,000, and his memory is revered in Sweden to this day. (A special visit to Guernsey by a Swedish warship was made in his honour in 1910, followed by another in 1936 to mark the centenary of his death). On his return from the Baltic he was made a full admiral.

Sir James Saumarez, who made generous donations to the schools of the Castel and St Andrew's in 1808 and 1823 respectively, in 1807 conceived the idea of providing a church where worship could be conducted in English, as a means of improving relationships between the garrison and the islanders — a project which came to fruition with the construction immediately behind his own town house of the church of St James the Less, which was consecrated in 1818 by Bishop John Fisher (q.v.). He also founded the Guernsey Savings Bank (now — 1984 — absorbed into the Trustee Savings Bank) on 25 January 1822. Universally esteemed when he retired in 1827, John Jacob in 1830 dedicated to him his *Annals of the British Norman Isles constituting*

the Bailiwick of Guernsey. Raised to the peerage in 1831, Lord de Saumarez died in 1836 at his country house in Saumarez Park. His funeral at the Castel church (in whose graveyard his body is buried) was attended by an enormous concourse.

On 4 September, 1975, a commemorative plaque to Lord de Saumarez was unveiled in Gothenburg City Hall in the presence of H.M. the King of Sweden and Earl Mountbatten of Burma.

SAUMAREZ, DR. RICHARD, F.R.S., F.R.C.S. (1764-1835). *The Guernsey surgeon of Newington Butts*. (D). Born in November 1764 as the fifth son of Matthew Saumarez and his wife Carteret le Marchant — and the younger brother of Admiral Lord de Saumarez and General Sir Thomas Saumarez (qq.v.) — Richard was orphaned while still a minor, whereupon responsibility for his sustenance was shouldered by his eldest brother John, who lived in the house in the Pollet which has since been converted into *Moore's Hotel*.

Reluctant to be a drag on his brother, Richard Saumarez applied for admission to the London Hospital as a medical student and on completion of his studies was admitted a Member of the Surgeon's Company on 7 April 1785. He was, however, only awarded a modified licence which did not allow him to practise in London or within seven miles of the City. On the Feast of the Epiphany 1786 he was married at the Town Church to Martha, the daughter of John le Mesurier (q.v.), 'Hereditary Governor' of Alderney. Shortly after the wedding the restrictions on his Licence were abolished and the newly-married couple settled in at Newington Butts near the Elephant and Castle — at that time a select venue with a fashionable clientèle.

In 1788 Richard Saumarez took up an appointment as Surgeon at the Magdalen Hospital in Streatham, remaining there for nearly 17 years. When he resigned in March 1805 he was made an Honorary Governor of the institution in recognition of his lengthy and valuable services. He then went into private medicine and rapidly built up a large and lucrative London practice. He also emerged as a prolific and polemical writer, with advanced ideas concerning medical education and the duties of medical corporations to their constituents.

Martha le Mesurier had died of consumption in November 1801 and after a time Richard married a wealthy widow named Elizabeth Enderby (who was the great-aunt of Gordon of Khartoum). At her suggestion he retired in 1818 to Bath, in which city he resided until his death in January 1835. A memorial tablet to Richard, his first wife Martha and their two sons, Admiral Richard Saumarez, R.N. and Captain

Thomas Saumarez, R.N., may be seen in Bath Abbey whither it was taken after removal from Newington Butts in 1879.

SAUMAREZ, GENERAL SIR THOMAS (1760–1845). *The double bearer of Guernsey's loyal salutations to the Crown.* (D). Born in July 1760 to Matthew and Carteret Saumarez, and the younger brother of James Saumarez (q.v.), Thomas joined the army as an ensign in January 1776 at the age of 15. It was not long before he had combat experience, as he was sent to North America and served throughout the War of American Independence, being present when Cornwallis surrendered on 19 October 1781 at Yorktown, where he was taken prisoner — remaining as such until released by the Peace of Versailles in 1783. While in captivity he had the unenviable experience of being one of the officers who had to draw lots to decide which of them was to be shot in reprisal for the execution of an American spy caught within the British lines. The man who drew the fatal lot was in the event reprieved in response to an appeal made to George Washington by Queen Marie-Antoinette of France, which country was in alliance with the Americans.

On the outbreak of the French Revolutionary War in 1793, Saumarez was appointed Brigade-Major of the Guernsey Militia, a post carrying responsibilities which were the greater because of the island's exposed position facing a hostile France itching to seize the operations base of the formidable local privateers. In this capacity he was accountable to the Lieutenant-Governor (General Sir Jonathan Small) for surveillance of emigrés from France and for the recruitment from among them of suitable agents for service on the French mainland. Two years later, in July 1795, he was knighted after being deputed to carry to London a Loyal Address from the States on the occasion of the marriage of the Prince of Wales (later King George IV). In 1799 Sir Thomas was made Inspector of the Guernsey Militia, a position he retained until his promotion to the rank of Major-General in 1811.

On the outbreak of war with the United States of America in 1812, Sir Thomas was dispatched to Nova Scotia where he assumed command of the garrison at Halifax, in addition to which during 1813 he also acted as Commander-in-Chief of New Brunswick. He relinquished his Halifax appointment with the conclusion of peace by the Treaty of Ghent in 1815.

With the advent of peace, Sir Thomas Saumarez became Groom to the Bedchamber to Edward, Duke of Kent, whose wife, Victoria of Saxe-Coburg, gave birth on 24 May 1819 to the daughter destined to be Britain's longest-reigning monarch. On the occasion of the coronation of Queen Victoria in June 1838, Sir Thomas was advanced to the rank of General. Six years later — in the summer of 1844 — after Major-General William Napier (q.v.) had landed troops in Guernsey 'to quell the island's insurrection', General Sir Thomas Saumarez was entrusted by the indignant Guernesiais with carrying an address to the Queen conveying the assurances of the islanders' immutable loyalty. This repetition of his duties of 1795 was destined to be the last public service he would perform. The following March the octogenarian General died at his residence of 'Belmont Lodge' (now infelicitously named 'Sausmarez Lodge', with an utterly inappropriate intrusive second 's') in La Petite Marche: a thoroughfare which the very next year was to become Queen's Road, in honour of the visit of the Sovereign to whom he had delivered his fellow-islanders' patriotic greetings.

DE SAUSMAREZ, BRIGADIER-GENERAL CECIL, C.B., C.M.G., D.S.O. (1870–1966). *A valorous soldier.* (E). Born on 29 September 1870 to Anne Priaulx (*née* Walters), the wife of the Reverend Havilland de Sausmarez — and hence the younger brother of Sir Havilland de Sausmarez (q.v.) — Cecil de Sausmarez was educated at Winchester College, whence he proceeded to the Royal Military Academy at Woolwich, entering the Royal Regiment of Artillery in 1889. Reaching the rank of captain by 1899, he served from 1900 to 1902 in the Boer War as Senior Transport Officer to the 1st Division and Western District of the South African Frontier Force. Mentioned twice in despatches in the course of hostilities, Captain de Sausmarez so conducted himself as to earn the Distinguished Service Order, in addition to which he was awarded the Queen's Medal with three clasps and the King's Medal with two clasps.

The conflict over, de Sausmarez was posted to what is nowadays Pakistan (but at that time part of the Indian Empire) where from 1904 to 1909 he was in command of the 2nd Derajet Mounted Battery. During this period he married (in 1905) Mildred, the daughter of the Reverend J. P. Morgan, rector of Llandyssil (now in Powys, though then in Montgomeryshire). Mentioned in despatches for his part in the Bazar Valley campaign of 1908 (during which he was promoted to brevet major), he served as Deputy Assistant Adjutant General to the Abbottabad Brigade for the years 1909 and 1910 and afterwards as General Staff Officer Grade II, 2nd (Rawalpindi) Division from 1910 to 1913.

Severely wounded while commanding the 108 Heavy Battery on the Aisne in the early stages of the First World War (when he was yet again mentioned in despatches and appointed brevet lieutenant-colonel), Cecil de Sausmarez thereafter served in the War Office from 1915 to 1920, in May of which year (having been promoted to Brigadier-General in 1917) he took command of No. 1 Pack Artillery Brigade, retaining this command until December. In 1918 the value of his services received recognition on his being made a Companion of the Most Distinguished Order of St Michael and St George; while in 1923 he was further rewarded by being created a Companion of the Most Honourable Order of the Bath.

Winding up his military career by serving from 1921 to 1925 as officer in charge of the Royal Garrison Artillery Records, Brigadier-General de Sausmarez in the latter year resigned his commission for what was to prove an extremely long superannuation. Widowed in 1937 and living at Sausmarez Manor into the Space Age, this last surviving grandson of Procureur Thomas de Sausmarez (q.v.) died on 20 August 1966, only a month short of his 96th birthday — leaving in the neighbourhood the memory of an octogenarian warrior-in-retirement diving into the sea off the rocks below the Pepper Pot at Fermain clad only in a pair of pyjama trousers cut short above the knee.

DE SAUSMAREZ, CECIL HAVILLAND, M.B.E. (1907–   ). *Academic and diplomat: the Seigneur who sponsored the 'Official War History' of the Channel Isles.* (E). Cecil Havilland de Sausmarez was born to Mildred (*née* Morgan), the wife of Captain (later Brigadier-General) Cecil de Sausmarez (q.v.) on 20 November 1907, in Rawalpindi, where his father was serving under Sir James Willcocks (1857–1926) who, promoted to Major-General the year before the baby's birth, the year after it commanded two expeditions on the North-West Frontier with a verve which so anticipated blitzkrieg techniques as to cause *Punch* to refer to 'Willcocks' Week-end Wars'.

Though born in what was destined to be Pakistan, young Cecil de Sausmarez was brought up in Hardy's 'Wessex', starting his education at Durnford Preparatory School near Swanage (where he later recalled that, much to his chagrin, he was bowled out first ball by Ian Fleming, the subsequent creator of James Bond); and going up from

there to Winchester College, first (in 1920) as an Exhibitioner and thereafter a Scholar from 1921 to 1926. From Winchester he went up to Oxford (Hertford) where, although Senior Classical Scholar, his addiction to the games of bridge and cricket resulted in his obtaining what he himself described as 'only' second class honours in Moderations and Litteræ Humaniores. A further memorable association in the realm of sport occurred during his university days when in the summer of 1929 he partnered Horst Wessel (he of the Nazi song: murdered the next February) in tennis doubles.

Rounding off his university career as a Laming Travelling Fellow of Queen's from 1930 to 1932. de Sausmarez then took up the position of assistant master at Wellington College in Berkshire, remaining there until January 1939 when he was appointed press attaché at His Britannic Majesty's Embassy in Brussels. Remaining at his post as the foe swept into Belgium in May 1940, he eventually made his getaway, together with the bulk of the British Expeditionary Force, through Dunkirk, from whence he was one of the very first to return. Back in London he served from May 1940 to September 1941 at the Ministry of Information, initially as Head of the Anti-Rumours Bureau and afterwards as Regional Specialist for Belgium and the Netherlands. Fate decreed that while at this ministry he was the duty officer at the time when the Bremen Radio transmission of a talk by Major — later Sir — Ambrose Sherwill (q.v.) was picked up by the B.B.C.: a broadcast to which he is on record as having reacted unfavourably. He also hastened to indicate the error in the transcript whereby reference was made to the 'Guernsey Potterer' instead of the Guernsey Procureur!

Moving in September 1941 to the Political Warfare Executive, he served first as deputy regional director and subsequently as regional director for the Low Countries region, remaining in this employment until September 1944 when, with Belgium liberated, he returned to the Embassy in Brussels with the rank of First Secretary, staying there until September 1946. It is interesting to note that, while at the Ministry of Information, Cecil de Sausmarez was one of the originators of the 'V' sign campaign and during his time at the Political Warfare Executive he was a member of Lord Ritchie Calder's 'V' Committee. While at the British Embassy in Brussels after the collapse of Germany and Japan, he was created a Member of the Most Excellent Order of the British Empire in acknowledgement of his valuable war services.

Cecil de Sausmarez spent the two years from October 1946 to October 1948 as the representative of the British Council for Belgium, at the same time discharging the duties of Chargé de Conferences at the Université Libre de Brusselles in English Poetry and History. In the course of these years, ás a result of the death on 15 March 1947 of his aunt-by-marriage, Lady Annie Elizabeth de Sausmarez, G.B.E. – who, as the relict of Sir Havilland de Sausmarez (q.v.), had been La Dame de Sausmarez during her widowhood – Cecil Havilland de Sausmarez, in accordance with the terms of his uncle's will, became Seigneur du Fief de Sausmarez, though his father resided at Sausmarez Manor as *'usufruitier'* until his death. He was well fitted for this rôle, having paid an annual visit to the manor during his summer holidays throughout his life, except for the war years. From October 1948 to January 1951 he withdrew temporarily from public service to enable him, in his own words, 'to complete his education' – following this up by serving for the seven years 1951 to 1958 as tutor at Wilton Park, an organisation for promoting better relations between Britain and West Germany.

The Seigneur de Sausmarez returned to Guernsey for good on New Year's Day 1959, and it was not long before he became prominent in the island's public life, serving as the Deputy representing St Martin's in the States of Deliberation from 1961 until 1979 and describing his main contribution in this capacity as that of a gadfly! During these years his most important speech, in his own estimation, was that made when, together with Sir William Arnold (the Bailiff) and Mr. (later Sir) John Loveridge – the Procureur – he presented Guernsey's case before the Royal Commission on the Constitution: a speech the gist of which was reflected in the subsequent Kilbrandon Report. While a member of the States, Deputy de Sausmarez, as President of the States of Guernsey History 1939-45 Committee, collaborated in 1970 with Senator C. S. Dupré, President of the States of Jersey Liberation Anniversary Committee, in commissioning the *Official History of the German Occupation* which, written by Dr. Charles Cruickshank, eventually appeared in 1975. Furthermore, as Guernsey's paramount Seigneur, he not only officiated as Seneschal of the Court of Seigneurs (as such leading the agitation which succeeded in bringing about a revision of proposals for the abolition of feudal dues which even a Labour Party Home Secretary described as 'confiscatory'), but also twice – in 1957 and 1978 – paid homage to Her

Majesty the Queen on behalf of the entire seigneurial body, the other Seigneurs and Dames standing while he did so. His duties as Third Butler to the Sovereign, of performing the office of cupbearer to the Monarch, were, however, remitted on each occasion.

From the time of his taking up permanent residence in Guernsey onwards, the Seigneur de Sausmarez gave enthusiastic support to La Société Guernesiaise, to which he contributed valuable papers (notably 'The Story of William le Marchant' and an examination of Lazare Carnot's Plan to invade the archipelago) and delivered much appreciated addresses, becoming President for the period 1964-65 and thereafter serving as a vice-president.

DE SAUSMAREZ, SIR HAVILLAND WALTER, BARONET (1861-1941). *The Bailiff who stood firm for the Islands' autonomy* (E). Born on 30 May 1861 to Anne Priaulx (*née* Walters), the wife of the Reverend Havilland de Sausmarez – and hence the grandson of Procureur Thomas de Sausmarez (q.v.) – Havilland *fils* was educated at Westminster School, whence he went up to Cambridge (Trinity), emerging therefrom in 1883 as a Senior Optime in the mathematical tripos. Called to the Bar as a Barrister of the Inner Temple in 1884, he embarked on a colonial career – at first setting up in private legal practice in Lagos, but later operating as Acting Attorney-General for Nigeria from 1890 to 1891.

Moving from the Bar to the Bench, Havilland de Sausmarez served as Assistant Judge in Her Majesty's Consular Court for Zanzibar from 1892 to 1897, in which latter year he was transferred to the post of Assistant Judge for the Ottoman Dominions under British control (i.e.: Egypt) – a post he retained until 1903. Knighted in 1905 after two years (1903-5) as a Judge of the Cairo Supreme Court, Sir Havilland proceeded to China (where British Courts at the time exercised extra-territorial jurisdiction) to take up appointment as Judge of His Britannic Majesty's Supreme Court for China, and he continued to serve in this capacity until he relinquished office in 1921.

Returning to Guernsey after withdrawing from the colonial service, Sir Havilland was back in the island in time for the visit on 11 July 1921 of King George V and Queen Mary. Being Seigneur du Fief de Sausmarez, he owed the duty as hereditary Third Butler to the Sovereigh, of performing the office of cupbearer to the monarch. This obligation was sensibly adapted to the usages of the 20th century by being commuted into the requirement that Sir Havilland should provide tea for Their Majesties.

In 1922, on the retirement of Sir Edward Ozanne (q.v.), Sir Havilland de Sausmarez was appointed Bailiff and he remained in this position for the next seven years. A twelvemonth after he assumed office the new Bailiff was faced with a very difficult problem which posed a threat to the Bailiwick's autonomy, arising as it did from a demand put forward by the British government to each of the two Bailiwicks for an 'annual contribution to the Imperial Exchequer' towards the cost of Imperial defence.

This demand provoked considerable bitterness, not only because of the excessive amount sought (£600,000 per annum), but also as the contribution from the Irish Free State had been cancelled, and finally because it was contrary to the Islands' Charters, in that the levying by the United Kingdom government of an annual charge would amount to the imposition of taxation, in derogation of the islands' fiscal autonomy. In these circumstances Sir Havilland attempted joint action with Jersey, but this approach unfortunately came to nothing. Eventually, on behalf of the States, he offered £220,000 as a 'final free gift' — but this offer was not even acknowledged by the British government.

In 1926, with Jersey now more responsive to Sir Havilland's blandishments, the States of the two Bailiwicks acted in close concert, replying to the revised United Kingdom suggestion for a reduced annual contribution by insisting that any remittance was to be seen as a 'once-for-all-gift'. In face of this intransigent united front the British government in 1927 accepted the 'gifts' and the lengthy controversy was at last settled.

Emerging triumphant from this prolonged confrontation, Sir Havilland (who had been awarded an honorary Doctorate of Law by the Université de Caen in 1927), was advanced to the rank of Knight Baronet in 1928. The following year he retired as Bailiff and was succeeded by Mr. Arthur William Bell. Enjoying tremendous prestige, the Seigneur de Sausmarez survived until the German Occupation, in the early stages of which, his sense of humour undiminished in the face of adversity, he gravely enquired whether the order whereby boats of every description had to be taken to St Peter-Port Harbour by 1 October 1940, applied to the punt which he kept on the pond at Sausmarez Manor to facilitate trimming its banks! The veteran stalwart by then had but a few months to live. He died on 5 March 1941, the tenure of Guernsey's most prestigious feudal holding passing to his widow (Lady Annie Elizabeth de Sausmarez, G.B.E.), who thus became La Dame du Fief de Sausmarez until her own death in 1947.

A man of considerable erudition, Sir Havilland de Sausmarez was elected President of la Société Guernesiaise for the period 1922 and 1923 and again for 1931 and 1932, contributing over the years several deeply researched papers to that organization's *Transactions*. Furthermore, during his last year as Bailiff and in the course of his subsequent retirement there flowed from his pen a monumental series of monographs which will long remain of inestimable value to the student of insular affairs. *The Earlier Charters of Guernsey* (1928) was followed by a disquisition on the great crisis of his years in office with the appearance in 1930 of *Guernsey and the Imperial Contribution*. Then in 1934 there came *The Extentes of Guernsey of 1248 and 1331* and finally, in 1936 (at the age of 75), *Captain Philip Saumarez: The Naval Uniform* — an examination of the part played by his illustrious ancestor in the establishment of a recognised uniform for the Senior Service.

DE SAUSMAREZ/SAUMAREZ, CAPTAIN PHILIP (1710-1747). *Global circumnavigator, intrepid seaman and sartorial trend-setter.* (D). Born in 1710 to Anne (*née* Durell) of Jersey, the wife of Matthew de Sausmarez, Philip in 1721 at the age of 11 was sent to a school in Southampton kept by Isaac Watts senior (1652-1737), the father of the great hymnologist Isaac Watts Junior (1674-1748), where he remained for a period of two-and-a-half years before going to another school in Greenwich. He then entered the Royal Navy in February 1726, initially serving on H.M.S. *Weymouth*, which was bound for the Baltic at the time she was joined by Midshipman Philip Saumarez (as he henceforth called himself, dropping both the prefix and the second 's').

Posted in 1727 to the Mediterranean, Saumarez served in Gibraltar under Captain John Byng (later — in 1757 — as Admiral Byng, to be executed on his own quarter-deck). Remaining under Byng until June 1734, Philip thereafter served first in the Channel and then on the Jamaica Station, where he was promoted to lieutenant. He returned to England in 1739. After the outbreak the same year of the 'War of Jenkins' Ear' against Spain, Philip Saumarez — together with his brother Thomas (q.v.) — joined H.M.S. *Centurion*, heading the squadron under Commodore George Anson (later Admiral Lord Anson) which sailed from Portsmouth on a mission to harry the enemy's galleons. Commanding *Tryal*, Saumarez led the squadron round the Horn and was in command of *Centurion* — Anson being ashore at the time — when she was torn from her cables at Tinian in the Marianas. It was only thanks to the Guernsey-man's supreme seamanship and power of command that the ship got back to her haven after an agonising absence of 19 long days. On 21 June 1743, after the capture of *Nostra Signora de Cabadonga* (the galleon plying between Manila and Mexico and hence sometimes referred to as the 'Manila Galleon' for short), Philip was made her captain. The prize was, however, later sold in China at Macao so that the new captain, retaining his rank, returned as a passenger on H.M.S. *Centurion*, which arrived back on 15 June 1744 after having circumnavigated the globe and seized treasure worth £600,000.

The share of the prize money from this exploit falling to Philip was sufficient to enable his brother John to buy back the Fief de Sausmarez from Charles Andros, whose family had held it since the mid-16th century and who only agreed to sell because he had no children. By a perverse fate his wife bore a son the next year: and in her bitterness cursed the mill of Sausmarez — 'Never again shall it grind the tenants' oats or the Seigneur's wheat'. The old mill was left to become derelict.

After commanding H.M.S. *Sandwich* from 1745 to 1746, Philip in September 1746 was given command of H.M.S. *Nottingham*, of 60 guns. Early in October of that year, during the War of Austrian Succession, *Nottingham* captured the French 64-gun ship *Mars*; but in a further action off Brest on the 14th of the month, Philip attempted to stay the flight of the *Intrépide* and the *Tonnant* and was killed by almost the last shot fired. His body was brought back to land and was buried in St Andrew's church in Plymouth. Had he lived, he would have seen his nephew (born to his brother Matthew's wife ten years after he fell) who later became Admiral Lord de Saumarez. Philip Saumarez was unmarried and only 37 years of age, but he had made his mark, both as a brilliant naval commander and also as the designer of the uniform selected by George II as the most suitable for officers of the Royal Navy. A monument to his memory by Sir Henry Cheere, giving details of his exploits, is to be seen in the north aisle of the choir of Westminster Abbey.

DE SAUSMAREZ/SAUMAREZ, CAPTAIN THOMAS (1713-1766). *The Captain who cap-*

tured the ship he commanded. (D). Born to Anne Durell, the wife of Matthew de Sausmarez, and hence the younger brother of Philip de Saus-marez/Saumarez (q.v.), Thomas also sailed with the squadron manned largely by Chelsea Pensioners (for want of other crew) which under Anson's command set out to vex the Spaniards in the 'War of Jenkins' Ear'. He thus shared the terrible hardships and innumerable perils of that epic four-year voyage around the globe. A month after his brother's death, Thomas was promoted to commander (November 1747) and a year later he attained the rank of captain.

In 1758, during the Seven Years' War, Thomas was commanding H.M.S. *Antelope* on the Bristol Station, when on 31 October he heard that the French 64-gun ship *Belliqueux*, with top foremast lost and short of water and provisions, was anchored off Ilfracombe. Despite having to contend with a strong head wind, *Antelope* steadily worked down the coast, reaching and capturing the *Belliqueux* on 2 November. The ship was added to the Royal Navy, with Thomas commanding her.

Three years later — in 1761 — H.M.S. *Belliqueux* was ordered to the West Indies. Shortly after arriving in the Caribbean, however, Thomas was forced by bad health to relinquish his command. He saw no further service and died in his early 50s on 21 September 1766.

DE SAUSMAREZ, THOMAS (1756-1837). *The father of 28 who fought a duel and was Law Officer for 56 years*. (D). He was born on 10 October 1756 to Martha (*née* le Marchant) second wife of John de Sausmarez (Procureur du Roi) and sister of William le Marchant (q.v.). Thomas, although originally intended for a military career (his Jersey relative Colonel Harry Burrard having offered to procure for him a commission in the Guards) accepted, at his mother's behest, appointment as Comptroller in 1774 at the abnormally young age of 18. This was brought about by his maternal uncle who, with his son Hirzel installed as Procureur in place of the recently deceased John de Sausmarez, thought to manipulate his callow nephew, dominating both law officers to tne enhancement of his own power as Bailiff. Immediately after his appointment Thomas went to Rouen where, entered as '*étudiant en droit*', he studied Norman Law. He returned to Guernsey in 1777 and commenced his professional career.

It soon became clear that uncle and nephew were destined to clash. As a suitor for the hand of

Martha Dobrée the young Comptroller was irritated by his uncle taking out a lawsuit against his prospective brother-in-law in 1777 — and nine years later he incurred his uncle's enmity by the help he gave to Zacharias Mahy, a Methodist whom le Marchant wished to send to prison for alleged perjury. By 1791 the animosity between Bailiff and Comptroller was such that de Sausmarez lodged a petition with the Privy Council for redress against his uncle, claiming that opprobrious remarks had been made against him in court when he was pleading for new Constables to be sworn in for St Peter-Port. Worse, however, was to come before the year was out.

The underlying tension between de Sausmarez and le Marchant erupted in October 1790. While pleading in court, the Comptroller was told by his Bailiff-Uncle that he was talking nonsense and by his Procureur-Cousin that he was impertinent; Thomas retorted with a 'tu quoque' in each case. Unfortunately the exchanges between the two cousins rapidly became more venomous, with each calling the other 'coward' and 'poltroon'. A similar unsavoury episode followed five minutes later when de Sausmarez' other cousin, Jurat Robert Porret le Marchant, in delivering his judgment, echoed his father's sentiments, remarking that 'the plea of the Comptroller was a tissue of nonsense' — thus provoking additional exchanges which once more ended with each cousin accusing the other of cowardice and poltroonery.

The outcome of this distasteful exhibition was, that through Mr. Carteret Priaulx as intermediary, de Sausmarez was challenged to a dual. Thinking his adversary to be Hirzel le Marchant, the Procureur, and knowing that both his cousins had for some time been practising with pistols, Thomas agreed to l'Hyvreuse as venue and chose the sword as weapon. Documentary evidence survives, incidentally, proving that it was to ensure that he would be the man challenged and hence entitled to this choice of weapons, that Thomas took care to hurl the final insult during the altercation in court.

At the time appointed, Jurat Robert Porret le Marchant appeared on the scene rather than the expected Hirzel, and after a dispute over the arms to be used conducted between the seconds (Carteret Priaulx for le Marchant and William Bell for de Sausmarez) the fight commenced, with de Sausmarez soon having le Marchant at his mercy. He spared his opponent's life, but refused to fight yet again with pistols. This resulted the following February in le Marchant posting up notices in various parts of the Town, reading, 'I hereby post up Thomas de Sausmarez, King's Controller, as a base lyar (*sic*) and a Coward'. By way of rejoinder de Sausmarez obtained no less than 76 signatures to a certificate that he had 'acted up to the principles of a Gentleman and a man of honour in declining to accept the second challenge of Mr. R. P le Marchant'. Thereafter both parties resorted to legal quibbles until on 24 February 1794 (three years and four months after the duel) Robert le Marchant was ordered by the Royal Court to pay a fine of 300 livres tournois to Thomas de Sausmarez and of three livres tournois to His Majesty the King for insulting an officer. He had to recognise Mr. de Sausmarez as a man of honour and to ask his pardon. Le Marchant complied.

The year when Robert Porret le Marchant made his apology also saw the death of his brother Hirzel, the Procureur. Normally the Comptroller succeeded to the office of Procureur, but in this case the Governor (Lord Amherst) was understandably hesitant to appoint someone who had so often been at loggerheads with the Bailiff, and he called on Thomas de Sausmarez to vindicate his claim to the post in view of these past animosities. Fortunately for Thomas, he was highly regarded by the new Lieutenant-Governor, Major-General John Small, who, referring to him in a letter to Amherst the following year said that 'his Merit, his Loyalty and his zeal are such as to lead me not to wish him to be long absent'. Thanks to the good offices of his patron de Sausmarez became Procureur, to William le Marchant's intense chagrin.

The year after Thomas became Procureur, his wife Martha Dobrée died, having borne him 12 children — and not long afterwards he married Catherine — the daughter of William le Marchant's other great antagonist, Peter de Havilland (q.v.) — who bore him a further 16! It is probably this element of uxoriousness in the personality of de Sausmarez which accounts for his never becoming Bailiff. In those days the Procureur, as well as receiving his salary as such, was also permitted to engage in private practice. His office, therefore, was more lucrative than that of the Bailiff — a potent consideration when one has sired 28 progeny! So it was that Thomas de Sausmarez' duelling adversary followed his uncle as Bailiff, to be succeeded in his turn by the Procureur's friend-cum-father-in-law. When Thomas de Sausmarez retired in 1830 he had been Procureur for 36 years following 20 as Comptroller: a total of 56 as Law Officer of the Crown, which must surely be a record !

A noteworthy feature throughout his career had been the warm friendship which existed between him and Daniel de Lisle Brock (q.v.). As Comptroller in 1789, Thomas pleaded Daniel's case before the Privy Council when Bailiff William le Marchant (q.v.) refused to confirm the young man's election as a Constable of St Peter-Port. A witness of the following year's duel, Brock was one of the signatories of the certificate upholding de Sausmarez' honour when he refused to fight a second time; while later in life the two worked in perfect harmony as Bailiff and Procureur, Brock going out of his way in a speech at the dinner given in 1826 to Sir John Doyle (q.v.) on his return to the island, to praise Thomas as 'the friend and defender of the poor '.

In addition to his legal and marital activities, Thomas de Sausmarez also wrote a short life of his paternal uncle, Captain Philip Saumarez (q.v.), based on the captain's personal papers which, sent to his father Matthew in Guernsey when he was killed, were on the latter's death inherited by Thomas' father John de Sausmarez, Procureur du Roi — the brother of Philip. This compilation by Thomas was used extensively by Jonathan Duncan (q.v.) as source material for his *History of Guernsey*. Thomas died of apoplexy on 1 April 1837.

SCHMETTOW, RUDOLF, LIEUTENANT-GENE-RAL GRAF VON SCHMETTOW (1891–1970). *An enemy of noble spirit.* Described by Sir Ambrose Sherwill (q.v.) as 'a man of great charm and humanity', Rudolf Bernhard Gottfried Karl, Lieutenant-General Graf von Schmettow, was born in Berlin on 8 January 1891. This Silesian aristocrat, whose father had been a personal friend of the Kaiser (visiting him each year during his exile at Doorn) was tall and erect, a fine horsemen and a lover of classical literature. Contemptuous of Nazi mores, he eschewed repressive measures and as Commander-in-Chief of the Channel Isles, made himself the laughing stock of the High Command by continually referring to the 'special circumstances' of the archipelago, for which he persistently solicited correspondingly 'special' treatment.

von Schmettow (who was awarded the German Cross in Gold) joined the Imperial Army as an Ensign (Fahnenjunker) on 1 September 1909, becoming a Lieutenant in the Cavalry on 27 November 1911. During the First World War he received a shrapnel wound when serving on the Eastern Front, and later lost a lung when gassed on the Western Front, where he commanded an infantry battalion. Promoted to the rank of Lieutenant-Colonel in November 1935, he was appointed to the command of the Breslau District on 1 October 1937 and advanced to full Colonel (Oberst) on 1 April 1938. On the outbreak of the Second World War he commanded the 164th Infantry Regiment from 1 September 1939 until 8 January 1940.

This soldier of the old school took up the post of Commander-in-Chief (Befehlshaber) of the Channel Isles on 28 August 1940, setting up his headquarters in Jersey; but on the arrival in June 1941 of the 319 Infantry Division, was supplanted by its Commander, Major-General Müller (q.v.*), who outranked him. He therefore served as Island Commandant (Inselkommandant) in Jersey until Müller's departure on 1 September 1943, when (having himself been promoted to the rank of Major-General on 1 April 1942) he replaced him as 319 Divisional Commander and resumed his responsibilities as Befehlshaber, at the same time moving his headquarters to Guernsey. He retained this appointment until ousted by the machinations of Vice-Admiral Friedrich Hüffmeier (q.v.) on 27 February 1945. During his term of office von Schmettow was promoted to Lieutenant-General on 1 April 1944.

Soon after assuming office, the new Commander-in-Chief in the autumn of 1940 showed his quality as a man of honour in the matter of Lieutenants Nicolle and Symes (qq.v.), the intelligence agents who gave themselves up after an amnesty had been offered to any British servicemen still at large who came forward before 21 October. Although General Schreiber at St Germain, an officer much senior to von Schmettow wanted an example to be made of the two subalterns and their accomplices, assurances of an amnesty notwithstanding, von Schmettow flew to Paris to see his own immediate superior (Count Brockdorf). He insisted that the promise made in his name be kept, asking to be relieved of his command should this not be done, and prevailed upon Brockdorf to approach Admiral Canaris, Chief of Counter-Intelligence, whose intervention finally saved the two young officers from the firing squad and secured the release of their helpers. The following May the Befehlshaber gave further evidence of his mettle by the courteous consideration he showed towards La Dame de Sercq, Mrs. Sibyl Hathaway (q.v.), personally crossing to Sark to offer his condolences when her eldest son Francis William Lionel Beaumont was killed during an air raid in Liverpool and saying, 'My sympathy is for mothers of all nations who grieve in the same way for their sons'. Two years later La Dame returned the gesture, showing similar humanity and compassion to von Schmettow (who, 'although he looked dour, was really very kind-hearted', as she herself said) when his own son was killed on the Russian Front.

Being a man of honour and kindliness did not mean that von Schmettow was in any way lacking in military ardour. He devoted considerable energy to the islands's fortifications programme and, having been appointed Festungskommandant when Allied invasion loomed in February 1944, with the charge to hold Guernsey to the last man and the last bullet, he was in France attending a conference of Corps and Divisional Commanders summoned by von Runstedt when the Allied assault on the Normandy beaches was launched. He hurried back to Guernsey, which he reached on 7 June and grimly held on, spurning an Allied approach under a flag of truce on 22 September, by signalling that he was fully informed of the war situation and did not want to discuss it with anyone. Moreover, he gave point to this reply by sending a series of raiding parties equipped for anti-tank fighting, to harrass the Allies. These raiders acquitted themselves well, especially around St Malo, and nearly always got back safely to the islands. As the situation worsened, von Schmettow showed himself a man of adamantine resolve, informing Victor Carey (q.v.) that Germans did not build mighty fortifications without holding them to the bitter end — and that he would do so even if it meant disaster for the islanders. He flatly refused any contact with the Protecting Power (Switzerland) to request food supplies, and only relented when overruled by direct orders from Naval High Command (West) (under which in October 1944 the islands had been placed for purposes of supply and administration) 'since the supply of food to the civil population has great bearing on our own ability to hold out'. Accordingly on 5 November Victor Carey was given permission to contact the International Red Cross over the German wireless transmitter.

Despite his determined — indeed stringent — measures which enabled him to report at the end of 1944 that he had accumulated sufficient food stocks to be able to hold out until the following June, von Schmettow's position was being rapidly undermined by the campaign of vilification against him waged by Vice-Admiral Hüffmeier who, alleging that the Befehlshaber was being 'too magnanimous' over civilian rations, so cogently advocated

far more draconian policies as ultimately to obtain the appointment he craved for as replacement of the Lieutenant-General who on 27 February 1945, was recalled 'for health reasons'. He had no sooner left Guernsey than he was summoned to report to Admiral Krancke, Commanding Navy Group West, who so berated him for his 'softness' towards the islands and taxed him with lacking National Socialist zeal, that von Schmettow thought that he was going to be 'purged'. Thanks, however, to the support of his uncle, General von Rundstedt, he was spared for the time being and later saved by the general confusion in Germany as the final collapse approached.

von Schmettow's lot after that collapse was not an enviable one. His Silesian home was included in the territory transferred to Poland, and he was overtaken by illness stemming from his lung damage in the First World War. So reduced were his circumstances after his release from internment in 1947, that he had to depend on charity until his pension was restored in 1951. Twelve years later he returned to the Bailiwick as a holidaymaker, on one occasion lunching with La Dame de Sercq, who welcomed him as an old friend. Rudolf, Graf von Schmettow died at Bad Wildungen on 28 June 1970.

SEICHAN, REVEREND LOUIS NAPOLEON (c. 1850–post-1922). *Sark's formidable Bonapartist of the Cloth.* Ecclesiastical records are silent regarding the birth of the Reverend Louis Napoleon Seichan (Vicar of Sark, 1897–1922), but an approximate date may be inferred from his ordination. This ceremony occurred in 1873, when this graduate of the Sorbonne was ordained both priest and deacon in the Roman Catholic church by the Archbishop of Paris. The presumption therefore would be that this Corsican Goliath (he was six feet six inches tall) was born about 1850.

Probably urged by Eros (he married soon afterwards) the Reverend L. N. Seichan forsook the Church of Rome in 1880, thereafter exercising his priesthood in the Church of England — initially as Curate of Grouville in Jersey (1880–1881), immediately followed by another curacy at St Helier from 1881 to 1885. After a spell as priest-in-charge at the Eglise Française Anglicane de St Julien in Southampton between 1885 and 1888, another curacy ensued at Guernsey's Town Church from 1888 to 1889. Then came six years in the Indian Ocean as Chaplain of St Paul, Vacoas, Mauritius, between 1890 and 1896 before this awesome character was finally installed as Vicar of Sark in 1897. This brief curriculum vitæ leaves no room for the myth that the Corsican cleric was chaplain at Devil's Island at the time of Dreyfus' incarceration (1894-1906) — a story which, besides failing to be 'vero', is not even 'ben trovato' either!

The new incumbent had not been in Sark for long before it became evident that he would make an eccentric Roland to match the bizarre Oliver of the Seigneur, William Frederick Collings (q.v.). Bonapartist in political sympathy as well as in name — as was to be expected of a son of Corsica — he took no cognisance of the Third Republic, his scorn for which he demonstrated by sartorial symbolism, wearing a black cloak flamboyantly thrown over his shoulder, together with the kind of hat popular in Paris during the Second Empire. When the re-trial of Alfred Dreyfus took place in 1899, the man of God emerged as implacably hostile to the unfortunate French officer, in contrast to Mademoiselle Mathilde des Essarts (the governess of the Seigneur's children) who passionately championed him: and violent arguments accompanied by threatening gesticulations frequently resulted between these two bitter opponents.

This ecclesiastical autocrat was a law unto himself. After the death of any islander who had incurred his disfavour, he would refuse to permit the church pall to be used on the coffin. In 1908, helped by his maidservant (who was too cowed to do otherwise) he pulled down a tombstone erected without his consent over the grave of Mr. Baker, a person of whom he disapproved. Although in the ensuing litigation William Baker, the son of the deceased, was given the legal right to replace it, this entitlement was not exercised as long as the intimidating presence of the 'turbulent priest' remained in the island. Furthermore, in contrast to the evangelically-minded Serquiais, Louis Napoleon Seichan (conditioned by his background) was Anglo-Catholic in his churchmanship, conducting services with a Tractarian ceremonial which so alienated an outraged flock that many of its members transferred their allegiance to the Ebenezer Methodist Chapel.

It was inevitable that priest and Seigneur would fall foul of each other. A feud speedily developed between the two arrogant personalities which lasted throughout the vicar's incumbency. In 1902 the redoubtable cleric sued the Seigneur for £140 damages, claiming that he had libelled him in a letter to the Bishop of Winchester, and in 1903 the feudal overlord first jostled the clerk in Holy orders with his horse and followed this up, while

still mounted, by chasing him on foot round and round the vicarage garden. Later the same year he threatened Mrs. Seichan with a stick, hurting her and frightening her so much that she fled to the shelter of the *Bel Air Hotel* and stayed there for the rest of the night. Visitors to the island would gaze on the inscription, 'Poor Sark, What a Vicar!' chalked by the Seigneur on a kiln (now demolished) near the harbour.

Only the removal of one or the other of the two antagonists could procure peace — and this did not come about until 1922 when, now in his seventies, the incarnation of the Church Militant at last left Sark for England. The absence of his name from the death records in London over the next decade and a half suggests however, the possibility of his having finally returned to his native Corsica for his declining years.

SHARP, ERIC WILLIAM (1890-1982). *The outstanding authority on matters maritime.* Eric William Sharp was born on 17 January 1890, to Emmeleine (*née* Sinnatt), the wife of William Sharp, who was the first headmaster of the Boys' Intermediate School, founded in 1883, which moved from its original home of Granville House in Mount Durand to premises in Brock Road when young Eric was three years of age. Educated at Elizabeth College from 1903 to 1907, Eric Sharp also taught there for the year 1910-11, before going on to the British School of Telegraphy in London, from which he emerged as one of the first wireless operators aboard merchant ships.

In the early stages of the First World War Eric Sharp served as wireless operator on various transports, one of which was the former Channel Isles mailboat *Caesarea*, of the fleet operated by the London and South-Western Railway Company. Later in the conflict he fought firstly in the Royal Naval Volunteer Reserve and subsequently in the Royal Flying Corps, seeing service in Belgium, Gallipoli and Greece. Between the wars he continued his career as a 'sparks' on ships plying in Far Eastern waters, so that his family took up residence in that part of the globe — with the unfortunate result that the spread of the Second World War after Pearl Harbour saw them interned by the Japanese. A few years after the defeat of the Japanese Mr. and Mrs. Sharp retired and returned to Guernsey.

It was during his retirement that Eric Sharp made the massive contributions to marine biology and historical research which assure the immortality of his name. An energetic and enthusiastic

member of the Council of La Société Guernesiaise (before which he read several papers), he was
active in leading excursions in the course of which
he would impart his unrivalled knowledge of life
on the island's shores, coupled with reflections
on Guernsey's maritime history. In recognition
of these valuable services he was in 1972 made an
honorary member of La Société and presented
by the Bailiff (Sir William Arnold) with an illu-
minated address couched in Patois, which the
recipient greatly treasured.

Eric Sharpe's especial interest was 19th century
cross-Channel shipping, with particular reference
to the many fine vessels built in Guernsey's ship-
yards. Informative articles on this history of
shipping services appeared in the *Channel Islands
Anthology* of 1972 and 1975. In addition this
maritime expert was the author of invaluable
papers on the history of the harbours of St Peter-
Port and St Sampson's. He extended his purview
further afield, however, investigating industrial
archaeology, the island's water supplies and life
in Victorian times.

As a veteran of the First World War, Eric Sharp's
last public appearances were among the Old Con-
temptibles—both at their inspection by Her Majesty
the Queen in 1978 and at the ceremony held at the
Town Church in 1979 when their standard was laid
up. Although advancing years thereafter kept him
mostly housebound, his intellect was still acute and
articles continued to flow from his pen — as well as
an authoritative booklet, *Lighthouses of the
Channel Islands*, which appeared in 1979 when he
was 89 years of age. Eric William Sharp died on 7
March 1982, at the fine old age of 92.

SHARP, GEORGE (1880–1962). *The Cyclops of
Brecqhou.* George Sharp was born in Aldershot
in 1880 to Mary (*née* Rowe-Buckingham), an
Alderney girl who in 1878 had married Archibald
Sharp, a soldier serving in the island during that
year with a detachment of the 75th Regiment of
Foot — later (in 1881) the Gordon Highlanders.
(The presence in the Bailiwick of this Scottish
Regiment, incidentally, gave the initial impetus
to the demand for the provision of the forms of
worship practised in the Kirk which by 1894
had grown sufficiently to warrant the building
of St Andrew's Presbyterian church in Grange
Road in Guernsey.) After his wife had presented
him with two more offspring (Archibald and
Mary), Archibald Sharp died and the young widow
brought her three children back to Alderney,
where they were brought up in her parents'
home at the Nunnery.

On reaching man's estate George Sharp took up
employment as a quarryman at Mannez, where he
suffered the misfortune of losing the sight of one
eye as the result of an explosion in the quarry.
One of his workmates was John Godfray, whose
son Daniel was later to marry George's younger
cousin Iris (his mother's niece). On a foggy day in
1902 the two men were hurriedly summoned by
Godfray's mother (Mrs. Mary Godfray) who
had made haste to fetch them after hearing the
loud rasping noise of a ship coming to grief on the
nearby Hommeaux Florains rocks. It was the
Liverpool — the world's largest sailing vessel at
the time — and the friends ran to the scene of
the disaster, George outstripping John Godfray
and so achieving the distinction of being the
first person to board the striken craft. He found
considerable confusion among the crew, the
captain thinking that he had in fact struck the
Casquets.

Aided by his maternal uncle, George Sharp in
1911 forsook Alderney for Brecqhou where,
having negotiated a 60-year lease at £20 per
annum with the Seigneur of Sark — William
Frederick Collings (q.v.) — he arrived on a small
steamer laden with furniture, farming equipment
and animals: which had to swim ashore for want
of other landing facilities. A gigantic task confronted the immigrant, together with the three
relatives and a carpenter friend who accompanied
him, as the islet, deserted for the previous five
years, had become a wilderness. As the legendary
Cyclops of old reputedly toiled to erect the walls
of Mycenæ, so did this 20th century monocular
pioneer labour to tame a bushland of heather,
gorse, bracken and brambles — not to mention
thistles six feet high. All was eventually cleared,
however, and Sharp (who is alleged to have introduced Belgian hares which interbred with the
indigenous rabbits to produce a vigorous strain
with the sleekest pelts and finest flavour in the
archipelago) farmed his domain until 1929,
becoming a distinguished Serquiais by settlement
and marrying the school teacher, Agnes Lanyon,
aunt of the wartime resistance hero Hubert
Lanyon (q.v.). In 1983 Mrs. Iris Godfray recalled
many happy childhood holidays during these years
spent with her adult cousin in his enisled abode.

One aspect of the difficulties with which this
colourful character had to contend in his colonisation of the islet was vividly recalled in 1983
by Mr. Hilary Carré, M.B.E., who by then had
become Sénéchal of Sark. The Sénéchal recounted
an incident in 1921 — which the records show as
the year of the great drought — when, as a boy

making his way to school, he espied a flag being flown at half-mast in Brecqhou. On arrival at the classroom he reported this to his schoolmaster who immediately informed the authorities. A boat was sent across the Gouliot Passage and it was discovered that the Sharp ménage was in sore straits, having completely run out of water!

By 1929 George Sharp was approaching his 50th birthday and found the physical exertion of farming Brecqhou an ever-increasing strain: a consideration which made him the more responsive to the financial inducements offered by La Dame de Sercq (who wished to dispose of the islet more profitably) as a *quid pro quo* for the surrender of his lease. Thus, although at first inclined – like Trojan Aeneas – to 'fear the Greeks when they bring gifts' ('*Timeo Danaos et dona ferentes*'), nevertheless the eventual upshot was that he and his wife moved to Little Sark, where for the next ten years they ran the *Bungalow Hotel*, and the lease of Brecqhou was sold to Angelo Clarke for £3,000. Mr. Clarke was also granted the seat on Chief Pleas attaching to La Moinerie de Haut.

Because of his birth in England, George Sharp and his wife were deported to Germany during the enemy occupation of the islands and returned after the Liberation to find that the *Bungalow Hotel* – their livelihood – had been destroyed by the foe, so that they were face to face with penury. With financial help extended by Chief Pleas, however, they had a small bungalow built near La Valette and Sharp – now in his mid-sixties – by his resolve yet again gave evidence of the courage which in his younger days had earned him the award of a Certificate of Commendation for rescuing an accident victim from drowning in the Thames. Maintaining his wife and himself by working as a gardener at l'Ecluse, this resourceful man once more assumed a prominent place in the life of Sark, being elected to serve as a Deputy in Chief Pleas. Death finally claimed him on 8 May 1962, with his wife following him to the grave precisely one year and one day later.

SHERWILL, SIR AMBROSE JAMES, K.B.E., M.C., K.St.J., L. en D. (1890–1968). *The rejected stone which became the head of the corner*. Born on 12 February 1890, at Les Landes, Castel, to Elizabeth Annie (*née* Roberts), the wife of James Edward Sherwill, Sir Ambrose Sherwill, one of the bravest men ever to be Bailiff of Guernsey, came of humble – and indeed penurious – origins. His father was the proprietor of a butcher's shop in a small and parlous way of business, so that his mother had to supplement the family income by working as a dressmaker, thereby bringing in a further five shillings a week. Despite these disadvantages young Ambrose, with grit and pertinacity reinforced by innate abilities of the highest order, contrived by dint of the utmost frugality to pursue at the Guernsey High School, followed by Elizabeth College and le Lycée de Cherbourg, studies eventuating in a Licence en Droit of the Université de Caen and a call to the Bar in 1920. Meanwhile, when serving with the Buffs (East Kents) on the Western Front during the First World War he had in 1917 been awarded the Military Cross after dashing out into the open, reckless of his own safety, to send an urgent signal with an Aldis lamp to a detachment which was cut off – with the virtually inevitable result that he was riddled by enemy fire, wounded in nine places, but still by a miracle alive. Nor did his sense of military duty cease with the end of hostilities. Serving in the Guernsey Militia as a captain, in 1931 he vigorously opposed current tentative proposals to discontinue its maintenance, urging that the force was the epitome of Guernsey's history and a bulwark of the island's constitution and insisting that 'the path of duty is sometimes irksome, but there is no other way'.

The verdict that 'a prophet is not without honour, save in his own country' certainly applied to Ambrose Sherwill. Despite his achievements and his gallantry, he was blackballed for the Grange Club because of his plebian background, while his fiancée (May Clabburn) was warned that marriage to this base-born and impecunious advocate would bring social ostracism – a warning which, to her credit, she contemptuously ignored. Furthermore, although he was made H.M. Comptroller in 1929 and became H.M. Procureur in 1935, Sherwill was passed over for appointment as Bailiff (the succession to which at that time was usually regarded as the perquisite of the Procureur) when the position fell vacant later the same year on the sudden death of Mr. Arthur Bell. In his place the patrician Victor Carey (q.v.) was advanced from the more lowly post of H.M. Receiver to the Bailiwick's supreme office.

Five years later, however, it was to this man that his fellow islanders turned for a 'shield in danger's hour' and whose 'shoulders held the sky suspended' when the greatest crisis in the Bailiwick's history came as a bolt from the blue. When, with an enemy landing imminent, it was suggested by Jurat (later Sir) John Leale (q.v.) that a Controlling Committee be formed as an emergency executive arm of the States to deal with the complexities of enemy occupation, Ambrose Sherwill was with one accord chosen as its President and he it was to whom 'the man in the street' instinctively looked for guidance. So it came about that he emerged as the 'uncrowned king of Guernsey' with the unenviable responsibility of having to negotiate with the victorious Germans. In doing this his task was somewhat eased by the fact that his soldierly bearing and magnificent First World War record evoked the respect of Major-Doktor Albrecht Lanz, the original German Commandant, and also of his Chief of Staff, Dr. Maass - who spoke fluent English.

Sherwill was soon to need - and imperil — his standing of esteem with the German authorities, as a result of military operations of which he naturally had no foreknowledge. About six o'clock one morning early in August 1940 he had gone to stoke up the boiler in his cellar when, on opening the back door in answer to a knock, he found himself face to face with Lieutenants Martel and Mulholland (qq.v.) who, left stranded after the fiasco of Operation 'Ambassador', had come to seek his aid. To save the two subalterns from being shot as spies Sherwill took a course of action which placed his own life in jeopardy. With the aid of a friend, Donald Bisset, he stole from the Town Arsenal two Militia uniforms whose buttons were replaced by British Army ones by Mrs. Dawes, the wife of the arsenal caretaker. He then produced the two young men, duly arrayed in uniform, before Dr. Maass and, when one of them admitted to Maass how long they had been in the island, muttered to them under cover of offering cigarettes, 'You bloody fools - just rank, name and number'. After prolonged interrogation in Dinard, the Germans eventually accepted the prisoners' story that they had landed in uniform and took civilian clothes from an empty house. They were treated as prisoners of war and Sherwill heard nothing more.

Despite his courageous help to Martel and Mulholland, Sherwill believed that the survival of the islands (which had been left by the United Kingdom to fare as best they could) depended on keeping good relations with the Germans. He also sought to allay the anxieties of Channel Island refugees in Britain. With the first object in mind, Sherwill in a speech to the first meeting of the States after the commencement of the Occupation (8 August 1940) expressed the hope that the Occupation would be a model to the world and that after it was over it would be possible

to say, 'We were civilians and we behaved as such in the strictest sense in accordance with the usages of war'. As for his second aim, in order to reassure the refugees in the United Kingdom Sherwill asked the Germans to arrange a Red Cross message system and, when this request was refused, recorded a speech which was broadcast by Bremen radio, referring to the 'correct and kindly attitude' of the Germans and their respect for the islanders' loyalty to the British Crown.

Sherwill's good relations policy apparently sank to the most craven sycophancy when on 31 July 1940 the Royal Court at his instigation issued an ordinance making criticism of the Germans a criminal offence - with retrospective application to the beginning of the Occupation. There was, however, more to this move than meets the eye. Sherwill had found two Germans about to arrest Mr. H. H. Collins, the manager of Le Riche's Stores, who had reproved a shop assistant for leaving a local customer to serve a German, and fearing that Collins, a sick man, would never survive imprisonment, he offered to obtain the retrospective legislation if the Germans would permit trial by the Royal Court. The bargain was struck and Collins was tried immediately after the issue of the Ordinance — and acquitted. The ordinance was never again invoked.

Sherwill's efforts to establish a *modus vivendi* with the occupying forces were destined yet again to be embarrassed by the presence of British spies to whom, at the dictates of patriotism, he extended help despite the danger to himself. This time he was to pay dearly for his quixotic conduct. Having learned through Emile Nicolle, the Controlling Committee's Secretary, of the presence of his son Lieutenant Hubert Nicolle (q.v.), together with Lieutenant James Symes (q.v.) as further British agents unable to get away from the island, he embarked on a cat-and-mouse game with the Germans. With the consent of the newly-appointed Commander-in-Chief, Oberst Graf von Schmettow, the local Commandant in Guernsey, Major Bandelow, hinted to Sherwill that British soldiers were in hiding and promised that if they gave themselves up they would be treated as prisoners of war. Sherwill contrived to have the time limit extended to 21 October (to give the two subalterns the maximum chance of escape in the meanwhile) and followed this up with a letter to Bandelow published in the *Evening Press*, the crucial part of which was: 'I have noted that you intend to arrange with me a time limit within which any personnel of the British Armed Forces in hiding in the island (if such there be) must surrender, and that if this direction is complied with, such personnel will be treated as prisoners of war and no measures will be taken against any of their relatives'. By the words in parenthesis Sherwill laid himself open to the charge of deliberately misleading the Germans. While these negotiations were in progress, Nicolle's uncle, Captain Frank Nicolle, discovered in his capacity as assistant harbour master that a stock of battle-dress had been stored in the harbour sheds and forgotten. Wearing the two uniforms thus stolen by Frank Nicholle, the two subalterns gave themselves up before the deadline on 21 October.

The question now was whether the Germans would keep their word. While a decision was pending, all who had been identified by the German counter-intelligence as having sheltered Symes and Nicolle were dispatched to solitary confinement in the Cherche Midi prison in Paris, where Louis Symes (James Symes' father) was later found dead in his cell. The Germans claimed that it was suicide, but it could well have been murder. To Sherwill's protests the Germans replied that their promise had been won by a trick, as Sherwill had pretended not to know that the spies were in the island. He was thus not altogether surprised when he too was arrested and had to face the gruelling experience of solitary confinement without heat in the month of December. First he was held at Versailles, where he occupied himself by assiduously cleaning every nook and cranny of his cell with a nailbrush and a razor blade. Then he was transferred to the Cherche Midi, of which he wrote, 'Never have I been in touch with so much misery at the same time' and where he kept his sanity by writing on any scrap of paper on which he could lay his hands. At last, in common with the other prisoners, he was saved by the sense of military honour of Graf von Schmettow (q.v.), who together with Colonel Schumacher and Major Bandelow, asked to be relieved if his post if the amnesty promises were not kept. He followed this up by a personal appeal to Count Brockdorf, who in his turn contacted Admiral Canaris, Chief of Counter-Intelligence. On the orders of Canaris, the proposed show trial in Paris was abandoned and all those in custody released.

Because of his part in the Symes–Nicolle affair, the Germans deposed Sherwill from the Presidency of the Controlling Committee and also from the office of Procureur. He was thus obliged to retire into private life, supporting his family as best he could, and devoting himself to keeping goats and growing vegetables – some of which he sold. In July 1942 he was allowed to resume his functions as Procureur on the death of Mr. G. J. P. Ridgway, but any reinstatement as President of the Controlling Committee was out of the question as far as the Germans were concerned.

After the Commando raid on Sark ('Operation Basalt') of October 1942, the Germans decided in January 1943 to deport all former officers of the British forces. The deportations took place the following month and although those in official positions were excused, the exemption did not extend to Sherwill, whose part in the matter of Nicolle and Symes still rankled with the German authorities. He thus spent the rest of the war in Laufen Internment Camp – but even there he played the rôle of saviour of fellow Channel Islanders, contriving by his representations to the Camp Commandant to procure the transfer thither of the Jerseyman, Stanley Green, who was in Buchenwald.

In the Occupation Honours List, published on 12 December 1945, 'A. J. Sherwill, H.M. Procureur, Guernsey' was among those made Commanders of the Most Excellent Order of the British Empire. It could well have been argued that a man who had risked his life and incurred prolonged incarceration at the dictates of patriotism deserved better. 'Better' did eventually come. In 1946 this natural leader became Bailiff and in 1949 he was knighted with advancement to Knight Commander of the Most Excellent Order of the British Empire. Receiving his accolade and looking back on the days when he was scorned as a parvenu, he could have been forgiven had he reflected on the dictum that 'the stone which the builders rejected, the same has become the head of the corner'!

After 14 years in Guernsey's supreme office, during which the Bailiwick was twice visited by H.M. Elizabeth II (in 1949 as Princess Elizabeth and in 1957 as Queen), and also by Field-Marshal Viscount Montgomery of Alamein, Sir Ambrose and Lady Sherwill in 1960 retired to Essex Castle in Alderney, where this brave and selfless man spent his declining years, dying in 1968, and followed to the grave two years later by his widow.

Guernsey mourned the loss of one of her most illustrious sons, whose memoirs, although remaining unpublished, nevertheless provided valuable source material for Dr. Charles Cruickshank in compiling his *Official History of the German Occupation*.

SIXTUS IV (FRANCESCO DELLA ROVERE) PONTIFEX MAXIMUS (1414-1484). *The 'Neutrality Pope'.* Born at Cella Ligure in July 1414, Francesco della Rovere in early manhood entered the Franciscan Order, of which he became Minister General in 1464. Three years later, in 1467, he was made a Cardinal by Pope Paul II, whom he succeeded on the Papal Throne in 1471 with the title of Sixtus IV. During the early years of his Pontificate Sixtus concentrated on foreign affairs — but with no more than indifferent success. Relations with Louis XI on France remained permanently strained, intent as that monarch was on maintaining the liberties of the Gallican church. The fleet dispatched by the Holy See in 1472 assailed the Moslem stronghold of Smyrna (present-day Izmir in Turkey), but a further expedition the following year met with failure. So too did the Pope's efforts in 1474 and 1476 to reunite the Russian church with Rome with the ulterior motive of enlisting Russian help against the Turks.

After these somewhat unfruitful experiences, Sixtus devoted his attention to matters nearer home, aiming at the aggrandisement of his family (which he greatly enriched) and also at increasing the power and extent of the Papal States. Thus, though he neither condoned (nor expected) assassination, he was privy to the anti-Medici plot as a result of which the agents of his nephew (Girolamo Riario), during Mass in Florence Cathedral in 1478 wounded Lorenzo the Magnificent and killed his brother Guilano de Medici. Sixtus seized the opportunity to excommunicate Lorenzo and put Florence under an interdict, following this up with fomenting war between Florence and Naples in the hope that the Papal States, contiguous to both antagonists, would thereby profit. This scheme, however, came to nothing. In 1480 a Neopolitan/Florentine Peace was concluded and Sixtus, realising the futility of further chicanery, removed the interdict on Florence and granted absolution to Lorenzo. Turning his attention further north, in 1482 he incited Venice to attack Ferrara (whose territory was coveted by the Papacy) and the next year, when Venice refused to discontinue the conflict (Sixtus again seeing that nothing was to be gained therefrom), the Queen of the Adriatic too found itself placed under and inderdict.

Such was the Supreme Pontiff who on 27 February (Ante Diem III Kal. Mart.) 1480/1 issued the Bull — preserved in the Vatican archives under Volume DCLXXIII, Folio 406 — protecting the Channel Isles from the incursions of pirates and reinforcing the agreement already reached between Edward IV of England (q.v.) and Louis XI of France that in the event of war between their two countries, the islands were to be regarded as neutral. The Bull started by recalling that papal intervention had been solicited because various pirates frequently attacked the Isles, imperilling both their inhabitants and also merchants coming to and going from them. These pirates had repeatedly carried off prisoners and booty, including chalices and ornaments meant for liturgical purposes — and had both wounded and killed people. The Bull therefore — under pain of excommunication, of anathema, of eternal malediction and of confiscation — ordered abstinence from such attacks upon the islands themselves 'or within sight of them, as far as human eye can reach'. It gave authority to the Archbishop of Canterbury, the Bishop of Salisbury and the 'Archpriest of St Peter at Rome' to publish its requirements and to see to its execution. Furthermore these executors were empowered to absolve those pirates who complied with the papal ordinance. On the other hand, the cities and castles of any who might defy this ruling were to be placed under an interdict, whatever the rank of the offending overlord, whose vassals would thereby be freed from all feudal obligations. Lastly, so as to ensure that the papal injunction was known to all, the Bull ordered that copies should be affixed to the doors of the Basilica of St Peter in Rome and the churches of Canterbury, London, Salisbury, Nantes, St Pol de Leon, Tréguier and St Peter-Port — which, with its invaluable roadstead, was indubitably the most important town in the Channel Isles at that time. The failure to include among these locations any on the Norman mainland gives rise to the speculation that the offending corsairs were not Norman, but either English or Bréton.

The conventional wisdom which held that the Bull of Neutrality was issued by Sixtus IV in 1483 rested on Letters Patent of Henry VIII, dated 6 February 1510, confirming a Bull of Sixtus IV relative to the security of the Channel Isles, the tenor of which was in all essentials identical to the papal edict just considered, but which according to the Letters Patent as quoted in *Jersey Church History* was given at Rome on 1 March 1483, *'la dixième année de son pontificat'*. As has been pointed out by Monsignor Bernard Jacqueline, however, March 1483 fell not in the 'dixième', but in the 'douzième' year of the pontificate of Sixtus IV — a fact which casts doubts on the dependability of the Letters Patent and favours a reliance on the evidence on the Vatican archives with their indication of 27 February 1480/1, the true 'dixième année' of this Pope's reign.

In the strictly ecclesiastical sphere Sixtus IV granted many privileges to the mendicant orders (especially his own Franciscans), instituted the Feast of the Immaculate Conception of the Blessed Virgin (1475), and condemned the abuses of the Spanish Inquisition (1482). A great patron of arts and letters, he commissioned such artists as Sandro Botticelli and his great memorial is the magnificent Sistine Chapel (named after him) which he had built — though of course a further one and a half centuries were to elapse before its breathtaking embellishments were created by the brush of Michaelangelo.

This Pope who created a state of affairs affording the islands immunity from external attack which lasted for two centuries died in August 1484. Thanks to the status given to the archipelago by his Bull, William Camden was able to write a hundred years later that 'here is alwaies a continual truce, as it were: and lawfull it is for Frenchmen and others, how hot soever the warre is, to have repaire hither too and fro without danger, and to maintain entercourse of trafficke in security'.

SPITZ, AUGUSTE (1901–1942). *Requiescat in Pace*. See *Jewish Victims of the German Occupation*.

STEINER, THERESIA (1916–1942). *Requiescat in Pace*. See *Jewish Victims of the German Occupation*.

STEVENS-COX, JAMES, F.S.A. (1910–   ). *A man of parts: tonsorial pundit, antiquarian, bibliophile and academic publicist*. Born in Bristol early in 1910, James Stevens-Cox was educated initially at Bristol Grammar School and subsequently at the Merchant Venturers' Technical College. Thereafter for 30 years a practising wigmaker and ladies' hairdresser in the family business founded in 1850 by his maternal grandfather, John Stevens, Stevens-Cox also emerged as an ardent bibliophile (who by the age of nine had already amassed some 400 volumes), as well as an antiquarian and archaeologist. He was a member of several archaeological societies and in 1951 was elected a Fellow of the Society of Antiquaries. He became, moreover, one of the world's leading authorities on the history of wigs and the hairdressing craft, and the possessor of a unique collection of books, manuscripts and pictures associated with matters tonsorial, as well as early tools of the trade.

At various times an extra-mural tutor of Bristol University, a contributor to the *Encyclopaedia Britannica* and a lecturer on hairdressing for the States of Guernsey Education Council, Stevens-Cox was Chairman of the Hairdressing Registration Council from 1960 to 1963 and also for many years an examiner in hairdressing both for the Hairdressers' Technical Council and for the City and Guilds of London Institute. A frequent visiting lecturer in Universities and Technical Colleges on both sides of the Atlantic and the author of many books on archaeology and history, he also established himself as an expert on Thomas Hardy, editing the *Thomas Hardy Year Book* in addition to a set of monographs on the Dorsetshire author's life, times and work.

James Stevens-Cox first engaged in publishing in 1931, originally under the imprint of The Coleridge Bookshop, but after 1960 as the Toucan Press; an enterprise which in 1969 came to be operated in partnership with Gregory Stevens-Cox, M.A. (Oxon.) — the son born in 1947 to his first wife Helen Hilson *veuve* Hotchkiss (*née* Whitton), after whose death he married Adèle Claire Senior.

Settling in Guernsey in 1965, Stevens-Cox enthusiastically identified himself with his island of adoption, becoming a member of La Société Guernesiaise in 1966, of the National Trust of Guernsey in 1969 and a sidesman at the Town Church in 1972. Besides serving from 1966 onwards as a lecturer for the States of Guernsey adult education classes in archaeology, folklore, local history and bibliography, in 1976 he wrote an invaluable *vade mecum* on *Guernsey's Prehistoric Monuments and Associated Folklore* and beginning in 1966, edited a set of *Guernsey Historical Monographs*, dealing with all aspects of Guernsey's past, with special emphasis on the details of everyday life and the folk-ways of our predecessors. In 1972 an attempt was made to launch an annual anthology comprising articles on the archaeology, history and folklore of the Channel Islands, but in the event demand only warranted one further issue, which appeared in 1975 — the year which saw the inauguration of a regular series of lectures on Guernsey given at the Old Government House Hotel every Monday during the summer months for the benefit of visitors to the island. This venture proved extremely successful.

With all these contributions to island life, not to mention sundry further publications such as a set of *Remarkables of Guernsey*, *The Life of Joshua Gosselin* and *The Mysterious Power of Linda Martel*, James Stevens-Cox's worth rapidly earned recognition and it was not long after his arrival before he came to be regarded as an 'honorary Guernseyman' and esteemed as a valued member of the insular community.

SYMES, MAJOR JAMES MICHAEL, M.C. (1919–   ). *The military member of an unfortunate family.* The family into which James Michael Symes was born on 24 October 1919, to Rachel (*née* Tostevin), the wife of Louis Morin Symes, was one doomed to suffer inordinately during the Second World War, with the baby's father destined to die under suspicious circumstances in the custody of the enemy and his elder cousin William Symes (q.v.) – a boy of 12 at the time of James' birth – fated to experience the horrors of a Hitlerite Concentration Camp; while the new arrival himself was to come within an ace of being short as a spy.

James Symes was educated at Elizabeth College and, after sampling the military life both in the Officers' Training Corps and in the Royal Guernsey Militia, he decided on the Army as a career. Entering Sandhurst in 1938, he was gazetted in the Hampshire Regiment in 1939. On 0300 hours on 4 September of the following year he landed secretly at Petit Port, together with Lieutenant Hubert Nicolle (q.v.), with orders to undertake an intelligence assignment – in his case with a special brief to watch the airport, so that he took shelter with Mr. and Mrs. Wilfrid Bird, who lived near it – and thereafter he shared in the adventures of his comrade. (See *Nicolle, Hubert Frank, M.C.*). When the sands were running out as the time limit approached for the amnesty offered by the Germans, Nicolle favoured surrender as he was anxious about the number of people they were likely to compromise; but Symes disagreed, advocating ignoring the amnesty offer, lying low and making further escape attempts later on. However, in deference to the advice given by Major-General Williams, a retired officer of the Hampshires, he finally fell in with Nicolle's point of view and as a consequence they both gave themselves up on 21 October.

The subalterns' long incarceration (and that of relatives and friends who had helped them) in the Cherche Midi Prison after their interrogation had convinced the Germans that they were spies deserving of death, was particularly harrowing for James Symes as his father, Louis Symes, was found dead in his cell on 23 December 1940. Although the Germans claimed that it was suicide, such would have been completely out of character for one of the tenacity and toughness of Louis Symes: murder seemed very likely.

Saved from execution (as was Nicolle), thanks to the code of honour of Graf von Schmettow (q.v.), James Symes spent the rest of the conflict as a prisoner of war, being awarded the Military Cross for his exploits on his release. The collapse of Germany and Japan, however, did not mean the end of war experience as far as this regular officer was concerned. Within a few years his regiment was involved in the 1948–55 campaign against the Malayan insurgents, in the course of which his courage earned the award of a Bar to his Military Cross. Eventually rising to the rank of Major, James Symes served in the British Army on the Rhine – and also on the British Mission to the Soviet Zone – before leaving the army and retiring into the privacy of civilian life.

SYMES, WILLIAM HENRY (1907–1982). *Macte virtute.* See *Underground Resistance Heroes of the Second World War.*

T

TARDIFF, ALFRED EDWARD (1902–   ). *Macte virtute.* See *Underground Resistance Heroes of the Second World War.*

TOMS, CAREL (1916–   ). *A photographer of surpassing excellence.* The son of Charles Henry Toms (1887-1957), an Associate of the Royal Photographic Society and President of the Guernsey Photographic Society, the quality of whose camera studies reflected an exceptionally high level of talent, Carel Toms inherited to the fullest degree his parent's flair with film, earning thereby wide repute as a photo-journalist. Born to Winifred Toms (*née* Baker) on 12 December 1916 and educated at Les Vauxbelets College, Toms took up employment with the Guernsey

Press Company on leaving school and served that newspaper throughout his adult life, working his way up from printer's devil to the position of Features Editor before retiring in 1979. The only break in his career was that of the years of the Second World War when, serving with the 51st Highland Division, he was taken prisoner in June 1940 at St Valery-en-Caux, remaining in captivity for the rest of the conflict.

Carel Toms' skill with the camera resulted in most books on Guernsey and her sister islands published after the Second World War (whether devoted to history, folklore, natural history or general interest) featuring his superb pictures, with his pictorial contribution to *The Guernsey House* by John McCormack (q.v.*) providing a particularly outstanding example of his supreme standard of craftsmanship. Furthermore, his own photo-history of the German Occupation, *Hitler's Fortress Islands*, appeared in 1967 and in addition he wrote many booklets of local interest and contributed hundreds of illustrated stories about the Channel Isles to magazines and newspapers on both sides of the Atlantic. After his retirement he produced in collaboration with Victor Coysh (q.v.) two photographic surveys of the Bailiwick's story (the first before and the second after, the pivotal year of 1914) in the shape of *Guernsey Through The Lens* and *Guernsey Through The Lens Again*. A consummate artist.

TOPLIS, WILLIAM ARTHUR (1857-1941). *The English artist who immortalised the glories of Sark*. Born in Sheffield in the spring of 1857, William Arthur Toplis, whose oil paintings were to capture so much of Sark's natural beauty, first became aware of the island as the result of a trip there during the course of a sojourn in Jersey on his honeymoon in 1878. So enchanted was he with the loveliness before his eyes on all sides that within five years of this original visit he and his wife had settled permanently as almost the only English-speaking people — the bizarre Seigneur William Frederick Collings (q.v.) apart — in a community whose members habitually conversed in Serquiais patois. Yet, despite the linguistic barrier, the couple soon made friends and as time went by Toplis became a revered and popular figure.

Toplis and his wife set up home (and established a studio) at 'La Maison Rouge', near La Seigneurie where they raised their family. The gifted islander-by-osmosis became a familiar sight about the cliffs and bays, painting the delightful scenes in which the Fief Haubert abounds. It was

Sark, rather than the Serquiais, however, which stimulated him — the islanders themselves are rarely featured in his work. His brush faithfully recorded Sark's scenic charms, meticulously portraying all the eye beheld — down to individual pebbles on a beach. His colouring was vivid and the passage of time after his death failed to diminish the demand for reproductions of such pictures as Port du Moulin's Natural Arch, the romantic circular pond with its 18 feet of translucent water which Toplis himself named 'Venus's Pool', or the 'Fairy Grotto' (again a name he gave) at Les Fontaines Bay.

In collaboration with John Oxenham (q.v.) — who provided the text — Toplis in 1908 brought out an ornate publication, *The Book of Sark*, which was limited to 500 copies, each of which was signed by both author and artist. A selection of Toplis' most celebrated pictures embellished the volume, copies of which are ever more keenly sought and fetch increasingly higher prices with every year that passes: an appreciation in face value by no means solely due to inflation.

William Arthur Toplis who, straddling the 19th and 20th centuries, had become the doyen of Sark's artists, elected — despite his English birth — to remain in the island as enemy occupation threatened in 1940. A year later, sharing the fate of the people whom he had made his own, he was saved by death from deportation to Germany as a non-islander and his body was committed to the soil of the isle, the history and geography of which he had studied and which had been his joy and inspiration for nearly threescore years.

TUGUAL OF TRÉGUIER, BISHOP AND SAINT (c. 490–c. 564). *The patron saint of Herm*. The career of St Tugual (alias Tudwal, Tutwal, Tugdual) to whom the attractive chapel in Herm is dedicated and whose Feast Day is 1 December, is steeped to the hilt in fable. The earliest extant documentary reference to this holy person occurs in a register of the churches of the archipelago compiled between 1251 and 1279, which shows Herm's chapel as dedicated to St Tugual. As this is 700 years after the supposed lifetime of the saint, it is not a great deal to go on. Not even the sex of St Tugual is certain, as one version of the story refers to a Welsh woman, killed by the Saxons, whose remains were transferred to Armorica. The main tradition, however, is to the effect that the saint was born in Wales in 490 as the son of Pompeia (Celtic name Coupeia), the sister of Riwal (or Rigwal), paramount chief of the Dumnonii (who inhabited south-western

Britain as well as Armorica). Like his contemporary St Sampson (q.v.), Tugual is alleged to have been brought up in St Illtyd's monastery at Llantwit. At some time between 520 and 530 (by which time his cousin, Deroch, had succeeded Riwal) he is said to have crossed to Armorica in the company of his mother and 72 monks. The religious house he set up was known as Lan Pabu ('Lan' denoting church land and 'Pabu' — or 'Father' — being the title accorded to the saint). Several evangelistic journeys ensued, and the folk memory of the inclusion in these travels of a visit to Herm might possibly account for the dedication of its chapel — though Tugual's influence is said to have been so considerable in the Armorican area generally that upwards of 50 churches or chapels were named after him. Local folklore in the Côtes du Nord also states that about the year 532 his establishment of another monastery (Lan Trecor) led to the growth around it of the city of Tréguier, of which he thus emerges as founder. King Childebert, when visited by Tugual, is said to have confirmed his right to the lands he held and to have had him consecrated bishop, so that Tréguier became a cathedral city. It is supposed that Tugual died in 564. Popular hagiography also credits the saint with being Bishop of Lexovium as well, and even claims that he made a pilgrimage to Rome, where he was elevated to the Papacy as Pope Leo V. (This tale most likely owes much to his appelation 'Pabu' becoming confused with 'Papa' or 'Pope', while the name 'Leo' is suspiciously similar to the district of Léon, where Lan Pabu was located. How the number 'V' came to be attributed to him, however, is baffling, as two-and-a-half centuries later the famous Leo who crowned Charlemagne was only the third of that name.) While in the ninth century Tréguier was being sacked by Norsemen under the Jarl Hasting, the Bishop (Gorennan) fled and, taking St Tugual's body with him, conveyed it to Chartres. Finally, it was bruited abroad that during Tréguier's eventual reconstruction a carpenter called Goeder fell from high scaffolding during the rebuilding of the cathedral — but escaped unscathed when his workmates invoked St Tugual.

TUPPER, FERDINAND BROCK (1795-1874). *Guernsey's historian par excellence.* (E). He was born in 1795 to Elizabeth (*née* Brock), the wife of John Elisha Tupper (1764-1845) and hence was the nephew of both Sir Isaac and Daniel de Lisle Brock (qq.v.), as well as the elder brother of Jurat Henry Tupper (q.v.). Ferdinand Brock Tupper came of old Huguenot stock known variously as Töpper in Germany, Toupard in France and the Low Countries and Tupper in the Channel Isles, Great Britain, North America and the British Commonwealth, his forebears having been exiled from their home in Hesse-Cassel by the Emperor Charles V in 1522 because of their Protestant beliefs. Ferdinand (whose family became armigerous — with the motto *'L'Espoir est ma force'* — as a result of the award granted by George IV to his father John Elisha in 1826) was not only descended from John Tupper (q.v.*), who had earned great distinction at Cap La Hogue in 1692, but was also kinsman to Martin Farquhar Tupper (1810-1889), of *Proverbial Philosophy* fame.

Ferdinand Brock Tupper earned undying renown as a result of his outstanding work as an historian during a decade of furious creative activity between 1845 and 1854. In the former of these years there appeared his memorial to his famous uncle in his *Life and Correspondence of Major-General Sir Isaac Brock*, which ran to a second edition in 1847. Then in 1849 came the *Chronicles of Castle Cornet*, followed in 1854 by his magnum opus, *The History of Guernsey and its Bailiwick*, which he described in the preface as a sequel to the *Chronicles*. A second edition (seen through the press by his daughter Henrietta in 1876) incorporated the many corrections, improvements and additions with which he had annotated the copy of his first edition which is preserved in the Priaulx Library. (It was during this same creative decade, incidentally, that Ferdinand, on the death of his mother in 1848, inherited his parents' residence of Les Côtils. Finding its upkeep beyond his purse, however, he sold it to his brother Henry.)

Besides enjoying the reputation of being the most accurate of Guernsey historians, Tupper also has the distinction of being the first native of the island to produce a Bailiwick history, all previous historical or annalistic contributions having been the work of English birds of passage, such as Peter Heylyn (q.v.: 1629), John Warburton (1682), Thomas Dicey (1751), William Berry (1815), John Jacob (1830) and Jonathan Duncan (q.v.: 1843). Moreover, his *History* has the merit of being extremely readable throughout its 600 pages, the literary style being invariably attractive.

Ferdinand Tupper performed his most important service as an historian in unearthing and editing the letters written to her true-love, Sir William Temple, by Dorothy (1627-1695), the spirited daughter of Sir Peter Osborne (q.v.), the perusal of which threw new light on the period of the Civil War. Besides making some limited use of these letters in his *History*, Tupper embodied them in his book *Chronicles of Castle Cornet*, which as a result not only deals very thoroughly with the general history of the fortress, but is especially rich in vivid detail of the prolonged (and seemingly interminable) siege when it stood out for the king from March 1643 until December 1651. Ferdinant Brock Tupper died in 1874, leaving his daughter Henrietta as his literary executrix.

TUPPER, JURAT HENRY (1809-1875). *A human dynamo of vision and verve*. (E). The youngest son of John Elisha Tupper and his wife Elizabeth (*née* Brock) and the brother of Ferdinand Brock Tupper (q.v.), Henry Tupper was born into a family about to experience a series of tragic traumas. The year 1812, when he was only three, saw his mother's famous brother Sir Isaac Brock (q.v.) killed in action in Canada, as was also the fiancé of his sister Henrietta (Lieutenant Jones) who fell in Spain; while his eldest brother John Elisha (aged 20) was drowned in the Mediterranean. When he was six — in 1815 — his 16-year-old brother Charles James was drowned at Spithead, while when he was a youth of 17 in 1826 yet another brother (William Elisha) died of wounds received in action against Greek pirates near Crete. His coming of age in 1830 was lugubriously marked by a further brother, William de Vic Tupper (29 years of age) being hacked to pieces by Indians while on service with the Chilean Army. During his early manhood his brother Brock (aged 30) died at sea while Henry was 24 — and three years later an identical fate befell his brother Frederick (aged 33).

In 1845 Henry Tupper, in his capacity as the Lieutenant-Colonel commanding the North Regiment of the Royal Guernsey Militia, was one of those officers who, involved in a confrontation with the unpopular Lieutenant-Governor Major-General William Napier (q.v.), resigned their commissions by way of protest, stating their readiness, if necessary, to serve in the ranks. In his case, however, a way out of this embarrassing eventuality was found by representing that the proportions of his somewhat ample frame were such that no private soldier's uniform was available big enough to fit him!

The year of this contretemps saw the death of Henry's father, John Elisha Tupper, and Ferdinand Brock Tupper inherited the family home of Les Côtils on the death three years later of John Elisha's widow Elizabeth. Not long after this Henry bought the property from his brother (who found it too expensive to maintain), pulled down the old house and built a new one which now forms the nucleus of the present-day complex — various additions having been made by Les Sœurs de la Présentation, who acquired the premises in 1904.

After settling in at Les Côtils, Henry performed the first of his many signal services for his fellow islanders. In 1851 he started to direct his energies towards expediting the creation of a deep-water harbour, proposals for which had been hanging fire since 1830 when Henry's uncle, Daniel de Lisle Brock (q.v.), the Bailiff of that time, had favoured such improvements. So enthusiastically did he throw himself into campaigning for the project, that he succeeded in persuading the States to sanction a scheme prepared by a well-known engineer named Rendel. The foundation stone was laid and work put in hand two years later (24 August 1853).

In 1857 Henry Tupper was elected a Jurat of the Royal Court and almost immediately he was again active in good works. Thanks to his initiative and persuasiveness, the following year saw the institution of a telegraph service via submarine cable between Guernsey and England, which was inaugurated on 7 September 1858, when a message was delivered in London within 40 minutes of dispatch in the island. In the same year the States, spurred on by this enlightened Jurat's forceful advocacy, approached Trinity House regarding the erection of a lighthouse on Les Hanois Reef. Trinity House responded by agreeing to build a lighthouse provided Guernsey came within the jurisdiction of the Elder Brethren and also undertook to pay the coasting rate instead of the overseas rate. Henry, however, did not relish the inroads into the Bailiwick's autonomy which such an undertaking might imply and launched himself into advancing arguments designed to demonstrate that in 1858 the overseas rate had actually come to more than the coasting rate — and was so convincing that Trinity House retracted this requirement. The foundation stone for the 100 foot lighthouse was laid on 15 August 1860, and the light first shone on 8 December 1862.

In 1860 Jurat Henry Tupper was elected President of the Royal Guernsey Agricultural and Horticultural Society, and remained until such until 1868. It was during his period of office — in 1866 — that the first mowing and harvesting machines were seen in action in Guernsey. He died in 1875, and his body was buried in the imposing vault on the left-hand side of the Monument Road Entrance to Candie Cemetery. He is commemorated by the Caen Stone Pulpit in the Town Church which was given by Major and Mrs. Charles le Mesurier Carey in his memory.

TUPPER, MAJOR-GENERAL JOHN (1727–1795). *Guernsey's illustrious Commandant of Marines.* (E). Grandson of John Tupper of Cap la Hogue fame (q.v.*) and great-uncle to the eminent historian Ferdinand Brock Tupper (q.v.), Major-General John Tupper was born in 1727 to Elizabeth (*née* Dobrée), the wife of Daniel Tupper. Later in life he became the first Guernseyman to attain the rank of major-general in the British forces, where he also became Commandant-in-Chief of the Royal Marines. He entered this corps by purchase in 1747 at the age of 20. Ten years later, during the Seven Years War, he served as a captain at Sir Edward Hawke's defeat of the French fleet at Quiberon Bay in 1757; while in the War of American Independence he commanded a battalion — now being a major — at Bunker's Hill in 1775. It was in this engagement (where Tupper was wounded) that the Marines so distinguished themselves as to win the laurel encircling their device. Later in the same war Tupper participated as a lieutenant-colonel on 12 April 1782 in Admiral Rodney's victory at the Battle of the Saints, having been especially sent from England to command the 4,000-strong Marine contingent in the event of its being landed on any of the enemy's West Indian Islands.

Major-General John Tupper died in London on 26 January 1795 at the age of 67, his vitality sapped by grief at the loss of his only son, Lieutenant Carré Tupper, R.N. This bereavement meant that for the short time thereafter remaining to him, the Major-General's nearest male kin was his brother, Elisha Tupper (1720–1802). This latter, after 40 years' prominence in Guernsey's commercial life, had on the eve of the French Revolution become so extensively involved in the trade which Jersey initiative had built up between that island and Newfoundland that a Jersey-built ship launched in June 1789 had been named *Tupper* in his honour.

V

DE VERNON, GUILLAUME (*c.* 1087–*c.* 1162). *The Seigneur of Sark who founded the Priory of St Magloire.* Guillaume de Vernon, who derived his name from his land-holding at Vernon-sur-Seine (an important Norman frontier fortress), was the second son of Richard de Reviers, to whom Henry I had granted lands in Devon, the Isle of Wight and the Cotentin (the last-named including Sark) in return for services rendered during his struggle for the control of England and Normandy culminating in his victory over his brother Robert at Tenchebrai in 1106. On the death of de Reviers in 1107, his elder son Baudouin inherited his English lands, and his younger son Guillaume his Norman ones. Such an inheritance coming to an adult in 1107 indicates the likelihood of birth *c.* 1086–87.

It was in all probability under Guillaume de Vernon that the creation occurred in Sark of the five sub-fiefs, of the existence of which there is a 14th-century record. One of these tenants (who had the obligation of providing boats for carrying the Seigneur's grain to the Norman mainland) was Oliver de Barneville, a knight who served under Guillaume. While Guillaume was Seigneur, several *hôtes* settled in Sark — villeins granted land on favourable terms to encourage them to migrate to peripheral areas. Proof of the existence of an island community at the time is furnished by the appointment of a parish priest to minister to the spiritual needs of the islanders.

About 1160, sensing the approach of death, Guillaume de Vernon donated to the Abbey of Montebourg in the Cotentin (the abbey where his father's body was buried) the revenue from the *enclos* and water-mill of Sark, as well as from five *vergées* of land outside the *enclos*, provided the abbey maintained a monk in the island responsible for saying masses for the soul of Guillaume, his wife Lucie de Tancarville, his parents and his children. Guillaume also gave straw for heating the cell and pasture land to support the anchorite, who became known as the Prior of St Magloire, with a chapel near the site of the present-day house of Le Manoir. Successive priors continued to be appointed for the next two centuries — until Sark was finally abandoned in 1373 following devastating French raids. The future welfare of his soul thus ensured, Guillaume de Vernon died *c.* 1162.

DE VERNON, RICHARD (*c.* 1135–*c.* 1206). *The Seigneur whose Sark holding twice escheated to the Crown*. The son and heir of Guillaume de Vernon (q.v.), Richard inherited his father's holdings on the latter's death, whereupon he confirmed his parent's grant to the Abbey of Montebourg and in addition supplemented the provision made for the solitary Prior of St Magloire with an annual remittance of 30 sols of Anjou, to be deducted by his *prévôt* from his Sark revenues and paid to the monk.

Richard de Vernon was a victim of the tumultuous circumstances of his day. The accommodation between Prince John – later King John (q.v.) – and Philip Augustus of France, arrived at after Cœur de Lion had been imprisoned in Austria in 1192, whereby the French monarch took into his hands the whole of Upper Normandy save for the town of Rouen, put Richard in a most embarrassing position as the area involved included Vernon-sur-Seine, to retain which he gave his allegiance to Philip. On the release of Cœur de Lion in 1194 the English king ordered the seizure of the fiefs of Néhon and Sark as the escheats of a traitor. After Prince John's reconciliation with his brother, however, de Vernon was reinstated. In this connection he found it necessary in 1196 to visit Sark for the purpose of clearing up difficulties arising from the loss and subsequent recovery of the fief. While in the island he signed a further charter – the ceremony taking place in the chapel of St Magloire – confirming his donations to the monastery and the anchorite, such reaffirmation being made necessary by the recent vicissitudes which had attended his land-holdings.

Richard de Vernon's recovery of his fiefs was short-lived. On John's loss of continental Normandy (and, for a short while, also of the islands themselves) to Philip Augustus in 1204, de Vernon once more made his submission to the victorious French monarch – to which John retorted by the seizure of Sark, which yet again escheated to the Crown, to be for all practical purposes (albeit unofficially) made over to Eustace the Monk (q.v.). The lone monk from Montebourg remained, however, though he was thenceforward required to say masses for the souls of the kings of England rather than for those of the de Vernons.

DE VIC, SIR HENRY, BARONET (1597–1672). *The Guernseyman who rose to 'walk with Kings', before whom he interceded for his island*. (F). Born in November 1597 to Elizabeth (*née* Pageot), the second wife of Jean de Vic (q.v.), who, however,

died during his infancy, Henry de Vic was brought up in the home of his stepfather, Henry Masham. As a youth, he was sent to England in the care of his second cousin William de Vic (1572–1615: previously Procureur), who was 25 years his senior. Thanks most likely to William's connections with Sir Thomas Edmunds (later in 1616 Ambassador in Paris and in 1624 Treasurer of the Royal Household), who was nephew-by-marriage to George Villiers (in 1618 created Duke of Buckingham), Henry de Vic became known to Buckingham and through him, to the royal entourage. As early as 1617, at the age of 20, Henry wrote to Villiers soliciting the release of various Channel Island ships, signing himself, 'Your affectionate friend'. He was obviously already moving in circles favouring advancement. In the same year, incidentally, he sold 'La Bigoterie' in Berthelot Street to Philip de Beauvoir.

After the failure of Buckingham's Ile de Rhé expedition of 1627, Charles I employed de Vic to negotiate with the Duc de Rohan and the Huguenots for cooperation in helping to raise the siege of La Rochelle. After marrying Margaret, the daughter of Sir Philippe de Carteret, Seigneur of Saint Ouen and of Sark (q.v.), Henry became a Gentleman of the Duke of Buckingham's Bedchamber, but after his master's assassination in August 1628 he was taken on as Secretary by Lord Conway. During this period he was called upon to defend Guernsey's liberties in the King's Court and also to buy and ammunition for the island's defence. Thanks to his intervention the martial law imposed by Sir Peter Osborne (q.v.) was done away with in 1628, though he was not able to secure any reimbursement from the Crown for the outlay of £1,393 incurred by the Guernesiais in billeting troops.

In 1638, while Henry was in Paris, his half-sister Martha, wife of Jacques de Havilland, obtained a Court Order on her brother's behalf forbidding anyone to tie his or her horse to his garden wall at La Plaiderie. The following year he petitioned the king for the grant of La Braye du Valle with a view to its reclamation – anticipating Sir John Doyle (q.v.) by two centuries – but the project was still-born, being overtaken by events. Shortly afterwards Henry was knighted by Charles I and appointed His Majesty's Agent in Brussels. He remained at this post for many years, during which, on 3 September 1649, Charles II, in exile at St Germain, created him a baronet: most likely as a sop to compensate for arrears of pay. Although reduced to sore straits, Sir Henry contrived to survive, remaining in Brussels until the Restoration — and in the meanwhile becoming a widower on the death of Lady de Vic in 1654.

At the Restoration Sir Henry had the delicate task of offering Charles II propitiatory congratulations on behalf of the States of Guernsey, who through him sought 'indemnity and oblivion' for the island's adherence to the Cromwellian cause. For his own unfailing devotion, the king made him Chancellor of the Garter to the See of Salisbury (an honour rarely conferred on a layman), as well as appointing him his Secretary for the French Tongue and Agent to the King of Denmark. In 1662 he was made Comptroller of the Duke of York's Household at a salary of £400 per annum. Shortly afterwards, in the light of what he himself described as *'l'affection que j'ay eu pour notre pauvre pays'*, the States begged him to persuade Charles to renew Guernsey's ancient charters, and to authorize the deportation of paupers, thieves and vagabonds to either the American plantations or to the Kingdom of Ireland. He did not succeed in obtaining permission to transport unwanted riff-raff, but in 1667 he ultimately managed to prevail upon the king not only to ratify and confirm previous charters, but also to amplify them. For this service the States in December 1667 voted that the island's gratitude to Sir Henry be officially recorded in the public register, to the effect that 'during the many years in which your talents raised you to honourable employments in the Courts of three of our Kings, you have repeatedly asked and obtained of their Majestys, whenever so desired, not only the renewal and amplification of our Charters and privileges, but all other decrees and ordinances which could contribute to the happiness of this poor island, and this without thought of personal advantage or private gain'.

At this time Sir Henry was living in London, where his daughter Anne Charlotte married Lord Frecheville, becoming later in life when a widow one of the Ladies of the Bedchamber to Queen Anne. After his daughter's wedding Sir Henry retired to Windsor where he made his will, bequeathing, *inter alia*, £10 to the poor of the parish of St Peter-Port and asking for burial in St George's Chapel. On the evening of 21 November 1672 (his 75th birthday), while talking to his nephew Jacques de Havilland and to Charles Andros, Seigneur d'Anneville, he 'was taken upon a sudden with a dimness of his eyes'. After saying, *'La Volonté du Seigneur soit faite'*, he became speechless with 'an apoplex' and died at half-past-three the next morning. Contrary to his wishes, his body was buried in Westminster Abbey on 24 November.

DE VIC, JEAN (*c.* 1550–*c.* 1601). *A chequered career: gaoled by the Governor and widowed by witchcraft!* (F). The son of Richard de Vic (one of the Jurats who fomented and led the anti-Huguenot street riots in April 1564), Jean de Vic on 15 March 1580 married Anne Careye, daughter of the Seigneur de Blanchelande and three years later, in addition to the children she bore him, he assumed responsibility as guardian of the offspring of his deceased eponymous cousin on the remarriage of his widow.

Appointed Greffier to the Royal Court soon after his marriage, de Vic was imprudent enough in 1589 to oppose the formidable Sir Thomas Leighton (q.v.), after which, apprehensive of the outcome of his temerity, he was so afraid to face the Governor that he fled into hiding and absented himself from a meeting to which he was summoned. On 18 October Leighton sent troops to force an entry into de Vic's house and, finding that he was not there, raised a hue and cry, requiring anyone who knew the fugitive's whereabouts to 'runne at him, apprehend him, or follow him with the cry of Haro', that he might be brought to the Governor dead or alive. At this juncture Jean de Vic, fearful of incriminating his friends, gave himself up, praying the benefit of the law. Leighton nevertheless consigned him to imprisonment without trial in Castle Cornet — and only released him after the Privy Council responded to an appeal by ruling that his prerogative extended only to martial offences and not to civil ones.

Becoming Procureur in 1593, Jean de Vic was left a widower on 28 June of the following year when his wife Anne Careye died suddenly and mysteriously. Witchcraft on the part of an ill-disposed agent of Satan was suspected and in his *Guernsey Folklore* Sir Edgar MacCulloch (q.v.) relates that four weeks to the day after Anne's death an unfortunate female scapegoat (Marie Martin, alias Salmon) was sentenced by the Royal Court to be burned at the stake forthwith 'until her body was reduced to ashes', for having 'compassed the death of the said Anne, as well as divers others, by her sorcery'. On 15 December of the same year, de Vic sought consolation in the arms of a new bride, Elizabeth Pageot, and two and a half years after this he was elected a Jurat of the Royal Court. He did not, however, live very long thereafter, dying about 1601.

By his first wife Jean de Vic had (*inter alia*) a daughter, Marguerite, who married William

Briard, the son of the privateer Jean Briard (q.v.). Their daughter Rachel married Jean de Sausmarez (q.v.*), the Dean who imposed Anglicanism in Guernsey. By his second wife he became the father of Sir Henry de Vic, Baronet (q.v.), who achieved fame and fortune as a courtier to Charles I and Charles II.

DE VIC, LOUIS (c. 1540–1607). *The Procureur who was assailed by cut-throats and left for dead in a Westminster gutter: but lived to become Bailiff.* (F). The date when Louis de Vic was born is uncertain, but bearing in mind that his father Laurent died in 1557, that his paternal aunt (his father's elder sister) married before 1537, and that his paternal uncle Thomas was a Jurat as early as 1520, plus the fact that he himself married in 1565, it is a reasonable assumption to place his birth around the year 1540. Marrying Perotine Guille in 1565, de Vic was serving as St Peter-Port Parish Constable three years later, when it was recounted that he broke the head of an insubordinate parishioner at a general muster. Two years after this incident in 1570, he was brought before the Church Court on a charge of adultery, but was acquitted.

On 24 July 1578 Louis de Vic was appointed as Procureur de la Royne, becoming the right-hand-man of the Governor, Thomas Leighton (q.v.), who described him as 'a very honest and sufficient man and the best servant to Her Majesty that ever I found in the isle'. Within three years this energetic official found himself at the centre of a storm arising out of an Order-in-Council of 1581 which provided that probate and the administration of the revenues of vacant benefices should be ordered by the Bishop of Winchester. In the light of this the Bishop appointed the Procureur as his Commissary to deal with Wills and other ecclesiastical business. Outraged by this episcopal intrusion into their Presbyterian establishment, the Ministers sought to discredit de Vic by indicting him as being 'a troubler of the Ministry and the Church'. Besides resuscitating the accusations of violence on his part when dealing as parish constable with an obstreperous parishioner (and also the adultery charge of which he had been cleared), it was alleged that he had refused to obey a summons before the Consistory and struck the elder who brought it — an assault that de Vic admitted, pleading strong provocation — and furthermore that he had roughly accosted a minister, charging him with preaching a factious and seditious sermon (who which the Procureur retorted that

the sermon had in very truth been seditious). Holding that 'whether all ministers should be on an egality or that a bishop should be a superintendant over them . . . is a thing that toucheth not salvation', Leighton sprang to his lieutenant's defence, telling Walsingham that the complaints stemmed from 'the office of Commissary that he holdeth under the Bishop rather than the vices of the man or his troubling of the Church or Ministers'. These representations convinced Walsingham of the hollowness of the accusations and de Vic was vindicated.

During this confrontation with the ecclesiastical authorities, Louis de Vic was busily engaged on a prolonged investigation into Guernsey's 'Droit Normand'. The indefinite and fluid state of local law on which Adrian de Saravia (q.v.) had commented disparagingly in 1565 ultimately led the Privy Council in 1581 to require the Royal Court and the Procureur to draw up a report as the laws, customs and usages of the Bailiwick, to the extent that they differed from the Grand Coutumier de Normandie from ancient times observed in the islands. This difficult task threw a heavy burden on de Vic's shoulders, for whereas its adequate performance called for a body of jurists, the fact of the matter was that none of the court apart from the Bailiff (Thomas Wigmore, who was Leighton's nephew), and himself had received any legal education — and even in their cases it was rudimentary. Nevertheless the undertaking was completed and the resulting compilation, approved, by Elizabeth I in 1582, forms the frequently cited *Approbation des Lois, Coutumes et Usages de l'Ile de Guernesey*.

A dispute which bade fair to cost Louis de Vic his life arose in 1586 when the Governor seized four French ships in St Peter-Port, believing them to have Spanish goods on board. The Royal Court immediately declared the seizure invalid on the grounds of the neutrality accorded to Guernsey a century earlier by the 1480 Bull of Pope Sixtus IV (q.v.). Leighton, however, declined to release the ships and the court appealed to the Privy Council — which upheld its ruling and instructed Leighton that no such arrest should again be made to the prejudice of the island's privileges. Leighton now complained to the Privy Council that his nephew the Bailiff and the Jurats had taken advantage of this dispute to levy slanderous charges of tyranny against him, and as a result the Bailiff and Jurats were summoned to London in 1587. To present the case for the Governor Louis de Vic also went to London in his capacity as Procureur. The accused having hired two men to murder de Vic, he was attacked in Westminster and left for dead, but recovered. The upshot was that the Bailiff and the Jurats were consigned to the Marshalsea, de Vic's chief assailant (a ruffian named Rousewell) was set in the pillory in Guernsey, and de Vic himself was appointed as the new Bailiff on 2 December 1588,

During his time in the Bailiff's chair, de Vic presided over the case in 1594 when it was alleged that the wife of his cousin Jean de Vic (q.v.) — who held his old post of Procureur — had died because of the evil spells of a witch. The following year he incurred the censure of the local hierarchy because of his refusal to pronounce a sentence when he disapproved of the Jurats' findings. The Jurats had in fact given a decision so obviously partial against the Crown that the Bailiff (still Leighton's man) 'stayed to pronounce a sentence so corrupt and prejudicial to the Queen's Royal Prerogative'.

After nearly 12 years in Guernsey's supreme office Louis de Vic resigned in 1600, '*à cause de sa maladie, faut d'usage de ses mains et faiblesse de sa vue et forces*'. In 1603 he sold to Jacques de Beauvoir the estate of Les Granges at the top of the Rohais — which as a result ultimately came into the hands of the famous 'Roundhead' leader, Pierre de Beauvoir (q.v.). Louis de Vic died in 1607.

W

WAHLSTATT, H.S.H. GEBHARD GUSTAV LE-BRECHT, PRINZ BLÜCHER VON WAHLSTATT (1836-1916). *Herm's Serene Highness*. In 1889 the lease of Herm was acquired by the West Bank Leignitz of Silesia, which had as one of its major customers the fabulously wealthy Prinz Blücher von Wahlstatt, the great-grandson of the Iron Duke's ally at Waterloo. Although he was the owner of gigantic estates at Krieblowitz and Wahlstatt in Prussia, as well as others at Radun, Stauding, Stiebnik, Brisdorf and Polanka in what was then Austrian Silesia, the prince nevertheless had a passion for islands and was thus attracted to Guernsey's satellite as a desirable retreat from the cares of the world. Accordingly His Serene Higness entered into an arrangement with the bank whereby he became sub-lessee of the island, where he took up residence in 1891. This nobleman, who on succession to his title in 1875 had become an hereditary member of the Prussian House of Lords, had been born on 18 March 1836, and after a course of private education had as a young man been the military attaché to the Prussian Legation, Vienna, from 1857 to 1859. During the Austrian-Prussian War of 1866 he had fought as a first lieutenant with the Cuirassiers of the Guard, serving at the battles of Skalitz and Königgratz.

The Prince wrought considerable changes in this tiny addition to his vast lands, planting pine and spruce groves and also surrounding the Manor House with tropical plants and eucalyptus trees, as well as laying two metalled roadways and restoring St Tugual's Chapel. Furthermore, he converted the house into a rambling castellated mansion, thereby prompting the next tenant — Sir Compton Mackenzie (q.v.*) — to remark that Blücher was 'less happy as a builder than as a planter and he made the Manor House what is externally as ugly a building as may be seen in Europe'. Four years after his first arrival in Herm (in 1895), Prince Blücher married as his third wife the beautiful Wanda, Princess Radzywill — only to be followed to the altar almost immediately by his son, Count Lothair, who promptly entered into wedlock with his new step-mother's elder sister, taking over the White House Hotel as a home for his bride and himself.

Herm's insularity offered plentiful scope for one of the Prince's favourite recreations — swimming — while its many rabbits catered for the other — shooting. In addition Blücher introduced a number of wallabies to the island, and 'acclimatized them so that they increased and multiplied. Members of aristocratic houses came from far and wide to share in the sport, which, however, was strictly controlled by their host in the interest of preserving stocks. Great, therefore, was the wrath of His Serene Highness (and far his departure from serenity) when his chef and butler took advantage of his absence on one occasion to engage in a shoot themselves, almost wiping out the entire marsupial colony. Indicted under the common law of larceny, the culprits served a month's hard labour, at the end of which each wrote a contrite letter to his outraged lord and master. There must, however, have been enough survivors of the slaughter perpetrated by these domestics to permit of further breeding, as during the First World War, when a detachment of the

South Staffordshire Regiment was stationed in the island, the beasts' nocturnal leapings led to a refusal by the men to go out patrolling at night alone, so convinced were they that one of them had been attacked by a ghost!

The outbreak of war in 1914 occasioned the departure of Herm's princely tenant (who in 1909 had considered linking the island with the outside world by telephone, only to reject the idea as too expensive). A degree of confusion reigns over the circumstances under which this tenancy ended. Raoul Lemprière in his *History of the Channel Islands* represents Blücher as having been interned as an enemy alien, while Sir Compton Mackenzie in Octave V of *My Life and Times* speaks of his being deported. On the other hand, the late C. P. le Huray maintained that 'the tenancy of Prince Blücher was terminated during the First World War because he was a sub-tenant of the West Bank of Silesia. The loyalty of the Prince and his family was never in question'. Such absence of suspicion would certainly have constituted a logical attitude, bearing in mind Blücher's opposition to contemporary German political policies and the fact that his sons had served as officers in the Royal Guernsey Militia — indeed, Count Lothair, as a British subject, served as a subaltern in a labour battalion later in the conflict (in the middle of which his father died on 12 July 1916). Two certainties emerge, however. One is that, despite the affection and regard in which the Prince was held by the people of Guernsey — and his disapproval of the Kaiser's assertiveness — he was never compensated for the loss of his tenancy. The other is the fact that the Princess Wanda, who was greatly attached to Herm, took very unkindly to be compelled to leave it — and several years later Sir Compton Mackenzie was told by her sister (the Countess Lothair) that she had 'solemnly prayed to the island spirits that they would bring misfortune to the next tenant'.

WAKLEY, CYRIL FRANCIS (1902–   ). *Macte virtute*. See *Underground Resistance Heroes of the Second World War*.

WARREN, JOHN PERCY, B.Sc., F.R.G.S. (1888–1972). *The stalwart of La Société Guernesiaise*. Born on 23 October 1888, in London, John Percy Warren came to Guernsey in 1912 (after taking the degree of Bachelor of Science at the University of London) with a view to taking up an appointment at the Boys' Intermediate School (later the

Grammar School), of which he eventually became Deputy Headmaster and where he remained until his retirement in 1948. Although primarily a geographer — in which subject he specialised during his teaching career — John Warren, as a man of wide culture, also took a keen interest in geology and history.

Soon after his arrival in the island which he was enthusiastically to adopt as his own, John Warren paid court to Helène de Garis Mauger, to whom he was married in 1914 on the eve of leaving for France to serve in the forces for the duration of the First World War. When he had originally come to Guernsey he had immediately joined the Society for Natural Science and Local Research — which in 1922 was to be re-named La Société Guernesiase — and on his return from the army he threw himself energetically into its activities, becoming a veritable pillar of the organisation from then until the late 1960s, leading scores of excursions arranged for its members and being thrice elected as its president.

During the inter-war years La Société, devoted as it is to the encouragement of 'interest in all aspects of Guernsey's natural and local history, geography and geology', was much beholden to John Warren for an invaluable series of erudite papers. 'Considerations upon Earthquakes' in 1926 preceded 'Alderney and Destiny' in 1928, which in its turn was followed by 'Suggestions for a Regional Survey' in 1929. Then came 'Extracts from the Journal of Elisha Dobrée' in 1930 and — in collaboration with Doctor A. E. Mourant — 'A Catalogue of Earthquakes felt in the Channel Islands' in 1936, while on the eve of the outbreak of the Second World War there appeared in 1939 'Guernsey in the 1820s'. In addition to these dissertations a geography of Guernsey entitled *Our Own Island* had also been published for general consumption in 1926.

When the German Occupation threatened, John Warren accompanied his school to its refuge in Oldham, where he shared his pupils' and colleagues' exile for the rest of the war. Becoming a member of the Channel Island Study Group, he contributed to the informed symposium, *Nos Iles*, which the Group, 'conscious of the important part which joint thought must play in shaping the future of the Channel Islands', published in March 1944.

Three years after the Liberation John Warren retired, in the sense that he no longer taught regularly at the Boys' Intermediate School, but this did not in any sense imply any cessation of exertion. Indeed, the post-Liberation period literally bristled with activity on his part. In addition to a valuable series of historical articles serialised in the *Star* newspaper, a whole stream of learned papers flowed from his pen for publication in the *Transactions* of La Société Guernesiaise, commencing with 'The Journal of John Robert' in 1946 and followed by 'The Streams of Guernsey' (1948), 'A Note on Peat in Guernsey' (1949), 'Partages des Communes de la Forêt' (1952), 'Fire Marks and Early Fire Fighting in Guernsey' and 'The Guille-Allès Library and Museum' (both 1955), 'More About Elisha Dobrée's Diary and Weather Journal' (in collaboration with Mr. J. M. David 1959), 'Torteval Church and La Seigneurie de Torteval' (1960) and 'The Evolution of the Map of Guernsey' (1961). In recognition of these massive contributions John Warren was made an Honorary Life Member of La Société. In these years also he served as a Douzenier of St Peter-Port (the Douzaine appointing him as its Representative in the States), before being elected as a Deputé du Peuple in the States in 1955 and serving as such until 1958. After ceasing to be a Deputy he was again chosen as St Peter-Port's Douzaine Representative from 1959 to 1960.

This energetic retirement was brought to a close by the poor health of his wife, which compelled John Warren to leave Guernsey in 1967 for Dundee in Scotland, the home of his daughter Elise, who was in a position to give her mother nursing care beyond the capabilities of a man of 79. There, just before Christmas in 1972, John Percy Warren died, three years after the death of his wife.

WILSON, JOHN (CHARLES?) (1780?-1866). *The outstanding figure in the architectural development of St Peter-Port*. Although Charles Brett in his *Buildings in the Town and Parish of St Peter-Port* considers that John Wilson's 'life and career remain a total mystery' (there being no trace of him in the records of the Royal Institute of British Architects); yet H. M. Colvin in his *Biographical Dictionary of English Architects* remarks that his design for a Place d'Armes in Alderney manifests the style of draughtsmanship of one trained by the Royal Engineers – and consequently postulates the likelihood of this main creator of St Peter-Port's architectural milieu being identical with the John Wilson who retired from the Royal Arsenal in 1845. This John Wilson appears to have been the son of a Cumbrian stone mason, born *c.* 1780, who may possibly have had the second Christian name of

Charles. He could also probably be the 'J. Wilson junior' who exhibited architectural designs at the Royal Academy between 1794 and 1796.

Whatever his background, John Wilson arrived in Guernsey at the end of the Napoleonic Wars and, as an experienced and sophisticated master of Greek and Gothic Revival architecture, he completely re-shaped the central area of St Peter-Port (with especial emphasis on Fountain Street and the markets) as well as designing many other important buildings in the Town. Although his first assignment was Torteval church (1816) with its naked stone, Wilson normally built in stucco (which he called 'Roman cement'), as in the Greek Revival church of St James the Less (1817-1818) and the Tudor Gothic Elizabeth College (1826-1829). In 1822 he undertook various alterations to the Royal Court House (of which the main feature consists of the spiral staircase and domed toplight), while the next three years (1823-1826) were devoted to extensive restorations to the Town Church. Much of the market complex in his creation, the Meat Market (1822) being followed by the States' Arcade and Upper Vegetable Market (originally intended for fish) – together with the refurbishment of Fountain Street – which were completed in 1830. In the meantime he had built Springfield House in Queen's Road (then La Petite Marche) between 1825 and 1828, in which latter year he was appointed Surveyor to the Guernsey Board of Works. On stylistic grounds, Wilson is usually also credited with four other distinguished buildings in the Town in the shape of Bonamy House, Clifton (1826), Summerland House, Mount Durand (1828), Castle Carey (1828) and Grange Lodge (1830).

On the basis of references in advertisements for tenders relating to building works, Mr. George Bramall has concluded that John Wilson lived in a cottage in Les Gravées which at the time was owned by the Board of Ordnance. He is also of the opinion that late in 1830 Wilson was ordered by the Board of Ordnance to leave Guernsey for Edinburgh in the capacity of a Clerk of Works. Added weight is given to this conjecture by the marked similarity between signatures appearing on applications for forage issued in Edinburgh after 1830 and those appended to documents drawn up in Guernsey before 1829. From Edinburgh he seems eventually to have moved to Woolwich, taking up a post at the Royal Arsenal. If Guernsey's John Wilson be indeed identical with the John Wilson who retired from the self-same Royal Arsenal in 1845, it would appear from

O. F. G. Hogg's *The Royal Arsenal* that on 12 June 1839 he was promoted to the rank of First Class Clerk of Works (thereby qualifying for a salary increase of 1s. 6d. — seven-and-a-half pence in decimal coinage — per day) and on 1 July 1845 was superannuated on a pension of £200 per annum. After a retirement of over 20 years he died at Cardew Villa, Shirley, Milbrook, Hampshire in January 1866, leaving £12,000 earmarked for the purchase of an estate in what was then called Cumberland (now part of the county of Cumbria) for the benefit of a great-nephew.

WOOD, MAJOR ALEXANDER GOUGH ('PETER') (1915–   ). *Herm's enterprising tenant from 'Down Under'.* Alexander Gough Wood, invariably referred to as 'Peter', was born on 4 April 1915 in North Island, New Zealand, where his boyhood was spent on a sheep farm. While he was in his early 'teens his family moved to England, taking up residence in a house named 'Ox Barn' near Warminster in Wiltshire. Here Peter Wood finished his education, eventually entering employment as a Civil Engineering Contractor in Devonshire. Then came the Second World War and military service with the Royal Engineers — mostly overseas — from which he emerged in 1945 honorably scarred and with the rank of Major. During the conflict he had become engaged, and in April 1946 at Linton-on-Wharfe (at that time situated in the West Riding of Yorkshire, though since 1974 located in the Metropolitan County of West Yorkshire) he married Joan Joyce ('Jenny') Appleyard, the sister of Major John Geoffrey Appleyard, D.S.O., M.C., who, after leading Commando raids on Sark and the Casquets in 1942, lost his life in the Sicilian campaign on 13 July 1943.

Early in 1947, the couple acquired a stretch of farmland adjacent to their house at Linton and embarked on small-scale farming as a supplementary pursuit to Major Wood's career in charge of an agricultural department at his father-in-law's firm of motor engineers. Dispirited by the refusal of the local authority to permit them the full occupancy of their home (on the grounds that the alternative accommodation they had provided for those sharing their roof would be better used to give homes to people on the waiting list), the Woods in the spring of 1949 went to see Mr. and Mrs. Wood, senior at Ox Barn and in the course or the visit fortuitously met Mr. A. G. Jeffries, the Tenant of Herm, who told them about the island and informed them that he was prepared to dispose of the lease.

Although a subsequent visit of inspection had made his wife and himself enthusiastic about the tenancy of Herm, Peter Wood, during the ensuing negotiations with the States Board of Administration, declined to have Jeffries' lease assigned to him, regarding its terms as too onerous. Eventually an agreement was reached for a provisional tenancy over a trial period at a peppercorn rent of £10 per annum, devoid of any lease and with the condition attached that he should maintain a set of accounts for annual scrutiny by the Board, with an official lease ultimately to be drawn up taking cognisance of the heavy cost of managing Herm as revealed in these accounts and covering a period of 66 years minimum and 99 years maximum.

This interim arrangement lasted until 1952, Wood claiming that over the three years concerned he had lost money at the rate of £5,000 per annum. The lease negotiated that year was for a period of 66 years and provided for financial assistance towards the capital cost of installing public services and repairing the various buildings reduced to dilapidation by persistent neglect since the outbreak of war in 1939. In addition, it was stipulated that the States should make available an allowance of £3,000 per annum to help maintain public public services — with reimbursement coming from the proceeds of the landing tax. The rent payable to the States of Guernsey was to be on a sliding scale, rising with any increase of profits made by the Tenant, with the proviso that the entire arrangement was to be subject to a seven-year break clause in the event of the lessons of experience showing the compact to be unsatisfactory from the States' point of view.

As things turned out the break clause was never invoked, and in 1962 a fresh agreement was reached whereby the lease was extended to 2029 (80 years from the original trial tenancy of 1949), though the subvention towards maintenance costs was thenceforth to be determined on a descending scale — a decision which made inevitable some degree of commercialisation of Herm, as beautiful scenery of itself would never support a community. Accordingly the Woods set out purposefully to make their holding a going concern, identifying themselves absolutely with the island as their only source of livelihood — and doing so to such effect that at last, in 1969, 20 years after first raising it to finance essential initial capital outlay, they were finally able to clear an overdraft which had been repeatedly extended by an indulgent bank manager.

Everything became grist to the mill for the insular monopsonist. A pottery industry was started, and thrived for a time but ultimately had to be abandoned as manpower shortage rendered it uneconomic. Despite the failure of a daffodil marketing venture, however, the farm proved an abiding asset. Two hundred and fifty *vergées* in extent (reputedly the largest in the archipelago), it was given over to dairying, with a herd numbering 150 which produced about 160 gallons of milk a day — ample for the tourist-swollen population of summer and in winter yielding a surplus for export to Guernsey. The other mainstay for the economy was provided by visitors to the island. In addition to self-catering accommodation, the *White House Hotel* (originally founded by Lieutenant-Colonel M. J. Fielden in the 1870s) was considerably enlarged, so as to be capable of housing 90 guests — but the main business came from day trippers, averaging about 100,000 a year, with their patronage of the *Mermaid Tavern*, the *Ship* Restaurant, the *Belvoir Bay* and *Shell Beach* tea houses and the shops on the Piazza, all operated by the Wood family.

Major Wood also organised a school for about a dozen pupils with a full-time teacher (Herm's first educational venture since that of the Reverend Henry Benwall (q.v.*) over a 100 years previously); arranged the generation of an island electrical supply; laid a ring water main fed from springs (after suffering severely from drought at the start of his tenancy); and installed an efficient sewage system. Until 1969 he issued (very profitably) his own 'carriage labels' for the conveyance of mail to Guernsey — and thereafter (the States' Postal Authority refusing to tolerate any such infringement of its philatelic monopoly) became the Sub-Postmaster for the Guernsey Post Office in the island. Furthermore, labouring seven days a week instead of six and, like St Paul, shouldering 'beside those things that are without, that which cometh upon me daily, the care of all the churches', this adaptable Antipodean undertook the conduct of worship in the lovely old chapel of St Tugual, which he also refurbished, providing a heavy Victorian bed-sheet carrying his grandparents' initials as an Altar Cloth, while the stained-glass window was supplied by his father-in-law. Deservedly did this resourceful and energetic man earn the sobriquet of 'King Peter'.

When in 1978 King Peter handed over the management of his realm to Crown Prince Simon (without, however, abdicating) his tenancy had endured for 29 years: a length equalled only once before when Peter Carey held the island from

1737 to 1766. Each year thereafter took him ever further past Carey's term: undeniably the holder of the longest tenancy in Herm's history and (with interests also embracing several hotels in Guernsey) unquestionably the most successful.

WOOTTON, LIEUTENANT-COLONEL PATRICK ALWEN (1919–   ). *The latter-day Baden-Powell of Lihou Island.* Born in Croydon on 16 August 1919 to Elizabeth (*née* Thrale), the wife of Thomas Wootton, Patrick Wootton was educated at Hazelwood Preparatory School, Limpsfield, Surrey and subsequently (1933–1937) at Lancing College. He joined the Inns of Court Regiment as a Territorial in February 1938, and on the outbreak of war was commissioned to the Lovat Scouts in December 1939 after cavalry training with the Scots Greys at Redford Barracks in Edinburgh. An abortive attempt to land in Norway during the spring of 1940 was followed by a spell of service in the Faröes. Later in the war his regiment provided the Royal Guard at Balmoral Castle in 1943, subsequent to which training as mountain and ski troops in Wales and the Canadian Rockies preceded its disembarkation at Taranto to fight with the Eighth Army in the Italian campaign — during the course of which Wootton was promoted to Lieutenant-Colonel in 1944 at the age of 25! On the collapse of Germany the Colonel's unit moved to Austria, and thence to Greece to oppose the E.L.A.S. forces near Salonika. In Greece he founded and commanded the 181 Brigade Training Centre (which developed into the 4th Indian Division Training School) at Khalkis, north of Athens. After VJ Day he extended his service on a short-term commission, studying psychological methods of teaching during the latter part of his army career.

Returning to civilian live in 1946, Lieutenant-Colonel Wootton was selected as prospective Conservative candidate for Stoke Newington and Hackney North in 1953 and 1954, in which latter year he became married to Miss Ann Mary Blake. After his marriage he served until 1957 as Chairman of Hurstpierpoint Parish Council, on which he had previously been a councillor for several years.

A man of deep Christian conviction, resolved to devote himself to promoting the moral welfare of youth, Lieutenant-Colonel Patrick Wootton (who had purchased a summer house in Alderney in 1958) acquired the lease of Lihou in 1961 with the specific idea of making use of Guernsey's western appendage for the furtherance of this design, convinced (as he himself later said) that the island's isolation would help youngsters 'to sort out the priorities in their lives in peace and quiet'. The gallant Colonel and his lady did not, however, actually take up permanent residence in the Bailiwick until 1964 — though once settled, no time was lost in implementing their plans which had already been formulated. The very next year the Lihou Youth Project was launched with the holding of the first of an annual series of summer camps for young people over the age of 17. The camps were normally of a fortnight's duration — with two usually held each summer — and were aimed both at training youth leaders and also at fostering a life-style based on a spiritual outlook, a scientific interest and a sense of social responsibility; with the ultimate intention that once trained, the leaders would organise similar groups in their own localities. The organisation was later re-named the Lihou Youth Fellowship and Colonel Wootton wrote *Lihou, the Holy Island* and *The Story of Lihou Island* to promote its ideals.

In pursuance of the Fellowship's aims, studies embracing ornithology, entomology, marine biology and meteorology were organised for the campers. Archaeology was also incorporated into the programme with the investigation of the ruins of the Priory of St Mary, the site of which was cleaned up during the very first season (1965), with débris and overgrowth removed, while the next year the floor area was cleared and a survey made of the general layout of the buildings. In 1978 Lieutenant-Colonel Wootton invited Mr. Ken Barton to direct an excavation of the ruins undertaken by the campers with the co-operation of La Société Guernesiaise and help from the Ancient Monuments Committee. Well aware, however, of what 'all work and no play' does to Jack, the Colonel made arrangements for recreational pursuits such as swimming and rock-climbing by day and campfire sing-songs of an evening, while from time to time parties of handicapped children were entertained.

The camps held in July and August 1982, attended by youth from Spain, Italy, Belgium and and United Kingdom, were honoured by a visit from His Excellency the Lieutenant-Governor and provided the occasion for the publication of an anthology of poems written by participants in the Project over the years since 1965 (and with a Foreword by the Bishop of Winchester) entitled *The Silence of Lihou is Wonderful to Listen To*. At the same time, however, Lieutenant-Colonel Wootton announced that the future of the Project was problematical, remarking that (despite the support accorded by the group called 'The Friends of Lihou Fellowship') the people of Guernsey

had 'never really grasped the idea' of the camps, and by and large the scheme had not been encouraged by the island's authorities.

In addition to his endeavours on behalf of youth Lieutenant-Colonel Wootton was also responsible for introducing sheep farming to Lihou with the importation thither of a hardy strain originating in the Orkney island of North Ronaldsay capable of subsisting on vraic. By July 1982 the herd consisted of 20 ewes, four rams and 25 lambs. Less successful was a Lihou Island stamp-issuing venture, terminated by the point-blank refusal of the States of Guernsey Postal Authority to tolerate infringement of its monopoly. Better fortune attended the enterprise which this imaginative philanthropist initiated on the Guernsey mainland with his foundation of the Tropical Gardens on a site including the Germans' Mirus Battery at Les Rouvets in St Saviour's. The gallant Colonel also founded Guernsey's Alternative Energy Society, of which he became the first Chairman and (later) the first honorary member.

In May 1980 Lieutenant-Colonel Wootton found himself at loggerheads with the Douzaine of St Pierre du Bois arising from his refusal to pay Occupier's Rate on Lihou Island. From the premise that the terms of his lease clearly identified Lihou as a separate island, he claimed that it no more came within the jurisdiction of any parish than did Jethou (also held on a 'fee-farm' lease). He therefore maintained that no rate payment was owed to St Pierre du Bois — and added that, even if parochial taxation *were* payable, the amount involved would be more than offset by compensation due to him for expenditure incurred in providing services for tourists, such as clearing up their litter, succouring those stranded by the rising tide, and even maintaining the causeway linking Lihou to Guernsey. For its part the Douzaine decided to submit a *requête* to the States to establish once for all whether or not Lihou Island fell within the parish of St Pierre du Bois.

The resultant ruling, made in 1981, was unfavourable to Colonel Wootton who, however, had by that time emigrated to Prince Edward Island in Canada, where he had purchased two islands off Murray Harbour on which he had set up a branch of the International Trust for Constructive Living — an organisation designed to promote the 'Lihou concept' internationally. Before leaving for the New World, he had presented La Société Guernesiaise with two fields in St Pierre du Bois of an area totalling seven-and-a-half *vergées* to be held in perpetuity for the people of Guernsey 'in recognition of the kindness I have received at the hands of many people in Guernsey and the happiness I and my family have enjoyed during 20 years in the island'. Back in the Bailiwick in 1982 for that year's camps he said that, even if the Project came to an end, Lihou Island might still be used as an 'occasional home' for himself, his family and his friends — but that it was likely that Les Rouvets Tropical Gardens would have to be put on the market because of their 'greater need for "on-the-spot" owner participation'. In the event, however, July 1983 saw the island's lease put up for sale: a chapter in its history had come to an end.

ADDENDA

MOULLIN, THOMAS (1831–1927). Born at Les Baissières in 1831, Thomas Moullin followed up a period of apprenticeship to a builder and carpenter by moving to London in 1854 in search of fame and fortune. Marrying Rachel Rose soon afterwards and still working as a builder and carpenter, Moullin, in order to eke out resources, took in as a lodger at his Stepney home another carpenter named Thomas Hurry, under whose influence he became attracted to the idea of promoting insurance. Such a project had especial appeal because of the prospects it afforded of helping the unfortunate — for whom, as a devout Methodist, Moullin felt a keen sense of compassion. The upshot was that in July 1864 Moullin, Hurry and five other associates each subscribed £50 and the Pearl Life Assurance Loan and Investment Company Limited came into existence: an organisation which (as Pearl Assurance P.L.C. with funds of £35 million) has grown to be one of the major concerns in the realm of insurance. Indeed, within Moullin's own lifetime — by the year 1918 when he retired — it already enjoyed an annual premium income in excess of £4¾ million. He visited his native isle regularly, staying at Annesley in Candie Road. Thomas Moullin died at his Ealing home in 1927 at the magnificent age of 96.

PHILLIPS, THOMAS (1635–1693). A military engineer whose cartographical work was praised by Lord Macaulay (1850–1859) for being 'so exact that the houses may be counted', Thomas Phillips was in the Channel Isles during 1679 and 1680 engaged in making maps and plans of the bays and probable landing places, as well as of defences both existing and required. His plans of Guernsey, Jersey, Sark and Herm, together with a description of the several harbours, bays, landing places and castles of Guernsey, illustrated by coloured plans and executed in 1680, are in the British Museum. He died on 23 November 1693, from the after-effects of a terrible explosion (what a later age called 'shell-shock'), on board H.M.S. *Norwich* (Captain John Benbow) anchored in Guernsey roadstead after an attack on St Malo during the War of the League of Augsburg.

SCALES, MICHAEL JOHN (1951–   ). *A dauntless life-saver, defying 'the raging winds and the roaring sea'*. Michael John Scales was born on 5 February 1951, to Lena Ivy (*née* Lowe), the wife of Edwin John Scales, and attended successively Amherst, the Castel and the Vale Primary Schools before completing his education at the Boys' Grammar School. He went from the classroom to the Merchant Navy, subsequently being employed on the Herm Ferries before taking up in 1973 the post of Boatman in charge of the launch *Lady Hayward*, with which the late Sir Charles Hayward (q.v.) maintained communications between Guernsey and his home in Jethou.

This courageous islander was to earn undying fame as a result of his daring feats while serving with Guernsey's lifeboat. After participating in the tricky and hazardous sortie to the oil rig *Orion* when it was stranded at Grandes Rocques on 1 February 1978, the exploit which made his name a household word occurred shortly before Christmas in 1981. On Sunday 13 December of that year the *Sir William Arnold* under his command as Coxswain answered a distress call from the Equadorian motor vessel *Bonita*, which reported that she was lurching helplessly in mountainous seas. A hurricane force wind was blowing from the south and driving snow reduced visibility to no more than 200 yards. Nevertheless the lifeboat pressed ahead at full speed, reaching the storm-tossed vessel at dusk and finding that, floundering amid 50 foot waves, the victim had a list of 45 degrees, it was thus compelled to go right up to her transom stern to effect a rescue. During the next three and a half hours, the turbulent seas notwithstanding and despite pitch darkness and bitter cold, the Coxswain and his heroic crew made no less than 50 approaches to the stricken craft, succeeding thereby in saving 29 lives. For his devotion and gallantry Michael Scales was awarded the Royal National Lifeboat Institution's Gold Medal — the highest award in its power to give. He and his comrades received their decorations from H.R.H. Princess Alice, Dowager Duchess of Gloucester, at a ceremony at the Royal Festival Hall on 1 May 1982, which was attended by His Excellency the Lieutenant-Governor who by his presence sought to demonstrate his admiration for the sterling qualities exhibited by these magnificent men on their perilous mission of mercy.

The intrepid Guernseyman gave further proof of his bravery and superb seamanship on Tuesday 24 January 1984, when his lifeboat dashed to the succour of the Liberian steamship *Radiant Med* which, battered by heavy seas, had been brought to the point of sinking by a shift in her cargo. Technically the vessel was in the French rescue area and was attended by a French ship which was attempting to take her into Cherbourg and had originally signalled that no aid was required. As a consequence the ability of the *Sir William Arnold* to be of help was severely curtailed, as by the time that she was summoned the situation had become desperate. Nevertheless Coxswain Scales and his crew retrieved nine survivors, half dead from exposure, who were found adrift in the wreck's boat, awash and sinking in a savage tempest south-west of Les Hanois; and brought them back to the Town Harbour where they were given emergency medical attention before being taken to the Princess Elizabeth Hospital.

APPENDIX ON THE SECOND WORLD WAR

JEWISH VICTIMS OF THE GERMAN OCCUPATION (1940-1945)

'If you prick us, do we not bleed'. In addition to the large but unascertainable number of Jews of various nationalities, who trod the terrible path from slavery and bludgeoning to death in the living hells of Alderney's concentration camps, a small group of Bailiwick residents also experienced the purgatory of merciless hounding which in two cases culminated in the gas chamber. *Requiem æternam dona eis Domine et lux perpetua luceat eis.* On 21 March 1941 Inspector W. R. Sculpher, Guernsey's Chief of Police, submitting a return which the Bailiff — Victor Carey (q.v.) — had demanded in deference to German requirements, reported the presence in the island of 'four known persons of the Jewish persuasion', two of whom were British by marriage, while the other two were of German nationality. This information Carey passed on to the Feldkommandant.

The Jewesses 'of German nationality' only fell into that category because of the Anschluss; both of them actually came from Vienna. They had come to Guernsey from Austria in 1937 with a view to learning English. The elder of the two was Auguste Spitz, born 25 August 1901 and the younger Theresia Steiner, born 22 April 1916. According to a further report called for by the Feldkommandant and forwarded by Louis Guillemette (the Secretary of the Controlling Committee) on 14 January 1942, both women worked at the Castel Hospital where Steiner was a nurse earning £48 10s. per annum and Spitz a wardmaid earning 15 shillings per week, in each case plus keep. A record at the Greffe shows that these two unhappy women 'left for France' on 21 April 1942: 13 months after their presence had first been notified to the Germans. Nothing further is known of these unfortunate martyrs, not even the precise concentration camp where they were ultimately butchered.

When Frauleins Steiner and Spitz first came to Guernsey they were accompanied by their friend Elisobet Fink (obit. 14 March 1983) who, like them, was a Viennese. Before the outbreak of war, however, Elisabet married Harry Duquemin, thereby acquiring the British nationality which possibly saved her life. Similarly, it is highly probable that being a British subject as the relict of a Guernseyman likewise saved the life of Elda Brouard (*née* Bauer) who came from Florence and was the fourth Jewess mentioned in Inspector Sculpher's report. She was a widow earning her living as a housekeeper at 10s. per week plus board and lodging, possessed of savings amounting to £250 in War Loan and £60 on deposit in Barclay's Bank. British or not, both these women suffered the humiliating and distressing disabilities ordained by the anti-Jewish measures which the Royal Court at the behest of the Occupying Power registered on 23 October 1940. As a consequence they were debarred from art galleries, museums, cafés, theatres, cinemas, concerts, telephone booths, public halls, beaches, swimming pools, libraries, exhibitions, camping sites, public parks and sporting events. In February 1943, in common with many other residents born outside the Bailiwick, the two women, together with Elisobet Duquemin's 18-month-old daughter Janet, were deported to the Internment Camp at Biberach. Unlike their camp-mates, however, who felt reasonably secure in their incarceration, these two Jewesses lived in perpetual fear of what might befall them at any moment — and looked on their eventual survival as a miracle.

Far more fortunate was the fifth person notified to the German authorities as being Jewish, but in regard to whom Carey wrote to the Feldkommandant on 31 October 1940 that the Seneschal of Sark (her island of domicile) reported her insistence that the 'J' on her passport had been entered through a misunderstanding. This was Annie Wranowsky, who claimed that neither her parents nor her grandparents were Jews and that she could go back five generations without encountering Jewish blood. These protestations did not, however, prevent Inspector Sculpher from reporting to the Germans at the end of the year that she was 'the only known person of Jewish extraction living within the Bailiwick outside Guernsey' and her fate might well have been tragic but for the support she received from La Dame de Sercq. According to the testimony of Mr. Wehrner Rang, the ex-Wehrmacht officer who returned to the island to marry the Serquiaise with whom he had fallen in love during the Occupation, it was only the vehement representations made by the forceful Mrs. Sibyl Hathaway (q.v.) — whose verbal onslaughts so often cowed the Germans — which procured for Annie Wranowsky exemption from deportation to Germany with potential ensuing consequences too horrible to contemplate.

UNDERGROUND RESISTANCE HEROES OF THE
SECOND WORLD WAR

'In defeat: defiance' — *Winston Churchill.* It is obvious that in the restricted confines of Guernsey it was impossible to set up any organised resistance movement such as that of, say, Marshal Tito in Jugoslavia with its vast mountain redoubts from which to operate. All the more honour is therefore due to those who, alone or in small groups, attempted opposition to the enemy war effort. Probably the first man in the island systematically to undertake such activity was William Symes, the cousin of James Symes (q.v.), to whom, before giving himself up, James had passed the information he had obtained, asking him to get it back to England. William ran *The Dive* in Fountain Street, a hostelry which was frequented by sailors from ships which brought supplies from France. Through resistance workers among them he smuggled out James's information and subsequent messages to a British agent in Spain. The French resistance called him 'Sandeman Bill', from the well-known brand name displayed outside his establishment.

Eventually one of the messages was intercepted, and Symes was arrested. Despite continual interrogation and maltreatment at the Cherche Midi prison in Paris, he denied any knowledge of the messages, and so avoided betraying any of his collaborators. Sentenced to imprisonment for the rest of the war, he was sent to Compiègne and later to Roumainville, the 'hostage' prison from which inmates were selected for shooting as reprisals. From Roumainville William Symes was sent to Buchenwald Concentration Camp in a cattle truck whose 100 occupants, because of an escape attempt, were forced to undress and heap all their clothes on one side, after which they travelled naked for four days with no means of sanitation. Symes owed his release from Buchenwald to a near miracle. He risked writing a postcard to his wife (who had been evacuated to Taunton in Somerset before the Occupation) and smuggled it out among the postcards with French prisoners, at rare intervals, were allowed to send to their families. By an incredible freak it was delivered in England, where its receipt led to an official demand from the British to the German government for Symes to be moved to conditions more befitting a British subject — with the result that he was transferred to join other Channel Island internees at Laufen, where much more humane circumstances prevailed.

By the autumn of 1944, as the result of Allied control of France, the food situation in Guernsey had become desperate and already (on 18 September) a directive from German headquarters had threatened a complete stopping of rations to the civilian population. There was widespread feeling that everything depended on getting the facts to London, to persuade the British government to relax the blockade and allow Red Cross supplies to come through. At this juncture Captain Fred Noyon volunteered to attempt to escape to England to acquaint London with the facts. Noyon was supplied with statistics from every States Department, which were rapidly collected, thanks to the initiative of Deputy C. H. Cross. On Friday, 3 November, Noyon, accompanied by his friend William Endicott, made his way to his boat, the *Littlewood* (for which he had accumulated eight cans of petrol, acquired by bartering fish) in St Sampson's Harbour, ostensibly to go fishing. After obtaining his fishing permit, Noyon dissuaded the German customs officer who should have accompanied them by saying that he was going to put out his net and then proceed to St Peter-Port for repairs to his engine pump, returning the next day. Not relishing walking back from St Peter-Port to St Sampson's, the customs officer returned ashore. Thus unsupervised, Noyon and Enticott put out their net and then carried on, pretending to be looking for longnose. When a drizzle sprang up they made for the Channel, hoisting sail as soon as it was dark. At 22.00 hours they were picked up by an American submarine chaser and taken to Cherbourg where Noyon handed over his valuable papers, while Enticott, who had driven a lorry for the Germans, gave details of their guns and defences. Noyon reached London on 12 November, his information confirming the British government in the decision it had provisionally made on 7 November on the account it had of his news from Cherbourg.

In January 1945 a daring escape was made by two brothers, John and Thomas le Page, together with a Frenchman called Golivet, the instigator of the exploit being the French Consul, Monsieur L. V. Lambert. Monsieur Lambert was anxious to acquaint Paris with the urgent need of French prisoners of war for Red Cross Parcels. He also wished to transmit to the Allies the information on German naval constructions and minefields which he had obtained from Golivet (who had worked for the German navy in St Peter-Port) in return for which he had promised to help him escape back to France. With these objectives in mind, Lambert approached the le Page brothers, and on their agreeing to make the attempt as soon as there was a misty day, he entrusted them with a sealed box containing his information, weighted so as to sink at once in the event of interception. In the meanwhile his accomplice, Golivet, accustomed the Germans to permit him to accompany fishermen, by representing himself as skilled in that pursuit and handing over to them part of his alleged catch (often, in fact, bought by Lambert). The misty day having arrived, Golivet, followed by the le Page brothers, went to the guard room at the Albert Pier. Golivet managed to get himself assigned to the le Pages' boat, the brothers feigning reluctance to take him so as to divert suspicion. At the last moment Golivet excused himself and went to the men's lavatory adjoining the Prince Consort's statue. Here Lambert handed over further documents and last minute news of German operational plans, including a projected raid on Granville ultimately launched by Vice-Admiral Hüffmeier (q.v.). Golivet returned with the papers in a fisherman's bag slung over his shoulder and the boat sailed — ostensibly to pick up lobster pots south of Jethou. Under cover of the mist they turned north between Herm and Sark, and were ten miles north of the latter island when, to their dismay, the sun came out — but they remained undetected. At 11.00 hours the following day Lambert saw a plane fly across to Guernsey, circle the island and fly back again to France — the signal he had asked for should the three men reach the Allies in safety. The testimony of the le Page brothers reassured London that Red Cross supplies were, in fact, going intact to the civilian population, so that they were allowed to continue.

The most sustained and widespread subversive activity carried on in the entire Occupation was the publication of a daily news-sheet giving the B.B.C. nine o'clock news bulletin plus a summary of the 08.00 hours news on the day of issue. The news-sheet, which appeared regularly from May 1942 to February 1944 under the title of *G.U.N.S.* (Guernsey Underground News Service) was the brainchild of Charles Machon, a linotype operator on the *Star* newspaper, though its actual title was suggested by Frank Falla, the assistant editor of the same newspaper and Machon's main collaborator. Other helpers were Cyril Duquemin, a greenhouse worker and near neighbour of Charles Machon, together with two carpenters, Ernest Legg and Joseph Gillingham. In June 1942 Hitler's 'Island Madness' led to a decree that all wireless sets should be confiscated, to prevent the islanders from receiving instructions from the B.B.C. when the British launched what the Führer regarded as their inevitable assault on the archipelago. The deadline for surrendering sets was 20 June. This development reinforced Machon's determination to publish his news-sheet, which he had started the previous month for the benefit of those who were too poor to own wireless sets. As many as 100 copies a day were turned out on thin tomato-packing paper, averaging 780 words a time. One appeared daily on the Bailiff's desk, disappearing mysteriously after he had read it. Another was placed in a pre-arranged book in the Priaulx Library, where those in the secret could consult it. Three were sent to Sark, taken by passengers who hid them behind hat-bands on in the heel of a shoe as a precaution against being stripped and searched at the harbour barrier. At Le Creux they were collected initially by Cyril Wakley, the carrier, by whom they were passed on in rotation to Alfred Tardiff, the lay preacher in charge of the Methodist church, or to William Giffard — an employee of Frank Falla's close friend Hubert Lanyon, who undertook the responsibility for distribution within the island. Should German surveillance at any time be particularly close, Tardiff and Giffard distributed independently, so as to divert attention from Lanyon. On one occasion Lanyon's young daughter Megan collected the incriminating consignment, hidden in the folds of a tomato 'chip' left at La Colinette corner.

Acting on information treacherously supplied by an Irishman whom Machon had unwisely treated as a friend and confidant, three officials of the Geheime Feldpolizei arrested Machon and Duquemin on 11 February 1944, finding his typewriter and past copies of *G.U.N.S.* (which he had been rash enough to keep) in Machon's house. The unfortunate Machon was subjected to physical violence and more suble means of eliciting information such as being placed in an overcoat before a red-hot stove and then thrown into an icy cell. Finally he was threatened that his 74-year-old mother, Mrs. Mary Ann Machon, would be sent to Germany if he did not talk. When his mother fell ill with shock Machon was incredibly allowed to visit her, guarded by an English-speaking German officer, who doubled the time allowed and informed Mrs. Machon that her son was a hero. Legg and Gillingham were next rounded up and finally, on 3 April 1944, Falla was placed under arrest. On 26 April they were tried and Machon was sentenced to two years and four months, Duquemin one year and eleven months, Legg one year and ten months, Falla one year and four months, and Gillingham ten months. These terms were meaningless as any commitment of six months or more involved leaving Guernsey, and once in Germany all sentences became *sine die*.

By the time of the trial Machon was already wretchedly ill, the effects of his maltreatment exacerbated by the refusal of his captors to allow him the special food essential to his ulcerated stomach. The severities of prison life in Potsdam rapidly took their toll and Charles Machon died on 26 October 1944. Joseph Gillingham, too, was far from robust and although he survived the ten months to which he had been sentenced, his stamina could not stand up to the extended rigours and brutal treatment which followed a point-blank refusal to release him, and he also succumbed in prison. Thus died two very gallant Guernseymen.

The other three survived by a hair's breadth. When the Americans liberated them from their prison at Naumberg-on-Saale, Legg was emaciated and limping as a result of injuries received from being hurled down a flight of stone steps; while Falla, who had not even been allowed an aspirin when ill with pneumonia, was considered by his liberators to have only a fornight to live. Only devoted and skilled nursing by the Americans pulled him through. The only leading member of the network to escape the horrors of imprisonment in Germany was Hubert Lanyon, who was caught as a consequence of an unwise decision to diversify his resistance activities. With the aim of killing two birds with one stone, he hit upon the idea of stealing flour from the German stocks held in the building constituting the present-day Post Office and using it to supplement the bread supply available to the Serquiais, who would thereby profit from his acts of sabotage of the enemy. While investigating these thefts (where Lanyon as the island baker was the obvious suspect) the Germans came across copies of *G.U.N.S.* which Lanyon, like Machon, had imprudently retained. The Geheime Feldpolizei grilled him mercilessly, beating him unconscious with brutal blows and knocking out two of his teeth in an effort to discover the names of his helpers. He staunchly refused to divulge anything or to incriminate Wakley, Giffard or Tardiff, maintaining that he had merely read copies of *G.U.N.S.* which he had come across and foolishly kept them as souvenirs. At his trial he received a sentence of six months, reduced to four on appeal, and so was not sent to the Continent.

PART II

ANECDOTAL JOTTINGS

ANCHETEL, VICOMTE DU BESSIN. Anchetel was Seigneur of one of the two original fiefs into which Guernsey was divided, the other Seigneur being Néel of the Contentin (q.v.*). This division and allocation was effected in 1020 by Duke Richard II, with Anchetel being granted the western half of the island, which thus became known as Le Fief du Bessin (a name which one hundred years later was changed to Fief Le Comte when Anchetel's descendant, Ranulf, was created Earl of Chester). In 1030 Anchetel was deprived of his fief by Duke Robert I, because of traitorous alliance with the Count of Brittany with whom Robert was at war. In 1042, however, Duke William II (the future conqueror of England), anxious for support to consolidate his succession in view of his bastardy, returned western Guernsey to Anchetel's son Ranulf.

ARLOTT, DR. LESLIE THOMAS JOHN, O.B.E. (1914-   ). Born at Basingstoke in Hampshire on 25 February 1914 and educated at that town's Queen Mary's School, this well-known broadcaster and wine correspondent (always known by his third Christian name) started his career as a clerk in a mental hospital from 1930 to 1934, after which he served in the police force (rising to the rank of Detective-Sergeant) from 1934 to 1945 before entering the employment of the British Broadcasting Corporation. He subsequently earned fame as 'the voice of cricket': a capacity in which his ever-increasing repute culminated in his being nominated Sports Journalist of the Year in 1979 and both Sports Personality of the Year and Sports Presenter of the Year in 1980, the year of his retirement. The author of numerous books on cricket, wines and cheeses and created an Officer of the Most Excellent Order of the British Empire in 1970, this gifted personality (who contested the Epping Division in the Liberal interest in 1955 and 1959) was awarded an honorary Master of Arts Degree by Southampton University in 1973, and gained a Doctorate of the Open University in 1981. Becoming acquainted with Alderney as the result of a holiday in 1951 and falling in love with the island, he paid regular return visits over many years and chose it as his place of retirement, settling for good near Longis as a 'naturalised Aurigniais' in September 1980.

BASIEL, SON OF TURBEL. Basiel the son of Turbel is, in the opinion of the eminent scholar, le Père Bourde de la Rogerie, the earliest Guernseyman of whom we have recorded knowledge — a sailor of the first century. Father de la Rogerie based this identification on a burial plaque unearthed in 1920 at Algaiola in Corsica which shows Roman citizenship as being granted on Basiel's demobilisation at Paestum on 5 April, 71 A.D. after 26 years' service with the Misene Fleet. He is described as 'Basiel, Turbeli F. Gallinaria Sarniensis', born c. 25 A.D. As Basiel appears to have come from Sarnia (which William Camden in the 16th century equated with Guernsey) and as, moreover, the name of his father — Turbel — persisted in the island until just before the First World War, Bourde de la Rogerie claimed that he must be the earliest Guernseyman whose existence has yet been established. Rejecting 'Sarniensis' as in any way connected with the River Sarnus south of Naples on the grounds that its two known adjectival forms are Sarnianus and Sarnensis, the scholarly Curé finally clinched his argument by urging that 'Gallinaria' survives in the Torteval location of Les Galliennes.

Strong dissent from this interpretation has been expressed by Dr. S. K. Kellett-Smith (q.v.) who, after a reminder that (whatever William Camden may have said) the weight of evidence suggests that Sarnia was the Roman name for Sark rather than for Guernsey, then pointed out that the scribe who fashioned the plaque misspelt the adjective 'Misenensis', rendering it as 'Miseniensis' — and therefore might well have intended 'Sarnensis' (referring to the River Sarnus) when he inscribed 'Sarniensis' Furthermore Dr. Kellett-Smith indicated that Basiel is a name of pure Greek origin and that, just north of Misenum (much nearer at hand than Torteval!) there was located Gallinaria Silva. On the basis of this analysis Dr. Kellett-Smith advanced the theory that a Celt named Turbel (possibly hailing from the Channel Isles, but more likely from Armorica) emigrated to the Sarnus basin, where he married a Greek wife who bore him a son given the Greek name of Basiel Sarn(i)ensis. Basiel on this hypothesis later moved to Gallinaria Silva near the home port of the Misene Fleet, on leaving which he identified himself as Gallinaria Sarn(i)ensis and spent his declining years at Algaiola in Corsica. Which of these rival views to adopt is left to the discretion of the reader.

BENWALL, REVEREND HENRY. The Revd. Henry Benwall was appointed as Chaplain to Herm in 1838 to cater for the spiritual needs of the labourers recruited to work the island's quarries. His arrival brought the Anglican Church to Herm for the first time and led to the restoration of the ancient chapel of St Tugual (q.v.). In addition to his cure of souls, this cleric also established Herm's first school with financial assistance from the townsfolk of St Peter-Port, in 1838. The quarrymen, however, who had no wish for their children to receive any education, refused to make any contribution. An approach to the States of Guernsey, asking for the diversion of part of the *impôt* on spirits to help support the school was also unsuccessful. The upshot was that although 40 children were in attendance, the little school was forced to close in 1840. A century was to elapse before it was replaced.

BÉUCHET, ADMIRAL NICOLAS. Admiral Nicolas Béuchet led the assault on Guernsey in 1338 which inaugurated a French occupation persisting for two years as far as the island was concerned — but seven years in the case of Castle Cornet. Two years afterwards (in 1340) he lost his life at the Battle of Sluys.

BRUEL, CAPTAIN FRANCOIS. Captain François Bruel was in command of the French forces occupying Sark after a fleet from Havre de Grace under Leon Strozzi, Prior of Capua, reinforced by a flotilla from St Malo under Captain Poulain, Baron de la Garde, had brought 200 men to the island in July 1549. This move was made in pursuance of the decision of Henri II of France that Sark's seizure would strike a useful counterblow against English fortification of the other islands. (A half-hearted attempt to land in Guernsey also was made following Sark's capture, but the hostile craft being perceived by some ships lying near Castle Cornet, an alarm was given and the Guernesiais, mustering the Militia, drove off the invading force.) Bruel consolidated his position with triple defence works, constructing Le Grand Fort to cover the landing places at l'Eperquerie and La Banquette in the north, Le Château de Quénevêts dominating Dixcart Bay — and a fort at Vermandaye to cover the approach across La Coupée. He was hard put to it, however, to retain his garrison (consisting mostly of convicts), which desertions had reduced to 90 by 1551, when he left Sark to the care of his brother,

himself assuming command of the garrison at Granville. Two years later the island fell to Adrian Crole (q.v.*).

BURGESS, COLONEL SIR ROBERT. Colonel Sir Robert Burgess was appointed as the Royalist Lieutenant-Governor of Guernsey under Henry, Lord Percy, as Governor, in 1649 — though his effective authority never extended beyond the confines of Castle Cornet, which he continued stubbornly to hold for Charles II. His position was, however, rendered impossible by his loss of all source of supplies after Jersey had been overrun by Parliamentary forces in the autumn of 1651. On 19 December of the same year he was forced to yield the castle — the last Royalist stronghold to surrender. He and his garrison of 55 men marched out with the honours of war, Burgess himself being granted an indemnity of £1,500 as an acknowledgement of the humane way in which he had treated some Parliamentary prisoners whom he had captured in an earlier abortive attack on the fortress.

C

CAEDWALLA OF GWYNEDD (died 634). Caedwalla succeeded to the throne of Gwynedd in 625. He invaded Northumbria in 629 in pursuance of a long-standing vendetta between his family and the Deiran royal house. At Morpeth, however, he was defeated by Edwin, who 'commanded all the nations of the English as well as of the Britons, save only Kent' and was driven back into Wales, where the Northumbrian king beseiged him on the island of Priestholm (better known as Puffin Island) near Anglesey, from which he narrowly escaped in 631. Many accounts give Ireland as Caedwalla's land of refuge, but in his *History of the Kings of Britain* Geoffrey of Monmouth (1100--1154) related that accompanied by his nephew Brian Caedwalla made for Brittany, en route for which the fugitives were shipwrecked on the coast of 'Garnereia'. It would seem that seventh-century Guernsey was not to be recommended as a health resort for its visitors, as the story goes on to relate that Caedwalla fell ill and Brian desperately searched for venison meat with which to restore strength to his uncle and lord. Failing to find any, this devoted nephew proceeded to roast a slice cut from his own thigh. His uncle pronounced it excellent and speedily recovered. This cannibalistic repast is the earliest meal consumed in Guernsey of which the menu survives! Fortified by this nepotic sacrifice, Caedwalla returned to Britain and in 633, in alliance with Penda of Mercia, defeated and slew Edwin at Hatfield near Doncaster. Merciless in victory, he ravaged and pillaged the countryside until he himself was slain by Edwin's nephew Oswald in 634 at Oswald's Cross near Hexham.

CALVERLEY, SIR HUGH (died 1393). Described as one 'who slept not on his business' and with a record of service dating back to involvement as Edward III's agent in the Bréton Succession War of 1341-64, during which he participated in the bloody 'Combat des Trentes' (or 'Bataille de Mi-Voie') in March 1351, an engagement between 30 leading knights of each side fought mid-way betwixt the strongholds of Josselin and Ploermel; Sir Hugh Calverley was appointed Warden of the Isles in 1376 and retained office until his death in 1393. He had hardly taken up his duties when the church was rent assunder by the Papal Schism, with Urban VI being recognised by the Cardinals in Rome, but Clement VII by those in Avignon. Edward III acknowledged Urban, whereas the Bishop of Coutances — and the Dean of Guernsey — took the Clementine side. Calverley took immediate steps to enforce his royal master's authority. Expelling the Clementine Dean and repudiating the Bishop of Coutances, he placed the islands' churches under the Urbanite Bishop of Nantes, who became resident in Jersey, being himself exiled from his own cathedral city by a Clementine rival — the first (but by no means the last) time that the archipelago was divorced from the See of Coutances. In 1830 an even more urgent crisis arose when the French under Admiral de Vienne occupied Jersey and captured Castle Cornet as well. Calverley, however, with promptitude and energy launched a counter-attack and drove them out. The isles remained unmolested for the rest of his term as Warden. His remains lie at Bunbury in Cheshire.

DE LA CERDA, LUIS. In 1343, while the French still held Castle Cornet, which had been taken in 1338 by Admiral Béuchet (q.v.*), they launched a further attack on the Bailiwick with an invasion of Sark led by Luis de la Cerda. Easily overcoming the puny garrison of one armed man and six archers allocated to the island's defence, de la Cerda's force was not dislodged until 1347, two years after the recapture of Castle Cornet.

COLLINGS, SIR WILLIAM (1781-1854). (B).
Brother-in-law to the eminent archaeologist Frederick Corbin Lukis (q.v.), of whom he was a near neighbour in Grange Road, Sir William Collings was active in good works, as evidenced by his association with the resuscitation of Elizabeth College from 1826 onwards and also his prominence among those responsible for the erection of the Victoria Tower in 1848. This public-spirited knight is chiefly remembered, however, for the 'Sir William Collings Fund' which he founded in 1849, with the stipulation that it be used 'for the benefit of the necessitous poor natives of this island, or naturalised inhabitants, and also of strangers who shall have resided in the island for seven years, who, through any accident whatever, or from any unforseen cause, may need relief'. This fund is still administered by the Royal Court.

CRADOCK, FANNY. Well-known for a series of telecasts stimulating pride and pleasure in the preparation of good food, and the authoress (sometimes pseudonymously) of over 80 books — which besides those devoted to the culinary art also include nine novels (especially the Lorne trilogy) as well as eleven children's books written under the nom-de-plume of Frances Dale — Fanny Cradock took up residence in Guernsey in the latter part of her career. She did not, however, become particularly identified in any way with the Bailiwick.

CROLE, ADRIAN. A Flemish corsair sailing under Letters of Marque issued by the Admiral of the Emperor Charles V, Adrian Crole quite fortuitously arrived in Guernsey waters in the summer of 1553. Thomas Compton, the Lieutenant-Governor of Guernsey, saw in this chance circumstance an opportunity — without any resort to open warfare — of regaining the island of Sark which for the past four years had been occupied by a French force initially under Captain François Bruel (q.v.*), and latterly under his brother. He accordingly suggested to the Fleming that an attempt should be made on Sark, offering unofficially to supply four pilots. Crole fell in with this proposal and on 7 September 1553 he landed at l'Eperquerie, overcame the depleted and unenthusiastic garrison and took possession of the island — though the story that, on the pretence that one of the ship's crew had died, the Flemings carried ashore a coffin filled with arms which they used to overpower the garrison, is pure myth bereft of factual foundation. Leaving a holding force of 50 men in Sark, Crole went to

London and reported his capture to the Ambassador of the Emperor Charles V, only to find that Charles was so little impressed by this miniscule addition to his vast dominions as to instruct his Ambassador to negotiate the island's transfer to the English for a cash payment. However, Mary I's preoccupation with domestic religious issues, coupled with a reluctance to antagonise the French, led to the failure of these negotiations. Charles therefore ordered Crole to abandon the island after removing the ordnance and demolishing the forts, paying him 1,200 livres as reimbursement for expenses incurred. Crole accordingly returned to Sark and removed some of the ordnance, but left in haste on the arrival of a body of men sent by the Captain of Jersey to destroy the forts, mistaking them for superior enemy forces. On his way home he sold some of the equipment he had removed to Captain Robert Turberville (q.v.*), commanding the forces in Alderney.

D

DOBRÉE, ELISHA. Elisha Dobrée, who was a Douzenier of St Peter-Port as well as being an Admiralty Pilot (and consequently particularly interested in naval matters) is famous for his *Journal* which he kept over many years. This record provides an invaluable source of information for the period from the War of American Independence to Waterloo, describing the embryonic stage of Sark's tourist trade when the island was a venue for fashionable picnic parties from Guernsey in the 1770s; besides giving details of the Battle of Jersey, prizes brought in by privateers, the exploits of James Saumarez (q.v.) and his ship, the *Crescent* — and the eventual celebrations when peace was concluded with France. Dobrée's diary was edited and accorded detailed examination by John Percy Warren (q.v.) in papers published in the *Transactions* of La Société Guernesiaise for 1930 and 1959.

E

EAGLESTON, ARTHUR JOHN, C.V.O. (1870--1944). Entering the Civil Service after a brilliant career at Oxford (where he took a First in both Moderations and Greats and was a Scholar of Balliol), Arthur John Eagleston was employed

from 1913 until his retirement in 1932 as an Assistant Secretary at the Home Office, where for some considerable time he headed the Division which provides the link between the Channel Islands and the Privy Council. The value of his services in this capacity received its recognition in his appointment as Commander of the Royal Victorian Order. The preparation of the reports called for by his duties led him into insular historical research which issued in an abiding fascination concerning the history of the archipelago, with particular reference to the 16th century — an interest manifested as early as 1924 in the paper, 'Parliamentary Analogies from the Channel Islands' which he wrote for the publication *History*. After his retirement, Arthur Eagleston threw himself energetically into the composition of a set of informed and penetrating monographs of insular history. For the *Bulletin Annuel* of La Société Jersiaise an article on Sir Hugh ·Vaughan preceded an examination entitled 'Les Chroniques de Jersey in the Light of Contemporary Documents'; while the *Transactions* of La Société Guernesiaise he contributed 'The Quarrel between the Ministers and the Civil Power, 1581-85', 'The Dismissal of the Seven Jurats' and 'Guernsey under Sir Thomas Leighton, 1570-1610'. All this time Eagleston's magnum opus was in gestation — his *Channel Islands Under Tudor Government, 1484-1642: A Study in Administrative History*. In typescript only at the time of his death, the book was eventually published in 1949 thanks to the initiative of his widow and generous support from the Guernsey Society, La Société Guernesiaise, the Jersey Society in London, La Société Jersiaise and Balliol College. It was seen through the press by Professor John le Patourel (q.v.), who in his preface said of its author that he 'had read more deeply in the State Papers and the records of the Council than any previous historian of the Channel Islands; nor did he neglect the records kept in the islands themselves, those records which have been so rarely disturbed by the historian'. Arthur John Eagleston, who was born at Headington in Oxfordshire in the autumn of 1870, died in January 1944 at Hendon, in the London Borough of Barnet.

F

LE FEBURE, PIERRE. The autumn of 1643 was attended by a series of setbacks for Parliament's supporters in the islands. In October Pierre de

Beauvoir (q.v.) and the other two Commissioners entrusted with the government of Guernsey were inveigled into captivity in Castle Cornet, while in November George Carteret (q.v.) seized Jersey for the king. In these circumstances the decision was taken as a matter of urgency to secure Alderney for the Puritan cause. Accordingly Pierre le Febure was sent there with orders to drive out all papists and to put the island in a state of defence against the Royalists. In order to discharge this trust effectively, le Febure had to take steps to overhaul the somnolent Alderney Militia. Tackling this task energetically and efficiently, he completely re-organised the force, with the result that Alderney was held firmly in the Roundhead interest, first by le Febure and — from 1656 onwards — by Captain Nicholas Ling (q.v.) until the Restoration.

LE FEBVRE, CAPTAIN CHARLES (1800–1867). The name of Captain Charles le Febvre, Seigneur de Blanchelande from 1854 to his death in 1867, is intimately connected with the picturesque fishing haven — Le Havre de Blanchelande — on the west side of Saints Bay. In 1866 41 local fishermen petitioned the Bailiff (Sir Stafford Carey) for the provision of a breakwater at Saints to protect their boats in this traditional anchorage. Their request was soon followed by a letter to the Bailiff from Captain Charles le Febvre in which he expressed his desire to co-operate in the project. He accordingly offered to contribute £500 towards the cost of undertaking and furthermore expressed his willingness to allow the builders to quarry stone within the Blanchelande fief to the extent of his seigneurial rights, provided that no damage was caused to adjacent property.

These benevolent intentions were doomed to frustration. Work was put in hand but at the end of 1868 (a year after Charles le Febvre's death) a terrible gale destroyed the partly-completed structure. Although the hopes of the Saints fishermen were thereby dashed, yet nevertheless a granite column was put up in memory of the would-be benefactor, inscribed, 'Charles le Febvre, Seigneur de Blanchelands 1854–67'. At last, in 1909, the States. taking pity on the fishermen who had no convenient dry-landing place, constructed a quay, about 50 feet long, at a cost of £750. At the same time the le Febvre memorial, which was in danger of being washed away, was moved to a safer place. So matters remained until the Second World War when the German forces, for reasons best known to themselves, overthrew the monument and tumbled it into the sea. There it remained for a further three

decades until it was finally recovered and re-erected on the occasion of Architectural Heritage Year — over a century after the passing of the generous Seigneur it commemorates. May it — and he — now rest in peace!

LE FEBVRE, GEORGE (1766–1854). In contrast to his successor as Seigneur de Blanchelande (who enjoys repute for his benevolence towards local fishermen) George le Febvre is remembered mainly for his connection with ill-starred mining ventures with consequences woeful enough to bring him within an ace of being involved in a lawsuit for damages brought by the St Martin Douzaine. This *cause célèbre* occurred in 1843. Some time previously the Blanchelande Mining Corporation, with the blessing of George le Febvre, had started mining for silver at Le Mont Durand — but unfortunately its operations led to the drying-up of wells, fountains and drinking-troughs, not only in the immediate vicinity of Le Mont Durand, but also at La Bouvée and Les Courtes Falaises. In these circumstances the Royal Court was approached on 4 January 1843, with a request for an order closing the mine. The Court banned the exploitation of the workings for a month to allow all parties concerned time for full investigation. In the breathing space thus afforded, an indignation meeting of the Chefs de Famille of St Martin's parish was held on 17 January with the outcome that the Constables and Douzeniers were authorised to seek the intervention of other parishes and of the States — and, as a last resort, to sue both the mining company and the Seigneur de Blancelande for damages, the expenses of litigation to be met from the proceeds of parochial taxation.

On 3 May the Constables and Douzeniers reported that legal proceedings had already been started, but in October the Chefs de Famille received a letter from the secretary of the Blanchelande Mining Corporation, offering to abandon the rights granted by the Seigneur du Fief de Blanchelande and also to contribute £15 towards the cost of blocking up the mine, providing the parochial authorities undertook the work and withdrew all legal action. This communication was accompanied by another letter from George le Febvre giving an undertaking not to exercise in future his right for research for precious metals in his fief save under sufficient securities given to the satisfaction of the Douzaine. It being thus obvious that both the Seigneur and the Mining Corporation were anxious to rid themselves of a white elephant, besides the fact that the preservation of water supplies was safeguarded, a settlement was agreed on the terms offered. The episode of Le Mont Durand was closed and the spotlight of history moved away from George le Febvre.

LE FEYVRE, GUILLAUME (executed 1357). (D). Guillaume le Feyvre is memorable on account of the consequences of his death far more than for anything that he achieved in life. In 1356 Castle Cornet was taken by the French, but they were driven out again the following year by a force consisting largely of Jerseymen led by Sir Reginald de Carteret of St Ouen, Ralph Lemprière (the Bailiff of Jersey) and Richard de St Martin, the Seigneur of Trinity. In the course of this relief operation the Jerseymen charged with treason, and executed, a prominent Guernseyman, Guillaume le Feyvre, who was 'slain as a traitor by the common consent of the armed men'. Nicolaa, *veuve* le Feyvre and sister of the eminent Guernsey Seigneur Matthieu de Sausmarez (both of them being the children of Matthieu de Sausmarez senior by his wife Alice de St-Remi) sought redress in the Guernsey Court, which ordered the arrest of those responsible for the death of her husband, found them guilty of wrongful execution and sentenced them to banishment. Lemprière and de Carteret, however, stood by their men, challenging the verdict of guilty which had been returned against them. 'Though they were not at the killing nor consenting thereto, considering that those impeached were in no way to blame, they told the Court that they were as much to blame as any of those impeached'. As a consequence the two leaders found themselves arrested and thrown into a dungeon in the very fortress they had taken, 'to be detained till justice was done'.

Fearing that the Jerseymen would be denied an impartial hearing in Guernsey, the Warden, Sir Otto de Holland, made representations to the Privy Council. In August 1357 he pleaded through his deputy, Thomas de Langhurst, on the prisoners' behalf and obtained an Order to supersede the processes, remitting the case coram rege, as 'Thomas de Langhurst has testified before the Council that Guillaume was a traitor at the time of his death'. Nicolaa le Feyvre, however, betook herself to London and in November 1347 prevailed upon Edward III to require the Warden to proceed with a trial locally, despite the bitter feelings obtaining in Guernsey, where the Jurats threatened to resign if justice were not done. Edward defended ·his revised Order by stipulating that Nicolaa had 'shown to the King that Guillaume, at the time he was slain, was under the

King's special protection and his liege man, and that he neither adhered to the King's enemies nor abode with them, and that he was killed out of ancient enmity and malice and not for treason'. On these grounds the Warden was commanded 'to take diligent information on the matter and, if he finds that Guillaume was the King's liege man and did not deserve death, to cause justice to be done'. The upshot was that the unfortunate Jerseymen languished in durance vile until March 1359, when they were at last granted the king's pardon 'in regard to the arduous task they had performed in recovering the island and the castle'. The episode aroused considerable inter-insular bad blood, and the opinion has frequently been voiced that the Montague and Capulet relationship which existed for many years between the two major islands of the archipelago had its genesis in this unhappy incident.

G

GARDNER, WILLIAM. William Gardner first distinguised himself as a map-maker in 1784 when, under contract to the Board of Ordnance, he drew up the six-inches-to-the-mile town plan of Plymouth which came to be recognised as the prototype of all future Board of Ordnance work. He thereafter became a salaried surveyor under the Duke of Richmond, Master-General of the Ordnance, being appointed Chief Surveying Draughtsman in 1787, after which he was in continual employment on military trigonometrical surveys — the forerunners of the Ordnance Survey, which was founded in 1791. This cartographer's first assignment after promotion to Chief Draughtsman was the famous. 'Accurate Survey and Measurement of the Island of Guernsey, surveyed by Order of His Grace the Duke of Richmond, Master-General of the Ordnance, by William Gardner, 1787'. For this undertaking he was paid twopence per acre. As *Whitaker* gives Guernsey's area as 15,654 acres, it would seem that Gardner earned £130 9s. 0d. for his labours. In return for this remuneration he produced a masterpiece of cartography on a scale of six inches to the mile, the plates of which have survived in so good a condition as to permit a further limited printing in the years 1981 and 1982, with each copy hand-coloured in accordance with the technique of Gardner's day. It was by reference to this survey that Sir John Doyle (q.v.) planned his defence dispositions and road works during the

Napoleonic Wars. In modern times this cartographic triumph was used by Sylvester White as the foundation for his Island Development Plan approved by the States of Deliberation in November 1967. More recently still the 1,040 individual buildings marked on this map formed the basis of the detailed study of vernacular architecture undertaken by Mr. John McCormack (q.v.*) and published in 1980 under the title *The Guernsey House*.

GEOFFROI LE GRAND SARRAZIN (9th-10th centuries). A persistent tradition claims that the Castel Parish takes its name from a castle alleged to have been built on the site of the present church by a Norse pirate leader to enable him to maintain a dominance over the island. Furthermore, a small dolmen at Le Paradis in the Vale, partially destroyed in 1810 — though the site was later excavated by F. C. Lukis (q.v.) prior to total destruction in the mid-19th century — was known as 'Le Tombeau du Grand Sarrazin'. While (as the popular name of the demolished dolmen indicates) this legendary sea-dog is invariably referred to as 'Geoffroi le Grand Sarrazin' ('Sarrazin' being the name given to marauders in general: witness also the town of Castle Sarassin in the Languedoc), there are two main varieties of the story as far as the identity of this warlord is concerned. One version depicts him as staging his forays in the early part of the reign of Duke William II of Normandy (1035-1087), holding that prior to his conquest of England the Duke sent a certain Sampson d'Anneville over from mainland Normandy to expel the sea-raider. It goes on to assert that this commission was successfully discharged and that Geoffroi was either killed or fled. To mark this victory the brigand's castle was demolished and a church erected on its site, dedicated appropriately to Our Lady of Deliverance.

This story can hardly be said to command credence. In the first place, to postulate attacks by Vikings half-way through the 11th century is an anachronism, as the wild Norse community around Cap La Hague had been brought under effective control in the early years of the century by Duke Richard II, who reigned from 996 to 1026. Secondly, the account bears many of the hallmarks of myth, with the various ingredients of the tale forming a neat pattern, displaying a precision rarely met with in real life. Moreover, suspicions as to its veracity are further aroused when one recalls that although there is a genuine record much later — in the early 13th century in fact — of a Sampson d'Anneville (from

Anneville in the Cotentin) whose support of Philip Augustus led to the confiscation of his Guernsey lands by King John (q.v.), the name is bandied about in considerably less reputable contexts. The spurious document concerning the origins of Guernsey's churches — 'La Dédicase des Eglises' — also features an obviously fraudulent Sampson d'Anneville (placing him for good measure in the 12th century) who is there portrayed as the son of Sir Richard d'Anneville in whose presence this bogus manuscript describes St Sampson's church as having supposedly been consecrated in 1111 — when we have convincing indications of its existence a 100 years earlier! Furthermore, this self-same forgery in its account of the consecration of the Castel church speaks of it being 'built on the site and in place of a certain castle called the Castle of Great Geoffrey'.

This first identification of Le Grand Sarrazin is thus thoroughly discredited, and far more likely is the second interpretation to the effect that he is the expression of a folk memory of the Jarl Godefroy, one of the many sons of Harald the Fair Haired (King of Norway from 860 to 933). Late in the ninth or early in the tenth century, as one of several Nordic contemporaries of Rollo (q.v.*), he could well have established a local hegemony which he sought to perpetuate by building a castle on a spot which occupies high ground almost exactly in the middle of the island — and which (witness the female statue menhir adjacent to the church) also seems to have been associated with worship from time immemorial.

DE GOLDINGHAM, SIR SYMON. At the outbreak of the Hundred Years War in 1338 the Constable, holding Castle Cornet was Sir Symon de Goldingham, who commanded a garrison consisting of his son, six men-at-arms and 50 archers and crossbowmen. The position occupied by the fortress was virtually unassailable, with the islet accommodating it too small to offer any lodgment for an attacking force. As a result Sir Symon was lulled into a false sense of security. He failed to perceive that his impregnability depended on sea power ensuring supplies, and consequently took no precautions to provide for a contingency where maritime dominance was lost. Thus when Admiral Nicolas Béuchet (q.v.*), by his sudden raid in the Spring of 1338, seized command of the seas, sweeping the English fleet into its ports, the castle was cut off from all chances of succour. Even so, de Goldingham held out until early autumn, not yielding up the stronghold until the following September. It was to remain in French hands for seven long years.

DU GUESCLIN, BERTRAND. In the year 1373 Bertrand du Guesclin, Constable of France, was beseiging the English in Brest. Wearying of the prolonged inactivity involved, du Guesclin decided to entrust the operation to his subordinates and sailed for the Channel Isles in search of more active pursuits. After subduing the whole of Jersey save Mont Orgueil, he exacted ransoms from the islanders which continued to be paid for three full years. Resuming his onslaught, the 'Black Dog of Brittany' wrought considerable damage in Guernsey and collected further ransoms. In Sark he caused such devastation, hard on the heels of the previous year's depredations at the hands of Owen of Wales (q.v.), as to induce the few inhabitants who had survived the 1372 attack to quit the island — which thenceforth remained abandoned for nearly 200 years, a haunt for pirates and smugglers. Thus leaving a terrible trail of havoc behind him, du Guesclin returned to Brest to receive the English surrender which before his departure had been pledged at the end of a month failing the arrival of any relief.

H

DE HARCOURT, GODFREY. Although Guernsey was freed from French occupation in 1340 by Walter de Weston (q.v.*), Castle Cornet remained in enemy hands for a further five years. In August 1345, however, mercenary forces led by the 'Captains of Bayonne' arrived in the island and took service under Godfrey de Harcourt. The castle was re-taken under de Harcourt's leadership and garrisoned by ten men-at-arms and 20 archers. One-third of this force consisted of Guernseymen — not feudal levies in the nascent Militia, but *bona fide* soldiers serving in the garrison and in receipt of pay.

HENRY, NICOLAS. In 1392 Nicolas Henry of La Perelle returned safely with his ships after service with the English navy. He obtained the consent of his Seigneur (the Abbé de Mont St Michel) for the endowment of a chapel in thanksgiving for his deliverance from the defeat the French had inflicted on the English fleet shortly after he had left it. The royal confirmation of the Abbé's permission to proceed (as required by

the 1279 Statute of Mortmain) was granted by Richard II in 1394, in a charter authorising Nicolas Henry to build the chapel of Notre Dame de la Perelle for the purpose of maintaining a chaplain to say Mass daily in perpetuity for Nicolas and his wife Philippa, for their souls after their deaths, as well as for the souls of all their ancestors and benefactors and those of Christian people generally. Later coming to be known as La Chapelle Ste Appoline, the building was rescued from irredeemable decay when the property was bought by the States in 1873 at the instigation of Sir Edgar MacCulloch (q.v.), its acquisition bringing to birth the Ancient Monuments Committee. After restoration it was in October 1978 jointly consecrated by Anglican, Roman Catholic and Nonconformist clergy as a Chapel of Unity for the promotion of ecumenicism in Guernsey.

L

LAKE, AIMÉE HENRIETTA. Mrs. Aimée Henrietta Lake (*née* Queripel, born 7 January 1888), of La Robergerie in St Sampson's, stood trial on 28 January 1914 for witchcraft — the last such case ever to be heard in Guernsey. The accused was charged with fortune-telling, interpreting dreams and practising witchcraft from August 1913 to January 1914, the main evidence against her being supplied by Mrs. Marie Outin. According to Mrs. Outin's testimony she had consulted Mrs. Lake on the advice of a neighbour after the death of her cattle the previous October and had been told by tea-cup divination that her husband (Jean Marie François Outin, who had died at the age of 61 on 14 April 1912) had been the victim of sorcery and that she herself was under a spell, to counteract which she had buried a number of 'charmed' packets later found to contain Brown and Poulson's Cornflour, Paisley Flour, brown starch, salt and baking powder — all of which she had bought for £3 10s. from Mrs. Lake, under whose influence she was also convinced that a metal box box she possessed was 'full of little devils' and that she would soon follow her husband to the grave unless she made a substantial payment for the protective powers of the sorceress. Offering to refund the monies she had received, Mrs. Lake pleaded that people came to her of their own free will and were normally quite satisfied when she 'read the cups' for them. She was sentenced to eight days imprisonment for disorderly conduct.

LAMBERT, MAJOR-GENERAL JOHN (1619–1683). Born at Calton near Malham Tarm (in what is now the county of North Yorkshire), where he was baptised on 7 November 1619, this famous Civil War commander was insufficiently adroit in his attempts to run with the Roundhead hares and hunt with the Royalist hounds after Oliver Cromwell's death in September 1658 had created a power vacuum. His machinations only led to his being among the few excluded from the general pardon extended by Charles II at the Restoration. A temporary sojourn in the Tower of London was followed by his being sent to Castle Cornet, where he landed in November 1661, destined to become one of the 'People in the Islands' Story' for the next nine years. In the late spring of 1662 (by which time the Royalist position had been consolidated) Lambert was shipped back to London, where he stood trial in June. The sentence was death, commuted to imprisonment for life and the prisoner was accordingly sent back to Castle Cornet under a warrant dated 25 July 1662. On 18 November of the same year the deputy governor (Nathaniel Darell) was ordered to allow him 'liberty and indulgence' (for which relief Lambert wrote thanking Clarendon, whose influence lay behind the concession), but it is unlikely that this clemency was in fact exercised, Darell reporting later the same month that 'I have caused him to be locked in a chamber with his three children and two others relating to them'. The position was eased in April 1663 when 'Honest John' was permitted the free run of the whole of Castle Cornet provided the porter was always with him. However, Lambert and his family felt such an antipathy towards this porter — who was none other than Jean de la Marche, the eponymous son of the formidable Presbyterian Pastor (q.v.) — that they preferred to remain locked in their quarters, their spirits cheered by visits from their fellow prisoner, the Reverend Thomas le Marchant (q.v.*).

Later in 1663 a further relaxation in the terms of his incarceration allowed the captive to visit the Guernsey mainland (where his wife had taken a house) during daylight hours, but in the event, 'wary and fearful to commit any errors by his liberty', he refused to go unless accompanied by the Governor, Lord Hatton of Kirby. In any case this indulgence was swiftly reversed the following year (1664), when Lambert's movements were again closely restricted following the discovery of the clandestine marriage between his daughter Mary and the Governor's son, Charles Hatton. Yet more stringent conditions were imposed in 1666, when Louis XIV having entered the lists against Charles II in support of the Netherlands in the Second Dutch War, the new Governor, Colonel Sir Jonathan Atkins, was ordered to shoot Lambert should the French ever land in Guernsey. He remained strictly confined to the castle (cultivating on a patch of land adjoining his cell the Guernsey lily which he had in happier days grown in his garden in Wimbledon) until September 1670, when he was removed to Drake's Island in Plymouth Sound, where he languished until his death in the winter of 1683.

LEGGE, COLONEL JOHN. In vindication of his assertion of the Dispensing Power, James II at Bath on 10 September 1687, overrode the Test Act and commissioned the Roman Catholic Colonel John Legge as Lieutenant-Governor of Guernsey under Christopher Viscount Hatton (q.v.) as Governor. When Legge sailed for Guernsey to take up his appointment, the king sought to strengthen his hand by simultaneously sending over Irish troops and Roman Catholic officers, together with their chaplains, to form a large part of the garrison — a move which gave rise to considerable consternation in Guernsey with its Calvinist traditions going back over one-and-a-quarter centuries. A year later when news of the landing at Torbay of James II's Dutch — and Protestant — son-in-law reached the Bailiwick in November 1688, the island leaders — in the absence (as usual) of the Jacobite Bailiff, Sir Edmond Andros (q.v.), who was in New England — contacted the senior Protestant officer in the garrison and a coup was jointly planned, to be executed on the day when it was this officer's turn to take command in Castle Cornet. When the appointed day arrived the Commander of the Town Militia Regiment, at the head of his men, seized and disarmed any Roman Catholic officers or soldiers to be found in St Peter-Port. At the same time the garrison was paraded at the castle and on a pre-arranged signal the Protestant troops, with loaded muskets, moved forward and swung to face their Roman Catholic comrades, intimidating them to lay down their arms. Legge was taken into custody and thereafter vanished from the stage of history. Guernsey was thus made safe for William III (q.v.*) and Roman Catholicism was completely obliterated from the Bailiwick's life for the next 100 years, only reappearing with the arrival of refugees from the Jacobin Terror during the French Revolution.

LOARING, RICHARD GEORGE (1937–   ). Born in the Vale on 2 February 1937, to Marjorie (*née* Short), the wife of William John Loaring, and with his boyhood home at Rougeval, St Peter-Port, Richard Loaring's first venture into show business came in 1962 with a series of appearances, together with his brother John, at Candie Auditorium. These performances could, however, be regarded as little more than an experimental apprenticeship and his true début came in 1970 when, after being noticed by an impressario's 'talent scout', he was offered a four-month contract for a part in 'The Boyfriend' at the Academy Theatre in Johannesburg, an offer which he accepted with alacrity. From then on Richard Loaring never looked back, with films and recordings following soon afterwards. An ensuing spiral of success reached its peak with 'Joseph and the Amazing Technicolour Dreamcoat' which proved to be the most widely acclaimed musical of all time in South Africa — where he continued his career after 'The Boyfriend' had launched it. Finally settling in South Africa — and marrying a model and beauty queen late in 1982 — Loaring scored repeated triumphs in all fields of entertainment: stage, cabaret, films — and television, in which he became famous throughout the country in the rôle of 'host' on a regular transmission of the 'Pebble Mill At One' genre, incorporating interviews, music and singing. Early in 1983, while in Guernsey with his wife on one of his periodical visits, this prominent personality expressed the hope eventually to return for good to the island where he felt his roots to lie and whither 'some strange sort of magnet draws us back'.

M

MACKENZIE, SIR EDMUND MONTAGUE COMPTON, O.B.E. (1883-1974). First Herm (where he was Tenant from 1920 to 1923) and then Jethou (where his tenancy lasted from 1920 to 1934) provided both home and inspiration for Sir Compton Mackenzie, whose *Fairy Gold* has a local setting, with his two insular retreats discreetly disguised as Roon and Carrakoon — offshore islands 'across the Sound from Penzawn in Lyonesse'; and with Sir Percival Perry — the author's successor as Herm's tenant — deftly caricatured as Sir Caleb Fuller. Although still remaining its tenant, Sir Compton (who is credited with the transportation thither from the Canaries of the giant blue echium) in fact left Jethou in December 1930 and confesses in Octave Six of his autobiography, *My Life and Times*, that as he

sailed he had such misgivings over 'forsaking that much-loved little island' that 'I felt a deserter'. However, he also relates in Octave Seven that when his wife, in view of the difficulties experienced in disposing of the lease before it was ultimately taken over by Mrs. Fortington in 1934, suggested a return thither, his reaction was that although 'Jethou was for me a vivid and cherished memory', yet 'it has been against my rule of life ever to go back to a place from which I felt I had exhausted all the creative urge it could give me. To have gone back to Jethou would have seemed a surrender'. He never set eyes on the island again.

MAÇON, SIMON (1572-1652). Born in Southampton to parents who formed part of the French Huguenot community which, fleeing from persecution in its homeland, had sought sanctuary in that port, Simon Maçon was trained for the Calvinist Ministry in the special school for that purpose which the colony had founded. A substantial contribution towards the cost of his training was made by the *Anciens* (Elders) of Alderney's Presbyterian establishment, who thereby hit back at William Chamberlayne (q.v.) who, as a fervent Roman Catholic, had from 1591 onwards attempted to eradicate the practices of Geneva from the island by withholding any clerical stipend, and allowing the Manse to sink into dilapidation. Maçon took up the Alderney living in November 1607 after the Royal Commissioners in Guernsey had ordered Chamberlayne to make an annual payment of 30 marks (£20) to a minister. It was during Maçon's incumbency that the name of the island township was changed from St Mary to St Anne — most likely not St Anne the mother of the Virgin, but St Anne the mother of St Sampson! Maçon remained in Alderney for the whole of the rest of his life, dying there in 1652.

MADOC OF WALES. A Welsh prince of this name is reputed to have been the local military commander during the French occupation of the archipelago between 1338 and 1340. (Although no such leader is known to the *Dictionary of Welsh Biography*, it was by no means uncommon for Welsh support to be given to the French as part of the national vendetta against the English after the conquest of Wales by Edward I.) A persistent tradition asserts that a resistance movement developed in St Martin's and that in 1339 a group of 87 St Martinais — hoping that their initiative would encourage the other parishes to rise also — attempted to ambush the enemy in a low-lying marshy area near Les Hubits. The venture was a failure and the defeated insurgents are said to have escaped from Petit-Port and to have taken shelter in Jersey at St Ouen. So runs the story. *Se non é vero é ben trovato*. A house in the area where this ill-starred attack is deemed to have been launched is undeniably known as La Mare Mado (or Madoc) to this day — allegedly in memory of the exploit. One cannot but wonder whether Le Mont Mado in the Jersey parish of St Ouen preserves a similar memory of this elusive Welshman postulated by the tradition.

MALESART, CAPTAIN. In the summer of 1558 this French soldier of fortune decided to take advantage of the defenceless condition to which Alderney had been reduced by the discontinuance of all attempts at fortification and the withdrawal of the 200-strong garrison in 1554. Accordingly, with a crew of volunteers from Cherbourg he swooped on the island, collected all the cattle and booty he could carry — and then returned whence he had come to auction his acquisitions on the quayside. Encouraged by his success, Malesart returned with yet larger forces and made another unopposed landing, but withdrew hastily when the English fleet was sighted. Eventually thinking that the coast was clear, the adventurer came back a third time, but a force dispatched by the Captain of Guernsey, Sir Leonard Chamberlayne (q.v.) — augmenting a naval expedition under Admiral Clinton — captured him and he was sent as a prisoner to the Tower of London.

LE MARCHANT, REVEREND THOMAS. (D). In 1650 Thomas le Marchant, a man of outstanding erudition and ability, became the incumbent of St Martin's as a *Ministre de l'Eglise Etablie Presbyterienne de Guernesey*. A few years earlier he had taken up the Castel living and five years later (in 1655) he was transferred to the Vale Parish. When Anglicanism was forcibly imposed after the Restoration by the assertive personality of Dean Jean de Sausmarez (q.v.*), le Marchant led those who clung fiercely to the island's long established Calvinist forms of administration and liturgy. As an immediate consequence of his stand, this fervent disciple of Geneva was deprived of his living, where in 1662 he was replaced by Philip Brashmart. As he still remained obdurate, le Marchant was subjected to imprisonment, first in Castle Cornet and subsequently in the Tower of London — his incarceration lasting two years. Although thereafter silenced on the

ecclesiastical plane, le Marchant now raised his voice in matters legal, publishing a critical study both of the 'Coutumier de Normandie' and of the famous 'L'Approbation des Lois' in his *Remarques et Animadversions sur l'Approbation des Lois et Coustemier de Normandie usitées ès Jurisdiction de Guerneze, et particulièrement en la Cour Royale de la dite Isle*. In this analysis (which one and a half centuries after his lifetime in 1826 was printed and published by authority of the Royal Court) the ejected Minister demonstrated the inadequacy of the credentials of 'L'Approbation des Lois' to be considered an authoritative statement of Guernsey laws and usages as differing from le Grand Coutumier, by arguing cogently that its authors, because of a lack of both enlightenment and of maturity of judgement, had produced a document beset with misunderstandings and contradictions. The fact that 'L'Approbation' never became a definitive legal code for the Bailiwick may be said in itself to endorse the validity of le Marchant's criticism. Thomas le Marchant married Olimpe Roland and his granddaughter Martha (1692–1714) became the wife of George Andros, who was briefly the Governor of Alderney between the death of Sir Edmund Andros (q.v.) in 1713 and his own demise the following year — which in its turn ushered in the era of le Mesurier governance in the island.

LE MARQUANT, THOMAS. Thomas le Marquant, together with his wife Janette Thelry, provided Guernsey with the first school of the foundation of which any record survives, when in 1513 they jointly made a gift to the parish of St Peter-Port of a house and garden on the north side of the Chapel of St Julien for use as the parish school. They also bestowed two quarters of annual wheat *rente* upon the schoolmaster who was to repeat with his charges daily an anthem of Our Lady, with a De Profundis and an Ave Maria, for the souls of the donors, of their friends, and for all souls in general. This school eventually came to be known as La Petite Ecole de la Ville to distinguish it from Elizabeth College (founded 50 years later) which was referred to as 'La Grande Ecole'. Rebuilt early in the 19th century near the point where the modern St Julian's Avenue debouches on Glategny Esplanade, La Petite Ecole de la Ville was demolished as a result of the creation of the Avenue, being replaced early in the 20th century by Vauvert School, which is thus its lineal descendant. *N.B.* — Please read this entry in conjunction with that on *'De Saint-Peyr, Pierre'* (also in Part II).

MARTEL, MARIE. Born Marie Robilliard, this young woman was the central figure in a dramatic and romantic episode between the years 1598 and 1600. Most likely at the insistence of her mother Perotine Robilliard (*née* Bréhaut) Marie in 1598 pledged herself before the Parish Consistoire of St Pierre du Bois as betrothed to Roger Langlois. When the time limit of three months — the maximum delay between betrothal and marriage permitted by the Calvinist Establishment — had elapsed, and no wedding had taken place, Roger Langlois testified before the Island Colloque that Marie refused to marry him, being enamoured of Jacques Martel of St Saviour's. Marie persisted in her defiance of ecclesiastical authority when the formidable Colloque forbade her to see any more of Martel and to marry Langlois forthwith. After a further six months had gone by and she still refused to wed Roger, her father Pierre Robilliard (who appears to have sympathised with his daughter and thanks to whose connivance the young lovers seem to have seen each other from time to time) was ordered to keep her under lock and key until she submitted. Despite this incarceration the maiden still remained obdurate, and in 1600 the Colloque released Roger Langlois from his betrothal pledge to Marie 'because of her sin'. She and Jacques Martel were permitted to marry provided that first of all they both did public penance in their respective parish 'temples'. Thus Marie, bare-headed and bare-footed and clad only in a chemise, was required to kneel in front of the congregation, a flaming torch in one hand and a Bible in the other, confessing her sinfulness and praying for pardon of God, the Queen and Justice; after which the expiation of her guilt was rounded off by the luckless demoiselle having to endure the verbal lashings of a scathing and prolonged commination. Her battle of wills with the Colloque finally won — an unparalleled defeat for this powerful body — the determined young St Pierraise at last married the man of her choice. Now Marie Martel, she had earned her place in history.

MARTIN, THOMAS (1839-1921). A parishioner of St Martin's who, born to Rachel (*née* Dowdney) the wife of Thomas Martin, in 1839, dwelt in Havilland Vale and earned his living as a labourer engaged on road maintenance, Thomas Martin *fils* is highly — and deservedly — esteemed for having by his writings preserved for posterity the St Martinais dialect of the Guernesiais language: a variant which since his death has become virtually extinct as a spoken tongue. In a collection of over 400 exercise books this extraordinary man, 'born to blush unseen', accomplished in exquisite handwriting unblemished by blot or erasure the remarkable *tour de force* of translating from English into St Martinais large sections of the Bible and the entire works of William Shakespeare — a feat performed at a time when very few people outside St Peter-Port knew any English. Rather more than 200 of these books survive as part of the archives of La Société Guernesiaise but, sad to say, the remainder of the set containing this humble workman's tremendous achievement has disappeared. The self-effacing scholar whose labours embellish these pages and whose worth was denied recognition during his lifetime, died on 11 November 1921.

McCORMACK, JOHN ALISTAIR (1939-   ). Born in Gillingham, Kent on 13 August 1939 and going up from Bushey Grammar School to the University of Wales (Swansea), where he took an honours degree in English and also a diploma in education, this islander by adoption originally came to Guernsey in 1961 on appointment to a post at the Boys' Intermediate School, but later gave up teaching in search of a less inhibitory life style giving scope for the pursuit of his interests in archaeology, old buildings and church architecture, which he eventually developed to the point of expertise. Earning his living by acquiring, refurbishing and subsequently letting, semi-derelict properties (and for a time supplementing his income by working for the Guernsey Telecommunications Board), John McCormack progressively extended his knowledge of the island's vernacular architecture to the point where he was able to produce *The Guernsey House* — a monumental study of over 1,000 houses shewn on the famous map drawn in 1787 by William Gardner (q.v.*). This survey not only reflects profound research but also undoubtedly constitutes one of the most important books on a Guernsey topic ever to have been written. A member of the National Trust of Guernsey, La Société Guernesiaise and the Vernacular Architecture Group, this accomplished expositor (who is also interested in church music, gardening and cycling) later turned his apparently inexhaustible energies to an investigation of the derivative relationship between Guernsey and Jersey churches and those of the Cotentin, the Bessin and Poitou, thus paving the way for the appearance of a further magnum opus.

LE MESURIER, REVEREND JOHN (1818-1903). (A). The son of Lieutenant-General John le Mesurier (q.v.) to whose wife Martha he was born seven years before his father's surrender of the grant of Alderney, the Reverend John le Mesurier (who later became an honorary Canon of Winchester) presented to the island the fine church of St Anne, designed by Sir George Gilbert Scott. The foundation stone of the church, built at the sole expense of this generous priest as a memorial to his parents, was laid in 1847, with the building being finally consecrated on 21 August 1850, by the Bishop of Winchester, Dr. Charles Richard Sumner. Beneath the west window the donor caused six brass plates to be affixed commemorating the successive members of his family who had served as 'Hereditary Governors' of Alderney.

MEWTIS, SIR PETER. Appointed as Governor of Guernsey in 1545 — an office he held until 1553 — Sir Peter Mewtis almost immediately addressed himself to the modernisation of Castle Cornet, which neglect had rendered vulnerable to attacks by pirates or privateers. Under the supervision of John Rogers, the King's Chief Engineer, this fortress was strengthened by the construction of a bastion and artillery emplacement. Erected at a cost of £492 17s. 10d., the installation was appropriately called the Mewtis Bulwark — a name which survives to the present day. Now, however, it would appear that the work was restorative rather than original, as the evidence of archaeological excavations conducted in 1982 points to a tower having existed on this site as far back as the late 13th century.

MONSARRAT, NICHOLAS JOHN TURNEY, F.R.S.L. (1910-1979). Resident in Guernsey from December 1966 to December 1968, this well-known writer was born in March 1910 to Marguerite (née Turney), the wife of the distinguished Liverpool surgeon Dr. Keith Waldegrave Monsarrat. After going up from Winchester College to Cambridge (Trinity) and taking an Honours Law Degree in 1931, Monsarrat subsequently discarded a legal career in favour of gaining by his pen a living that remained precarious until his war-time experiences as a Lieutenant-Commander in the Royal Navy (when he was, incidentally, mentioned in despatches), inspired *The Cruel Sea* which, published in 1951, earned him the Heinemann Foundation Prize for Literature and also election as a Fellow of the Royal Society of Literature. He and his wife Ann lived in the Forest, at Le Paradou, Les Nicolles, and during his time in the island Monsarrat wrote *Richer Than All His Tribe*. Unfortunately, however, he

did not emulate Hugo or Oxenham (qq.v.) or MacKenzie (q.v.*) in writing a novel with an insular setting. Moving to Malta, he died in London in August 1979. The Monsarrats loved Guernsey and paid frequent return visits for the rest of the author's lifetime — a practice continued by his widow after his death. This affection is reflected in an Introduction to a guide book* which the famous novelist wrote in 1971: 'I recently lived in Guernsey for two happy years, and it is always a joy to return to its meandering country lanes with their intricate dry-stone walls of marvellous pink granite (and a blessed speed limit of 35 miles an hour); to the incredibly luxurious green fields and those beautiful long-eyelashed cows which supply the richest cream and the most gorgeous butter to be found anywhere'.

* Peter Haining: *The Channel Islands* (1972).

MOONEY, WILLIAM. An English visitor to Guernsey in 1798, William Mooney kept a diary which provides valuable information about the privateering, *entrepôt* trading and smuggling activities of the period. From his jottings one learns of a lilliputian privateering schooner of two tons, called *Hat and Wig* (Captain Queripel) which engaged a French vessel of 700 tons with easily foreseeable results. Not only were the Guernseymen taken prisoner, but their craft was actually hoisted on board the enemy ship! Regarding the *entrepôt* trade Mooney records that thanks to the island's geographical situation near so many French ports, Guernsey by his time had become an 'Emporium of a Universal Trade', its exports to England paying £1½ million pounds into Customs and Excise during 1796–97. He furthermore describes how he watched from his window a 'free trader' (smuggler) taking on board a cargo of spirits and tobacco before sailing for the Sussex coast. Added piquancy attaches to Mooney's accounts when one reflects that the ventures of which he tells took place while the Revolutionary War between France and Britain was being waged.

MOURANT, PETER. The reflection that whereas the seventh letter of the alphabet stands for Guernsey, it also stands for 'greenhouse', emphasises an economic fact of life of prolonged applicability to the island which derived originally from the initiative of Peter Mourant. This father of modern Guernsey horticulture had Candie House (now the Priaulx Library) built in 1780, establishing an ornamental pleasance in what is now called the Upper Candie Gardens and growing fruit and vegetables in what is now known as the

Lower Gardens. The better to grow his grapes and pineapples, Mourant in 1793 erected in the Lower Gardens the first glassshouses ever seen in Guernsey — structures which survive to this day. His success produced an ever--increasing number of imitators and thus ultimately precipitated the proliferation of cultivation under glass which is now so dominant a feature of the island's 'growing' industry. Mourant eventually sold Candie House to Jonathan Priaulx, who re-sold it to his brother Osmond de Beauvoir Priaulx (q.v.), the founder of the present library.

MÜLLER, LIEUTENANT-GENERAL ERICH (1889-1962). Described by the late Dame de Sercq, Mrs. Sibyl Hathaway (q.v.) as 'a bombastic gentleman who would have made a perfect music hall character', Erich Müller came to Guernsey with the rank of Major-General as Commander of 319 Infantry Division in June 1941. On arrival he automatically became *Befehlshaber* (Commander-in-Chief) in place of Oberst Graf von Schmettow (q.v.) whom he outranked. With a passion for equitation, the new Commander-in-Chief was apt to call on young officers at random to ride with him — with woeful consequences for any who fell below the standard he expected. Red-faced and irascible, Müller (who was promoted to Lieutenant-General on 16 June 1942) was notorious for pouncing on bodies of troops to scatter castigations and punishments. On one occasion he even stopped a column on the march and ordered that all boots be removed to enable him to catch those with holes in their socks! It was therefore completely in character for him to reject the appeal made in February 1943 by Freiherr von Aufsess (q.v.) for Mrs. Sherwill and her two children to be exempted from a deportation to Germany which strictly speaking only applied to ex-officers of the British Forces, reiterating the order that they should go: an order which von Aufsess courageously ignored. Relinquishing command of 319 Division on 1 September 1943 to von Schmettow (who thereby resumed the office of *Befehlshaber*), Lieutenant-General Müller went to the Eastern Front in command of 603 Division. Taken prisoner in August 1944, he remained in Russian hands until 10 October 1955. The following year he revisited the Bailiwick in company with his sister and seemed quite surprised at the somewhat tepid welcome accorded him!

N

NÉEL, VICOMTE DU COTENTIN. Néel de St Sauveur became Seigneur of the fief comprising the south and east of the island at the time of Guernsey's original enfeoffment by Duke Richard II in 1020, the grant of the western part being made to Anchetel, Vicomte du Bessin (q.v.*). As a result of this infeudation the area concerned became known as Le Fief du Cotentin. Although he forfeited his fief for rebellion against Duke William II (by whom he was defeated at the Battle of Val-ès-Dunes in 1047), Néel was reconciled with William in 1054 and the fief was later restored to him. He retained it until his death and it remained in his family until the whole of Guernsey came into the hands of Geoffrey of Anjou (q.v.) during the struggles of the mid-12th century.

O

D'ORON, SIR GERARD. A nephew of Sir Otto de Grandison (q.v.), one of whose sisters was his mother, Sir George d'Oron was Sub-Warden of the Isles from 1321 until late December 1323, when Edward II dispatched him on a mission to Burgundy and Savoy. Sir Gerard, who, on taking up his appointment found the islanders in open revolt against the depredations of his uncle as Lord of the Isles, initially withdrew to Sark, but later tried to quell unrest by deposing the Bailiff of Guernsey, John le Marchant. This *démarche* was an utter failure, resulting as it did in the selfsame Bailiff, together with the Court over which he presided, throwing d'Oron into jail for attempting an improper exercise of authority on the grounds that his appointment was invalid for lack of any commission to rule according to insular 'laws and customs'. The Guernsey Donkey had begun to kick against its oppressors!

P

PICOT, REVEREND ELIE. Originally appointed as the Calvinist incumbent in Alderney in 1654, the Reverend Elie Picot was transferred at the time of the Restoration to St Andrew's in Guernsey, his place in Alderney being taken by the Reverend W. J. Germain. In February 1662, however, Germain died and the following November Elie Picot was re-appointed, retaining the living until his death in December 1696. The imposition of Anglicanism on the Bailiwick with the appointment as Dean of Jean de Sausmarez (q.v.*) initially met with considerable resistance from the Aurigniais, but Picot's conscience was sufficiently pliable for him to accept the adaptations involved, and it was mostly thanks to his tact and popularity that the transition was ultimately effected reasonably smoothly. During his first tenure of office Elie Picot inaugurated Alderney's register of baptisms, marriages and burials. The original record was lost during his absence from the island but its successor, which he started on his return from St Andrew's, has been maintained until the present day.

DE PRÉAUX, PIERRE. In 1200 King John (q.v.) granted Pierre de Préaux the Lordship of the Islands of Jersey, Guernsey and Alderney, together with a rent in England drawn on 60 librates of land at Alton in Hampshire and a further rent to be drawn from market stalls in Rouen. On 13 August 1203, with the archipelago under threat, John required the Lord of the Isles to take 20 per cent of their annual income from all persons, lay or clerical, who had land or rents in Jersey or Guernsey, to 'maintain the knights and sergeants who are protecting the said islands'. It would seem that the implementation of this royal order was left in the hands of subordinates such as Sub-Warden Gregory Balizan, as de Préaux himself was actively involved in operations on the Norman mainland, later being personally in command of Rouen when it was beseiged by Philip Augustus in May 1204. He yielded to Philip in June under terms whereby all knights and burgesses present in the city could retain their lands provided they did homage for them to the French king. The implication is thus that the islands were surrendered to Philip Augustus and granted back to Pierre in return for homage — though access to them on his part was now denied by the activities of Eustace the Monk (q.v.). In June 1206 Pierre de Préaux crossed to England under safe conduct after having switched his allegiance back to King John. He did not, however, recover the Channel Isles, over which his lordship had for all practical purposes ceased in 1204. By way of compensation in March 1207, John granted him lands in Essex and Cambridgeshire.

PRIAULX, WILLIAM ARTHUR (1870-1946). Born in Allez Street on 31 January 1870 to Amelia (née Whitford), the wife of John Dickson Priaulx, William Priaulx takes his place among the immortals thanks to his prowess on the rifle range, where he established himself as the finest shot Guernsey has ever produced. In 1891, as a private in the 1st Regiment of the Royal Guernsey Militia, he won the Lieutenant-Governor's Prize at the Guernsey Rifle Association Meeting, subsequently being 'chaired' and carried around the camp, acclaimed by an enthusiastic crowd. His greatest triumph, however, came in 1899, during that year's competitions at Bisley organised by the National Rifle Association. On 22 July Private Priaulx won the Queen's Prize, which was presented to him by H.R.H. the Duke of Connaught, Commander-in-Chief of the British Army. To gain this award — founded by Queen Victoria in 1860 and worth £250, and carrying with it the Gold Medal of the National Rifle Association — the contest is severe. All entrants fire seven shots at 200, 500 and 600 yards, with the best 300 among them being selected to fire ten further shots at 300, 500 and 600 yards — after which the surviving best 100 fire fifteen shots at 900 and 1,000 yards to discover the best of all. At the same meeting, in the competition for the Kolapore Cup — open to teams throughout the Commonwealth (at that time Empire) and involving ten shots with service rifles at 300, 500 and 600 yards — Priaulx again distinguished himself, making the highest individual score. (The Guernsey Team as a whole, however, only came third: a disappointing result after that of the previous year when Guernsey had won, with England second, Victoria [Australia] third and Canada fourth.) Greeted on his return to the island by the combined Militia Bands playing 'See the Conquering Hero Comes' as he stepped ashore at the White Rock, William Arthur Priaulx is commemorated for all time by his statuette in silver preserved in the Militia Museum at Castle Cornet. A builder by career, he died at Mount Row Nursing Home on 25 February 1946.

PRICE, DENNISTOUN JOHN FRANKLYN ROSE (1915-1973). Born at Twyford in Berkshire on 23 June 1915 to Dorothy Patience (née Verey), the wife of Brigadier-General Thomas Rose Caradoc Price (and baptised Dennistoun, though as an adult invariably known as Dennis) this famous actor was educated at Radley College, going up thence to Oxford (Worcester) and while there participating in amateur theatricals as a member of the Oxford University Dramatic Society. After studying for the stage under Ronald Adam and Eileen Thorndyke at the Embassy Theatre School of Acting, he first trod the boards professionally at Croydon Repertory Theatre in 'Behind Your Back' during June 1937, with his first West End performance occurring the following September at the Queen's Theatre. During the Second World War Dennis Price served in the Royal Artillery from March 1940 until he was invalided out in June 1942. Back on the stage by August 1942, the following year he played Charles Condamine in 'Blithe Spirit' (his favourite part) at the Duchess Theatre. He appeared in films (including the uproariously funny 'Kind Hearts and Coronets') from 1944 onwards and on television (especially as Jeeves in 'The World of Wooster') from 1965 onwards. This well-known player became one of the 'People in the Islands' Story' from 1966 until his death. Taking the part of Mr. Andrew Bennett in 'Not in the Book' at Guernsey's Little Theatre in May 1966, he thereafter made his home in the Bailiwick, living in several houses in Sark, but mostly at Le Clos du Vivier. His closing years clouded by acute financial worries, he fell victim to pulmonary oedema and cirrhosis of the liver and died at the Princess Elizabeth Hospital on 6 October 1973. His remains lie in Sark cemetery to the south of St Peter's church.

R

ROBERT I, DUKE OF NORMANDY (died 1035). Robert I (known as the Devil or the Jerusalemite), who wore the ducal coronet from 1027 to 1035, when he met his death on crusade at Nicaea, is reputedly the only Duke of Normandy ever to have set foot in Guernsey. The largely apocryphal story goes that in 1030, while en route for England to support his cousins Alfred and Edward (the sons borne by his aunt Emma to Ethelred the Unready) against Canute, he was driven by adverse winds to put ashore in Guernsey, the name 'L'Ancresse' allegedly deriving from the 'ancrage' where his ships took shelter. Equally doubtful are the anachronistic legends that during his enforced sojourn in the island the Duke built the viaduct across La Braye du Valle ('Le Pont du Diable': the original St Sampson's Bridge) and also the Vale Castle and Le Château des Marais — both of which in fact betray 13th to 18th century constructional characteristics. While a storm-induced landfall is obviously possible, the main factual foundation for these legends would seem to be the grant of the western half of Guernsey made to Mont St Michel the self-same year

(1030) by the Duke on the occasion of a peace treaty between him and Alain, Count of Brittany, concluded at the great Benedictine monastery — together with the associated Charter making over four Guernsey churches to this religious house.

ROLLO THE VIKING (c. 846–c. 930). The ninth century was the great era of Viking raids, most of the invaders (as far as France was concerned) coming from Denmark. Some penetrated the Loire Valley (where, after varying fortunes, they were finally defeated by the Bréton leader Alan Barbetorte at Trans near Pontorson in 939), but the main thrust was up the Seine where the Norsemen wintered in 850. In 885 they sailed up the river and beseiged Paris. Taking advantage of a fleeting victory over the insurgents near Chartres secured by his vassal Count Robert of the Bréton March, King Charles the Simple (898–929) in 911 reached the agreement with the Norse leader Rollo traditionally known as the Treaty of St Clair-sur-Epte. Despite the predominantly Danish nature of his forces, this commander himself was Norwegian. He was the son of Ragnvald the Strong, Jarl of Marr (nowadays Moere, in Western Norway) who was possibly the ancestor of the Guernsey family of Mauger and also that of the present writer — see Appendix at the end of Part III — to whom the Orkney Islands were awarded as a gift. Rollo (or Rolv) was the younger brother of Einar Dal-Koll, King of the Orkneys and Pictia (West Scotland), one of whose descendants — through the Norwegian Bonde family — is the Princess of Wales. Prior to his incursions up the Seine Valley Rollo had spent some time in Scotland, marrying two of his daughters to Scottish kings and thereby obtaining the further accession of strength to the forces under his command which facilitated the success of his onslaughts on northern France.

By his accord with the French king Rollo (who, being in his mid-sixties — he was born *circa* 846 — was by then ready for an accommodation) undertook to accept Christianity and a token political subordination to Charles in return for the grant of the city of Rouen, together with a number of *'pagi'* (administrative areas comparable to counties) in its vicinity. Charles for his part obviously hoped that Rollo would now have a vested interest in blocking the Seine Valley against other raiders, and furthermore that with a stake in the country the erstwhile pillagers would ultimately be tamed and absorbed into the Frankish social and political order. On the other hand Rollo, who by the treaty became in effect the first Duke of Normandy (though no such title as yet officially existed), regarded the compact as providing an operational base for further expansion at a later date — and indeed, in 924, when about 80, the old war lord after a series of raids secured an additional grant of territory to the west of his original acquisitions around Rouen. It was not, however, until the grant to his son William Longsword (or Longbeard) by Charles's successor Rudolf in 933 of 'the land of the Brétons by the sea-coast' (Cotentin and Avranchin), that the Channel Isles came within the Norsemen's domains. (Hence, incidentally, the doubt attaching to Max Gilbert's speculation in his *Pierres Mégalithiques en Normandie* that Rollo may have assembled his assault force in L'Ancresse Bay before launching his final attack up the Seine estuary which culminated in the famous Treaty of 911 with Charles the Simple).

S

DE SAINT-PEYR, PIERRE. In 1361 Pierre de Saint-Peyr (who later in 1376 was a Jurat and later still in 1388 Lieutenant-Bailiff) built a chapel attached to a hospital or alms house dedicated to St Julian and located at the lower end of the Truchot. He had obtained Crown permission to found a hospital for a Master and an unspecified number of brethren and sisters, situated near Bosq in the parish of St Peter-Port (commemorated by the modern Bosq Lane) and to endow it with 20 *vergées* of land and 80 quarters of wheat *rente*. Although the conventional wisdom credits Thomas le Marquant (q.v.*) and his wife Janette Thelry with the foundation of Guernsey's first school 'near the Chapel of St Julian', it is nevertheless a tenable speculation favoured by some historians that an earlier educational establishment connected with Pierre de Saint-Peyr's foundation might have existed, it being possible to interpret the terms of le Marquant's 1513 Deed of Gift as implying such a previous institution.

DE SAINT-REMI, GUILLAUME (killed 1294). During the greater part of the 13th century the subordinates of the Lord of the Isles — or the Warden, as the case might be — were indiscriminately described as *ballivi*, *custodes* or *subcustodes* and were functionaries with general responsibility for all aspects of administration. As the century approached its end, however, the expression *ballivus* increasingly came to be applied to an officer concerned exclusively with the Court,

whose authority was limited to one island. Thus in 1290 Denis of Tilbury was sent from England to audit the accounts of Guillaume de Saint-Remi, 'Bailiff of Guernsey'. This individual (who in another capacity was Seigneur du Fief Mauxmarquis and whose authority was limited to Guernsey) emerges in 1278, when he first became *ballivus*, holding his appointment on this occasion until 1282. Resuming office in 1288, he behaved in so oppressive and extortionate a manner as to evoke a complaint by the islanders, which led to the enquiry and audit conducted by Denis of Tilbury in 1290. Although as a result of these investigations, he found it prudent temporarily to leave the island, Saint-Remi was back in 1292 when he assumed office yet again, this time becoming the first person to be specifically appointed Bailiff of Guernsey by Royal Patent. The same year he acquired the Fief de Sainte Helène of which he became Seigneur by purchase of the holding from the Abbey of Cormery — a transaction to which Edward I gave his approval by a Charter dated 24 April 1292. His tenure of neither position was destined to last very long, however, as he was one of the 1,500 people slain in the murderous French raid of 1294.

DE LA SALLE, GAUTIER (executed 1320). In 1304 Pierre le Marchant, Bailiff of Guernsey, accompanied by Ranulph Gautier, set out for the Priory of Lihou Island to arrest Thomas le Roser, who had murdered one of the monks, Brother Jean del Espin. Le Roser resisted arrest and in the ensuing skirmish was killed by Ranulph Gautier, who thereupon sought sanctuary in St Sampson's church and subsequently escaped from Guernsey entirely. After having obtained Edward II's pardon, Gautier returned several years later to Guernsey where (on the testimony of his nephew, Gerard Philippe, in a petition to the king) he was held in Castle Cornet by Gautier de la Salle and there tortured and finally done to death by de la Salle and a number of accomplices. The accomplices escaped but de la Salle himself was apprehended and stood trial at the General Eyre held in 1320, which sentenced him to death. The execution took place at le Courtil du Gibet in St Andrew's (approximately where the States' Dairy now stands), where de la Salle was hanged after having halted to make his last confession — and possibly receive his viaticum — at the wayside cross still referred to as the 'Bailiff's Cross' — not because he had at any time been Bailiff in the modern sense of the word, but because in the late 13th and early 14th centuries any official of the

Lord of the Isles was frequently so designated. His *villa* or holding, 'La Petite Ville', was forfeit to the Crown as the estate of a felon and is to this day known as 'La Ville au Roi'. As for the cross itself, this is a simple incision in a flat stone located over the years on the footpath beside the road between Le Vauquiédor and Les Ruettes, but latterly removed and set in an upright position adjoining the hostelry at the top of Le Vauquiédor. Possibly originating as a memorial to mark the site (not far from his Fief of Mauxmarquis) of the 1294 murder by French raiders of Guillaume de Saint-Remi (q.v.*) — an alternative (and equally plausible) reason for its name — its reputed association with the 'Wicked Bailiff' seems to have led the 16th-century reformers to regard it as endowed with an historical significance outweighing its taint as emblematic of 'popish superstition': so that, alone among Guernsey's mediaeval wayside crosses, it survived the iconoclastic zeal of the Calvinist Establishment. Beloved of raconteurs is the story in connection with de la Salle which tells of a Bailiff (in the present-day sense of the word) coveting a neighbour's well and hiding some silver cups in a hayrick to incriminate the well's owner, whom he was on the point of condemning to death when his perfidy was uncovered. Needless to say, this tale 'is a fond thing vainly invented and grounded upon no warranty', possibly deriving from the account in 1 Kings 21 of the inculpation of Naboth by King Ahab of Samaria, who thereby contrived to obtain his victim's vineyard.

SARCHET, THOMAS — and family. In 1806 a party of 26 Guernsey folk — men, women and children — decided to emigrate to the New World and sailed under the leadership of Thomas Sarchet, a Methodist lay preacher whose grandfather had come to the island as a Huguenot refugee from France. Prominent among those accompanying Thomas were his brothers Nicolas, Jean and Pierre and his brother-in-law Daniel Ferbrache. Thomas' qualities as leader were demonstrated almost as soon as the emigrants set out. The first stage of their journey took them to Jersey, en route for which their ship was boarded by the press gang and two of its company pressed into the Royal Navy. Immediately on landing in Jersey Thomas proceeded to lay information whereby the Royal Court of that island was able to obtain the release of this pair of unfortunate seafarers on the grounds that impressment was obviously a gross infringement of insular privileges.

After crossing the Atlantic the islanders landed at Norfolk, Virginia, and made their way up Chesapeake Bay to Baltimore in Maryland, whence they set out in covered wagons with the intention of making for Cincinnati in Ohio, which had been admitted to statehood in the Union three years previously (1803). After 30 days' travelling the immigrants camped in West Virginia near what nowadays in Wheeling, the bulk of them resting there while Thomas Sarchet rode ahead on horseback to Childicothe, Ohio, inspecting the newly-blazed trail. On his return the party resumed its journey, crossing the Ohio River and eventually reaching the nascent township of Cambridge. The day after their arrival being a Sunday the wayfarers rested and worshipped in the morning, while during the afternoon they were visited by some of the settlers in the neighbourhood, with whom they made friends through Jean Sarchet (the sole member of the group to speak a little English). The morrow — Monday — happened to be a day appointed for the sale of lots and, weary of wandering, the Guernesiais bought eleven lots and settled permanently in the vicinity, Pierre Sarchet building a two-storey log-house for winter shelter in what is now the heart of Cambridge Town.

In the spring of 1807 the group was joined by a further body of Guernsey immigrants led by William Ogier, a preacher licensed by the Methodist Episcopalian Church who cooperated with Thomas Sarchet in conducting divine worship. The expatriates were typical Channel Islanders of the day who, although sober and devout, nevertheless believed in witchcraft, with some of them even claiming to be white witches, capable of frustrating evil spirits. Despite these oddities, however, they soon came to be highly regarded in the locality, with the Sarchets emerging as the dominant family. Thomas opened the settlement's first store, which he provisioned from Pennsylvania by bringing in by packhorse supplies obtained in Pittsburgh and Philadelphia. He also supplied his fellow-settlers with salt from salt springs which he leased in Muskingum County, as well as planting orchards of fruit-trees which he bought near Marietta. Later on he established an arboreal nursery from which he sold young fruit trees. Jean — a blacksmith — arranged for the pack-horses commissioned by his brother to bring from Pittsburgh consignments of iron which he made into nails, horseshoes, mattocks, and axes. Pierre's services as a carpenter were constantly in demand for building homes and making doors, puncheon floors, hinges, latches and various items of furniture. In the year 1810 the State of Ohio created a new county around

Cambridge and, at the suggestion of Jacob Gomber, named it in honour of the islander immigrants. Guernsey County had come into existence.

DE SAUSMAREZ, HENRY. (A/D/F). The son of Jean de Sausmarez, Dean of Guernsey (q.v.*) by his wife Rachel Briard, Henry de Sausmarez is memorable for having invented a device intended to supersede the log-line and to record distances sailed by a dial and a gong. In 1715 the invention was submitted to Sir Isaac Newton, who referred it to the Elder Brethren of Trinity House, by whom it seems to have been shelved. Henry's concern with matters maritime also led to his making a chart of the area of the Channel Isles, including and emphasising the dangerous Casquets Rocks.

DE SAUSMAREZ, VERY REVEREND JEAN (died 1697). (A/D/F). In early manhood a Calvinist divine (first of St Saviour's from 1653 and from 1655-56 of St Martins), Jean de Sausmarez was pliant enough with the collapse of Richard Cromwell to accommodate himself to the usages of the Church of England, receiving episcopal ordination at the Restoration and, like Amias Andros (q.v.) becoming known as a 'boon companion' of Charles II. In 1662 (the Book of Common Prayer having been translated into French by the Jersey cleric, the Reverend Jean le Vavasseur dit Durel (1625-1683)) the Bishop of Winchester appointed de Sausmarez as Dean of Guernsey, while at the same time a body of troops was sent to the island to repress any resistance to the introduction of Anglicanism. The new Dean joined battle with the Presbyterian organisation, threatening the use of these troops and employing the authority of the Royal Court to compel submission. Despite the opposition of Guernsey's equivalent of Scotland's Covenanters, led by the redoubtable and repeatedly imprisoned Reverend Thomas le Marchant (q.v.*), de Sausmarez won to the extent that the outward structure of Anglicanism was secured, though adherence to it was perfunctory and the mode of worship in the island's churches remained largely unaltered. Indeed, the Dean himself in his parish of St Martin retained the pew distribution whereby the pulpit was the centre of attention, with the Communion Table relegated to obscurity. Surviving for a very long time, this seating arrangement fostered an amusing spectacle in Victorian days when General George de Sausmarez and his wife were to be seen facing each other when reciting the Creed –

a confrontation arising from the fact that the lady, as a staunch High Churchwoman in this evangelical ambience, insisted on facing east, while her spouse, out of respect for the magnificent fighting qualities of his beloved Sikhs, was determined to turn his back on Mecca! Jean de Sausmarez married Rachel Briard (1626-1719), the grand-daughter of Guernsey's first privateer Jean Briard (q.v.) and their daughter Rachel in 1682 bore her husband Thomas le Mesurier a son, John, from whom stemmed the le Mesurier dynasty of 'Hereditary Governors' of Alderney. Guernsey's Dean prospered within the Church of England, becoming a Prebendary of Windsor. His body was accordingly buried in the prestigious St George's chapel on his death in 1697.

SLOWLEY, ROBERT (and descendants). (G). A Devonian hailing from Totnes, Robert Slowley as a young man in his hometown met Jean Chevalier, a member of the family which had been granted La Rondellerie tenement by Helier de Carteret (q.v.) and who had come to Devonshire to ply his trade as a shoemaker. As a result of this acquaintanceship Robert came to Sark, marrying Marie Chevalier of La Rondellerie and taking over the tenancy of Le Grand Dixcart in 1589 after it had been vacated by its original holder – the butcher and brewer William Smith. On 16 July 1594, Robert Slowley became Juge of the Court which the acting Seigneur Amice de Carteret (q.v.) that day caused formally to be installed in accordance with the Order-in-Council of 24 April 1583 which his brother Philippe (the previous Seigneur) had for 11 years seen fit to ignore. The Juge steadily built up a strong position for his family, which was long to remain dominant in the life of Sark. In 1606 he bought from the Seigneur – Sir Philipppe de Carteret (q.v.) – the tenement of La Jaspellerie (a later holder of which – his eponymous descendant Captain Robert Slowley – married into the powerful le Gros family and in the wars against Louis XIV emerged as a prominent privateer bringing in many prizes with his sloop, *Runner*). The family's influence was further increased on 8 November 1626 when the Juge's daughter Susanne married the formidable incumbent Elie Brévint (q.v.); while the following year it possessed itself of still more property when Robert's son Philippe, on its sale by his father-in-law Noel Vaudin, acquired Le Grand Beauregard by retraite '*à cause de sa femme*'. (Please see note at end of entry.) Juge Robert Slowley died in 1634, his daughter Judith (the wife of Lucas le Masurier in which name the tenement was thenceforth held) inheriting Le Grand Dixcart. A century later yet another Robert Slowley (the nephew of the privateering captain) held office as Sark's Prévôt and was also appointed Captain of the Island Militia under the ultimate command of the Governor in Guernsey. By this time the family was prospering exceedingly from the profits of privateering, thanks to which Prévôt Robert was able in 1736 to rebuild his inheritance of Le Grand Beauregard. A few years previously — in 1728 — both La Ville Farm and La Moinerie (the tenants of which were married to Slowley wives and so shared in the kindred's prosperity) had likewise been rebuilt.

　　N.B.: Retraite — Known in full as *Retrait Lignager* and possibly deriving from Mosaic Law (see Leviticus 25, 25), this is an ancient usage whereby the near relatives of the vendor of a property enjoy the right to retrieve it by paying the purchase price to the buyer within a year and a day (Guernsey) or 40 days (Sark) — as his cousin Hanameel bade Jeremiah to do in regard to the field at Anathoth (Jeremiah 32, 7).

DE SOULIES, REVEREND ALEXANDRE. The Reverend Alexandre de Soulies, who was rector of St Saviour's from 1680 until 1692, is noteworthy for having established that parish's first school — a church day school which he started in 1687. In June that year the Ecclesiastical Court approved of his nominee, Jacques de Quemin, for the post of school master and also authorised his salary of two quarters of wheat *rente* per annum, half to come from a legacy by Jacques Rougier and half from church funds. The following November du Quemin was sworn in by the Court after he had publicly subscribed to the Thirty-nine Articles of the Church of England and to the Act of Uniformity. The fortunes of the enterprising rector's venture must have waned, as the record shows that half a century later — in 1736 — a parish school was established, with Daniel le Prevost as the first school master, St Saviour's having been without any place of instruction for some years. It is, however, interesting to discover that the contribution from Jacques Rougier's legacy towards the income of de Soulies' appointee Jacques du Quemin survived as part of the emoluments of the headmaster of St Saviour's until the school finally ceased to operate with the transfer of its pupils (together with those of St Pierre du Bois) to the new school at La Houguette in 1976.

SUTTON, MAJOR-GENERAL RICHARD. Major-General Richard Sutton, who was Governor of

Guernsey from 1735 to 1737, was led by his experience in office to become extremely critical of the custom whereby the Crown had regularly let on a short-term basis tracts of waste and marsh located on Fief Le Roi. This arrangement he found to be woefully inefficient as 'here to-day, gone to-morrow' tenancies gave no incentive to holders to make any outlay on improving and draining these areas. With the object of rectifying this unsatisfactory state of affairs, Major-General Sutton petitioned the Crown in 1737 for permission to grant leases 'for and during the term of sixty-one years, renewable every one-and-twenty years at a fine certain of three years value of the Reserved Rent'. The resultant Order-in-Council creating such 'Fee Farm Leases' (as they came to be called) ushered in a form of land-holding of feudal derivation which is Guernsey's nearest approximation to leasehold in the United Kingdom. The system thereby introduced gives tenurial security, with no risk of disappropriation providing the annual rent is paid, plus the renewal fine every 21 years of three times the annual rent; while at the expiry of 61 years a new lease may be negotiated with identical terms and conditions. Finally, there is no bar to the holder of the lease alienating all or part of the land involved. Consequently Major-General Sutton's initiative has had the effect of promoting considerable improvements in the areas affected, reflected in major enhancements in their market values. The islands of Jethou and Lihou are well-known examples of fee-farm leases.

T

LE TOCQ, JEAN. Remembered in Guernsey as are the sacred geese on Rome's Capitoline Hill, the 'prentice boys in Londonderry, or Paul Revere in Lexington; Jean le Tocq who, so the story goes, lived at La Houguette in the Castel, was allegedly abroad at an early hour on the fateful day in 1372 when the island was invaded by Owen of Wales (q.v.), so that he is reputed, from the vantage point of his abode, to have seen the insurgents making landfall at Vazon, and thereupon raised the alarm — though in his case the warning unfortunately did not suffice to enable the defenders to repel the onslaught threatening them.

TUPPER, JOHN (1620–1696). — (E). The privateering era proper (as far as Guernsey was concerned)

consisted of the one-and-a-quarter centuries following the repudiation by William III (q.v.*) of the archipelago's neutral status deriving from the 1480/1 Bull of Pope Sixtus IV (q.v.). Nevertheless a foretaste of the daring deeds of the island mariners during that period was provided by the career of John Tupper who, in the course of the Second Dutch War (1665-1667) operated as a privateer in the early months of 1667, his achievements earning an accolade from the Governor, Colonel Sir John Atkins: 'How bravelie the men of St Martyn's have behaved themselves at sea. They have brought in a prize of sixty Ton, of Amsterdam, laden with wine, tobacco, figs and rosin'. There was more significance to Tupper's activities than first meets the eye. The French — who in this conflict were allied with the Netherlands (strange bedfellows indeed!) against Charles II — had hoped that Guernsey, with its Calvinist traditions and its resentment over the imposition of Anglicanism, would prove to be a British Achilles heel, rallying around General Lambert (who was a political prisoner in the island) in revolt against the Crown. John Tupper's exploits demonstrated unequivocally that any such hopes were doomed to disappointment.

TUPPER, JOHN (1660-1720). (E). The eponymous son of the John Tupper of the Second Dutch War (q.v.*) and, like his father, a privateer, John Tupper was in 1692 presented by William III (q.v.*) and Mary II with a massive gold medal and chain in recognition of signal service rendered on 16 May of that year which precipitated the Battle of Cap La Hogue. It fell out that Tupper, commanding the *Monmouth Galley*, was crossing from Guernsey to England when, thanks to a temporary lifting of the prevailing fog, he espied the French fleet under Admiral Tourville. Proceeding with all haste to St Helen's in the Isle of Wight, he alerted Admiral Russell regarding the enemy's presence in the Channel — thereby providing intelligence which led to the great naval victory and the ruin of James II's hopes of regaining the throne. In the engagement itself Tupper gained further distinction, destroying four French ships as they tried to escape through the Race of Alderney and thus earning a public citation. The Tupper Medal and Chain (which John's descendants are permitted to wear as an honourable augmentation to their arms and crest) are on permanent loan to the Island Museum — though for security reasons only replicas are ever displayed. The Tupper Portrait, in which the intrepid islander is shown wearing his medal and chain, is also on permanent loan to the same institution.

TUPPER, JURAT JOHN (1743-1810). (E). Great-nephew of the John Tupper who distinguished himself at Cap La Hogue (q.v.*) and grandfather to the poet Martin Farquhar Tupper (1810-1889) of *Proverbial Philosophy* fame, John Tupper (whose residence was in Le Pollet) became a Jurat of the Royal Court and during the War of American Independence operated as a privateer with no mean success. With three ships in the fray, he brought in during the course of the conflict prizes worth nearly £60,000 — about £2,000,000 at modern (1984) prices.

TURBERVILLE, CAPTAIN ROBERT. At the end of Henry VIII's reign the Privy Council, realising Alderney's potential as a base for harrying Channel shipping and as a haven of refuge from French privateers, decided to fortify its main anchorage at Longy. As a result Captain Robert Turberville was sent to the island in 1547, with the title of Marshall of Alderney, to take command of the garrison of 200 troops as well as of the 200-strong labour force. Although building operations after the fall of Protector Somerset in October 1549 were spasmodic, the project remained alive for the next four years, so that in 1553 Turberville was willing to buy from Adrian Crole (q.v.*) the equipment which the Fleming had removed from the French installations in Sark. The Aurigniais, however, disliking the influx of labourers and soldiers, and resenting Turberville's attempts to exercise authority over them, complained to the Privy Council, with the outcome that in 1554 the 'Marshal of Alderney' was recalled, never to return — and leaving the island a prey to the tender mercies of Captain Malesart (q.v.*).

V

VIGNOL, SAINT (?). Gracing La Grande Vallée to the west of La Petite Blaye is a charming garden commemorating all involved in the conversion of Alderney and named after St Vignol (Latin: *Vignalis*). This evangelistic wraith, so insubstantial as to be unknown to the Calendar of Saints, is supposed by common (but ill-informed) report to have brought Christianity to Alderney c. A.D. 575; and is identified by one school of thought with Herm's St Tugual (q.v.). Another opinion attributes Alderney's introduction to the Faith to St Guénault (q.v.), for whose existence there is far more credible evidence.

W

WAKE, SIR BALDWIN. Sir Baldwin Wake — who replaced Sir Peter Osborne (q.v.) as Royalist Governor of Guernsey at Castle Cornet in 1646 following representations made to Charles, Prince of Wales by Sir George Carteret (q.v.) when the prince visited Jersey in April of that year — was most likely the third son of Sir Baldwin Wake, of Clevedon, Somerset, who was created a baronet on 5 December 1621. His eldest brother (the second baronet Sir Edward Wake), raised a troop of horse for the king and also attended Charles II when he took refuge in Jersey in September 1649. Sir Baldwin appears to have been both a naval and a military officer. It is recounted by that peerless Guernsey historian Ferdinand Brock Tupper (q.v.) that he made an honourable answer to Colonel Russell when called upon to surrender the castle in January 1647. He was away in England early in September 1648, but returned the same month, reporting his safe arrival back in Castle Cornet to Prince Rupert on 14 September. His relations with Sir George Carteret were, however, as strained as had been those between the eminent Jerseyman and Sir Peter Osborne, and as a consequence he declined to allow Sir George into the castle with more than six men — a refusal that rendered impossible any plan by Carteret to invade Guernsey in the Royalist interest. Sir George complained to the new king when he arrived in Jersey in September 1649, and Wake thereupon followed in the footsteps of his predecessor, to be replaced by Colonel Sir Robert Burgess (q.v.*) who, however, was only appointed to act as Lieutenant-Governor under Henry, Lord Percy, as absentee Governor. Sir Baldwin's subsequent fate is unknown.

WESLEY, REVEREND JOHN (1703-1791). This renowned revivalist, whose parish was the world, braved the stormy seas in August 1787, at the age of 84, to visit the Bailiwick in support of the proselytising efforts initiated the previous year by his fervent disciple, Jean de Quetteville (q.v.). Staying at Mon Plaisir, the home of Henri de Jersey, which had become the local headquarters of his movement, Wesley preached from a nearby *perron* (mounting block) still to be seen in the

Green Lanes (alias Les Camps Collette Nicolle), attracting large numbers both there and in the Assembly Rooms (now the Guille-Allès Library), where he also spoke. The indefatigable octogenarian subsequently went on to Alderney (where another of his followers, Dr. Adam Clarke, had introduced Methodism earlier the same year) and proclaimed his message at the Old Forge near Braye Harbour, as well as from an upstairs window at La Maison Jeanette, off Marais Square. He stayed at the house in Braye Street now known as the *Diver's Inn* where, according to his *Journal*, he and his companions were accommodated in a room with five beds where he 'slept in peace'.

DE WESTON, WALTER. Walter de Weston had the unique experience of being Sub-Warden of the Isles on no less than four occasions. The first was from 1334 to 1336, and the second in 1338, in which year the French under Admiral Béuchet (q.v.*) over-ran the entire archipelago save only Mont Orgueil. In 1340, after Edward III's naval victory at Sluys had robbed the enemy of control of the Channel, de Weston returned at the head of a relief force which liberated the islands. He was, however, unable to subdue Castle Cornet, which the foe continued to hold until 1345 when it was finally retaken by Godfrey de Harcourt (q.v.*). With the recovery of the islands, de Weston resumed his duties as Sub-Warden pending the appointment the following year of Thomas de Hampton as Warden. Between the years 1343 and 1347, however, de Weston served as Sub-Warden yet again for a fourth term — this time under Sir Thomas de Ferrers as Warden.

WHITE, TERENCE HANBURY (1906-1964). Born in Bombay on 29 May 1906, this Aurigniais by adoption was educated at Cheltenham College whence he went up to Cambridge (Queens') — where he published a book of poems while still an undergraduate. On coming down he taught at Stowe School until 1936 when — *Farewell Victoria* having already appeared in 1933 and heedless of the danger of penury involved in the step he was taking — he decided to devote himself entirely to writing, living initially in a gamekeeper's cottage near the school. Terence Hanbury White's main claim to fame rests on the quartet, *The Once and Future King*, the first novel of which (*The Sword in the Stone*) was produced in 1939. Despite further works such as *Mistress Masham's Repose* (1946), *The Age of Scandal* (1950) and *The Goshawk* (1951) — a classic account of a struggle of wills between man and beast — White's pen never brought him more than a bare competence. Finding the larger islands deficient in the seclusion he sought and eschewing Sark because of its ban on bitches, he settled in Alderney in June 1947, setting up house at 3, Connaught Square (for which he paid £800) and candidly admitting his impecuniosity in a contribution made during 1955 to a publication entitled *Twentieth Century Authors: A Biographical Dictionary*, in which he wrote, 'I now live in a small house on an island in the English Channel and funds are beginning to run low'. Terence Hanbury White remained domiciled in Alderney for the rest of his days and died on 17 January 1964.

WILLIAM III, KING OF ENGLAND, SCOTLAND AND IRELAND (1650–1702). This monarch's single-minded dedication to his struggle to save his native Holland from Louis XIV was to have momentous repercussions for the Channel Isles, precluding as it did any toleration on his part of the possibility of their being used by the French as a haven of refuge. He accordingly repudiated unilaterally the status of neutrality which since 1480/1 had given security to the archipelago. He did this by an Order-in-Council of 8 August 1689 which, although apologetic in tone and with the superficial appearance of being provisional, nevertheless effectively put a stop to the local franchise which had been a major formative influence on island development for over two centuries: 'His Majesty in Council is this day pleased to declare that (being at this time strictly obliged in his treaties with his allies and confederates to prohibit in all his dominions all trade and commerce whatsoever with France) he does not think it fit or expedient to dispense with the execution of this said Order in this present and extraordinary juncture of time; yet, it is not the intention of His Majesty in any manner whatsoever to revoke or infringe any privileges that may have been granted by his royal predecessors to the inhabitants of the said island of Guernsey'. An epoch had come to an end.

PART III

FAMILY TREES

NOTE

As already stated in the explanatory notes following the preface, these tables do not attempt to provide complete genealogies, but (as their name implies) seek only to illustrate relationships. BLOCK CAPITALS are employed for anyone accorded an entry in Part I. The name of any person who is the subject of an entry in Part II is *italicised*. The name of any woman who, because of marriage, appears twice in the same Table, is BOXED . Note in particular the distinction between de Sausmarez, Saumarez and de Saumarez. Matthew, the father of Admiral Lord de Saumarez—and himself a naval surgeon—in emulation of his brothers Philip and Thomas dropped from his name both the prefix and the second 's'. All of his lineage have continued this practice, except for each generation's peer who, upon succession, resumes the 'de' while continuing to forego the second 's'. On the other hand, the descendants of the Procureur John de Sausmarez (the remaining son of Matthew de Sausmarez and Anne Durell) have retained both features of the ancient name of this house.

KINSHIP TABLE A

Andros/le Mesurier/de Sausmarez/Briard/Dobrée/Perchard links

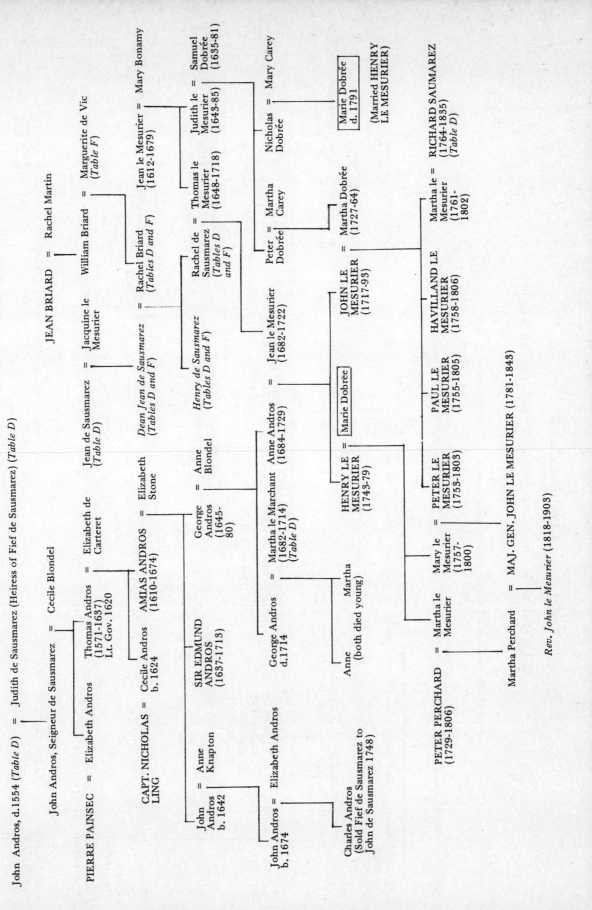

KINSHIP TABLE B

Lukis/Mansell/de Guerin *and* Collings/Lukis/Gosselin/Carey links

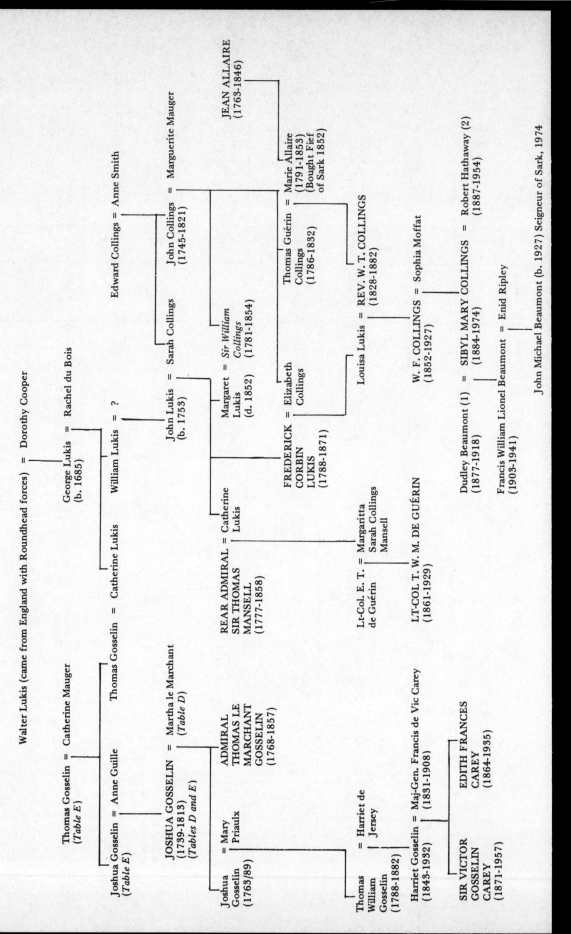

KINSHIP TABLE C

Guille (Castel)/Métivier links *and* Guille (Saints)/Harvey/Neve links

Castel Family

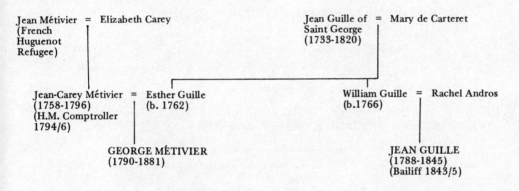

Jean Métivier = Elizabeth Carey
(French
Huguenot
Refugee)

Jean Guille of = Mary de Carteret
Saint George
(1733-1820)

Jean-Carey Métivier = Esther Guille
(1758-1796)   (b. 1762)
(H.M. Comptroller
1794/6)

William Guille = Rachel Andros
(b.1766)

GEORGE MÉTIVIER
(1790-1881)

JEAN GUILLE
(1788-1845)
(Bailiff 1843/5)

Saints Family

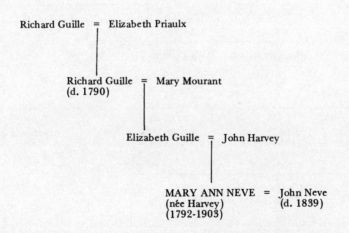

Richard Guille = Elizabeth Priaulx

Richard Guille = Mary Mourant
(d. 1790)

Elizabeth Guille = John Harvey

MARY ANN NEVE = John Neve
(née Harvey)   (d. 1839)
(1792-1903)

KINSHIP TABLE D

Andros/de Sausmarez/Saumarez/le Marchant links

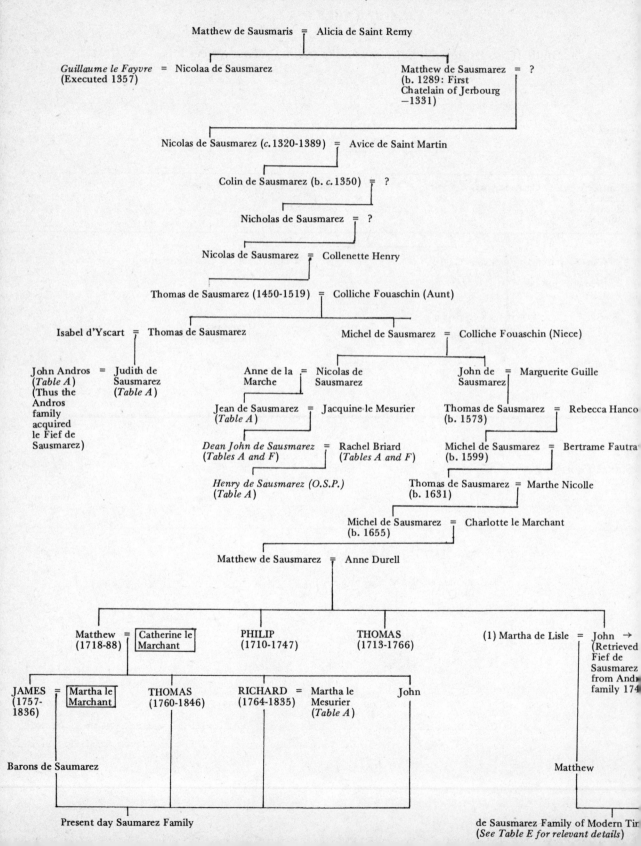

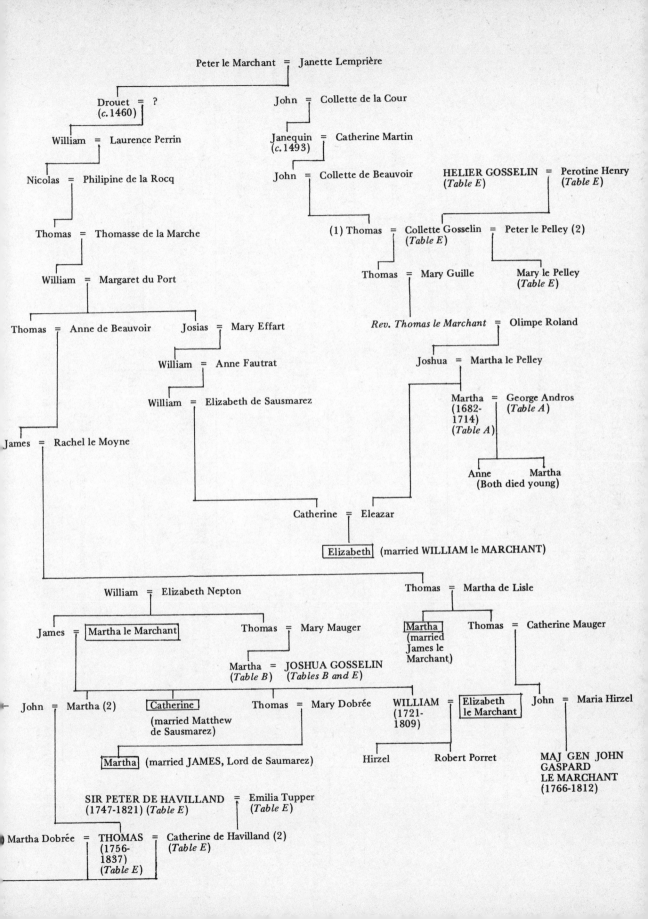

KINSHIP TABLE E

Gosselin/Tupper/Brock/de Sausmarez links

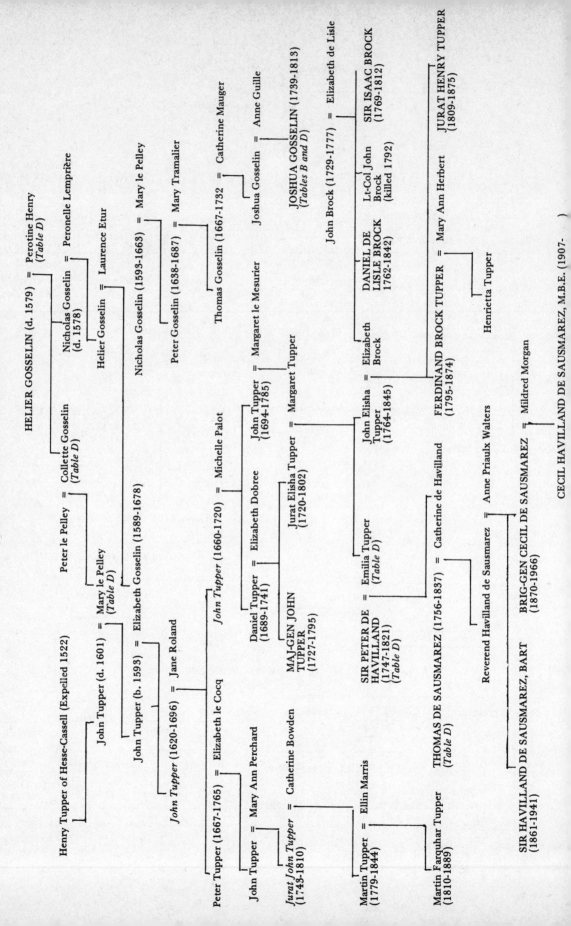

KINSHIP TABLE F

de Vic/de Carteret/le Roy/Briard/de Sausmarez/le Mesurier links

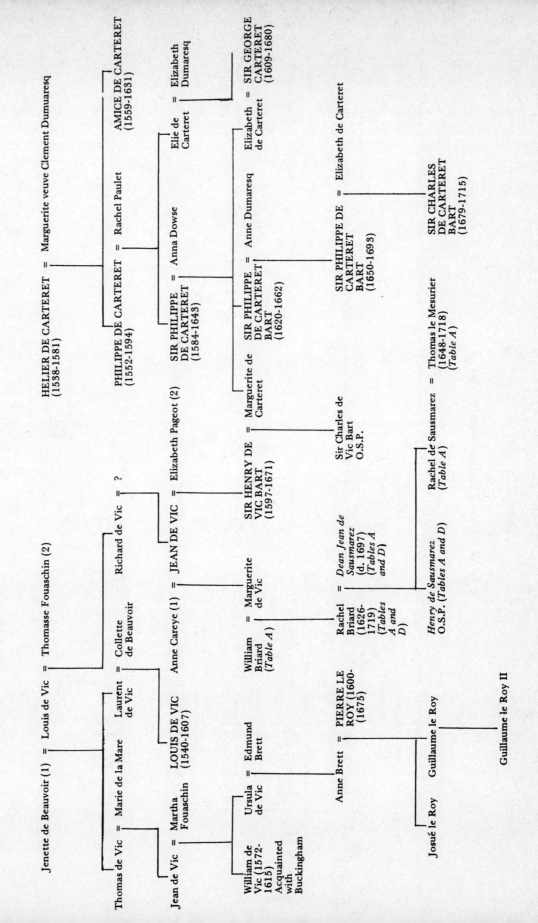

KINSHIP TABLE G

le Pelley/le Gros/Brévint/Slowley links

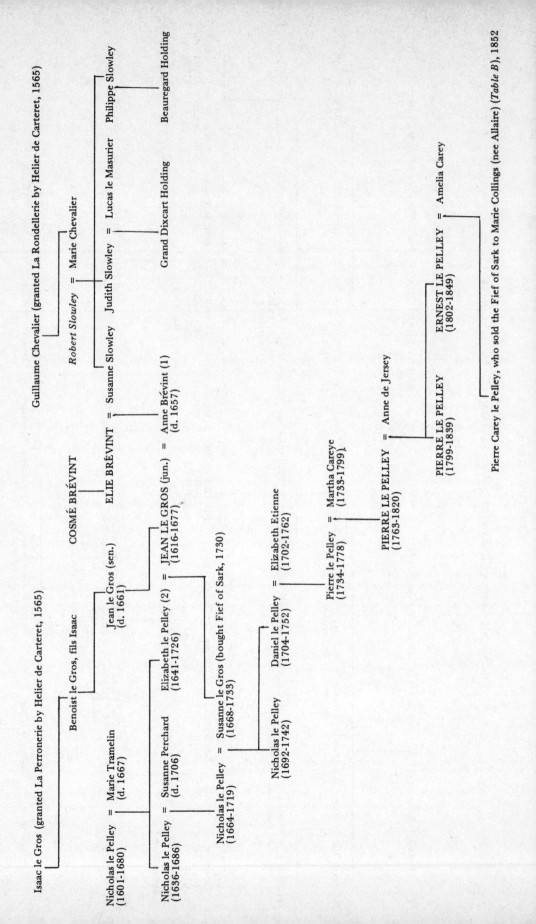

Isaac le Gros (granted La Perronerie by Helier de Carteret, 1565)

Guillaume Chevalier (granted La Rondellerie by Helier de Carteret, 1565)

Benoist le Gros, fils Isaac

Robert Slowley = Marie Chevalier

COSMÉ BRÉVINT

Jean le Gros (sen.) (d. 1661)

ELIE BRÉVINT = Susanne Slowley   Judith Slowley = Lucas le Masurier   Philippe Slowley

Anne Brévint (1) (d. 1657)

Grand Dixcart Holding

Beauregard Holding

Nicholas le Pelley (1601-1680) = Marie Tramelin (d. 1667)

Elizabeth le Pelley (2) (1641-1726) = JEAN LE GROS (jun.) (1616-1677)

Nicholas le Pelley (1636-1686) = Susanne Perchard (d. 1706)

Susanne le Gros (bought Fief of Sark, 1730)

Nicholas le Pelley (1664-1719) = Susanne le Gros (1668-1733)

Daniel le Pelley (1704-1752) = Elizabeth Etienne (1702-1762)

Nicholas le Pelley (1692-1742)

Pierre le Pelley (1734-1778) = Martha Careye (1733-1799)

PIERRE LE PELLEY (1763-1820) = Anne de Jersey

PIERRE LE PELLEY (1799-1839)

ERNEST LE PELLEY (1802-1849) = Amelia Carey

Pierre Carey le Pelley, who sold the Fief of Sark to Marie Collings (nee Allaire) (*Table B*), 1852

PART III: APPENDIX

I have received the following amazing letter from Norway, from a specialist in Norwegian history. Because of its local interest would you kindly publish in the Dear Sir column.

Mrs. Ronald Mauger
Rosenheim,
La Gibauderie Road,
St Peter Port.

My 30th cousin (or maybe a little less) in agnatic lineage (as his ancestor, Walter St Clair, Normandie, born approximately 1180/90, seems to be the son of a grandson's grandson of my ancestor, Thorrin Vasse, of Orkney descent, born 1001), Col Stig Adeler, Canary Islands, has given me your address, probably because he very flatteringly regards me to be some kind of a specialist on the first Earls of Marr, Mauger ancestors in the first millenium.

Mauger is really an old Norwegian word (megir) meaning sword. The son of Rollo (Gange-Rolv Ragnvaldson), William, is in our sagas given the epithet Langsverd (equals Long-sword), while other sources are said to name him Mauger; obviously correct.

Rollo, born 846 according to Frankish sources, came from Marr, a county in western Norway today called More (Moere). His father was the very famous and historically important Earl of Marr, Ragnvald the Strong, who got Orkney as a gift.

He was the son of Eysten Glumra, also mentioned at Marr, son of Ivar, Earl of Oppland (a district north of Oslo), son of King Halvdan Hvitben (White-foot), who had his seat at Vest, mar, also spelt Westmaur, a part of Vestfold, today a county west of the Oslo Fjord, at that time the Kingdom of Westarfolda, which was the whole of southern and western Norway.

It was also, in foreign sources, called Mauringania, meaning Gania of the Ocean (Norway was often called the Ocean, or the Sea, by Latin sources, and for instance, the legends about King Arthur of the Round Table equals King Thor in saga.

Halvdan Hvitben is in Ynglinge Saga mixed up with an earlier king, Halvdan Hvitlegg (White-leg) and given his pedigree there. Hvitben was the son of a Norwegian king (Saxo) Gote, in sagas called Eysten Gotske (Gote) of Vestfold, of known Ring lineage.

Marr is in heraldry depicted in different ways: 1. A bend (equals mare in Norwegian); 2. Wavy lines (equals sea equals mare in Latin and marr in old Norwegian); 3. Seagull (equals mar in old Norwegian); 4. Black man or head (equals maur, moor); 5. Brick or stone wall (equals mar in Norwegian).

But family lines have at all times also flourished their own coats of arms, like boat, eagle, raven, crow (corona), crown (corona) and bar.

William Langsverd (Mauger), second Duke, had the son Richard the Fearless, father of a new Richard, fourth Duke, ancestor of Maugers. This Richard had, however, at least three brothers, a count of Corbeil, Robert, Count of Evreux (he is in sagas called Earl Valland), and a third, Viljalm (William), also Earl of Valland, as their mother was a Capetienne of France.

Both Snorre and Sicilian history mention him, the last because he was ancestor to a Sicilian royal house, being the father of Tancred of Hautville, the father of Robert Guiscard, who took Italy etc.

It is less known that the elder brother of Rollo, King Einar Dal-Koll of Orkneys and Pictia (West Scotland), became ancestor of important royal houses all over Europe after Norman time, even a Czar line in Russia (the Romanovs), and also the Washington family of England.

Strangely enough the present Princess of Wales, formerly Lady Diana Spencer, is also one of his descendants, through a Norwegian line, the Bonde (Colon) family.

Also Rollo spent some time in Scotland, with his brother, and two of Rollo's daughters were married to Scottish kings, according to P. A. Munch. Rollo did not get his strength from Norway, but from Scotland.

SVEIN GRODYS
Leil. 101,
Brekkevei 23, 1430 As,
Norway.

(Reproduced by permission of the Guernsey Evening Press and Star, *edition of Tuesday 18 May 1982)*

PART IV

EARLY BAILIWICK NAMES

by

DR. S. K. KELLETT-SMITH

INTRODUCTORY REMARKS

The following, in contrast to the preceding sections, is concerned mainly with humbler folk living in the Middle Ages within the Bailiwick of Guernsey. It is intended to chronicle some 550 names of people ranging from pauper to inn-keeper, from landowner to poor fisherman, from oppressed farmers and their wives to thieves and murderers, with a trifle of information about each.

These names have been abstracted from five sources — the Rolls of the Assizes held in 1309, Ancient Petitions of the Chancery and the Exchequer, the Extente of 1274, the Cartulaire de Jersey Guernesey etc., and 'Herm and Jethou' — all works available in the Priaulx Library. The names are arranged in alphabetical order under each of the above reference-headings; originally it was planned to record each person under his or her parish, but as only the Extente gives us the required parish, and this in some cases only, this plan had to be shelved and the present layout adopted.

The vast majority of Christian names are of Germanic (Frankish) and Biblical origin, with one or two that are now virtually obsolete, e.g.: Scholastica, Emmelotta. Just about the only — yet frequent — Scandinavian Christian name persisting is Ranulf, with its derivatives Raoul, Renouf, and Ralph. Scandinavian surnames nowadays form but a small percentage of what one regards as typical Guernsey names, but bearers of these names constitute a far larger proportion of the traditional Guernsey population. Torodes, Ogiers, Renoufs, etc., are numerous and surely of ancient origin, as witness in our list Thoroude (Torode) from 'Thorvald', Ode (Ogier) from 'Odin' (via intermediate forms such as Otger); Turgeys from 'Thorgils'; Tostain from 'Thorstein'; Chetill father of Torald, from 'Ketil'; all this bears out a general truth that of all Scandinavian names to survive in foreign lands, those derived from Thor are commonest, followed by Ketil.

One may enumerate some 160 surnames which are commonly accepted as being Guernsey names — though naturally these are by no means confined to the Bailiwick — and of these about one-half may be found represented under the several reference-headings. In a few instances the same individual, i.e. a person bearing the same Christian and surname, appears under two or more headings, but it is not always possible to be certain that we are dealing with just the one person, and scrutiny of the original sources is probably the only, and not always satisfactory, solution to the problem. Lastly, some interest may be derived from the short informative précis that follow each entry; one wonders what tragedies lie behind the numerous murders and assaults by night; how came poor Geoffrey le Cu to hang himself and the Chapelle men to be such a family of utter rascals, and what was John Lalowe's general reputation among his neighbours. Interested readers may find further information in the references, to which this list pretends to supply no more than a guide.

1. Rolls of the Assizes held in the Channel Islands ... A.D. 1309

A

ABRAHAM, ROBERT; a Crown juror in Pleas of of the Crown in Sark.

ADAM, JOHN; a taverner, fined for selling contrary to the Assize; also accused of theft from Ralph Adam.

ADAM, RALPH; accused John Adam of theft; associated with Robert Adam in the crime of burglary.

ADAM, ROBERT; associated with Ralph Adam in the crime of burglary.

ALEXANDER, OSBERT; fined 19 sols for wounding Helen Restaud, thereby causing her death.

ALIANOR, ALICE; accused of harbouring Matilda Lohir, who had abjured the islands; see Eminer, Emmeline.

AMELOT, PETER; 'broke the assize of bread'.

ANEYNE, WILLIAM; wounded by night by William Toytin, but later shown to have himself wounded said William Toytin in the first place.

ANGOT, RICHARD; his daughter Joan taken off by Richard du Port.

219

AUNYS, PETER; with others, accused Oliver Galan of theft.

AVOINE, EMMA D' and AVOIN, LUKE GRAIN D'; Emma gaoled for stealing from Luke, her husband.

B

BALAN, GERVAISE; juror of the Vale.

BALAN, WILLIAM; accused of kidnapping John Robert's wife; in fact her husband was cuckolded 'as he lay with her'.

BALIGAN, AVICE; owes 2 bushels of wheat.

BARBER, JOAN LA; holds 1 messuage and 1 virgate worth 2 bushels wheat.

BARBER, JONETT LE; with Jonett le Plemonceys and Colin Denys, broke open by night the doors of the widow of Peter Larker, and same of William le Neveu; gaoled.

BARBER, WILLIAM; was assaulted by night by Ralph de Boure.

BARENTIN, JOHN DE; with others, claims wreckage rights at Jerbourg, and right of warren.

BARNARD, PETER; with WILLIAM LE GROS, pays 2 loaves and 2 capons for the messuage 'towards the sea'.

BASSETT, WILLIAM; attacked by night by Jonett Pian.

BAUDEWYN, PETER; representative of Ralph of Rouen, ship-owner, whose vessel was wrecked on Guernsey.

BAUGE, COLIN; indicted for inciting robbery and for stealing from the king's mill.

BEALASSIS, OLIVER; taverner, fined with others for selling contrary to the assize.

BEAUCHAMP, THOMAS DE; one of several holders of udal land, who sold his land to the king for an annual pension to himself and his heirs.

BEAUVER, FLORIA DE; accused of stealing hens, etc., from Haundevil and from Joan Rolaunt.

BEAUVER, RALPH DE; the King's Serjeant; compounded for 100 sols for allowing Colin Blondel, a prisoner, 'to wander free in the village', whereas he should have been in gaol.

BELASSET, OLIVER; had sheaves stolen by John Forlot; also himself accused of stealing one pig.

BENET, RICHARD; see Durel, Nicolas, priest.

BENNES, JOHN; one of several bakers fined for 'breaking the assize of bread and wine'.

BERNARD, JOHN; with partner William Bernard, fined for encroaching on the king's highway.

BERNARD, WILLIAM; see Bernard, John.

BESOIGNE, MATTHEW DE; with John de Rocheford and Johanettus de Genas, abjured the islands for the murder of Johanette Naom.

BETE, RICHARD DE LA; his sheaves of wheat stolen by Michel de Graunceys and Thomas Elyes, who were first found not guilty, but later gaoled.

BLAUNCHE, GILLOT; assaulted Richard le Mouner in the king's mill; later put on trial for theft.

BLENLOK, WILLIAM; a Sark man; one of his sheep was taken by Ralph Ode: during their dispute it fell over a cliff and was killed.

BLONDEL, COLIN; see Duvel, Richard; and Beauver, Ralph de.

BLONDEL, JOHANNET; compounded for 100 sols for beating the son of John of Cobo on the seashore.

BLONDEL, MATTHEW; fined for 'pleading with the twelve without License'.

BLONDEL, RALPH; returned to Sark with king's letter of pardon after abjuring the islands; his lands were improperly restored to him by the Bailiff who had no proper authority.

BLONDEL, RICHARD; fined for stealing rayfish.

BLONDEL, WILLIAM; accused of making off with William Melege's wife.

BLUNDEL, COLIN; fined for wrongly raising the Clameur de Haro against William Truant; Nicolas Durel, priest, attempted to extort money from him and others.

BOLE, THOMAS; wounded in the head by William Corlu; a taverner; fined with others for 'breaking the assize of bread and wine'.

BONAMY, MATILDA; thrown to the ground by Jordan Clouett whereby she was delivered of an abortive child who died.

BOSCO, NICOLAS DE; as per Beauchamp, Thomas de.

BOT, PETRONELLA LE; fined for concealing from the king's receiver a small chest taken from a wreck; a Sark woman.

BOTILLER, WILLIAM; hanged. See Carteret, Jean de, p. 231.

BOUCE, JORDAN; fined for encroaching on the king's highway.

BOUGRE, ADAM DE; one of the electors of St Peter-Port.

BOURE, RALPH DE; see Barber, William le; was assaulted by night by William de Câtel.

BOUTILLIER, JORDAN; owes 2 loaves and 2 capons for his property.

BOYA, RICHARD DE; forcibly 'rescued' an ox from William le Count.

BOYE, WILLIAM; gaoled and pilloried, in that he indicted 3 men for theft, then sat as 'one of the twelve' who acquitted them.

BRETON, JOHN LE; wounded by Johannet Clouett.

BRETON, JOHN LE, Senr.; one of several standing as guarantor for Nicolas Durel when he compounded his crime for 30 livres.

BRETON, JONETT; assaulted by night by Jonett Clouett.

BRETON, THOMAS DE; fined for encroaching on the king's highway.

BURNEL, COLIN; a juror of St Samson's parish; assaulted by night by Guillot de la Chapelle.

BURNEL, RALPH; the king claims from him and others 1 mill in the Forest.

BURNEL, WILLIAM; murdered; see Vigor, Peter.

C

CACHER, COLIN LE; pilloried for being found 'in the chamber of Raulina Isonde wishing to have dinner there by stealth'.

CALEZ, JOHN; see Durel, Nicholas.

CANS; his (or her?) daughter had her overtunic, etc., stolen by William May and William Durel.

CARDET, JOHN; the Bordage hangman.

CARETTE, RAYMUND LA; accused of theft, took sanctuary in St Saviour's church, and abjured the islands.

CAPOUN, MATTHEW; accused of furtively broaching a wine cask belonging to William le Lumbard; not guilty.

CARPENTIER, NICOLAS DE; wrongfully fenced off some common land.

CARTERET, JOHN DE; held the wreckage rights of Brecqou.

CARUPEL, COLIN; 'owes of relief for the death of his father 9 sols'; a Sark man.

CARUPEL, WILLIAM; one of the jurors witnessing that the advowsons of 5 parishes belong from time immemorial to Marmoutier.

CASTEL, AUGUSTINE DE; assaulted by Matthew du Prael.

CASTEL, MATTHEW DE; fined for beating by night William Lynot.

CASTRO, WILLIAM DE; accused of serious assault by night.

CATEL, ROBINET DE; prosecuted Helen le Vecchere 'concerning lay chattels'; the latter compounded.

CATEL, WILLIAM DE; fined for night assault on Ralph de Boure.

CELER, ROBERT DE; a king's man; murdered by Thomas d'Estefeld.

CHAPELLE, GUILLOT DE LA, Senr.; gaoled for keeping for 2 weeks a steer of the widow of Henry Turgis.

CHAPELLE, GUILLOT DE LA; fined for assaulting by night Colin Burnel; together with his brothers Henry and Ralf, gaoled for being found throwing stones at each other.

CHAPELLE, RICHARD DE LA; a thief; outlawed.

CHAPELLE, WILLIAM DE LA, Junr.; accused of stealing a washbasin and hens from Ralph Forlot, chaplain, with William Robeys.

CHAPELLE, WILLIAM DE LA; gaoled for theft of a horse belonging to the widow of Henry Turgis; with partners, owned a mill in the Forest; and see Vivier, Raulina du.

CHAPELLE, WILLIAM DE LA, Senr.; accused of stealing a horse belonging to Henry Turgis; not guilty.

CHARNETHOUS, JOHN; a Herm man; stole money from John de la Ville; fled and therefore outlawed by the justices of the Abbot of Cherbourg. [The crime would therefore have occurred on Herm, where the Abbot's ecclesiastical law obtained].

CHOFFIN, BENEDICTA; murdered her husband Peter Oar, abjured the islands.

CHOFFIN, JORDAN; a representative of the Forest in re Les Landes market.

CHUAN, PETER DE; representative of St Saviour's parish in re Les Landes market.

CLOET, JONETT; gaoled for harbouring thieves and taking conies from the king.

CLOUET, JOHN; 'broke the assize of bread and wine'.

CLOUET, JORDAN; abjured the islands for killing an abortive child by throwing Matilda Bonamy to the ground. Pardoned.

CLOUETT, JOHANETT; accused of wounding Richard le Faucouner on the king's highway, 'wherefore blood etc.'; his crime compounded for 36 sols; same accusation in re John le Breton.

COBO, JOHN OF; his son beaten on the seashore by Johannet Blondel.

COLHAELET, STEPHEN; one of the Crown jurors in Pleas of the Crown in Sark.

CORBYN, COLIN; assaulted by night by John Jordan (who later died), and by John Esturnel and Jonett Esturnel, who were both fined.

CORLU, WILLIAM; wounded Thomas Bole in the head; fined.

CORNAILLE, PETER LA; with Robert Dagenas, Luke le Corner and Richard le Herice detained half the cargo of a ship wrecked on Guernsey, belonging to Ralph of Rouen; fined for absence from the Court of assize.

CORNER, LUKE LE; see Cornaille, Peter la.

CORNER, PETER LE; guilty of suing Luke Larcher in the Court of Christianity instead of in the king's court; compounded prison sentence for 80 livres.

COUNT, WILLIAM LE; see Boya, Richard de.

COURT, RICHARD DE LA; fined for night assault on Salvatus Martin.

COUTURE, WILLIAM DE LA; to rebuild at his own cost a bridge that he accidentally demolished.

CROIX, RALPH DE LA; a Sark landowner.

CU, GEOFFREY LE; 'moved by poverty and grief, hanged himself'.

CURLA, WILLIAM; one of those fined for 'breaking the assize of bread and wine'.

D

DAGENAS, ROBERT; see Cornaille, Peter la.

DARCIZ, DARTIS, PETER; as per Carupel, William; a juror; representative of the Abbot of Blanchelande in dispute over the advowson of St Martin's church.

DAVY, BAUDEWYN; representative of St Samson's parish in re Les Landes market.

DEN, JOHN LE; fined for 'breaking the assize of bread and ale'.

DENYS, COLIN; gaoled; with Jonett le Plemonceys and Jonett le Barber broke open by night the doors of the widow of Peter Larker and of William le Neveu.

DENYS, MATTHEW; see Gilbert, Floria.

DIONIS, GEOFFREY; his son accidentally killed by a pig; value of one hog to be donated by him to provide a quay by the sea.

DIRE, JORDAN; the king claims 1 mill in the Forest from him and others.

DISCART, JORDAN; a representative of the Forest in re Les Landes market; apparently later a juror of St Martin's parish.

DISME, JOHN; his wife and all her goods taken away by Ralph Mengis; assaulted John le Key; sentence compounded.

DOREE, PETER; fined for encroaching on the king's highway.

DUCHEMIN, JOHN; his necklace allegedly stolen by Richard Marche.

DUREL, NICOLAS; priest; accused of extorting money from Colin Blundel and William le Gaufre, accused of 'causing to be cited out of the kingdom and extorting money from . . .' Colin Blundel, Robert Osmund, Richard Galiot, John Calez, Richard Benet, Oliver Juliene, Gregory Fitzsimmon, Robert de Vic, Peter de Vic, and William Genemies.

DUREL, WILLIAM; 'of tender age' gaoled for taking the king's conies; not guilty of stealing an overtunic from the daughter of Cans, together with William May.

DYE, RICHARD; owes 2 hens to the king for unlawful enclosure.

DYMOKE, JAMES; murdered John le Orfevre, sought sanctuary and abjured the islands.

DYRE, JORDAN; the king claims 1 mill in the Forest from him, along with Ralph Burnel and William de la Chapelle.

E

ELYES, THOMAS; see Graunceys, Michael de.

EMINER, EMMELINE; sheltered Matilda Lohir, who had abjured the islands; therefore herself abjured the islands.

ERNAL, PETER; as per Carupel, William, i.e. juror.

ESMITET, WILLIAM; as per Beauchamp, Thomas de.

ESPIN, JEAN DEL; priest on Lihou, murdered by Thomas le Roser.

ESTFELD, ALICE D' and ESTFELD, THOMAS D'; both fined, together with Matthew de Saumarez, for allowing sailors to remove a wrecked ship from their land; Thomas murdered Thomas de Celer, sought sanctuary and abjured the islands; his land therefore escheated.

ESTUR, JOHN; had 1 wether stolen by William Germayn, who however was found not guilty.

ESTURNEL, JOHN and ESTURNEL, JONETT; see Corbyn, Colin.

EVELYN, THOMAS; a juror of St Peter's parish.

F

FABER, JOHN; gaoled for night assault on William le Rey.

FALAISE, ALICE DE LA; her land — 4 virgates — escheated.

FAUCOUNER, RICHARD LE; wounded by Johannet Clouett.

FAUSILIOUN, DROGO; a Sark man; obtains restoration of 6 virgates of land in Sark (obscure).

FEROUN(D), RALPH; accused of stealing his own father's sheep; not guilty; committed night assault on William le Rey, assisted by Peter du Mont; holds part of the escheated land of Joan la Hocheresse.

FEUVRE, WILLIAM LE, Senr.; a baker; fined for 'breaking the assize of bread and wine'.

FEVRE, NICOLAS LE; a jurat accused by Gerard Philip of withholding the king's dues, and trying to bribe him; sentenced to gaol, but compounded for 100 livres.

FEVRE, RALPH LE; with his wife, Juliane, seems to have abjured the islands; their land now held by Robert le Gay.

FITZSIMMON, GREGORY; see Durel, Nicolas.

FLOINES, ROBERT; a udal landowner as per Beauchamp, Thomas de.

FLORINCENT, JOAN; murdered by Matthew le Besoigne, John de Rocheford and Johanettus de Genas.

FLOYNES, ROBERT; as per Carupel, William.

FONTANELLE, JOAN DE LA; 'took her married daughter into a certain small house called La Cote belonging to Ranulph Gautier in order that a stranger might lie with her in adultery'; imprisoned and pilloried.

FORLOT, JOHN; accused of stealing sheaves from Simon le Mesurier and Oliver Belasset; not guilty.

FORLOT, RALPH; chaplain; see Chapelle, William de la, junr., and Robeys, William.

FOURNER, PETER LE; 'broke the assize of bread and wine'.

FRANKET, RICHARD; accused of stealing one anchor and plough-irons, along with Johannet Moulin; both gaoled.

FRAUNCEYS, WILLIAM; a Crown juror in Pleas of the Crown in Sark.

FRAUNKET, PHILIPPA DE; accused of receiving Simonette, daughter of John le Marchant, and stolen goods; at first found not guilty, then gaoled.

G

GALAN, OLIVER; accused of theft from Peter

Aunys, John le Graunt and Cicely Salekyn; not guilty.

GALIOT, RICHARD; see Durel, Nicolas.

GARRYS, PETER DE; deputy King's Receiver; see Gerard, Philip.

GASTEIN, PETER LE; a Sark elector.

GAUFRE, WILLIAM LE; see Durel, Nicolas.

GAUTIER, Juliana; robbed by Richard Lestornel, q.v.

GAUTIER, RANULF; see Fontanelle, Joan de la, and Roser, Thomas le.

GAY, ROBERT LE; holder of the escheated land of Ralph and Juliane le Fevre.

GAYDON, JOHN; killed by a fall of stones while working in a quarry.

GEFFREY, ROBERT; his land escheated to the king.

GENAS, JOHANNET DE; see Besoigne, Matthew la.

GENEMIES, WILLIAM; see Durel, Nicolas.

GERMAYN, WILLIAM; acquitted of stealing a sheep from John Estur; and see Huberland, William.

GERMEYNE, —— ; a Sark man; landowner.

GILBERT, FLORIA; requires execution of judgment previously given in her favour against Matthew Denys.

GILBERT, GEMINUS; fined for assault on William Melege.

GILBERT, JOAN; abjured the islands 'in the church' for receiving Emelote (? harbouring a criminal).

GOBBE, RALPH; infant; suffocated in his cradle by a pig.

GOBBE, RALPH LE; outlawed for theft.

GODELAND, MATTHEW; a juror of St Martin's parish.

GOLBE, RALPH LE; ? same as Gobbe, above; not guilty of theft.

GORREYS, ROBERT DE; his sheaves stolen by John de la Mare.

GOSTE, RICHARD; representative of St Martin's parish in re Les Landes market.

GOYE, GILLOT; abjured the islands after theft.

GRAUNCEYS, MICHAEL DE; gaoled with Thomas Elyes for stealing sheaves of Richard de la Bete, and of Robert Turgeys; elsewhere however found not guilty in re the former.

GRAUNT, JOHN LE; see Galan, Oliver.

GREINDEVINE, EMMA; accused with her daughter Philippa of stealing her husband's hens.

GROS, WILLIAM; a representative of St Peter-Port in re Les Landes market.

H

HADDY, or HADY, PETER DE; fined for obstructing the king's highway; later heavily fined for dishonesty and for failing to appear at the suit of William Laloel.

HADDY, or HADY, WILLIAM DE; burgled by Richard Waclyn and his brother Robert and Robert de Oronge.

HAMELIN, RICHARD; stole from the house of Peter le Marchant, bailiff, acquitted by jury, ? on technicality; re-arrested by the king's orders.

HAMON, JOHN; murdered John Jordan, sought sanctuary in Castel church, abjured the islands.

HANE, EMMELOTTA; fined for striking the wife of Philip Tostein.

HANELET, JOHN and WILLIAM: as per Carupel, William.

HARPHAT, RICHARD; representative of Torteval in re Les Landes Market.

HARPYN, JEAN; fined for encroaching on the king's highway.

HAUNDEVIL; see Beauvoir, Floria de.

HAVELAND, RALPH; an elector of St Peter-Port.

HERICE, RICHARD LE; a juror and jurat; representative with Peter Dartys of the Abbot of Blanchelande; and with John du Vivier or Henry Trent representative of the Guernsey commonalty; see also Cornaille, Peter la.

HIDOUS, or HYDUS, JOHN; owed the king 1 bushel of wheat for one-third virgate of land.

HOCHERESSE, JOAN LE; her land partially escheated; part of it held by Ralph Feroun(d).

HOMET, PETER; warned to pay his dues — 1 bushel of wheat — to the king.

HOUEL, WILLIAM; a Sark man; 'owes of relief for the death of his father 9 sols'.

HOWE, HENRY; attacked by Joanetta Wylon, who compounded for 18 sols.

HUBERLAND, WILLIAM DE; accused of buying a wether from William Germayn who had stolen it from John Estur; not guilty, but later gaoled.

HUNGIER, EMMA; abjured the islands for theft.

HUREL, WILLIAM LE; fined for taking the king's rabbits.

I

ISONDE, RAULINA; see Cacher, Colin le.

J

JEREMEYE, WILLIAM; a juror of St Samson's parish.

JEUNE, WILLIAM LE; a representative of St Peter-in-the-Wood in re Les Landes market.

JOEVENE, RALPH; fined for building a wall out onto the king's highway.

JOEVENE, STEPHEN; accused of stealing overtunic from Ralph Ledevin; not guilty; see Ledevin, Ralph.

JOEVENE, WILLIAM; raised Clameur de Haro for night attack on himself.

JOLIET, REGINALD; 'of tender age'; gaoled for taking the king's rabbits.

JORDAN, JOHN; committed night assault on Colin Corbyn; killed by John Hamon.

JULIANE, SIMON; a baker; fined for breaking the assize of bread and wine.

JULIENE, OLIVER; see Durel, Nicolas.

K

KARITEY, RALPH; fined for encroaching on the king's highway.

KATERINE, RALPH; hanged.

KAYNEL, SCHOLASTICA; owes 1 bushel of wheat to the king.

KEMBOUN, SARRA; obstructed the king's highway, by her cottage roof falling in.

KEY, JOHN LE; see Disme, John la.

KEYMAN, ——; as per Carupel, William.

L

LALOEL, WILLIAM; owes 2 bushels of wheat for his land; called Peter de Haddy as witness in a lawsuit, who failed to appear and was fined. Unjustly gaoled by the Abbot of Cherbourg; Abbot therefore fined.

LALOWE, JOHN; his young geese eaten by William le Tellier's cat; kidnapped the cat, and kept William prisoner in his house till he paid 14 large Tournois; compels poor soldiers to pay for his drinks.

LANDES, RICHARD MICHEL DES; owes 2 hens to the king for unlawful enclosure.

LARCHER, LUKE; see Corner, Peter le.

LARKER, PETER; see Denys, Colin.

LAYKER, LUKE; as per Carupel, William.

LEDEVIN, RALPH; accused Steven le Joevene of stealing his overtunic; later accused of stealing his own overtunic so as to accuse Steven le Joevene of theft; not guilty.

LESTAK, HENRY DE; assaulted William Melege by night; compounded for 15 sols.

LESTORNEL, MICHAEL; a juror of St Saviour's parish.

LESTORNEL, RICHARD; hanged; had abjured the islands for theft; on his return, rampaged by night through St Samson's, Vale — there robbing Juliana Gautier — , Câtel, St Saviour's Lihou, and St Peter's church, and re-abjured.

LESTUR, MICHAEL; a representative of Castel parish in re Les Landes market.

LEVESQUE, COLIN; owes 4 years' service to the king for land.

LEVESQUE, NICOLAS; a canon on Herm.

LEVESQUE, PETER; outlawed for stealing.

LISTARC, JORDAN; the king's granger; suffered loss by exchange of currency with Peter de Parvafiaco.

LOHIR, MATILDA; see Eminer, Emmeline.

LOMME, RICHARD; owes 1 bushel of wheat on his land.

LORFEVRE, GILBERT; fined for obstructing the king's highway.

LUMBARD, WILLIAM LE; see Capoun, Matthew.

LUPE, PETER; ship-owner, Spaniard; his ship once wrecked on Guernsey, and division of cargo as then made thought of as a precedent for the future.

LYNOT, WILLIAM; assaulted by night by Matthew de Castel.

M

MACEON, JOHN; master of the ship mentioned under Cornaille, Peter le.

MACHON, PETER LE; an elector of St Peter-Port.

MALEGUE, ALICE; abjured the islands after stealing.

MALMAR, EMMELOTTA; stole a fleece, and abjured the islands.

MANERS, GEOFFREY DE; a udal landowner as per Beauchamp, Thomas de.

MARCHANT, COLIN LE; forces simple paupers to pay for his drinks in taverns; stole a sheep from Colin Nicole; failed to appear at his trial, so his guarantors gaoled.

MARCHANT, PETER LE, a fisherman; owes for his property 1 bushel of wheat.

MARCHANT, PETER LE; Bailiff; see Hamelin, Richard.

MARCHANT, RALPH DE; fined for 'breaking the assize of bread and ale'.

MARCHE, RICHARD; accused of receiving William Renouf after his abjuration of the islands; see Duchemin, John.

MARE, JOHN DE LA; fined for encroaching on the king's highway; see Gorrys, Robert de.

MARKS, WILLIAM; assaulted by night by Colin Renouf, who died before he could be tried.

MARTIN, SALVATUS; assaulted by night by Perrot le Roy, who afterwards compounded.

MAUNCEYS, RICHARD; owes 2 hens to the king for making an unlawful enclosure.

MAUNS, JOHN and JORDAN DES; arraigned for unjustly abstracting part of the estate inherited by Gilbert and Perotte, children of Dionisia.

MAY, WILLIAM; with William Durel, stole an overtunic and other goods from the daughter of Cans; not guilty.

MELEGE, WILLIAM; see Lestak, Henry de; also assaulted by Geminus Gilbert; see Blondel, William.

MENGIS, RALPH; did a wrong to John la Disme — compounded; also accused of taking John Disme's wife and all her goods; found not guilty, but later fined.

MESURIER, RAULIN DE; caught red-handed taking conies in the king's warren with nets and ferrets; fined.

MESURIER, EMMA; hanged.

MESURIER, SIMON LE; assaulted William le Rey. Accused of sheep-stealing — not guilty, a taverner; fined with others for selling contrary to the assize; his sheaves stolen by John Forlot.

MIRESSE, COLETTELA; abjured the islands for receiving Matilda Lohir.

MOIGNE, GEOFFREY LE; died without heir; his lands escheated.

MOIGNE, RALPH LE, JOHN LE, OLIVER LE; sued by the king for dues on land in several parishes.

MONT, PETER DU; fined for night assault on William le Rey; and same upon Guillot le Rey.

MOULIN, JOHANNET; see Franket, Richard.

MOULIN, JOHN DU; abjured the islands for furtively concealing a neighbour's sheep, stealing an anchor, and making iron instruments for picking locks.

MOULLIN, JONETT DU; indicted for stealing wheels, tires, and fleeces, 'furtively clipped'.

MOUNER, RICHARD; a Norman; the king's miller; assaulted by night by Guillot Blaunche.

MUSTENG, —— DE LA; arraigned for unjustly seizing the land of Henry Payncaud.

MUSTENG, JOHN LE; fined for encroaching on the king's highway.

MYNOT, RALPH; a Sark landowner.

N

NAOM, JOHANETTE; murdered by Matthew la Besoigne, John de Rocheford and Johanettus de Genas.

NEEL, RALPH; was improperly summoned to the Court of Christinity; a Sark man.

NEIRJOIE, JOHN; a juror of St Peter-in-the-Wood.

NEVEU, WILLIAM LE; see Barber, Jonett le.

NEWENT, JOHN DE; a Sark landowner.

NICOLE, PETER; a representative of Torteval in re Les Landes market; ? a juror of Castel.

NICOLLE, COLIN; had 2 sheep stolen by Colin le Marchant.

NOEL, PETER; an elector of St Peter-Port; as per Carupel, William.

O

OAR, PETER; murdered by his wife Benedicta Choffyn.

ODE, RALPH; compounded for 10 livres for taking a sheep from William Blenlok; during the argument the sheep fell over the cliff and was killed; disputed over ownership of land with John du Val; both men fined. A Sark man.

ORFEVRE, JOHN LE; murdered by James Dymoke.

ORLYENS, WILLIAM DE; concealed in Herm thieves who had stolen a sail; fined. A Herm Man.

ORENGE, ORONGE, ROBERT DE; accused with others of stealing from the house of William de Hady.

OSMOND, ROBERT; see Durel, Nicolas.

OZANNE, RICHARD; encroached onto the king's highway.

P

PARMENTIER, PETER LE; a Sark taverner.

PARVAFIACO, PETER DE; the king's receiver.

PARYS, SCHOLASTICA DE; abjured the islands for the death of her infant.

PASTER, GEOFFREY DE; assaulted by night by Robert le Peletier.

PATRICK, JOHN; his land worth 2 quarters of wheat escheated to the king.

PAYN, JOHN; accused of sheep-stealing, and of taking a four-wheeled wagon from a shipwreck.

PAYNCAUD, HENRY; see Musteng, —— de la.

PELETIER, ROBERT LE; gaoled for night assault on Geoffrey le Paster.

PELLETIER, PETER LE; hanged.

PESSOUN, RALPH; a taverner; fined for selling contrary to the assize.

PETEVIN, COLIN and PHILIP; Colin had his teeth knocked out by his brother Philip.

PEVERIL, GODFREY; held the escheated land of Jordan Simon — to pay arrears thereon.

PEYTEVIN, WILLIAM LE; encroached onto the king's highway.

PHILIP, GERARD; accused jurat Nicolas le Fevre (q.v.) of withholding the king's dues, and trying to bribe him.

PIAN, JONETT; indicted for assault by night on William Basset.

PLEMONCEYS, JOHN DE; gaoled for wounding a Norman.

PLEMONCEYS, JONETT DE; see Barber, Jonett le.

PONT, WILLIAM DU; an elector of St Peter-Port.

POPECTE, EMMELOTA; many thefts; lands escheated.

PORT, RICHARD DU; accused of kidnapping Joan, Richard Angot's daughter.

PORT, WILLIAM DU; a Crown juror in Pleas of the Crown in Sark.

PRAEL, MATTHEW DE; wounded Augustine de Castel; assaulted by night William de Vinot.

PYAN, JOHN; accused of serious assault by night.

PYNERE, JOHN; a Sark landowner.

R

RALPH, PETER; stole a boat; outlawed.

RATEYS, ROBERT LE; abjured the islands after theft.

RENALD, ROBERT; a representative of St Samson's parish in re Les Landes market.

RENOUF, COLIN; indicted for night assault on William Marks; died before the trial.

RENOUF, WILLIAM; abjured the islands, harboured by Richard Marche.

RESTAUD, HELEN; wife of William Restaud; beaten by Jordan Thoroude; wounded by Oscar Alexander who was fined 19 sols; her wound proved fatal.

RESTAUD, HENRY; encroached onto the king's highway; fined.

REY, GUILLOT LE; assaulted by night by Peter du Mont.

REY, WILLIAM LE; assaulted by night by Simon le Mesurier, John Faber, Ralph Feroun(d) and Peter du Mont and John de Rocheford; fined for breaking his wife's teeth.

RIORY, RALPH; ex-serjeant of Ralph the Provost; abjured the islands for theft; Ralph the Provost fined for improperly appropriating his land.

RIVIÈRE, WILLIAM DE LA; a representative of St Samson's parish in re Les Landes market; wrongfully fenced off some common land, therefore fined.

ROBERT, JOHN and JORDAN; 'broke the assize of bread'; former accused of theft; not guilty.

ROBEYS, WILLIAM; with William de la Chapelle, accused of stealing hens and a wash-basin from Ralph Forlot, chaplain; not guilty.

ROCHEFORD, JOHN DE; gaoled for night assault on William le Rey; with Matthew la Besoigne, abjured the islands for the murder of Johanette Naom; involved with John de Genas in the murder of Joan Florincent; later returned, ordered to stand trial, imprisoned, but freed on producing the king's pardon.

ROGER, RALPH; hanged.

ROGER, WILLIAM; a representative of St Peter-in-the-Wood in re Les Landes market.

ROKER, PETER DE; as per William Roker Junr.; bought part of Fantosme bordage without the king's consent; fined.

ROKER, WILLIAM DE, Junr.; gaoled for breaking by night the windows of the widow of Robert Sarre, along with Peter de Roker.

ROLAUNT, JOAN; along with Haundevil, had her hens stolen by Floria de Beauver.

ROSER, THOMAS LE; servant of Jean del Espin, monk on Lihou, whom he murdered; in turn killed by Ranulph Gautier.

ROSEYE, —— LE; a Sark taverner.

ROUEN, RALPH DE; ship-owner; ship wrecked on Guernsey.

ROY, PERROT LE; compounded for night assault on Salvatus Martin.

S

ST MARTIN, HENRY DE; summoned, with Avice de Wyk, for taking 'royal aid' from their men and tenements.

SALEKYN, CICELY; allegedly robbed by Oliver Galan.

SARRE, ROBERT; see Roker, William.

SARRE, WILLIAM; fined for obstructing the king's highway with stones.

*SAUZMAREYS, JOAN DE; with Matthew and Nicola, claimed wreckage rights at Jerbourg, and right of warren.

SAY, PETER LE; poached the king's fishing rights by night.

SERKOF, WILLIAM; imprisoned and hanged in Castle Cornet.

SIMON, JORDAN; a Crown juror in Pleas of the Court in Sark.

SIMON, JORDAN; after theft, sought sanctuary, abjured the islands; land escheated.

SOUS-MOULIN, AUGUSTINE DE; indicted for robbery, inciting robbery, and stealing from the king's mill, with Colin Bauge.

STEVEN, ROBERT; fined for encroaching onto the king's highway.

*See note to Part III: here the spelling used is that most commonly found in MS.

T

TARDIF, GUILLOT; holds land worth 2 small bushels.

TELLIER, WILLIAM LE; see Lalowe, John.

THOROUDE, JORDAN; found not guilty of beating Helen, wife of William Restaud, whereby she died.

THOUME, JORDAN; fined for encroaching onto the king's highway.

TOSTEIN, PHILIP; see Hane, Emmelotta.

TOYTIN, MARGERY; wife of William Toytin; claims for assault on the king's highway, leading to 'effusion of blood'.

TOYTIN, WILLIAM; husband of Margery Toytin; accused of wounding William Aneyne by night, but the latter shown to have wounded him first.

TRENTE, HENRY; a representative before the king of the commonalty of Guernsey, along with Richard le Herice.

TRUANT, WILLIAM; see Blundel, Colin.

TURGEYS, HENRY; his horse stolen by William de la Chapelle, Senr.; see Guillot de la Chapelle Senr.

TURGEYS, ROBERT; a thief; abjured the islands; his sheaves stolen by Michael de Graunceys.

V

VACHERE, HELEN; assaulted Robinet du Vivier; the latter fined for suing her in the ecclesiastical court.

VAL, ANDREW DU; with Matthew du Val, sought sanctuary (? reason) then abjured the islands; their land escheated; the present occupiers to pay arrears; see Nicolas du Val.

VAL, COLIN DU; assaulted at sea Robert le Venous of Herm; died before trial.

VAL, JOHN DU; compounded for 40 sols for seeking permission 'to kill the English in his village'; with John de Vauvert, fined for mixing water with wine.

VAL, JOHN DU; a Sark man; in dispute with Peter du Val over land in Sark, both parties fined.

VAL, MATTHEW DU; see Val, Andrew du.

VAL, NICOLAS DU; appears associated with Andrew du Val; both returned to Sark where Nicolas died; Sark commonalty fined for harbouring them.

VAL, PETER DU; a Sark elector in Pleas of the Crown in Sark.

VAUVERT, JOHN DE; fined for mixing water with wine.

VECCHERE, HELEN LA; prosecuted by Robert de Castel 'concerning lay chattels'; compounded.

VENOUS, ROBERT LE; a Herm man; assaulted at sea by Colin du Val.

VERE, BALDWYN DE; received wreckage rights from Robert, Earl of Mortain.

VIC, HENRY DE; 'forces simple paupers to pay for his drinks in taverns'.

VIC, PETER DE; see Durel, Nicolas.

VIC, ROBERT DE; see Durel, Nicolas.

VIGOR, PETER; accused of aiding in the murder of William Burnel; not guilty; questioned the authority of the king's court over him because he was a crusader; compounded for 10 livres.

VILLE, JOHN DE LA; a Herm man; see Charnethous, John.

VINOT, WILLIAM DE; assaulted by night by Matthew du Prael.

VIVIER, JOHN DU; fined for assuming right of chase and taking conies; a representative before the king of the Guernsey commonalty.

VIVIER, RAULINA DU; the king claims 1 mill in the Forest from her, Jordan Dire, John Dyre, Ralph Burnel and William de la Chapelle.

VIVIER, ROBERT DU; gaoled for seizing a wreck at Cobo; summoned for trespass and contempt of court.

VIVIER, ROBERT DU; gaoled for suing Helen Vecchere in the ecclesiastical court.

W

WACLYN, RICHARD and ROBERT; gaoled for stealing 10 livres from the house of William de Hady.

WITECLYN, RALPH; a Forest landowner; as per Breton, John le Senr.

WYK, AVICE DE; with Henry de St Martin, summoned for taking 'royal aid' from their men and tenements.

WYLON, JOHANETTE; compounded with 18 sols for attack on Henry Howe.

2. Ancient Petitions of the Chancery and the Exchequer (covering the dates 1290–1454)

ALLEN; provost of Guernsey; attacked by Richard German, whose companion Rauf de Guethehon was killed in the struggle by said Richard German.

APAREL, RAULYN DE; compelled to abjure Alderney by Raoul Eudes for having stolen a sheep and eaten it, now prays the king to pardon him this abjuration (1291).

APPLEBY, THOMAS D'; Guernsey Bailiwick Receiver 1374-1477; asks the king for his guerdon in return for his services, he having performed his duties competently, yet has been impoverished and twice gaoled.

B

BASQUIES, PETER LE; one of the 'twelve honest and lawful men' of Guernsey at an inquisition into the holding of Jerbourg Castle by Matthew de Sauzmareys (1330).

BEAUVER, RADULFUS DE; as per Basquies, Peter le.

BERNARD, JOHN; with Gerveys Cleremond, John Feuer Senr., and Gylot Feuer, charged with making 'divers towers and fortresses' in Guernsey without the knowledge of the king or of his lieutenant (1302).

BLONDEL, COLIN; as per Basquies, Peter le (1330).

BLONDEL, RAUF; a Sark man; begs the king's pardon for abetting burglary there.

C

CARPENTIER, WILLIAM LE; as per Basquies, Peter le.

CAUCHEYS, PETER LE; as per Basquies, Peter le.

CLEREMOND, GERVAYS; see Bernard, John.

CLIDEROWE, RICHARD DE; the king's nominee for office in St Peter-Port church (1382); and see Pussin, Lawrence.

CUEUL, JOHN LE; see Basquies, Peter le.

CUMBERWELL, ROBERT DE; complains that the Prior of Wenlock seized his ship and goods in Guernsey; before the ship was returned to him, it was burnt by the enemies of the king; wherefore he begs the king to order the prior to compensate him (1297).

D

DENIS, RICHARD; killed in the defence of Guernsey (c. 1300).

E

ENGINOUR, WILLIAM LE; seigneur of Alderney 1172; together with Christian Hert and John Justice abjured the islands in connection with the hanging of Gautier de la Salle, who in turn had murdered Ranulph Gautier; see also Cartulaire de Jersey . . . , fasc. 4, 5, and 6.

ESTAC, PETER DE L'; see Basquies, Peter le.

ESTEFELD, THOMAS D'; his wife Alice was the sister of William de Remigio; and see Vivier, John — Moigne, Oliver le — St Martin, Henry de.

ESTUR, JOHN; prays to be excused being a jurat; cannot afford it. (14th c.)

F

FUEUR, GYLOT, and JOHN, Senr.; see Bernard, John.

FOURE, JOHN LE; with Richard de Port, their ship with cargo of wine seized by the men of St Malo; pray for remedy (1342).

G

GAUTIER, RANULF; with Peter le Marchant, bailiff, arrested Thomas le Roser who had murdered brother Jean del Espin on Lihou; killed le Roser, sought sanctuary in St Samson's church, abjured the island, returned with the king's pardon, but killed by Gautier de la Salle in Castle Cornet (1304 et seq.).

GERMAN, RICHARD; instigated attack with companion Rauf de Guethehon on Allen, Provost of Guernsey; abjured the island and now asks for return to his land; see Allen.

GODELENT, MATTHEW; see Basquies, Peter le.

GUETHEHON, RAUF DE; see German, Richard, and Allen.

H

HERT, CHRISTIAN; see Enginour, William le; was not pardoned.

J

JANQUIN: temp. Richard II; being granted the king's peace in the island of Guernsey, begs the king to be 'restored in his bailiwick according to the purport of his patent, and that he may not be aggrieved again by any malice'.

JEUNE, ROBERT LE; see Basquies, Peter le.

JORDAN, HENRY; temp. Richard II; fled the island having stolen 6 sheaves of corn; begs the king's pardon for 'this flight'.

JUSTICE, JOHN; see Enginour, William le; pardoned December 1320.

L

LALOWE, JOHN; temp. Edward III; complains of being beaten and fined by the Guernsey Bailiff.

LENGINOUR, WILLIAM; same as Enginour, William l'.

LORUEL, COLIN; associated with John du Vivier, q.v. in respect of imprisonment and fine.

LYOUT, ROBERT; appointed to the church of St Peter-Port by the bishop of Coutances, the king withdrawing his candidate Robert de Leysset (1295).

M

MARCHANT, DIONYSIUS LE; with his wife Petronilla, holder of the land of William de Remigio during its forfeiture; see St Martin, Henry de, and Sauzmareys, Matthew de.

MARCHANT, PETER LE; see Gautier, Ranulf.

MARCHANT, ROBERT LE; temp. Edward I; having obtained supplies for the castle in the late war, by order of the Prior of Wenlock, begs for payment; the Prior later sued for this.

MOIGNE, JOHN LE; temp. Edward I; complains of being treated contrary to the custom of the Court of Christianity, while under the king's protection; together with Dionysius and Petronilla le Marchant, and his own brother Ralph, a holder of land forfeited by William de Remigio; see also St Martin, Henry de.

MOIGNE, OLIVER LE; provost of Guernsey; associated with Thomas d'Estefeld in asking the king for an inquisition into the alleged withholding of certain benefits in St Andrew's parish, belonging to William de Remigio following the latter's pardon; was nephew of said William and is now his heir (1331).

MOLEPU, WILLIAM DE; temp. Richard II; see Rosel, Richard du.

N

NICOLAS, ROBERT; with his wife Joan and son John, holds a mill in fee of the Abbot of Marmoutier (early 14th c.).

O

ORENS, GERARD DE; see St Martin, Henry de.

P

PHILIP, GERARD; temp. Edward II; complains against the ministers of Sir Otto de Grandison for the murder of his uncle Ranulf Gautier, q.v., in the castle of Guernsey.

PORTE, EDWARD DE; a partner John Le Foure.

PUSSIN, LAWRENCE; the Apostolic See's appointee to the living of St Peter-Port; probably removed in favour of the king's nominee Richard de Cliderowe, q.v. (1382).

R

ROHAIS, WILLIAM; temp. Edward I; begs writ of confirmation from the king for 'a little serjeantry called the franchise of Rohays in the parish of St Andrew, the justices having already granted it to him'.

ROSEL, RICHARD DU; temp. Edward II; having received a charter of peace for the death of William Molepu, begs the king 'to give him that which to you belongs for the fee of the said charter'.

ROSER, THOMAS LE; see Gautier, Ranulph.

S

SACTE, WILLIAM; as per Basquies, Peter le.

ST MARTIN, HENRY DE; associated with Gerard de Orens in an accusation by Thomas d'Estefeld, Dionysius le Marchant, and John le Moigne, that they had disseized them of the Champart called the fee of St Ellens, St Andrew's parish (1324).

SAUZMAREYS, MATTHEW DE; temp. Edward II; associated with Denys le Marchant as part holder of William de Remigio's tenements complains that the bill he and his partner delivered into Parliament has been held up.

SOLLEZ, SR. GERARD; died 5 March 1368; incumbent of St Peter-Port.

SPISSA, WILLIAM DE; the king's nominee for the living of St Samson's parish, but this interdicted by the bishop of Coutances (1298).

T

TONGER, WILLIAM; a Jerseyman; begs the king's pardon for stealing a surcoat from the king's manor in Guernsey, seeking sanctuary, and fleeing the islands.

TURGEYS, ROBERT; stole a sheep, fled to the church, and adjured the islands (1307).

V

VAL, RICHARD DU; *see* Basquies, Peter le.

VINCHELEZ, PHILIP DE; *see* Vivier, John du.

VIVIER, JOHN DU; associated with Thomas d'Estefeld and Philip de Vinchelez in seeking the king's protection against false rumours sent to the English court about themselves; they seek the king's protection against the wife and son and relatives of Gautier de la Salle (1320); imprisoned and fined by Sir Henry Spigurnel 1323.

3. Extente des Iles . . . 1274 — Edward I

A

ARCHER, —— LE; imprisoned by Jean Arnaud for non-payment of dues which he claims were paid.

ARNAUD, WILLIAM; with Pierre Arnaud de la Sawe, accused of blacking the eye of Colin de Wyncelys' wife, throwing her down, so she raised the Clameur de Haro; claims she called them outrageous names; to remain arrested till they give her satisfaction; a St Martin's man.

ARTUR, FLORIA; holds land from the escheat of Raoul Vimin; a St Martin's woman.

AUDEVILLE, SAMSON DE; forfeited land on account of taking the side of the Normans; a St Samson's man.

B

BALLARD, JOURDAIN; his son forfeited land to the king; a Torteval man.

BEAUCHAMP, JOHN DE; commune holder by the seaside; a St Peter-Port man.

BOTILER, WILLIAM LE; landowner; hanged, land forfeited to the king; a St Andrew's man.

BOULANGER, RICHARD DE; landowner of St. Peter Port, who took the side of the Normans; land presumably forfeited.

BREIARD, WILLIAM; *see* Chauncebrun, Peter.

BULLYE, WILLIAM DE; a St Samson's man; with Raoul le Sage and others gaoled for removing timber from the house of Jourdain Greyn-d'Avene at request of rector of St Samson's.

BURGEYS, ANDRE; *see* Vivier, Robert du.

BURNEL, PETER; a St Peter-Port man; *see* Vivier, Robert du.

BURNEL, RAOUL; a St Peter-Port man; *see* Herice, Richard le.

C

CARTERET, JEAN DE; holder of house belonging to Eglentine Bastard; a St Peter-Port man.

CARTERET, JEAN DE; a St Andrew's man; holds the land of Arnaud Johannes, i.e. the land of Guillaume le Boteler who was hung.

CHAUNCEBRUN, PETER; a Forest man; deputy of bailiff Hugh de Trubleville; accused of many injustices; gaoled Colin le Sueur and his wife whereby she suffered miscarriage; beat William Breiard, jurat of St Andrew's, and Henry de Cynqueleys.

COUR, THOMAS DE LA; *see* Vivier, Robert du.

COK, RAOUL LE; holds the escheated land of the bastard son of William Isolde; a St Samson's man.

D

DENISE, JEAN; a St Andrew's man; imprisoned by the Guernsey bailiff because he sought remedy against wrongs done to him by the bailiff.

DUREL, RAOUL; fined 60 sols while in prison; received the escheated land of Karupel Mordant.

E

ENGLES, PHILIPPE LE; a St Peter-Port man; holds the land forfeited by Peticonsal.

ESCOT, B. LE; a St Peter Port man; with Arnaud Gallycen, threatened to burn land belonging to the king; servant of the bailiff.

F

FORLOO, HENRY; fined unjustely 60 sols by the bailiff; a St Peters-in-the-Wood man; *see* Herice, Richard le.

FORTESCUE; a Norman; land forfeited to the king.

G

GALLYCEN, ARNAUD; a St Peter-Port man; *see* Escot, B. le.

GERESI, THOMAS DE; banished, property escheated to Richard Witeclyn.

GERNUN, MATTHEW; holds with his partners the escheated land of Jean Peerles; a St Peter-Port man.

GILLEBERD, RICHARD; holder of escheated land 'le legat'; a Vale man.

GORGES, THOMAS DE; a St Martin's man; forfeited land to the king.

GREYN-D'AVINE, JORDAN; timber removed from his house by William de Bullye and others.

GUNNOR, GEOFFREY; householder; a St Peter-Port man.

GUNNOR, Geoffrey; householder; a St Peter-Port man.

H

HERICE, RICHARD LE; with Raoul, councillors of the Bailiff; accused of misleading the court enquiring into alleged misdeeds by themselves, and obtaining 20 sols unjustly from Henry Forloo.

HOUGUE, RICHARD DE LA; banished, land forfeited to the king; a St Andrew's man.

HYDUS (HIDOUS); forfeited land to the king; a St Peters-in-the-Wood man.

I

ISOLDE, WILLIAM; *see* Cok, Raoul, le.

J

JOHANNE, PETER; holder of land forfeited by Hydus; a St Peters-in-the-Wood man.

K

KARITE, DIONYSIUS; fined 2 oxen for accidentally wounding a boy by running him over; a St Peter-Port man.

L

LAUNDES, NICOLETTE DES; as for Norman, Richard, but sum paid 40 sols.

LEISONT, PETER; accuses Robert du Vivier of seeking double payment by appealing to the bishop of Coutances as well as to the king.

M

MACHUN, WILLIAM, and WIFE; imprisoned unjustly by the bailiff who stole 100 sols from them.

MANNERE, WILLIAM; his heirs own land escheated from Orenge Maselyne; a St Peters-in-the-Wood man.

MARTYNVAST, RICHARD DE; his land escheated for taking the side of the Normans; a Torteval man.

MASELYNE, ORENGE; *see* Mannere, William; a St Peter'-in-the-Wood man.

MAUNT, AMICUS LE; holds the escheated land of Emelote Selvestre, banished; a St Peter-Port man.

MAUTALENT, ——; forfeited land for taking the side of the Normans; a Câtel man.

MERYENE; holds land forfeited by the wife of Raulin Mesurier; a St Peters-in-the-Wood man.

MESURIER, RAULIN; *see* Meryene; a St Peters-in-the-Wood man.

MEYNNIER, RICHARD; pays 2 chickens annually for 'the increase on his land'; a Vale man.

MOLEPY, GIRAUD; suicide; held land in Moyllepe; a St Martin's man.

MORDANT, CARUPEL; landowner; a St Peter-Port man.

MURIEL, COLIN; a Forest man; holds escheated land of David de Vieles.

N

NORMAN, RICHARD; gaoled by the Bailiff, though acquitted by 24 jurats after he had paid them 40 livres for an enquete; a Forest man.

O

OSBORNE, GEOFFREY; hanged; a St Peter-Port man.

P

PAISANT, RAOUL; *see* Forloo, Henry; a St Peters-in-the-Wood man.

PERLES, JEAN; *see* Gernun, Matthew; a St Peter-Port man.

R

ROBILARD, HENRY; holds the escheated land 'Sigod'; a Torteval man.

ROGER, RAOUL; forfeited his land to the king.

S

SAGE, RAOUL LE; as per Bullye, William de; a St Samson's man.

ST MARTIN, DROUET DE; with Thomas de Wyk, usurped property from 80 individuals in the time of Drouet de Baretin; a Torteval man.

ST PLAUNKEYS, THOMAS DE; forfeited land to the king; a St Peters-in-the-Wood man.

SAWE, PETER ARNAUD DE LA; *see* Arnaud, William; a St Martin's man.

SELVESTRE, EMELOTE; *see* Maunt, Amicus le; a St Peter-Port man.

SEUE, JULIE and THOMAS; retired to Brittany after accusation of theft; land forfeited; St Martin's folk.

SICCAVILLE, SIMON DE; holds escheated land of Geoffrey Osborne, who was hanged; a St Peter-Port man.

SURCOUF, PETER; unjustly fined 2 sols.

SUWARD, RICHARD; forfeited land for taking the side of the Normans; a Câtel man.

T

TUSCHEN, PETER; unjustly fined 5 sols by the Bailiff.

V

VIELES, DAVID DE; *see* Muriel, Colin; a Forest man.

VIELESE, LA; a Norman; forfeited her land to the king. a St Martin's woman.

VIMIN, RAOUL; *see* Artur, Floria; a St Martin's man.

VIVIER, ROBERT DU; holds land forfeited by Thomas de Gorges; accused of confiscating part of Andre Burgey's estate; of taking money from Peter Burnel by demanding double tax on wine; accused by Thomas de la Cour on matters appertaining to the Court; and *see* Leisont, Peter; a St Martin's man.

W

WEREVILLE, WILLIAM DE; landowner; a St Saviour's man.

WIBERD; holder of escheated land; a Vale man.

WIKE, THOMAS; *see* St Martin, Drouet de; holds escheated land of Raoul le Fevere and Julie his wife; a St Samson's and Torteval man.

WILDELIGNAGE; householder; a St Peter-Port man.

WITECLYN, Richard; holds escheated land of Thomas de Gersei; a St Samson's man.

WYNCELYS, COLIN DE; *see* Arnaud, William; a St Martin's man.

4. *Cartulaire de Jersey, Guernsey etc. . . . Fasc. 1-6*

A

ALRENOIO, VINCENZIO DE; Alderney man; a charter witness in 1172.

ANGOT, WILLIAM; bought from Mont St Michel a house at Ville Bauda and land nearby (1309).

B

BOUTILLER, ROBERT LE; gives Blanchelande Abbey an annual return from his mill in Guern-sey; gave 'the land of the old Grange' in Guernsey to . . . (MS incomplete).

BOUTILL(I)ER, RICHARD LE; uncle of Robert B., v.s.; a canon.

C

CALIDO BOSCO, JOHANNES DE; the Cartulaire editor considers that the place name Cobo is derived herefrom.

D

DIDIER, PETER, son of; donor to Mont St Michel of land in Guernsey on becoming a monk (1330).

E

ENGINOUR, WILLIAM LE; *see also* under *Ancient Petitions*; seigneur of Alderney; grants land in Alderney to Cherbourg Abbey, which at present is held from him by Richard le Gallais (Walensis); also land at Hamon Thore in Alderney with three other small parcels of land therein.

ESTUR, WILLIAM; lessee of land at Hamelin Estur fief in Guernsey from Mont St Michel, *c.* 1270; owner of Le Grand Clos in Castel parish.

F

FOLLOT, WILLIAM; owner of a field next door to that bought by William Angot; 1309.

FORLOT, JEAN; *see* Prevost, Alain le.

G

GAIUN, WILLIAM; priest of St George's chapel, Câtel, became a monk in 1156.

GALLAIS, RICHARD LE; *see* Enginour, William le; (1772).

GARIS, PETER DE; a Gascony merchant; in 1313 bought from Mont St Michel the land at Hamelin Estur fief; rented the esperqueries in Guernsey for 5 years on payment of 15 sols for each 100 congers caught; renewed this in 1319; in 1318, to pay at regular intervals for 6 years commencing 1319, 160 livres Tournois to Trinity Abbey, Caen.

GUERIN, JEAN; appointed Prior of the Vale (1369).

GUILLAUME; priest of Yvetot; sold to Mont St Michel certain rights he possessed in respect of tithes at Perelle (1157).

H

HAVILLAND, ROBERT DE; a witness to a letter of restitution of property to Mont St Michel in Guernsey (1219).

HOUGUE, PETER DE LA; lessee of land called La Source in Castel parish, from Mont St Michel, *c.* 1239.

HUGUES, brother of NEEL of the Cotentin; grants land at Pleinmont to Mont St Michel (mid-11th c.).

J

JACQUELINE; owner of a house next door to that bought by William Angot (1309).

L

LAMBERZARD, GIRARD; Guardian of the Islands; witness to a restitution of land in Guernsey to Mont St Michel (1238).

M

MALMARCHE, RICHARD; grants the land called Grand Moullin to Mont St Michel; he previously reclaimed it, and hence was excommunicated; he now seeks to make amends.

MOUCHE, WILLIAM LE; owner of a field next door to the land bought by William Angot; (1309).

P

PASTEY, PETER and RENAUD; *see* Prevost, Alain le.

PICHENOHT, WILLIAM; donor of land to Mont St Michel at Perelle, on becoming a monk (1130).

POINGDESTRE, JOURDAIN; an arbitrator in dispute about tithes on parsnips between the Vale Priory and the Vale parish (1331).

POLIERS, GILBERT DE; obtained a corrody from Mont St Michel in return for services to the Vale Priory and goods given thereto, 1286; fell into arrears 1306.

PREVOST, ALAIN LE; complains to the king that his house in Guernsey was damaged and himself wounded by Peter and Renaud Pastey,

Prior and monk respectively of the Vale Priory. Together with Jean Forlot, he asks that the parishioners of the Vale, Castel, St Saviour's of St Peters-in-the-Wood and Torteval be allowed to leave their tithes in the fields and not be forced to transport them; and that they be allowed to perform the annual chevauchée around the 'monastery of St Michael of the Vale' (1324).

S

SALINELLES, WILLIAM DES; as per Havilland, Robert de (1219).

T

THORE, HAMON, Alderney landowner in 1172.

TORALD, son of CHETELL; a charter witness; note name of father Ketil, which along with

Thor and derivatives, persisted longer than any other Scandinavian name (c. 1060).

TORAUD, RICHARD; sold property in Guernsey to Marmoutier Abbey for 7 livres.

V

VIVIER, GODEFROI; succeeded Gaiun as priest of St George's chapel.

W

WAC, HUGHES and RICHARD; donors of land in Guernsey to Longues Abbey (pre-1309).

A long list of medieval Guernsey names appears on p. 370 of the Cartulaire; among them are: Baileul, Baugy de, Carey, Durand, Fallaize, Girard (Giraud), Gosselin, Guille, Hauteville de, Maindonal, Mauger, Putron de, Rue de la, Tardif, and Jehan.

5. Herm and Jethou (Priaulx Library)

ASTHORP, WILLIAM D'; given a sort of mandate to administer the islands of the Bailiwick as he saw fit, to devote the proceeds to fortifications (1373).

BUDWAL, LOIESCON, NIVO: 6th c. landowners in the Bailiwick; semi-legendary.

DOUBE, FRERE JO; head of the Cordelier monks who inhabited Herm from 1440–1458.

GUYFFART, JEAN; installed as incumbent of Herm 1480.

JOLIS, JEAN LE and PLACE, RICHARD DE LA: incumbents of Herm immediately before Jean Guyffart.

SOURCES OF QUOTATIONS

Entry of Occurrence	*Source (Authorized Version if Biblical)*
Explanatory Notes	Thomas Osbert Mordaunt, 'Verses Written During the War, 1756–1763'.

PART I

le Boutillier, George	Tomb of Sir Christopher Wren, St Paul's Cathedral.
Brévint, Cosmé	Henry II, referring to Becket.
de Carteret, Amice	Judges, 7, 18.
Chamberlayne, Sir Francis	Charlotte Elliott: Hymn 'Just As I Am'.
Collings, Rev. W. T.	(a) John Mason Neale: Hymn 'Christian, Dost Thou See Them?'
	(b) Luke 11, 21.
David Family	William Shakespeare: *Twelfth Night*, Act 1, Scene 1.
French, Frederick George	Mark 6, 4.
de Garis, Marie	(a) Virgil: Eclogues X, 69.
	(b) Saint John 1, 47 – adapted.
Geoffrey of Anjou	(a) Anglo-Saxon Chronicle.
	(b) Chronicles of Abbey of Fontenelle.
	(c) Anglo-Saxon Chronicle.
Hatton, Sir Christopher	(a) Diary of Pierre le Roy.
	(b) Roger North: *Lives of the Norths*, Volume II.
Jewish Victims	William Shakespeare: *Merchant of Venice* Act 3, Scene 1.
Kellet-Smith, Dr. Stanley	Luke 5, 31.
Leighton, Sir Thomas	(a) Book of Common Prayer – Litany.
	(b) William Shakespeare: *Othello*, Act 3, Scene 3.
	(c) Deposition of Guernesiais recorded in *Calendar of State Papers, Domestic – Addenda 1574-65*.
le Lièvre, Peter	Matthew 6, 19.
Lindsay, Lieutenant-Colonel	Robert Browning: 'Andrea del Sarto'.
le Marchant, William	Louis XIV.
Osborne, Sir Peter	Robert Browning: 'Cavalier Tunes – Marching Along'.
le Patourel, Brigadier. H. W.	Geoffrey Chaucer: *Prologue to Canterbury Tales*.
le Pelley, Ernest	Acts of the Apostles, 3, 6.
Pym, Lieutenant-Colonel J. B.	(Both quotations) Rudyard Kipling: 'Soldier an' Sailor too'.
Scales, Michael	Book of Common Prayer: Forms of Prayer to be used at Sea.
Sharp, George	Virgil: Aeneid 11/49.

Entry of Occurrence   *Source (Authorized Version if Biblical)*

Sherwill, Sir Ambrose   (a) Mark 6, 4.
                                (b) William Whiting: Hymn, 'Eternal Father'.
                                (c) Alfred Edward Housman: 'Epitaph on an Army of
                                    Mercenaries'.
                                (d) Matthew 21, 42

de Vic, Sir Henry   Rudyard Kipling: 'If'.

PART II

Caedwalla of Gwynedd   Anglo-Saxon Chronicle.
le Feyvre, Guillaume   (All quotations) *Bulletin Annuel de la Société Jersiaise*
                                    Volume IX.
de la Salle, Gautier   Twenty-second Article of Religion of the Church of
                                    England.
Martin, Thomas   Thomas Gray: 'Elegy Written in a Country Churchyard'.

INDEX OF PERSONS

Prefixes (which have been ignored in arranging the alphabetical sequence) are placed immediately after Christian names, so that — for example — Gautier de la Salle will be found under 'S' as 'Salle, Gautier de la'. Further the inclusion against a name of a letter or letters among the page references indicates the Kinship Table(s) in Part III where the person concerned is featured.

LIST OF SUBSCRIBERS

Cyril A. Adam
Laurence Adkins
W.B. Adlard
John R. Allan
Joan Allenet
Patricia Anderson
Rosemary Ashley
C.N. Aubin
Philip M. Bailhache
Monica M. Ball
Jeanne & Alan Barber
Miss G.M. Barnett
Stanley W. Beale
Richard & Sue Bellinger
F.J. Benest
Mr & Mrs M.E. Best
Maurice B. Bisson
R.H. Blanchford, OBE., GM.,
K. St. J., LFIBA.
Gordon Blatchford
Laurence S. Blundell
M.H. & J. Le Boutillier
Sieur Kenneth Bradford
Lawrence Bradshaw
Mrs Phyllis Brehaut
R.N. Brehaut
Neville & Elizabeth Brouard
Robert W. Brown
P.K. Burgess
H.C. & G.I. Burr
Mrs M.F. Carey
Mr & Mrs W.J. Carman
P. Malet de Carteret
Mr & Mrs P.R. Castle
D.A. Le Cheminant
Air Chief Marshal Sir Peter
Le Cheminant
P.J.H.de L. Le Cheminant
Edward Choppen
Mrs Barbara Clarke
Raymond Clark
Mrs Rhoda Cohu
D.M. & M.F. Collas
The Revd. Canon V.J. Collas
Mr & Mrs D.A. Le Conte
D.O. & D.A. Le Conte
D.C. Cook
Simon B. Coombe
G.V. Cossanteli
Mr & Mrs John Court
P. E. Le Couteur

Lt.-Col. C.C. Davey
Mrs H.P. Davey
Mr & Mrs John David
W.G. Davis
Revd. C.F. Davison
Mr & Mrs W.J. Denning
Emile & Joan Digard
Leonie B. Dorey
L.M. & B.D. Dorey
M.S. Douglas
Edward C. Druée
Erica Drummond
Richard A. Falle
Patrick J. Fennelly
Joan Flood
Pamela J. Le Gallez
Mr & Mrs D.A. Gardiner
Helen B.T. Gardiner
N.J. Gaudion
Mr & Mrs W.J. Gaudion
Mrs D.M. Gill
Peter J. Girard, B.Sc.
Mr & Mrs John D. Goodwin
A.S. Green
Mrs D.F. Gregg
Revd. John A. Guille
Graham W. Gumbley
D. Hands
P. de B.C. Hart, R.D.
Martin Harvey
Revd. Vincent A. Harvey
Dr. Ruth Hawker
Lord Coutanche Library,
Société Jersiaise
Edward J. Hotton
Mary G. Hughes
Mr & Mrs M.D. Hutchings
Miss M.C. Jackson
R.O. Falla
Mr & Mrs Nigel Jee
P.J. Kenton
Norman A.B. King
S. Kinn
G. Michael Lambert
Raoul Lemprière
R.E.K. Levett
K.G.H. Lewis
R. & M.L. Long
Bernard B. Lovell
I.W. Lovell
Jurat Max Lucas (Jersey)

Mrs L.M. Lucas
Mrs A. Macartney
Niall D. McCathie
David McClintock
A.J. & R.M. McDade
D.J. McLeod
Capt. William Machon
James W. Maingay
P.S. Mansell
Mr & Mrs R.J. Marquis
Mr & Mrs R. Martin
Eleanor Maslin
Miss D.C. Meldrum
Marie-Louise Mendham
Colin Le Messurier
Alan Middleton
Mrs M.N. Mimmack
Ian Monins
Mrs M. Monk
Doreen P.E. Mooney
Miss N.C. Moore
Mrs J.E. Moullin
Dr R.O. Murray
Dr M.E. Ogier
Adele M. Ozanne
Mr & Mrs P.J. Ozanne
K.E. Le Page
Keith J. Le Page
The Hon. Mrs Llewellen Palmer
Hugo Parsons
Paul R. Le Pelley
Mrs D.W. Le Pelley
D. H. Phillips
Mr & Mrs B.J. Pill
Alfred S. Pipon
Nicholas Le Poidevin
Priaulx Library
D.L. Purdy
C. J. Rabey
Mr & Mrs M. Radford & family
Lt.-Col. Brian A. Rankilor
M.W. Le Ray
R. Reddall
Kenneth C. Renault
Mrs H.B. Roach
John C. Robilliard
Miss Y.J. Robilliard
Deputy J. Roche
Miss Lucille B. Le Rougetel
Mr & Mrs G.R. Rowland
Richard E. Ruggle

Viscountess Sandon
David Sarre
J.W. Sarre
Mr & Mrs L.W. Sarre
Mr & Mrs R.F. Simons
John Le Couteur Simon
O. J. Simpson
L. Chester Smith, M.A.
J.C.S.F. Smithies

P.F. Stanton
Mrs Joan Stevens
M.-C. Swann
Jane L.Syvret
Philip W. Syvret
F.W. & D.F. Thompson
Mr & Mrs L.C. Le Tocq
Miss M.E. Tooley
Brian E. Torode

Frederick M. Towers
C.A. Travers
Mlle. B. Feuillerat
Philip M. De Veulle
Adrian A. Walton
E. C. Wavell, D.F.C.
Doreen G. Wilcock
Dorothy J. Wilson
H.R. Windridge

Endpapers: (*left*) Certificate containing the signatures of many famous Guernseymen supporting Tnomas de Sausmarez in his refusal to fight a second duel with Robert Porret le Marchant; (*right*) Pierre Levrier's letter to Bishop John Thomas asking that Jean de la Noye be appointed as his Curate.

Guernsey 23ᵈ February 1791

We the undersigned Gentlemen are of opinion that Mr Thoˢ De Sausmarez (Kings Comptroller) has acted up to the principles of a Gentleman and a Man of Honor in declining to accept the second challenge of Mr R. P. Le Marchant after what passed in the Duel between them on the 23ᵈ October last ——————

Js Saumarez   Aⁿ P DePeyster   Martin De Havilland
John Brock   Samuel le Cocq
Charles Bell—   W Carrut   Nicholas Dobrée
Danˡ Tupper.—   Jⁿ Armstrong   Peter Thou—
    John le Cocq   Geo: Armstrong   George Bell
    Peter de Jersey Durell Saumarez   Edw. Lefebvre jr
    Daniel de Lisle Brock Roedt. Pollard   Nathˡ Brock
    John Saumarez   Thoˢ P Geo Armstrong Charles Guille
    Jos Le Marchant Jean Alexʳ Duke   Wm Le Marchant Esq
    Wm Bell Junr.   G A Armstrong   John Savery Brock
    John Carey son of Thoˢ Bn Armstrong   George Lefebvre
    Nathaniel le Cocq jun. Jⁿ Booth   W John Bonamy
    James Brock   Daniel Hardy
    William de Jersey Bryan McMinⁿS   John Dobrée
    John Elisha Tupper Arthur Collins   John De Lisle
    William Peter le Cocq Thomas Andros Wm Condamine
    William Brock   Richᵈ De Beauvoir. John Bowden
    Isaac Carey—   Peter Ludlam
    Isaac Dobrée   Danˡ Dobrée   Elisha Dobrée
    W. L. Brock   Peter De Lisle   Wm Bainbrigge
    H Le Mesurier   Osmond De M. earvois Josˢ Dobrée Junr.
    Thomas Dobrée   John Le Marchant   Nichˢ Le Mesurier
                    William Coutart   Thoˢ Le Marchant
                    P M Carey